Before Adam Smith

Before Adam Smith

The Emergence of Political Economy, 1662–1776

Terence Hutchison

Basil Blackwell

First published 1988

Basil Blackwell Ltd
108 Cowley Road, Oxford, OX4 1JF, UK

Basil Blackwell Inc,
432 Park Avenue South, Suite 1503
New York, NY 10016, USA

British Library Cataloguing in Publication Data

Hutchison, T.W.
Before Adam Smith: the emergence of political economy, 1662–1776.
1. Political science——History——17th century 2. Political science——History——18th century
I. Title
320'.01 JA83
ISBN 0-631-15898-7

Library of Congress Cataloging in Publication Data

Hutchison, T.W. (Terence Wilmot)
Before Adam Smith: The emergence of political economy, 1662–1776
Terence Hutchison.
p. cm.
Bibliography: p.
Includes index,
ISBN 0–631–15898–7
1. Economics——History—18th century. 2. Economics——History—17th century. I. Title.
HB83.H8 1988
330'.09'032—dc19

87–29368
CIP

Typeset in 10 on 11 pt Bembo
by Photo·graphics, Honiton, Devon
Printed in Great Britain by TJ Press Ltd, Padstow, Cornwall

For C

Somewhere about the middle of the seventeenth century European life was so completely transformed in many of its aspects, that we commonly think of this as one of the great watersheds of modern history, comparable with the Renaissance, or the Reformation, or the French Revolution.

Sir George Clark, *The Seventeenth Century*

It does not necessarily follow that, because a man treats of a subject by itself, his remarks will be wiser than those of his predecessors who dealt with it in conjunction with other matters.

Sir William Ashley, *Surveys Historical and Economic*

We still underestimate pre-Smithian achievement.

J.A. Schumpeter, *History of Economic Analysis*

. . . l'intervalle qui existe entre les mercantilistes et les classiques – intervalle où l'on trouve ce qui constitue probablement la perfection de l'intelligence économique.

Louis Salleron, *Pierre de Boisguilbert ou la Naissance de l'économie politique*

Contents

Acknowledgements

I am very grateful for the financial assistance, with regard to travelling and typing expenses, which I received, at an earlier stage, from the Leverhulme Foundation and from the Faculty of Commerce and Social Science of the University of Birmingham.

I am grateful to the Cambridge University Press for permission to reproduce, with slight revisions, most of pp. 2–25 and 127–35 of *On Revolutions and Progress in Economic Knowledge* (1978).

The author of a book such as this must obviously be very dependent on the libraries available and the facilities and services they provide. I am much indebted to the staff of the library of the University of Birmingham, especially those of the Inter-Library Loan Service, and the Rare Book Room, who, in a period of severe stringency, have been helpful well beyond the call of duty. On the other side of the Atlantic, it has been a great boon and blessing to be able to use the magnificent libraries of Yale University. In London, the British Library of Political and Economic Science, and the Goldsmith's Library have assisted regarding some vital items. I am also grateful to the Fitzwilliam Museum in Cambridge for permission to examine the papers of General Henry Lloyd, and to the University of Glasgow for information regarding the manuscripts of Gershom Carmichael.

I am deeply indebted to many individuals and especially to the following for advice and criticism: Mr Roger Backhouse of the University of Birmingham has read almost the entire typescript, and his wise and discerning comments and criticisms have been very helpful at many points. Professor Stephan Böhm of the University of Graz kindly sent me copies of the important writings of his predecessor in Graz, Anton Tautscher, on the subject of Ernst Ludwig Carl. Professor Gilbert Faccarello generously supplied me with copies of his authoritative writings on Boisguilbert, and made a number of important, corrective criticisms of my sections on Nicole and Boisguilbert. Professor Peter Groenewegen has generously made available to me advance copies of his valuable contributions to *The New Palgrave Dictionary of Economics* which deal with a number of the main writers discussed in this book. Professor Pier Luigi Porta of the University of Milan kindly read, and commented helpfully on, the chapters on Italian economists, as well as sending me copies of valuable unpublished papers on Galiani and on Smith's theory of value. Finally, M. Philippe Steiner, of the University of Paris VII, read the chapter on the physiocrats and made several searching comments and criticisms, which I have taken gratefully into account. For the errors and misinterpretations which, I fear, remain, I must take entire responsibility.

An invitation to deliver in July 1987 the Bateman lecture at the University of Western Australia provided an occasion for formulating more clearly and cogently the Postscript. My warmest thanks are due to the Chairman of the Economics department, Robin Ghosh, and to other members, for their generous hospitality.

Finally, I cannot adequately express my indebtedness to my wife. Her stylistic and grammatical advice has enabled me to remove numerous mistakes and infelicities. In addition, she has provided constant encouragement and many other kinds of practical support and assistance.

T.W.H.

PART I
Introduction

1
The Period and its Starting-point

I

Important pioneer scholar of economic thought though Karl Marx undoubtedly was, his version of its history seems – to this writer, at any rate – to contain much that calls for criticism. What remains, however, of the highest value, is Marx's *aperçu* regarding the outstanding creative impetus given to the advance of political economy in the seventeenth century by Sir William Petty. Similarly valuable is Marx's recognition of the great merits of the writings of Petty's successors in the 100 years or so before the appearance of *The Wealth of Nations* in 1776.

On the other hand, though Marx's verdict on Petty as 'one of the most gifted and original of economic investigators', seems entirely just, his nomination of Sir William as 'the founder of modern political economy' (1951, 15) is not very helpful. To claim that any one individual – Aristotle, Petty or Adam Smith – was 'the founder' of political economy is bound to be highly questionable, since it is difficult to accept that any one person alone *could* have founded the subject. Nor do we agree that Petty's brief suggestion of the idea of an economic 'surplus' either played a very important role in his work or constitutes a main reason for holding that Petty's writings mark a major turning-point in the history of political economy. Nor, moreover, do we accept Marx's conception of 'classical' political economy as beginning with Petty, and running on through Locke, Hume, Steuart, Quesnay, Smith, James Mill and Ricardo, down to about 1830 – that is, until just before Marx himself took up the subject. The view, or definition, widely adopted today, according to which the ascendancy of classical political economy in Britain lasted slightly less than 100 years from, roughly, 1776 until 1871, seems reasonably adequate and justifiable. For it was with the publication of *The Wealth of Nations* in 1776 that the rise to dominance can be traced of the first major, modern theoretical orthodoxy, which, in Britain, largely excluded, or obliterated, some of the most significant ideas regarding utility and value, aggregate demand and employment, and expectations and uncertainty, which had emerged in the preceding century of theoretical pluralism.

This book is concerned with what may be called the pre-classical period of slightly over 100 years before 1776, which may be said to have begun with the appearance of Petty's first and most important work in 1662.[1] Of course, there is bound to be something arbitrary and artificial in trying to mark out any periods of history, inevitable though it is that such attempts should be made. There are obvious dangers in seeking to lay down such demarcations with much rigidity or precision. But 1662, like 1776 and 1871, seems a reasonably significant and suitable year to take as marking the opening of a new period in the history of economic thought.

II

Marx's emphasis on the originality and importance of Petty's work, and on the value of the contributions of his successors over the next century or so, has much merit, not simply because it does justice to Petty. The fuller recognition of the work of Petty and his successors makes possible a much more balanced and illuminating view of the history of economic thought before 1776 – and indeed of the whole history of the subject.

First, Marx's recognition of Petty's major importance implies a rejection of the classical view proclaimed by J.B. Say, and still alive and well today, that political economy had no history, or virtually no history, before 1776, or only a disconnected pre-history.[2]

Secondly, Marx's observation clears out of the way much of the obfuscation created by the excessive and indiscriminate use of the term 'mercantilism', which has so confused the history of economic thought and policy ever since Adam Smith, mainly for polemical purposes, introduced the idea of 'the mercantile system' as a comprehensive description of the policies of his predecessors.

The term mercantilism need not, however, be regarded as so fatally confusing as to be completely unusable. We are not following the example of the late T.S. Ashton who completely banished the word from his book on the economic history of the eighteenth century (1955). But there is a danger of suggesting highly inadequate and misleading conclusions if this term 'mercantilism' is used in generalizations about the history of economic thought and theory, and not confined to doctrines about economic policy or policy recommendations.[3]

Heckscher described mercantilism as 'the economic policy of the time between the Middle Ages and the age of *laissez-faire*' (1955, vol. 1, 20). It may – or may not – be adequate to describe the economic policies of several centuries, and countless régimes, following the end of the Middle Ages, in terms simply of 'mercantilism' and '*laissez-faire*'. It is certain, however, that such a dichotomy involves a highly unsatisfactory oversimplification when applied to the economic thought and theories of much of the seventeenth and eighteenth centuries. This is particularly the case when this oversimplification is applied to the period between 1662 and 1776. For in this period the formation was taking place of what was to emerge as the independent subject of political economy; and the economic literature and theories of this formative phase are much too complex and richly variegated to be categorized as belonging either to the fag-end of mercantilism, or to an early phase of *laissez-faire*. It is especially inadequate and misleading to try to force particular economists of this period into either one compartment or the other of a mercantilist – *laissez-faire* dichotomy. Many, or most, of the major writers, from Petty, via Mandeville and Cantillon, to Steuart, simply cannot be categorized at all adequately in such terms.

Certainly the advance of economic theory, from the seventeenth through the first half of the eighteenth century, was closely interconnected with the growing advocacy, and advance, of free-market economic policies, away from a direction generally describable as 'mercantilist', towards what might be called 'classical liberal'. But the two developments, one of the growth and advance of positive economic theories, and the other of a transformation in attitudes to policy, are analytically distinguishable, and should be kept distinguished, if a clear historical account, either of policies or of theories, is to be achieved. Of course, in terms of 'mercantilism' and '*laissez-faire*' our starting date of 1662 is of little or no significance.

Moreover, throughout the seventeenth and much of the eighteenth centuries, there were at least two distinct streams of economic thought and literature which flowed mainly independently of one another. The history of economic thought at this time does not consist simply and solely of the mercantilist literature, mostly in pamphlet form, on current policy problems. There was another stream of ideas which eventually was to prove, arguably, of greater significance for the theoretical foundations of political economy. These were the ideas of the natural-law philosophers, which were of fundamental importance for the formation of the subject, not only because they introduced the concepts of a natural order and of natural law but also for the nucleus of value and price theory which the writings of these philosophers contributed, a nucleus which had come down from Aristotle via the scholastics. Hugo Grotius (1583–1645), shortly before the beginning of our period, and Samuel Pufendorf (1632–94), shortly after its beginning, continued this tradition.

Any attempt, therefore, to cover, or categorize, the economic thought of this period by an all-embracing application of the term 'mercantilism' would disregard a vitally important element in the economic theory of this time. A further inadequacy which the term 'mercantilism' is apt to encourage, is a general disregard of the intellectual or epistemological quality – or lack of it – of the widely varying writings to which it is applied. Such an uncritical attitude is specially unjust regarding writers like Petty and Cantillon, who embarked on a serious attempt to raise intellectual standards by the explicit introduction of new methodological distinctions and criteria.

III

It hardly seems necessary to defend further the selection of 1776, or of some neighbouring year, as marking the end of one period and the beginning of the next. This great year (1776), or another near by (such as 1790, adopted by Schumpeter), has frequently been used by historians of economic thought as marking a major dividing line. There is more to be said, however, regarding the choice of 1662 as a starting date.

Periods in the history of economic thought are usually most appropriately marked off by the dates of epoch-making works, rather than by the dates of important events in political or economic history. But the case for selecting any particular year as signifying the starting-point, or end, of a period, can be reinforced if the date of a major work coincides with what is recognized as an important turning-point in political or economic history, the events of which have sometimes significantly influenced economic ideas.

In fact, the first year or two of the 1660s saw various very important new developments in political and economic history, as well as in the history of economic thought. In England, 1660 saw the opening of a new political era with the restoration of the monarchy. Petty's *Treatise*, two years later, was, in fact, primarily directed at examining the principles which should underlie public expenditure and taxation in the new régime – always (if not *the*) central issue in the political upheavals of the seventeenth century in England. In 1661 a new and remarkable phase in economic policy began in France, when Jean Baptiste Colbert assumed the direction of the French economy under his young sovereign, Louis XIV.

Equally important was the influence on political and economic thought of the profound philosophical and scientific developments of the seventeenth century. William Petty (1623–87) came shortly after Bacon (1561–1626), Hobbes (1588–1679) and Descartes (1596–1650) and shortly before the great example of Newton (1642–1727).[4] Just as the philosophical ideas of such men were giving a vital impetus to the study of the natural sciences, so, also, the study of 'trade', or of economic problems, received an important stimulus in the form of new methodological foundations and criteria. It is not entirely devoid of significance that Petty's first and most important work was published in the same year as the incorporation of the Royal Society for the Improving of Natural Knowledge. Just as Petty was profoundly influenced by Bacon and Hobbes, so also was North influenced by Descartes.

Thus there are reasons, not only from the internal history of economic thought, but from various external directions, including political and economic history and the development of philosophy and the sciences, for regarding the middle of the seventeenth century, and, in particular, the early 1660s, as marking the opening of a new period.

As regards, however, the narrower perspectives of the history of economic thought, it might be maintained that a significant turning-point had already been reached in the 1620s, when a great depression of English trade produced a remarkable outburst of debate which included the important contributions of Mun, Malynes and Misselden. Indeed, the 1620s *might* be regarded as providing the first example – on a much smaller scale, of course, than on subsequent such occasions – of one of those major creative controversies and turning-points, stimulated by pressing real-world problems, such as the Ricardian years in England in the second decade of the nineteenth century, and the Keynesian decade in the 1930s. But apart from the huge contrast in scale, a profoundly significant change in intellectual quality must be noticed, between the works of Mun and his contemporaries, and those of Petty. Both writers were primarily, and almost entirely, concerned with policy; and, of course, almost inevitably there were theories, of some kind, underlying the policy doctrines of both Mun and Petty. The vital difference in quality between Mun's work in the 1620s and Petty's work from 1662 onwards, is to be found in the fact that such theories as could be said to underlie Mun's policy conclusions were almost completely inchoate and inexplicit, while Petty, on the other hand, made a forthright, pioneering attempt to raise the quality and reliability of his policy contributions by basing them on much more explicit methodological criteria and theoretical foundations. For however Petty's methodological and theoretical ideas may be assessed or criticized, he was seeking to introduce new intellectual or epistemological standards, in which he was followed, in differing directions, by a number of successors: Locke, North, Gregory King and others. It is for this challenging fundamental methodological innovation, just as much as for its theoretical ingenuity and policy interest, that Petty's work may justifiably be regarded as marking a new starting-point in the history of economic thought and theory, as contrasted with the writings of Thomas Mun and his contemporaries some forty years earlier.

IV

Having roughly defined its boundaries, we turn briefly to the secondary literature covering this period of economic thought. There is a fairly impressive range of scholarly editions and monographs dealing with many of the leading individual writers and their writings, though quite a number of these, especially of English works, are now fifty to 100 years old – such as, for example, the fine editions by C.H. Hull of Petty's writings (1899), by F.B. Kaye of Mandeville's (1924), and by H. Higgs of Cantillon's *Essai* (1931). There are also a number of important studies of particular aspects or branches of the economic thought of this period, to two of which I am very much indebted: Douglas Vickers' *Studies in the Theory of Money, 1690–1776* (1959), and William Letwin's *The Origins of Economic Science* (1963).[5]

But a striking contrast is apparent between, on the one hand, the great number of monographs, partial studies, and scholarly editions of individual writers, and, on the other hand, the paucity of reasonably comprehensive historical accounts of the period as a whole. With the outstanding exception

– especially valuable on our period – of Henry W. Spiegel's *The Development of Economic Thought*, many, or most, one-volume histories of economic thought start by giving the impression that the author is eager to hurry on to the physiocrats, and/or Adam Smith and the English classicals. For, as Mark Blaug puts it, in the first chapter – entitled 'Pre-Adamite Economics' – of his masterly work: 'There is great convenience' – which there certainly can be – 'in looking comprehensively at the predecessors of Adam Smith much in the same way that he did' (1985, 10). The question is how far convenience may be purchased at the expense of adequacy, and how far Smith's methods of referring to contemporaries and predecessors are acceptable today.

It should go without saying that Schumpeter's chapters on our period are characterized by the illuminating profundity which distinguished all his writings (see 1954, part II, chapters 3–7, 143–376). But within this part of his great book, covering the years from about 1550 to 1790, chronological order goes largely by the board. In fact, in these chapters, the reverse of chronological order is much more evident than chronological order itself. For example, the main treatment of Adam Smith and *The Wealth of Nations* comes near the beginning of this part (181 ff.), while the discussion of the mercantilists, opening with Sir Thomas Gresham (1519–79), comes near the end (342 ff.).[6]

Of course, it would be almost impossible always to give absolute priority to chronological order, unless one were to content oneself with a *catalogue raisonée*, arranged strictly chronologically. Other principles of arrangement, in terms of particular branches, subjects, national groupings, or schools, must often be conceded an overriding claim, as well as, naturally, the bringing together of an individual's works. But in sacrificing chronological order, whatever the gains, or convenience, *something* of historical significance is lost, insofar as it becomes more difficult to follow the general development of the subject through time. Moreover, in this earlier period of economic thought, when specialization in particular branches of the subject was much less developed, there would seem to be less to gain from following out separate themes or sub-divisions, than when one is dealing with later periods, when specialization had developed further.

Indeed, it appears that in some recent treatments of the more intensely cultivated passages in the history of the subject – such as those of the English classicals, or of 'the Keynesian Revolution' – the chronological development of economics and economic literature becomes almost completely lost from view behind the dense undergrowth of often highly speculative, and sometimes tendentious, interpretations, re-interpretations, and misinterpretations, of what certain charismatic writers must have 'really meant'.[7] Of course, there is plenty of interpretation – and, perhaps, misinterpretation – in this volume: but our primary aim is to provide a useful chronological account rather than to argue for any particular (or general) interpretation.

V

The contrast just noted in the secondary literature between the considerable range of valuable editions, monographs, and partial studies, on the one hand, and the absence of more comprehensive accounts, on the other, may point to difficulties in composing a reasonably connected history of the economic thought of our period, difficulties which mostly do not exist, to quite the same extent, with regard to subsequent periods. The problem is one of composing, or stringing together, a connected historical account. Undoubtedly, between 1662 and 1776 there were writers on trade, commerce and political economy of the highest quality and interest. Petty, Locke, Boisguilbert, Mandeville, Cantillon, Galiani, Hume, Quesnay, Turgot, Steuart and Smith, together with many other distinguished writers such as Barbon, North, Becher, Law, E. L. Carl, Hutcheson, Montesquieu, Tucker, Beccaria, Verri and Condillac, constitute an array of talent which goes some way towards justifying the claim of Louis Salleron (see page v) that this was the most brilliant period in the history of the subject – just before it came fully into independent existence. There is, undeniably, a row of superb, scintillating beads. But there is a question about the supply of reliable thread for stringing them together as a necklace. Our first answer to this problem is, that even if there were a shortage of adequate thread for connecting together the works of such writers into a closely integrated historical account, it would surely be well worthwhile to discuss the writings of these great minds in a roughly chronological order.

Certainly in this period, especially in its earlier phases, down to about 1750, the transmission of ideas from one writer to another, whether between contemporaries, or from writers of an earlier generation to their successors, was much more intermittent and irregular. A great growth in the communication and transmission of economic ideas, especially from the late 1740s to the end of our period in 1776, is one of the important features of its history.

In the earlier phases, however, writers, or groups of writers, were generally thinking and writing more on their own, with not only a much smaller literature, past and present, to study, but also with less of the current literature easily available. Moreover, even when writers were certainly, or almost certainly, aware of some earlier or contemporary work, there was no regularly observed code of scholarly practice by which they felt obliged to mention their debts to predecessors. So the extent of the debts of one writer to another may often be extremely difficult – or impossible – to trace.

There was not, therefore, in the field of political economy, to the same extent as later, what might be described as a scholarly or scientific community, either within national or linguistic frontiers, or outside them. For political economy – as it was subsequently to be called – was still, at this time, as we have stressed, an inchoate, incompletely formed subject, conducted along at least two largely separate lines of enquiry, with little communication, or interpretation, between them. Especially in the first part of our period, from about 1660–1700, dominated by the advance in the subject led by Petty in England, though there seems to have been some acquaintance with the work of other leading writers in the field, most of whom were based on, or published in, London, there was very little awareness of works appearing in other countries. As the eighteenth century wore on, however, communication with, and knowledge of the work of, other writers, in the same country and to some extent in others, gradually increased. The great Cantillon showed the way, in his *Essay* (or *Essai*) by citing Petty and Locke. Then, in the third phase of our period, which opened in the late 1740s, and which we have called 'the mid-century efflorescence', communication and contacts grew enormously, especially across the Channel. Indeed, for some years in the late 1750s and 1760s an international flow of ideas and influences took place which was seldom, if ever, equalled in the following two centuries.

VI

Although in the literature of the seventeenth and early eighteenth centuries it is more difficult than with regard to later periods to trace threads and influences, it is still possible in some very important cases. Schumpeter put great emphasis, for example, on one vital thread, or sequence, running through our entire period: 'Few sequences in the history of economic analysis are so important for us to understand and to fix in our minds, as is the sequence Petty – Cantillon – Quesnay' (1954, 218). There could hardly be a more profound contrast, philosophically and methodologically, than that between Petty and Quesnay. There is certainly, however, an important line of development, regarding method and the theory of value from Petty to Cantillon, and, again, in Cantillon's *Essai*, there is a clear anticipation of the main physiocratic theories and doctrines of Quesnay. Following out this great sequence one could also trace out the main developments in the idea of the surplus.

A second fundamentally important line of thought, on a central question of theory, which runs through the seventeenth and eighteenth century, and which can be traced back to Aristotle and forward to Adam Smith and Léon Walras, is that of the natural-law analysis of value and price. In our period, Pufendorf, Hutcheson and Burlamaqui were among the most notable exponents of this body of doctrine. Smith inherited from Hutcheson this analysis, but in *The Wealth of Nations* mixed it with other ideas, while, on some points – for example, the nature of utility, and labour as a measure of value – he introduced a very different emphasis.

Another variant of the scholastic doctrines on value and price, which prevailed in Italy, and also with the school of Salamanca, put an even greater emphasis on subjective utility as a determinant of value. This line of thought, which was later to prove very fruitful, was followed by Davanzati (1529–1606) in his brilliant '*Discourse*' of 1588. In our period Montanari, Galiani, and later Turgot, further developed this analysis which subsequently emerged, in its full form, in the neo-classical theories after 1870.

So, continuing threads and themes are clearly discernible running through our period, though not always in the form of acknowledged influences. What can also be traced are the common interests, questions and responses to major persisting problems, of different writers of the same, or successive generations. *In fact, most of what were to become, and have so long remained, the central, perennial issues and questions of political economy, together with most of the persisting, conflicting viewpoints regarding these issues and questions, of method, theory and policy – (mostly still unsettled and often vigorously debated today) – can be found to have been broached in the writings of our period*: for example, conflicts over method, between more empirical and quantitative approaches, on the one side, as against more *a priorist*, geometric or deductivist postures, on the other; the conflict between explanations of value and price based on utility and demand, and explanations based on cost and labour; the perennially fluctuating argument between an exclusively, or predominantly, 'quantity' approach to the theory of money, as contrasted with opposing theories based rather on income and aggregate demand; the issues between monetary theories of the rate of interest and 'real' theories; the fundamental question as to whether the economic system, as a whole, should be regarded as ('macro-economically') self-adjusting, or not; and the many and various questions concerned with the nature and sources of economic progress.

Although these fundamental, perennial theoretical questions were plainly raised in our period, with cogent statements forthcoming from contrasting points of view, no consensus was reached, or even approached, regarding the answers. Certainly no orthodoxy was able to assert itself either in England or Europe. Almost at the end of our period the physiocratic school attempted to establish a kind of theoretical supremacy, but such orthodoxy as the physiocratic doctrines may have achieved was confined mainly to Paris and only lasted a few years. It was not until the classical period in England, in the early nineteenth century, that a claim to orthodoxy was more or less successfully established by the Mills, Ricardo and McCulloch, on behalf of a particular system of theory which was held to provide a fairly clear-cut set of answers to most, or all, of the general, fundamental methodological and theoretical issues listed above, – (though the dominance of this orthodoxy on some fundamental questions, such as value and price, was confined mainly to Britain). In our pre-classical period, on the other hand, methodologically and theoretically, pluralism ruled. In fact, it was largely in order to strengthen the influence of the new subject, with regard to policy, that some of the leading English classicals sought, and claimed to replace pluralism with an authoritative theoretical orthodoxy, buttressed by their own version of the history of the subject, according to which the works of almost all their predecessors had been based on profound errors.

Finally, regarding policy, the degree of 'mercantilist' consensus (if that is what it may be called) which may have prevailed earlier, began to dissolve as the eighteenth century wore on. The debate between the advocates of government regulation and the champions of free markets, took on a specially intense and politically vital form with regard to the market for grain, the subsistence foodstuff of the people. The conflict was particularly bitter in France in the late sixties, between the physiocrats and Galiani. Over the latter part of the eighteenth century, Galiani, Steuart and Bentham were on the side of government intervention, while the physiocrats, Pietro Verri and Adam Smith advocated freedom of the grain market, as of other markets.

VII

During our period, from 1662 to 1776, the leading role in the advance of what came to be called political economy, was taken by different countries at different times. As an inspection of our chronology indicates, the lead was, more than once, taken over quite suddenly by a particular country, only to be relinquished, just as abruptly, after a brief phase of pre-eminence. As already mentioned, our period as a whole seems to divide into four phases:

The first phase, of just about forty years, from 1662 until the opening years of the eighteenth century, was characterized predominantly by the notable English advance initiated by the work of Petty, who was followed by Locke, Barbon, North, King, Martyn, and a number of other important writers. But the English advance slowed down with remarkable suddenness, and, throughout almost the entire eighteenth century, England's role – as contrasted with those of Scotland, France and Italy – was very modest indeed.

In the second phase, from the opening years of the eighteenth century until the late 1740s, no one country moved markedly to the fore. Though Paris supplanted London as a main source of new ideas, important works were forthcoming from writers of several different nationalities: Boisguilbert, a Rouen magistrate; Dr Mandeville, a Dutch immigrant in London; together with such cosmopolitan figures as John Law, Ernst Ludwig Carl, Richard Cantillon and Daniel Bernoulli. The works of these writers were, on the whole, concerned rather more with fundamental ideas and theories, and less directly with immediate policy problems, than had been the case with the English writers in the latter part of the seventeenth century. The beginnings of a new systematization become discernible in the works of several writers at this time.

Then, again comparatively suddenly, in the later 1740s, a kind of great thirty-year boom opened, which lasted until the end of our period in 1776. Initially, for about a decade (1747–56), what may be called an international, mid-century efflorescence – our third phase – took place, with major works appearing in one country after another from Scotland to Italy. In the second half of the fifties, a fourth phase could be said to have begun with the publication in 1756 of the first economic article by Dr François Quesnay, at which point pre-eminence in the subject passed to France, where, for about fifteen years, political economy, and in particular the doctrines of Quesnay's physiocratic school dominated, to an extraordinary extent, the public mind. But, just as the English advance had slowed down so suddenly some seventy years earlier, so the decline and fall of the physiocratic school, and of French leadership in the subject, was as abrupt as its rise had been. At the end of our period, with the appearance of *The Wealth of Nations* ascendancy in the newly emerging subject passed, almost unquestionably, to Scotland, at least for the rest of the eighteenth century.

2
The Century before Petty: Some Outstanding Writings (*c.*1560–1660)

CHRONOLOGY

1526	Copernicus	*Monetae cudendae ratio*
c. 1544–*c.* 1556		The School of Salamanca
1576	Bodin	*Les six livres de la république*
1581	Smith	*A Discourse of the Commonwealth*
1588	Davanzati	*Discourse upon coins*
1588	Botero	*A Treatise concerning Cities*, etc.
1613	Serra	*A Brief Tract*, etc.
1615	Montchrétien	*Traité de l'économie politique*
1621	Culpeper	*A Tract against Usury*
1621	Mun	*A Discourse of Trade*, etc.
1622	Misselden	*Free Trade*, etc.
	Malynes	*The Maintenance of Free Trade*
1623	Misselden	*The Circle of Commerce or the Balance of Trade*
162?	Mun	*England's Treasure by Foreign Trade* (published 1664)
162?	Rice Vaughn	*A Discourse of Coin and Coinage* (published 1675)
1642	Hobbes	*De Cive*
1651	Hobbes	*Leviathan*

I

Before beginning the history of our period with Petty and his writings, let us try to obtain some impression of the state of the partially formed subject of 'trade' and political economy, at the time of our starting-point, by undertaking a rapid survey of some of the outstanding works of the preceding 100 years or so.

Some four more or less distinct streams of economic thought and literature may be discerned at this time. *First*, there were the writings of the later scholastics (notably the School of Salamanca), and of the natural-law philosophers, who analysed mainly what would today be called 'micro-economic' questions of value, price and interest, as a small sub-section of their comprehensive treatises of moral philosophy, which included ethics, law and politics. Different branches of the scholastic and natural-law philosophy put slightly different degrees of emphasis on the role of utility in determining value and price. In Holland, Hugo Grotius (1583–1645) expounded a rather different version of the natural-law doctrines on value and price from that of the Salamancans. *Second*, there were several notable writings, from different parts of Europe, concerned with the problem of the great rise in prices throughout the Continent, in the middle and later decades of the sixteenth century, following the influx of the precious metals. The central idea of the quantity theory of money was suggested by several writers. *Third*, there were some remarkable contributions, on different branches of the subject, from Italy, the leading country in the field at this stage. *Fourth*, and especially in England, there was, from the latter part of the sixteenth century, a growing literature, mostly in pamphlet form, focused on current controversial problems of economic policy. This stream, and also, to some extent the second and third, represented the emergence and growth of a separate treatment of economic questions outside the moral-philosophical framework to which such issues had been confined in the works of the scholastics and the natural-law philosophers.

Most writers in the scholastic tradition had put their primary emphasis, as regards the explanation of value and price, on utility and scarcity, though labour and cost (or difficulty) of production was also sometimes included in the analysis. In the middle of the sixteenth century the scholastic tradition had reached one of its peaks, in the treatment of economic questions, in the writings of the School of Salamanca. The Salamancan writers, as their historian has emphasized, put forward a 'markedly subjective theory of value' (Grice-Hutchinson, 1952, 48). One of its early representatives, Luis Saravia de la Calle, comprehensively rejected cost of production as a determinant of the just price:

> Those who measure the just price by the labour, costs, and risk incurred by the person who deals in the merchandise or produces it, or by the cost of transport or the expense of travelling to and from the fair, or by what he has to pay the factors for their industry, risk, and labour, are greatly in error, and still more so are those who allow a certain profit of a fifth or a tenth. For the just price arises from the abundance or scarcity of goods, merchants, and money, as has been said, and not from costs, labour and risk. If we had to consider labour and risk in order to assess the just price, no merchant would ever suffer loss.
>
> (1544, see Grice-Hutchinson, 1952, 81–2)

It is of some interest to find, at this comparatively early stage, such an emphasis on an *ex-ante* approach to the analysis of economic phenomena, which rejected the exclusion of errors and imperfect foresight and the kind of simplification which often came to be involved in cost-of-production theories of value and price, with their pseudo-objective *ex-post* approach.

Another leader of the Salamancan School, Diego de Covarrubias (1512–77), who was later quoted by two of the greatest Italian economists, Davanzati and Galiani, stressed the subjective element in value by maintaining that 'the value of an article does not depend on its essential nature but on the estimate of men, *even if that estimate be foolish*' (see Grice-Hutchinson, 1952, 48, italics added).

The emphasis, in the italicized clause, on the subjectivity of value, was often to be repeated by some of the most important writers in our period (though it was to be disregarded by Adam Smith at a crucial point in Book I, Chapter 4, of *The Wealth of Nations*).

Jumping ahead chronologically, we may mention here, as an important contribution from another branch of the scholastic tradition, the treatment of value and price by the great Dutch philosopher of natural law, Hugo Grotius (1583–1645), in his *De jure belli et pacis* (1625). Grotius restated the main scholastic doctrines and contributed a fundamentally important emphasis on the idea of natural laws in human affairs. Regarding value, he maintained that, 'the most natural measure of the value of each thing is the need of it, as Aristotle has rightly shown' (see translation by Kelsey, 1925, 351). But Providence has brought it about 'that the most necessary things are of less value because of their abundance' (351). Some cognisance was taken of the cost side when it was stated that, 'with respect to the current price, account is ordinarily taken of the labour and expenditure of the dealers' (352).

II

We come next to early ideas about the quantity of money and its value. Sometimes such ideas amounted to little more than an application to the case of money of the general theory or notion that an increasing abundance of a good led to a fall in its value, and scarcity to a rise. With the influx of precious metals into Spain in the second half of the sixteenth century, and their dispersion through Europe, the idea of the quantity theory of money followed this dispersal, from Spain to France and to England, to explain the rise in prices. There had, however, been one remarkable presentation of the idea of the quantity theory before the European price inflation began, that of the great Copernicus (1473–1543), who included among his encyclopaedic range of interests the subject of money and monetary reform. He began his report, *The Reason for Coining Money* (*Monetae cudendae ratio*, written in 1526, but not published until the nineteenth century), by maintaining that of the four evils or afflictions which destroy kingdoms and republics, i.e. strife, deadly plagues, barrenness of the soil, and the deterioration of money, the last was perhaps the most disastrous, going on to observe that 'money above all falls in value when it has been multiplied too abundantly' (Wolowski, 1864, 49 and 53).[1]

When the great rise in prices got under way, it seems to have been in Spain (as might have been expected) that the idea of the quantity theory first appeared. Martin de Azpilcueta Navarro (1493–1588) of the Salamancan School, in his *Comentario resolutorio de usuras* (1556), observed that 'money is worth more where and when it is scarce than where and when it is abundant' (Grice-Hutchinson, 1952, 95).

In France, the leading contributor to the theory of money in the sixteenth century was the political philosopher of absolutism, Jean Bodin (1530–96). His statement of the idea of the quantity theory of money came as a reply (1568) to a pamphlet (by de Malestroit) in which it was claimed that prices had not risen over the previous 300 years in terms of gold and silver, but simply in terms of the devalued currency units which, with successive debasements, contained less and less of the precious metals. Bodin included his reply in his major work *Les six livres de la république* (1576) in the latter part of which he discussed issues of public finance and money. Bodin attributed the rise in prices to a number of causes, but maintained: 'The principal reason which raises the price of everything, wherever one may be, is the abundance of that which governs the appraisal and price of things ... It is therefore necessary to demonstrate that there was not as much gold and silver in this Kingdom three hundred years ago ... as there is now: which is evident at a glance' (Monroe, 1924, 127–8).

It depends on one's conception, or definition, of a 'theory' whether Bodin's statement – and those of Copernicus and Navarro – amounted to a formulation of the quantity theory of money. But certainly the germ of the idea was there that a close relationship existed between the quantity of money and its value.

One other French contribution from this period deserves notice. This was a book of little merit apart from its title, which first introduced a term which had a great future: the *Traité de l'économie politique* (1615) by Antoine de Montchrétien (1575–1621).

III

A third stream of economic thought and literature at this time came from Italy, the leading country in the sixteenth century in the advance of our subject (as of so many others). Here the influence was still strong of that branch of the scholastic philosophy which emphasized especially strongly the role of subjective utility in value and price, as in Bernardo Davanzati's outstanding *Discourse upon Coins* (1588). Davanzati was a distinguished classical scholar and historian. His brief lecture started with a brilliantly clear statement of the fundamental nature of an economy as rooted in mutuality, specialization and exchange. Individuals cannot exist by themselves. Everybody needs things,

> . . . which no body can procure by himself alone; and this is the reason why we live together in cities, to help one another . . . no person is born fit for all sorts of business, some have a genius for one thing, and some for another; nor can any climate currently produce all the fruits of the earth . . . Hence it is that one man labours and toils not for himself alone, but also for others, and they reciprocally for him. So one city helps another, and one country parts with its superfluities to another, in *lieu* whereof it is from thence again supplied with what it wants.
>
> (English translation by John Toland, 1696, 9)

Davanzati recognized that inevitably knowledge was scarce: 'Now it was difficult to know who stood in need of what you could spare' (9). To meet this need for communication and commercial knowledge, markets, and then money ('the medium and fountain of the universal value of things') came into existence (10). Davanzati combined a 'metallist' with a 'consensus' view of money, which he described as 'gold, silver, or copper coined by public authority at pleasure, and by the consent of nations made the price and measure of things, to contract them more easily' (12).

Turning to the subject of value and price, Davanzati described the role of scarcity, and emphasized the particular circumstances of the individual in forming his preferences. He used an example – subsequently quoted and unfairly criticized by Galiani – of a man starving in prison, who would, if he could, exchange all the gold he could lay hands on for a single egg: 'A natural calf is far more noble than a golden one, yet how much inferior in price? An egg that was bought for half a grain of gold, kept Count Ugolino alive in the castle for ten days, which all the treasure in the universe could not do' (14). On the other hand, water could not usually command a price because, though 'we could not well live without it, . . . everyone may have enough of it for nothing' (16).

Davanzati's lecture was an outstanding achievement as a presentation of fundamental economic ideas, and was clearly influenced by the Italian scholastic tradition. His analysis of value, price and money was later built on by Montanari and Galiani, and has been described as 'initiating, some would say, modern economics' (Langholm, 1979, 143). It was unfortunate that the English translation of his *Discourse* apparently exercised no influence.

Another important Italian work on a very different theme, published in the same year as Davanzati's *Discourse*, was the *Treatise Concerning the Causes of the Magnificence and Greatness of Cities* (1588) by Giovanni Botero (1544–1617), which put forward important views on the subject of population. From the sixteenth to the eighteenth century, overwhelmingly the majority view, in all the leading countries regarding population growth, might be summarized as the more the better, both politically and economically. A growing population was regarded as both the aim of governments and a criterion of the success of their policies. Sometimes the tendency was noted of population to expand up to the limits of subsistence, but no harsh or pessimistic conclusions were drawn. Botero's, therefore, was a lone voice on this subject, 'the first to sound that note of pessimism' (as Schumpeter put it, 1954, 255), which, over 100 years later was to be struck so resonantly by Malthus in the first edition of his *Essay*.

Botero contrasted what he called 'the virtue generative of men' with 'the virtue nutritive of cities' (translation by R. Peterson, in D. Waley (ed.), 1956, 276). It was maintained that 'the virtue generative' had long been constant: 'So that if there were no other impediment or let therein, the propagation of mankind would increase without end, and the augmentation of cities would be without term. And if it do not increase in infinite, I must needs say it proceedeth of the defects of nutriment and sustenance sufficient for it' (276).

It was this pressure of the constant 'virtue generative' on the limited 'virtue nutritive' which led to expansionist war-making, and, on a smaller scale to theft and murder, on top of which disease, plagues, earthquakes and floods were 'the let and stay that the number of men cannot increase and grow immoderately' (279).

Actually, Botero went too far in maintaining that world population had remained largely unchanged for 3000 years. But there is a close similarity with the doctrines of Malthus' first *Essay*, which were to become so highly influential. Botero's deductive, *a priorist* method also resembled the procedure of Malthus in his *Essay* of 1798.

A third highly important Italian work, which somewhat resembled a mercantilist pamphlet, was Antonio Serra's *A Brief Treatise on the Causes which can make Gold and Silver Plentiful in Kingdoms where there are No Mines* (1613). Little seems to be known about Serra, not even the dates of his birth and death, except that he spent some time in prison in Naples. The title of his pamphlet encapsulated the prime concern of 'mercantilist' writers, but his work contained some important theoretical advances. Serra devoted no time to asking *why* it was desirable for a kingdom to have a plentiful supply of gold and silver. Like many or most writers of the period, he assumed from the start the serious damage to an economy which could be inflicted by an inadequate supply of money or of the precious metals. He concentrated rather on how a sufficient supply was to be achieved. His answer was essentially in terms of 'real' productive resources. A kingdom would ultimately come to possess ample supplies of gold and silver if it had a diligent and ingenious labour force and developed its industries. It was to industry rather than agriculture that one should look for the export surplus which would bring in a supply of the precious metals. For industry was subject to less uncertainty than agriculture, and, furthermore, in industry, 'there can be extension and thus the profit can be increased, which is not possible in the case of [agricultural] produce, this not being subject to increase' (translation in Monroe, 1924, 147). Someone with a piece of land on which only 100 bushels of wheat could be grown, would be unable to expand production to 150 bushels. But, as regards industries, 'it is just the other way, since they may be multiplied not only two-fold but two hundred-fold, and with proportionately less expense' (147). Serra seems here to be suggesting the important idea that, as contrasted with agriculture, increasing returns could be expected in industry.

Serra also contributed notably towards clarifying the concept of the balance of trade, and he included 'invisible' items in the balance. Though he suggested that wise policies could help bring in a plentiful inflow of gold and silver, Serra was opposed to prohibitions on the export of money. People would only export money if they expected a profit. If the gold exported was used to buy commodities abroad, these commodities would be paid for by people who wanted or needed them. Interesting similarities may be noted with the arguments, about ten years later, of Thomas Mun of the East India Company, who also opposed prohibitions on the export of specie. On some important points, Serra seems the more perceptive writer.

IV

Most of the more important English writings at this time (*c.* 1560–1660) belong with the literature of policy pamphlets, or tracts for the times about current economic problems. In this class may be counted *A Discourse of the Commonweal of this Realm of England; or A Compendious or Brief Examination of Certain Ordinary Complaints*, published by 'W.S.' (William Smith) in 1581, having first been written (as now seems established) by the publisher's father, Sir Thomas Smith in 1549.[2] The work consists of three dialogues between five representatives of different ranks and occupations, led by a doctor and a knight.

The *Discourse* was devoted to the great economic problem of the day, the severe rise in prices, or 'price revolution', and to the distress and injustices which had resulted. Various causes were put forward for the inflation, including debasement of the coinage. The *Discourse*, however, first broached in English the basic idea of a quantity theory of money in order to explain, or partially explain, the severe rise in prices, especially from about 1540 to 1560. Among a number of reasons for the rise was included: 'The great store and plenty of treasure which is walking in these parts of the world, far more in these our days than ever our forefathers have seen in time past' (Dewar, 1969, 145).

On foreign trade, the *Discourse* took a conventionally mercantilist line to the effect that 'we must always take heed that we buy no more of strangers than we do sell them'. But a notable emphasis was placed on the power, and also on the potential beneficence, of the individual profit motive. 'Every man', it was maintained, 'will seek where most advantage is' (54). So the wise policy for government was generally to let this powerful force have its head, and to guide it 'by allurement and reward', rather than to try to regulate it by laws and prohibitions. For, 'that thing which is profitable to each man by himself, so it be not prejudicial to any other, is profitable to the whole Commonweal' (52). Moreover, it was 'hard to make a law', with regard to trade, with 'so many as profit by that matter resisting it' (51).

This *Discourse* constituted a notable example of how economic problems were gradually coming to be discussed in detachment from the philosophical and moral framework in which they had long been confined as a small, minor compartment. Here was an early indication that an important independent subject might, eventually, emerge. In the next century, this development was, of course, to be taken much further, in the first instance in the controversies of the 1620s.[3]

V

In 1620 the English economy was suffering from a serious crisis. A heavy fall in exports had been followed by an outflow of money and precious metals, and a severe economic depression ensued. There was a notable and virtually unprecedented outburst of public controversy regarding causes and remedies, the first significant, modern occasion when a problem of current economic policy had produced a debate of tracts or pamphlets.[4]

The three major protagonists were Gerard de Malynes, Edward Misselden and Thomas Mun (1571–1641; the vital dates of Malynes and Misselden are not known). All three agreed that the outflow of gold and silver, with the consequent contraction of the money supply, was the prime cause or substance of the crisis, or, as Malynes put it: 'The want of money . . . is the first cause of the decay of trade, for without money commodities are out of request' (1622, 37). It was also broadly agreed that the outflow of specie followed from the excess of imports over exports. But there was sharp disagreement as to how and why this imbalance had come about and as to the remedies that should be sought.

In subsequent centuries, Malynes might have been regarded as something of a crank. Over nearly a quarter of a century he had repeated his diagnosis, and favourite remedial policy, in a series of writings which suggested that England was being exploited by foreign financiers. A writer, however, can hardly be dismissed as a crank when no coherent orthodoxy exists. Malynes maintained that the trade deficit was due to the undervaluation of English money on the exchanges, which were being manipulated by foreign operators. Here was what Malynes described as 'the Canker of England's Commonwealth', bringing it about that the English were receiving too little for their exports and paying too much for their imports. If the exchange rate was fixed at its 'true par', receipts for exports would increase and payments for imports would decrease, thus restoring the balance of trade and halting the outflow of the precious metals and the contraction of the money supply. The government should therefore pass a law prohibiting the exchange of English money 'under the true par', thus 'keeping the price of exchange at a certainty' (1603, 101). Malynes apparently assumed that the demand for English exports and the supply of imports were appropriately inelastic.

In 1622, in the midst of the depression, Edward Misselden published his first, rather verbose and polemical pamphlet, *Free Trade, or the Means to Make Trade Flourish* (1622). Agreeing with Malynes as to the shortage of money, and maintaining that 'money is the vital spirit of trade' (1622, 28), Misselden also emphasized the deflationary role of the trade deficit.

He first attacked the export of bullion by the East India Company – a charge which he was to withdraw the following year. Misselden proposed to combat the depression by an expansion of the money supply, to be brought about by 'raising the coin', or depreciation, which would raise prices:

> . . . that which is equal to all, when he that buys dear shall sell dear, cannot be said to be injurious to any. And it is much better for the kingdom to have things dear, with plenty of money, whereby men may live in their several callings: than to have things cheap with want of money, which now makes every man complain.
>
> (1622, 107)

Also, as regards high interest rates, Misselden maintained that 'the remedy for usury may be plenty of money' (116). By 'free trade' he meant little more than the breaking down of monopolies.

Misselden's attack on Malynes brought a prompt reply (Malynes, 1622), which Misselden countered with *The Circle of Commerce or the Balance of Trade* (1623). This time the East India trade was defended by Misselden on the grounds that what was purchased from the Indies was, in large measure, re-exported at a considerable profit. Misselden went on to denounce the proposal of Malynes for government regulation of the exchange rate, proclaiming:

> . . . trade hath in it such a kind of natural liberty in the course and use thereof as it will not induce to be forced by any. If you attempt it, it is a thousand to one that you leave it worse than you found it . . . Natural liberty is such a thing . . . as will not endure the command of any, but God alone.
>
> (1623, 112)

Misselden's pamphlet of 1623 is notable for the first use of the phrase 'the balance of trade'. His writings helped to publicize the idea, which he compared with a pair of scales, describing the concept as: 'an excellent and politic invention to show us the difference of weight in the commerce of the kingdom with another: that is, whether the native commodities exported, and all the foreign commodities imported, do balance or overbalance one another in the sales of commerce' (1623, 116).

Thomas Mun had traded for some time in Italy (where he may perhaps have read Serra's work). Later he became a director of the East India Company and in his first pamphlet (1621) was specially concerned to defend its interests, maintaining that the re-export, at a large profit, of most of the Indian goods purchased, immensely benefited England's trade balance. He did, however, emphasize the 'real' forces which would strengthen England's position in foreign trade: 'Industry to increase and frugality to maintain are the true watch words of a kingdom's treasury' (1621, 2).

Mun's general case was expounded in his celebrated pamphlet *England's Treasure by Foreign Trade*, the classic statement of English mercantilism, which was written in the middle or late twenties, but not published until 1664. Mun started from the principle: 'The ordinary means to increase our wealth and treasure is by foreign trade, wherein we must ever observe this rule; to sell more to strangers yearly than we consume of theirs in value' (1664, 5). International economic relations were envisaged as a strictly zero-sum game. Mun went on to set out twelve policy maxims which included the reduction of imports; the development of resources so as to expand exports; the development of shipping and foreign trade; and no probitions on the export of money and specie. He explicitly rejected the policy, advocated by Malynes, of alterations in the foreign exchange rate, which could not be effective since it was 'plenty or scarcity' which determined exchange rates. Mun recognized, to some extent, the effects of price changes on exports and imports, without, however, discerning in, or ascribing to, such effects any corrective influence on the balance of trade.

Another remedy for the crisis of the early 1620s was put forward by Sir Thomas Culpeper (senior) in *A Tract against Usury* (1621). This pamphlet went through several editions in the ensuing decades, including one produced by his son (also Sir Thomas), who weighed in on the same theme *A Discourse, showing the many advantages which will accrue to this kingdom by the abatement of Usury (1668)*. The Culpepers were concerned with a question which became one of the main issues of policy and theory in the latter part of the century, especially after the subject had been taken up by the influential Sir Josiah Child (in pamphlets of 1668 and 1693, see chapter 5).

'The high rate of usury decays trade', complained Culpeper senior at the start of his *Discourse*. He sought to support his case by introducing another frequent theme in English economic debates, through much of the seventeenth century: that of the economic success of the Dutch and the reasons for it. As Josiah Child was to do, Culpeper ascribed the prosperity of 'our industrious neighbours the Dutch' not to their industry but to the low interest rates they enjoyed, thanks to government measures reinforced by the people's frugality. Culpeper wanted English interest rates to be restrained by law to the levels prevailing in Holland.[5]

The writers of the 1620s were mainly and primarily practical businessmen, concerned with mainly short-term remedies for current difficulties, rather than with theoretical explanations. But it is unjust to maintain that they were ignorant of the main characteristics of the problems they faced. Some of the concepts and ideas which they developed in embryo form were to prove fruitful when applied with more intellectual discipline than these writers, at this stage, were ready to bring to bear. By the time, however, of the next major crisis in English economic and financial policy, some seventy years later in the 1690s, something of an intellectual transformation had taken place. The writings of Petty, Locke, Barbon, North and King were on a different, more disciplined, intellectual level compared with those of Malynes, Misselden, Culpeper and Mun.

VI

Finally a brief mention should be made of Thomas Hobbes, whom William Petty for some time served as secretary. In his works on political philosophy Hobbes broached, in passing, some fundamental ideas which were subsequently to wield a profound influence in English political economy, and perhaps most importantly on Adam Smith. Indeed, if one were to attempt to summarize *The Wealth of Nations* in thirteen words the following sentence of Hobbes would probably perform such a feat better than any other: 'There are two things necessary for the enriching of subjects, labour and thrift' (1642, 164). Certainly Hobbes then went on to mention a third productive factor 'which helps', that is, 'the natural increase of the earth and water'. His account, indeed, of the two basic productive factors of labour and nature strongly suggested that put forward by Petty eleven years later: 'As for the plenty of matter, it is a thing limited by nature, to those commodities, which from (the two breasts of our common mother) land and sea, God usually either freely giveth, or for labour selleth to mankind' (1651, 130).

Hobbes's emphasis on the original factors of labour and nature in the production of wealth was developed by Petty in his cost-of-production approach to value. A somewhat similar approach was to be followed by Locke, in his *Second Essay of Civil Government* (1690) in formulating his labour theory of property and in his treatment of the relationship between labour and value.

The Hobbesian view of man as motivated above all by individual self-interest posed the basic political problem, which, he maintained, could only be solved by an all-powerful state. Subsequently, as we shall see, Nicole, Domat, and Boisguilbert in France, and the Dutchman Mandeville in England – though, all of them, no less convinced than Hobbes of the aggressive selfishness of human beings – showed how, through competitive markets, dangerous and 'vicious' self-interest could be tamed and canalized towards the public good.[6]

PART II

Advance in England (1662–*c.*1700)

3
Petty on Policy, Theory and Method

I

William Petty came of a humble family engaged in the clothing trade in the small town of Romsey, Hampshire.[1] He was a youth of wide-ranging curiosity and prodigious abilities: literary, scientific, and practical. Romsey was soon much too small to hold him, and, aged thirteen, he went to sea as a cabin-boy in a coastal vessel, apparently making some money on the side by hawking cheap jewellery. Having been put ashore on the coast of Normandy with a broken leg, he applied, in Latin, for a place at the Jesuit College in Caen, where, in the ensuing years, he acquired a rigorous education in Latin, Greek, French, mathematics and astronomy. Leaving Caen in 1640, he seems to have spent some three years in the Royal Navy. In 1643 he departed for Holland to study medicine, anxious, presumably, to keep clear of involvement in the Civil War at home. In the Netherlands he would have gained not only a grounding in medicine, but also a first-hand acquaintance with the impressive achievements of the Dutch economy. He moved on to Paris, where, for a year or so, in 1645–6, he acted as secretary to Thomas Hobbes, by whose theory of knowledge and political philosophy he was deeply influenced.

After a brief sojourn back in Romsey, busy with the invention of a machine for double writing which he patented in 1647, Petty proceeded to Oxford to complete his medical studies. His progress there was phenomenal. By 1650 (*aet.* twenty-seven) he was Professor of Medicine and Vice-Principal of Brasenose College, with the reputation of having supposedly raised from the dead a woman who had been hanged for child murder. At Oxford he became acquainted with a circle of scientists, including Samuel Hartlib and Robert Boyle, whose leaders a decade later, were to form the Royal Society. In 1651 Petty acquired a new title, Professor of 'Music' – in just what sense remains unclear – at Gresham's College, London, where he met John Graunt, his fellow pioneer of population statistics.

Thus, fifteen years after having been dumped ashore as a broken-legged, small-town cabin-boy, Petty had risen to the top of the university world. But his ambitions for power and money were far from satisfied. Instead of settling down to an academic career, he headed adventurously westward as chief physician of the army in Ireland, where, over the next six or seven years, he acquired a fortune in land of millionaire proportions. Much of the land of Ireland was lying unoccupied, or depopulated by the butcheries of Cromwell's army, and was thus 'up for grabs' – the slang is not inappropriate. Much had been promised to the soldiers, but before any distribution could be undertaken, a vast survey was necessary. In 1654 Petty put himself forward for the job of surveyor, and accomplished his tremendous task with extraordinary promptness and efficiency. As Strauss puts it:

> The organisation of the Down Survey was on any account a remarkable feat of foresight, administrative ability and penetrating common sense; it was particularly striking for a man of thirty-one with Petty's background and interests, who embarked on this scheme in opposition to the express opinion of practically all the experts, and who had bound himself to perform the task within a period which the experts regarded as grossly insufficient and in a country where the ordinary machinery of government had completely broken down. Only a man of boundless self-confidence could have undertaken such a project, only a man of infinite resource could have designed the bold plan of campaign and improvised the great organisation which it required, and only an administrator of genius could have ensured its practical execution within the stipulated period. The maps of the Down Survey prove that Petty possessed this combination of rare qualities on a very high level.
>
> (1954, 65)

Petty proceeded to use the money he had earned and the special knowledge he had gained to acquire for himself a huge fortune in land, and to become one of the greatest land magnates in Ireland.

By the end of the fifties Petty was back in London, serving briefly as a member of Parliament, and re-establishing contacts with his scientific friends and acquaintances in London and Oxford. It was at this time that Petty and his colleagues were forming the Royal Society of London for the Improving of Natural Knowledge, of which he was one of the original charter members on its incorporation in 1662. The programme of the Society, inspired by the ideas on scientific method of Francis Bacon, was to apply the empirical processes of observation and experiment, in the first instance to the study of the natural world and technology, and then to the study of society, which was Petty's own main interest. Throughout his life he remained a very active member of the Royal Society, contributing especially to its studies of the history of trades and technology. He completely agreed with the emphatically practical bent in the Society's programme. Petty saw his own work in 'political arithmetic', or economic and social statistics, as an application of the empirical research programme of the Society to the human and social world.

Petty seems to have learnt little or nothing from previous or contemporary economic writings. His own first major publication was on economics, in the same year as the incorporation of the Royal Society. This was his

Treatise of Taxes and Contributions (1662), a survey of current problems in public finance, which, however, ranged widely over fundamental questions of economic theory and policy. He subsequently expressed dissatisfaction with this work, presumably because it did not bring him the influence and office he wanted, though the monarch had recently bestowed a knighthood on him. Anyhow, the *Treatise* remains his most important work and deserves to be regarded as a major achievement and landmark in the history of economic thought. A number of editions of the *Treatise* appeared in Petty's lifetime (in 1662, 1667, 1679 and 1685).

Petty produced many more essays and pamphlets, though a number thereof appeared only posthumously, for he wrote, mostly, not for publication but for circulation in the corridors of power or with a view to acquiring influence and jobs – which he never managed to obtain. Apart from his writing, much of his time was spent in journeys to, and sojournings in Ireland, in endless litigation in defence of his properties, and in furthering his inventions, notably that of a double-bottomed boat. Somewhat late in life, in 1667, he married, and, through his daughter, became the founder of the later politically celebrated Shelburne and Lansdowne family. So, though Karl Marx's claim that he was the founder of political economy may be questionable, Petty was certainly one of the founders both of the Royal Society, and of an important political dynasty.

Petty's main economic writings fall into three chronological groups (see Hull, 1900, 311ff.). *First*, there were his two works of the early 1660s, the *Treatise* and the brief *Verbum Sapienti* (written 1665, published 1691). *Second*, in the early 1670s, he produced two statistical studies, *The Political Anatomy of Ireland* (written 1671–2, published 1690), and his *Political Arithmetic* (written 1672–6, published 1690) which was concerned with the economic strength of England relative to that of her main rivals, France and Holland. Then, *third*, there were several works on population, including further *Essays in Political Arithmetic*, in which, among other themes, Petty sought to follow up the *Observations on the Bills of Mortality* (1662) of his friend John Graunt. These works date from the eighties, as does his pamphlet *Quantulumcunque concerning Money* (written 1682, published 1695). All his writings are so packed with ideas which so tumble over one another in constant digressions and asides that the task of giving an account of them is considerably complicated.

In the history of economic thought Petty is probably most widely known as an advocate and exponent of the empirical, quantitative method, or of 'political arithmetic'. But the lasting influence of his *Treatise* was almost as great through its challenging pronouncements on fundamental questions of economic theory, notably on the subjects of value, price and money. Certainly the *Treatise* also contained frequent and bold attempts at rough quantification. But it is the stimulating methodological and theoretical ideas which stand out in this work, though these, like the quantitative estimates, were introduced primarily instrumentally, in order to provide a firmer basis for policy conclusions. In all his writings, Petty's overriding purpose, no less than was the case with his mercantilist predecessors and contemporaries, was centred on justifying his policy proposals. What constituted the vital new departure in Petty's work and achievement was the introduction of a general theoretical and scientific foundation for sounder policy-making, together with the endeavour to estimate quantitatively the elements involved.

Let us now survey briefly Petty's main ideas and doctrines under the headings of policy, theory and method, and then return to the main conclusions of his essays in political arithmetic.

II

In his *Treatise of Taxes and Contributions* Petty was concerned with laying down the principles of public finance for the recently restored monarchy. He urged that 'when there is opportunity', governments should 'pass into positive law whatsoever is right reason and the law of nature' (Hull, 1899, 9). He started by examining the main heads of public expenditure, or 'the several sorts of public charges', turning subsequently to the principal types of taxation. The first charge on a state was 'that of its defence by land and sea of its peace at home and abroad'. Next came 'the maintenance of the governors, chief and subordinate' (18). A rather grudging and pragmatic acknowledgement was included of the need to provide for the established church, as a kind of adjunct of law and order, or for 'the pastorage of men's souls and the guidance of their consciences' (19). Then came education and provision for schools and universities, though Petty was doubtful about religious instruction, remarking 'whether divinity etc. ought to be made a private trade, is to me a question' (19). He acknowledged that schools and colleges were mostly privately funded, but claimed that this biased their selection of pupils, which should be on merit, and not 'according to the fond conceits of their own parents and friends'. The overriding aim should be rather: 'to furnish all imaginable helps unto the highest and finest natural wits, towards the discovery of nature in all its operations' (20).

The next branch of expenditure was that devoted to the maintenance of the destitute: orphans, foundlings, 'impotents of all sorts', and 'such as want employment'. Under this last heading Petty had much of economic significance to say. Hard-headedly, he explained that to permit begging was more wasteful than government provision for those 'whom the law of nature will not suffer to starve, where food may possibly be had'. It was, moreover, unjust to let those starve whose wages had been controlled, 'so that they can lay up nothing against the time of their impotency and want of work' (20). The last item for government expenditure was that of public works, including highways, bridges, harbours, etc., 'and other things of universal good and concernment' (20).

Such, according to Petty, should be the main headings for public expenditure: defence, law and order, government, the religious establishment, education, provision for the destitute and unemployed; and public works. This list did not differ, very importantly, from that drawn up 114 years later, in *The Wealth of Nations*, except for the inclusion of provision for the destitute, and for 'such as want employment', as an explicit, major commitment. Here lay the crucial distinction regarding the *internal* economic duties of government – as distinct from the regulation of *external* economic relations – between Petty, the 'mercantilist' liberal, and Smith, the 'classical' liberal. For Petty, unlike Smith, did not hold that the economy adjusted, of itself, or could fairly easily be made to adjust, to a high level of employment, or that involuntary unemployment was never a serious problem. Moreover, as we shall observe, Petty was more of a *dirigiste* regarding the manpower and recruitment of the leading professions, which he was certainly not willing to leave entirely to market forces.

The *Treatise* went on to consider why this list of items for government expenditure was absorbing a heavier burden of taxation than was necessary. First, the difficulties of collection were aggravated by the inconvenient times at which taxes were demanded, and by the scarcity of money or coins. The military budget was inflated by the pretence that England needed more territory, a view denounced by Petty as totally erroneous. He denied that 'our country is full peopled, or that if we wanted more territory, we could take it with less charge from our neighbours, than purchase it from the Americans' (21–2).

Provision against internal disturbances and the danger of civil war could be improved by reducing the concentration of wealth in too few hands, and by preventing, for all the population, the 'necessity either to beg, or steal, or be soldiers' (23). Turning to the charge for the religious establishment, Petty's main recommendation was fewer and larger parishes. He saw even more scope for reductions in the legal establishment than in the church. He estimated that the amount of litigation could have been reduced to one-tenth of its then level if land registers and banks of deposit had been set up, as in Holland. As regards physicians, Petty maintained that it was 'not hard ... to calculate how many physicians were requisite for the whole nation, and consequently, how many students in that art to permit and encourage' (27). A rather rough-and-ready estimate of the number of sick in London could be derived from the number of deaths as given by the bills of mortality – recently examined by his friend Graunt. With such sweeping reductions in the numbers of lawyers and divines, and probably also of physicians, there could be considerable retrenchment in the universities.

Petty then turned to his most important and interesting heading – one very little mentioned in *The Wealth of Nations* – that is, the care of the poor and unemployed. In another somewhat cavalier calculation he suggested that there was a considerable permanent percentage of mainly involuntarily unemployed, who should be put to work:

> When all helpless and impotent persons were ... provided for, and the lazy and thievish restrained and punished by the Minister of Justice, it follows now that we find certain constant employments for all other indigent people ...
>
> ... In the next place it will be asked, who shall pay these men? I answer everybody; for if there be 100 men in a territory, and if 1000 of these can

> raise necessary food and raiment for the whole 1000; if 200 more make as much commodities as other nations will give either their commodities or money for, and if 400 more be employed in the ornaments, pleasure, and magnificence of the whole; if there be 200 governors, divines, lawyers, physicians, merchants, and retailers making in all 900, the question is, since there is food enough for this supernumerary 100, also how they should come by it?
>
> (29–30)

Petty mentioned public works such as road-building and afforestation, as well as mining, quarrying and iron manufacture, and he proposed investment in new trades to replace cloth-making, 'which we have almost totally lost' (30). He ruled out starvation and begging, and, emphasizing how lengthy idleness may indispose people to labour, he concluded: 'Now as to the work of these supernumeraries, let it be without expense of foreign commodities, and then 'tis no matter if it be employed to build a useless pyramid upon Salisbury Plain, bring the stones at Stonehenge to Tower Hill, or the like' (31). It is clear that Petty entertained no idea of a self-adjusting mechanism bringing about a full, or high, level of employment.

Petty next considered the question of the burden of taxation, claiming that unnecessary impositions were often levied because of quantitative ignorance regarding budgetary estimates of expenditure, and of receipts from taxation. If a rule of proportionality was observed, the burdens would hardly be felt, because of the relativity of wealth: 'Let the tax be never so great, if it be proportionable unto all, then no man suffers the loss of any riches by it. For men . . . if the estates of them all were halved or doubled, would in both cases remain equally rich' (32).

Petty remarked here, incidentally, on the benefits of a larger population, arising from economies of scale in respect of government and administration: 'Fewness of people is real poverty; and a nation wherein are eight millions of people are more than twice as rich as the same scope of land wherein are but four. For the same governors, which are the great charge, may serve near as well for the greater as the lesser number' (34).

He proceeded to reject complaints against luxury expenditure by the state, which, he claimed, reduced unemployment. In fact, government expenditure, and fiscal policy, had a major part to play with regard to the money supply. If the money supply was excessive, a budget surplus, or government hoarding, would be in order; but if, on the other hand, the money supply were insufficient, then, excess taxation, or a budget surplus, would 'leave less money than is necessary to drive the nation's trade; then the mischief thereof would be the doing of less work' (36).

Petty then began a review of the different kinds of taxes, beginning with those on land, rents and houses. He thought that the last of these had been overtaxed in order to discourage building. This was an erroneous policy. In particular, the expansion of London westward should have been encouraged, as should the growth of cities generally. For Petty maintained that there were increasing returns to population density.

On the subject of customs and excise duties, Petty suggested that these had originated, or first been justified, as a charge 'for protecting the carriage of goods both inward and outward from the pirates' (54). He then put forward the usual mercantilist proposals for import duties: *first*, goods for final consumption should be made dearer than the same things produced at home; *second*, all luxuries should be heavily taxed, though not so heavily as to encourage smuggling; and *third*, raw materials and semi-manufactured goods 'ought to be gently dealt with' (56). But Petty opposed too much intervention to exclude goods from abroad. The main aim should be to keep down the cost of food and so improve the country's competitive power. It was better

> ... to take away burdensome, frivolous and antiquated impositions and offices.
>
> I conceive even this were better than to persuade water to rise of iteslf above its natural spring.
>
> We must consider in general, that as wiser physicians tamper not excessively with their patients, rather observing and complying with the motions of nature, than contradicting it with vehement administrations of their own, so in politics and economics the same must be used.
>
> (60)

The exclusion of imports was unnecessary 'until they much exceeded our exportations' (60). In fact exports might suffer from shutting out foreign imports. It was much better to admit the import of 'debauching wines' in return for our cloth, than to cease making the cloth. It was 'better to burn a thousand men's labours for a time, than to let those thousand men by non-employment lose their faculty of labouring' (60).

As regards poll taxes, Petty condemned them as regressive, while he dismissed lotteries as 'a tax upon unfortunate self-conceited fools' (64). After a rapid but detailed survey of many different kinds of taxes and impositions, Petty discussed the 'raising' of the coinage, by making more coins out of the same quantity of gold or silver; or by 'debasing', by mixing copper or silver with gold, or copper with silver, thus, in either case, trying 'to make it pass for more than it did before' (84). Petty maintained that such depreciations of the coinage were 'a very pitiful and unequal way of taxing the people', a 'breach of public faith', and a 'burden upon all that live on pensions, established rents, annuities, fees, gratuities, etc.' (84).

Finally, Petty laid it down that 'men should contribute to the public charge but according to the share and interest they have in the public peace; that is, according to their estates or riches' (91). He favoured, apparently, a proportional tax on consumption expenditure as best satisfying this principle, since 'every man ought to contribute according to what he taketh to himself and actually enjoyeth' (91). This implied a tax, or excise, on final consumption goods, which might be difficult to administer for some goods, so that 'we ought to enumerate a catalogue of commodities both native and artificial, such whereof accounts may be most easily taken ...' (91).

III

It was when he came to the subjects of rent and the valuation of property for tax purposes, that Petty became involved with fundamental analytical and theoretical questions. Regarding the concept of rent, he was a pioneer in treating it as a surplus:

> Suppose a man could with his own hands plant a certain scope of land with corn . . . I say that when this man hath subducted his seed out of the proceeds of his harvest, and also what himself hath both eaten and given to others in exchange for clothes and other natural necessaries, that the remainder of the corn is the natural and true rent of the land for that year.
>
> (43)

Next the question arose as to 'how much English money' this corn or rent is worth? Petty's answer again anticipated the classical idea that value was in accordance with labour embodied. In terms of money this corn surplus, or rent, would be equal to the amount of silver which could be produced by the same quantity of labour, allowing for costs of subsistence and transport. That is, the rent or corn surplus was worth:

> so much as the money, which another single man can save, within the same time, over and above his expense, if he employed himself wholly to produce and make it . . . I say, the silver of the one, must be esteemed of equal value with the corn of the other; the one being perhaps twenty ounces and the other twenty bushels.
>
> (43)

In this analysis Petty was simply concerned to suggest a practical method of assessing for tax purposes the rents of owner-cultivated land – though whether, in fact, this method was operationally very practical and unambiguous seems questionable. He was not concerned with any profound or penetrating theory of value or with explaining or predicting exchange or market behaviour. He acknowledged that this approach was a very simplified one: 'This, I say, to be the foundation of equalising and balancing of values; yet in the super-structures and practices hereupon, I confess there is much variety and intricacy' (44).

In fact, Petty further complicated his initial answer, in terms of labour embodied, by adding the element, or input, of land, and by maintaining that 'all things ought to be valued by two natural denominations, which is land and labour; that is, we ought to say, a ship or garment is worth such a measure of land, with another such measure of labour' (44).

As he put it in a significant phrase, perhaps derived from Thomas Hobbes: 'Labour is the father and active principle of wealth, as lands are the mother' (68). So Petty can hardly be said to have maintained a labour theory of value, but rather a loosely formulated cost-of-production theory. Later, in *The Political Anatomy of Ireland*, Petty was to describe as 'the most important problem in political economy' as: 'how to make a par and equation between lands and labour, so as to express the value of anything by either alone' (181).

Petty's solution was to estimate how many days' food an area of pasture land would produce, without the application of labour, simply by leaving a calf to feed on it, and by observing how much weight the animal had put on at the end of a year. Then this additional meat could be compared with the number of day's food which the same area would yield with a man working on it for the year (181). Certainly this was rather a rough-and-ready procedure, which suggested numerous knotty questions.

Petty, however, did not confine his cost theory simply to the two original factors of labour and land. He sought to make another difficult 'par and equation' between capital equipment and labour – or 'art and simple labour', as he put it:

> . . . for if by such a simple labour I could dig and prepare for seed a hundred acres in a thousand days; suppose then, I spend a hundred days in studying a more compendious way, and in contriving tools for the same purpose, but in all that hundred days dig nothing; but in the remaining nine hundred days I dig two hundred acres of ground; then I say that the said art which cost but one hundred days invention is worth one man's labour for ever; because the new art, and one man, performed as much as two men could have done without it'
>
> (182)

Indeed, Petty recognized the productivity of capital instruments and what he called 'the facilitations of art', and he emphasized also the value of the research which discovered such 'facilitations' (118–19).

Before Petty, the theory of value had been examined mainly by followers of the scholastic or natural-law traditions, primarily in terms of utility and scarcity, though labour was sometimes assigned a role. So on value and price Petty started out on comparatively fresh lines. Although his observations on labour, land and value hardly amount to a systematic theory, they may have influenced Adam Smith.

Petty then took up the question of interest, comparing the exchange of sums of money at different places, or 'local usury', with 'usury upon time', as he put it, which he saw no reason for trying to limit by law, emphasizing 'the vanity of making civil positive laws against the laws of nature' (48). Subsequently, he defined interest as: 'A reward for forbearing the use of your own money for a term of time agreed upon, whatsoever need your self may have of it in the meanwhile' (446).

It was with regard to interest and rents that Petty implicitly introduced demand, though generally he gave very inadequate recognition in his writings to this fundamental economic force. He observed how just as 'the great need for money', at a particular place, raised the exchange rate, or price, so, would a greater demand raise the rent and value of land: 'for as great need of money heightens exchange, so doth great need of corn raise the price of that likewise, and consequently of the rent of the land that bears corn, and lastly of the land itself' (48). He explained how the stationing of an army on the outskirts of London would raise the demand for and the price of food, and, in particular, of 'perishable commodities': 'Hence it comes to pass that lands intrinsically alike near populous places ... will not only yield more rent for these reasons, but also more years purchase than in remote places' (49). Thus rent was higher not only because of higher food prices, resulting from a higher demand for food, but also because of the advantages of location, or 'by reason of the pleasure and honour extraordinary of having lands there' (49).

As part of his discussion of depreciation or debasement of the coinage, Petty included an interesting distinction between 'natural' and 'political' dearness and cheapness. 'Natural' cheapness depended on competitive, efficient cost of production, or on 'the few or more hands requisite'. On the other hand, 'political' cheapness, or the 'political' price, might include inefficiencies, as 'where are 200 husbandmen to do the same work which 100 could perform'.[2] Petty pointed out the range of possible factors affecting market prices, and how it was the function of merchants or entrepreneurs, to foresee the changes which such factors, and opinions about them, produced:

> But forasmuch as almost all commodities have their substitutes or *succedanea*, and that almost all uses may be answered several ways; and for that novelty, surprise, example of superiors, and opinion of unexaminable effects do add or take away from the price of things, we must add these contingent causes to the permanent causes above mentioned, in the judicious foresight and computation whereof lies the excellency of a merchant.
>
> (90)

The pamphlet *Verbum Sapienti* (1665) contained an original analysis of the velocity of circulation of money, and of the institutional factors which determined velocity. Petty observed that less money would be needed if the velocity was higher, or if 'the revolutions were in such short circules', as would be the case if wages and salaries were paid weekly rather than quarterly. He concluded: 'For money is but the fat of the body-politic, whereof too much doth as often hinder its agility, as too little makes it sick' (113).

Subsequently, in his *Quantulumcunque concerning Money* (1682), Petty produced another of his bold estimates, based on supposed average velocities of circulation, of 'how much money is sufficient for a nation':

> I think it may pretty well be guessed at; *viz*. I think that so much money as will pay half a year's rent for all the lands of England and a quarter's rent of the housing, and a week's expense of all the people, and about a quarter of the value of all the exported commodities, is sufficient for that purpose.
>
> (446)

Such attempts at estimating a 'sufficient' quantity or supply of money have sometimes been regarded as stemming from the fallacies of 'mercantilism'. But somewhat similar attempts are made today to estimate the appropriate additional percentage for the money supply in a growing economy.

IV

In his *Treatise*, Petty had attempted various rough-and-ready quantitative estimates. Any practical account or analysis of the items of government expenditure almost inevitably require some such estimates, and *some* attempt at quantification. Petty's two main works, however, of the early 1670s, the *Political Anatomy of Ireland* and *Political Arithmetic*, were much more comprehensively quantitative and explicitly proclaimed a thoroughgoing quantitative method and programme. In the preface to the *Anatomy*, Petty cited his master, Francis Bacon, regarding the parallels between medical and politico-economic studies, that is,

> ... between the Body Natural, and Body Politic, and between the arts of preserving both in health and strength; and it is as reasonable, that as anatomy is the best foundation of one, so also of the other; and that to practice upon the politic, without knowing the symmetry, fabric and proportion of it, is as casual as the practice of old women and empirics.'
>
> (129)

This statement implied also another markedly Baconian principle, that knowledge should be *useful*. As far as Petty was concerned, the politico-economic knowledge which he sought was aimed at providing useful policy guidance, which required quantitative estimates.

The *Anatomy* was a highly statistical, social and economic survey of Ireland, directed at guiding and improving politico-economic policy in that island. From a political viewpoint Petty was strongly in favour of the union with England.

His other main work of this period, his *Political Arithmetic*, was concerned with the economic condition of England and, in particular, with the comparative politico-economic strength of the three leading rivals of the day, England, France and Holland – a concern which was, at about this time, occupying the mind of the great Colbert, across the Channel. In his *Preface* Petty delivered his fullest and best-known statement of the methodological principles of *Political Arithmetic*. Having made clear his view that the pessimists were wrong, and that he was showing that 'the affairs of England' were 'in no deplorable condition', he continued:

> The method I take to do this, is not very usual; for instead of using only comparative and superlative words, and intellectual arguments, I have taken the course (as a specimen of the political arithmetic I have long aimed at) to express myself in terms of number, weight, or measure; to use only arguments of sense, and to consider only such causes, as have visible foundations in nature; leaving those that depend upon the mutable minds, opinions, appetites, and passions of particular men, to the consideration of others.
>
> (244)

This was very much the programme of the Royal Society.[3] Petty seems to have been rather over-confident about the possibility of the government using its authority to collect reliable statistical data. In any case, he claimed that, even if his observations were inaccurate, they were 'not so false as to destroy the arguments they are brought for; but at worst are sufficient as suppositions to show the way to that knowledge I am at' (245). Petty's attitude was that any quantitative estimates were, for budgetary or policy purposes, better than none, a view which might be regarded as defensible if no high-risk policies were based on such questionable, or hypothetical, foundations – which could hardly be said to have been the case with regard to his drastic suggestions that the bulk of the populations of Ireland and Scotland, in their own interests, should have been moved to England so as to obtain economies of scale and a rise in rents (289).

V

One of Petty's more important earlier attempts at 'political arithmetic' had appeared in his brief essay *Verbum Sapienti* (1665), in which he supplemented his *Treatise* of three years earlier by taking into account the heavy extra expenditure incurred as a result of the first Dutch war. He produced some further quantitative estimates, including one of the population of England and Wales (*c.* six million), and one of total national expenditure (£40 million), giving an average annual expenditure per head of £6$\frac{2}{3}$. In another estimate he put the reduction in trade due to the war at about one-eighth. He concluded that England was much wealthier in land and people than the Dutch, and, on balance twice as rich, in spite of the Dutch advantage in money, housing, and shipping.

In his *Political Arithmetic* (written 1672–6, published 1690) Petty went on to formulate some bold comparisons between the political and economic resources of the three leading economic powers of Western Europe. To explain the economic success of the Dutch, he emphasized liberty of conscience, as encouraging the settling of skilled immigrants and minorities; the registry of land, which improved the security of property and reduced litigation; low customs duties; and efficient banks, which increased the circulation of money, and so enabled a smaller quantity 'to drive the trade of the nation'. Finally, the Dutch economy was strengthened by good water transport. All these factors helped, directly or indirectly, to reduce interest rates. They also, incidentally, added up to a set of policies, approved by Petty, which might be said to have had a more liberal than mercantilist emphasis.

Turning to the question of the kind of tax policies which favoured economic progress, Petty attempted to lay down a distinction somewhat on the lines of that subsequently developed by the physiocrats, on the one hand, and by the English classicals, on the other, between productive and unproductive labour and investment:

> If the stocks of laborious and ingenious men who are not only beautifying the country ... but are also increasing the gold, silver, and jewels of the country by trade and arms; I say, if the stock of these men should be diminished by a tax and transfered to such as do nothing at all, but eat and

> drink, sing, play and dance; pay to such as study the metaphysics, or other needless speculation; or else employ themselves in any other way, which produce no material thing, or things of real use and value in the Commonwealth: in this case the wealth of the public will be diminished otherwise than as such exercises are recreations and refreshments of the mind; and which being moderately used, do qualify and dispose men to what in itself is more considerable.
>
> (270)

Petty's distinction had a similarity with – and seems no more problematic or questionable than – subsequent attempts, by some physiocrats and classicals to define 'productive' and 'unproductive'.

A point, however, introduced by Petty at this stage, which was emphasized by a number of seventeenth- and eighteenth-century writers, but which was not always maintained by the classicals, related to the desirability of keeping down wages, because of the backwardly sloping supply curve of labour. He even recommended governmental support of corn prices when harvests were abundant, to prevent the rise of real wages:

> It is observed by clothiers, and others who employ great numbers of poor people, that when corn is extremely plentiful, that the labour of the poor is proportionably dear; and scarce to be had at all (so licentious are they who labour only to eat, or rather to drink) ... it seems not unreasonable that this common blessing of God, should be applied to the common good of all people ... much rather than the same should be abused by the vile and brutish part of mankind, to the prejudice of the Commonwealth; and consequently, that such surplusage of corn should be sent to public store-houses; from thence to be disposed to the best advantage of the public.
>
> (274–5)[4]

Petty expressed great confidence in the power and wealth of England, which, he asserted, had grown significantly in the previous decades. He maintained, moreover, that if the considerable number of unemployed were put to work, national output would rise 'by many millions of money' (312). Also, if people in England 'superlucrated' more – or saved and invested more – then national wealth might double in five or six years (308). In fact, rejecting the views of the pessimists, Petty arrived at the optimistic conclusion, by means of his 'political arithmetic': 'that it is not impossible, nay a very feasible matter, for the King of England's subjects, to gain the universal trade of the whole commercial world' (312).

A later essay in political arithmetic examined the growth of the city of London.[5] Petty estimated the population of the city to be 670,000 and that of England and Wales 7,369,000 (460). Favouring large cities, Petty cited the advantages of specialization and the division of labour in cloth-making, and in shipping and ship-building where there was a large sea trade: 'cloth must be cheaper made, when one cards, another spins, another dresses, another presses and packs; than when all the operations above mentioned, were clumsily performed by the same hand' (260). The case was similar with regard to shipping and ship-building. Because of their command of the sea trade, Petty observed, the Dutch could afford a particular sort of vessel for each particular trade (261).

In a subsequent *Essay in Political Arithmetic* (1682), concerned with the growth of London, Petty went into more detail in providing one of the most penetrating accounts of the division of labour before that of Ernst Ludwig Carl:

> . . . the gain which is made by manufactures will be greater, as the manufacture itself is greater and better. For in so vast a city manufactures will beget one another, and each manufacture will be divided into as many parts as possible, whereby the work of each artisan will be simple and easy; as for example: in the making of a watch, if one man shall make the wheels, another the spring, another shall engrave the dial-plate, and another shall make the cases, then the watch will be better and cheaper than if the whole work be put upon any one man.
>
> (473)

There were also external economies:

> . . . we also see that in towns and in the streets of a great town, where all the inhabitants are almost of one trade, the commodity peculiar to those places is made better and cheaper than elsewhere. Moreover, when all sorts of manufactures are made in one place, there every ship that goeth forth can suddenly have its loading of so many several particulars and species as the port whereunto she is bound can take off.
>
> (474)[6]

VI

On policy, theory and method, Petty's ideas and writings were as stimulating as they were wide-ranging. Though often methodologically controversial, and sometimes extravagantly bold in his estimates, Petty was the outstanding economist of the seventeenth century. His work provided an impetus and stimulus, which was powerfully effective, not only in the intellectual 'boom' of the 1690s in England, but also for the rest of our period, throughout much of the eighteenth century; in particular, on Richard Cantillon, on the efflorescence of the 1750s, and on Quesnay and the physiocrats.

On the principles of domestic economic policy, Petty, like many of the writers of his time, supported government action against involuntary unemployment via public works and monetary and fiscal measures. He advocated the imposition of wage restraint against *voluntary* unemployment. In his rather *dirigiste* ideas regarding the reform of the leading professions and their manpower levels, Petty may have showed the influence of Hobbes. Regarding the regulation of foreign trade, he supported some of the usual 'mercantilist' measures. He argued, however, for moderation by government in intervening in foreign trade and in other areas, and he appealed to the beneficent workings of 'natural' forces, meaning the forces of individual self-interest. At one point he described the duty of statesmen, in their positive law-making, as that of implementing beneficent natural laws. Such ideas contributed later to the development of a basis and justification for the thoroughgoing, free-market policies of economic individualism.

As regards the fundamental questions of economic theory, Petty was a comparatively early and influential exponent of the cost-of-production and labour approach to the analysis of value and price, as contrasted with the natural-law theory of Samuel Pufendorf, in terms of utility, demand and scarcity, which had come down from the scholastics. But Petty can hardly be said to have stood for a labour theory of value. He was primarily concerned with practical, rough-and-ready assessments of real incomes and property for tax purposes. On the theory of money, Petty's version of the quantity theory, with its emphasis on the velocity of circulation, and the institutional determinants thereof, was an important contribution.

Finally, there were Petty's powerfully expressed methodological ideas, with his advocacy of quantification and of a Baconian, natural-scientific approach – which will hardly be regarded as an advance by those inclined to a more abstract, deductive, Cartesian stance, or to one that distinguishes, sharply and totally, between the appropriate criteria and methods for the natural sciences and those for social studies. We do not, however, at this point, wish to raise any fundamental methodological issues. It may simply be maintained that, even if Petty's methodological views were to be regarded as somewhat one-sided and over-optimistic, it must, at least, be conceded that to have been the first economist to have raised, in a challenging way, fundamental, critical questions about economic knowledge and methods, was to have been the first to take a vital step. Though he did not go deeply into them himself, he suggested profound questions of both method and theory.

A fuller assessment of 'political arithmetic' can only be attempted when an examination has been made, in the next chapter, of the work of other able exponents of quantitative methods in the closing decades of the seventeenth century, in particular that of John Graunt, to which Petty may have made a significant contribution.

4
English Pioneers of Social and Economic Statistics

I

John Graunt (1620–74) was the most important pioneer, in England or elsewhere, of population statistics; and he was also the most important friend in the first half of Petty's life (Strauss, 1954, 159).[1] He came of a family of drapers of some standing in the City of London. The friendship between the two started around 1651, at the time when Graunt helped Petty to obtain a professorship at Gresham's College. Later on, however, the favours seem to have flowed more in the other direction. Petty helped Graunt to a Fellowship of the Royal Society, and also assisted him after the disastrous losses he suffered in the great fire of 1666. Subsequently, there seems to have been some cooling off between the two, possibly for religious reasons, after Graunt became a Roman Catholic. He died in poverty.

The key controversial question, however, regarding the relations between Graunt and Petty has been that regarding the authorship of the *Natural and Political Observations made upon the Bills of Mortality*, which was published in 1662, a few months before Petty's *Treatise*. A fascinating controversy has lasted over some decades. Arguments can be produced on both sides, though the strongest claims on behalf of Petty's authorship have been put forward by his descendant, the Marquess of Lansdowne, and so might possibly be suspected of smacking of dynastic chauvinism. But there now seem to be no adequate reasons for rejecting the conclusions reached some time ago by the two editors, C. H. Hull in his edition of Petty's writings (1899), and W. F. Willcox in his introduction to the reprint of Graunt's *Observations* (1939). Hull concluded that: 'it seems almost certain that neither Graunt nor Petty was the exclusive author of all parts of the *Observations*' (1899, LII), but that 'the essential and valuable part of the *Observations* seems to be Graunt's'. As regards Petty's role, Hull maintained that he

> ... perhaps suggested the subject of the inquiry; he probably assisted Graunt with comments upon medical and other questions here and there; he procured the figures from Romsey for the 'Table of the Country Parish'; and he may have revised, or even written, the Conclusion and possibly, also, the curious 'Epistle Dedicatory to Sir Robert Moray', commending the book and its author to the Royal Society.
>
> (LII)

Willcox also maintained that: 'According to the overwhelming weight of argument and expert opinion Graunt was the main but not the sole author' (1939, VII). Willcox agreed with Hull regarding the parts which were possibly, or probably, contributed by Petty.

The Epistle Dedicatory – perhaps by Petty – begins, like Petty's Preface to the *Political Anatomy of Ireland*, by invoking Sir Francis Bacon. The *Observations*, as their title stated, were partly '*political*', in being concerned with trade and government, and, at the same time, partly '*natural*' in that they were concerned with ... 'seasons, fruitfulness, health, diseases, longevity, and the proportions between the sex and ages of mankind' (6). Bacon, it was claimed, considered such subjects to belong to 'natural history', like the observations of 'heat, wetness, and windiness', which were also being collected by the Royal Society. In other words, the *Observations* started with a thoroughly 'naturalistic' approach to their subject.

Graunt explained how his interest in the bills of mortality, collected by parishes, arose initially from mere curiosity. But he then found that conclusions were suggested which were at variance with prevailing opinions, and which might yield significantly useful knowledge, not merely 'idle and useless speculation' (18). He went on to describe his sources, the bills of mortality, and the records of burials and christenings, kept by the parishes. There was an obvious possibility of ambiguities or errors regarding the causes of death reported by the 'searchers', who were 'ancient matrons', who 'repair to the place where the dead corpse lies, and by view of the same, and by other enquiries, they examine by what disease, or casualty the corpse died' (26). Graunt was reasonably critical of very confident or precise conclusions regarding the different causes of deaths, and of changes in these diagnoses, especially those involving allegedly new diseases.

He remarked, however, on how few deaths were reported as being caused by starvation, and was prepared to observe 'that the vast numbers of beggars, swarming up and down this city, do all live, and seem to be most of them healthy and strong' (33). He concluded that it was preferable that they should live by state provision, rather than by begging.[2]

The effects of plagues were obviously then of major importance. Graunt observed that christenings declined during plagues. But in spite of plagues resulting in more burials than christenings, he estimated that the population was restored in two years, so that considerable immigration into London, from other parts of the country, was taking place. Graunt's next observation was that slightly more males were born than females. But more young men died violent deaths of one kind or another, and more men remained celibate, with the happy result that 'every woman may have an husband, without the allowance of polygamy' (58). There was a suggestion here, in one socially important respect, of the Divine Order which the great German demographer, Süssmilch, was to proclaim some eighty years later (see chapter 14).

The high point of the *Observations* was reached with the so-called Life Table (which would more accurately be described as a Death Table). Since the London bills of mortality did not state the age of death, this was a rather bold construction. Graunt found that some 36 per cent of the deaths were caused by children's diseases, which, he assumed, must have killed off their victims before the age of six. He also assumed that the 7 per cent of deaths stated as being due to old age, came after the age of seventy. There has been considerable discussion as to how the intermediate figures, regarding deaths between the ages of six and seventy, were arrived at. It was suggested by Willcox that the more audacious Petty may have assisted the more cautious Graunt in completing the table.

Further examination led to the observation that London was significantly 'more unhealthful' than the countryside (76). This was attributed partly to environmental pollution caused by the burning of coal, and, partly, simply to the fact that London was 'more populous' and to the variety of health hazards which a denser population brought about. The population of London was estimated at 460,000 and that of the whole country at 6,440,000.

The 'Conclusion' (77ff.) was in a markedly different mood, or style, to most of what had gone before. Undoubtedly Graunt was a more cautious and critical worker than Petty, who was boldly and impatiently out for results of practical, policy significance. The 'Conclusion' began by asking the purpose of 'all this laborious buzzling and groping', to establish 'the number of the people', how many males and females, etc. The pure pleasure of the exercise, 'in doing something new', was not taken seriously. More seriously, a telling criticism was put forward of the aggressive 'mercantilist' assumption of politics and political economy as a zero-sum game, or process. He complained that the study of the art of government and politics should be devoted to 'how to preserve the subject in peace and plenty', instead of being directed at one-sidedly teaching 'how to supplant and overreach one another, and not by fair out-running but by tripping up each other's heels to win the prize' (78).

On the other hand, 'honest, harmless policy' must be based on a knowledge of the economic geography of the country. Moreover:

> It is no less necessary to know how many people there be of each sex, state, age, religion, trade, rank, etc., by the knowledge whereof trade and government may be made more certain and regular; for if men knew the people as aforesaid, they might know the consumption they would make, so as trade might not be hoped for where it is impossible.
>
> (78–9)

Such information was required, of course, not only by governments, but by individual entrepreneurs, if their expectations, or predictions, about markets were to have a reasonable basis.

It has been said, in a glowing and authoritative tribute, that Graunt was 'the first person to whom it occurred that numerical information on human populations could be of more than ephemeral interest' (Sutherland, 1963, 554). As his editor, Willcox, has claimed, Graunt suggested the uniformity and predictability of certain social phenomena taken in the mass, and thus opened the way to the later discovery of other such uniformities (see Graunt, 1662, XII–XIII). Peter Laslett has maintained that Graunt's work 'ranks as one of the great contributions by Englishmen to the foundation of scientific enquiry during the century of their genius' (Laslett ed., introduction, n.p.).

The next pioneer contribution to the development of population statistics, following up the *Observations* of Graunt (and Petty), also came from a Fellow of the Royal Society, the ultra-versatile Edmund Halley (1656–1742) (of the comet, of course). His multifarious interests, extending over both 'natural' and 'political' (or social) subjects were typical of the Royal Society, and its members, in its early decades. So too was his application of the same criteria and methods to the problems of both the natural and the 'political' world. Apparently Halley made his name at the age of twenty-one, when he sailed to St Helena to study the astronomy of the southern hemisphere.

Halley's brief papers, *Degrees of Mortality of Mankind*, were published in the Transactions of the Royal Society in 1693, and based on records of births and deaths for the City of Breslau, in Silesia, for the years 1687–91. It seems that this material had been forwarded, via Leibniz, to the Royal Society because of the interest and achievements of its members in this field. The information from Breslau was fuller than that provided by the London bills, since it included both the age at death, and figures as to the total population. Moreover, the Breslau population was approximately stable, with no significant immigration or emigration. At the start of his paper, Halley noted the superiority of his material over that of Graunt.

Halley then proceeded to set out a table stating the number of persons dying yearly at each age. As in Graunt's estimates for London, mortality in childhood was very heavy, though it fell markedly in the teens. He described the main contribution of his paper:

> From these considerations I have formed the adjoined table, whose uses are manifold and give a more just idea of the state and condition of mankind, than anything yet extant that I know of. It exhibits the number of people in the City of Breslau of all ages, from the birth to extreme old age, and thereby shows the chances of mortality at all ages, and likewise how to make a certain estimate of the value of annuities for lives, which hitherto has been only done by an imaginary valuation: also the chances that there are that a person of any age proposed does live to any other age given.
>
> (1693, reprinted 1942, 6)

Halley then drew a number of conclusions from the table, for example:

(a) the number of males of military age – i.e eighteen to fifty-six – was about one-quarter of the total population; (b) mortality and expectation of life at different ages were estimated (e.g. the odds were 80 : 1 against a person of twenty-five dying within a year); (c) also the odds were given against a person attaining a particular age. Halley further demonstrated, assuming a particular interest rate, what the purchaser, at any particular age, ought to pay for an annuity, and how the price of insurance could be regulated.

In an additional note, he stated his views on what it was that held back the increase of population. His diagnosis was that population was checked by 'the unequal distribution of property' (20). He described the mass of poor people, not as losing their offspring through disease or starvation, but as holding back 'from the cautious difficulty most people make to adventure on the state of marriage, from the prospect of the trouble and charge of providing for a family' (20). Halley would seem to be maintaining that a kind of 'moral restraint' was actually being practised – such as Malthus was to urge in his *Essay* more than a century later.

Incidentally, Halley's work in drawing on material sent from Silesia provided an example of Anglo-German co-operation among the pioneers of population statistics, which was to be repeated, half a century later, when Johann Peter Süssmilch, in his great work on *The Divine Order* (1741), started from the achievements of Graunt and Halley, and drew, for his ideas regarding divine beneficence, on the writings of another Fellow of the Royal Society, Rev. William Derham (1657–1735). Derham, in his *Physico-theology: or a Demonstration of the Being and Attributes of God from his Works of Creation* (1713), claimed that the Divine Order was manifest in the regularities shown in the vital statistics of human population produced by Graunt and Halley.[3]

II

Gregory King (1648–1712) was a genealogist, accountant, and perhaps the most accomplished economic and social statistician of his time. Born at Lichfield, at fourteen he became Clerk to the antiquary, Sir William Dugdale (1605–86). King's most important work – and almost his only published work in the field – was his *Natural and Political Observations and Conclusions upon the State and Condition of England* which was not published until 1802 (by George Chalmers). Charles Davenant, however, a close political ally, knew well King and his work, and referred to it at several points in his writings. No writings by King on economic and social statistics were published in his lifetime.

King explained his purpose in the Preface to his *Observations*:

> If to be well apprized of the true state and condition of a nation, especially in the two main articles of its people and wealth, be a piece of political knowledge, of all others, and at all times, the most useful, and necessary; then surely at a time when a long and very expensive war against a potent monarch ... seems to be at its crisis, such a knowledge of our own nation

> must be of the highest concern: but since the attaining thereof (how necessary and desirable soever) is next to impossible, we must content ourselves with such near approaches to it as the grounds we have to go upon will enable us to make.
>
> (ed. Barnett, 1936, 13)

King claimed that 'having better foundations than heretofore' had enabled him to come 'very near the truth'. It may be of some incidental interest that the kind of estimates which King was attempting included some of national income, the first of their kind, which, he claimed, were especially useful for a country at war, for it was during a war crisis, nearly two and a half centuries later, that regular, official national income statistics were first published in England, when the need for reliable – or as reliable as possible – quantitative information was specially acute.

King's *Observations* also contained estimates of national capital (covering both its composition and growth) and of population, which he calculated via an estimate of the number of houses, and put at five and a half million, a rather lower estimate than Petty's. One of King's most striking estimates was his table of ranks and degrees in his 'Scheme of the Income and Expense of the several Families of England calculated for the Year 1688'. This table has received much acclaim and approval from economic and social historians, while his national-income estimates have been described by Professor Phyllis Deane as 'in advance of any calculations made in this field until the mid-twentieth century' (1968, 385).

Recently, however, King's work has come in for some criticism. Though acknowledging that King was 'one of the cleverest, most original men of his day', Professor Geoffrey Holmes goes on to emphasize 'his frustrated ambition; his deep conservatism; his obsessive ensnaring passion for figures; and yet with all this, a certain underlying humility' (1986, 284). Professor Holmes criticizes King for seriously underestimating the country's ability to finance the war against France by taxation, and charges him with failing to foresee England's great economic potential, on which point Petty proved himself the more far-sighted. On the other hand, in another paper ('Of the Naval Trade of England at 1688'), King looked back to the Stuart period and sought to establish 'this great fundamental truth that the trade and wealth of England did mightily advance between the years 1600 and 1688' (61). Though some of King's estimates were very wild indeed (e.g. regarding the population of New England) he was, on the whole cautious and modest. Professor Holmes remarks, however, on how 'King's highly conservative over-reaction against the more euphoric assumptions of recent years frequently led into contrary error' (293). Holmes especially attacks King's 'Scheme of the Income and Expense' of English families in 1688, by which, he claims, many economic and social historians have been misled.

Among economists, King is probably best known for what has been called variously the King–Davenant or Davenant–King law of demand. Two fascinating problems surround first the authorship and second the interpretation of this proposition.

As regards authorship, it should be emphasized that, as Jevons long ago pointed out (1871, 154–6), the 'law' does not appear (contrary to what Schumpeter and others have stated) in King's *Observations*. Though King almost certainly played an important or vital role, Evans concluded that 'Davenant's role in the formulation of the Law of Demand . . . has been much undervalued' (492), which perhaps should be known as the Davenant–King Law of Demand.[4] Anyhow, it has been Davenant's formulation which has so often been described as 'the Law of Demand' and attributed to King. In his *Essay upon the Probable Methods of Making a People Gainers in the Balance of Trade* (1699) Davenant stated:

> We take it, that a defect in the harvest may raise the price of corn in the following proportions:

Defect		Above the Common Rate
1 Tenth	raises the price	3 Tenths
2 Tenths		8 Tenths
3 Tenths		1.6 Tenths
4 Tenths		2.8 Tenths
5 Tenths		4.5 Tenths

> so that when corn rises to treble the common rate, it may be presumed that we want (i.e. lack) above a third of the common produce; and if we should want (i.e. lack) 5 tenths, or half the common produce, the price would rise to near 5 times the common rate.
>
> (*Works*, 1771, vol. II, 224–5)

(Clearly, '1.6 tenths' etc. equals 1 and 6 tenths.)

The second problem surrounding the 'law', that of its interpretation, has some bearing on the question of authorship.[5] Most earlier authorities, including Jevons, appear to have assumed that the 'law' was empirically based on observations or estimates. It appears to have been the polymath William Whewell (1794–1866) who first suggested that the Davenant–King proposition was hypothetically based on a mathematical formula. The validity of this interpretation has been demonstrated most recently and most thoroughly by Professor Creedy, who interestingly suggests that Isaac Newton may have been responsible for the approach adopted (1986, 209–10). The demonstration of the mathematical character of the 'law' probably indicates a greater role for King than for Davenant in its formulation.

III

Charles Davenant (1656–1714), perhaps a grandson of William Shakespeare, was the eldest son of Sir William Davenant (or D'Avenant), poet laureate and dramatist, and of a French mother. He was the grandson of the proprietor of the Crown Inn at Oxford, who had known Shakespeare when he stayed at his inn on his way to and from Stratford and London.[6] In 1671 Charles Davenant was at Balliol College but left without a degree. Subsequently he studied law and acquired an LLD from Cambridge. He made a career in politics and government, was in and out of Parliament several times, and held various governmental posts, including that of Secretary to the Commission negotiating the Union with Scotland, and, from 1705 until his death, that of Inspector-General of Exports and Imports. Davenant was an able political and economic pamphleteer, but has the reputation of having been something of a political opportunist – and an unsuccessful one at that – who shaped his economic and political opinions and arguments to further his political ambitions. Ashley described him as the most important of the Tory Free-Traders, who, he suggested, advocated free trade for party-political, and foreign-political, reasons, rather than on any firmly or profoundly held economic grounds.[7] Motives may, however, be regarded as ultimately irrelevant: Davenant wrote well and discerningly on the economic problems of the day and he left behind some important economic papers containing well-formulated ideas of lasting value. With due acknowledgement, he drew considerably on the work of Gregory King, and, though not uncritical of Petty, was obviously much indebted to the pioneer of *Political Arithmetic*.

In one of his first economic writings Davenant proclaimed the existence of law in the economic and political world, overriding any law of government, and based, ultimately, on the self-interest of the individual:

> Nor can law interpose in this matter with any effect, for in the natural course of trade, each commodity will find its price . . .
>
> The supreme power can do many things, but it cannot alter the Laws of Nature, of which the most original is that every man should preserve himself.
>
> This thought of self preservation drives him to supply his necessities from others, which he cannot do but upon equal foot and value for value, which must be determined by common usage, and consent, and this, in a matter of trade, must be the common consent and usage of trading people.
>
> (1695–6, 21)

Davenant maintained that in a politically free society competitive market forces would dominate, though in a state of serfdom, governmental power might prevail:

> Perhaps in a tyranny, the sanctions of the prince might prevail to alter this course of trade in some particular things; but this cannot well be done in a mixed government, where the legislative and executive authority are in different hands, and not near and ready always to help one another upon ali disputes that shall arise. . .
>
> (21)

Davenant warned, generally, against drastic governmental measures, such as a major reform of the currency involving debasement or depreciation. He resorted to a medical analogy, in rather different terms from those of Petty: 'In sharp diseases of the body bold and empirical remedies are often applied with good success, but the body politic should not in this manner be tampered with, and will find at last a more certain cure for its distempers from time, steady conduct, wholesome laws and discretion in the rulers' (29).

Davenant also contributed significantly to the discussion of trade policy and of the trade with India, in his *Essay on the East India Trade* (1697 [1771]) in which he took a notably free-trade stance. He argued that the trade with India 'greatly benefited England', and he opposed prohibitions on Indian silks, and other oriental luxuries in order to help the English woollen industry and raise wool prices: 'The only way beneficial to England of making wool yield a good price, is to have it manufactured cheaply' (1771, vol. I, 100). He was against an 'unnatural' price for wool, or for anything else, and proclaimed the case for freedom of trade in the following well-known declaration:

> Trade is in its nature free, finds its own channels and best directeth its own course; and all laws to . . . limit and circumscribe it, may serve the particular ends of private men, but are seldom advantageous to the public.
>
> Governments are to take a providential care of the whole, but generally to let causes work their own way; and considering all the links and chance, by which they hang together, peradventure it may be affirmed that, in the main, all traffics whatsoever are beneficial to a country.
>
> They say few laws in a state are an indication of wisdom in a people; but it may be more truly said, that few laws relating to trade are the mark of a nation that thrives by traffic.
>
> (I, 98–9)

However questionable Davenant's motives may have been, or however opportunistic his professed allegiance to free-trade principles, these paragraphs provide a notable statement of an important doctrine on trade policy, which was then beginning, very briefly, to gain ground:

> Wisdom is most commonly in the wrong, when it pretends to direct nature. The various products of different soils and countries is an indication that providence intended that they should be helpful to each other, and mutually supply the necessities of one another.
>
> And as it is a great folly to compel a youth to that sort of study to which he is not adapted by genius and inclination, so it can never be wise to endeavour the introducing into a country either the growth of any commodity, or any manufacture, for which, nor the soil, nor the general bent of the people is proper.
>
> (104)

Davenant went on to lay down a general principle echoed some sixty years later by Adam Smith, in his *Theory of Moral Sentiments*:

> For the laws of all countries must be suited to the bent and inclination of the people; and (I am loath to say), there is sometimes a necessity they should be a little accommodated to their depraved manners and corruptions.
>
> (114)

> He that frames his polity upon what mankind should be, will find himself almost ever in the wrong . . .
>
> (392)

In the first of his *Discourses on the Public Revenues* (1698 [1771]) Davenant explained and defended political arithmetic, which he defined as 'the art of reasoning by figures, upon things relating to government' (128). He maintained that: 'The abilities of any minister have always consisted chiefly in this computing faculty; nor can the affairs of war and peace be well managed without reasoning by figures upon things' (1771, vol. 1, 131).

Political arithmetic was very ancient, he claimed, going back to the Greeks and Romans, and even to King David's numbering of the Israelites. He observed that Petty had first applied this art to revenue and trade, but he lacked the 'right materials'. Moreover, Davenant accused Petty of bias in underestimating the power and wealth of France, and in overestimating those of England in order to flatter and curry favour with the monarch.

Political arithmetic was needed not only by governments and statesmen, but also by merchants in making their business decisions. He warned against concentrating only on the immediate, primary effects of economic policies and decisions, and emphasized the complexities and interdependence of economic relationships. Regarding foreign trade:

> In the first appearance those traffics seem hurtful which export money, but when we come to reason upon things by figures, we find that such trades are beneficial, when they bring in one way more bullion than they carry out another . . . So that to object against the motion of one wheel, without seeing how the whole engine moves, is to no manner of purpose.
>
> (147)

Political arithmetic was necessary for balancing out the different effects of policies: 'And perhaps this art alone can show the links and chain by which one business hangs upon another, and the dependence which all our various dealings have upon each other' (147). Davenant presented political arithmetic as a kind of cost–benefit analysis. A statesman needed 'a computing head', to arrive at the balance of advantage, 'by summing up the difficulties on either side, and by computing upon the whole' (135).

It was in *An Essay upon the Probable Methods of Making a People Gainers in the Balance of Trade* (1699 [1771]) that Davenant's statement of what has so often been called 'King's Law' occurs, in a section entitled 'Of the Land of England and its Produce'. He was discussing the question of policy arising out of the fluctuations in harvests and corn prices, and whether, or how, government should intervene. The regulation of the corn trade was to be a major issue in several European countries in the eighteenth century, notably in France in the third quarter of the century. Davenant estimated that in normal years England only had five months' stock of grain in hand, at the time of the new harvest. He then presented his calculation of how prices would rise in response to various percentage shortfalls in the harvest (II, 224, see above). Observing that the Dutch had granaries and store-houses, Davenant suggested that in England the government should take similar precautions to even out supplies and prevent rises in price which would bring starvation to the poor. He concluded:

> It is true, in those matters men are apt to follow what they think their particular profit; but the influence of good laws would go a long way towards inclining them more to pursue what is for the general advantage; and indeed the private concerns of men should be always made subservient to the public interest.
>
> (II, 229)

On the problem of the coinage (to be discussed more fully in the next chapter) Davenant maintained that the nation's seriously unfavourable trade balance, and the outflow of specie, had first to be corrected, if any reform of the coinage was to be lastingly successful. He was opposed to attempting such a drastic measure while the war with France lasted. Meanwhile, loans from Holland should be obtained to tide over the crisis. Regarding the nature of money, Davenant was a 'cartalist' rather than a 'metallist', maintaining that money needed to be generally acceptable, without necessarily possessing value from the metallic, or any other physical properties, it contained. He emphasized the major role of paper credit:

> Of all things that have existence only in the minds of men, nothing is more fantastical and nice than credit. 'Tis never to be forced; it hangs upon opinion. It depends upon our passions of hope and fear. It comes many times unsought for and often goes away without reason, and when once lost, is hardly to be recovered . . . no trading nation ever did subsist and carry on its business by real stock. That trust and confidence in each other is as necessary to link and hold a people together, as obedience, love, friendship or the intercourse of speech.
>
> (1696, in Usher, 1942, 75–6)

In fact as far as England was concerned: 'the general trade of this country has been more carried on by credit, than managed with the species of money, which when it was most plentiful amongst us could not have the fifth part of our foreign and domestic commerce' (68). For, 'money is at bottom no more than the counters with which men, in their dealings, have been accustomed to reckon' (1771, vol. I, 355). Davenant maintained that the value of money, like the value of everything else, was determined by needs, supplies, and by the overriding force of competition:

> Therefore in all formed societies consisting of great numbers, the worth of money will always take its rule from the necessity men have of other commodities . . . But why must so much corn be worth such a weight in silver? Because if B will not give it, the same may be had from C and D, or if neither of them, it will yield such a price in foreign countries; and from hence arises what we commonly call intrinsic value. Nor can any law hinder B, C, and D from supplying their wants; nor will any law (in discretion) prevent such transportation when the plenty admits it.
>
> (1695, Usher, 1942, 20)

It was her foreign trade which had immensely assisted England's tremendous economic growth throughout much of the century, Davenant asserted. But he showed his 'mercantilist' inclinations at a number of points, for example when he eulogized the policies of Colbert. He attacked as misconceived concerns about the balance of trade in particular commodities, but emphasized the importance of the 'main' balance: 'To enquire whether we get or lose by this or that branch of trade is an endless and uncertain speculation; the only question of importance, and which indeed should employ the thoughts of considering men, is, in the main, do we get, or lose? (1771, I, 386).

In fact, like many important writers, in the century or so with which we are concerned in this volume, Davenant did not perceive, or believe in, the sufficiently effective operation of self-adjusting forces in international trade, though he supported, and cogently expounded, the general case for economic freedom.

IV

William Fleetwood (1656–1723) does not quite belong with the statisticians and 'political arithmeticians' discussed in this chapter. The problem of price index-numbers, which he was a pioneer in addressing, though it was eventually to become the subject of a major branch of economic statistics, had not been identified, or examined, in seventeenth-century writings. It is, however, convenient, at this point, to mention Fleetwood, and his highly original work, the *Chronicon Preciosum; or an Account of English Money, the Price of Corn and other Commodities for the last 600 years.*

A Fellow of King's College, Cambridge, who subsequently became Bishop of Ely, Fleetwood had been set the problem, in an inquiry from Oxford, of determining what the then present equivalent, in 1706, would have been, of an income of £5 per annum, which had been fixed on the foundation of a College 260 years previously, i.e. *c.*1450. As part of this task, Fleetwood collected prices of a wide range of commodities, claiming that, 'the observations of these little things may be of good use in the consideration of great affairs' (8). As he posed the problem: '. . . the plain, literal and grammatical sense of five pounds is not the same as it was 260 years ago' (11). But the Founder of the College had, presumably, 'intended the same ease and favour to those who should live in the College 260 years after his decease' (11). According to Fleetwood's estimate: 'A degree might be taken 260 years ago at five times less charge, than it can be at this day' (12). He concluded that '£5, 260 years ago, was equivalent to £28 or £30 now'.

Fleetwood recognized the problem of short-term fluctuations in prices of agricultural products in making long-range comparisons. He observed: 'You must neither take a very dear year to your prejudice, nor a very cheap one in your favour' (167).

He recognized, also, that individual prices do not change in the same ratios, but offered no answer to the problem of 'weighting'. Edgeworth described Fleetwood's work as 'the earliest treatise on index-numbers and one of the best' (see Keynes, 1930, vol. I, 55). This may still be a valid appraisal.

VI

Political arithmetic and the study of economic statistics, after Fleetwood's remarkable work, went into a sharp decline in England, a decline which lasted through most, or all, of the eighteenth century. Indeed the study of political economy generally, as far as English writers were concerned, fell away in the eighteenth century. This sudden withering, after the brilliant flowering in the latter part of the seventeenth century, is not easy to explain. Certainly the political arithmeticians were ahead of their time. Petty had advocated the creation of a government statistical office, which would gather reliable basic material. But no such body came into being, and it must be rather doubtful as to how much such an office might have achieved in the eighteenth century, had it existed.

The achievements on population statistics of the seventeenth-century pioneers were more firmly based than those concerned with wealth and income. No very sophisticated or problematic analysis was required with regard to such categories as 'births' and 'deaths', 'males' and 'females' – (in spite of some marginal ambiguities creeping into these concepts 300 years later). Concepts like 'wealth', however, 'national income', and 'national capital' are obviously fraught with problems that needed more analysis than was available in Petty's day – though he showed little or no sign of appreciating these difficulties.[8]

Though political arithmetic so largely and so suddenly faded away in the eighteenth century, it seems to have had a follower in one of the two greatest economists of the century (or of any century), Richard Cantillon. Very unfortunately, however, the loss of the statistical supplement to his *Essay* has prevented our appreciating how far, and in what ways. Cantillon built on, or followed up, the work of the seventeenth-century quantifiers. At some points, he was severely critical of Petty. His own reference to statistics was rather tantalizing, but also rather optimistic: 'There is no branch of knowledge in which one is more subject to error than Statistics when they are left to imagination, and none more demonstrable when they are based upon detailed facts' (Cantillon, n.d., 133).

The other of the two greatest economists of the eighteenth century was responsible for the celebrated dismissal: 'I have no great faith in political arithmetic' (Smith, 1776, 535). But then just what and how much non-trivial economic knowledge should one have '*great* faith' in? There does not seem to be very much agreement on this point, and when, or where, there has been, it does not seem often to have lasted very long. If the fruits of Petty's pioneering, but perhaps rather naively empirical and Baconian methods, hardly deserved to have *great* faith invested in them, neither, it might be argued, did the naively Cartesian, deductive dogmas of some of Smith's classical contemporaries and successors. But though he was justifiably sceptical regarding the reliability of political arithmetic and economic statistics, Smith did consider it worthwhile to cite the estimates of King, Davenant and Fleetwood at a number of points in his massive historical and descriptive investigations.

5
John Locke and the 1690s

I

The development of economic thought has been marked at several major turning-points by outbreaks of intense debate concentrated into a particular decade or so, and centred on some pressing, controversial, real-world policy problem, or some epoch-making work by one of the great masters of the subject. The Quesnaysian phase in France in the late 1750s and much of the 1760s, the Ricardian years from about 1814 to 1823, and the Keynesian decade of the 1930s, are obvious examples of such outstanding passages in the history of the subject. As already suggested, the 1620s might, perhaps, be identified as the earliest such phase, when a serious depression in British trade gave rise to fierce and profound arguments over monetary and commercial policies and inspired the important contributions of Malynes, Misselden and Mun. The 'boom' of the 1690s was on a much larger scale, and included a comparatively new, explicit, methodological and theoretical dimension. The 1690s might well be regarded as the first *major* concentrated burst of development in the history of the subject, comparable with such subsequent great decades, or phases, as those associated with Quesnay, Ricardo, and Keynes.

The 'boom' of the 1690s was almost entirely confined to England, the only major writing originating elsewhere in that decade being Boisguilbert's *Détail de la France* (1695) – certainly a work of the highest importance (discussed in the next chapter). It had been Petty, thirty years earlier, who had initiated the great English advance, which had been steadily gathering momentum until it came to a peak after the revolution of 1688–9. A glance at our chronology will suffice to show the remarkable cluster of important publications in the 1690s. In our period, the only comparable concentration was to come in the 1750s, and then on an international scale. We have already mentioned that a number of Petty's pamphlets first appeared posthumously in the 1690s, and we have also discussed the works of Halley, King and Davenant, which appeared in that decade. This chapter is devoted to the writings of Locke, Child, Barbon, North and Martyn, with, unfortunately, only brief mention, or no mention at all, of interesting contributions from several others, for which space is not available.

By way of partially explaining this burst of creative thought and argument in the still rather unformed subject, it might be observed, first, that there was, at this time, a great deal to discuss regarding the trade and economy of England. Economic change had been gradually quickening throughout much of the century, with expanding markets at home and overseas. There were serious and controversial issues of policy regarding foreign trade, first with England's two great Western European rivals, the French and the Dutch, and also with regard to trade with India.

By the 1690s, moreover, two fundamental issues of policy had come to a head. The question, first, of the legal regulation of interest rates, which had long been simmering, was now acute; second, the silver coinage had so deteriorated, from many years of clipping, that its reform constituted an urgent, though highly controversial, issue. Both these problems, regarding interest and money, raised basic perennial questions of policy and theory, which went far beyond the immediate, local problems. Also, thanks initially mainly to Petty, critical philosophical principles and distinctions, together with new ideas regarding scientific method, were being applied to problems of trade and political economy. In particular, the distinction between normative and positive, or between the moral and the technical, was gradually gaining ground, as part of a search for more reliable and unbiased solutions to policy problems than had been previously been available.[1]

So the challenging economic problems were there, together with the philosophical challenge of new ideas regarding scientific criteria and method. In other leading countries, however, which were facing difficult economic problems, and in which new philosophical and scientific ideas were circulating, there was no similar advance in the subject of trade or political economy. What was crucially different in England, as compared with other countries, was the much greater freedom of discussion and publication on controversial issues of policy. To some extent this had been the case before 1689, but it became very much more so after the revolution, in the opening years of the new régime. Finally, as part of the growth of the economy, the London publishing industry had expanded enormously. As Professor Joyce Appleby has observed:

> Because much of the conflict among the contending parties during England's century of revolution was waged through the printed word, there developed in England a vigorous public press and an equally novel phenomenon, a reading public. London, which has been praised as a place for conspicuous consumption, and a lever under the kingdom's latent productive powers, should also be celebrated as a publishing center. Here were gathered the presses, the bookstores, the writers, and the readers to sustain a rapid acceleration of printed communication. Pamphlets and books streamed from the city's presses, in runs between 500 and 2000 ... Debates that were once argued exclusively in face-to-face encounters began to take shape through written words addressed to unseen audiences ... there grew up a new kind

> of forum, where the absence of the immediate presence of a speaker or listener made possible a freer, more impersonal kind of exchange.
> (1978, 5)[2]

Unlike subsequent 'booms' in the subject, with their clusters of important new works, the developments of the 1690s were not centred on one particular overriding problem, or a single epoch-making publication. John Locke, with his tremendous prestige as a philosopher and political theorist, and his high position in the government, was the most important figure at this time. But his contribution to economic theory and method was at least equalled by those of North and Barbon, while there were works of other writers which were of considerable importance. It might, indeed, reasonably be held, that at no other period have English writers been so outstandingly in the lead on the subject of trade, political economy and economics.

II

The first important controversial issue of current policy to emerge in England in our period which raised fundamental theoretical questions, was that of the regulation of the rate of interest. This problem had been intermittently under discussion at least since the debates of the 1620s, when Sir Thomas Culpeper had published *A Tract against Usury* (1621), a work which may have influenced the reduction of the maximum legal rate of interest from 10 to 8 per cent in 1624. Culpeper's *Tract* was republished in 1641, and again in 1668 as an appendix to another powerful pamphlet on the subject, Josiah Child's *Brief Observations concerning Trade and Interest of Money*. Child's work gave a notable impetus to the discussion of the regulation of the rate of interest because, as a result of its publication, John Locke was asked to examine the problem, his unpublished report being his first essay in the field of trade and political economy.

Josiah Child (1630–99) came of a merchant family and soon amassed a large fortune, making his career in the East India Company, of which he eventually became governor. He campaigned for the interests of his company, both during several spells as a Member of Parliament, and also in his publications – not unsuccessfully perhaps, for he was made a baronet by Charles II in 1678. His *Brief Observations*, a pamphlet of eighteen pages, started with what was a frequent concern of the time, namely: ' the prodigious increase of the Netherlands in their domestic and foreign trade, riches, and multitude of shipping ... the envy of the present and maybe the wonder of all future generations' (1668, 41).[3] Child proceeded to give fifteen reasons for the economic success of the Dutch, which included 'their parsimonious and thrifty living'; the education of their children; their employment of the poor; religious toleration, which attracted industrious immigrants, notably Jews; and finally 'the lowness of interest of money' in Holland. This was 'the *Causa Causans* of all the other causes of the riches of that people; and that if interest of money were with us reduced to the same rate it is with them, it would in short time render us as rich and considerable in trade as they are now ...' (45).

Child claimed that England had made a great economic advance in the previous fifty years, and that the step-by-step reduction in interest had been responsible. It was now time to carry this reduction further, from 6 to 4 per cent (47–8). He added several other interesting points. Though not calling for a free market in loans, Child pleaded that the reduction was natural, and that 'nature must and will have its course' (55). He attempted to answer, rather dubiously, the objection that Holland's low interest rate was an effect rather than a cause of prosperity, by arguing that though they had no legal limitation on interest, the Dutch would have held down interest by law if their market rate had not fallen so low. Child also added an early attempt to distinguish between productive and unproductive labour – though he described 'productivity' in terms of the production of exports:

> It is (I think) agreed on by all, that merchants, artificers, farmers of land, and such as depend on them ... *viz.* seamen, fishermen, breeders of cattle, gardeners etc., are the three sorts of people, which by their study and labour do principally, if not only, bring in wealth to a nation from abroad; other kinds of people, *viz.* nobility, gentry, lawyers, physicians, scholars of all sorts, and shop-keepers, do only hand it from one to another at home. (54)

After the Glorious Revolution, Child again took up the cause of a legal reduction in the interest rate, publishing *A Discourse about Trade* (1690) and (virtually the same work) *A New Discourse about Trade* (1693). This was a much longer and more wide-ranging booklet than the *Brief Observations* of a quarter of a century before. A number of additional themes and arguments were introduced, some on the side of economic freedom, some upholding highly restrictive, or otherwise mercantilist views, and some neutral between the two. On the mercantilist side should probably be included Child's emphasis on the benefits of a large population and his call for the employment of the poor. He maintained: 'That it is our duty to God and nature, so to provide for, and employ the poor. That by so doing one of the great sins, for which this land ought to mourn would be removed' (1693, 56). Obviously Child believed that there was much involuntary unemployment, though he emphasized, too, the strong leisure preference of labourers, when their real wages rose, complaining that the poor 'will not provide for a hard time, but just work so much and no more, as may maintain them in that mean condition to which they have been accustomed' (19). Child also approved the restrictions of the Navigation Acts on economic grounds, and argued that the trade of the colonies should be strictly regulated by the mother country, if the 'plantations' were not to become a burden – as that in New England, he maintained, already was.

More on the side of freedom, Child argued for liberal naturalization laws, and recognized the force of competition:

> ... they that can give the best price for a commodity shall never fail to have it by one means or another, notwithstanding the opposition of any laws, or interposition of any power by sea or land.
>
> (129)

> Where the market is free, they shall be sure to have the trade that can sell the best pennyworth.
>
> (184)

Perhaps rather more neutral, though far from unbiased, was his rejection of arguments about the balance of trade in terms of one particular commodity, or type of trade, and that it was only the general balance which might be significant. He also pleaded that though the East India Company 'import much more goods into England than they export', and that 'to purchase the same they carry out quantities of gold and silver annually', nevertheless this trade was beneficial to the English economy (143).

Child was an unsystematic writer, obviously heavily biased by his own special financial interests, and is comparable in intellectual style and standards with Thomas Mun. But he gave pointed, if brief, expression to some important emerging ideas. Moreover, as Professor Letwin has remarked, 'with frequent reprinting of the *New Discourse*, Child came to be the most widely read of seventeenth-century English economic writers' (26). The influence and stimulus of his work continued into the second half of the eighteenth century, not only in England, but in France, when his *New Discourse*, and the pamphlet of Culpeper were translated by Vincent Gournay (1754). So, whatever its precise merits or demerits, Child's work was not without importance for the history of economic thought, in that it not only provided the cue, or stimulus, for the contribution to political economy of the great John Locke, but continued to arouse wide interest for well over half a century.[4]

III

John Locke (1632–1704), the son of a lawyer in the Somerset village of Wrington, came from a Puritan family and started life in a rather higher stratum of the middle class than had William Petty. In contrast with Petty's adventurous, nomadic youth, Locke's was spent first at Westminster School and then at Christ Church, Oxford, to which he proceeded in 1652, just when Petty was departing. In studying at Oxford, and in turning to medicine, as well as in being later elected to the Royal Society, Locke, though a man, in other ways, of a very different intellectual type, followed, at an early vital stage, somewhat similar paths and interests to those of Petty. In his early years at Christ Church, Locke pursued his classical studies and lectured in Greek and Rhetoric. One of his courses of lectures at Oxford was on the Law of Nature, which was important for his later economic writings. But, for a time, medicine became his main interest and study. Though he also worked briefly in Robert Boyle's chemistry laboratory, he began to practise as a doctor. It was as his personal physician that Locke's important association began with Anthony Ashley Cooper, later the first Earl of Shaftesbury, whom he joined in London in 1667, and who in 1672 became Lord High Chancellor. Subsequently, Locke acted as his Lordship's secretary and assistant. Shaftesbury was keenly interested in commercial development and in the expansion of colonial and international trade, and has been described by Locke's biographer as 'the complete progressive capitalist in politics; he might almost have been invented by Marx' (Cranston, 1957, 107).[5]

There then followed the first of the two periods in Locke's life (aet. *c.*35–42) when problems of 'trade' and political economy became his main interest. In 1668 he prepared a report for Shaftesbury on a proposal to reduce the rate of interest by law to 4 per cent – a measure, as we have seen, strongly supported by Josiah Child in his pamphlet of that year. Nearly a quarter of a century later Locke was to follow up his early unpublished paper with the most important of his economic writings, published in 1691.

In 1673–4 Locke served briefly as secretary to the Council of Trade and Plantations, which was a forerunner of both the Board of Trade and the Colonial Office, and took within its scope much of the field of economic policy. But following the fall of Shaftesbury in 1674 Locke spent almost fifteen years out of government, and mostly out of England, in precautionary exile in France and Holland. It was in these years that he wrote his epoch-making works, as the master of empirical philosophy and of liberal political theory. His *Essay on the Human Understanding* was finished in 1686, and his *Two Treatises of Civil Government*, was written about 1681 (both works being published in 1690 [1812]).

With the revolution of 1689, Locke sailed back from Holland, on the same ship as the Queen, and, among other activities, began his second spell as a consultant administrator in the field of trade and economic policy, becoming one of the Commissioners for Trade. He advised the government on the two important current issues concerned with interest and money. The first was that on which he had reported to Shaftesbury over twenty years before, which was the proposal of Sir Josiah Child and others, for a reduction by law in the rate of interest to 4 per cent. The second main issue of economic policy, one on which Locke made a decisive, though perhaps misguided, contribution, was that of recoinage.

Formed, as they were, between his early studies of classical literature and philosophy, and his later masterpieces on philosophy and political theory – and also his works on education, toleration, and religion – Locke's economic ideas were, to some extent, shaped by those of the natural-law philosophers. His economic writings, on the other hand, might rather be classified with those of the topical pamphleteers, since they begin and end as direct contributions to current problems of policy – though they were certainly also important, methodologically, for introducing the idea of natural laws into political economy in England.

In his *Essays on the Law of Nature* (written in 1663–4), Locke described natural laws as existing both normatively and positively. Normatively, 'a law of nature can be derived from men's consciences; from the fact that "no one who commits a wicked action is acquitted from his own judgement"' (1954, 117). In a positive sense, the existence of natural laws was:

> ... derived from the very constitution of this world, wherein all things observe a fixed law of their operations and a manner of existence appropriate to their nature ... This being so, it does not seem that man alone is independent of laws while everything else is bound. On the contrary, a manner of acting is prescribed to him that is suitable to his nature.
>
> (177)

The combined normative-positive quality of natural laws derived from their divine source: God's creation was based on justice. Locke conceived of natural laws in trade and economics as similar in kind to those discovered in chemistry and physics by his friends Boyle and Newton.[6] He held that it was the duty of the policy-maker to formulate positive laws which corresponded with the divinely framed natural laws. Otherwise, policies were bound to be damaging, and to fail in their purposes. There existed, for example, a 'natural' rate of interest, which it was vain, or harmful, for the statesman to attempt to override by legislation, or to supplant by a lower or higher rate. Locke, however, did not deduce, as Adam Smith and later economists did, more general *laissez-faire* conclusions, certainly not regarding foreign trade.

It may seem to many economists today that, in the economic world, no propositions have been discovered which may validly be described as 'laws', in the same strong sense as the laws of physics and chemistry. In the seventeenth century, however, it may have been a helpful hypothesis, or presupposition, to start from the idea of natural laws operative in the economic world, though Locke, like subsequent writers, never stated with much precision the laws which he claimed to exist. Subsequently, in the eighteenth century, the idea of economic laws, was, for the most part, not so strongly or widely asserted. Adam Smith, though he applied the term 'natural', in a somewhat ambiguous normative-positive manner, to particular levels of prices, wages, etc., did not go as far as Locke in emphasizing the role of laws in political economy. It was Quesnay and the physiocrats who insisted, with a vengeance, on the existence and role of natural laws, and it was the Ricardians and Marxians who brought back the idea of economic laws, even of 'iron' laws, on a par with the laws of physics and chemistry. In some circles, this pretentious terminology lasted well on into the twentieth century.

IV

As already mentioned, the first economic problem which Locke confronted was that raised by Sir Josiah Child's proposal to reduce, by law, the maximum rate of interest from 6 to 4 per cent. In his own paper of 1668 (first published in Letwin, 1963, 273ff.) Locke began by comparing the effects of such a legal reduction on the lender and on the borrowing merchant:

> It will be gain to the merchant: for if he borrow at 4 per cent and his returns be 12 per cent, he will have 8 per cent and the usurer 4, whereas they divide it now equally at 6 per cent. But this neither gets nor loses to the Kingdom in the trade, supposing the merchant and user to be both Englishmen.
> (Letwin, 1963, 273)

Thus Locke at once introduced the idea of the rate of return to the borrower from his investment, and compared it with the rate of interest paid for the loan. But he maintained that forcing down the interest rate by law would 'hinder trade', by discouraging lending and promoting hoarding: 'Now 'tis to be expected that where the venture is great and the gain small (as is lending in England upon low interest) many will choose rather to hoard up their money than venture it abroad on such terms' (274).

Already in this early paper Locke introduced the concept of 'the natural rate', or 'the natural use', and urged that it would be 'better to the advantage of the country, if the legal use were raised pretty near to the natural (by natural use I mean that rate of money which the present scarcity of money makes it naturally at)' (277).

In his *Considerations*, twenty-three years later, Locke very much amplified and improved his argument. He defined interest in purely monetary terms, as 'the price of the hire of money' (*Works*, 1812, vol. V, 4). This price, like other prices, could not effectively be regulated. Such a measure was not only likely to be far from completely successful, it could also have damaging effects. Certainly, in a free market, a low rate of interest would be beneficial: 'I grant low interest, where all men consent to it, is an advantage to trade, if merchants will regulate their gains accordingly, and men be persuaded to lend to them' (69). But attempts at regulation by law simply would not work; for 'the skilful, I say, will always so manage it, as to avoid the prohibition of your law, and keep out of its penalty, do what you can' (5). Moreover, the country had earlier been very prosperous, when, in the reigns of Elizabeth I and James I, interest rates had been at 8 and 10 per cent, which had been no hindrance to trade when the rate of return was high (66; see Leigh, 1974, 214). Attempts to force down the rate of interest by law would encourage hoarding, and monopolistic practices by bankers, which would depress trade: 'Whatsoever, therefore, hinders the lending of money, injures trade; and so the reducing of money to four per cent which will discourage men from lending, will be a loss to the Kingdom in stopping so much of the current money, which turns the wheels of trade' (14). Locke argued that 'the natural interest of money' was raised by a shortage of money, first in proportion to debts, and secondly in proportion to trade, that is either because borrowers were requiring more money to repay loans, or because more money had to be borrowed to support the level of trade.

If the market for loans was left free, then the rate of interest would settle at 'the true and natural value, which the present state of trade, money, and debts, shall always raise interest to' (5). Some regulation might, however, be desirable if a bankers' monopoly came about:

> If money were to be hired, as land is; or to be had as corn, or wool, from the owner himself, and known good security be given for it; it might then probably be had at the market (which is the true) rate, and that rate of interest would be a constant gauge of your trade and wealth. But, when a kind of monopoly . . . has put this general commodity into a few hands, it may need regulation, though what the stated rate of interest should be, in the constant change of affairs, and flux of money, is hard to determine.
> (64)

Regarding the right level of the interest rate, Locke went on to put forward,

> . . . as a reasonable proposal, that it should be within such bounds, as should not, on the one side, quite eat up the merchant's and tradesman's profit, and discourage their industry; nor, on the other hand, so low, as should hinder men from risking their money in other men's hands, and so rather choose to keep it out of trade, than venture it upon so small a profit.'
> (64; quoted by Vickers, 1959, 51)

But the general conclusion was: 'It was in vain, therefore, to go about effectually to reduce the price of interest by a law; and you may as rationally hope to set a fixed rate upon the hire of houses, or ships, as of money' (10).

V

Locke believed profoundly that money must possess intrinsic value, based on the qualities which the precious metals were generally recognized as embodying. Although otherwise practically useless, gold and silver had, outstandingly more than other goods, the qualities necessary for serving as money, or as a medium of exchange and store of value:

> For mankind, having consented to put an imaginary value upon gold and silver, by reason of their durableness, scarcity, and not being very liable to be counterfeited, have made them, by general consent, the common pledges, whereby men are assured, in exchange, for them, to receive equally valuable things, to those they parted with, for any quantity of these metals . . .
> (*Works*, 1812, vol. V, 22)

No governmental laws could give intrinsic value to paper bills:

> . . . A law cannot give to bills that intrinsic value, which the universal consent of mankind has annexed to silver and gold; and hence foreigners can never be brought to take your bills or writings, for any part of payment, though perhaps they might pass as valuable considerations among your own people, did not this very much hinder it, *viz.* that they are liable to unavoidable doubt, dispute, and counterfeiting, and require other proofs to assure us that they are true and good security, than our eyes, or a touchstone.
> (23)

As Locke stated at the start of his *Further Considerations* (1695): 'The intrinsic value of silver, considered as money, is that estimate which common consent has placed on it, whereby it is made equivalent to all other things, and consequently is the universal barter, or exchange . . . and thus, as the wise man tells us, money answers all things' (139).

Locke's deeply rooted belief in the intrinsic value of money was to shape his views on the second major policy issue of the 1690s, that of re-coinage, on which he expressed influential views. In the second of his *Two Treatises of Government* Locke had put great emphasis on the original function of money as a store of value: 'And thus came in the use of money, some lasting thing that men might keep without spoiling, and that by mutual consent men would take in exchange for the truly useful, but perishable support of life' (365). In the *Considerations* Locke was concerned more with money as a medium of exchange, and with the need for a certain quantity of money to sustain the volume of trade:

> So that it is requisite to trade, that there should be so much money, as to keep up the landholder's, labourer's, and broker's credit and therefore ready money must be constantly exchanged for wares and labour, or follow within a short time after.
>
> This shows the necessity of some proportion of money to trade; but what that proportion is, is hard to determine; because it depends not barely on the quantity of money, but the quickness of its circulation.
>
> (23)

The vital element of 'quickness of circulation' would be enhanced by more frequent payments: 'it were better for trade, and consequently for everybody (for more money would be stirring and less would do the business) if rents were paid by shorter intervals than six months' (27). Certainly, insofar as he was concerned about the dangers of hoarding and stagnation, Locke was more of a mercantilist-Keynesian than a classical.

As regards the value of money, this, like all values, depended on quantity and vent: 'That which regulates the price, i.e. the quantity given for money (which is called buying and selling) . . . is nothing else but their quantity in proportion to their vent' (36). Locke offered no special explanation of the 'vent' of money, though he defined the term 'vent' as: 'nothing else but the passing of commodities from one owner to another, in exchange; and is then called quicker, when a greater quantity of any species of commodity is taken off from the owner of it, in an equal space of time' (43).

For Locke, the determinants of the value of money were quantity as modified by 'quickness of circulation', together with 'trade', or transactions: 'the value of money in any one country, is the present quantity of the current money in that country in proportion to the present trade' (49). Locke then went on to apply his analysis, in the first instance, to an abstract case, that of an isolated island, 'separate from the commerce of the rest of mankind', where 'any quantity of that money . . . would serve to derive any proportion of trade, whether more or less' (48).

The case was not the same, however, in a country 'that hath open commerce with the rest of the world'. If this country 'uses money made of the same materials with their neighbours, any quantity of that money will not serve to drive any quantity of trade' (49). Here Locke put forward a kind of purchasing-power-parity theory:

> ... to keep you going without loss, your commodities amongst you must keep an equal, or at least near the price of the same species of commodities in the neighbouring countries; which they cannot do, if your money be far less than in other countries: for then either your commodities must be sold, very cheap, or a great part of your trade must stand still, there not being money enough in the country to pay for them ...
>
> (49)

Trade imbalances, with inward or outward flows of specie, would make, respectively, for higher or lower prices. An inflow would bring higher prices and less favourable terms of trade; an outflow would bring lower prices, stagnation, and probably the emigration of skilled labour. Locke either did not perceive the possibility of a self-adjusting mechanism, or did not believe that it would actually work out effectively. He apparently did not discern how, in deficit countries, lower prices would probably reduce imports and increase exports, or, in the surplus countries, higher prices would tend to increase imports and reduce exports. A clear exposition of the self-adjusting mechanism was not developed until the eighteenth century.[7]

The second major issue of current policy, at which Locke's economic writings were directed, was that of the re-coinage in the 1690s. He took up this question towards the end of his *Considerations*, and devoted his *Further Considerations* (1695 [1812]) to a full statement of his views. In the early 1690s English currency and English credit were in a bad way. The currency consisted partly of old silver coins which, through much clipping, had lost a large part of their silver content, while the newer unclippable coins rapidly disappeared from circulation, to be melted down into bullion and disposed of at a considerable profit. Nor did it pay to take silver to the mint for coining. In 1694 the critical situation was aggravated by a burst of inflation brought about by the issue of bank notes by the newly founded Bank of England, created in that year to raise money for the hard-pressed government.[8]

The problem was to re-establish confidence by producing a new, trustworthy currency without, in the process, seriously contracting the coinage in circulation. A senior Treasury official, William Lowndes (1652–1724) was asked by the Privy Council to put forward a scheme. In his *Report* containing an *Essay for the Amendment of the Silver Coin* (1695), Lowndes proposed that the debasement that had taken place should be accepted, and that new shillings should be issued with some 25 per cent less silver content. Locke was then invited to present his views, and categorically, though courteously, denounced Lowndes' proposals as dangerous and unjust.[9]

We have noted the principles from which Locke started: an assertion of the 'real' intrinsic value of money, and a belief that attempts by government to interfere with 'natural' values, in the domestic economy, would generally be either damaging, ineffective, or unjust. So Locke proceeded to denounce the proposal to depreciate, or 'raise the coin' (as it was then described). Reducing the amount of silver in the shilling, or debasing it by adding copper, or some baser metal, was, according to Locke, simply trying to conjure with names. For him, the reality was the amount of silver in a shilling coin, not that the coin was still called a shilling. It was fraudulent for the government to put the same face value on a coin with a 20–25 per cent smaller silver content. Locke implored the government 'to preserve every one their right', and that it should 'not be for such lessening our coin, as will, without any reason, deprive great numbers of blameless men of a fifth part of their estates' (134).

Locke did not examine at all searchingly the positive effects of the proposed reform, or of his own doctrine, but harped rather on the moral issue:

> The reason why it should not be changed is this; because the public authority is guarantee for the performance of all legal contracts. But men are absolved from the performance of their legal contracts, if the quantity of silver under settled and legal denominations be altered . . . the landlord here and creditor are each defrauded of twenty per cent of what they contracted for and is their due . . . and whether this will not be a public failure of justice thus arbitrarily to give one man's right and possession to another, without any fault on the suffering man's side, and without any the least advantage to the public, I shall leave to be considered.
>
> Raising of coin is but a specious word to deceive the unwary.
>
> (144–51)

Locke's moral stance appealed to the interests of the court and the landowners, and carried the day. The consequence was a serious deflation, with the quantity of silver coinage almost halved. Much of the new coinage was melted down and sold as bullion. A severe shortage of coins ensued.

Probably a majority of economists today, like, apparently, majority opinion at the time, would be opposed to Locke's view, which, however, remained remarkably persistent. A survival of the Lockean doctrine might be traced even in the decision of 1925 to return to the gold standard at the traditional gold parity. As Feavyearyear observed: 'Largely as a result of Locke's influence, £3 17s 10½d an ounce came to be regarded as a magic price for gold from which we ought never to stray and to which, if we did, we must always return' (1963, 149; quoted by Appleby, 1978, 239).

But it was not only Locke's tenets regarding intrinsic and natural value, but also his liberal political principles, which were at the basis of his rigid opposition to depreciating the currency: the government should not have the power to alter the value of money. As Professor Appleby has put it: 'The definition of what constituted money was integral to the struggle for power that had gone on in England since the beginning of the century' (1978, 237).

VI

On the subject of value and price, Locke, in his *Considerations*, followed the analysis of the natural-law philosophers, notably Grotius and Pufendorf, whose works were well known to him. He regarded their natural-law analysis as possessing general validity, and applied it in formulating his theories of interest and money. The natural-law analysis was, basically, a supply-and-demand analysis. On the one side, there was the essential element of usefulness, utility, or service to human needs and conveniences; and, on the other side, there was scarcity, or difficulty of acquisition. Locke used the terms 'quantity' and 'vent' which were approximately, but not precisely, equivalent to supply and demand. According to Locke: 'He, that will justly estimate the value of anything, must consider its quantity in proportion to its vent, for this alone regulates the price' (1812, vol. V, 40). He insisted that everything which affected the values and prices of goods and services could be regarded as working through quantity and vent, and that it was the *proportion* between quantity and vent which determined values and prices. 'Vent', as Professor Vaughn has observed, should be defined as 'rates of sales per unit of time' (1980, 25). Tastes, the price of the good, and the prices of substitutes all affected vent. As Locke put it: 'The vent of anything depends upon its necessity or usefulness; as convenience or opinion, guided by fancy or fashion, shall determine' (30).

Thus, with his concept of 'usefulness', Locke followed, as had the natural-law theorists, a subjective approach to value. He proceeded to deal effectively with the water-and-diamonds paradox. Though a good may possess the utmost usefulness, this alone would not give it a price:

> What more useful or necessary things are there to the being, or well-being of men, than air and water? And yet these have generally no price at all, nor yield any money: because their quantity is immensely greater than their vent in most parts of the world. But, as soon as ever water (for air still offers itself everywhere, without restraint or inclosure, and therefore is nowhere of any price) comes anywhere to be reduced into any proportion to its consumption, it begins presently to have a price, and is sometimes sold dearer than wine.
>
> (41)

In his *Considerations*, therefore, Locke based value on demand and subjective usefulness, and insisted on its relativity. He would have regarded the search by some of the classicals for an absolute standard of value as a waste of time:

> ... the intrinsic, natural worth of anything, consists in its fitness to supply the necessities, or serve the conveniences of human life; and the more necessary it is to our being, or the more it contributes to our well-being, the greater is its worth. But yet ... there is no such intrinsic, natural, settled

> value in anything, as to make any assigned quantity of it constantly worth any assigned quantity of another.
>
> (42)

It may be noted that, according to Locke, it was usefulness, or service to human needs and conveniences, that determined 'intrinsic, *natural worth*' – not cost of production, or labour embodied. Locke was simply following the natural-law analysis (which we shall be examining further in the next chapter, when discussing the contribution of Samuel Pufendorf).

Elsewhere, however, in the second of his *Two Treatises of Government* (written *c.*1681, published 1690), Locke approached the problem of value from a very different angle, in fact from virtually the opposite direction to that which he had followed in his *Considerations*. In chapter V, 'Of Property', in his *Second Treatise* Locke was concerned, in the first instance, to present a labour theory of property, which he argued partly in positive and partly in normative terms: that is he sought to show how, in fact, property rights had been established, and, also, that they had been *justly* established. He began by proclaiming the human right of self-preservation, 'and consequently to meat and drink and such other things as Nature affords for their subsistence' (1812, vol. V, 352). God, Locke maintained, had 'given the world to men in common', to make use of to the best advantage for their life and convenience. Every one had a property in his own person and labour: 'Whatsoever, then, he removes out of the state that Nature hath provided and left it in, he hath mixed his labour with it, and joined to it something that is his own, and thereby makes it his property' (354). Locke then asked how much any individual had the right to appropriate? The answer may seem, even in the spacious conditions of the state of nature, quite a generous one: 'As much as any one can make use of to any advantage of life before it spoils, so much he may by his labour fix a property in' (356). Moreover, an individual might appropriate not only what he himself had laboured on, but also what an employee of his had laboured on: 'Thus, the grass my horse has bit, the turfs my servant has cut, and the ore I have digged in any place, where I have a right to them in common with others, become my property without the assignation or consent of anybody' (354).

Locke was assuming that there was 'land enough in the world to suffice double the inhabitants' (359). But then, the invention of money, and the tacit agreement of men to put a value on it, introduced the possibility of much larger possessions, and immensely extended the right to property and the possibility of accumulating it. At this point, however, Locke went on to a different and distinct point, in that he proceeded from a labour theory of property to a labour theory of value. Not only, he suggested, did labour confer a right of property, it was also the (almost) sole source of value. In fact, Locke enunciated what *might* be called a 99 per cent labour theory of value: 'if we will rightly estimate things as they come to our use, and cast up the several expenses about them – what in them is purely owing to Nature and what to labour – we shall find that in most of them ninety-nine hundredths are wholly to be put on the account of labour' (361).

Locke claimed to justify his labour theory by pointing to the example of the Americans, who, though Nature had furnished them 'as liberally as any other people with the materials of plenty', nevertheless 'have not one hundredth part of the conveniences we enjoy' (362). For land 'would scarcely be worth anything' without the application of labour, not only to final consumption goods, but in all the intermediate stages:

> ... for it is not barely the ploughman's pains, the reaper's and thresher's toil, and the baker's sweat, is to be counted into the bread we eat; the labour of those who broke the oxen, who digged and wrought the iron and stones, who felled and framed the timber employed about the plough, mill, oven, or any other utensils, which are a vast number, requisite to this corn, from its sowing to its being made bread, must all be charged on the account of labour ... Nature and the earth furnished only the most worthless materials as in themselves.
>
> (363)

Locke concluded his chapter by emphasizing how the invention of money gave people the opportunity to continue to enlarge their possessions without encroaching on the limited supply of land, or acquiring more land than they could use. In fact, Locke's primary explanation of the invention of money was in terms of its services as a store of wealth, rather than as a medium of exchange.

Though Locke mentioned labour as 'in great part the measure' of value, he did not attempt to explain how the measurement might be made, or how, precisely, relative values were determined in terms of quantities of labour of different qualities. So it could be held that Locke did not propound a labour theory of relative values and prices; and, therefore, that there was no outright contradiction between the natural-law analysis of value in his *Considerations*, and his treatment of labour and value in the *Second Treatise*. But there were some untidy loose ends between the two treatments. It cannot very cogently be argued that the analysis in terms of labour in the *Second Treatise* was somehow in more profound or long-run terms, because Locke had emphasized in his *Considerations* that 'intrinsic' and 'natural' values depended fundamentally on usefulness. Though, however, there were some important contrasts between Locke's treatment, or treatments, of value and price, and that of Adam Smith, it seems that the influence, on this subject, of Locke on Smith may have been considerable. Of still broader significance was Locke's economic account of the formation of political societies, in terms of the right to economic self-preservation by individuals via the acquisition of private property.

VII

Locke did not attempt any systematic exposition of economic policy and of the principles thereof, such as Petty had sketched out in his *Treatise*.

He confined himself, almost entirely, to the two specific questions which faced him during his time as a consultant administrator, though he sought to base his answers to these questions on the general principles of the natural-law analysis. Certainly Locke was one of the great masters of liberal political philosophy. He also firmly upheld the right of the individual to private property as the basis of the politico-economic order. He assumed, too, the existence of beneficent natural laws, underlying economic activity. Nevertheless, Locke did not expound or maintain any general principle of freedom or *laissez-faire* in economic policy-making. Certainly he believed that, on the whole, governments lacked the knowledge and foresight to intervene, other than ineffectively or harmfully, in the field of prices and interest rates. As regards money, 'it is as little capable to have its yearly hire fixed by law, as land itself' (*Works*, 1812, vol. V, 33). As for attempts to fix the rent of land:

> The absurdity and impracticalness of this every one sees, at the first proposal, and readily concludes within himself, that things must be left to find their own price; and it is impossible, in this their constant mutability, for human foresight to set rules and bounds to their constantly varying proportion and use, which will always regulate their value.
>
> (34)

But Locke saw the need for regulation where a harmful monopoly might exist, as in the case (already mentioned) of bank lending, where, apparently, monopoly practices had come about by agreement.

Moreover, Locke did not believe, either that the economic system automatically adjusted to a full or high level of employment, or that a country's balance of trade was effectively self-regulating. In his published writings Locke did not propose the comprehensive regulation of imports, and subsidies on exports, which were called for by many of his mercantilist contemporaries. He did, however, maintain a zero-sum view of international economic relations, holding that what counted was the percentage or proportion of specie held by a country compared with that held by other countries, and not absolute quantities. This view, Heckscher maintained, was the view 'most characteristic' of mercantilism. According to Locke:

> Riches do not consist in having more gold and silver, but in having more in proportion than the rest of the world, or than our neighbours, whereby we are enabled to procure to ourselves a greater plenty of the conveniences of life than comes within the reach of neighbouring Kingdoms and states, who sharing the gold and silver of the world in a less proportion, want the means of plenty and power, and so are poorer.
>
> (*Works*, 1812, vol. V, 13, quoted by Heckscher, 1955, vol. II, 23)

Heckscher even went so far as to draw a comparison between Locke and Colbert (27).

It seems that, much more than was suggested in his published writings, Locke's influence as a Commissioner of Trade (1696–1700) was at a number of points exercised in a markedly mercantilist direction, that is, in favour of extensive government intervention on behalf of narrowly nationalist objectives. Professor Joyce Appleby, after describing Locke as 'the great architect of political liberalism' (1978, 203), went on to maintain that 'Locke has frequently been claimed as a critic of mercantilism where in truth if English mercantilistic policies date from 1696, he must be considered their principal architect' (254).

On at least one issue of policy Locke advocated the most drastic government intervention to suppress, or destroy, the Irish woollen industry, because it competed with the English industry. At the same time, he proposed that help be given to develop the linen industry in Ireland. In a paper of 1697, accepted by the other Commissioners,[10] Locke argued:

> To hinder, therefore, the growth of the woollen manufacture in Ireland, so wholly incompatible with the fundamental trade of England, on which the prosperity of this nation so much depends, we are humbly of opinion that the exportation of all sorts of woollen manufactures out of Ireland to any parts whatsoever . . . be restrained and discouraged with impositions, penalties and all other ways which together may be sufficient to hinder it.
>
> (Fox-Bourne, 1876, vol. II, 364)

In another paper of the same year – described by his biographer, Professor Cranston, as 'an appalling document' – Locke presented a rigorous and detailed plan for the reform of the Poor Law. These proposals, which might be considered profoundly illiberal, included rounding up adult males found begging 'in maritime counties', and sending them for compulsory service and hard labour at sea for three years, together with whipping and compulsory labour for children under fourteen found begging outside their parish, as well as a series of similar measures involving conscription and regimentation of the poor and unemployed (377ff.).

Perhaps Locke might be described as more liberal and less mercantilist in theory, and more mercantilist and less liberal in practical policy-making. Perhaps, also, Keynes was justified in describing 'the great Locke' as 'standing with one foot in the mercantilist world and with one foot in the classical world' (1936, 342–3).[11] Perhaps, however, 'mercantilist' and 'classical', as a dichotomy, are seriously inadequate when attempting to categorize most writers of any depth or sophistication in this period or, perhaps, in any other.

Locke was a great philosopher-economist. But 'trade', or political economy, was not one of the subjects to which he made the most distinguished of his contributions. He did not, like Hume in his *Essays*, select his own leading, major topics for masterly and illuminating treatment; nor, of course, did he ever devote himself, as did J. S. Mill, to a comprehensive treatment of the principles of the subject. Locke's economic questions were selected in accordance with what emerged for him, as a temporary consultant administrator, as the leading policy issues at the two periods during which he worked at the subject. This rather intermittent concern with problems of political economy may explain, in part, certain ambiguities, loose ends, and even, as some have said, inconsistencies in his economic writings, to which the contrasting interpretations which have been placed on parts of his theories, seem to point.[12] Though Locke's economic writings hardly possess the stimulating and forthright originality of those of Petty, they rendered three major services to the emerging subject of political economy:

First, Locke's economic work contributed immensely to the merging of the two main disparate types of economic literature, the writings of the natural-law philosophy, traceable back to Aristotle, and the stream of topical pamphlets on current policy issues. Locke's work, in fact, exemplified that developing merger.

Second, together with Petty and North, Locke contributed importantly to the methodology of the subject. While Petty had introduced the challenge of quantification, and of critical, Baconian, natural-scientific empiricism, and while the brothers North had advanced the claims of *a priorist*, Cartesian deductivism, Locke significantly fostered the application of the idea of natural law to the economic world.

Third, the weight of his great philosophical and political authority lent an importance to Locke's economic writings which continued well on into the middle decades of the eighteenth century. His work was active as a stimulus during the great efflorescence of the subject after 1750, not only in England, but, through translations, in France and Italy. Finally, for better or for worse, the influence on Adam Smith of Locke's labour theories of property and value seems to have been important. It was this influence which Marx had in mind when he described Locke as 'the classical exponent of bourgeois society's ideas of right and wrong', and Locke's philosophy as having 'served all subsequent English economists as the foundation for all their ideas' (1951, 29; quoted by Winch, 1978, 18).

VIII

Nicholas Barbon (1637–98) was born in London, the son of the Anabaptist preacher Praise-God Barbon (or 'Barebones'). Like Petty and Locke, Barbon studied medicine, and, like Petty, he did so at Leiden, Holland. Also like Petty and Locke he did not make a career of medicine, becoming a business tycoon, or projector, in the first instance in large-scale building, by seizing the opportunities which resulted from the great fire of London of 1666. He was also a pioneer of the insurance industry, and later of banking, with the establishment of his Land Bank. In the nineties he was twice a Member of Parliament.

His best-known economic work is his *Discourse of Trade* (1690). His *Apology for the Builder* (1685) is also interesting, though it is mainly a boost for the building industry, in particular in London, which, Barbon claimed had grown by one-third in the previous twenty-five years, and had become 'the Metropolis of Europe' (1685, 2). The concept of riches was defined as follows:

> The rich are fed, clothed, and housed by the labour of other men, but the poor by their own; and the goods made by this labour are the rents of the rich men's land (for to be well fed, well clothed, and well lodged, without labour either of body mind, is the true definition of a rich man).
>
> (1685, 5)

Such was the growth of wealth that much more labour was devoted 'to things necessary to make up the general distinctions of men' than to necessities.

Barbon's *Discourse of Trade* is a compact, but wide-ranging pamphlet of some thirty-six pages, which opens with an emphasis on the political importance of recent rapid economic growth: 'Trade is now become as necessary to preserve governments, as it is useful to make them rich' (1690, reprinted 1934, 5). But men's thoughts and writings on the subject had gone astray. This was because

> . . . they apply their thoughts to particular parts of trade, wherein they are chiefly concerned in interest; and having found out the best rules and laws for forming that particular part, they govern their thoughts by the same notions in forming the great body of trade, and not reflecting on the different rules of proportions betwixt the body and parts.
>
> (7)

After some brief preliminaries about the various types of trade and goods (or 'wares'), Barbon was soon tackling the subject of value and price, on which his contribution was outstanding.[13] He followed the general lines of the natural-law approach in terms of usefulness and scarcity, but stressed the subjective elements even more explicitly. Barbon began: 'The value of all wares arise [*sic*] from their use; things of no use, have no value . . . they are good for nothing' (13).

'Use' derived from the power to satisfy wants, which were generally of two kinds, wants of the body and wants of the mind. Most goods, Barbon insisted, supplied wants of the mind, rather than of the body. Wants of the body consisted of bare physical necessities, largely food. On the other hand, Barbon emphasized the great significance of goods that supplied wants of the mind:

> The wants of the mind are infinite; man naturally aspires, and as his mind is elevated, his senses grow more refined, and more capable of delight; his desires are enlarged, and his wants increase with his wishes, which is for everything that is rare, can gratify his senses, adorn his body, and promote the ease, pleasure, and pomp of life. (14)

> It is not necessity that causeth the consumption; Nature may be satisfied with little, but it is the wants of the mind, fashion, and desire of novelties, and things scarce, that causeth trade.
>
> (35)

Barbon remarked on the desire for distinction, especially in clothing: 'for no creatures adorn the body but man; beside the decking of the body doth not only distinguish man from beast, but is the mark of difference and superiority betwixt man and man' (14).

Barbon then turned to price and scarcity, implicitly introducing the idea of diminishing utility:

> The price of wares is the present value; and ariseth by computing the occasions or use for them, with the quantity to serve that occasion; for the value of things depending on the use of them, the overplus of those wares, which are more than can be used, become worth nothing; so that plenty, in respect of the occasion, makes things cheap; and scarcity, dear.
>
> (15)

Prices were constantly changing because the uses and scarcities of goods were constantly changing. Their scarcities changed because of natural factors, such as dearths, famines, and years of great plenty; and their 'uses' because these, 'proceeding from imagination, the mind changeth; the things grow out of use, and so lose their value' (15). With values and prices always in a state of change, they had to be 'guessed at'. There were two guidelines for such guesses: 'the price of the artificer and the price of the merchant'. The price of the artificer was arrived at 'by reckoning the cost of the materials, with the time of working them'. Barbon noted, however, that the cost of labour time varied widely with art and skill. For the merchant, interest was the most important cost. But it was not costs, but supply and demand in the market that were the decisive determinants. '. . . the market is the best judge of value; for by the concourse of buyers and sellers, the quantity of wares, and the occasion for them, are best known: things are just worth so much as they can be sold for, according to the old rule, *valet quantum vendi potest*' (16).

Next Barbon turned to money, credit and interests, taking a view fundamentally different from that of Locke. While Locke insisted on the full, metallic value of currency, Barbon, as Professor Douglas Vickers has observed, was a 'cartalist'. Vickers observes that Barbon's work, though not always consistent, provided 'the first statement in systematic form of the cartalist position, which in the eighteenth century, was to be developed by Law, Berkeley and Steuart' (1959, 75n.). The cartalist view of money was that general acceptability was the essential quality of money, which did not need to possess any intrinsic, metallic value, provided that it was generally acknowledged as legal tender, not because of a value derived from the value of precious metals, but because of the stamp put on it by government:

> Some men have so great an esteem for gold and silver, that they believe they have an intrinsic value in themselves, and cost up the value of everything by them: the reason of this mistake, is, because money being made of gold and silver, they do not distinguish betwixt money, and gold and silver. Money hath a certain value, because of the law; but the value of gold and silver are uncertain, and varies their price as much as copper, lead, or other metals.
>
> (18)

Thus, following the strongly subjective line he took in his value theory, Barbon denied any absolute or objective value in gold or silver: 'It is only the scarcity that keeps up the value, and not any intrinsic virtue or quality in the metals . . . nothing in itself hath a certain value; one thing is as much worth as another: and it is time and place that give a difference to the value of all things' (18).

Barbon put great emphasis on credit: 'Credit is a value raised by opinion, it buys goods as money does; and in all trading cities, there's more wares sold upon credit, than for present money' (19). He went on to call for the establishment of 'public banks of credit' in England, as existed in Amsterdam and Venice. He recognized that a public bank might be abused by a 'despotical' government. Rather optimistically, however, Barbon maintained that:

> . . . in England, where the government is not despotical; but the people free; and have as great a share in the sovereign legislative power, as the subjects of any state have, or ever had . . . and where the flourish of trade is as much the interest of the King as of the people, there can be no such cause of fear.
>
> (20)

On the subject of interest Barbon made another important contribution, emphasizing the 'real' rather than the monetary aspect of interest, which he compared with rent: rent was the return on natural, or 'unwrought' stock, or capital, while interest was the return on man-made, 'wrought', or 'artificial' capital: 'Interest is commonly reckoned for money; because the money borrowed at interest is to be repaid in money; but this is a mistake; for the interest is paid for stock: for the money borrowed is laid out to buy goods, or pay for them before bought' (20). Schumpeter (1954, 329–30) saw this as 'a new departure', and 'a momentous statement', in that Barbon was foreshadowing the 'real' analysis of saving, investment and interest, which – via Joseph Massie and David Hume in the eighteenth century – became such a vital element in the work of the English classicals. Schumpeter may have exaggerated somewhat the significance of Barbon's words, but they remain noteworthy.[14] What, in any case, seems rather inconsistent on Barbon's part, was his acceptance of the fixing of interest rates by law – but even Adam Smith was in favour of some intervention in this area.

Barbon waxed enthusiastic regarding the benefits of trade, or of economic progress. Trade not only produced plenty, but made for peace. Peoples which might be unfavourably endowed by nature, instead of resorting to war to raise their standard of living, learned to achieve prosperity through trade. Moreover, again rather optimistically, Barbon observed that, 'trade allows a better price for labourers than is paid by fighting. So it is become more the interest to live at home in peace, than to seek their fortunes abroad by war' (23).

Barbon produced a remarkably prophecy regarding the British Empire. After discussing the prospects of the Dutch and the French, Barbon continued:

> But England seems the proper seat for such an empire: it is an island, therefore requires no military force to defend it. Besides, merchants and soldiers never thrive in the same place; it hath many large harbours fitting for a large dominion: the inhabitants are naturally courageous ... the monarchy is both fitted for trade and empire. And were there an act for a general naturalization, that all foreigners purchasing land in England, might enjoy the freedom of Englishmen it might within much less compass of time than any government by arms at land, arrive to such a dominion ... (31)

Barbon optimistically envisaged for England 'an empire not less glorious and of much larger extent, than either Alexander's or Caesar's' (31).

Regarding the chief causes that promoted trade, or economic growth, Barbon emphasized 'industry in the poor and liberality in the rich', together with good government, peace, and a favourable geographical situation (31). He anticipated Mandeville in the latter's *Grumbling Hive* (first published five years later) by proclaiming the public economic benefits of prodigality, 'a vice that is prejudicial to the man, but not to trade' (32). The 'covetous' or miserly man was a public enemy: 'a conspiracy of the rich men to be covetous, and not spend, would be as dangerous to a trading state as a foreign war' (32). Fashion was the spirit and life of trade 'because it occasions the expense of clothes before the old ones are worn out' (32). Barbon also claimed that building, his own trade, did much to promote the prosperity of the whole economy.

The principal causes of the decay of trade were restrictions and high interest rates. Restrictions on imports, or 'the prohibiting of any foreign commodity doth hinder the making and exportation of so much of the native, as used to be made and exchanged for it' (35). Moreover, restrictions on imports from other countries stimulated retaliation, which made for general impoverishment. Barbon followed Child in maintaining that high interest rates were damaging English trade, while Dutch trade was benefiting immensely from low interest rates. Among other benefits, low interest rates would encourage the holding of stocks and bring greater stability of prices. He denied that lowering interest would make money more scarce, or would reduce the supply of funds for lending.

The third of Barbon's pamphlets, well worthy of mention, was his *Discourses concerning Coining the New Money Lighter* (1696), which contained a fundamental refutation of Locke's views on re-coinage, published in the previous year. Barbon confronted Locke's arguments head-on, denying his basic principle regarding the intrinsic value of silver (or of any other good). Barbon restated, sometimes *verbatim*, the subjective value theory of his earlier *Discourse*: 'Nothing has a price of value in itself. The price or value of everything arises from the occasion or use for it. Plenty and scarcity, in respect to their occasion, makes things of greater or lesser value' (10).

Barbon posed the fundamental question regarding money as follows: 'Whether money has its sole value from the quantity of silver in each piece of coin? Or whether money has not some value from the authority of the government where it is coined, above the value of the silver in each piece?' (12). According to Barbon, 'Men do not buy and sell by the quantity of silver in the coin' (23). Money derived its value from being made legal tender (28): ''Tis the current and lawful money of England that men contract for, and oblige themselves in their bonds to pay' (29).

Re-coining the money at the old standard, as recommended by Locke, would cause a vast deflation: 'For if all the money should be new coined to the old standard, it would not produce much above half the quantity of the money before it was coined' (94). Barbon concluded:

> If nothing in itself has a certain price or value; if gold and silver are commodities of uncertain values; if money has its own value from the authority of the government, which makes it current, and fixes the price of each piece of metal; then the money will be as good value to all intents and purposes when it is coined lighter. For the authority being the same, the value will be the same. It will buy as much goods: the landlord will have as much rent; and the nation will save a million of money at a time when they have so great occasion for it; besides the preventing those fatal consequences that follow coining the money too weighty; as the loss of the money; decay of trade; the fall of rents; and a general poverty and clamour all over the nation.
>
> (96)

Up to a point, Barbon provided an effective answer to Locke, and was mainly correct in his dire predictions regarding the effects of Locke's proposals. But Barbon's views were one-sided in that he made no reference to the dangers of inflation which could follow from the propensity of governments to debase the coinage.

Barbon may also be regarded as an early advocate of freer trade. He attacked the balance-of-trade doctrine as vigorously as Adam Smith, eighty years later, as based on 'this supposition that gold and silver are the only riches' (36). On the contrary, one sort of commodity was as good as another. Certainly Barbon maintained that 'a well-regulated and proportioned duty laid upon foreign wares, may be very useful to a trading nation' (42), but he balanced this with the view that the freer its trade, the better the nation will thrive. Barbon categorically denied Mun's comparison of a nation's trading accounts with the accounts of a private individual.

The assessment of Barbon's economic theories and writings seems sometimes to have been unduly affected by his reputation as a wealthy and unscrupulous businessman who refused to pay his debts, and also by elements of special pleading at some points in his works. In the last analysis, however, such defects may seem irrelevant in view of the basic merits of his ideas and theories, which, at important points, were in advance of their time.

IX

Sir Dudley North (1641–91), one of five brothers, came from a talented noble family, which, in the eighteenth century was also to produce a well-known (or notorious) Prime Minister. Born in the year in which Mun died, Dudley North spent much of his career as a merchant in the Levant trade and resided for some time in Turkey. Returning to England in 1680, he occupied a succession of posts in the Tory government of James II, including that of Commissioner of Customs. His remarkable *Discourses upon Trade* (1691) were produced right at the end of his life, having been stimulated by the proposal to reduce the maximum interest rate by law, and also by the debates about the coinage.

Two points about North's *Discourses* should be noted before we examine their content. First, the pamphlet seems to have disappeared from view almost completely very soon after its publication. Later, it was disinterred and its merits publicized by James Mill and McCulloch. Mill described North as one of the few writers who 'at a comparatively early period had attained wonderfully correct notions on the principles of commerce' (*Encyclopedia Britannica*, 1818, quoted by Letwin, 1963, 254). It does not, however, seem necessarily to have been the case that, at the time of its publication, North's work was ignored as completely as it came to be later. But it is not for any considerable early influence, which it may or may not have exercised, that it is today of such great interest.[15]

There is, second, a question as to the authorship of parts of the pamphlet, which has been expertly examined by Professor Letwin (1963, appendix IV, 251ff.). It appears that the preface, and perhaps one or two other paragraphs, were written by Dudley's brother Roger, who revised the work for publication, which probably took place, not, as stated on the title page, in 1691, but early in 1692, soon after Dudley's death at the end of 1691. Roger's enthusiastic exposition and summary is in close agreement with his brother's line of argument, but runs somewhat beyond it in the challenging, comprehensive boldness of its doctrines regarding both method and policy.

The *Discourses*, a pamphlet of about thirty pages of text, but packed closely with content of fundamental significance for economic method, theory and policy, consisted of a preface, two *Discourses*, one on interest and one on coined money, and a brief postscript, adding or re-emphasizing one or two points. We may take first the two Discourses, unquestionably Dudley's work, and then go on to the postscript, and finally to the preface, which was clearly written after the rest, presumably by Roger.

The first *Discourse* was concerned with 'the abatement of interest'. As posed by North, the question was: 'Whether the government have reason by a law, to prohibit the taking more than 4 per cent interest for money lent, or to leave the borrower and lender to make their own bargains' (1691, 15). North started with some basic generalizations regarding the nature of exchange: 'Trade is nothing else but a commutation of superfluities: I give of mine, what I can spare, for somewhat of yours, which I want, and you can spare' (16). As regards the source and nature of wealth

> ... he who is most diligent, and raiseth most fruits, or maketh most of manufactory, will abound most in what others make, or raise; and consequently be free from want, and enjoy most conveniences, which is

truly to be rich, although there were no such thing as gold, silver, or the like among them.

(16)

It was plenty that made for cheapness, whether with regard to corn, wool, or loans of money:

> ... it will be found, that as plenty makes cheapness in other things, as corn, wool, etc., when they come to market in greater quantities than there are buyers to deal for, the price will fall; so if there by more lenders than borrowers, interest will also fall; wherefore it is not low interest makes trade, but trade increasing, the stock of the nation makes interest low.
>
> (18)

If interest was lower in Holland, it was not because of any laws by government to reduce it, but because the Dutch had more 'stock' available for lending.

According to North, only one-tenth of all loans in England were to 'trading people' for financing their business, the other nine-tenths being for luxury consumption, often to landowners who 'spend faster than their lands bring in' (20). No legislation could prevent such transactions. Therefore, North concluded, 'it will be found best for the nation to leave the borrowers and the lenders to make their own bargains, according to the circumstances they lie under; and in so doing you will follow the course of the wise Hollanders' (29). A general conclusion followed regarding supply and demand. It was 'an universal maxim, that as more buyers than sellers raiseth the price of a commodity, so more borrowers than lenders will raise interest' (21).

North's second *Discourse* attacked the idea that it was lack of money that depressed trade. Gold and silver were exchanged, like all other goods, and were, 'in no sort different from other commodities, but are taken from them who have plenty, and carried to them with as good profit as other merchandises. So that an active prudent nation groweth rich, and the sluggish drones grow poor' (25).

North went on to anticipate Mandeville's argument, in *The Fable of the Bees*, to the effect that it was 'private vices' that were the great stimulus behind economic activity: 'The main spur to trade, or rather to industry and ingenuity, is the exorbitant appetites of men, which they will take pains to gratify, and so be disposed to work, when nothing else will incline them to it; for did men content themselves with bare necessaries, we should have a poor world' (27).

In fact, 'there is benefit from the very person of a covetous man', while countries which had sumptuary laws were generally poor:

> ... the growth of wealth in the nation is hindered; for that never thrives better, than when riches are tossed from hand to hand.
>
> The meaner sort seeing their fellows become rich, and great, are spurred up to imitate their industry. A tradesman sees his neighbour keep a coach, presently all his endeavour is at work to do the like, and many times is

> beggared by it; however the extraordinary application he made, to support his vanity was beneficial to the public ...
>
> (27–8)

North expressed doubts about re-coinage, which he considered would be too costly. He stressed the difficulty of making estimates of the quantity of money, which were liable to be exaggerated because the velocity of circulation was not allowed for – or rather the converse thereof – the time for which people hold money was not taken into account:

> We are apt to make over-estimates of the quantities of current money; for we see it often, and know it not again, and are not willing to consider how very little time it stays in a place; and although every one desires to have it, yet none, or very few, care for keeping it but they are forthwith contriving to dispose of it; knowing that from all the money that lies dead, no benefit is to be expected, but it is a certain loss.
>
> (32)

Here North was anticipating the Smithian and classical idea that no one wanted money for its own sake, or that hoarding was irrational, and not a serious problem. This second *Discourse* concluded with some confident, unqualified generalizations, which also have quite a Smithian ring, and in which Professor Letwin detects the hand of Roger:

> ... I doubt not but we shall join in one uniform sentiment; that laws to hamper trade, whether foreign or domestic, relating to money, or other merchandises, are not ingredients to make a people rich, and abounding money and stock. But if peace be procured, easy justice maintained, the navigation not clogged, the industrious encouraged ... the stock of the nation will increase, and consequently gold and silver abound, interest be easy, and money cannot be wanting.
>
> (33)

The postscript restated North's fundamental maxim 'that plenty of anything makes it cheap' (34), and went on to discern the operation of self-adjusting forces in the money supply and in the economy:

> This ebbing and flowing of money, supplies and accommodates itself, without any aid of politicians. For when money grows scarce, and begins to be hoarded, then forthwith the mint works, till the occasion be filled up again. And on the other side, when peace brings out the hoards, and money abounds, the mint not only ceaseth, but the overplus of money will be presently melted down, either to supply the home trade, or for transportation.
>
> (36)

The authors, however, were not apparently convinced that this self-adjusting ebbing and flowing, or self-equilibration, always operated smoothly and conveniently, without damaging fluctuations. For one of the conclusions of the preface stated: 'That money is a merchandise, whereof some may be a glut, as well as a scarcity, *and that even to an inconvenience*' (14, italics added). The postscript ended, however, with a restatement of the great principle: 'Thus we may labour to hedge in the cuckoo, but in vain; for no people ever yet grew rich by policies; but it is peace, industry, and freedom that brings trade and wealth, and nothing else' (37).

In the preface it was claimed that the author of the *Discourses* was 'of a temper different from most who have meddled with this subject in public' (10), in that, though possessing knowledge and experience of trade, 'he speaks impartially of trade in general, without warping to the favour of any particular interest' (10). This provided a contrast with most merchants, whose views about trade were biased by their interests, so that 'when opposite interests were concerned, they differed *toto coelo*' (10). But it was asserted that any charges of partiality against the author of the *Discourses* were unfounded, because he stated his reasons, when maintaining, for example, that 'no laws can set prices in trade, the rates of which must and will settle themselves' (13), and that interest 'should be left freely to the market, and not be restrained by law' (10). The author's method, moreover, of starting 'from principles indisputable true', apparently guaranteed the impartial quality of his conclusions. For it was observed that his work was based on a method of reasoning introduced by 'the new philosophy', as expounded by Descartes in his 'excellent dissertation *de Methodo*' (11). By this method 'knowledge in great measure is become mechanical', by being 'built upon clear and evident truths'. The preface closed with some thirteen conclusions, arrived at by this new and infallible method, which included: 'That the whole world as to trade is but as one nation or people, and therein nations are as persons . . . That there can be no trade unprofitable to the public; for if any prove so, men leave it off; and wherever the traders thrive, the public, of which they are a part, thrives also' (13).

Dudley and Roger North were, therefore, pioneers of the Cartesian, rationalistic, deductive or geometric, method, subsequently deployed in the nineteenth and twentieth centuries, in slightly varying ways, by, among others, Senior and Mises. Those specializing in this method in political economy and economics, have usually been vigorous upholders of individualistic, free-market principles, though sometimes claiming, like the Norths, the impartiality of their conclusions, based on 'indisputable' axioms, or 'clear and evident truths'. One request, which it seems reasonable to press, especially in such a politically controversial field, is for a very clear, full and precise statement of these indisputably true and self-evident principles or axioms. Such a statement has often been rather difficult to obtain. It might further be noted that Descartes' *Discourse on Method*, which the Norths claimed to be following, has been cited by Friedrich Hayek as the methodological fount and origin of what he has called 'false individualism' and of a kind of 'intellectual hubris' underlying historicist claims to having discovered inevitable laws of development. Perhaps the Norths may not have followed out to the full the Cartesian method, which, according to Hayek, was to bear such dangerous fruit.[16] Anyhow, they were certainly intellectual innovators, and their brief pamphlet, however negligible its influence in its own day, presented a vigorous statement of doctrines, on both economic method and economic policy, which were to be mightily powerful in subsequent centuries.

X

North's *Discourses* have been widely regarded as providing the most forthright general statement forthcoming from English writers of the seventeenth century of the case for unrestricted markets and economic freedom. But some of the most important arguments undermining the cruder bullionist, protectionist, balance-of-trade doctrines were put forward by those concerned with the East India trade. Thomas Mun, widely regarded as the archetypal English mercantilist, an officer of the East India Company, could be said to have initiated a dilution of bullionism and protectionism, by arguing for some freedom for the export of precious metals. The case for greater freedom of trade, both in terms of the East India trade, and more generally, was taken significantly further by Charles Davenant – as noted in the previous chapter. But the most distinguished and penetrating of the writers concerned with the East India trade, who provided important general arguments and ideas regarding freedom of trade, was the author of the anonymously published *Considerations on the East-India Trade* (1701), a work not unworthy of being placed beside North's *Discourses*, which, at some points, it surpassed. The author is now generally believed to have been Henry Martyn.

Considerations on the East-India Trade is a pamphlet of eighty pages, in the first instance concerned with the case for the unrestricted import of Indian silk and cotton materials. But the work went on to present powerfully formulated general ideas and arguments in support of freedom of trade. The author began by echoing Petty on method. After alleging that his pamphlet was arguing 'directly contrary to the received opinions', Martyn claimed to base his case 'on the clearest evidence', apparently seeking somehow to combine Petty's quantitative empiricism with the Cartesian, *a priorist*, geometric method of the Norths:

> ... instead of using only comparative and superlative words to amuse the reader, the author has endeavoured, after the manner of the *Political Arithmetic*, to express himself in terms of number, weight, and measure; and he hopes, he shall not be thought to speak with confidence of anything that is not as certain as the very principles of geometry.
>
> (*Considerations on the East-India Trade*, in McCulloch, 1856 and 1952, 543)

The author first dealt with the bullionist argument against exporting gold or silver in return for Indian silk and cotton goods, by maintaining that the Indians would not be prepared to import, in return, English manufactures, which were too costly. Martyn went on to insist,

> ... that the exportation of bullion for Indian manufactures, is an exchange of less for greater value; that 'tis the most likely way to import more bullion; that the kingdom is not more impoverished by the consumption of Indian than by that of English manufactures.
>
> (556)

> ... in general we may be assured, that more or better will not be sent abroad for any quantity of bullion, than can be bought for the same in England.
>
> (557)

The forces of competition, unleashed by freedom of imports, would benefit the English economy as a whole, although some people might suffer initially: 'The East-India trade does not so much diminish the riches of some private persons, as it increases the riches of the kingdom ... The East-India trade procures manufactures at less price, and by less labour than the like would be made in England' (568). A country should only produce what it can make more cheaply than other countries. The author placed a major, pioneering emphasis on comparative costs, or cost-effectiveness in terms of labour: 'If the same work is done by one, which was done before by three; if the other two are forced to sit still, the Kingdom got nothing before by the labour of the two' (569). Martyn proceeded to claim that allowing the free export of bullion would increase the nation's import of bullion: 'By the export of this into India for manufactures, we have more of these than were carried out to procure this bullion; we are therefore enabled to export more manufactures, and consequently to import more bullion' (571). His emphasis on cost-effectiveness in terms of labour led the author to attach great importance to technological advance and to the introduction of machinery, the effects of which he compared with freedom of trade:

> A saw-mill with a pair or two of hands will split as many boards as thirty men without this mill; if the use of this mill shall be rejected, that thirty may be employed to do the work, eight and twenty are employed more than are necessary ... So, if by any art, or trade, or engine, the labour of one can produce as much for our consumption or other use, as can otherwise be procured by the labour of three; if this art, or engine shall be rejected, if three shall rather be employed to do the work, two of these are more than are necessary ... Wherefore, the people employed to make manufactures here, more than are necessary to procure the like from India, are people employed to do the work that may be done as well without 'em ...
>
> (580)

As has been observed, a stress on technological advance as a means of achieving higher productivity is rarely met with until much later in the eighteenth century (see Macleod, 1983, 228).[17]

Martyn had no qualms about increasing unemployment, or its effects on the unemployed. He may have been referring to, and denouncing, Petty's insistence on the possibly considerable benefits from useless public works, such as carrying the stones of Stonehenge to Tower Hill, when he proclaimed: 'A people would be thought extravagant and only fit for Bedlam, which with great stir and bustle should employ itself to remove stones from place to place, at last to throw 'em down where at first they took 'em up' (581). The argument from comparative labour costs was presented as follows:

> If nine cannot produce above three bushels of wheat in England, if by equal labour they might procure nine bushels from another country, to employ these in agriculture at home, is to employ nine to do no more work than might be done as well by three . . . is to employ six to no profit, which might be employed to procure as many bushels of wheat to England; is the loss of six bushels of wheat; is therefore the loss of so much value.
>
> (583)

The author was much concerned with the effects on wages of free imports. He admitted that, for some workers, money wages would be reduced, but that this would not necessarily mean a fall in real wages, and certainly not for most workers, who might obtain a real rise. Similarly, though obviously some workers would be displaced, it was apparently implied that they should find other employment, though elsewhere the author had assumed the existence of considerable unemployment (552).[18]

The author continued his comparison of freedom of trade with the introduction of improved machinery, or with improved skills, distinguishing labour costs from the level of wages: 'The East-India Trade by the importation of cheaper, must needs reduce the price of English manufactures; nevertheless it is matter of fact, that the wages of men are not abated . . . so that the East-India trade by reducing the price of manufactures, has not yet abated wages' (589).[18] Martyn argued that freedom of trade with the East Indies brought 'more order and regularity into our English manufacturers' (590), by which he seems to have meant that it improved the allocation of labour, or resources, in that 'it must put an end to such of them as are most useless and unprofitable; the people employed in these will betake themselves to others' (590).

The next major step was to introduce the vital concept of specialization and the division of labour, and their accompanying economies of scale (which had been so clearly emphasized by Petty). Martyn argued that English manufacturing should, and, when stimulated by freedom of imports, would, develop a labour force which was more specialized and varied in its skills. In cloth-making, for example, the work was divided into carding, spinning, weaving, etc., so that 'the weaver must needs be more skilful and expeditious at weaving, if that shall be his constant and whole employment, than if the same weaver is also to card and spin and make the loom . . .'. (591) Martyn developed the example of watch-making, and related the extent of specialization to the demand for the product:

> A watch is a work of great variety, and 'tis possible for one artist to make all the several parts, and at last to join them altogether; but if the demand of watches should become so very great as to find constant employment for as many persons as there are parts in a watch, if to every one shall be assigned his proper and constant work; if one shall have nothing else to make but cases, another wheels, another pins, another screws, and several others their proper parts . . . this man must needs be more skilful and

> expeditious in the composition of those several parts, than the same man could be if he were also to be employed in the manufacture of all these parts.
>
> (591–2)

The same analysis, in terms of specialization, the division of labour, and economies of scale, was applied to the key industry of shipbuilding.

Pursuing the question of the effects of economic progress brought about by specialization, Martyn observed that the relative share of wages might decline while the absolute level of the individual's wage rose. In a primitive economy – as Adam Smith was to observe almost three-quarters of a century later – the labourer got virtually the whole product. But in England, though labour received a much smaller share, the individual labourer was much better off:

> Among the wild Indians of America, almost everything is the labourer's, ninety-nine parts of an hundred are to be put upon the account of labour: in England, perhaps the labourer has not two thirds of all the conveniences of life, but then the plenty of these things is so much greater here, that a King of India is not so well lodged, and fed, and clothed, as a day-labourer of England.
>
> (594)[19]

We have seen how a number of writers, from Petty onwards, among those sometimes described as 'liberal mercantilists' put forward general viewpoints or maxims, as well as some parts of the case in favour of free markets and free trade.[20] With North and Martyn, 'liberal mercantilism' became, rather, 'mercantilist liberalism', with the liberal element predominating over the mercantilist in the *Discourses* and the *Considerations* – the latter pamphlet constituting a striking and culminating achievement in a long movement in England. But at this point, at the start of the eighteenth century, this movement received a check, the reasons for which are somewhat obscure. North and Martyn had no immediate successors developing the case for economic freedom along similar lines, or in the same style. In the eighteenth century the arguments for economic freedom, together with the more positive analysis of equilibrating, self-adjusting processes, were to start from a more general, systematic foundation, in a philosophical and moral analysis of the nature of man. This development is traced in chapter 7. The English advance in the closing decades of the seventeenth century had come to a halt, or had very much slowed down. But, before concluding this part of the story, a brief examination must be made of the economic literature of other countries in the latter part of the seventeenth century, while the English advance was still in progress.

6
Continental Alternatives: Colbertism and Cameralism: Natural Law and Moral Philosophy

I

In the latter part of the seventeenth century when, in England, Petty, Locke, North and others were making such important and, in some cases, highly original advances in economic method, theory and policy, a very different kind (or kinds) of economic discourse was prevalent on the mainland of Europe, in France, Germany and Austria. Clearly the differences in economic policies, pursued in the different countries at this time, were related, even more closely than is usually the case, to the very different political frameworks, and very different institutions and philosophies prevailing in those countries, and especially to the existence or non-existence of the freedom to proclaim and discuss ideas about policy. In France, Jean Baptiste Colbert (1619–83), the son of a cloth merchant of Reims, and a protégé of Mazarin, became, on the death of his patron in 1661, the most powerful minister of Louis XIV, especially in economic affairs. His policies and ideas dominated the economic life of France until his death. Thus Colbert's career as the supreme economic policy-maker of his country coincided, chronologically, very closely with Petty's career (roughly 1660–87) as a writer and political arithmetician (though none of Petty's works would ever have got published in the France of that time).

Colbert was neither a thinker nor a theorist. Sir John Clapham maintained that Colbert had 'no single original idea' (1940, p. 389). He is not known to have read about, or studied, economic or commercial subjects. He simply absorbed the current, established ideas of his time, and used them to explain or justify his policies. Indeed, presumably largely because of the censorship, no economic writings of much importance seem to have been published in France in our period, until those of Boisguilbert and Vauban; and these two men both suffered for their boldness in criticizing the policies of the régime, not even Vauban's great prestige, and the mildness of his comments, saving him from royal disfavour. It might, perhaps, be objected that Colbert should have no place in this volume. But his policies, and his ideas, as presented in his letters, instructions, and memoranda, epitomize so forcefully what is often understood by 'mercantilism', that French mercantilism has, not inappropriately, been described as 'Colbertism'. As Heckscher claimed:

> Colbert's achievements hold a special interest chiefly because he, more than any other mercantilist statesman, formulated his programme as a complete whole and realised the connection between measures taken in different spheres. His work consequently indicates with peculiar clarity how the abolition of internal tolls was just one part of the general attempt at economic unity within the state and fitted in with the whole mercantilist system of trade – with its policy of hindering imports, encouraging exports, and free trade within the country, attracting precious metals and having a rapid circulation of money within the country.
>
> (1955, vol. I, 81)

Colbert started from a political belief in the absolute monarchy of Louis XIV, whose rule, ordained by God, it must be the supreme, overriding aim of policy to strengthen and glorify, first in France, and then abroad, by expanding the power of the greatest monarch in the world. The living standards of the people were hardly significant, except insofar as they affected tax revenues and the availability of suitable military or naval manpower.

Richelieu and Mazarin had unified France politically, but not economically. Local restrictions could bring it about that a famine in one part of the country coincided with abundance in another part. Colbert set out to unify the country economically, but was only partially successful. Externally, for Colbert, as an exponent of 'your-loss-my-gain' mercantilism (see Clapham, 1940, 390), international trade and commerce, like political power, was a relative, zero-sum game. He agreed with Montaigne that '*le profit de l'un est dommage de l'autre*' and he explicitly assumed in a memorandum to the king of 1670, that the total amount of international trade in Europe was fixed, as well as the total number of ships in which it was carried (see Clement (ed.), 1869, vol. VI, 269–70; and vol. VII, 239–40). The development of any new trade was assumed by Colbert to be 'highly uncertain'. Therefore, an expansion of trade by one country could only be at the expense of a contraction by another country. The same assumptions were applied to the stock of the precious metals: 'Commerce causes a perpetual struggle, both in peace and war, between the nations of Europe, over whom can gain the largest share. The Dutch, the English and the French are the contestants in this struggle' (op. cit., vol. VI, 266). This triangular, zero-sum relationship between Holland, England and France was Colbert's constant concern.

It was vital, moreover, to keep increasing the quantity of silver, or money, in the country, or to '*attirer l'argent*'. Though tax policies could help, the main method of achieving this growing money supply had to be through the balance of trade, by constantly striving to reduce imports and expand exports. Colbert allowed imports of essential raw materials, but summed up: 'The whole business of commerce consists in facilitating the import of those goods which serve the country's manufactures, and placing embargoes on those which enter in a manufactured state' (1869, vol. VII, 284, quoted by Heckscher, 1955, vol. II, 146).

Of course, the export of the precious metals must generally be strictly prohibited. Colbert, though more uncompromising on this point than Thomas Mun in England, nearly half a century earlier, was, however, not totally inflexible with regard to the financing of some kinds of trade, such as that with the Levant.

Self-sufficiency for France was an ultimate objective. Production and employment were to be raised to the highest levels. Idleness of any kind, whether among adults or children, had to be countered by keeping down wages and providing employment in manufacturing. The labour force was to be expanded by measures to encourage the growth of population, such as the offer of tempting tax advantages to those who married young. Immigration of skilled workmen was subsidized, and emigration was to be prohibited or prevented. The most ruthless methods were employed for rounding-up manpower for the galleys of Colbert's navy.

Many examples of ideas and policies such as these could be found in other leading countries at the time. One feature, however, of Colbert's programme was carried to extraordinary lengths. This was his intensely detailed regulation of industry by the central administration, which was hardly equalled anywhere else. An immense system of controls was built up, which laid down precise specifications regarding, for example, the measurements and qualities of textiles. These regulations prescribed uniform methods of production, specifying how raw materials were to be treated and the exact processes to be adopted at each stage of production. Severe penalties, in the form of fines and confiscation, were exacted for any goods not precisely in accord with the central government's regulations.

With regard to the development of trading companies for overseas trade, in Colbert's system the initiative, as usual, came entirely from the state, and was in the hands not of merchants, but officials. This was very different from England and, to some extent, Holland, where such companies owed their foundation and development much more to private initiative. Mention should, however, be made of one new policy direction, potentially liberal in nature, which Colbert fostered: that of furthering the commercial education of merchants and businessmen.

It was Louis XIV's wars which gave Colbert's policies little or no chance of any such solid success as they *might*, with peace, have achieved. But it was the aggressive nationalism of Colbert's own policies which had helped to bring on war. As the major study of Colbert and his achievements observes: 'Colbert's mercantilism needed peace for its progress, but it made war inevitable' (Cole, 1939, vol. II, 551). Moreover, while Colbert himself was constantly striving for economy, he was the willing tool of an exorbitantly extravagant monarch.

Towards the end of the century, Boisguilbert (as is discussed in chapter 7) was to charge Colbert with having brought about a catastrophic decline in the French economy. Though Quesnay later supported this charge, it has been categorically dismissed by a contemporary economic historian (see Hamilton, 1969). In this century also, a number of highly centralized, authoritarian régimes have attempted to raise the level of economic development by concentrating on the planned expansion of industry. But neither the normative issues raised by the policies of Colbert's twentieth-century followers, nor the historical questions of the correctness of the charges which Boisguilbert brought against these policies, can be reviewed here.

II

The word 'cameralism' seems to have been adopted in English because the original German term 'Kameral-wissenschaft' is more or less untranslatable, being derived from the word 'Kammer', which has a wide range of possible meanings and connections. In the cameralist Wilhelm Schröder's treatise, *Fürstliche Schatz- und Rent-Kammer*, the meaning is 'treasury'. But 'administrative and policy studies' would give a fuller indication of what was covered by 'Kameral-wissenschaft', which was certainly much more than simply political economy and economic policy. Political institutions, constitutional law and education policy were all included, as were not only economic policy and public finance, but the whole field of state policy. The economic policies of the cameralists had some similarities with those of the 'mercantilists'. But both the conditions and problems which they faced, and the political framework and philosophy which shaped cameralist ideas and policies, were to a large extent peculiar to Germany, as Colbert's were to France. For the German and Austrian cameralists were mostly not the supreme administrators of a large and powerful nation state, like Colbert. Nor were they wealthy and influential merchants, like a number of the English 'mercantilists', such as Mun and Child. Indeed, some French and German 'mercantilists' seem to have regarded merchants and businessmen highly unfavourably – Wilhelm von Schröder, for example. The cameralists in Germany and Austria were, for the most part, well described by Schumpeter's term 'consultant administrators', being part experts, part executives, often in the service of rather small principalities – apart, that is, from Austria. Though to some extent concerned to justify the absolutist claims of their princes, most cameralists seem to have held a considerably more qualified version of the absolutist doctrine than had Colbert in respect of Louis XIV. Moreover, the smaller scale of these principalities may have helped in keeping their rulers less remote from their subjects, and in inclining them towards a more genuinely benevolent paternalism. Though a supreme objective of economic policy was the raising of tax revenue for the prince, it was appreciated by most cameralists that the well-being of his subjects was essential for this purpose (and was also of value for its own sake). Cameralist policies, more than those of the majority of mercantilists, were directed, in the first instance, rather at internal unification, social cohesion, and the strengthening of the state within its own territory, than towards external ambitions. The cameralists were consultant administrators who assisted their prince in running his territory like a rather paternalist business enterprise.

One of the earlier, and certainly the most original of the cameralists was Johann Joachim Becher (1635–82). Born in Speyer, the son of a clergyman, he became an itinerant autodidact, polymath, projector and consultant administrator of extraordinary versatility, in a baroque age of versatility. He devoted much of his energy to the natural sciences, especially chemistry, metallurgy and alchemy, and to practical applications ranging from a perpetual-motion machine to the cultivation of the potato. Among his earliest posts was that of a teacher of medicine at the University of Mainz (which provides a parallel with Becher's near contemporary William Petty). After Mainz, Becher worked in Munich as an economic adviser and then moved to Vienna as a *Kommerzialrat*, or Commercial Counsellor, where his career and influence reached its peak. He also sojourned, at various times, in Sweden, Holland and England.[1] Becher has been described by Heckscher as not only 'the most original thinker among German mercantilists', and as 'the most important' of them, but even as 'the most remarkable personality in the whole economic literature of that time' (1955, vol. II, 205).

The politico-economic situation confronting Becher was dominated by the catastrophic devastation brought about by the Thirty Years War, in which, it has been estimated, something like 40 per cent of the population of some German states – in some even more than that – had perished from slaughter or disease. Becher was concerned, therefore, with a programme of revival and reconstruction, and he was especially prolific in projects for new industries. His main cameralistic work had the lengthy title *A Political Discourse on the Real Causes of the Rise and Decline of Cities, Provinces and Republics* (1668). Further prolonged sub-titles spelled out the main framework and topics of the *Discourse*. First, the problems were examined of 'how a country can be rendered populous and well fed, and made into a truly civilized community'. From this statement of overriding aims, Becher passed, secondly, to the three great classes, or social strata ('*Stände*'), into which the community, or economy, was divided: namely, the peasants, or agricultural workers, those working in manufacturing, and the traders or merchants. These 'classes' corresponded with the three main sectors of the economy, the food and raw-material sector, the manufacturing sector, and the distribution sector. The food and raw-material sector was basic, but was matched in importance by merchandizing and distribution, which had a vital role in keeping the economy in balance and in promoting its development. The importance and beneficence of such intersectoral balance and interdependence – it would, perhaps, be premature or anachronistic to use the term 'equilibrium' – was much emphasized by Becher, who explained how 'the people must take one another by the arm and, by ordinary trade and exchange help one another to get their daily bread' (1668, 3).

Moreover, each class must maintain its 'proportion', one to another, if a genuine 'human community' was to be achieved. Perhaps there was here something of a hint of the corporate state, as much as the idea of economic equilibrium. But some suggestion of the latter is present, as was certainly the notion of mutuality as the basis of a more developed economy. Anyhow, Becher pointed out the economic uselessness of the nobility, and expressed his opposition to extremes of inequality, including among his principles that taxation should bear more heavily on goods consumed by the rich than on those used by the poor (261). In fact, the idea of progression in taxation, and support for progression, is to be found in cameralist writings some time before proportionality became the general maxim of the English classicals (as may also be observed later in the work of Justi, discussed in chapter 14).

A further theme announced by Becher on the title page of the *Discourse* identified the three enemies of the economic well-being of the community. *First*, there was *monopoly*, which promoted inequality and prevented the growth of a prosperous population. Indeed, Becher maintained that 'it is preferable to have many moderately well-off people in a community, than a few super-rich' (112). *Secondly*, there was *polypoly*, or an excessive number of impoverished producers and sellers, whom Becher did not regard as adjusting sufficiently swiftly or equitably to changes in demand. The *third* 'enemy' was '*propoly*', which corresponded with the medieval idea of 'engrossing', forestalling, or cornering – a kind of special case of monopoly.

Among Becher's overriding policy objectives a large population came first, primarily on economic grounds, though considerations of power and military strength were also relevant (see Sommer, 1920–5, vol. II, 47). As Becher put it: 'Just as one swallow does not make a summer, so a few people cannot make a community . . . What has made Paris, London, Amsterdam and similar populous cities so powerful? Nothing other than the large numbers of people who mutually support one another, so that the more there are, the more want to come' (op. cit., 305–6).

Becher seemed, however, for the most part, to have envisaged his objectives in terms of an average-sized town of his time, together with its surrounding countryside, whose inhabitants had been catastrophically reduced by war, both in numbers and in food supply. Population and food supply must rise together. The number of people must be neither too large, nor too small, and must always be proportioned to the food supply (115). Moreover, Becher's reference to building 'a truly civilized community' showed that his objectives extended well beyond the narrowly economic.

The aim of increasing population and food supply required also a high level of employment, and this, according to Becher, necessitated an ample money supply. In fact, in another formulation of his policy objectives, Becker laid down that: 'The fundamental conditions for the well-being of a country consist of an abundance of common people and of money, which is to be obtained by commerce and trade' (584).

He went on to describe money as 'the nerve and soul of a country' (269), and set out – as Mun had done – a list of policy rules for attaining his money-supply objectives. The first of these rules was that: 'One must always see that money is kept in the country and that still more is brought in from abroad' (260). The fundamental rule of trade policy was: 'It is always better to sell goods to others than to buy goods from others, for the former brings a certain gain, while the latter brings inevitable damage' (261).

Nevertheless, Becher put rather less emphasis on 'mercantilist' trade and tariff policies. Of central importance for Becher was consumption, or consumption spending, which formed, as the other side of the coin, so to speak, the incomes of the community. For Becher, raising and maintaining consumption was the vital task for policy, for he regarded consumption as at once the prime mover and main substance of economic life and activity. Indeed, Schumpeter described as 'Becher's Principle' the proposition that one man's expenditure is another man's income. This is one of those fundamental truisms, out of the analysis of which economists have attempted to draw and construct significant conclusions. In the case of this truism, it was, among others, Quesnay and Keynes who used it as a starting-point. Schumpeter even goes so far as to suggest that Becher was one of the most important forerunners of Keynes (1954, 283–4).

A high level of consumption, or economic activity, was, for Becher, a vital economic and social objective, and he certainly entertained no idea that this might come about spontaneously, in a self-adjusting system without state regulation. For Becher, saving, frugality, or parsimony, were the opposite of the major economic virtues, which they were to become for Smith and the classicals – who held that not only one man's spending, but one man's *saving* was another man's income. It was the *spender* who was the public benefactor.

One kind of mercantilistic policy to which Becher was enthusiastically, even romantically, devoted was the establishment of colonies to expand trade. This was one of his main interests in his Vienna period, and not surprisingly ended in total failure, which may in part have been responsible, together with what seems to have been an abrasive temperament, for his departure from Austria and his move to Holland and England, where he attempted to continue his scientific researches and projects. But, at the age of 47, Becher died in London, a poor and lonely man. Almost all his German and Austrian cameralist followers, over the next 100 years or more, were indebted to his work – some heavily. Becher's stature, and the continuity of cameralist ideas may be indicated by his biographer's description of him as the Friedrich List of his century (Hassinger, 1951, 253).

III

Philipp von Hörnigk (1640–1714) was Becher's brother-in-law and probably the best-known and most typical cameralist and German mercantilist of his own day, when his work *Oesterreich über Alles wann sie nür will* went through many editions. Because of the English translation of this flamboyantly entitled work, von Hörnigk's remains today the most familiar name among the cameralist writers of his time. The lengthy sub-title offered the pamphlet as 'a well-intentioned proposal for raising the imperial territory above all others in Europe'. The work originally appeared anonymously, perhaps because the author feared that his message of 'Austria Over All, if She Only Wants to Be', might be less favourably received (as had been his brother-in-law's) if it had been known that it came from a German, born in Frankfurt.

Von Hörnigk was an itinerant publicist and pamphleteer, writing in the service of various princely authorities in Germany and Austria. He had studied in Mainz, where he had met Becher, from whose *Politische Discours* he learnt much, though Hörnigk became rather more narrowly nationalist and 'mercantilist'. Whatever conclusions may be reached about his economic doctrines, the political background and assumptions on which Hörnigk based them must be recognized. At that time not only had much of Central Europe still to be rebuilt following the catastrophic destruction of the Thirty Years War, but, while Germany was threatened by the annexationist, military aggression of Louis XIV, Austria's territory was under siege from the Turks. So if the economic policies put forward by Von Hörnigk have many similarities with those of Colbert, on the one hand, and Thomas Mun, on the other, these policies could be said to be based on a justifiably defensive, embattled position, one dominated by political power rivalry, which might well be seen as a *relative* situation, or zero-sum game. Anyhow, that was Hörnigk's starting-point, as it was Colbert's, with regard to trade, with wealth and well-being (and not only political power) regarded as relative to that enjoyed by neighbouring countries: 'Whether a nation be today mighty and rich or not depends not on abundance or scarcity of its power or riches, but principally on whether its neighbours possess more or less than it. For power and riches have become a relative matter, dependent on being weaker or poorer than others' (Hörnigk, 1684, ch. 7, quoted by Heckscher, 1955, vol. II, 22). Heckscher regards this as 'stating explicitly that riches do not make a country rich'. But riches, however massive, will not *keep* a country rich, so long as aggressive, annexationist neighbours remain politically or militarily stronger.

Hörnigk put forward a series of nine 'rules' for developing the economy of Austria, most of them closely similar to the twelve formulated, more than fifty years previously, by Thomas Mun. Hörnigk stressed especially his aim that the economy of Austria should operate 'without dependence on others', or 'with as little dependence as possible on foreign countries'. First, Hörnigk extolled the resources of Austria as adequate for economic independence. He insisted on a thorough exploration of the country's agricultural and mineral resources, urging that 'above all, no trouble or expense should be spared to discover gold and silver', regarding which Hörnigk did not share Mun's incipiently liberal notion of the permissibility of exports of precious metals. All materials, he maintained, 'should be worked up within the country'. For this a large labour force must be encouraged, and, therefore, 'attention should be given to population, that it may be as large as the country can support'. Hörnigk's fourth rule may be quoted in full:

> Fourth, gold and silver once in the country, whether from its own mines or obtained by *industry* from foreign countries, are under no circumstances to be taken out for any purpose, so far as possible, or allowed to be buried in chests or coffers, but must always remain in *circulation*; nor should much be permitted in uses where they are at once *destroyed* and cannot be utilized again. For under these conditions, it will be impossible for a country that has once acquired a considerable supply of cash, especially one that possesses gold and silver mines, ever to sink into poverty; indeed, it is impossible that it should not continually increase in wealth and property.
>
> (224)[2]

This fourth rule of Hörnigk has been described by Heckscher as 'a concentrated expression of the practical monetary programme of mercantilism, with the circulation aspect ... at the heart of the whole conception. One cannot possibly overrate the importance of the circulation of money in the ideology of the mercantilists ... (1955, vol. II, 217).

In pursuit of this aim, imports, and especially luxuries, must be cut to a minimum, and when indispensable must be exchanged for exported goods and not gold or silver. Some goods must be excluded altogether, in particular 'everything included under the name French manufactures' (Monroe, 1924, 228). Hörnigk implored Austrians 'to be content for a while with their own goods, with their own manufactures, however bad they may be at first, and to refrain from foreign ones, keeping their good gold and silver in their pockets' (226). Imports may be accepted only in the form of raw materials to be worked up within the country. The export drive must be pursued 'night and day', and markets sought 'in the farthest ends of the earth'. Hörnigk's final stern injunction was again to prohibit the import of any goods obtainable from home production.

Wilhelm von Schröder (or Schrötter) was the author of *Fürstliche Schatz- und Rent-Kammer* – i.e. roughly, *The Prince's Treasury and Revenue Office* – first published in 1686. Schröder succeeded Becher as director of manufactures in Vienna. In his political philosophy he was much more unconditionally absolutist and monarchist than most cameralists, and rejected the idea that the prince's powers were qualified by any contract, or that there was any limit to the sums he was entitled to raise by taxation. But in his preface he recognized that 'the prosperity and welfare of his subjects is the foundation on which all the success of a prince, as ruler of his subjects, is based'. He wrote, explicitly, of the prince as a 'father' of his subjects. Schröder also showed strong hostility to businessmen ('*Kaufleute*'), whom he described as 'pests', whose advice should never be heeded. Schröder had, however, visited England, and was considerably influenced by Mun, Child, Malynes and others, and he placed more emphasis on the balance of trade, and on policies for rendering and keeping it favourable, than had Becher. Though not identifying wealth and the precious metals, Schröder maintained that the acquisition and retention of precious metals was of the greatest importance for a state. '*Pecunia est nervus rerum gerendarum*', or 'money is the sinews of business' was one of his precepts. *First*, the prince himself must have a full treasure chest, or he will be courting disaster (as he proclaimed in his opening sentence): 'The prince who has no treasure in his chest and relies only on his lands, and the goodwill of his subjects, is walking on stilts' (1737, 1).[3]

Second, the precious metals were essential for maintaining the circulation or money supply. Indeed, Schröder warned against the hoarding of precious metals by the prince (as Petty had done) because it kept money out of circulation. Though frugality is a virtue 'it should be practised within reason and with prudence' (28). Miserly hoarding, in fact, was 'the root of all evil', and had more damaging and disastrous results than prodigality. The prince, or government, especially, must 'keep frugality within limits', and must not squeeze all the money into his own coffers, or he would reduce to beggary, his country, his subjects, and himself. Schröder strongly favoured public investment and luxury expenditure, as had Petty, and is approvingly cited by Keynes in his *General Theory* (1936, 359).

As part of his trade policies for acquiring gold and silver, Schröder, like most, or all, cameralists and mercantilists, supported the encouragement and development of manufactures, which should use, preferably, domestic raw materials, and seek to export the finished products. Every attempt should be made to keep down interest rates, to the low level of which he attributed (like Child) the economic success of the Netherlands. Another possible indication of English influence was shown in Schröder's recommendations regarding the collection of trade statistics. He also called for the establishment of a national bank. With Becher's and Hörnigk's, Schröder's ideas exercised a considerable influence on Austrian policy in the ensuing decades.

In conclusion, we may return for a moment to our comparison between the economic writings of such English masters at this time as Petty, Locke and others, and those of Colbert and the three leading German-Austrian cameralists discussed in this chapter. Certainly some of the main doctrines on money and foreign trade, put forward by Colbert and the cameralists, could be found in a milder and more flexible form in the writings of the contemporary English economists. But, in the first place, Petty, Locke, and obviously North, glimpsed more clearly some of the possibilities of private, individual initiative, and of a self-adjusting mechanism potentially at work – as the continental writers, for the most part, did not. Secondly, and more fundamentally, Petty, Locke, North and others were pioneers of basic theoretical, conceptual, analytical and methodological ideas hardly to be found in the works of Colbert and the cameralists (except, to some extent in Becher). Most importantly the island-based English and the continental Germans based their ideas on a fundamentally quite different political framework and on sharply contrasting geographical conditions.

Political economy in Germany continued to be dominated mainly by cameralism, and the conception of the subject which it represented, through most of the eighteenth century, and even, to some extent, into the nineteenth, and we shall be returning, in chapter 14, to its leading exponents in the middle and later eighteenth century, Justi and Sonnenfels.

IV

A kind of economic discourse quite distinct from either that of the English liberal mercantilists (apart from Locke) or from that of Colbert and the cameralists, was represented by the writings of the natural-law philosophers. The contribution was discussed earlier (chapter 2) of Hugo Grotius (1583–1645), the great exponent in the first half of the seventeenth century of the ideas and doctrines of the natural-law school. It was remarked how, in Grotius' *The Law of War and Peace* (1625), some of his economic teachings about value, price, money and interest can be traced back, through the medieval philosophers and Roman lawyers, to their original source in the works of Aristotle. Half a century after Grotius, early in our period, the natural-law doctrines were magisterially restated by Samuel Pufendorf (1632–94), most fully in his *De jure naturae et gentium* (1672, English translation, 1934) and more briefly in his widely used and much translated textbook, *De officio hominis et civis* (1675, English translation, 1927), and his earlier *Elementorum jurisprudentiae universalis* (1660, English translation, 1931). Each of these three works has a chapter on value and price. In fact, the economic analysis of the natural-law philosophy was concerned mainly with the foundations of what today is called 'micro-economics'.

Born in Saxony, in the same year as John Locke, Samuel Pufendorf was the son of a Lutheran clergyman. He became one of the great seventeenth-century polymaths, at once philosopher, lawyer, historian and statesman. He tutored, lectured, and advised in Denmark, Sweden and Holland, and was later professor in Heidelberg. In his economic analysis, Pufendorf followed Grotius very closely in fundamentals, but added a great deal of detail in his *De jure naturae et gentium*. Like Grotius, he drove home most of the points he made with a quotation from, or reference to, an ancient Greek or Latin authority, or to a medieval philosopher, so that his chapter on value and price illustrated the continuity of the tradition he was expounding.

Pufendorf started his analysis of price with a distinction which might, at first glance, appear to suggest those subsequently drawn by Cantillon, Smith and others between 'natural' (or 'intrinsic') price and market price: 'The correct understanding of the nature of ordinary price is markedly aided by considering as separate things first its foundation in itself and then why the same rises or falls' (1672 [1934], 676). But it must be noted that, for Pufendorf, the 'foundation' of price is to be found not on the cost of production or labour side, but in 'aptitude' (or utility). *Moreover, as subsequently in neo-classical analysis, the prices of 'actions', or services, were derived from the same foundation (i.e. 'aptitude') as goods themselves.* Here is Pufendorf's version of the basic, natural-law doctrine of the values and prices of goods and services ('actions'): 'The foundation of price is the aptitude of a thing or action, by which it can mediately or immediately contribute something to the necessity of human life, or to making it more advantageous and pleasant. This is the reason why in ordinary speech things of no use are said to be of no value' (675).

In his earlier treatise Pufendorf had explicitly recognized the subjectivity of this 'use' (or utility) which is the foundation of value (and not some true, or real, use as Adam Smith was to introduce): 'Now the use of a certain thing is defined not merely from the circumstance that it truly helps to preserve or to make pleasurable our existence, but in addition that it contributes some pleasure or ornament *even though this be in the sole opinion of certain men*' (1931 [1660], 65, italics added).

Pufendorf's explicitly subjective emphasis regarding 'use' is notable. He also maintained that the stimulus to economic activity, and, at the same time, what bound a social economy together, came from the demand side:

> For if men had need of nothing, or of another thing no more than what they have, there would be no commerce and no exchange, since each man would keep what was his own and enjoy that. For Aristotle expressly says ... 'The fact that it is demand which is like a principle of unity binding society together, is evident because, if there is no mutual demand on the part of two persons, if neither of them or only one needs the services of the other, they do not effect an exchange'.
>
> (1934 [1672], 677)

Turning to the causes of the rise and fall of prices, Pufendorf emphasized the concept of scarcity:

> There are various reasons why the price of one and the same thing rises or falls, and why, therefore, one thing is preferred to another, although the latter apparently affords as much or greater service in the life of men. For here the need of the article, or the distinction of its use, does not always form the first consideration, and so we observe that those things are the cheapest which men are least able to do without, and this for the reason that by a special provision of God nature bestows them in great abundance ... Therefore, the chief factor in high price is scarcity, the maintenance of which is considered by some to be one of the secrets of business.
>
> (680)

Pufendorf recognized, some time before Mandeville, the strong and pervasive forces of snobbery, envy, luxury and 'irrationality' in human demand: 'So also in general men scarcely ever consider a thing valuable which does not yield to the holder some distinction and position above that held by the rest of men ... Consequently the overweening luxury of men has set enormous values upon things which they could very easily do without' (681). Hence a high price may willingly be paid for a good or service just because its price is high: 'Nay the folly of men fancies that some great value lies in anything that has had a high value placed upon it' (682).

Pufendorf was aware of what are today described as differences in elasticities of demand and how scarcity may drive up the prices of what are usually the cheapest, basic commodities: 'But things of daily use, and such as concern primarily food, clothing, and arms, experience the greatest rise in price when scarcity of them is joined with necessity, such as is seen in times of famine' (683). Other factors which, Pufendorf observed, influenced the level of prices for services, were 'the difficulty of the work, the abundance and scarcity of workmen, and the like . . . Finally, the price of labour and actions is raised by their difficulty, the dexterity required in them, their usefulness, necessity, the scarcity of workers, their renown or position, their freedom to work when they choose and similar considerations' (684).

Finally, Pufendorf turned to the emergence of money as a measure of value and means of exchange. He started with a quotation from Aristotle which emphasized the relation between the holding of money and ignorance or uncertainty:

> When need introduces the exchange of commodities, of course the immediate need could be met by their exchange, when it was simple. But since we cannot know at the present what we will want in the future, and how much of it, νόμισμα, or money, was introduced in order that we would have thereafter the means to secure what we should need in the future; and this money is a sort of ἐγγυητής, sponsor or surety; and so by this agreement between men, every individual is endowed with such a power that when he presents this he can get anything that is for sale.

Pufendorf observed that, for this common measure and means of exchange, gold, or a precious metal is usually most convenient. But it is 'by the imposition and agreement of men', and not 'by necessity', that money is given this function. Stability in value was very important. He noted, however, that, in the course of the previous 200 years, 'so great a quantity of gold and silver has been brought into Europe . . . that little by little the value of money has notably fallen' (692–7).

In conclusion, Pufendorf called attention to a fundamental distinction, later emphasized by Carl Menger: 'Therefore, when the price of one and the same thing is said to be changed, a careful distinction must be drawn as to whether the value of the thing is changed, or the value of money' (698).

Some English economists and historians of economic thought have failed to recognize the central, fundamental importance of the economic analysis of the natural-law school, of which Pufendorf's chapter was the culminating expression. For example, James Bonar once asserted that Pufendorf's place 'was a humble one in the history of economic theories' (1922, p. 86n.). Hasbach, the German historical economist, on the other hand, was probably rather nearer the mark when he maintained that: 'The germ, or embryo ('Keime') of systematic theoretical economics is to be found in another science, or subject, that of Natural Law. It was from a branch of Natural Law that the systematic theory of our subject developed' (1891, 139).

Certainly the natural-law doctrines expounded by Pufendorf, comprising ethics, law, politics and economics, amounted to a comprehensive theory of society. More particularly, his chapter on value and price has a key position in the history of economic thought, not so much for its originality, but because it acted as authoritative transmitter of a long tradition of analysis of fundamental economic concepts concerned with value and price, the central element in which, the idea of scarcity, included the elements of the supply and demand framework, as well as a subjective concept of utility.[4]

As we shall see, through Gershom Carmichael and Frances Hutcheson in Glasgow, Pufendorf's formulation of the economic concepts of the natural-law analysis passed on to Adam Smith; while through Jean-Jacques Burlamaqui (an almost exact contemporary of Hutcheson) they passed to Auguste Walras, and so to his son Léon. Incidentally, Auguste Walras was amply justified in complaining how neglected the natural-law concept of scarcity had become in the nineteenth century. In any case, however, a writer among whose intellectual grandchildren may be counted both Adam Smith and Léon Walras surely possesses a notable place in the history of the subject.[5]

V

In chapters 3–5 we saw how a number of writers in England in the closing decades of the seventeenth century, such as Petty, Child, Davenant, Barbon and others were arguing, rather briefly and unsystematically, on the side of economic freedom, and against the intervention of government in the economy. North and Martyn certainly put forward a more systematic case. A crucial advance was, however, to take place when the foundations were laid for a more profound, comprehensive, systematic case, derived from a fundamental, philosophic view of the nature of man. This case was to be developed right at the end of the seventeenth and at the beginning of the eighteenth century, by Boisguilbert in France, and, soon after, by Mandeville, in his adopted country, England. These two great writers, however, were both importantly indebted, directly or indirectly, to a common source: the French moralist Pierre Nicole (1625–95) and, to a lesser extent, the legal philosopher Jean Domat (1625–96).

Pierre Nicole was a leading Jansenist, that is, he was a moral 'rigorist', who heavily stressed the sinfulness of mankind as a result of the Fall and the special grace required if people were to free themselves sufficiently from their vice and depravity to achieve salvation.[6] Nicole was a prolific and widely read writer. Especially popular were his *Essais morales*, the first two volumes of which appeared originally in 1670–1, the third in 1675, and the other fourteen volumes some time later. Of particular relevance to the theme of this chapter are the essays 'De la grandeur', and 'De la charité et de l'amour propre'.[7]

In his view of human nature Nicole agreed with Hobbes, seeing man as basically selfish, greedy and aggressive. Though Nicole, of course, deplored Hobbes' moral tolerance of sinful human nature and behaviour, he relented sufficiently to express his acceptance of, or even some admiration for, how, through an *enlightened* ordering of society, ordinary men, though profoundly wicked and uncharitable, and intent primarily on the pursuit of their own self-interest, could nevertheless be brought to cooperate in achieving a peaceful, orderly and prosperous existence, based on commercial mutuality in serving and exchanging with one another. The problem was to reconcile the aggressively selfish nature of individuals with their economic interdependence in meeting one another's multifarious needs and wants. The answer was to be found in channelling self-interest in enlightened directions. It was self-interest that brought people together in societies, and in economic life, and Nicole conceded that self-interest could be so tamed and directed as to become relatively enlightened. He observed: 'Although there is nothing more opposed to charity, which renders everything to God, than self-interest, which renders everything to oneself, nevertheless there is much that is similar in the effects of charity and self-interest. They proceed by closely similar paths' (1715 edn, vol. III, 103).

Nicole maintained that it was a divine law that one should do unto others what one would have done unto oneself:

> One gives in order to receive. That is the source and basis of all commercial practices among men, which take on a thousand diverse forms. For exchange not only takes place when goods are exchanged for other goods, but in work, services, attentions and favours ... Thus, by means of commerce, all the needs of life are in some way met without any intervention of charity. (107–8)

Nicole concluded that in order to banish the grosser disorders from society, and to render men happy in this life: 'One must only, assuming no charity exists, grant each person an enlightened self-interest, which can discern its true interests, and attain them, by routes which right reason will discover' (139). In his essay on 'Grandeur', Nicole went further:

> It must be born in mind that men, being devoid of charity, because of their depraved sinfulness, remain, nevertheless, full of needs, and are dependent on one another for an infinite number of goods. Cupidity, therefore, takes the place of charity for the meeting of our needs, and it does this in a manner which is not sufficiently appreciated – for they cannot be met by charity.
>
> (135)

Nicole then proceeded to anticipate precisely Adam Smith's famous observation, at the outset of *The Wealth of Nations*, as to how, 'it is not from the benevolence of the butcher, the brewer, or the baker that we expect our dinner, but from regard to their own interest. We address ourselves, not to their humanity but to their self-love, and never talk to them of our own necessities but of their advantages' (1776, 26–7).

Just a century previously, Nicole had made the same remark with regard to the inn-keeper:

> One finds, for example, almost everywhere when travelling in the country people ready to be of service to those who are passing, who have lodgings ready for them, to make use of as is desired. One gives one's orders and they are obeyed. These people believe that one is bestowing a pleasure on them by accepting their services ...

> What could be more admirable if these people had been animated by the spirit of charity? But it is cupidity which makes them act with such good grace.
>
> (1715, vol. II, 135)

Nicole took another example: 'What sort of charity would build a complete house for another person, furnish it, lay down carpets, and put the key into one's hands? Cupidity does this gladly . . . Thus there is nothing from which greater services can be obtained than from the cupidity of men' (135).

The cupidity of men must, however, be firmly regulated and canalized:

> For if one leaves cupidity to itself, it knows no limits or measure. Instead of serving human society it destroys it. There is no excess of which it is not capable. Its inclination and tendency are directly to robberies, murders and injustices . . .
>
> A way must, therefore, be found to regulate cupidity, and this consists of the political order, which reins it back by fear and punishment, and gets it applied to things useful to society . . .
>
> Who would not admire a man who has discovered the art of taming lions, bears, tigers, and other wild beasts, and of making them serve life usefully? That is the marvellous feat which the political order of a state achieves. For men, full of cupidity, are worse than tigers, bears, and lions. Each would devour the other. But by means of laws and policy these ferocious beasts are tamed, so that one obtains from them all the services which the purest charity might provide . . .
>
> The political order, therefore, is an admirable invention for procuring, for all, the commodities which the greatest kings could not enjoy, however many their officials and whatever riches they possessed, if this order were to be destroyed.
>
> (136–7)[8]

Nicole's political inclinations were thoroughly conservative and authoritarian in that he accepted the political order and the mercantile economic policies prevailing in France in his day. So also did Jean Domat, also a friend of Blaise Pascal,[9] who, in the Introduction to his vast legal treatise, *Lois civiles dans leur ordre naturel* (1689, an influential work which went through several editions and was translated into English in 1722), summed up the paradox of what Mandeville, soon after, was to describe as 'private vices, public benefits'. Domat's summary is worth quoting in full:

> Religion teaches us the infinite good which God hath drawn out of so great an evil as the state to which sin hath reduced mankind: and that the incomprehensible remedy which God has made use of to draw him out of it, hath raised him to a state of greater happiness than that which he enjoyed before his fall . . .
>
> We see in his government of society, that from so bad a cause as our self-love, and from a poison so contrary to mutual love, which ought to be the foundation of society, God hath made use of it as one of the remedies for preserving it in being. For it is this principle of division that he hath made a tie which unites men together in a thousand manners and supports the greatest part of engagements . . .

> The fall of man not having freed him from his wants, and having on the contrary multiplied them, it hath also augmented the necessity of labour and commerce, and of ties; for no man being sufficient of himself to procure the necessaries and conveniences of life, the diversity of wants engages men in an infinite number of ties, without which they could not live.
>
> This state of mankind induces those who are governed only by a principle of self-love, to subject themselves to labour, to commerce, and to ties which their wants render necessary. And that they may reap advantage from them, and preserve in them both their honour and their interest, they observe in all these intercourses, integrity, fidelity, sincerity: so that self-love accommodates itself to everything, that it may reap advantage from all things. And it knows so well how to adapt its different steps to all its views, that it complies with all duties, and even counterfeits all virtues ...
>
> We see, then, in self-love, that this principle of all the evils is, in the present state of society, a cause from whence it derives an infinite number of good effects, which in their nature being true and real goods, ought to have a better principle. And thus we may consider this venom of society as a remedy which God makes use of for supporting it, seeing that although it produces in those persons whom it animates only corrupted fruits yet it imparts all these advantages to society.
>
> (1722, XX)

It was this analysis of Nicole and Domat of the mutuality of a commercial society, based on a realistic, if pessimistic, view of human nature, which laid the foundations of the case for commercial freedom and economic liberalism, developed by Boisguilbert and Mandeville, and elaborated later in Scotland and France. But it must be emphasized that Nicole and Domat themselves stood for a severely illiberal, authoritarian *political* order, although providing a philosophical or moral basis for a liberal *economic* order. Professor Gilbert Faccarello has emphasized how profoundly the doctrines of Nicole influenced the work of Boisguilbert.[10] It seems probable, also, that some influence from Nicole's work may have come through later, directly or indirectly via Boisguilbert, to the German cameralist Ernst Ludwig Carl. As regards Mandeville, Jacob Viner observed that he was significantly indebted to Pierre Bayle and Nicole.[11] Indeed, the parallels are clear and fundamental. But while Nicole was profoundly serious in his condemnation of human cupidity, the Dutch doctor seems, most of the time, to have had his tongue in his cheek in denouncing the viciousness of 'luxury' (defined as anything above subsistence). Mandeville, however, followed Nicole in pointing out the vast growth of commercial prosperity which originated in the basic human vice of cupidity.

In the next chapter and part II of this book we turn to Boisguilbert and Mandeville, and examine how they formulated their ideas regarding the harmony of interests in the economic world, as between self-seeking individuals and public benefits.

PART III
Fundamental Ideas and Theories (*c.* 1700–*c.* 1746)

7
Economic Harmonies, Equilibrating Tendencies and Freedom of Trade

I

In the second half of the seventeenth century the great advance in economic theory and method had been concentrated mainly in England. The appearance of the first writings of Pierre de Boisguilbert, notably his *Détail de la France* (1695), can be taken as a sign that eventually, in the course of the eighteenth century, pre-eminence in political economy would pass to France – before subsequently being assumed by Scotland. As regards France, the title of the definitive edition of Boisguilbert's writings (1966) is well justified: *Pierre de Boisguilbert: où la naissance de l'économie politique*.[1] According to Marx, 'classical political economy', which began in England with Petty, in France began with Boisguilbert (1859, 52). Petty and Boisguilbert embodied respectively the 'perpetual contrast between typically English and typically French political economy'. Anyhow, this section follows straight on from the closing section of the previous chapter on Nicole and Domat. For Boisguilbert's economic doctrines were rooted in the ideas of Jansenism, which provided him with the moral, or theological, foundations for his theory of political economy and economic freedom.

Boisguilbert (1646–1714) was born at Rouen of an aristocratic family. After study at the École de Droit in Paris, he indulged, for some years, a taste for history and literature, before taking over a high magisterial office in his native city.[2] It seems that his economic works may have been written some years before they were published. Certainly, Boisguilbert regarded the economic situation of France as one of disastrous decline and widespread poverty, and he began to study, with mounting passion, the causes and policies in the preceding decades which had brought this about. The depression seemed to have been specially severe in agriculture, which had suffered from Colbert's policy of favouring industrial development.[3]

France's supposedly appalling economic condition was the opening theme of Boisguilbert's *Détail*, the subtitle of which, in some editions, was *La France ruinée sous la règne de Louis XIV*. In numerous letters and memoranda to government officials, including the Controller-General, Chamillart, he was constantly attacking government policies. Thanks, perhaps, to his own influence, there seems to have been greater freedom of publication in Rouen than elsewhere in France. But Boisguilbert was himself, in 1707, sentenced to six months in exile from his home city, because of the sharpness of his criticism. For he had begun his work by claiming that income had halved in France in the preceding thirty years. Vauban who, on *some* points, was an ally of Boisguilbert, made a no less pessimistic diagnosis.[4]

Whether or not his alarming assessment of France's economic decline was correct, Boisguilbert, in seeking to analyse and establish the causes of what had happened, made general, theoretical and conceptual contributions of fundamental importance, including, among others, such monetary, or macro-economic, concepts, clearly though imprecisely formulated, as: the propensity to consume or save, the velocity of circulation, the state of confidence, the expectations of businessmen, multiplying or cumulative effects, and, especially, the fundamental notion of equilibrium. His writings were often imbued with an almost missionary fervour. But Boisguilbert's style, though he had a sharp turn of phrase, was often obscure, repetitious, and not without ambiguities, which have led to contrasting interpretations of his ideas on money, and even regarding his support for freedom of trade.

Boisguilbert started from the idea of the fundamental interdependence of men in an exchange economy. Men cannot survive alone but must engage in exchange, and by mutual help provide reciprocal utility (*l'utilité réciproque*). In the contemporary economy, 'men are divided entirely into two classes', one being that of rich rentiers, 'which does nothing and enjoys every pleasure', and the other that of the labouring class 'which works from morning to evening for its necessities, of which it is often entirely deprived'. For God, since the Fall, had decreed that men shall live 'by the sweat of their bodies' (*Dissertation*, 1707b, 979 and 994). Here the Jansenist influence on Boisguilbert is especially obvious.

As an economy develops, with the production not only of necessities, but of luxuries and superfluities, exchange becomes more and more complex and economic life takes on a larger dimension. Barter, therefore, becomes increasingly and impossibly difficult, because of ignorance as to where to find the goods which one wants in return for those one has to offer. Such a search would necessitate 'an infinity of sales and resales one after the other' (*Factum*, 1707a, 888). In describing how the introduction of money is necessary for the development of an exchange economy, Boisguilbert's originality, as Professor Faccarello has observed, lay in his perception of the role of ignorance in economic life. It is with the monetarization of the economy, as a partial counter to human ignorance, that a circulation of payments comes into being.

Boisguilbert's macro-economic analysis was based on the fundamental truism of Becher's Principle, that one man's expenditure was another man's income – while he certainly did not accept Smith's classical addition to, or transformation of, that principle to the effect that one man's *saving* was *equally* another man's income. For Boisguilbert, wealth consisted in the consumption of useful goods and services, including instrumental goods and services, the value of which was determined by demand and supply. Consumption spending, for Boisguilbert as for Becher, was at once a fundamental objective and motivating force for the economy. What was seen as the economic decline of France had consisted in the destruction of consumption and consumption-spending:

> Thus to find the causes of the ruin of France, it is only necessary to discover those of the ruin of consumption.
>
> (1695, 590)

> Consumption and income (*revenu*) are one and the same thing and the ruin of consumption is the ruin of income.
>
> (602)

The causes of this 'ruin' were certainly not to be found in a shortage of money or precious metals. On this point Boisguilbert proclaimed his emphatically anti-bullionist stance, in denouncing 'this lamentable idolatry of money, the source of all difficulties' (1707b, 975).

Money was, or should be, simply a medium to facilitate exchange: 'Money is only a means; it is useful goods which are the end and objective. Thus a country can be rich without much money, and a country which has only money will be very miserable, if it can only with difficulty exchange it for goods' (1695, 618).

It was not simply the *quantity* of money which was important, since, to counter a shortage, the velocity (*célerité*) of its circulation could rise. In a letter of 1704 Boisguilbert wrote: 'It is not a question of making a country rich by having a lot of money, but by having the money always active and circulating' (306). Money, moreover, could be supplemented, or replaced, by a vast progeny of substitutes, in the form of bills of exchange. Again, therefore, it was not a large quantity of money, but a high level of consumption, or consumption-spending, which made for, or constituted, wealth, and, when consumption was paralysed, poverty in the midst of plenty was the result. Then, a country 'is and appears wretched amid an abundance of all sorts of goods, like Tantalus, who perished of thirst when surrounded by water' (1707b, 997). In such a situation, Boisguilbert insisted on the benefits of paper money:

> We have in use continually in Europe the easiest and cheapest device to bring the metals to reason and, destroying their usurpation, to place them in their proper sphere, which is to be solely the servants and slaves of commerce, and not its tyrants: ... a simple piece of paper, which costs nothing, and performs nevertheless, all the functions of money, for millions in quantity and for an indefinite length of time.
>
> (Quoted and translated by Roberts, 1935, 183, from 1707b, 977)

The velocity of circulation of money, Boisguilbert emphasized, and the propensity to hoard, differed greatly, both between rich and poor, and between prosperity and depression:

> A coin with a poor man, or with a very small trader, has a hundred times more effect in creating income, than it does with a rich man. With the poor man this small sum is being renewed continually, each day. This does not happen with the rich man, in whose coffers large sums of money may remain useless for months and whole years at a time, either through corruption or blindness or avarice, or through waiting for a more favourable market.
>
> (1707b, 1006)

As regards the differences between prosperity and depression, he described money as 'the slave of consumption alone, following step by step its destined route, moving or halting accordingly, with a coin passing through a hundred hands in a day when there is plenty of selling and re-selling, and remaining for entire months in one place when consumption is ruined (1707a, 954). While the more rapid circulation of money raised incomes, uncertainty, on the other hand, caused a failure to invest by the rich, and so depression. Here was where Boisguilbert, by implication, denied the classical Smithian postulate that one man's saving was another man's income:

> What is true of the merchant applies equally to all who live on incomes from property, either from landed estates or invested funds. Receiving their returns they are unable to reinvest them for lack of security ... because of the destruction of consumption. Also, they would rather lose the interest than risk the capital, and so they cut down their expenditure, which further increases the loss for the country as a whole.
>
> (Quoted and translated by McDonald, 1954, 407; from 1695, 619)

Boisguilbert identified the cause of this paralysis as the crushing burden and arbitrary uncertainty of taxation, in the first place of the *taille* (property tax), but also of the many local and indirect taxes and levies, together with export duties and other barriers to trade. Moreover, official interference in agriculture and industry had also contributed to the reduction of consumption spending. The further consequence was the fall in prices to excessively low levels. He urgently and repeatedly warned against the dangers of low prices.

The system of taxation also produced a mal-distribution of income from poor to rich, which further slowed down the velocity of circulation of money and further reduced consumption and incomes. This was because of the much higher propensity of the poor to spend and consume, as compared with the rich, who had a much greater propensity to hoard:

> From this hoarding the King and the state get no utility, for it amounts to theft from them both.
>
> But such a sum, of a thousand *écus*, distributed among a thousand people of small means, would pass through a hundred thousand hands in less time than it remained in the coffers of a rich man, and, consequently, a hundred thousand *écus* of consumption expenditure would be generated.
>
> (Quoted and translated by McDonald, 1956, 406, from 1707b, 1006)

Boisguilbert condemned hoarding as, in his day, a constant menace, just as he condemned the falling prices caused by it. Somewhat like J. A. Hobson, 200 years later, he combined under-consumption and the mal-distribution of income in his explanation of economic depression (though he was also against labour combinations which pushed costs above prices). Regressive taxation was especially damaging in its effects on consumption expenditure. If the rich understood their own interests they would remove taxation from the poor.

There was also another, even more important, kind of disturbance, and that was the damaging distortion of prices, which upset 'that equilibrium between all goods, which is the unique preserver of general opulence' (1707b, 995). For, as Boisguilbert saw it, prosperity involved keeping all sectors of the economy moving reciprocally in support of one another, like the parts of a watch:

> For wealth is only this continual exchange, from one person to another, from region to region, and even from kingdom to kingdom. It is appalling blindness to seek the cause of poverty elsewhere than in the reduction of commerce brought about by the disturbance of the proportions between prices, which are no less essential to the prosperity of all states than to the very maintenance of their existence and formation.
>
> (1707b, 991)

> It is necessary for all things and all goods to be continually in equilibrium, and that prices are kept in proportion with one another and with the costs necessary for creating the goods.
>
> (993)

But Boisguilbert does not seem to have regarded equilibrium as always very stable. It required for its maintenance a balance between the two sides of the market: 'To maintain this equilibrium, the unique conserver of general opulence, it is necessary always to maintain an equal balance between sales and purchases, with an equal obligation, or necessity, on either side, without which is all lost' (quoted by Faccarello, 1983b, 177, from 1707b, 993).

II

Boisguilbert started from the assumption of the unrelenting, maximizing pursuit of their own self-interest by individuals:

> It is this reciprocal utility which makes for the harmony of the world and the maintenance of the state; each individual cares only for procuring his personal interest to the maximum extent, and with the greatest possible ease; and when he goes four leagues from home to buy a good, it is because it is not for sale three leagues away, or because it is better value and worth the extra distance.
>
> (Quoted by Faccarello, 1983, 180 from 1705b, 749)

It was the discipline established by nature and Providence, by means of a balanced, or competitive market, which brought about the harmonious reconciliation of self-interest with the good of society.:

> There is no worker who does not try, with all his strength, to sell his goods at three times more than they are worth, and to get those of his neighbour at a third of what they cost to produce.
>
> It is not at the point of the sword that justice is maintained in these transactions. But it is cared for by nature and Providence. Just as they have established safe refuges for the weaker animals, so that they do not become the prey of the stronger, who are by birth equipped to live by carnage, so, in the business of human life, nature has created an order – provided one leaves it alone – under which even the strongest, when buying a good from a poor person, has not the power to prevent him from obtaining his subsistence from the sale. . . .
>
> We have said 'provided nature is left alone' ('*pourvu qu'on laisse faire la nature*'), that is to say that one leaves nature free, and only intervenes to procure protection and prevent violence.
>
> (1707a, 891–2)

Boisguilbert went on to emphasize how each individual, though constantly moved solely by his own private interest, contributed to the general good: 'All are occupied night and day with their own particular interests, but, at the same time, although it is what they care about least, they are contributing to the general good, while, nevertheless, attending to their own individual utility' (1707b, 991).

There was, however, an essential role for government:

> A policy principle is necessary in order to have peace, and the laws of justice observed by so large a number of men, who are seeking only to destroy, deceive, and trick one another from morning till night; and who aspire continually to establish their wealth on the ruin of their neighbours.
>
> But it is nature alone which can create order and maintain peace. All other authority spoils everything when it interferes in business, however well-intentioned it may be.
>
> (1707b, 992)

Thus, as Professor Faccarello has observed, Boisguilbert perceived nature, or Providence, as working through competition, or a balance between sellers and buyers, to establish order and discipline:

> Nature, or Providence, alone can preserve justice, provided, once again, that no one interferes; and this is how they achieve it. They establish first an equal need to sell and to buy with regard to every sort of good, with the moving spirit, in all markets, both with sellers and buyers, being solely the desire for profit. It is with the aid of this equilibrium, or balance, that the seller and the buyer alike are equally forced to listen to reason and to submit to it.
>
> (1707b, 992)

Boisguilbert did not, however, seem to envisage that equilibrium always came about smoothly, or was stable when achieved. There was too much ignorance and too many wrong expectations. He maintained that many were ignorant of their own interests, and that there was a lack of communication, which he likened, at one point, to the tower of Babel, and to 'a confused mob which is pulling at the cord with which it is strangling itself' (1704, 828 and 859). The economy was subject to cumulative processes of expansion and contraction, and during the latter, 'bankruptcy is so contagious that a single one can lead to an infinity of others' (1704, 839).

Moreover, wage flexibility, which Boisguilbert regarded as vital for maintaining equilibrium, hardly existed in industry, and was resisted by violent strike action:

> One sees in centres of commerce seven or eight hundred workers for a single manufacturer suddenly walk out, in a moment, leaving their work unfinished, because he wanted slightly to reduce their pay, when the price of their products had fallen four times over; while the most mutinous of the workers use violence against those who would be reasonable.
>
> (Quoted by Faccarello, 1983b, 239, from 1704, 875)

Boisguilbert likened the economy to a top which could be left alone when spinning swiftly and smoothly, but which must be stimulated when it slowed down (1705, 708).

While believing generally in the beneficent self-equilibration of free, competitive markets, Boisguilbert was exceptionally concerned with the agricultural sector, and, in particular, with the market for corn, or the people's subsistence. The price of grain had a fundamental role in the economy. The market for grain was both of the greatest social importance and also one which suffered the most extreme fluctuations of prices: 'Extreme dearness makes the worst lands workable at a profit, which is followed by a lowering of price . . . so that even the best lands can only be managed at a loss' (1705, 707).

The two extremes were equally damaging. Moreover, uncertainty, and erroneous information and expectations, aggravated the fluctuations. In fact, Boisguilbert recommended the establishment of public stocks of corn, at a number of towns round Paris, so that the intervention of public buyers and sellers in times of crisis could stabilize prices. He seemed highly optimistic about the effects of such governmental operations (1705, 738). This, however, was an exceptional proposal to his general rule of '*laisser faire la nature*'. In fact, whether or not there should be government intervention to regulate the price of grain – a vital, subsistence good, the price of which was liable to extreme changes – remained a recurring crucial issue, both for economists and for governments, through much of the eighteenth century. In France the debate was to rage especially fiercely in the late sixties, with the physiocrats on one side and Galiani on the other. The issue was also a burning one in Italy at that period. In Britain, Sir James Steuart, and later, during the Napoleonic wars, Jeremy Bentham, supported government action to set up buffer stocks, or 'magazines', to stabilize prices. Most of the German cameralists, as might be expected, supported similar policies by governments. On the other side, at various times, were Benjamin Franklin, Pietro Verri, Smith and Burke, in favour of making no exception, in the vital case of grain, to their general support for free markets. But Boisguilbert, Galiani, and even Steuart and Bentham, who, from differing viewpoints, advocated intervention, can hardly be regarded simply as benighted 'mercantilists', or social planners.

The main reform advocated by Boisguilbert was a complete reshaping of the tax system, including a reform of the *taille*, which would establish certainty rather than arbitrariness, and which would be based on convenience of collection and ability to pay, with no concessions to particular classes, and especially not to the better off. What he advocated was a reform based on principles of taxation fairly similar to those later proposed by Adam Smith. But Boisguilbert went further in supporting progression, with complete exemption for the poor, and emphasized that taxation must support, and not upset, the equilibrium and proportionalities in an economy.

III

Boisguilbert's ideas regarding the economic decline of France attracted some contemporary attention in England, though there seems to be no strong evidence of any significant influence either way between him and English writers.[5] His influence seems, however, plainly apparent subsequently in the work of the great German cameralist, Ernst Ludwig Carl. In France, though he was indebted to Bodin, Boisguilbert has the position of a founding father, whose ideas were drawn on by most of the major French economists of the eighteenth century. First, his emphasis on agriculture was followed by Cantillon, as also, probably, was his concept of the velocity of circulation of money and his criticism of an unqualified quantity theory. Secondly, Quesnay and the physiocrats were explicitly and considerably indebted to Boisguilbert, not only with regard to the primacy of agriculture, but also as to the central importance of the circular flow of payments, and regarding the principle of *laisser-faire*, of which he was recognized by Mirabeau to have been a pioneer champion. This phrase, which originated more as a slogan of protest than as a philosophical formula, was used by Boisguilbert only in the infinitive form. As regards agriculture, he did not assign it exclusive claims to productivity, or hold, like the physiocrats, that manufacturing was 'sterile'. But he did maintain that the vital flow of payments originated from the land. Quesnay, also, explicitly agreed with Boisguilbert's analysis of the causes of the decline of the French economy in the closing decades of the seventeenth century, and as to the destructive role played by the burden of taxation.[6] Mirabeau, in fact, hailed Boisguilbert as 'the true and sole precursor of the *Économistes*' (quoted by Hecht, in Boisguilbert (1695–1707, 217–18), and he was also highly praised by Dupont de Nemours in the *Ephémérides* (1769, see Faccarello, 1983b, 14).

Subsequently, Karl Marx made an interesting comparison between Boisguilbert and Petty. Though holding the highest opinion of Petty as a great economist, Marx (1859 [1969], 55) described him as 'a frivolous adventurer' and 'plunderer without character', in contrast with Boisguilbert's high-minded and courageous defence of the oppressed classes. Today, Boisguilbert can be regarded, to an important extent, as a precursor of both Adam Smith and Keynes – though, of course, differing from these in significant respects. He was also the first to emphasize the importance of information and misinformation, and of correct or erroneous expectations, and was, therefore, a precursor of Condillac (see chapter 18). As Professor Faccarello summarizes Boisguilbert's achievements: 'The theory he constructed brought together the idea of general equilibrium and of the circulation of payments, of social classes and of the market, of a micro-economic and a macro-economic approach, of information and expectations, and of fixed and flexible prices in the analysis of prosperity and depression' (1986, 16).

IV

Bernard Mandeville (1671–1733) was born in or near Rotterdam in 1670. The son of a doctor, he himself qualified as a doctor of medicine in 1691, specializing in nervous and digestive diseases. In order to learn the English language, of which, on paper at any rate, he became a consummate master, he went to London, married an English woman in 1699, and settled there. While practising as a doctor he began to publish a number of literary and philosophical essays, including a translation of fables by La Fontaine. Somewhat in this vein, he published in 1705 a sixpenny pamphlet of twenty-six pages in verse called *The Grumbling Hive: or Knaves Turned Honest.* Out of this brief poem there grew his major work *The Fable of the Bees: or Private Vices, Public Benefits*, which first appeared in 1714. The new volume included the original verses together with some twenty prose 'Remarks', or elaborations of themes and arguments in the poem. This expanded the work some ten times over, and it was more than doubled in length in subsequent editions of 1723, 1724 and 1725, further 'Remarks' and essays being added, including, notably, 'An Enquiry into the Origin of Moral Virtue', a very sharp and interesting 'Essay on Charity and Charity Schools', and 'A Search into the Nature of Society'. With the edition of 1723, Mandeville's book came in for severe criticism, being denounced as immoral and outrageous, and condemned as a public nuisance by the Grand Jury of Middlesex. He sought to vindicate himself in *The Fable of the Bees, Part II 1714–29*, and also in his last publication, *A Letter to Dion* (1732), an answer to George Berkeley's criticisms in *Alciphron, or the Minute Philosopher* (1732).

Mandeville, like most of his contemporaries, made few references to other writers – apart from mentioning Graunt's *Observations on the Bills of Mortality*. As regards his doctrine of the economic beneficence of luxury spending, this had been proclaimed previously by, for example, Petty, Barbon and North, and even, to some extent by Pufendorf. Heckscher refers to the deep-rooted belief in the utility of luxury and the evil of thrift, in the writings of this period (1955, vol. II, 208). Mandeville's *Fable* certainly gave an additional, extravagant thrust to the idea.

The Grumbling Hive: or Knaves Turned Honest starts with a description of a flourishing, affluent, rapidly growing economy and society: 'A spacious hive well stocked with bees/That lived in luxury and ease ... Was counted the great nursery/Of sciences and industry' (1714, 63).[7] But, of course, the bees did not feel secure in their happiness: 'No bees had better government/More fickleness or less content' (63). Everything was on a large and growing scale: big was beautiful: 'Vast numbers thronged the fruitful hive;/Yet those vast numbers made 'em thrive – /Millions endeavouring to supply/Each other's lust and vanity;' (64). The affluence was far from equally distributed: 'Some with vast stocks, and little pains/ Jumped into business of great gains;/And some were damned to scythes and spades,/And all those hard laborious trades;/Where willing wretches daily sweat,/And wear out strength and limbs to eat' (64). Mandeville, however, confidently, if paradoxically, concluded: 'Thus every part was full of vice,/Yet the whole mass a paradise;' (67). Everybody's efforts were somehow beneficently directed or canalized: 'The worst of all the multitude/Did something for the common good' (68). Even burglars provided employment for locksmiths. Moreover, economic growth was surging ahead, with affluence 'trickling down'. For even '... the very poor/lived better than the rich before' (69).

Then suddenly a puritanical, moral revolution broke out. Luxuries were spurned, extravagance shunned, robbery and fraud ceased and armaments were abolished: 'But, oh ye Gods, what consternation/How vast and sudden was the alteration!' (70). Unemployment soared. Whole industries collapsed. Millions fled away from the hive. The community's defences against rivals and its power in the world disappeared. The moral was plain:

Then leave complaints: fools only strive
To make a great an honest hive,
To enjoy the world's conveniences,
Be famed in war, yet live in ease
Without great vices, is a vain
Utopia seated in the brain

So vice is beneficial found,
When it's by justice lopped and bound;
Nay, where the people would be great,
As necessary to the state
As hunger is to make 'em eat.

(76)

Mandeville's theories and doctrines were shaped, fundamentally by his view of man, or by what he believed human beings were like. His view came partly from Hobbes, and also, as we have seen, from the Jansenists Pierre Nicole and Jean Domat – who also influenced Boisguilbert – as well as from the sceptical moralists Pierre Bayle (1647–1706) and La Rochefoucauld (1613–80), from whose 'Maxim 305' Mandeville may well have drawn inspiration: 'Self-interest, which is accused of all our crimes, often deserves to be praised for our good actions.' His special contribution consisted in his blending of the ideas of English economists with those of French moralists.

These intellectual influences were reinforced by Mandeville's detestation of, and contempt for the religious movement for moral reform, very active in his day, which held that Christian virtues were what held society together, and called for legal curbs on vices, private and public. Mandeville's 'Enquiry into the Origins of Moral Virtue' opened by observing: 'One of the greatest reasons why so few people understand themselves is, that most writers are always teaching men what they should be, and hardly ever troubled their heads with teaching them what they really are' (77).[8]

Telling men 'what they really are', or appealing from norms to facts, was, of course, what Mandeville claimed to be engaged in – though huge generalizations about 'the nature of man' often seem to lie on the margin of testable, empirical factuality, and to come nearer to statements of the writer's own temperament, mood or creed. Anyhow, for Mandeville:

> . . . no species of animals is, without the curb of government, less capable of agreeing long together in multitudes than that of man . . . But being an extraordinary selfish and headstrong as well as cunning animal, however he may be subdued by superior strength it is impossible by force alone to make him tractable, and receive the improvements he is capable of.
>
> (81)

As Mandeville put it elsewhere:

> Men are naturally selfish, unruly creatures, what makes them sociable is their necessity and consciousness of standing in need of others' help to make life comfortable: and what makes this assistance voluntary and lasting are the gains or profit accruing to industry for services done to others, which in a well-ordered society enables every body, who in some thing or other will be serviceable to the public, to purchase the assistance of others.
>
> (1720, 254, quoted by Home, 1978, x)

So, just as man's vicious tendencies have to be 'lopped and bound' to be rendered beneficent, so, in 'a well-ordered society', people will be *induced* in the right direction by pride and avarice. Pride is in man 'so inseparable from his very essence', that politicians have used it to foster 'the first rudiments of morality'. In fact: 'The moral virtues are the political offspring which flattery begot upon pride' (1714 [1970], 88). Thus, by playing on his pride and greed, man can be induced to serve the public good. As Mandeville remarked: 'It may be said that virtue is made friends with vice, when industrious good people, who maintain their families and bring up their children handsomely, pay taxes and are several ways useful members of the society, get a livelihood by something that chiefly depends on, or is very much influenced by the vices of others' (117).

Respectable locksmiths and sword-makers were cited as examples of 'industrious good people', whose comfortable incomes depended on the vices of others. Here Mandeville, anticipating Carl Menger and Friedrich Hayek, emphasized the importance of recognizing the often unnoticed and unforeseen consequences of human actions: 'The short-sighted vulgar, in the chain of causes seldom can see further than one link; but those who can enlarge their view, and will give themselves the leisure of gazing on the prospect of concatenated events, may, in a hundred places see *good* spring up and pullulate from *evil*, as naturally as chickens do from eggs' (123).

This complexity 'in the chain of causes' makes for great difficulty in the art of statesmanship: 'it is a great while, before that nature can be rightly understood; and it is the work of ages to find out the true use of the passions, and to raise a politician, that can make every frailty of the members add strength to the whole body, and by dextrous management turn *private vices into public benefits*' (1714–29 [1924], vol. II, 319). The regulations, by which such 'dextrous management' operated, were 'the result of consummate wisdom', not so much conscious and deliberate, but the fruit of experience and long traditions:

> There are very few, that are the work of one man, or of one generation, the greatest part of them are the product, the joint labour of several ages . . . the wisdom I speak of is not the offspring of a fine understanding, or intense thinking, but of some deliberate judgment, acquired from a long experience in business, and a multiplicity of observations. By this sort of wisdom and length of time it may be brought about that there shall be no greater difficulty in governing a large city, than (pardon the lowness of the simile) there is in weaving of stockings. . . . There is something analogous to this in the government of a flourishing city that has lasted uninterrupted for several ages. There is no part of the wholesome regulations belonging to it, even the most trifling and minute, about which great pains and consideration have not been employed as well as length of time.
>
> (322)

Mandeville distinguished sharply, however, between the qualities which, ideally or optimally, are needed in government, and those which will, in fact be forthcoming: 'it would certainly be best, that none but men of good lives, and known ability, should have any place in the government whatever: but to expect that this should ever happen, or to live in hopes of it in a large, opulent and flourishing kingdom, is to betray great ignorance in human affairs' (335). Though insisting that he was 'far from encouraging vice', Mandeville strongly upheld the realism of accepting the lesser evil: 'The passions of some people are too violent to be curbed by any law or precept; and it is wisdom in all governments to bear with lesser inconveniences to prevent greater' (1714 [1970], 127). So it is with prodigality, 'that agreeable good natured vice that makes the chimney smoke and all the tradesmen smile'. In fact, 'the prodigal is a blessing to the whole society' (a doctrine the exact opposite, of course, to that which Adam Smith and his followers were to make a fundamental tenet of classical economics).

Mandeville sought to protect his doctrine of the economic beneficence of luxury by employing an extremely broad definition, according to which 'everything is to be a luxury (as in strictness it ought) that is not immediately necessary to make man subsist ...' (136). He defended his definition on the grounds that: 'once we depart from calling everything luxury that is not absolutely necessary to keep a man alive ... then there is no luxury at all' (137).

The luxury debate, in which economic and moral arguments were often mixed together, continued through much of the eighteenth century, until Smithian orthodoxy took over, which denounced luxury and maintained the unconditional beneficence of frugality and parsimony. The great philosopher-economists, Berkeley, Hutcheson, and Hume, all reacted with fundamental criticisms of Mandeville's provocative thesis, and their views are discussed in due course. But, in the eighteenth century, Mandeville had formidable defenders, notably Voltaire and Dr Johnson, and his views were represented by subsequent French writers, such as Melon and Montesquieu, and in Italy by Genovesi.[9]

In Mandeville's time the luxury issue was often involved with questions of international trade policies. Here, in two closely adjacent paragraphs, Mandeville showed himself as both for and against 'mercantilist' views. First, he was against prohibiting luxury imports, as he was against sumptuary laws, on the ground that this would reduce English exports: 'If we continue to refuse taking their commodities in payment for our manufacturers, they can trade no longer with us, but must content themselves with buying what they want of such nations as are willing to take what we refuse' (139). On the other hand, Mandeville supported the most thorough-going 'mercantilist' policies with regard to the regulation of foreign trade by government:

> Every government ought to be thoroughly acquainted with, and steadfastly to pursue the interest of the country. Good politicians, by dextrous management, laying heavy impositions on some goods, or totally prohibiting them, and lowering the duties on others, may always turn and divert the course of trade which way they please ... But above all, they'll keep a watchful eye over the balance of trade in general, and never suffer that all the foreign commodities together that are imported in one year, shall exceed in value what of their own growth or manufacture is in the same exported to others.
>
> (141)

> But what I have insisted on the most and repeated more than once is the great regard that is to be had to the balance of trade, and the care the legislature ought to take that the yearly imports never exceed the exports: and where this is observed .... I still continue to assert that no foreign luxury can undo a country.
>
> (257)

Returning to his central theme of pride and emulation, Mandeville emphasized their role as the mainspring, or driving force, behind economic activity:

> To this emulation and continued striving to outdo one another, it is owing, that after so many various shiftings and changing of modes, in trumping up new ones and renewing of old ones, there is still a *plus ultra* left for the ingenious; it is this, at least the consequences of it, that sets the poor to work, adds spurs to industry, and encourages the skilful artificer to search after further improvements.
>
> (154)

He then attacked the fallacy of composition with regard to saving:

> As this prudent economy, which some people call saving, is in private families the most certain method to increase an estate, so some imagine, that whether a country be barren or fruitful, the same method, if generally pursued (which they think practicable) will have the same effect upon a whole nation and that, for example, the *English* might be much richer than they are, if they would be as frugal as some of their neighbours. This, I think is an error.
>
> (199)

On the question, much argued over at that time, as to the reasons for the remarkable economic progress and prosperity of the Dutch, Mandeville was quite emphatic that frugality played no part (as had been alleged, for example, by Sir William Temple):[10]

> The Dutch may ascribe their present grandeur to the virtue and frugality of their ancestors as they please; but what made that contemptible spot of ground so considerable among the principal powers of Europe has been their political wisdom in postponing every thing to merchandise and navigation, the unlimited liberty of conscience that is enjoyed among them, and the unwearied application with which they have always made use of the most effectual means to encourage and increase trade in general.
>
> (202)

Mandeville also called attention, as he had originally done in *The Grumbling Hive*, to the immense long-term economic progress, which had so raised the living standards of the mass of the people, including the poor: 'If the ancient Britons and Gauls should come out of their graves, with what amazement would they gaze on the mighty structures everywhere raised for the poor ... Those who were once the greatest and richest of the land would have reason to envy the most reduced of our species now' (190).

For Mandeville, the main factors promoting such a vast increase in wealth could hardly have included saving and investment, or technical progress, as mostly understood in the twentieth century, unless this referred to specialization and the division of labour, of which he emphasized the major importance:

> ... if one will wholly apply himself to the making of bows and arrows, whilst another provides food, a third builds huts, a fourth makes garments, and a fifth utensils, they not only become useful to one another, but the callings and employments themselves will in the same number of years receive much greater improvements, than if all had been promiscuously followed by every one of the five.
>
> (1714–29 [1924], vol. II, 284)

Mandeville continued by citing the example of clocks and watches: 'I am persuaded that even the plenty we have of clocks and watches, as well as the exactness and beauty they may be made of, are chiefly owing to the *division* that has been made of the art into many branches' (284, italics added).

In spite of, or perhaps because of, the huge rise in the living standards of the poor, there remained the need to hold down the rise of wages. For Mandeville distinguished sharply between the motivation of labourers, who were not so effectively stimulated by pride and avarice, and what drove the other classes in society. Like many writers in the seventeenth and eighteenth centuries, Mandeville believed in the reverse-sloping supply curve of labour: 'Everybody knows that there is a vast number of journeymen weavers, tailors, clothworkers, and twenty other handicrafts; who, if by four days labour in a week they can maintain themselves, will hardly be persuaded to work the fifth' (208). He proceeded to explain how all men

> are more prone to ease and pleasure, than they are to labour, when they are not prompted by pride or avarice, and those that get their living by their daily labour are seldom powerfully influenced by either: so that they have nothing to stir them up to be serviceable but their wants which it is prudence to relieve, but folly to cure. The only thing that can render the labouring man industrious, is a moderate quantity of money; for as too little will, according as his temper is, either dispirit or make him desperate, so too much will make him insolent and lazy.
>
> (210)

Certainly Mandeville's views seem to possess the same capacity for shocking late-twentieth-century egalitarians as they did early-eighteenth-century optimistic philosophers and divines: 'If nobody did want nobody would work ... To make the society happy and people easy under the meanest circumstances, it is requisite that great numbers of them should be ignorant as well as poor. Knowledge both enlarges and multiplies our desires, and the fewer things man wishes for, the more easily his necessities may be supplied' (294).

But employment had to be available. Mandeville was quite clear that there was a distinction between voluntary and involuntary unemployment, and that involuntary unemployment constituted a problem that the legislature had to face: 'We ought not to confound those who remain unemployed for want of an opportunity of exerting themselves to the best advantage, with such as for want of spirit, hug themselves to their sloth, and will starve rather than stir' (250).

Mandeville insisted that the involuntarily unemployed poor cried out for employment: 'the labour of the poor, is so far from being a burthen and an imposition upon them, that to have employment is a blessing which in their addresses to heaven they pray for, and to procure it for the generality of them is the greatest care of every legislature' (360).

V

Thus, although Mandeville advocated (at another point) leaving the proportion, or numbers of workers in each particular trade, to free market forces, like other leading writers of this period, however, he did not entertain the idea of the level of employment as a whole settling itself adequately at a high level, through market mechanisms and without government action. In fact, he held that 'most employments of the poor' were 'overstocked', and that: 'The great art then to make a nation happy, and what we call flourishing, consists in giving everybody an opportunity of being employed' (211–12).

In order to achieve this, a favourable balance of trade must ensure that 'the quantity of circulating coin in a country ought always to be proportioned to the number of hands that are employed; and the wages of labourers to the price of provisions' (209). But, going beyond this, Mandeville recommended governments to 'promote as great a variety of manufacturers arts and handicrafts as human wit can invent; and second to encourage agriculture and fishery in all their branches' (212). He also urgéd the authorities to 'promote navigation, cherish the merchant, and encourage trade in every branch of it; this will bring riches, and where they are, arts and sciences will soon follow, and by the help of what I have named, and good management, it is that politicians can make a people potent, renowned and flourishing' (201).

He seemed, moreover, to envisage an important scope for the kind of 'public works', which Adam Smith himself regarded as a duty of government: 'There is above three or four hundred years work, for a hundred thousand poor more than we have in this island. To make every part of it useful, and the whole thoroughly inhabited, many rivers are to be made navigable, canals to be cut in hundreds of places' (321). For Mandeville insisted on the government's duty to posterity:

> It is the business of the public to supply the defects of the society, and take that in hand first which is most neglected by private persons ... The legislature ought to resolve upon some great undertakings that must be the work of ages as well as vast labour, and convince the world that they did nothing without an anxious regard to their latest posterity.
>
> (323)

Furthermore, in spite of his belief in the healthy effects of ignorance in keeping the poor industrious, Mandeville recommended a big expansion in the public provision of schools and universities: 'In every county there should be one or more large schools erected at the public charge. I would have nearly double the number of professors in every university of what there is now' (298 and 301). This great expansion was to come, of course, in the subjects in which Mandeville himself was specially interested, such as anatomy, botany, pharmacy and 'physic'.

So the role Mandeville assigned to the 'dextrous management' of 'good', or 'skilful' politicians went beyond that of establishing and maintaining the legal and institutional framework for a free market economy. He maintained that the government should include among its duties the care both of the balance of trade and the level of employment. But his vision of dextrous and skilful management by politicians contrasted with his sceptical view regarding their objectives. He concluded: 'Unhappy is the people, and their constitution will be precarious, whose welfare must depend upon the virtues and consciences of ministers and politicians' (206).

Though 'great and good' politicians would, however, represent the optimal solution, such paragons were not always available:

> The best of all then not being to be had, let us look out for the next best, and we shall find, that of all possible means to secure and perpetuate to nations their establishment, and whatever they value, there is no better method than with wise laws to guard and entrench their constitution and to contrive such forms of administration, that the commonweal can receive no great detriment from the want of knowledge or probity of ministers, if any of them should prove less able and honest than we would wish them.
> (1714–29 [1924], vol. II, 335, quoted by Hayek, 1978, 259n.)

No one before him, and few since, have stated so effectively the fundamental case for the free market economy as did Mandeville in his enthusiastic eulogy of money and freedom of exchange. After agreeing that money is 'deservedly called the root of all evil', he continued:

> . . . it has done more mischief in the world than any one thing besides. Yet it is impossible to name another that is so absolutely necessary to the order, economy, and the very existence of the civil society; for as this is entirely built upon the variety of our wants, so the whole superstructure is made up of the reciprocal services, which men do to each other. How to get these services performed by others when we have occasion for them, is the grand and almost constant solicitude in life of every individual person. To expect that others should serve us for nothing is unreasonable; therefore all commerce, that man can have together, must be continual bartering of one thing for another . . . Which way shall I persuade a man to serve me, when the service, I can repay him in, is such as he does not want or care for? Nobody, who is at peace, and has no contention with any of the society, will do anything for a lawyer; and a physician can purchase nothing of a man, whose whole family is in perfect health. Money obviates and takes away all those difficulties, by being an acceptable reward for all the services men can do to one another . . . To procure all the comforts of life, and what is called temporal happiness, in a large polite nation, would be every whit as practicable without speech as it would be without money . . . There are great blessings that arise from necessity; and that everybody is obliged to eat and drink, is the cement of civil society. Let men set what high value they please upon themselves, that labour, which most people are capable of doing, will ever be the cheapest. Nothing can be dear, of which there is great plenty, how beneficial soever it may be to man; and scarcity enhances the price of things much oftener than the usefulness of them . . .

Relative scarcities ruled:

> . . . it is evident why those arts and sciences will always be the most lucrative that cannot be attained to, but in great length of time, by tedious study and close application; or else require a particular genius not often to be met with. It is likewise evident, to whose lot, in all societies, the hard and dirty labour, which nobody would meddle with, if he could help it, will ever fall.

Mandeville became almost rhapsodical:

> The invention of money seems to me to be a thing more skilfully adapted to the whole bent of our nature than any other human contrivance. There is no greater remedy against sloth or stubbornness; and with astonishment I have beheld the readiness and alacrity with which it often makes the proudest of men pay homage to their inferiors . . . Nothing is more universally charming than money; it suits with every station; the high, the low, the wealthy, and the poor; whereas honour has little influence on the mean slaving people and rarely affects any of the vulgar; but if it does, money will almost everywhere purchase honour; nay, riches of themselves are an honour to all those, who know how to use them fashionably.
>
> (1714–29 [1924], vol. II, 349–53)

One can see why such a rather unattractive, but penetrating, and not unrealistic, picture of the market economy and society won the admiration of Karl Marx, who described Mandeville as 'infinitely bolder and more honest than the philistine apologists of bourgeois society' (Marx, n.d., vol. I, 376). If it is insisted that Mandeville must be counted a 'mercantilist', because of his advocacy of government action with regard both to the balance of payments and the level of employment, it must be acknowledged that he also put forward one of the earliest and most brilliantly penetrating cases for the market economy.

We have noticed the sharply opposing views held in the eighteenth century regarding Mandeville's ideas, and that while vigorously condemned by some authorities, they attracted much support from others, especially in France. In England, no less a figure than Dr Samuel Johnson, while maintaining that 'the happiness of society depends on virtue' (the diametric opposite, of course, of the message of *The Fable*), nevertheless admitted that Mandeville had 'opened my eyes into real life very much' (Boswell, 1791 [1906], vol. II, 211). In the nineteenth century there was much more agreement, among the supporters of the prevailing orthodoxies, in condemning Mandeville's teachings, especially his economic doctrines as to the dangers of saving and frugality and the beneficence of luxury spending, both described as 'glaring absurdities' by Leslie Stephen, for example (1876, vol. II, 35).

In the twentieth century there has been wide agreement as to the quality and importance of Mandeville's writings, to which, from their contrasting points of view, Keynes, Viner and Hayek have all paid tribute. But there is fundamental disagreement, and apparently complete disarray, as to how Mandeville should be interpreted, or categorized, in particular as to whether he was a significant precursor of Adam Smith, and even an advocate of *laissez-faire*, or whether, on the other hand, he was a 'mercantilist'.[11] In fact, in provoking, or eliciting, such flatly contradictory interpretations, Mandeville has, perhaps, been surpassed, among writers on political economy only by David Ricardo. Mandeville, however, was surely, a very lucid writer. Comparatively few of his sentences or paragraphs are seriously opaque or ambiguous. So there hardly seems to be much excuse for such sharply conflicting interpretations from leading commentators and admirers. Moreover, in the nearly thirty years (1705–33) over which he was developing, elaborating, and defending his arguments, no significant modifications or shifts of view seem to be discernible, which might give rise to differing opinions as to what he 'really meant'. It may be, however, that, in countering a number of penetrating critics, Mandeville had to tack into the wind somewhat, and contrasts, or shifts in direction and emphasis, may have crept in here and there: with regard, for example, as to what could reasonably be hoped for, in the way of 'dextrous management' from politicians. At some points a certain optimism seemed to be permissible, which at other points was represented as rather unrealistic.

Historians of ideas often get involved in what seem virtually irreconcilable conflicts of interpretation, partly because they insist that economists maintain unrealistically, or unnecessarily, high standards of consistency, so that only one interpretation is possible; and/or because their interest in some much-admired figure is fuelled mainly by a desire to enlist him as a distinguished ancestor of their particular viewpoint, so that they need to discount, or explain away, whatever passages or arguments in his writings do not fit in with the ancestral role which they wish him to play. It is clear why Keynes and Hayek both hailed Mandeville as an ancestor. But the most serious conflict in interpretations seems to have been brought about by an excessively rigid and exclusivist use of the categories 'mercantilist', and support of *laissez-faire*; or by too sharply black-and-white definitions of the supporters thereof. There is nothing necessarily contradictory in recognizing, generally, the efficacy and beneficence of free market forces, or *laissez-faire*, over wide areas of the economy, while, at the same time, supporting government intervention with regard to this or that issue or sector – even in respect of the closely linked problems of foreign trade and the money supply. Such a balanced attitude has become fairly widely held in the twentieth century, as it was by a number of leading writers in the late seventeenth and eighteenth centuries, such as Petty, Locke, Law, Galiani, Hutcheson, Steuart and others. Mandeville belongs with this group. It is seriously inadequate to categorize him simply as a 'mercantilist', in the same pigeonhole as Mun, Hörnigk, Colbert et al., someone who presented such a brilliant pioneering version of the power and public beneficence of free markets, and the pursuit of individual profit. It is also seriously misleading to describe him simply as an advocate of *laissez-faire* and a precursor of Adam Smith, when he argued for government management of foreign trade, as well as policies to promote employment, and while he so scathingly denounced the Smithian virtue of frugality and parsimony. Mandeville, without fundamental inconsistency, was *both* a 'mercantilist' and a prophet of economic individualism and market freedom, and any satisfactory account of his work must recognize both aspects. His fundamental contribution may, in conclusion, be re-emphasized as that of acting as a transmitter, from France to England, of the ideas of French moralists, especially Nicole and Domat, which were to influence so fundamentally the doctrines of Adam Smith and *The Wealth of Nations*.

V

The work of Isaac Gervaise (vital dates unknown) consists of a single pamphlet of about twenty to thirty pages. But packed into this tract is a powerful and remarkably formal analysis of international exchange and payments which concludes with a comprehensive plea for universal free trade. Though from one angle Gervaise's achievement may be seen as a major contribution to fundamental economic concepts and theory, from another it may be regarded as complementing valuably the work of Boisguilbert and Mandeville as a pioneer presentation of the case for economic freedom. For international trade had been only rather tangentially treated in Boisguilbert's writings, while Mandeville's ideas on that subject hardly represented any significant shift from the earlier, and still prevailing, nationalistic or 'mercantilist' doctrines of restriction and regulation, and had failed to recognize the possible external elements of harmony and self-adjustment which he had discerned in the domestic economy. Second, in his insistence on the limitations of credit expansion as a means towards fostering growth, Gervaise was at once a critic of John Law's ideas, and, at some points, an anticipator of classical doctrines.

Gervaise was born in Paris of a French Protestant father who moved to London, where he and his son were employed in the family firm engaged in the manufacture of, and trade in, silk or lustring.[12] The Gervaise firm had acquired certain monopoly privileges from Parliament, and one might therefore have expected that if Isaac Gervaise were to put pen to paper on the subject of trade, he would have produced a 'mercantilist' pamphlet arguing for protection and special privileges against foreign competition. In fact, his tract presented a succinctly reasoned, and decisively argued analysis, almost Ricardian in its formalism, and methodologically quite remarkable for its time, which was directed at establishing, from first principles, a general case for universal free trade. Unfortunately, for readers today Gervaise's tortuous and archaic terminology constitutes something of an obstacle, though no strongly rose-tinted spectacles are required for discerning the logic and structure of the argument.

At the time he was writing (presumably 1718–20), the wild extravagances of credit expansion in Paris would probably have been much in his mind. Anyhow, Gervaise started by attacking the 'unnatural' use of credit, and the notion that the expansion of credit increased commerce. At once Gervaise was intent on claiming the 'natural' character of the principles from which he was arguing, so much so that he invoked this rather highly charged adjective twice in one sentence: 'I draw those principles from the natural bent of man; and the remarks and conclusions I infer from them, appear to me most natural' (1720 [1954], 3). Moreover, these principles were general and indeed universal, for Gervaise entitled his work: '*The System or Theory of the Trade of the World*, because it contains such principles as seem to me capable of answering any event in trade' (3).

Human desires provided the mainspring of economic activity, or 'labour'; but a balance was constantly being sought between the desire for (or the utility of) the product of labour, and the desire for ease (or the disutility of labour). Nations, constituted of a number of individuals thus motivated, were more or less advantageously endowed or situated, and their commerce or trade was directed, in the first instance, at acquiring gold and silver, which Gervaise called 'the grand real measure or denominator of values' (5–6).

Each nation, according to the labour, or the number and productivity of its inhabitants, could attract to itself a certain 'proper' proportion of gold and silver. If it gained possession of a greater proportion 'than its proper share', it would not be able to retain this excess, which would constitute a surplus of imports over exports. This surplus would have to be paid for by the excess of precious metals, or of 'the denominator': 'There enters in that nation, more labour than goes out of it . . . And as the end of trade is the attracting gold and silver, all that difference of labour is paid in gold and silver until the denominator be lessened, in proportion to other nations' (7).

Credit came into existence because people wished to clinch transactions in advance of payments:

> Man, generally speaking, being eager and greedy of gain, is impatient in trade; so that when he cannot have the value of things, as soon as he would, he chooses rather to allow unto the buyer, more or less time, at once to force the vent, and to prevent any others supplanting him.
>
> That time which is allowed in trade, is called credit.
>
> (8)

The expansion of credit would have a similar effect on a nation's international trading position as an addition of gold and silver, for consumption would rise leaving less for exports, which must fall. The 'balance of trade' was defined by Gervaise as follows: 'When a nation exports more or less labour, than is imported into it, that difference between exports and imports of labour is called Balance of Trade' (9).

Gervaise then set out a highly simplified arithmetical model of the foreign trade of 'a nation composed of four million souls', with a national product of forty million per annum. He proceeded to show that a nation's exports and imports, if out of balance, would 'return, into the proportional and equilibrium of the rest of the world' (11).

In a passage couched emphatically in terms of the 'real' analysis deployed by Adam Smith, Gervaise argued that the 'unnatural' expansion, or 'swelling', of credit cannot bring any lasting gain:

> All the profit a nation gains by unnaturally swelling its denominator, consists only in the inhabitants living for a time in proportion to that swelling so as to make a greater figure than the rest of the world, but always at the

> cost of their coin, or of their store of real and exportable labour. For as the whole creation is in a perpetual motion, and as God made man for labour, so no thing in the world is of any solid or durable worth, but what is the produce of labour; and whatever else bears a denomination of value, is only a shadow without substance, which must either be wrought for, or vanish to its primitive nothing, the greatest power on earth not being able to create anything out of nothing.
>
> (12)

Gervaise then summed up his argument in a series of conclusions, the most striking of which asserted a long-run equilibrium in international trade: 'That if trade was not curbed by laws, or disturbed by those accidents that happen in long wars, etc. which break the natural proportion, either of people, or of private denominators; time would bring all trading nations of the world into that equilibrium, which is proportioned, and belongs to the number of their inhabitants' (15). The classical full employment assumption seemed to be implied by the conclusion that:

> No nation can encourage or enlarge its proportion of any private and natural manufacture, without discouraging the rest; because whether an allowance be given, either to the manufacturer, or transporter, that allowance serves, and is employed to attract the workmen from those other manufacturers, which have some likeness to the encouraged manufacture: so that what is transported of the encouraged manufacture, beyond nature, only balances the diminution of others.
>
> (17)

Moreover, taxes or restrictions on imports distorted the 'natural' allocation of labour:

> When the natural proportion of one, or more manufacturers, although necessary, is not large enough to answer the entire demand of the inhabitants, the best and safest way is freely to suffer their importation from the rest of the world; taxes on imports being no more than a degree of prohibition, and prohibition only forcing those manufacturers to extend themselves beyond their natural proportions, to the prejudice of those, which are, according to the disposition of the country, natural beyond the entire demand of the inhabitants; which lessens or hinders their exportation, in proportion to the prejudice they receive by the increase of those manufactures, which are but in part natural and whereof the importation is prohibited.
>
> (17)

Gervaise then put forward his universal policy generalization: 'We may conclude that trade is never in a better condition, than when it's natural and free; the forcing it either by laws, or taxes being always dangerous; because though the intended benefit or advantage be perceived, it is difficult to perceive its countrecoup; which ever is at least in full proportion to the benefit' (17–18). Gervaise concluded with a final appeal for freedom and 'nature': 'Man naturally seeks, and finds, the most easy and natural means of attaining his ends, and cannot be diverted from those means, but by force, and against his will' (18).

Gervaise's tract seems to have long remained almost completely unknown. Eventually Foxwell got possession of a copy and noted in his catalogue (now in the Kress Library) that this was 'one of the earliest formal systems of political economy, and stating one of the most forcible practical arguments for free trade'. But the full discovery of Gervaise's work, and its importance, was due to Jacob Viner (1937, 79–83).[13]

Gervaise's pamphlet seems to have had little or no effect on his contemporaries or successors, while public and political opinion in Britain remained firmly opposed to free-trade ideas. Nevertheless, it may be discerned how, latently, by the first quarter of the eighteenth century, following the works of Boisguilbert, Mandeville and Gervaise, the case for economic individualism and the free market economy was beginning to strike deeper roots and acquire more structured arguments. But Gervaise's criticism of credit expansion was by no means sufficient to halt in its tracks the kind of 'paper money mercantilism' which John Law had represented so ably in theory, though so disastrously in practice. Well before Cantillon and Hume, however, Gervaise had put forward a well-worked-out theory of the self-adjusting mechanism in international trade and payments, but in terms of income rather than price effects. His editor went so far as to maintain that Gervaise's treatment of income effects and his general equilibrium analysis of the international mechanism of adjustment are in many respects superior to those prevalent in the twentieth century (Letiche, 1952, 34). However that may now appear, there can be no doubt about the conclusion: 'In effect, Gervaise outlined the first theory of general equilibrium in the international field' (34).

VI

It may have some significance that all three of those discussed in this chapter as contributing, in English, to the development of ideas about the beneficence of free economic processes, were foreign-born immigrants. Gervaise from France, and Mandeville and Jacob Vanderlint from the Low Countries. Little is known about Vanderlint (d.1740) except that he described himself as a businessman, and that his vigorous, but rather repetitious essay, *Money Answers All Things* (*Ecclesiastes* x, 19) appeared in 1734.

Vanderlint was not as aprioristically categorical regarding the rightness of free trade as Gervaise, but he began by asserting with considerable methodological confidence 'as the principles of trade I proceed on, are founded in the nature of things and constitution of the world itself, so I doubt not that they are capable of strict demonstration in which way I should be glad to see them handled by such as have abilities for it' (1734, 10).

Vanderlint's work contains an interesting blend of ideas. Starting from a somewhat 'mercantilist' emphasis on the need for a positive balance of trade, and hence a growing money supply, as necessary for a high level of trade and employment, he combined these notions with a physiocratic insistence on the primacy of land, while leading up to a clear statement of the self-adjusting mechanism in international trade, together with a plea, anticipatory of Richard Cobden, for peace and free trade as mutually promoting one another.

Like Boisguilbert in France, Vanderlint was motivated by what he believed was England's catastrophic economic decline and decay over the previous half century, in particular since 1688. He thus offers another example of an economic writer who began from what may have been a factually quite false starting-point, but who nevertheless produced valuable concepts and insights. According to Vanderlint, the first indication of England's economic decline was persistent unemployment, although wages were too low, and provided for scarcely half a family's needs. At the same time, the country had an unfavourable trade balance, even with Spain – not to mention many empty houses and growing crime. He attempted to sustain these far from conclusively established assumptions by quoting Sir William Petty on the rate of population growth. Vanderlint dismissed luxury as a cause of the decline, though he was not as enthusiastic a eulogist of the role of luxury demand as Mandeville, favouring the reduction of inequality and the diffusing of property among the people, on the grounds that 'that community will always be most powerful, and most happy, that abounds most with middling people' (100).[14]

The first essential in promoting economic recovery was a growth in the money supply, which Vanderlint described as 'the tradesman's only tool' (94n.). Countries without mines could only achieve this growing supply of previous metals by a favourable trade balance. For Vanderlint, as for many others, a money-supply policy (e.g. a growing money supply for a growing economy) *implied* a balance-of-trade policy, since he was a metallist who saw considerable dangers in paper money. Moreover, this favourable trade balance was emphatically not to be sought by any governmental regulations or restrictions, but by competitive efficiency and low costs, which, again very emphatically, were not to be achieved by reducing real wages:

> This must not be done by making the poor fare harder, or consume less than their reasonable wants in that station require; for they being the bulk of mankind would in this case affect the consumption of things in general so mightily, that there would be a want of trade and business amongst the other part of the people, which will affect the rents so much the more as the people this way shall be distressed; but this must be done by employing the poor the right way (i.e.) in tillage and cultivation of land to make the plenty so great that they may have their wants properly supplied for that station of life, and yet work so cheap as to make our produce and manufactures so cheap, as any of our neighbouring nations make anything whatsoever.
>
> (64n.)

Vanderlint emphasized the vital importance of reductions in labour costs: 'Reducing the present rates of labour appears to me so absolutely necessary to increase our foreign and domestic trade' (9). Insisting that taxes be removed from goods consumed by workers, Vanderlint continued:

> By this making the necessaries of life cheaper to such a degree as shall be found effectual to reduce the present rates of labour, and thereby the price of everything else, so much that the money, now circulating amongst the people, may extend a vast deal further than it now will do.
>
> We shall hence be enabled to make, and export our manufactures at much lower prices. (16).
>
> . . . there is no other way in nature to compass this end, or recover the trade of the nation: for those nations that can work cheapest, must have the money, as sure as they always will have the trade.
>
> (37)

Vanderlint's analysis has been well summarized by Professor Douglas Vickers:

> Relatively speaking, the produce of the land was scarce; its price was accordingly high; consequently the subsistence wage of labour was high; the minimum supply price of manufactures was therefore high; the demand for them was at the same time deficient and manufacturing industries and all non-agricultural trades were depressed owing to the resulting squeeze of profits; and unemployment was structurally high. The thing that was needed if profit margins were to be restored and industry and trade reactivated was a general all-round lowering of the cost structure . . . The subsistence level of wages was to be lowered by increasing the output of agriculture and this was to be accomplished by increasing the area of land under cultivation.
>
> (1959, 172–3)

Doubts, however, suggest themselves regarding the adequacy of the proposals put forward by Vanderlint for increasing the amount of land under cultivation by enclosures, and by appeals to the monarchy to release crown lands.

In his emphasis on the primary role of land and nature, Vanderlint anticipated Quesnay: 'All things that are in the world, are the produce of the ground originally; and thence must all things be raised' (15), and 'The land gives all we have' (109). On value and price, however, Vanderlint followed the scarcity theory of Pufendorf and the natural-law school, while putting great emphasis on the role of demand:

> The plenty or scarcity of any particular thing, is the sole cause whence any commodity or thing can become higher or lower in price; or, in other words, as the demand is greater or less in proportion to the quantity of anything, so will such things, whatsoever, it is, be cheaper or dearer. Nor can any arts or laws make this otherwise, any more than laws or arts can alter the nature of things.
>
> (15)
>
> . . . it is the demand alone, which gives the value and fixes the price to everything.
>
> (87)

Vanderlint expressed a strong belief in the overriding power and beneficence of market forces, internally and externally, and he gave a clear account of the self-adjusting mechanism in international trade:

> But no inconvenience can arise by an unrestrained trade, but very great advantage; since if the cash of the nation be decreased by it, which prohibitions are designed to prevent, those nations that get the cash will certainly find everything advance in price, as the cash increases amongst them. And if we, who part with the money, make our plenty great enough to make labour sufficiently cheap, which is always constituted of the price of victuals and drink, our manufactures, and every thing else, will soon become so moderate as to turn the balance of trade in our favour, and thereby fetch the money back again.
>
> (49, see Viner, 1937, 83)

Vanderlint was generally and strongly opposed to restrictions: 'In general, there should never be any restraints of any kind on trade, nor any greater taxes than are unavoidable' (33). Freedom of trade enabled countries to specialize in the production of goods for which they had particular advantages: 'All nations have some commodities peculiar to them, which therefore are undoubtedly designed to be the foundation of commerce between the several nations' (97). Restrictions by one country inevitably led to reprisals and the whole process becomes self-defeating:

> And as other nations, for want of looking thoroughly into the foundation of the trade of the world, will certainly make reprisals by prohibitions, as we know they actually do, the calamity of every nation, that is no wiser, will increase; since they cut off so much trade and employment from mankind as these mutual prohibitions can affect.
>
> (48)

Equally misguided were prohibitions on the export of coin, as well as attempts to fix the prices of the precious metals 'for it's no less absurd for the government to fix the price they will give for gold and silver brought to be coined, than it would be to make a law to fix and ascertain the prices of every other commodity' (54).

Vanderlint, like Cobden more than a century later, looked to the beneficent, complementary combination of peace and freedom of trade: 'Peace, therefore being the only natural foundation of happiness to any nation, and trade the particular means whereby the people can be employed and subsisted, the promoting and improving trade should be always consulted, and especially in times of peace, which is favourable to such a design' (33). In a period of constant war-making, or preparations for war, often largely for economic reasons, Vanderlint insisted:

> Yet we should not easily be drawn into a war, it being one of the greatest calamities to which mankind can be subjected; the end of which none can well foresee, and the burdens of which (i.e. public debts and taxes) are seldom discharged in one generation . . .
>
> (61)

> And if there really be this way, as there undoubtedly is, for every nation, that will be so prudent sufficiently to pursue it to preserve peace, and extend

> their trade, and avoid war; how absurd as well as wicked is it to go to war about trade, which we hence see may be more effectually promoted by the arts of peace.
>
> (62)

> ... it's monstrous to imagine, the author of this world hath constituted things so, as to make it any ways necessary for mankind to murder and destroy each other.
>
> (122)

After Vanderlint's work of 1734, there was a gap in the succession of important contributions on the side of economic liberty and freedom of trade until the appearance in mid-century of the writings of Josiah Tucker and David Hume.[15]

8
Paper Money, Employment and the Increase of Wealth

I

By 1700 the distinction between the 'mercantilist' pamphlet literature, directed primarily at current problems, and the works of the philosophers (of natural law, or otherwise) was beginning to fade away. This distinction, as applied to the literature of the earlier part of our period, also runs roughly parallel, for some of the way at least, with the modern distinction between microeconomics and macroeconomics. Writings in the tradition of the natural-law philosophy tended mainly, though not entirely, to be concentrated on the fundamental analysis of value and price, together, to some extent, with the conditions of monopoly and competition, that is, with the subject area which modern 'microeconomics' has developed. The topical pamphleteers, on the other hand, whether or not they may have been mercantilistically inclined, tended to be concerned, as regards internal or domestic economic problems, with issues of money and employment, or what have come to be called 'macroeconomic' problems. In between are the subjects of international trade, and the rate of interest, which may be treated either from a microeconomic or a macroeconomic standpoint. Domestically or internally, most of the writers of our period, especially in its earlier decades, were centrally concerned with problems of the money supply, on the one hand, and the level of employment, on the other hand. That was certainly the case with Petty in England and also Becher in Germany, and it was also true of the two leading writers considered in this chapter, John Law and George Berkeley.

The ancestors of John Law (1671–1729) had included an Archbishop of Glasgow, but the religious divisions in Scotland had led to his father leaving the church and starting in business in Edinburgh as a goldsmith, at which he was highly successful, particularly in developing the banking side. So the eldest son, John, grew up with a keen interest in, and an acute grasp of, the methods, functions, uses and abuses of banking. On his father's death, however, John was bequeathed a considerable inheritance, with which he proceeded to set himself up as a gambler and 'beau' in

London. This soon led to the fatal event in 1694 which profoundly affected his subsequent life, when a rival in a duel was killed, and Law was sentenced to be hanged. The precise degree of his guilt was unclear, and, securing a reprieve from execution, he managed to escape from prison and flee abroad. Thus began Law's career as an itinerant adventurer, gambler and financier.[1]

He spent nearly ten years in exile in France, Italy and Holland. In Holland he must have been much impressed by the success of the Bank of Amsterdam (of which, from a distance, George Berkeley subsequently also expressed much admiration).[2] Then, reprieved but not pardoned, Law returned to Scotland, where, before the Union with England, he was safe from arrest. It was in Scotland, from about 1703 to 1706, that Law devoted himself to his monetary project for developing the Scottish economy, then in an acute depression. He submitted his scheme to the Scottish Parliament, which debated it but turned it down. Law would undoubtedly have pursued his campaign further, had he not, in 1706, felt compelled to flee his native land when the Union with England approached, for this put him under threat of arrest and prosecution. He had, however, published his ideas in his remarkable tract, *Money and Trade Considered; with a Proposal for Supplying the Nation with Money* (1705). We cannot pursue much further here Law's extraordinary career as a financier and banker in Paris and elsewhere. In 1716 he established in Paris his *Banque Générale*, which was nationalized as the *Banque Royale*, and which later provided the prototype for the Bank of France. He then set up the Mississippi Company to develop Louisiana. To float the new issue, Law resorted to inflation, which was followed by a speculative mania and total collapse in 1720. He is said to have lost all his own money and property and to have died a poor man, though this is disputed. It may simply be added, at this point, that the sub-title of Mr Hyde's biography of Law, *An Honest Adventurer* (1948), seems, according to the judgements of worthy contemporaries, and of more recent scholars, to be well justified. Comparisons have been drawn between Law's Mississippi scheme and the excesses of the South Sea Bubble in England. But Law was never corrupted as were the South Sea directors, though he allowed himself to be pressed towards disaster by the extravagances of the French Regent and Court. His claim that the South Sea directors had 'worked against England', while he had 'worked for France' (Hyde, 1948, 168), seems not unjustifiable. But Law's naiveté – like that of other would-be reformers – regarding the moderation, good sense, and good faith of princes and politicians, as well as his misjudgements regarding the psychology of mob speculation, seems extreme to the point of culpability.[3]

In *Money and Trade Considered*, Law presented fundamental insights into the nature and functions of money, which, according to Schumpeter, have 'a brilliance, and yes, profundity, which places him in the front rank of monetary theorists of all time' (1954, 295). The work was written primarily as a memorandum directed at the improvement of the Scottish economy, in particular with regard to raising the level of employment and production, and has a trenchant brevity and the appearance of rather hurried composition. The author, in fact, concluded with an apology for 'omissions', and for 'not having had time to put my thoughts in order'.

Law started with the basic problem of value and price, and followed the natural-law tradition on the subject, dealing very effectively with the water-and-diamonds paradox:

> Goods have a value from the uses they are applied to; and their value is greater or lesser, not so much from their more or less valuable, or necessary uses: as from the greater or lesser quantity of them in proportion to the demand for them.
> *Example*: water is of greater use, yet of little value; because the quantity of water is much greater than the demand for it. Diamonds are of little use yet of great value, because the demand for diamonds is much greater than the quantity of them.
>
> (1705 [1934], vol. I, 2)

Law went on to correct Locke's use of the awkward term 'vent' and pushed the analysis a little further towards the concept of a demand schedule, without attaining full clarity:

> Mr Locke says, '*The value of goods is according to their quantity in proportion to their vent*'. The vent on goods cannot be greater than the quantity, but the demand may be greater: (*Ex*) If the quantity of wine brought from France be a 100 tunn, and the demand be for 500 tunn, the demand is greater than the vent; and the 100 tunn will sell at a higher price, than if the demand were only equal to the vent. So the prices of goods are not according to the quantity in proportion to the vent, but in proportion to the demand.
>
> (4)

Law then described the convenience of silver as a means of exchange, as contrasted with the awkwardness of barter, and maintained that it was adopted spontaneously as money by the public, before it was coined or minted by princes or governments.[4] The liberating advantages of money, as compared with barter, were stated by Law in terms of the increase in employment and production, rather than as fostering the division of labour: 'As money increased, the disadvantages and inconveniencies of barter were removed; the poor and idle were employed, more of the land was laboured, the product increased, manufactures and trade improved . . . ' (14)

Law then laid down what may be regarded as his central, or favourite, proposition, which he emphasized and repeated several times, regarding the fundamental importance of the money supply: 'Domestic trade depends on the money: a greater quantity employs more people than a lesser quantity. A limited sum can only set a number of people to work proportioned to it and 'tis with little success laws are made for employing the poor or idle in countries where money is scarce . . .' (14).

In conditions of very high unemployment, which Law seemed to assume for the Scotland of his day – as did many other writers regarding their own countries in this period – he claimed, very questionably, that an expansion of the money supply would not threaten the balance of trade:

> If one half of the people are employed, and the whole product and manufacture consumed, more money, by employing more people, will make an overplus to export: if then the goods imported balance the goods exported, a greater addition to the money will employ yet more people, or the same people before employed to more advantage; which by making a greater, or more valuable export, will make a balance due. So if the money lessens, a part of the people then employed are set idle, or employed to less advantage, the product or manufacture is less, or less valuable, the export of consequence less, and a balance due to foreigners.
>
> (16)

Law even linked the increase or decrease of population with the money supply: 'As trade depends on money so the increase or decrease of the people depends on trade. If they have employment at home, they are kept at home: and if the trade is greater than serves to employ the people, it brings more from places where they are not employed' (24). He went on to explain how a rise in the exchange rate, with an over-valuation of a country's currency (or 'undervaluing foreign money'), could have a depressive effect on the economy and should be countered by draw-backs on exports and an expansion of the money supply:

> . . . Such an alteration in the exchange, or undervaluing of foreign money, should lessen the export of goods. It may not be advisable, unless a fund were given, out of which draw-backs might be paid to encourage exports, and an addition be made to the money, whereby the people may be set to work. For without some addition to the money, 'tis not to be supposed next year's export can be equal to the last: it will lessen as money has lessened; a part of the people then employed being now idle, *not for inclination to work*, or for want of employers, but for want of money to employ them with.
>
> (46, italics added)

It should be noticed that Law, like other writers of our period, believed that an important amount of idleness, or unemployment, was involuntary.

Law then came to his main proposal: the setting up of a commission to issue and regulate a paper currency for Scotland. He now emphasized the defects of silver in that it was uncertain in value and might be debased by 'the magistrate'. The forty commissioners should be answerable to Parliament, and should lend notes on the security of land. Law claimed, with doubtful justification, that this paper money would not fall in value:

> This paper will not fall in value as silver-money has fallen, or may fall: goods or money fall in value, if they increase in quantity, or if the demand lessens. But the commission giving out what sums are demanded, and taking back what sums are offered to be returned: this paper money will keep its value, and there will always be as much money as there is occasion, or employment for and no more.
>
> (120)

Observing that 'money is not the value for which goods are exchanged but the value by which they are exchanged', Law went on to claim that paper possessed the qualities necessary in money to a greater extent than silver, including homogeneity, portability and storability. He maintained, moreover, that paper, secured by land, would be more reliable in value than silver: 'It has a better and more certain value than silver money, and all other qualities necessary in money in a much greater degree, with other qualities that silver has not, and is more capable of being made money than anything yet known' (130). He asserted again that: 'Trade and money depend naturally on one another; when trade decays, money lessens; and when money lessens, trade decays' (138). Law then further emphasized the advantages of a paper money supply:

> Money not being liable to be lessened directly, nor consequentially; so the power and wealth of that country will only be precarious, from what may be directly hurtful to trade.
>
> The paper money proposed being always equal in quantity to the demand, the people will be employed, the country improved, manufacture advanced, trade – domestic and foreign – will be carried on and wealth and power attained. And not being liable to be exported, the people will not be set idle etc. And wealth and power will be less precarious.
>
> (138)

With an expanding money supply: 'This addition to the money will employ the people [who] are now idle and those now employed to more advantage: so the product will be increased, and manufacture advanced' (144).

Law explained that the rate of expansion, or precise size, of the desirable money supply for a growing economy cannot be estimated in advance, though he assumed that it had always been inadequate in Scotland: 'It cannot well be known what sum will serve the occasions of the nation, for as manufactures and trade advance, the demand for money will increase; but the poor we have always had, is a great presumption we have never had enough' (158).

Law was warmly optimistic as to the economic potential of Scotland, as contrasted with its actual condition:

> Scotland has by nature many advantages for trade; a large territory; of easy defence; plenty of people, a wholesome air, mines, [etc.] . . . This country is more capable of an extended trade than any other country of Europe, yet it is reduced to a very low state. Trade is ruined; the national stock is wasted; the people foresake the country; the rents of land are unpaid; houses in towns, and farms are thrown upon the owners' hands; the creditor cannot have the interest of his money to live upon; and the debtor's person and estate are exposed to the law.
>
> (153–4)

The criticisms to which Law's ideas are open are not, mainly, with regard to his vision of theoretical possibilities, a vision which went along with a clear grasp of some of the fundamental functions and *desiderata* of a monetary and banking system. Where, of course, he is open to attack

– as have been so many reformers – is with regard to the actual, inbuilt, human limitations, which would so hinder the practical establishment, and so complicate the management, of his schemes and of the institutions he proposed.

Law, at one point, stated the objectives of his proposals in terms which might be described as 'mercantilist':

> National power and wealth consists in numbers of people and magazines of home and foreign goods. These depend on trade and trade depends on money. So to be powerful and wealthy in proportion to other nations, we should have money in proportion with them; for the best laws without money cannot employ the people, improve the product, or advance manufactures and trade.
>
> (80)

At least Law disposed here – as far as he was concerned – of the rather pointless debate as to whether it was power or plenty which was the prime objective of the kind of policies often proposed at this and previous periods. Clearly it was both. Heckscher, indeed, described Law as 'the man who took the decisive step towards paper money mercantilism' (1955, vol. II, 234). But it may well be asked what precisely it means to call Law a 'mercantilist'? Of course, he favoured some regulation of foreign trade. But he is to be found relatively frequently, or preponderantly, *opposing* governmental regulation. He opposed the legal reduction of the rate of interest (26). He supported the free export of wool (20). He was against prohibitions on the export of bullion and money (32). More generally, as we have seen, he put the prime emphasis in his proposals for raising employment and growth in the Scottish economy, on the establishment of a monetary constitution rather than on 'laws', or regulations, intended to raise the level of employment. Politically, Law, like Mandeville and others, ascribed the economic successes of the Dutch to religious toleration and freedom. If Law was a 'mercantilist' he was so liberal in his 'mercantilism' as to raise some questions about the meaning of the term.

II

In the early decades of the eighteenth century the idea of paper money, and proposals for its introduction or expansion, were forthcoming in a number of countries, and in more than one continent. Among the many attributes or accomplishments of Benjamin Franklin (1706–90) was that of being – according to some authorities – the first American economist. Anyhow, soon after moving, as a young man, from Boston to Philadelphia, Franklin, in one of his earliest writings, added his support to the popular demand in that city for an expansion of paper money. Since gold and silver were so difficult to obtain, or retain, in the colonies, various monetary arrangements had been undertaken in the different states, with paper money being made legal tender in some cases.

At the age of twenty-two, Franklin wrote the brief tract, *A Modest Inquiry into the Nature and Necessity of a Paper Currency* (1729, in *Works*, 1844). Like many writers of the period, Franklin attributed all sorts of evils to the shortage of money: it reduced demand, made for high interest rates, discouraged employment, and (rather paradoxically) Franklin argued that it made for more consumption of English and European goods. Anyhow, it was quite excessively difficult, especially for colonies without mines, to obtain and retain adequate quantities of the precious metals. He saw that 'money as a currency has an additional value by so much time and labour as it saves in the exchange of commodities'. He maintained: 'There is a certain proportionate quantity of money requisite to carry on the trade of a country freely and currently; more than which would be of no advantage in trade, and less, if much less, exceedingly detrimental to it' (1729 [1844], (255). Franklin argued, somewhat dubiously, that if the security of an issue of paper money were based on land, this security would increase as land rose in value with the increase in population (see Dewey, 1900, 129).

Franklin seemed very reluctant to recognize any possible danger from the over-issue of paper money (or he hardly did so until nearly half a century later when he described the inflation brought about by conditions during and after the War of Independence). An over-issue of money, he appeared to suggest, would simply have no effect. It certainly seems, however, that paper money had been successfully managed in the American colonies, and George Berkeley, six years later, was to support his proposals for paper money in Ireland partly on the basis of his first-hand knowledge during his sojourn in Rhode Island from 1728 to 1731.

Incidentally, Franklin, when complaining of the variability in the value of silver, which fluctuated 'according to scarcity or plenty', put forward a labour-commanded theory of value on Smithian lines: 'The riches of a country are to be valued by the quantity of labour its inhabitants are able to purchase' (1729, 265), and not by the quantity of silver and gold they possess.[5] Trade is 'nothing else but the exchange of labour for labour', by which the values of all things are 'most justly measured'. Observing that silver could vary in value, Franklin then switched to the idea of labour embodied as an absolute measure: 'Suppose one man is employed to raise corn, while another is digging and refining silver, at the year's end . . . the complete produce of corn and that of silver are the natural price of each other' (1729 [1844], 265).

Subsequently, in 1764, the British Government prohibited further issues of paper money in the colonies. The following year, when he was in London, Franklin expressed his opposition to this measure in a pamphlet *Remarks and Facts Relative to the American Paper Money* (1765, in *Works*, 1844). He restated his view that the lack of gold and silver made paper money essential, and that money or coins did not have to possess intrinsic value. Franklin maintained his interest in economic affairs throughout his long life, and kept in touch with leading economists in Britain and France. We shall return to Franklin as an economist in chapter 13.

III

A greater contrast in style and philosophy of life would hardly seem possible than that between the duelling, gambling, speculative financier, John Law, and Bishop George Berkeley. Nevertheless, in their responses to somewhat similar economic problems, as seen by Law in Scotland (*c.*1705), and as confronted by Berkeley in Ireland about thirty years later, these two men propounded the same kind of explanations and analyses, and argued for, certainly in one major respect, a very similar remedy, i.e. the setting up of a National Bank and a system of paper money.[6]

Berkeley studied at Trinity College, Dublin, and stayed there as a Fellow until 1713, by when he had produced the great philosophical works for which he is most celebrated (*A New Theory of Vision*, 1709; *Treatise Concerning the Principles of Human Knowledge*, 1710; and *Dialogues*, 1713). He then moved to London, where, in 1721, the scandal of the South Sea Bubble moved him to write *An Essay Towards Preventing the Ruin of Great Britain*, in which he attacked excesses of economic liberty. Soon after he began to be absorbed by his project for a Christian College on the other side of the Atlantic. He invested to the full his own time and resources, spending nearly three years in America (1728–31), mostly near Newport, Rhode Island on a project which ended in failure.

In 1734, when Berkeley returned to Ireland on his appointment as Bishop of Cloyne, that island had long been suffering from a combination of conditions which economists today would distinguish as those of a chronically depressed economy, of a distressed area, of an under-developed country, and of an exploited colony. Currency changes had rendered monetary conditions chaotic, and exports were further crippled by the English prohibition of Irish woollens in 1698–9 – which had been proposed or supported by Locke. Berkeley described the condition of the people around him in his diocese in terms somewhat similar to those of La Bruyère's account (quoted in note 3 to chapter 7) of the French peasantry under Louis XIV and Colbert:

> The house of an Irish peasant is the cave of poverty; within you see a pot and a little straw; without, a heap of children tumbling on a dunghill . . . In every road the ragged ensigns of poverty are displayed; you often meet caravans of poor, whole families in a drove, without clothes to cover or bread to feed them, both of which might be easily procured by moderate labour.
>
> (*Works*, ed. Jessop, vol. VI, 1953, 236)

Berkeley set out to combat such conditions both by practical measures in his own diocese – one in which it was apparently then unusual for the Bishop to reside – and by undertaking an analysis of Ireland's problems and putting forward proposals for overcoming them in his pamphlet *The Querist*, published in three instalments in 1735, 1736 and 1737. Berkeley defended his concern with economic problems in his foreword to the second edition (1750): 'I anticipate the same censure on this, that I incurred upon another occasion, for meddling out of my profession. Though to feed the hungry and clothe the naked by promoting an honest industry, will, perhaps, be deemed no improper employment for a clergyman, who still thinks himself a member of the Commonwealth' (1953, 103).

In its original form *The Querist* consisted of nearly 900 searching and provocative queries, apparently haphazardly arranged. A consistent and comprehensive analysis becomes, however, clearly discernible, although the conclusions were built up from particular practical proposals, suggested by his close observation of the evidence around him, rather than deduced downwards from a set of axioms or 'assumptions'. Berkeley started with a minimum of equipment in the form of analytical and conceptual refinements. Like his contemporaries, he hardly distinguished between the short-term raising of employment and production, and the longer-term growth of resources. He adopted the kind of demand-and-supply approach to value and price widely followed by predecessors and contemporaries: 'Whether the value or price of things, be not a compounded proportion, directly as the demand and reciprocally as the plenty?' (I, 24). Berkeley also accepted a quantity approach to the theory of money – introducing the *ceteris paribus* postulate: 'Whether, *ceteris paribus*, it be not true that the prices of things increase, as the quantity of money increaseth, and are diminished as that is diminished?' (III, 157).

But, like nearly all seventeenth- and eighteenth-century pamphleteers – apart, perhaps, from the exceptional Isaac Gervaise – Berkeley was concerned, primarily and predominantly, with practical measures rather than analysis.

There is little or nothing in Berkeley's writings in the form of specific references indicating the sources of his ideas, or the writers (if any) who influenced him, apart from William Petty and, especially, John Law. The staccato, interrogative procedure of *The Querist* may have been suggested by Petty's monetary tract *Quantulumcunque* (1682). More significantly, Berkeley, at one point, recommended the methods of 'political arithmetic' for obtaining a quantitative grasp of the unemployment problem (II, 199). With regard to John Law and his ideas, it is clear that Berkeley had followed attentively the course of Law's experiment in Paris, and had not allowed its disastrous conclusion to blind him to the penetration and relevance of some of the underlying theoretical ideas (I, 276). It is clear also, from numerous references, that Berkeley had made a close study of certain European banks, including the Bank of Amsterdam.

The two main features of economic conditions in Ireland which obviously provoked Berkeley most fundamentally, were those about which numerous other writers of that period, in Britain and elsewhere, including John Law, had frequently complained – though these two problems may well have taken on an even more severe and abject form in Ireland. (It may be noted, however, that Berkeley had been struck by the contrasting absence, or mildness, of these ailments in the American colonies.) These two major problems were, of course, (a) chronic and widespread unemployment or under-employment, and (b) a disastrously inadequate and unreliable money supply.

There is no doubt that, as in England, Scotland and elsewhere at this time, as it always is, and has been, 'unemployment' was at least to some extent 'voluntary', that is, in moralistic terms, due to slothfulness, or, technically, due to a perverse, backward-sloping supply curve of labour. Berkeley's proposals for combatting this awkward perversity combined the use of both sticks and carrots. On the one hand, the creation of new wants should provide incentives to work:

> Whether the creating of wants be the likeliest way to produce industry in a people? And whether if our peasants were accustomed to eat beef and wear shoes they would not be more industrious?
>
> (I, 20)

> Whether comfortable living doth not produce wants, and wants industry, and industry wealth?
>
> (I, 20)

On the other hand, however, Berkeley was prepared to propose compulsory workhouses: 'Whether it would be a hardship on people destitute of all things, if the public furnished them with necessities which they should be obliged to earn by their labour?' (II, 213). Berkeley cited St Paul: 'The shortest and most effective lesson is that of St Paul: "If any man would not work, neither should he eat (2 *Thess.* III, 10)"' (VI, 237).

Berkeley did not attempt to lay down the frontier line, so important administratively, but so difficult to draw in practice, between voluntary and involuntary idleness or unemployment. But, like Boisguilbert in France, Berkeley was provoked by the paradox of poverty and unemployment side-by-side, and it was perfectly clear to him that there was a large amount of chronic, *in*voluntary unemployment:

> Whether we are not in fact the only people who may be said to starve in the midst of plenty?
>
> (III, 101)

> Whether the public hath the right to employ those *who can not*, or who will not, find employment for themselves?
>
> (II, 216, italics added)

Berkeley also called attention (as had Law, with regard to Scotland) to the already considerable emigration of Irish labourers in search of a livelihood overseas, which suggested a serious lack of employment at home: 'Whether there can be a worse sign than that people should quit their country for a livelihood ... Whether this be not exceeding bad, and showeth some peculiar mismanagement?' (II, 103).

Berkeley's fiscal policies were aimed at curbing luxury expenditure and aiding the poor by raising employment. To some extent he agreed with Mandeville: 'Whether the industry of the lower part of our people doth not much depend on the expense of the upper?' (II, 229). But Berkeley emphatically disagreed with Mandeville's conclusion that the extravagance and luxury of the rich should have free rein, fiscally, when the majority of the population were starving, or in the most abject poverty: 'Whether necessity is not to be hearkened to before convenience and convenience before luxury?' (I, 63). Berkeley believed in 'trickling' (or pumping) *up*, rather than 'trickling down', and suggested something of the later Hobsonian-Keynesian diagnosis of how the unequal distribution of wealth may depress aggregate demand:

> Whether to provide plentifully for the poor, be not feeding the root, the substance whereof will shoot upwards into the branches, and cause the top to flourish?
>
> (I, 64)

> Whether as seed equally scattered produces a goodly harvest, even so an equal distribution of wealth doth not cause a nation to flourish?
>
> (I, 220)

He supported sumptuary laws and cutting down luxury imports to protect the Irish balance of payments, while Irish exports were cut back by English restrictions. The expenditure of the few Irish rich could and should be canalized to provide employment at home, into houses and furniture rather than foreign clothes and liquor. Berkeley followed Nicholas Barbon regarding the beneficence of expenditure on building, in order to reduce unemployment. However, Berkeley held that some imports from abroad should be encouraged: 'Whether foreign imports that tend to promote industry should not be encouraged and such as have a tendency to promote luxury should not be discouraged?' (III, 274).

Like Petty, Berkeley favoured a programme of worthy public building: 'Whether it would not be of use and ornament, if the towns throughout this Kingdom were provided with decent churches, town-houses, work-houses, market-places and paved streets, with some order taken for cleanliness?' (II, 248). In fact, in his essay of 1721, Berkeley proposed, in terms very similar to those of Petty, expenditure on 'triumphal arches, columns, statues, inscriptions, and the like monuments of public services' (vol. III, 1901, 205).

Berkeley's main emphasis, however, was on his proposals for thorough-going monetary reform, that is, for a national bank and a paper currency. Here, obviously, he was following John Law, while noting, and trying to correct, the errors in Law's experiment. Berkeley's remarks on the nature and functions of money were also very similar to those of Law.

The principal aim of monetary institutions and policies must be to maintain a high level of economic activity, and above all to prevent the paradox of poverty and unemployed resources existing side-by-side:

> Whether money be not only so far useful, as it stirreth up industry, enabling men mutually to participate [sic] the fruits of each others labour?
>
> (I, 5)

> Whether all regulations of coin should not be made, with a view to encourage industry, and a circulation of commerce, throughout the kingdom?
>
> (III, 140)

If the main error of 'mercantilism' was that of believing that the precious metals were the ultimate, real form of wealth, no-one could have exposed this error more vigorously and comprehensively than Berkeley:

> What makes a wealthy people? And whether mines of gold and silver are capable of doing this? ...
>
> (I, 31)
>
> Whether there be any virtue in gold or silver, other than as they set people at work, or create industry?
>
> (I, 32)

Berkeley was one of the first to describe money as a kind of 'ticket'. In the then prevailing conditions, the uncertain and unstable supply of the precious metals did not provide a steady and reliable money supply in the form of tickets of convenient dominations:

> Whether it doth not much import to have a right conception of money? And whether it's true and just idea be not that of a ticket, entitling to power and fitted to record and transfer such power?
>
> (III, 89)
>
> Whether business at fairs and markets is not often at a stand, and often hindered, even though the seller hath his commodities at hand, and the purchaser his gold, yet for want of change?
>
> (III, 179)

Such being the most important function of money, it was clear that a paper money supply could be much more conveniently and purposefully regulated that one consisting of the precious metals:

> Whether it be not agreed that paper hath, in many respects, the advantage above coin, as being of more dispatch in payments, more easily transferred, preserved, and recovered when lost?
>
> (I, 207)
>
> Whether there are not to be seen in America fair towns, wherein the people are well lodged, fed, and clothed, without a beggar in their streets, although there be not one grain of gold or silver current among them?
>
> (I, 284)

To issue and regulate the paper currency a National Bank should be established. Such banks, Berkeley claimed, were already operating successfully in Venice, Amsterdam and Hamburg, and such an institution had already been under discussion for Ireland:

> Whether a National Bank would not at once secure our properties, put an end to usury, facilitate commerce, supply the want of coin, and produce ready payments in all parts of the kingdom?
>
> (I, 12)
>
> Whether, therefore, a National Bank would not be more beneficial than even a mine of gold? (I, 23)
>
> Whether all things considered, a National Bank be not the most practicable,

> sure, and speedy method to mend our affairs, and cause industry to flourish among us?
>
> (I, 129)

> Whether in the rude original state of society, the first step was not the exchanging of commodities, the next a substituting of metals by weight as the common medium of circulation, after this the making use of coin, lastly a further refinement by the use of paper with proper marks and signatures? And whether this, as it is the last, so it be not the greatest improvement?
>
> (III, 100)

Berkeley held that it was necessary for the National Bank to be publicly owned, considering the great power that was concentrated in it:

> Whether a bank in private hands might not even overturn a government?
>
> (I, 214)

> Whether by a *National Bank*, be not properly understood a bank, not only established by public authority as the Bank of England, but a bank in the hands of the public, wherein there are no shares: whereof the public alone is proprietor and reaps all the benefit?
>
> (I, 222)

He went into considerable detail in his proposals for a National Bank, but insisted that any scheme, or constitution must be treated as experimental. He was well aware of the crucial importance of fostering public confidence:

> Whether there should not be great discretion in the uttering of bank notes, and whether the attempting to do things *per saltum* be not often the way to undo them?
>
> (II, 138)

> Whether the main art be not by slow degrees and cautious measures to reconcile the bank to the public, to wind it insensibly into the affections of men, and interweave it with the constitution?
>
> (II, 139)

Berkeley may, of course, have been rather too inclined to assume – like other reformers – that the arrangements and institutions that he was proposing would always be directed by people as wise and benevolent as himself. But he was well aware of the dangers of the excessive concentration of power, and also that the French régime had destroyed Law's scheme by its folly and greed. He certainly could not have been unaware of the dangers of inflation, and of the excesses of speculation in view of the monstrous recent examples both in London and Paris. He suggested, in fact, a vital rule for regulating the money supply in a growing economy: 'Whether therefore bank-bills should at any time be multiplied, but as trade and business were also multiplied?' (II, 124). In fact, Berkeley warned:

> Whether it was not madness in France to mint bills and actions, merely to humour the people and rob them of their cash?
>
> (II, 125)
>
> Whether we may not profit by their mistakes, and as some things are to be avoided, whether there may not be others worthy of imitation, in the conduct of our neighbours?
>
> (II, 126)

Finally, there was the need for a full study, and sound understanding, of so vital a subject as the monetary arrangements of a nation: 'Whether that which employs and exerts the force of a community deserves not to be well considered, and well understood? (III, 317).

In addition to emphasizing Berkeley's indebtedness to John Law, it is also interesting to compare his doctrines with those of Mandeville, on the one hand, and, on the other, with those of Francis Hutcheson – a fellow Irish Protestant, though from the north of the island – who joined Berkeley in severe moral criticism of Mandeville, but differed profoundly from both Berkeley and Mandeville on a fundamental point of economic theory. Berkeley's criticism of Mandeville comes in Dialogue II of *Alciphron or the Minute Philosopher* (1733). Regarding luxury expenditure 'Euphranor' (representing Berkeley's own views) answers 'Lysicles' (a Mandevillian) as follows:

> I would fain know whether money spent innocently doth not circulate as well as that spent upon vice? And if so, whether by your own rule it doth not benefit the nation as much? ... Should it not seem, therefore, that building, gardening, and agriculture would not employ men more usefully than if tailors, barbers, perfumes, distillers, and such arts were multiplied?'
>
> (1910, II, 72)

This criticism does not completely answer Mandeville's basic argument, which started from the assumption that some of what is not spent on luxuries would be *saved*, or hoarded, rather than spent on anything else, luxuries or non-luxuries. Berkeley's criticism seems, up to a point, to resemble very closely that which Francis Hutcheson had levelled against Mandeville, to the effect that until everyone was fully provided with the necessaries of life, and with all 'innocent conveniences and pleasures', consumption expenditure not merely *could*, but 'would', be fully maintained, without any 'vicious' luxury. But, as pointed out above, there is a vital distinction between 'could' and 'would' in this context, and Berkeley is confining himself simply to stating the *possibility*, not the actuality, or likelihood, that all income not spent on luxuries would be spent on non-luxuries. Anyhow, in complete contrast with Hutcheson, who had no such measures to propose, Berkeley, while urging that private luxury expenditure by the rich should be reduced, was demanding (a) redistribution in favour of the poor, (b) a vigorous programme of government expenditure on public works and buildings, and (c) a comprehensive reform of monetary and banking institutions and policy; all of which policies were aimed directly at raising and maintaining aggregate demand and employment.

In conclusion, two intellectual traditions may be noticed of which George Berkeley was an ornament. One was that, once mentioned by Keynes, of the eighteenth-century churchmen, who wrote on political economy, such as Fleetwood, Paley, and Malthus, to which Josiah Tucker's name should certainly be added, together with those of a number of lesser figures (see Iremonger, 1948, 439). The second, more celebrated tradition, of which Berkeley was a prominent member, was that of the great British philosopher-economists, notably Locke, Hume, and J. S. Mill. Although his economic writings did not possess the same long-run weight as those of the preceding trio, Berkeley may be regarded as one of the most distinguished exponents of this great tradition.

IV

Both Law and Berkeley were centrally concerned with what, two-and-a-half centuries later, would have been described as the problems of a comparatively 'less-developed' economy, those of Scotland and Ireland respectively. It would, however, be somewhat anachronistic, and perhaps misleading, to describe their ideas and questions in such mid-twentieth-century terms. Most of the main types of processes which would today be discussed in the context of 'development', and 'under-development', were simply not explicitly envisaged by Law, Berkeley, Franklin, and the vast majority of their contemporaries: such as, notably, saving for productive capital investment and technological progress. The division of labour was gradually coming to be recognized as a means of increasing production and productivity (as by Petty, Martyn, Mandeville, and Ernst Ludwig Carl), but it was not given a significant role by many writers (including Law and Berkeley). Quite a number of writers wanted to encourage the growth of population, as a means to a growing economy, while probably entertaining some inexplicit and imprecise notion of increasing returns to scale. The most widely advocated idea for bringing about a growth in production and wealth was that of securing an adequate and growing money supply in order to sustain a high level of aggregate demand and employment. It was with this aim in view that Law and Berkeley advocated the introduction of paper money as a means to maintaining either (or both) a high level of luxury demand, and higher living standards for the poor. In the seventeenth and eighteenth centuries, economic progress and the growth of production was seen as depending to an important extent on promoting higher levels of employment. The reduction of unemployment was regarded as the main means by which a growth in the production of wealth could be brought about. Distinctions between shorter-term expansion and longer-term growth were scarcely envisaged.

APPENDIX: KEYNES AND THE MERCANTILISTS[7]

In discussing the writers of the seventeenth and eighteenth centuries we do not wish to get involved in generalizations or arguments about 'mercantilism', 'the mercantilists', or 'mercantilist thought'. These are concepts which involve generalizing about both thought and policy, in different countries, over two or three centuries, lumping together the ideas and arguments of original and disciplined thinkers, such as Petty, Cantillon, or Steuart, with the outpourings of ephemeral special pleaders.

Anyhow, Keynes's attempt at a new interpretation of pre-Smithian writings met with immediate condemnation even from his most enthusiastic disciples.[8] Furthermore, Heckscher, on whose work Keynes had copiously drawn, strongly rejected his attempt 'to rehabilitate' what they both called 'the mercantilist doctrine' (1955, vol. II, 340ff).

Regarding Heckscher's strictures it should be noted that they are directed at both 'the mercantilist' and Keynes's own doctrines. Heckscher did not argue that the 'mercantilist' ideas and Keynes's were really quite dissimilar, as some subsequent critics of Keynes's interpretation of 'the mercantilists' have done. On the contrary, according to Heckscher, they resembled one another all too closely: 'Keynes's view of economic relationships is in many ways strikingly similar to that of the mercantilists' (340).

Moreover, according to Heckscher, neither Keynes's theories, nor those of 'the mercantilists' (*nor, incidentally, the classical theories*) were founded on the facts of their own or any other period: 'There are no grounds whatsoever for supposing that the mercantilist writers constructed their system – with its frequent and marked theoretical orientation – out of any knowledge of reality however derived. There is nothing to indicate that they were any different in this respect from the classical economists' (347).[9]

Professor Mark Blaug has criticized Keynes's interpretation of 'mercantilism' in terms to some extent similar to Heckscher's, though more particularized. He agrees, apparently, that the seventeenth- and eighteenth-century writers were concerned with unemployment, but holds, like Heckscher, that they quite misconceived the problems of their day in advancing diagnoses and remedies similar to those of Keynes. For the kind of unemployment which they faced in the century or two before Adam Smith was – according to Professor Blaug – of a completely different nature from that with which Keynes was confronted:

> The kind of unemployment which caused great concern was either disguised under-employment or else voluntary unemployment in the sense of a marked preference for leisure over earnings ... It may be conceded that a chronic shortage of currency impedes economic growth and that an increase in the stock of money can promote investment if it results in forced saving, but Keynesian remedies in a dominantly agrarian economy merely produce inflation without leading to full employment. If this be accepted, it follows that most of Adam Smith's predecessors were 'monetary cranks' not prescient Keynesians.
>
> (1964, 115)

It is fortunately unnecessary to argue at length over what kind of unemployment caused, or should have caused, greatest concern in the seventeenth and eighteenth centuries. Perhaps 'voluntary unemployment', and unemployment due to shortages of capital, were relatively more important in the seventeenth and eighteenth centuries than in the twentieth century, and even conceivably were then the most important kind of unemployment. All we need to maintain is that involuntary industrial or manufacturing unemployment due to instabilities and deficiencies of aggregate demand was *a* major, serious problem, with which many of the writers of this time were justifiably concerned, in the context of which it was reasonable for them to have advocated government policies, such as public works, fiscal policies, and policies to maintain the money supply. Anyhow, hardly any of these writers are to be found implying, like Smith and Ricardo later, that there was virtually no unemployment problem at all, or none with which government should attempt to deal. It also seems to be suggested that because 'Keynesian' policies cannot cure all, or nearly all, unemployment in some poorer, or 'less-developed' countries today (or in more developed either) therefore, writers of the seventeenth or eighteenth centuries, who suggested policies against unemployment in Britain, like those suggested by Keynes, must have failed to grasp correctly the problems of their time and place: for Britain at that time was also at a 'less-developed' stage. Such an argument seems unsatisfactory for two reasons: (a) it implies a crudely over-simplified, 'linear' conception of economic development, to suggest that all economies, in culturally quite different countries and continents, pass through the same stages, with processes and institutions working in the same way, only at different dates: that is, that the labour supply, labour market, and unemployment in India in 1970 can be assumed, in their institutions and processes, to be comparable or similar to those of a more 'developed' economy (e.g. that of Britain) at some earlier date, say 1670, or 1770, or 1870.

(b) Even if unemployment at some times and places may not be completely or approximately curable by Keynesian policies, this certainly does not mean that it cannot be seriously reduced or increased by wise or unwise government stabilization policies: in fact, when any sector of an economy has risen appreciably above a primitive agricultural level there may be a Keynesian problem of maintaining an appropriate level of aggregate demand and employment, even if a serious unemployment problem of a kind not curable by Keynesian methods may persist. It seems to involve considerable oversimplification to assume that at any one time and place *all*, or anything like all, unemployment must be of the same type. In fact, at most times and places, different types of unemployment will be existing side by side.

With regard to the 'voluntary' or 'involuntary' nature of the employment problem in the seventeenth and eighteenth centuries, it may be observed that one writer after another makes it abundantly clear that though sometimes *also* concerned with 'voluntary' unemployment, or laziness – which presumably exists in all times and places – the problem of involuntary unemployment was for them a major concern.[10] Of course, for Heckscher and those who agree with him, this means little because they hold that these writers had no knowledge of the realities of the economy which confronted them. However, a number of more recent economic historians have maintained that involuntary industrial unemployment, due to instabilities of demand, which were to a serious extent of monetary origin, was a major problem in seventeenth-century England.

First, Mr R. W. K. Hinton has emphasized the extent to which many of the seventeenth-century English writers were concerned with *depression* (like Keynes, incidentally):

> The writings from which we infer the so-called mercantilist ideas at present under discussion were largely a product of economic depressions. Most of Thomas Mun's classic exposition was written apropos of the depression of 1620, like the famous tracts of Malynes and Misselden. Nearly all the works cited in Professor Viner's bibliography to *English Theories of Foreign Trade* and most of the English legislation cited in the index to Professor Heckscher's *Mercantilism* fall in or near the periods of bad trade identified by W. R. Scott. The seventeenth century commissions of trade, whose instructions embody mercantilist thought and whose enquiries encouraged it, were established in crises.
>
> In the seventy years of Mun's lifetime from 1571 to 1641 there were only thirty-six years of good trade, according to W. R. Scott; the rest he calls either depressed or bad; he counts seven severe crises of varying duration. (1955, 284)

Professor B. E. Supple has also emphasized the extent to which seventeenth-century English writers were concerned with depression, and he strongly defends their realistic grasp of what were the significant problems of their day:

> There is incontestable evidence that it is impossible to dissociate some mercantilist writing from the problems of the day, and that it was usually a time of economic distress which provided an environment of urgency within which economic views first became fully articulate. Whatever the theoretical shortcomings and blatant oversights of contemporary pamphleteers, *their appreciation of the significant areas for economic investigation cannot be questioned*. If these men had their faults then they are largely those of any group desperately involved in an economic crisis. The whole tenor of what has come to be known as mercantilist literature owes not a little to this involvement.
>
> (1959, 221, italics added)

Professor Supple also strongly defends the concern of these writers with 'the scarcity of money', implying that it was not they who were the 'monetary cranks', who completely misconceived the problems with which they were faced, but rather, perhaps, the classical 'cranks' of facile self-adjustment who assumed away 'hoarding' and the problems of securing a growing money supply, because money didn't really matter:

> In large part the modern approach has been to discount contemporary theories of an independent shortage of currency on the grounds that they were products of a confused mercantilist view of the significance of treasure,

and that any economic problems posed by a drain of specie would quite naturally be solved by the speedy readjustment deriving from deflationary pressures on prices, costs and the demand for imports.

> *But such analyses presuppose economic mechanisms quite remote from the reality of the early seventeenth century* ... The operations of the seventeenth-century economy were not frictionless, and economic pressures which, in the perfect models of classical economics, lowered monetary values while maintaining full employment of resources, were likely, in Stuart society, to provoke chronic unemployment or underemployment as they met the relatively rigid line of prices and costs. *For an economy whose market values contained a significant traditional element and which depended so much on the availability of metallic coin for its continuing activity, fluctuations in the physical supply of liquid assets could impose long-term strains which cannot be measured by an exercise in formal logic.* For this reason it was quite possible, after 1611, for a shortage of money to be the cause of continuing dislocation and incipient deflation. It would therefore be misleading to claim that all such complaints of a shortage arose from a 'confused economic analysis'.
>
> (177, italics added)

Finally, Professor Supple has emphasized the importance of the unemployment problem *and of the problem of industrial unemployment due to deficiency or instability of effective demand*:

> The most critical element of instability as far as the government was concerned was the possibility of chronic unemployment. And it has already been indicated that in this last respect the textile industry played an almost unique role at this time. Thus variations in the effective demand for cloth were the principal causes of outbreaks of unemployment for people who might, at such times, find few alternative sources of income ...
>
> ... Since the prevention of social unrest by the maintenance of employment in textiles was a major aim of policy, governments were clearly forced to consider the relationships between commercial crises and the structure of the cloth industry.
>
> (234)

Unless Professor Supple can be shown to be very seriously wrong, we have here some quite massive support for the kind of interpretation of this literature which Keynes originated.

More recently (1969) this kind of interpretation has been supported in an article on Malynes – one of the writers cited by Keynes – who was much concerned with the instabilities of the money supply as a cause of unemployment:

> It was because of the impact of a monetary drain on spending and demand that he feared a specie outflow. 'The want of money', he wrote, 'maketh a dead trade'. In fact, if sixteenth- and early seventeenth-century observers were correct, the money supply, rather than habits of saving or methods and intensity of investment, was a major source of economic fluctuations. The early Stuart economy rested upon a rather stolid agricultural base, and the visible origin of the economic growth urgently needed to absorb the troublesome body of unemployed was the foreign sector, or more specifically, the textile industry.
>
> (Muchmore, 1969)

Professor Muchmore concludes that: 'The habit of continually assigning events a subordinate role has jeopardized the assessment of pre-Smithian economics. Malynes was immersed in the peculiar problems of his period.' Certainly the 'assigning of a subordinate role' to a massive unemployment problem, and the over-simplification of the nature of that problem, will not conduce to a just interpretation of seventeenth- and eighteenth-century economists.

As regards the eighteenth century, the prevalence of instability and unemployment throughout a wide range of industries has been noted by Ashton (1959).[11] In fact, in marked contrast with Heckscher's attitude, a number of economic historians have more recently recognized Keynes's contribution. For example, Professor van Klaveren has written of the 'important steps' in the understanding of mercantilist theorizing which 'have been properly acknowledged only since John Maynard Keynes' (1969, 141).

Professor C. H. Wilson has observed that 'it was John Maynard Keynes who first initiated a re-examination of orthodox attitudes here' (1967, ix). Professor Wilson accuses Keynes of 'perpetrating an anachronism' in 'trying to isolate the purely economic element in "mercantilist" thought and policy'. But this must be an error perpetrated by many historians of economic thought. Professor Wilson himself has sought to defend and rationalize 'mercantilist' theories and policies with regard to the balance of trade, against their dismissal as the work of 'cranks' and 'ignoramuses'.[12]

It could certainly be argued that Keynes in his chapter in *The General Theory* concentrated rather too narrowly on theories about the rate of interest in the seventeenth- and eighteenth-century economists, and that he might have also given more attention to the direct concern of writers, from Petty to Steuart, with the problem of unemployment, as one which called for government policies and would not beneficently settle itself by a self-adjusting mechanism. In fact 'full employment' has been described as 'the economic objective of mercantilist policy, as distinct from its political objective which was national power'.[13]

Regarding the role of monetary theory in this period Professor Douglas Vickers concludes his very thorough study:

> Its relevance in particular was to the problems of growth or development on the one hand and to the level of employment and activity on the other. The strands of thought at these points are clearly intermixed – yet it is necessary to conclude that *the more important considerations for the development of the theory of money were those of employment rather than those of economic growth* ...
>
> In moving, however, to the theory of employment, the theory of money here derives a clearer stimulus to analytical development, and it finds here its primary application. In the realm of policy again, the cause for concern was the chronic tendency to unemployment, poverty, and distress, and the social and human problems which these occasioned. Population, production, and activity were increasing during the eighteenth century, but the expansive trend was associated with a tendency to unemployment which was structural in part and which depended, moreover, on a dragging deficiency of the

means of exchange. Employment, therefore, was itself a prerequisite of the healthy functioning and development of the economy and the objectives of monetary analysis became consistently those of the effects of the money flow on the level of employment and trade.

(1959, 294, italics added)[14]

In his discerning study of the balance of trade doctrine Suviranta emphasized how 'the question of employment came to be of paramount importance in economic policy' (1923, 136).

Suviranta, writing long before Keynes, went on:

> Much in the appreciation of money by mercantile writers does not, therefore, appear unreasonable . . .
>
> As long as paper currency had not been introduced, there existed permanently, even at the time of the largest supply of money, a *potential* scarcity of money. A stoppage or even a substantial slackening in the supply of the precious metals would have, by the steadily growing demand for money, changed, sooner or later, the imminent danger of a scarcity into a painful reality. It is against this background that the mercantile psychology must be seen and that *the anxiety for a steady supply of money only becomes fully intelligible for us, who are living in greatly changed conditions* . . .
>
> Instead of reproving them for a theory, fallacious, and insufficient, we may, on the contrary, grant that we find in their writings much common sense and also, often, fine theoretical judgment.
>
> (77,95, and 166)[15]

It should be noted that Keynes claimed neither that the theories of the seventeenth- and eighteenth-century writers were devoid of errors and inadequacies, nor that they were identical in form and content with his own. Certainly economists in the seventeenth and eighteenth centuries had not developed the specialized, 'professional' terminology and the analytical and conceptual precision and refinement of the twentieth century. But they were able to discern the existence of unemployment, hoarding, and an erratic and often insufficient money supply as serious problems.

We are concerned with arguments which are apt to run in highly imprecise terms as to whether, or how far, the 'mercantilists', as some kind of generality, were 'precursors' or 'forerunners' of Keynes.[16] Keynes himself wished to claim that he had 'predecessors'. We would, however, claim that considerable evidence can be produced for the following propositions of Keynes:

1. 'Mercantilist thought' (or, as we would prefer to say, the leading and more typical writers in the century and a half before *The Wealth of Nations*) 'never supposed that there was a self-adjusting tendency by which the rate of interest would be established at the appropriate level' (1936, 341).
2. 'As a contribution to statecraft which is concerned with the economic system as a whole and with securing the optimum employment of the system's entire resources, the methods of the early pioneers of economic thinking in the sixteenth and seventeenth centuries may

have attained to fragments of practical wisdom which the unrealistic abstractions of Ricardo first forgot and then obliterated' (340).

3 Keynes was justified, in replying to the charge of 'glorifying imbeciles' in maintaining: 'What I want is to do justice to schools of thought which the classicals have treated as imbecile for the last hundred years, and, above all, to show that I am not really being so great an innovator, except as against the classical school, but have important predecessors and am returning to an age-long tradition of common sense' (1973, vol. XIII, 552).

9
Fundamental Ideas and Concepts: the Emergence of Systematic Theories

I

John Law was not the only important writer on political economy of foreign birth who was residing in Paris around 1720. There was, as already mentioned, the Irishman Richard Cantillon; and there was also the German, Ernst Ludwig Carl (1682–1743). Carl and Cantillon have each been credited with the authorship of the first systematic treatise on political economy, and even with having been the founder or '*Begründer*' of the subject. In the case of Cantillon, these high claims have, since Jevons's rediscovery of him over a 100 years ago, been widely accepted. But, though such a claim may seem much less justifiable with regard to Carl, he was undoubtedly a most interesting and original thinker, who developed the vital, fundamental idea of the division of labour and elaborated some of its implications earlier and more fully than anyone else before Adam Smith (and not less fully, in some respects, than the Scottish master himself). Certainly, Carl's work deserves very much more recognition than it has received.[1]

Ernst Ludwig Carl was born at Öhringen in Franconia, the son of an apothecary, and studied (1700–6) theology, philosophy, law and the cameralist subjects at the University of Halle, then one of the most advanced and distinguished universities in Germany. There he seems to have been influenced by the legal philosopher Christian Thomasius (1655–1728), a follower of Grotius and Pufendorf. Carl would probably also at Halle have got to know Becher's work. After leaving the university he entered the service of the Margraves of Bayreuth and Ansbach, and was sent, in 1720, to Paris to study French ideas on political economy and cameralist subjects, and to report on economic and manufacturing policy. He produced a three-volume work, *Traité de la Richesse des Princes et de leurs États*, which appeared anonymously, the first volume in 1722, and the second and third in 1723.[2] This was Carl's only published work. He stayed on in Paris as an official until 1731, subsequently entering the employment of Prince Eugen in Vienna. Much of the rest of his life was spent amid frustrating law suits against his former princely employer, in which he sought to recover money owed to him during his service in Paris.

Carl's *Treatise* was written in the French language because, as he maintained, 'most educated people prefer reading French'. But, in substance and intention, it was written, in the tradition of the German cameralist literature, as reasoned advice for a paternalist, princely ruler, or, in this case, for the education of the young successor to the Margrave of Ansbach. Carl's political presuppositions were also traditionally cameralist, for the most part very similar to those of Becher: that is, in terms of an enlightened, qualified absolutism, of a highly paternalist character. What is of the greatest interest, however, is the manner in which Carl combined his cameralist inheritance and assumptions with the ideas of Boisguilbert, whose influence he acknowledged. If not directly, then through Boisguilbert, the influence of Pierre Nicole would have been felt, as well as that of the politically more congenial ideas of Vauban on taxation. With these influences, there went also some elements of the natural-law tradition from Pufendorf.

The aim of policy, for Carl as for Becher, was to promote the wealth and welfare of the people, and, very importantly, the increase of their numbers. All people desired wealth, and their wealth always outran their desires: 'The Creator has inspired men with a love of abundance, and the wish to push wealth to an excess, with no limit on their desire to enrich themselves' (I, 131).

Wealth depended on land and labour, and was increased through specialization and 'the separation of functions' (or division of labour). Carl recognized the existence of an underlying, beneficent *ordre naturel*. But he took a very pessimistic, Hobbesian view of human nature, and maintained that the free activities of greedy, short-sighted and ignorant individuals obstructed the attainment of the natural order, and so must be overruled and regulated by princely government. Whereas the gradually emerging champions of economic freedom were, to an increasing extent, to see this natural order as attainable through the freedom of individuals in competitive markets, which would guide the selfishness of individuals into publicly beneficent channels, Carl, on the contrary, maintained that the prince must be responsible for directly establishing, and constantly and comprehensively regulating, the natural order. As for the difficulty and complexity of the task of economic management thus posed for the princely government, Carl may today seem rather blandly optimistic. But one mitigating circumstance should be noticed: that is, the comparatively very small scale of the economy, or estate, which, in many cases, would have been assumed by the cameralists, with populations often, probably, numbered in thousands, or tens of thusands, rather than in hundreds of thousands or millions. Within such a comparatively small framework, the paternalist assumption of the princely ruler as the beneficent head of a family and of his estate, might seem rather less far-fetched than it would with regard to a major modern economy, on a vastly larger, mass scale.

The three volumes of Carl's *Treatise* cover (1) the concept of wealth and how to increase the wealth of the people; (2) applications to the three main sectors of the economy: agriculture, manufacturing, and commerce (together with money and credit); and (3) public finance. The author was, to some extent, justified in claiming that what was new about his work was its systematic treatment, or 'method'. But though Carl went some way toward separating off political economy from the other ingredients of cameralism, he remained a cameralist, and did not go nearly as far as his Parisian contemporary, Cantillon, in stripping away ethical and political issues, or in presenting a more positive study of economic processes.

Carl's concept of *richesse* is thoroughly non-materialist, and even subjective, which he defines as 'an easy enjoyment of necessary, convenient, and superfluous goods for the support and pleasures of life' (I, 8). In this three-fold classification of goods, Carl was following Boisguilbert. But he emphasized that it was not simply the physical availability of goods which made someone rich. Freedom, and the ability to use and enjoy goods, as and when needed or wanted, was essential for 'wealth'. As Carl later put it: 'Nothing is wealth unless enjoyed; and only according to the number, power and will of those who enjoy something does it become valued and precious' (II, 460–1).

The accumulation of wealth was possibly only in society:

> It is absolutely impossible for a man to amass riches and enjoy them, without the cooperation of an infinite number of others. It is certain that if this multitude of persons does not combine their will with his, he will not attain his end. One need only consider the number of people needed to produce a shoe, or a pin – the least of our needs; or one need only calculate the number of all those who cooperate to dress fully one man . . . If a single link in this chain breaks, it is useless. The result is the inescapable obligation on whoever wishes to enjoy complete wealth, that the will of this multitude of others is united with his, to the fullest extent. It requires that he contribute to their satisfaction, in proportion to the extent it labours for his.
>
> (I, 17–18)

Thus, cooperation and reciprocity were the essential prerequisites for, and characteristics of, a wealthy economy and society. As it had been for Pierre Nicole, the principle of mutuality was fundamental for Carl:

> This is where the moral law of our Lord is demonstrated in all its force, that we must do unto others what we would have done unto us.
>
> (I, 103)

> Thus has the Creator made man for society.
>
> (I, 107)

Carl went on to emphasize further the subjective element in wealth by insisting on the 'infinity of different opinions with regard to the needs of life' (I, 40), and, as he later emphasized: 'What seems convenient and agreeable to one, is regarded as inconvenient and disagreeable by another, because of the infinite diversity of people's inclinations and sentiments' (I, 111). This diversity of tastes has brought about 'a prodigious quantity of different professions and occupations' (I, 119). For we are quite unable to satisfy our needs and desires in isolation, and thus live in what Carl called 'our natural poverty'. That is: 'We are not poor because of our needs ... but because we cannot satisfy them in isolation' (I, 101). This state of basic economic interdependence implied that it was in our own interest that those with whom we do business, or cooperate, should also be prosperous. For to reduce their wealth would impoverish ourselves (I, 141–3). The wealth of the prince depended on the wealth of his people. He could not remain rich without his people being rich. Loading the people with taxes, when they hadn't the means to pay, impoverished not only the people, but the prince, who, as a paterfamilias, must give back full value in services for the taxes he levied.

Increasing the number and wealth of the population must be the supreme objective of policy. Carl corrected Boisguilbert for not recognizing that the cause of France's economic decline was the loss of population, caused by war, plagues, and by expulsions and emigrations resulting from religious intolerance (I, 177). Falling population brought falling prices and economic depression. Carl laid down the basic principle: 'The wealth of princes and of a state resides only in the number of their people and their increase' (I, 201).

Carl showed a remarkable propensity for blending with his highly paternalist, regulatory cameralist principles, occasional expressions in favour of economic freedom. He went so far as to identify a people's 'easy enjoyment of the necessities and conveniences of life' with the promotion of 'what the English boast of under the name of liberty and private property, and which they regard, more than any other nation, as the principle basis for the happiness of a state' (I, 227).

Carl did not, however, believe that markets tended to provide adequate stability, and he was very concerned that fluctuations in the money supply, and in the supply and prices of essential foodstuffs, made for intolerable insecurity. He claimed that the remedy was 'neither mysterious nor difficult'. By examining costs and the labour involved, the prince could discover the price which balanced supply and demand. He maintained that a prince, 'in fixing the price of grain, in a judicious manner, would prevent both famines and an excessive abundance of such an essential commodity' (I, 252). He called for 'a just price' for basic necessities, maintaining that the prince must prevent monopolies forcing up prices, especially of necessities.

Carl repeatedly emphasized, with Hobbesian pessimism, the blindness and short-sightedness of individuals, consumers and merchants alike, in perceiving their own interests. For Carl, self-interest was certainly not regarded as likely to be 'enlightened': 'Insurmountable difficulties would arise in a state if the prince or the whole society, was not ready to intervene, but left each individual to judge and act according to his conscience with regard to natural law' (I, 416)

It would seem, however, that the intervention by the prince, which Carl called for, would have supported market tendencies, rather than that they would have overruled the market. At one point Carl observed that it might be thought that he was urging contradictory propositions in, on the one hand, seeking to make secure the economic condition of individuals, and, at the same time, urging them to enrich themselves. He explained that what he intended was 'to facilitate their commercial prosperity by promoting a certain equilibrium [*équilibre*] which brings them wealth at a steady and proportionate rate' (II, 52–3). For, as Carl concluded, both for producers and consumers: 'It would be infinitely better, for the one as for the other, that the balance should remain always in equilibrium, and that there should never be extremes of dearness or cheapness in any line of production, whatever the trade or craft' (II, 271). Carl continued: 'I could put forward further examples, proved from daily experience, that commerce can be damaging to all those contributing to the wealth of a state, and can destroy itself, when the government leaves unrestricted liberty to business men to do whatever seems good to them' (II, 304). The prince, therefore, must bring about the 'right proportions' in the economy.

To promote the improvement in knowledge which would help bring about the natural order, Carl was a great enthusiast for education at every level, especially on modernist lines, in the form of commercial and technical education for the young and for all branches of workers in the economy. Textbooks of every kind should be available. Every youth should be prepared for, and guaranteed a trade. As well as the usual public goods and services of roads and schools, public granaries should be maintained to reduce instability in the prices and supplies of essential foods. In fact, Carl called for a kind of welfare state, with social security for all, or 'an eminent degree of certainty and assurance of always enjoying easily, and without fear of interruption by *force majeure*, everything which contributes to the necessities and conveniences of life, in the same proportion, and to the same degree, that is contributed to those of others' (II, 4).

II

Volume II of Carl's *Treatise* is concerned with the three main sectors of production: agriculture, manufacturing, and commerce – the three-fold classification set out by Becher. He laid a primary, though less than physiocratic, emphasis on agriculture as fundamental in providing the basis of the wealth of others by supplying food and raw materials. But, in all three sectors of the economy, specialization and the division of labour (or '*séparation des fonctions*', or '*des professions*') constituted the essential means or process for advancing wealth. Nature herself showed the way by providing different qualities in the soil of different villages. Thus, 'an agricultural worker, having the advantage of a favourable climate and quality of soil, and by applying himself only to the cultivation of the particular product most suitable, produces a greater quantity, more economically' (II, 133). Also in manufacturing: 'A single man, for example, who makes only pins and needles . . . by applying himself to a single good, produces it more easily and more cheaply' (II, 132). Similarly for someone engaged in commerce and exchange: 'His intelligence, working on a sole product, provides him regularly with new means for improving it' (II, 133).

Carl broached the theme, subsequently developed mainly by German economists, of location and the proximity of raw materials. He recommended the concentration of artisans and their crafts, and of manufacturers (shoemakers, smiths, butchers, etc.), in particular streets, or parts of a town, in order to encourage specialization, which was apt to occur more in large towns than in smaller ones: 'the larger number of people increases the number of professions, in dividing each trade into several branches' (II, 242). As for the worker: 'The facility with which he works produces a double advantage to the public and to the worker. The public has more goods at a lower price, and thus grows richer; while the worker works with less effort and earns a higher income when he applies himself to a sole, small object' (II, 243). For example, separating off the trade of nail-making from that of locksmiths and iron-workers ensured that 'one man whose whole workshop is equipped for making nails only, and who applies himself without interruption from morning to evening, will make a much greater quantity at a much cheaper rate' (II, 244).

Carl was aware that the degree of specialization, or '*séparation*', which was possible in large towns, could be useless in less populated areas, where there would not be sufficient demand or consumption to keep so many specialized units in operation. But some degree of specialization and separation would be feasible even in small towns, and should always be carried as far as it profitably could (II, 248–9). Increasing population was desirable because it made possible the increasing specialization and 'separation' of occupations. For 'the separation of trades and professions makes a marvellous contribution' (II, 254), because:

> The more the object of an art is small and limited, the easier and more perfect it becomes, and the greater the production. This is confirmed by an infinity of experiences ... this separation of each trade into several branches makes each one more skilful, and produces a larger number of products, when it is applied to a single object.
>
> (II, 242)

On the other hand, specialization and separation had its limits:

> For what would be the use of perfecting agricultural production for producing a great quantity of goods for feeding people, and of perfecting arts and crafts, so that there is an abundance of manufactures, and of having merchants ready to distribute the goods, if there was not a sufficient number of people with the will and power to consume them? That is why consumption is the soul of human commerce.
>
> (I, 461)

In volume III, Carl went on to emphasize the benefits of international specialization, in terms fundamentally opposed to the mercantilist doctrines of beggar-my-neighbour rivalry, according to which international trade was a zero-sum game:

> We wish to draw for our needs on all nations, on condition that they equally have need of us.
>
> (II, 80)

> The common interest of all states in the world is to trade as far as possible with all peoples.
>
> (III, 254)

> Every interruption of this universal commerce is felt by each state in a considerable reduction in its wealth.
>
> (III, 255)

Comparative advantages must be exploited to the full:

> Each state has its particular gifts, either of situation, or climate, or of the distribution of primary materials when the world was created. The result is that each state can always transfer something to its neighbours . . . It is, therefore, a general maxim, for all states in the world, never to refuse its superfluities, of whatever kind they are, to foreigners.
>
> (III, 256–7)

But Carl was prepared for restrictions on trade in the case, for example, of industries not fully employed.

Carl attached great importance to the development of credit, based on confidence in a person's words, and ultimately on good faith and morals. On the subject of money, he held that intrinsic value was not essential, though he outlined the advantage of the precious metals. Banks could and should promote 'circulation'. Carl strongly emphasized Boisguilbert's (and Becher's) principle of the importance of consumption and the circulation of money, and, in condemning hoarding, he used almost the same words as Boisguilbert to describe how 'an *écu* with a poor man is much more effective than in the hands of a rich man' (I, 448).

In volume III, on public finance, Carl enumerated four principles of taxation fairly similar to the four of Adam Smith: (a) easiness of transmission from people to government; (b) (very similar to the first) that the money passes immediately from those who owe the taxes to those to whom they are due; (c) proportionality – subsequently explained as in accordance with ability to pay; and (d) that taxes do not damage or destroy the wealth of the state by their disproportionality, multiplicity, or uncertainty (III, 98). Carl favoured a single, simple tax on the lines of Vauban's Royal Tithe.

He identified peace and security at home and from outside attack, as public goods of inestimable value for which all citizens should pay (III, 10). But for Carl the economic role of government went far beyond the promotion of these fundamental public goods, and beyond also the provision of roads and health and educational services. He recommended the encouragement of immigration, and the establishment by the state of manufacturing industries. Finally, as we have seen, Carl favoured comprehensive regulation of prices, in particular the prices of basic foods. This widely regulatory and paternalist role for government, recommended according to cameralist principles by Carl, was combined with his insight into the importance of extending the division of labour, and into the comparative advantages of different countries, together with, up to a point, a strongly anti-mercantilist view of foreign trade.

Professor Anton Tautscher, to whom all students of Carl's work, and of the political economy of this period, are immensely indebted, went so far as to describe Carl as the founder (*Begründer*) of political economy, and suggested that Adam Smith must have known Carl's *Treatise*. Certainly Tautscher cited a considerable number of passages from Carl, especially on the subject of 'the separation of functions', or the division of labour, but also on taxation and other subjects, which show many resemblances to passages in *The Wealth of Nations*. Of course, it is quite possible that, though Carl's *Treatise* was not in his library, Smith saw a copy of the anonymous, three-volume work during his sojourn in France, and that he took note of some points and passages, especially on the division of labour. But there is no compelling evidence that this possibility actually occurred, for there were various other sources available in the half-century between the publication of Carl's *Treatise* and that of *The Wealth of Nations*, from which Smith *could* have derived some of his account of 'the separation of functions', as well as the example of pins and needles.[3]

But the great importance and interest of Tautscher's rediscovery, or perhaps rather his discovery of Carl, cannot be denied and should not be diminished. Carl's work has been overlooked for much too long. His *Treatise* is remarkable as one of the earliest comprehensive and systematic expositions of the subject, and, more specifically, for its early and important insights into the nature and implications of the division of labour. As such, it deserves an important place in the history of economic thought.

III

Among all the various and brilliant writers and writings of this formative period, Richard Cantillon (16??–1734?) and his *Essay* must surely be assigned an outstanding position, describable in merit as 'not unadjacent' to that of Adam Smith and *The Wealth of Nations*. For nearly a century after his death, except for a brief phase of a decade or two immediately after its publication in French in 1755, Cantillon's *Essay* was almost entirely lost to view. Then, in 1881, came Jevons's rediscovery, justly compared by Higgs with the unearthing of 'a statue silted by the sands of time' which was at once recognizable as a masterpiece (1931, 365). In the century or more since the pioneer revelations of Jevons, and also since the English edition of Higgs, some important facts have been confirmed. Much is still, and probably always will be, uncertain or unknown. Though established, unquestionably, as one of the greatest masters in the history of the subject, Cantillon remains, and seems likely to remain, a fascinatingly shadowy, elusive figure.

He was born – the date remains in doubt – into a Catholic family which had long been settled in a castle in the west of Ireland.[4] Following the defeat of James II, the Cantillons, or some of them, as Irish Jacobites, moved to Paris, where Richard's uncle was active as a banker in the years following the death of Louis XIV. Then came the Law experiment and, in a few days or so, in 1720, Richard Cantillon, correctly assessing and predicting the outcome, made himself a multi-millionaire. Apparently, at this juncture he is said to have had a confrontation with John Law, when the Scotsman, then a very powerful man in Paris, threatened the Irishman with immediate incarceration in the Bastille. Of these two cosmopolitan adventurers, both, for a time, millionaires, one (Law) was reputed to have died in poverty in exile, and the other was murdered or disappeared almost without trace. Both were monetary theorists of the highest order, though they differed fundamentally on the nature of money and its essential characteristics.

Cantillon apparently soon withdrew prudently from Paris to Amsterdam. A kind of Euro-citizen, with a passion for secrecy and anonymity, he had houses in seven leading cities and was constantly on the move. He also, like Keynes 200 years later, made large sums by speculating on the foreign exchanges, of the theory of which he was a masterly pioneer.[5] (It may be of some reassurance to find, occasionally, a possible connection between brilliant economic theorizing and immense financial success.) It has been widely held that Cantillon died on the night of 13 May 1734, killed by his recently dismissed cook, who burned down the house in Albemarle Street, in London's West End, on top of his victim, without succeeding in concealing the traces of his crime, though probably destroying masses of priceless documents in the blaze.

The facts as to just when Cantillon wrote his *Essay*, and as to the language in which he originally wrote it, still do not seem to be definitely established.[6] As regards the language, the question remains as to whether Mirabeau was correct in asserting that Cantillon himself was responsible for the translation into French, in which it first appeared in complete form in 1755. This was twenty-one years after the author's death, during which period hardly anything about him had appeared in print. In the meantime, however, the *Essay* had been partially 'leaked', or plagiarized, in publications by Malachi Postelthwayt, and probably by other writers in English. These rather baffling obscurities may be mainly explicable in terms of the Cantillon family's passion for anonymity, and/or of the inadequacies in the eighteenth century, by today's standards, of the acknowledgement of intellectual debts. Even the imprint of London as the place of publication of the French edition of 1755 seems almost certainly to be false.[7]

Cantillon's own intellectual debts do not seem very large, measured against the magnitude of his achievement. But what he owed to Petty was vital, and his indebtedness to Locke, and to some of the English quantitative writers, such as King, Davenant and Halley, was far from negligible, in spite of his sometimes derogatory criticisms of his English predecessors. Cantillon also made an interesting acknowledgement of discussions on currency with Sir Isaac Newton, though just when these may have taken place remains, like so much else, obscure.[8] Of French writers, only Vauban, and Jean Boizard, get a mention, though a very important influence from Boisguilbert appears to be traceable, and it seems almost certain that Cantillon must have known the work of the Rouen master.[9] Doubtless also the ideas and policies of John Law were a tremendous stimulus, though predominantly in a negative direction.

If Cantillon's debts were mainly to English writers of the previous century, his subsequent influence, in the middle decades of the eighteenth century, was much more important in France. Influence in France seems largely to have been exercised through the enthusiastic Mirabeau, who had somehow come into the possession of a (or *the*) manuscript of the *Essay*. Most important was Cantillon's influence on Quesnay, in providing him with his basic principle regarding agriculture as well as the idea of a *Tableau*. Quesnay quoted Cantillon, though not quite accurately, in his article on 'Grains' (1758). Later, Condillac also acknowledged a debt to Cantillon. In England Joseph Harris, in his *Essay on Money and Coin* of 1756 seems to have drawn, with no acknowledgement, on Cantillon's work, while, later, Sir James Steuart, on the question of the foreign exchanges, was explicitly indebted. Adam Smith made a single, brief reference to the greatest of his economist predecessors. Important, however, though its influence very briefly was, Cantillon's work can hardly have been widely known, so that Higgs' description of him, as 'the economists' economist', has much justification.

IV

Cantillon's title is worth noting. His *Essay* is about the nature of commerce (or trade) *in general*. The most obvious implication is that his work is concerned not with particular branches of commerce or trade – though it is rich in specific, factual detail – but in *general* characteristics. The title indicates, however, a more significant kind of generality regarding the 'nature' of trade, in that the *Essay* not only abstracts from the countless detailed differences between particular trades, but also from shifting local, temporal, historical and institutional peculiarities, in order to focus more on general, 'natural' uniformities. In fact, Cantillon repeatedly called attention to his abstractions, by noting, for example, that he was putting 'aside these considerations so as not to complicate our subject' (1931, 17),[10] or by explaining that he was abstracting from foreign trade when 'considering only at present a state in relation to itself' (25); or when he left out of account fluctuations in prices due to good or bad harvests, or to other accidents, 'so as not to complicate my subject, considering only a state in its natural and uniform condition' (65). The use may be noticed of the adjective 'natural' to signify some abstract, even ideal condition. Subsequently, Cantillon explained: 'My subject does not allow me to enlarge on the effects of these accidental causes: I confine myself always to the simple views of commerce lest I should complicate my subject, which is too much encumbered by the multiplicity of the facts which relate to it' (265).

Cantillon thus deliberately introduced a degree of abstraction which was to be carried, subsequently, to much greater lengths by his successors, notably by that other highly successful money-market operator, Ricardo, who claimed to be focusing on 'the long run'. Anyhow, Cantillon's justifiable abstractions – unlike those of some other practitioners of this method – were combined with a most impressive grasp of, and avidity for, facts about real-world processes and institutions. His empirical interests and understanding covered not only money and foreign-exchange markets, but much of the social and economic real world, from family budgets and population trends, to the detailed workings of different kinds of markets and institutions, including, in particular, the foreign exchanges and banking. His interest in, and grasp of, empirical data was both historical and statistical. A glimpse of Cantillon as a fact-gatherer, and social and economic field-worker, is provided by Mirabeau:

> The least knowledge to acquire or calculation to verify made him cross the Continent from one end to another. One of his friends told me that he found him at home in Paris in his dressing gown with Livy on his desk. 'I am going', he said, 'to make a little trip. There has always been a blunder as to the value of the coins with which the Romans ransomed their city from the Gauls. One of these coins is in the collection of the Grand Duke and I am going to verify its weight and alloy . . .' In these voyages he made certain of everything, got out of his carriage to question a labourer in the field, judged the quality of the soil, tested it, drew up his notes, and an accountant whom he always took with him put them in order when they stopped for the night.
>
> (382)

As shown above, however, Cantillon was also a pioneer of abstraction in economic theorizing, and he pushed abstraction, or detachment, in another fundamental, and, indeed, essential direction long before most other economists had begun to do so, going much further than his predecessors, and than many successors, including Adam Smith, in seeking to abstract, or detach himself and his theories, from moral, ethical or political judgements. His work may validly be described as an essay on economics, rather than political economy. As Higgs puts it, in a striking phrase, Cantillon, 'brushes Ethics and Politics aside as imperiously as a referee orders the seconds out of the ring before a prize fight. The isolation of the conception of material wealth which is claimed as one of the original merits of Adam Smith, is strikingly true of Cantillon' (388).

For example, the ethics of profit maximization were dismissed by Cantillon as 'outside my subject' (55). Later he raised the utilitarian conundrum, which subsequently fascinated Edgeworth, as to 'whether it is better to have a great multitude of inhabitants, poor and badly provided, than a smaller number, much more at their ease' (85). But he promptly ruled such a question as, again, 'outside of my subject'. Cantillon's programme, however, and to some extent, his practice, of *Wertfreiheit*, did not prevent him from discussing economic policies and their effects, or from indicating what policies, on certain value premises, were required. As Jevons concluded about the 160-page *Essay*: 'It is a systematic and connected treatise, going over in a concise manner nearly the whole field of economics, with the exception of taxation. It is thus, more than any other book I know, the first *treatise* of economics' (342, in Cantillon, ed. Higgs, 1931).

The *Essay* was divided into three parts, of seventeen, ten and eight chapters. The first part began with a definition of wealth and a rapid survey of the social framework of economic activity in villages, towns, cities, and capitals, and continued with a discussion of classes and population. Then came the basic analysis of value. Part II covered prices, money and interest; while part III dealt with international trade, the foreign exchanges, banking and credit. Thus the book laid down an outline of topics recognizable as that followed by countless treatises and textbooks in the nineteenth and twentieth centuries.

The opening statement presented a challenge regarding the source of wealth, though hardly regarding its nature: 'The land is the source or matter from whence all wealth is produced. The labour of man is the form which produces it: and wealth in itself is nothing but the maintenance, conveniences, and superfluities of life' (1931, 3). Thus Cantillon went further than Boisguilbert towards the exclusively agricultural emphasis of Quesnay, while holding the balance less unevenly than the physiocrats regarding the productivity of land and labour. As to the ownership of land, Cantillon remarked that 'most ancient titles are founded on violence and conquest' (31). But he also observed that if a prince were to redistribute land equally, it would 'ultimately be divided among a small number', because of differences in people's industriousness, frugality, inheritances, etc. (5).

In these opening chapters Cantillon put great emphasis on costs of transport in explaining the location and growth of towns and cities. He recognized Mandeville's argument as to how in cities luxury expenditure gives employment – though he was later to warn as to the role of luxury in bringing on economic decline. He also suggested the classification into primary, secondary and tertiary employments.

From land and location Cantillon turned to labour, and to explaining differences in wages between agricultural labourers and craftsmen in terms, in the first instance, of the costs of apprenticeship (19). In an analysis which anticipated much of Adam Smith's, Cantillon explained how different rates of pay for craftsmen of different kinds, in different circumstances, were based on 'natural and obvious reasons': 'The crafts which require the most time in training or most ingenuity and industry must necessarily be best paid' (21). But other important factors are trustworthiness, the risks and dangers involved, and special skills. The next chapter (IX) is entitled 'The number of labourers, handicraftsmen, and others who work in a state is naturally proportioned to the demand for them'. Demand fluctuates and Cantillon clearly envisaged a considerable margin of involuntary unemployment, and the need for a high degree of labour mobility.

Next came the analysis of value and price. Here Petty's starting-point was introduced, but somewhat refined: 'The price and intrinsic value of a thing in general is the measure of the land and labour which enter into its production' (27). Thus Cantillon laid down a cost-of-production theory for goods 'in general'. He then pointed out the widely varying proportions in which land and labour enter into cost of production, contrasting a small part of a watch with a quantity of hay in a field.

In orderly societies, market prices might not fluctuate much, though they often diverged from intrinsic values, or cost of production: 'But it often happens that many things which have actually this intrinsic value are not sold in the market according to that value: that will depend on the humours and fancies of men and on their consumption' (29). Cantillon thus recognized the element of subjective utility in market prices, without giving it the fundamental position it should occupy, while irrelevantly stressing as 'intrinsic' the results of bygone decisions which might well have been erroneously based:

> If a gentleman cuts canals and erects terraces in his garden, their intrinsic value will be proportionable to the land and labour; but the price in reality will not always follow this proportion. If he offers to sell the garden possibly no one will give him half the expense he has incurred. It is also possible that if several persons desire it he may be given double the intrinsic value, that is twice the value of the land and the expense he has incurred.
>
> (29)

In fact, Cantillon reached the strange position that 'there is never a variation in intrinsic values', and that 'in well-organised societies the market prices of articles whose consumption is tolerably constant and uniform do not vary much from the intrinsic value'. This approach to the problems of values and prices, based on this concept of 'intrinsic value', may seem too static, and does not cope with problems of uncertainty as effectively as the analysis in terms of scarcity and use, of the natural-law tradition. Such an approach is also at odds with Cantillon's recognition of the importance of uncertainty and expectations elsewhere in his *Essay*. Anyhow, it seems somewhat unnecessary and misleading to insist on calling cost of production 'intrinsic value'.[11]

Cantillon then passed to a detailed and lengthy analysis of Petty's concept of 'the par or relation between the value of land and labour' (the two components of 'intrinsic' values). He was critical of Petty's calculations as 'fanciful and remote from natural laws'. Certainly Cantillon seems to have based on much research into living standards his own conclusion that 'the daily labour of the meanest slave corresponds in value to double the produce of the land required to maintain him' (35). Subsequently, however, Cantillon introduced many qualifications, observing how wide the variations may be in different times, places, and cases, so that the concept of some general or standard 'par' appears as something of a mirage, of limited operational applicability.

Having laid down the fundamental physiocratic proposition that 'all classes and individuals in a state subsist or are enriched at the expense of the proprietors of land' (43), Cantillon described farmers as entrepreneurs (or 'undertakers'),[12] and launched on a masterly analysis of profit and of the entrepreneurial function, which played a decisive and pivotal allocative role in a market economy. Many people, Cantillon explained, set up in a city as merchants or entrepreneurs 'to buy the country produce from those who bring it', whether or not they then work on this produce further as raw materials for manufacturing. In fact, they buy at a given, certain price, and sell at an uncertain price: 'These entrepreneurs are the wholesalers in wool and corn, bakers, butchers, manufacturers and merchants of all kinds ... These entrepreneurs can never know how great will be the demand in the City ... All this causes so much uncertainty among these entrepreneurs that every day one sees some of them become bankrupt' (51). As regards their profits, Cantillon later noted that 'the subsistence and upkeep of entrepreneurs must always be deducted before arriving at their profit' (207).

The number of entrepreneurs in each trade or occupation is determined by consumption or demand:

> All these entrepreneurs become consumers and customers one in regard to the other, the draper of the wine merchant and *vice versa*. They proportion themselves in a state to the customers or consumption. If there are too many hatters in a city or in a street for the number of people who buy hats there, some who are least patronised must become bankrupt: if they be too few it will be a profitable undertaking which will encourage new hatters to open shops there and so it is that the entrepreneurs of all kinds adjust themselves to risks in a state.
>
> (53)

Cantillon then used the distinction between fixed and unfixed incomes to classify the population of a state:

> It may be laid down that except the prince and the proprietors of land, all the inhabitants of a state are dependent; that they can be divided into two classes, entrepreneurs and hired people; and that all the entrepreneurs are as it were on unfixed wages, and the others on wages fixed so long as they receive them, though their functions and ranks may be very unequal.
>
> (55)

Courtiers and army generals, along with domestic servants are all in the 'fixed income' category, while the rest are entrepreneurs, whether they possess capital, other than their own labour, or not, like beggars and robbers 'living at uncertainty'.

V

Cantillon's analysis of uncertainty and of the functions of entrepreneurs is hardly paralleled in the writings of the English classicals, but, in his main discussion of population, something resembling the Malthusian theory, in its softer and more ambiguous form, was put forward. It was observed that 'men multiply like mice in a barn if they have unlimited means of subsistence', and Cantillon predicted that, in the colonies, population would grow as much in three generations as it would in thirty in England

(83). But standards of living were not rigidly fixed, and might, and did, rise. In fact, after criticizing the estimates of Petty, Davenant and King, Cantillon maintained that the population of England had fallen while consumption had risen: 'We see daily that Englishmen, in general, consume more of the produce of the land than their fathers did, and this is the real reason why there are fewer inhabitants than in the past' (83).

As to the provision of employment for the population, Cantillon seems hardly to have entertained the notion that this could be held at a high or full level if left to 'natural' forces, as could the distribution or proportions of employment between different trades and occupations; that is, he seems to have assumed the existence of considerable involuntary unemployment. He claimed to have estimated, in his statistical supplement, that 25 per cent of the population sufficed to provide themselves and the rest with 'all the necessaries of life according to the European standard'. Thus, with 50 per cent treated as outside the labour force, the remaining 25 per cent 'would have nothing to do' (87). In fact Cantillon, like Petty, was prepared to encourage the provision of employment, even when it might be more or less useless;

> If enough employment cannot be found to occupy the 25 persons in a hundred upon work useful and profitable to the state, I see no objection to encouraging employment which serves only for ornament and amusement ... How little soever the labour of a man supplies ornament or even amusement in a state, it is worthwhile to encourage it unless the man can find a way to employ himself usefully.
>
> (91–3)

Thus, at this point, Cantillon went some way towards conceding Mandeville's case for luxury expenditure.

To close part I, and prepare the way for part II, Cantillon turned to the subject of money and the precious metals. The real or intrinsic value of metals 'is like everything else proportionable to the land and labour that enters into their production' (97). Likewise, the market value of metals may be sometimes above and sometimes below their 'intrinsic value' and 'varies with their plenty or scarcity according to the demand' (97). The familiar qualities which make gold and silver the most suitable for adoption as money are then summarized: 'Gold and silver alone are of small volume, equal goodness, easily transported, divisible without loss, convenient to keep, beautiful and brilliant in the articles made of them, and durable almost to eternity' (111).

Cantillon maintained an explicitly 'realist', or metallist, conception of money, rejecting fundamentally the views of the paper-money advocates, such as Law and Berkeley:

> Money or the common measure of value must correspond, in fact and reality, in terms of land and labour to the articles exchanged for it. Otherwise it would have only an imaginary value. If, for example, a prince or a republic gave currency in the State to something which had not such a real and intrinsic value, not only would the other States refuse to accept it on

> that footing but the inhabitants themselves would reject it when they perceived its lack of real value.
>
> (111–13)

VI

Having opened part II by asserting the 'absolute necessity' of finding a substance which met adequately the requirements for money, Cantillon turned to market prices, claiming that this was the only aspect of value which Locke, 'like all the English writers on the subject', had considered – in ignorance, it appears, of the discussion of labour and value in Locke's *Second Treatise of Civil Government.* Cantillon remarked, regarding the haggling, or *tâtonnements*, of markets, that though 'this method of fixing market prices has no exact or geometrical foundation' – perhaps hankering after some omniscient price-fixer – nevertheless, 'it does not seem that it could be done in any more convenient way' (119). (Here is the crucial difference with Ernst Ludwig Carl, who thought that a well-advised prince certainly could improve on market processes.) Cantillon then described the circulation of payments in an economy, outlining a process very similar in essentials to that later set out in Quesnay's *Tableau*:

> The circulation of this money takes place when the landlords spend in detail in the city the rents which the farmers have paid them in lump sums, and when the entrepreneurs of the cities, butchers, bakers, brewers, etc. collect little by little this same money to buy from the farmers in lump sums, cattle, wheat, barley, etc.
>
> (125–7)[13]

Next comes Cantillon's estimate of the amount of money which will be required in a state to provide for these payments – a transaction rather than a cash-balance approach, as Professor Douglas Vickers has pointed out (1959, 196). Cantillon concluded that 'the proportion of the amount of money needed for circulation in a state is not incomprehensible', but it would depend on the 'mode of living and the rapidity of payments'. He emphasized that it was always necessary, in estimating either the required amount of money or that actually in circulation, 'to take into account the rapidity of circulation' (131). Cantillon then gave his estimate that 'the real cash or money necessary to carry on the circulation and exchange in a state is about equal in value to one third of all the annual rents of the proprietors of the said state' (131). Of course, this can only be a rough estimate, but 'it is enough if it is near the truth' (133).

He then set out some of the factors on which the rapidity of circulation depended, such as the number of independent stages of production between raw materials and finished product. The notes of goldsmiths could also contribute to velocity. On the other hand, there were various motives for holding cash or slowing down circulation:

> All the classes in a state who practise some economy, save and keep out of circulation small amounts of cash till they have enough to invest at interest or profit. Many miserly people bury and hoard cash for considerable periods.
>
> Many landowners, entrepreneurs and others, always keep some cash in their pockets or safes against unforeseen emergencies and not to be run out of money . . .
>
> The capital of minors and of suitors is often deposited in cash and kept out of circulation.
>
> (147)

Indeed, Cantillon admitted that in view of all these factors 'it seems impossible to lay down anything precise or exact as to the proportion of money sufficient for circulation'. With regard to the effects on prices of an increase in the quantity of money, Cantillon concluded:

> . . . by doubling the quantity of money in a state the prices of products and merchandise are not always doubled . . .
>
> The proportion of the dearness which the increased quantity of money brings about in the state will depend on the turn which this money will impart to consumption or circulation. Through whatever hands the money which is introduced may pass it will naturally increase consumption; but this consumption will be more or less great according to circumstances. It will be directed more or less to certain kinds of products or merchandise according to the idea of those who acquire the money. Market prices will rise more for certain things than for others however abundant the money may be . . .
>
> (179)

> I conceive that when a large surplus of money is brought into a state the new money gives a new turn to consumption and even a new speed to circulation. But it is not possible to say exactly to what extent.
>
> (181)

Subsequently Cantillon settled for the general proposition: 'The quantity of money circulating in exchange fixes and determines the price of everything in a state, taking into account the rapidity or sluggishness of circulation' (287).

Cantillon's account of the effects of an increase or decrease in the money supply is an illuminating example of process (or disequilibrium) analysis (part II, 6; see Vickers, 1959, 185ff). The analysis started from the assumption of a new mine being opened. It was observed, on the basis of an expenditure approach, that the process began with the owners of the mines, and all those who worked there increasing their expenditure or lending: 'All this money, whether lent or spent will enter into circulation and will not fail to raise the price of products and merchandise in all the channels of circulation which it enters' (161). Apparently, the rise in prices would occur in spite of the margin of unemployment which Cantillon seems generally to have assumed. He commented, however, on Locke's more static or formal version of the quantity theory, which:

> . . . lays it down as a fundamental maxim that the quantity of produce and merchandise in proportion to the quantity of money serves as the regulator of market price . . . *he has clearly seen that the abundance of money makes*

> *everything dear, but he has not considered how it does so. The great difficulty of this question consists in knowing in what proportion the increase of money raises prices* ... an acceleration or greater rapidity in circulation of money in exchange, is equivalent to an increase of actual money up to a point ... On the other hand money flows in detail through so many channels that it seems impossible not to lose sight of it, seeing that having been amassed to make large sums it is distributed in the little rills of exchange, and then gradually accumulated again to make large payments.
>
> (161–3, italics added)

In fact, new money will affect different prices in different ways, depending on who spends it and what it is spent on, for elasticities of supply differ. With an increase in demand the price of meat will rise more than the price of bread (173). Anyhow, following an increase of 'actual money', there comes, first, a corresponding increase of consumption which gradually brings about rising prices. The effects multiply. For by increasing their consumption the owners of, or workers in, the mines 'will consequently give employment to several mechanics who had not so much to do before and for the same reason will increase their expenses' (163).

The higher level of prices forces reductions in consumption on others, or 'diminishes of necessity the share of the other inhabitants of the state who do not participate at first in the wealth of the mines in question' (163). It will be 'landowners during the term of their leases', and 'fixed wage earners', who suffer. Some workers will be sacked by the landowners and may 'emigrate to seek a living elsewhere'. Those remaining 'will demand an increase of wages to enable them to live as before' – so wage flexibility is uncertain. But the higher prices 'will determine the farmers to employ more land ... in another year' (165).

As the increase in the money supply continued, imports of manufactures would become relatively cheaper, and, Cantillon assumed, would eventually replace domestic production. In fact, Cantillon saw the discovery, or influx, of precious metals as disastrous, bringing both excessive rises in wages, and a flood of cheaper imports, which in turn, ruined manufacturing industries, and encouraged the emigration of workers displaced by the imports. At the same time, the increased imports had to be paid for by sending the new money abroad. Cantillon was very severely, and perhaps rather too comprehensively anti-inflationist. He claimed that 'this is approximately what has happened to Spain since the discovery of the Indies' (167) – a process which had been taking place, of course, for nearly two centuries. So it was a fairly long-term phase which Cantillon was describing, more one in which inflation of the money supply played a role in long-run decline, than the down-swing of a business cycle.

Cantillon then considered an increase in the money supply resulting not from new mines at home but from 'a balance of foreign trade'. This also would result in an increase in consumption and a rise in prices. But in this case, based, presumably, on some technical superiority in production, the favourable balance might be maintained: 'In this situation the state may subsist in abundance of money, consume all its own produce and also much foreign produce, and over and above all this maintain a small balance of trade against the foreigner or at least keep the balance level for many years. (169). In particular, a maritime state, with the advantages of cheap transport (always an important factor for Cantillon), might be able to compensate for higher costs. So it is clear that, though Cantillon clearly perceived how a favourable balance and an influx of precious metals would tend to be reversed, the process might not be, by any means, an entirely smooth, rapid, painless, or complete one, like those sometimes portrayed in classical models.[14] He seemed to envisage an inevitable cycle, with economic success ineluctably and fatally followed by decline. But the decline might be more cyclical than secular, and could be reversed:

> When a state has arrived at the highest point of wealth ... it will inevitably fall into poverty by the ordinary course of things. The too great abundance of money, which so long as it lasts forms the power of states, throws them back imperceptibly but naturally into poverty. Thus it would seem that when a state expands by trade and the abundance of money raises the price of land and labour, the prince or legislator ought to withdraw money from circulation, keep it for emergencies, and try to retard its circulation by every means except compulsion and bad faith, so as to forestall the too great dearness of its articles and prevent the drawbacks of luxury.
>
> But it is not easy to discover the time opportune for this, nor to know when money has become more abundant than it ought to be ...
>
> Such is approximately the circle which may be run by a considerable state which has both capital and industrious inhabitants. An able minister is always able to recommence this round ... as to Italy, Spain, France and England, however low they may be fallen, they are always capable of being raised by good administration to a high degree of power by trade alone. (195)

Cantillon's confidence in 'able ministers' and 'good administration' is significant. For him, however, in complete opposition to Mandeville, Melon, Montesquieu, and many others in the eighteenth century, luxury was the supreme evil,or danger. Finally, the decline and fall of the Roman Empire was cited (an example denied by David Hume): 'Thus the Roman Empire fell into decline through the loss of its money before losing any of its estates. Behold what luxury brought about and what it always will bring about in similar circumstances' (199).

VI

Cantillon treated the rate of interest as determined, like any other price, by 'the altercations of the market' between lenders and borrowers of loanable funds. The main demand for loans came from entrepreneurs. He denied any steady relationship between the quantity of money, or increases and decreases thereof, and the rate of interest and its movements. Changes in information, or the news, were constantly acting on the rate of interest, which 'rises and falls every day upon mere rumours' (215). Heavy expenditure by landlords and the nobility, or by the prince or his government, will raise interest. But attempts to regulate interest by law would certainly prove 'futile', unless it was fixed according to the current market rate.

Cantillon's theory of foreign trade was emphatically 'mercantilist' in its presuppositions, implications and policy objectives. As regards the export of manufactures:

> It will always be found by examining particular cases that the exportation of all manufactured articles is advantageous to the state, because in this case the foreigner always pays and supports workmen useful to the state: that the best returns or payments imported are specie, and in default of specie the produce of foreign land into which there enters the least labour.
>
> (233)

On the other hand, it would not, he maintained, be profitable to export large quantities of raw produce in return for foreign manufactures: 'It would be to weaken and diminish the inhabitants and the strength of the state at both ends ... Enough to say that it should always be endeavoured to import as much silver as possible' (235). If, however, by means of a successful policy of improving the trade balance, this import of the precious metals was continued, it would, as already noted, lead almost inevitably to luxury and decline. Though 'steps might be taken', such gains were likely to be fleeting:

> The wealth acquired by a state through trade, labour and economy, will plunge it gradually into luxury. States who rise by trade do not fail to sink afterwards. There are steps which might be, but are not taken to arrest this decline. But it is always true that when the state is in actual possession of a balance of trade and abundant money, it seems powerful, and it is so in reality so long as this abundance continues.
>
> (235–7)

Finally, Cantillon emphasized the importance of a state's supporting its own shipping services, as a part of the measures 'which must always be taken to maintain the balance against the foreigner' (243).

He approached the problem of the foreign exchanges by examining inter-regional payments and balances thereof, and the cost of remittances from one town to another 'where the same money is used'. Cantillon continued: 'But when exchange is regulated between two cities or places where the money is quite different, where the coins are of different size, fineness, make, and names, the nature of exchange seems at first more difficult to explain, though at bottom this exchange differs from that between Paris and Chalons only in the jargon of bankers' (255). He explained the 'long-run' determinants of exchange rates: 'The exchanges are regulated by the intrinsic value of specie, that is at par, and their variation arises from the costs and risks of transport from one place to another when the balance of trade has to be sent in specie' (257).

Throughout his *Essay* Cantillon noted the role of expectations and uncertainty, as here with regard to exchange rates (see also ch. 5 of his book III). Speculation and credit could cause temporary variations in exchange rates, when it was foreseen that the balance of trade might swing appreciably in one direction or another. However, 'in the long run we must get back to this balance which fixes the constant and uniform rule of exchange. And though the speculation and credits of bankers may sometimes delay the transport of the sums which one city or state owes to another, in the end it is always necessary to pay the debt and send the balance of trade in specie to the place where it is due' (259).

Cantillon next considered the question of the relative prices of gold and silver. After a lengthy historical review he concluded that any kind of 'intrinsic' value or price was irrelevant: 'the market price is alone decisive: the number of those who need one metal in exchange for the other, and of those who are willing to make such an exchange, determines the ratio. It often depends on the humour of men: the bargaining is done roughly and not geometrically' (279).

The *Essay* concluded with the subject of banking. Cantillon explained how banking and bank-notes had evolved out of the operations of goldsmiths, who had to decide on the proportion of cash to loans. The contribution of banks was 'to accelerate the circulation of money and to prevent so much of it from being hoarded as it would naturally be for several intervals' (305). On the other hand, Cantillon recognized 'that there are cases where it is better for the welfare of the state to retard the circulation than to accelerate it' (307). In conclusion, however, he reaffirmed his metallist view that, though

> ... the paper and credit of public and private banks may cause surprising results in everything which does not concern ordinary expenditure for drink and food, clothing and other family requirements, but ... in the regular course of the circulation the help of banks and credit of this kind is much smaller and less solid than is generally supposed. Silver alone is the true sinews of circulation.
>
> (319)

It has been pointed out (see Bordo, 1983) how adherents of most of the main schools of monetary thought and theory have found something to admire in the contributions of Cantillon's *Essay*. He has been hailed as a developer of the quantity theory, though he was certainly a critic of its more simplified forms. Upholders of the gold standard and of 'hard' money have emphasized Cantillon's insistence on 'real' metallic money, as against John Law's paper schemes. On the other hand, Professor Vickers (1959, ch. 10) has stressed a Keynesian element in Cantillon (as in Petty) directed at the objective of raising the level of employment. Professor Hayek (1931) has called attention to Cantillon's anti-aggregative approach, and his recognition of how monetary expansion affected different prices differently in the countless 'little rills of exchange' through which it passed. All these perceptions have some validity. But the widest agreement in assessing Cantillon's great contribution to monetary theory might probably be found with regard to his realistic, dynamic, disequilibrium and process analysis, with its recognition of uncertainty and the role of expectations and its emphasis on the 'general' interdependence of the markets for goods, labour, and bonds, together with the balance of payments.

VII

Finally, we turn to Cantillon's views on policy. Here there is considerable further evidence of his mercantilist outlook, especially with regard to imports and exports – in spite of his exposition of one of the first models of a kind of self-adjusting mechanism in foreign trade. For example, Cantillon suggested – as did George Berkeley in *The Querist* shortly after – that the nobility and landowners should, on infant industry grounds, confine their expenditure to the manufactures of their own country. For, as regards these industries, 'bad as they might be at the outset, they would soon become better, and would keep a great number of their own people to work there instead of giving this advantage to foreigners'(77). Cantillon held that 'gold and silver are the true reserve stock of a state, and the larger or smaller actual quantity of this stock necessarily determines the comparative greatness of kingdoms and states . . . It is needful to discourage all foreign manufactures and to give plenty of employment to all the inhabitants' (91). He concluded, moreover: 'After all it seems to me that the comparative power and wealth of states consist, other things being equal, in the greater or less abundance of money circulating in them *hic et nunc*' (191). Though recognizing the existence of certain self-adjusting processes in foreign trade, Cantillon was not prepared to rely on them, or let them operate uncontrolled. The state must 'have a care to bring about the influx of an annual, a constant and a real balance of trade' (193). Just as Mandeville recommended 'good management', or what could be achieved by 'good politicians' and 'dextrous management' – and Cantillon would probably have known Mandeville's work – so Cantillon himself held that an 'able minister', or a 'good administrator', could help promote a favourable balance of trade, which could be usefully regulated, and for the achievement of which it was 'needful to encourage as much as possible the export of goods and manufactures of the state, in exchange, so far as may be, for gold and silver in kind' (233). But Cantillon was also well aware that if ministers were sometimes 'able', they could also be 'corrupted', in particular when dealing with 'public stock' – as he observed in the very last paragraph of his *Essay* (323).

Adam Smith was to support England's Navigation Acts because defence was more important than opulence. Cantillon supported such legislation because it *promoted* opulence, irrespective of defence considerations. His conclusion was quite uncompromising:

> I will conclude then by observing that the trade most essential to a state for the increase or decrease of its power is foreign trade, that the home trade is not of equally great importance politically, that foreign trade is only half supported when no care is taken to increase and maintain large merchants who are natives of the country, ships, sailors, workmen and manufactures,

> and above all that care must always be taken to maintain the balance against the foreigner.
>
> (243)

It may, however, be noted that, like Thomas Mun, who was writing a century before, Cantillon opposed prohibitions on the export of gold and silver, maintaining that 'the only way to keep them in a state is so to conduct foreign trade that the balance is not adverse to the state' (267).[15]

It is clear, therefore, that this great creative genius in the field of economic theory and quantitative economics remained to a large extent a 'mercantilist' on policy issues. The same might be said of the greatest figures in this period, from Petty and Mandeville to Sir James Steuart. There is, however, nothing paradoxical, which needs explanation, in maintaining that though, to some extent, Cantillon was at once a 'mercantilist', a physiocrat and a classical liberal, he was not fully committed in any of these directions. Nor can he be described as an eclectic, if this implies that he selected *ex post*. For Cantillon was an original, striking out for himself. Like many in our period, he perceived certain self-adjusting forces, or tendencies, to be at work, or potentially at work, in this or that sector of the economy, but was not prepared to rely solely on these processes, or to leave them entirely alone to work themselves out in their own way.

At whatever age Cantillon wrote his *Essay* he may not have had an opportunity to revise it for publication. Moreover, the statistical supplement was lost. His work must undoubtedly be counted among the greatest and most creative of all time in the literature of political economy or economics. How thankful economists and all those interested in economic literature must be that – whatever may have happened to its statistical supplement, and to its author – the *Essay* itself escaped the blaze in Albemarle Street.[16]

VIII

A further fundamental idea which began to emerge early in the eighteenth century was that of applying mathematics to economic theory and analysis. Here, as in other aspects of the subject at this time, Italy was the leading country. Most of the pioneers in the application of mathematics to economics were concerned with using the mathematical methods applied to the explanation of the physical world for investigating economic and social problems. There are some parallels, though not precise, with the work and ideas of Petty and his school, though the Englishmen were more concerned with empirical quantification, while the Italians attempted rather to apply algebraic or geometrical treatment to the formulation of economic theories. Among these was Giovanni Ceva (1648–1734), professor of mathematics and hydraulic engineering at Mantua, and the author of a number of works on mathematics, who, comparatively late in life, published his pamphlet *De re numaria quoad fieri potuit geometrice tractata* (1711).

Ceva attempted to apply to economics the geometric method of precise abstraction and deduction from basic postulates or axioms. He has been described both as 'the first mathematical economist', and as 'a precursor of Econometrics' (see Masè-Dari, 1935).[17] In seeking to reduce to geometrical formulae, or theorems, the elements which regulated money and monetary transactions, he introduced the size of the population as a factor in propounding a kind of quantity equation (1711, 40). Ceva, however, seems to have been far from successful in achieving clarity and consistency. (See the criticisms in Masè-Dari, 1935.) But he may well be recognized as having initiated an approach which sought to apply mathematical analysis to economic theorizing, and which was followed, later in the century in Milan, by Verri and Beccaria.

Easily the most outstanding early application of mathematical methods to economics was that of Daniel Bernoulli (1700–82), who is now recognized as the first to have applied calculus to an economic problem in his work *Specimen theoriae novae de mensura sortis* (1738). He was, of course, a member of the brilliant Swiss family of mathematicians and philosophers, a cosmopolitan, European figure, who was born in Groningen, studied in Italy, and became professor of physics and philosophy in Basel, as well as a member of the academies of Paris, Berlin and St Petersburg, and of the Royal Society of London. His father, Jean Bernoulli (1667–1748) was the author of an important work on calculus, and his uncle, Jacques (1654–1705), wrote a pioneering study of probability (*Ars conjectandi*, published posthumously in 1713).

Daniel Bernoulli's paper of 1738 was, for over a century and a half, with a single distinguished exception, almost completely disregarded by economists, not even being recognized as concerned with an economic problem. Both as regards ancestry and descendants, however, Bernoulli's work has some important affinities with the Italian ideas of our period on utility, value and price. For he was probably indebted to Italian writers, and, moreover, his work was fairly promptly, though very briefly, recognized by one of the greatest Italian economists, Ferdinando Galiani, who had, among his many original ideas, arrived at some of the major propositions regarding utility and value, which Daniel Bernoulli had been the first to formulate explicitly and precisely (see chapter 15).[18]

Bernoulli's work arose out of the discussion of what came to be known as the St Petersburg paradox, that is, the discrepancy between the mathematical value of a chance, or lottery ticket, and the actual value which people are observed often to place on it, or reveal themselves as ready to pay for it.[19] His explanation put important emphasis on how the circumstances of an individual, especially including the quantity which he already possessed of money, or of a particular good, might determine the utility to him of more money, or more of the good. Thus were opened up the idea of the subjectivity of utility, together with the concepts of diminishing utility, and of the marginal utility of an additional unit. As Bernoulli put it:

> Somehow a very poor fellow obtains a lottery ticket that will yield with equal probability either nothing or twenty thousand ducats. Will this man

> evaluate his chance of winning at ten thousand ducats? Would he not be ill-advised to sell this lottery ticket for nine thousand ducats? To me, it seems that the answer is in the negative. On the other hand I am inclined to believe that a rich man would be ill-advised to refuse to buy the lottery ticket for nine thousand ducats. If I am not wrong then it seems clear that all men cannot use the same rule to evaluate the gamble.

At that point Bernoulli proposed a subjective rather than an objective concept of 'value':

> . . . the determination of the value of an item must not be based on its *price*, but rather on the *utility* it yields. The price of the item is dependent only on the thing itself and is equal for everyone; the utility, however, is dependent on the particular circumstances of the person making the estimate. Thus there is no doubt that a gain of one thousand ducats is more significant to a pauper than to a rich man though both gain the same amount.
> (1738 [1954], 24)

Bernoulli then laid down the proposition that, 'in the absence of the unusual, the utility resulting from any small increase in wealth will be inversely proportionate to the quantity of goods previously possessed' (25). After illustrating this proposition geometrically, Bernoulli added that 'everyone who bets any part of his fortune, however small, on a mathematically fair game of chance acts irrationally', and concluded: 'it may be reasonable for some individuals to invest in a doubtful enterprise, and yet be unreasonable for others to do so' (29).

Finally, Bernoulli emphasized the empirical basis of his conclusions: 'since all our propositions harmonize perfectly with experience it would be wrong to neglect them as abstractions resting upon precarious hypotheses' (31).

Galiani's passing reference did not take Daniel Bernoulli's ideas any further. It would, however, be quite unfair to criticise one of the most original and brilliant writers of his century for not having developed further the ideas in Daniel Bernoulli's paper of 1738 (if, in fact, that was the work to which he was referring). But he did keep the torch alight, leaving it to readers of his own masterpiece, and his successors, to take up the torch – which they almost completely failed to do. So Daniel Bernoulli had to wait for another century and a half, until well on in the neoclassical period, before he was recognized for his highly important and original contribution to economic ideas.[20]

We end here our account of this second part of our period, covering, roughly, the first four decades of the eighteenth century. This phase has something of the character of a gestation period in which fundamental concepts and ideas were emerging which led on gradually to the build-up of a systematic body of theory.

On strictly chronological grounds, there are several other important works which should be included here in part II. In particular, the work (already mentioned in chapter 6) of Gershom Carmichael, the founder of the Glasgow school, belongs chronologically in this part, as well as those of one or two French and Italian writers. But the balance of advantage seems, at this point, to lie with a slight abandonment of strictly chronological order, so as to include these writers and their works in the appropriate chapters of part III, which deals with developments, nation by nation, in the last three decades of our period.

PART IV

The Thirty-year Boom: Phase I: The Emergence of a Subject (*c.* 1746–1756)

10
Mid-Century Efflorescence, French Enlightenment and the Thirty-year Boom

I

As was observed earlier, a cursory inspection of the chronology for our period (1662–1776) shows two notable decades, or phases, which stand out as containing particularly rich clusters of important publications on the subject of 'trade' and 'commerce', or 'political economy' as it was eventually to be known. The first of these decades, or phases, was that of the 1690s, when the advance in England, earlier given such a decisive initial impetus by Petty, culminated in a remarkable concentration of important writings. With the turn of the century, the English advance rather suddenly and markedly slowed down, and there followed, for much of the first half of the eighteenth century, a longish phase (covered in the last three chapters) when the leading achievements in the subject came from widely different parts of western Europe. Paris, to a significant extent, replaced London as the place of publication of major works, though the authors, in several notable cases, were not French. But varied or cosmopolitan though the leading writers were in national origin, a certain convergence in approach and objectives is discernible as compared with the economic literature of the seventeenth century, when the divergences in interests, objectives, and criteria, between the philosophers and the policy pamphleteers, were much wider. This convergence was centred upon certain fundamental ideas and theories and was marked by the emergence of a new kind of systematization.

The later 1730s and the early 1740s were rather lean years in terms of important publications in our field. But in the later 1740s a remarkable boom in the subject began rather suddenly to gather momentum, this time on a much wider scale than in the case of its English predecessor of just over half a century earlier. In fact, what may be called a great international efflorescence took place. Among outstanding publications were, first, in 1747, an English translation from the original Latin of the *Introduction to Moral Philosophy* by Francis Hutcheson, the teacher of Adam Smith, and pupil of Gershom Carmichael. In the following year came

Montesquieu's epoch-making *L'Esprit des lois*, a landmark not as a contribution to political economy, but as a new philosophical approach to political and social enquiry. Between 1749 and 1752 there appeared the first economic writings of Josiah Tucker (Dean of Bristol), together with, in successive years, from opposite ends of western Europe, Galiani's *Della moneta* (1751) and Hume's *Political Discourses* (1752), two works which are surely among the peak achievements in political economy of the eighteenth century.[1]

Certainly a great deal was happening in these mid-century years. In the same year as the publication of Hume's *Political Discourses*, Adam Smith succeeded to the chair of Moral Philosophy at Glasgow. This was a decisive step in his career, and therefore in the history of what was soon to become 'political economy'. The year 1754 was marked by the appearance of the first of a number of translations from English into French, instigated by Vincent de Gournay, a series which included works by Child, Tucker and Hume, and which encouraged, and signified, a rapidly growing interest in economic problems in France, the country which, for a decade or so from the later 1750s, was to assume a dominant position in the subject. Finally, 1755 was, internationally, another remarkable year, which saw the appearance of Tucker's weightiest work, the *Elements of Commerce*, along with the *Staatswissenschaft* of Johann von Justi, one of the most accomplished publications of German cameralism. The outstanding event, however, for the history of economic thought, of 1755, was the appearance, in full and in French, of Cantillon's *Essay*, though through mysterious plagiarisms and leakages, this masterpiece had already exercised some influence before its publication. So, with the addition of Benjamin Franklin's important pamphlet on population (*Observations concerning the Increase of Mankind and the Peopling of Countries*, 1751), almost all the leading countries were represented, with varying degrees of distinction, in this near decade of mid-century efflorescence (*c.*1747–55).

There were one or two sharp differences with the boom of the 1690s. First, there was the contrast between the high degree of concentration in a single country, England, in the earlier decade, and, on the other hand, the international breadth of the mid-century boom. Secondly, there was the remarkable transformation as between the number and quality of the English contributions in the 1690s, and those of the mid-century years. In the mid-century phase, if Dean Tucker is counted as, by birth, a Welshman, the leading English-born contributors were two writers, to be discussed in chapter 13, Joseph Massie and Malachi Postelthwayt. Harris and Lloyd were also Welshmen, while Franklin, needless to add, was American. In fact, the outstanding and original contributions at this time, and during much of the eighteenth century, came from Italy, Scotland, and, from the late 1750s onwards, France. Indeed, after almost a decade of important publications from most of the leading countries, the phase of French pre-eminence was now at hand.

At this point, however, it should be emphasized and re-emphasized, that neither the mid-century efflorescence, nor the great phase of French pre-eminence which followed directly after, could have happened without the intellectual platform provided by the work of Petty and of the writers, mostly English, of the latter part of the seventeenth century.

As regards this great mid-century efflorescence, there hardly seem to have been any sufficiently important external events and problems in the preceding decade or so which could have stimulated, or brought to a head, such a remarkable burst of intellectual advance. No external stimuli, in the form of pressing policy problems, such as had existed in England in the 1690s, seem to have been present in any sufficiently significant form; though soon, in France, behind the great phase of French interest and advance in economics, there was, in the state of the country's agriculture, the stimulus of a very profound politico-economic problem. There were questions, of course, regarding the expansion of trade, and of colonial rivalries, as there had been for decades. The pace of economic growth may have been quickening. But such longer-term trends could hardly be said to have reached some markedly stimulating level of intensity at the middle of the century.

The mid-century international efflorescence of economic theorizing must have been created and shaped more by the internal condition of the subject; and it could not have happened, and cannot be understood, apart from the advance initiated by the work of Petty, nearly ninety years earlier. Without the achievements, first of Petty, Locke, and their English contemporaries, and, after these, without the works of Montanari, Nicole, Boisguilbert, Mandeville, Law and Cantillon, the advances achieved by Galiani, Hume, Tucker, Quesnay and Turgot could not have taken place, or brought about the emergence of an independent subject.

By the middle of the century certain fundamental general-theoretical questions regarding values and prices, and money and trade, with their ramifications and interdependencies, had come more clearly and explicitly into focus. A kind of critical intellectual state had been reached regarding a nexus of basic theoretical issues concerned with values and prices, money, the circular flow of payments, and the nature and extent of self-adjusting processes in the economy or in this or that sector or market. Up to a point, there was *some* measure of agreement regarding the answers, though primarily what was important was a clarification of such fundamental questions as the determination of value and price, and of the value of money, or of interest rates, or regarding the main forces making for economic progress. Certainly there existed fundamental disagreements regarding the answers, and these were to become much sharper in the nineteenth century, with some of the main issues persisting, in an acute form, ever since.

In the 1690s in England the primary interest and stimulus had been predominantly practical, and had been concentrated on important, current problems of policy concerned with the rate of interest and the coinage, though a significant measure of general theoretical and conceptual clarification was going forward at the same time. Half-a-century later the emphasis had shifted somewhat. Although practical policy relevance was still of prime importance and seldom, if ever, remote from the writer's interests – as it was often to be in the second half of the twentieth century – the balance had tilted, gradually but significantly, in the direction of a more explicit focus on general-theoretical and conceptual questions. From another angle, this shift of balance might be seen as part of the continuing convergence of the two earlier much more disparate streams of economic thought: that of the analysis of the philosophers, and that of the current policy pamphleteers.

Let it be emphasized that suggestions that external factors, such as the stimulus of current policy problems and debates, were not of prime importance applies only to the international, mid-century flowering (*c.*1747–55), and not to the immediately subsequent phase of French pre-eminence (*c.*1756–70). In France, the long-running problems of agriculture were coming to a head and were bringing about a fundamental crisis of the régime. Unquestionably this mounting politico-economic crisis in France provided the paramount stimulus to the intense, if short-lived, burst of interest on the part of the French intelligentsia in the problems of political economy and in the answers to those problems by François Quesnay and the physiocratic school.

But another kind of external stimulus was at work in both phases, less intensely in the mid-century efflorescence, but very powerfully indeed in France in the 1750s and 1760s: this was the intellectual stimulus imparted by the ideas and philosophy of the French Enlightenment. We shall turn briefly to this subject after first reviewing some features and expressions of the great advance of the subject, and of the interest in it, in France at this time.

II

The two phases, that of the international, mid-century efflorescence (*c.*1747–55) covered in part III, and that of French pre-eminence (*c.*1756–70), covered in part IV, can, and should, be distinguished, though they merged into one another and are not very sharply separable. Of course, during this phase of French pre-eminence, very important writings were appearing elsewhere, notably in Scotland, with the publication of Adam Smith's *Theory of Moral Sentiments* in 1759 and Sir James Steuart's *Principles of Political Economy* in 1767. There were also, in the sixties and early seventies the major contributions of the leaders of the Milanese Enlightenment, Pietro Verri and Cesare Beccaria.

The decade or so of French ascendancy might be said to have begun in 1756 with the publication of the first economic article by Dr Quesnay, who, together with Turgot, was the dominant figure in this great French phase, of which four features may here be noted. These new features all contributed towards creating the beginnings of an international scholarly community. Though none of these four developments was confined exclusively to France, in three of the four, France and Paris were unquestionably in the lead.

First, the international communication of ideas was much enhanced by a marked increase in the number of translations of works on trade and commerce. We have already referred to the important series of translations from English into French inspired by Gournay in the early fifties. Somewhat later, mostly during the sixties, a number of English and French works were translated into Italian. There were also translations into German (e.g. of Hume's *Political Discourses*). In England, though some earlier writings were republished (e.g. by Petty, Child, Law and others) there were few translations into English. Perhaps this was an indication of an intellectual insularity which was to harm the subject in this country, in due course.[2]

Second, the growth of the subject, and of interest in it, was demonstrated by the appearance, in France, of a number of semi-specialist journals. First, there was the *Journal Oeconomique* (1751–72). There were also the *Journal du Commerce* (1759–62), the *Journal de l'Agriculture, du Commerce, et des Finances* (1762–4), and, most importantly, the celebrated organ of physiocracy, the *Éphémérides du Citoyen* (1765–72, very briefly revived in 1774).[3]

Third, there was a significant increase in international visits and contacts between leading writers on 'commerce' and political economy. This increasing flow of international travel culminated in the decade of the 1760s and was concentrated especially, though not exclusively, on Paris. Contacts between economists reached, perhaps, a relatively higher level than they were to attain for 100 years or more, until the neoclassical era before World War I. Following the earlier sojourns in Paris, around 1720, of Cantillon, Law and Carl, this city was again, or still, in the 1760s, the major intellectual centre of attraction. Sir James Steuart, during his wanderings in exile, was in Paris, meeting other economists in 1754. Later there came Galiani (1759–69), Hume (1763–6), Adam Smith (Dec. 1765–Oct. 1766), Beccaria (1766), and Benjamin Franklin (1767 and 1769). The appearance of a number of Scottish – though not English – names in this list is indicative not only of what great travellers the Scots were, but also of the importance, at this time, for the development of political economy, of a kind of Franco-Scottish intellectual axis. Benjamin Franklin was, as an international personification of the Enlightenment, typical of this phase. Though economic problems comprised only one comparatively small section of his multifarious interests, he corresponded with many of the leading writers on political economy and was especially friendly with, among others, David Hume and Dupont de Nemours. He may have met both Hume and Adam Smith in Edinburgh – 'the Athens of the North' – in 1759, and, in 1769, he met some of the leading physiocrats in Paris, and contributed to their journal, the *Éphémérides*. But perhaps the most remarkable international contact between economists was that in Italy between Pietro Verri, the leader of the Milanese Enlightenment, and the Welsh adventurer 'General' Henry Lloyd, author of *An Essay on the Theory of Money* (1771), a work notable for a pioneer attempt at a mathematical formulation of the quantity theory, an approach which was also developed by his friend Verri (see chapter 15).

Fourth – and this development took place mainly, or entirely, outside of France at this time – several of the first academic chairs in economic subjects were founded. Already in 1727 a chair of 'Oeconomie, Policey und Kameralsachen' (Cameralism) had been established at the University of Halle in Prussia; while a similar chair was created soon after at the University of Frankfurt. In Italy, Antonio Genovesi was appointed in Naples in 1754–5, and Beccaria briefly occupied a chair of 'Cameral Sciences' in Milan in 1768–9; while, in 1763, Joseph von Sonnenfels took over a new chair in Vienna.[4]

III

In the 1690s the boom in the subject had had, as its philosophical background, the new ideas about quantification and the empirical methods of the natural sciences developed by the founders of the Royal Society, together with the philosophical empiricism and liberal political thought of John Locke, who also introduced some of the ideas of the natural-law philosophy. There had also been the Cartesian deductivist ideas championed by Dudley North. The international, mid-century expansion of the subject, soon to become the more-or-less distinct field of political economy, was, however, part of the much wider intellectual movement of the Enlightenment by which most writings on political economy, throughout much of the eighteenth century, were influenced. In the phase of French ascendancy in political economy, when this subject briefly dominated the interests of French intellectuals and philosophers, the influence of the ideas of the Enlightenment was especially intense, and there was a great outpouring of philosophical, political and scientific ideas in France. We have already emphasized the great stimulus of Montesquieu's *L'Esprit des lois*. Subsequently, from 1751 onwards, cam the *Encyclopédie*, edited by Diderot and d'Alembert, together with many of the greatest and most influential works of Voltaire, Rousseau and Helvetius.[5]

In spite of profound contrasts and conflicts, this was a time, generally, of intense intellectual optimism regarding the progress and potential of human knowledge, and the tractability of human, or social, problems to its application. As Tocqueville was to remark about the French Enlightenment: 'All thought it was agreed that simple and elementary rules founded in reason and natural law could be substituted for the complicated and traditional customs which ruled the society' (1856 [1955], 205).

Though not universally shared, confidence was high that the methods which had achieved, through Sir Isaac Newton, such a comprehensive understanding of the physical universe, would soon provide a comparable intellectual mastery in the social, political and economic spheres. Deeply conflicting notions were, however, maintained as to the principles and methods on which Newton's supreme achievements had been based.

It was as a small part of this broad intellectual movement, as it reached a peak in France at mid-century, that the crucial advance of political economy towards more-or-less independent subject-hood, took place. The intellectual atmosphere of somewhat pretentious, scientistic optimism in which political economy took these important steps towards its independence – sometimes regarded as consummated in 1776 – long left its traces on the subject.[6] Certainly a healthy, balancing scepticism was forthcoming from, most notably, Ferdinando Galiani and also from David Hume. Indeed, there could hardly have been a more fundamental methodological contrast than that between the *a priorist*, universal, and deductivist abstractions of Quesnay and his school, and the empirical, historical, relativist scepticism of Galiani and Hume. But the philosophical and methodological claims and pretensions of the physiocratic 'economists' long exercised a powerful underlying influence. The report may not be entirely without significance that if only the aged Dr Quesnay had lived a year or so longer, *The Wealth of Nations* would have been dedicated to him.

French pre-eminence did not last quite to the end of our period in 1776. By the early 1770s the physiocratic school was in sharp decline. Certainly as late as February 1776 there appeared in France the work of Condillac, a fundamental opponent of physiocracy, who was well ahead of his time and long unduly neglected. But by June of that year *The Wealth of Nations* had appeared.

We proceed now to a fuller survey, country by country, from the beginnings of the mid-century efflorescence (*c.*1747) to the end of our period in 1776 – a phase in the history of economic thought, which might well be described as 'the thirty-year boom'.

We turn first to Scotland, taking up our account where we left it with Gershom Carmichael when we were discussing the natural-law ideas and the origins of the Glasgow school of moral philosophy. Following Francis Hutcheson's *Introduction to Moral Philosophy* (1747) came Hume's *Political Discourses* (1752).

It was, however, nearly a quarter of a century later that the *magnum opus* of Scottish political economy appeared. By then the thirty-year intellectual boom, including the international mid-century efflorescence and the French Enlightenment, had, as regards political economy, run its course. It was almost as though Adam Smith had waited for the whole intellectual turmoil and hubbub to settle and simmer down before producing his own definitive statement. The thirty-year boom broke abruptly. As a kind of temporary last word, *The Wealth of Nations* was followed by a long and fairly barren lull of nearly a quarter of a century. Intellectually there was a great deal to digest. Then, around the turn of the century, the appearance of important works by Malthus (1798), Lauderdale, James Mill, Thornton and J. B. Say signified the arrival of a new creative phase.

11
Moral Philosophy and Political Economy in Scotland

I

The contribution of the Scottish Enlightenment to – what was to become – political economy may be said to have begun with the lectures of Gershom Carmichael and his edition of Pufendorf's *De officio hominis et civis* (1718, revised 1724). It was Carmichael who introduced into Scotland the work of Samuel Pufendorf and the ideas of the natural-law philosophers. As such, he played a vital role in both the history of Scottish philosophy and the history of economic thought. Sir William Hamilton stated that Carmichael 'may be regarded, on good grounds, as the true founder of the Scottish school of philosophy' (1872, vol. I, 30n., quoted by Taylor, 1955, 253). More recently, among historians of political economy, W. L. Taylor appears to have been the first to have given Carmichael some of the attention he deserves.[1]

Carmichael (1672–1729) studied at Edinburgh and taught philosophy, first, very briefly, at St Andrews, and then, from 1694 to the end of his life, in Glasgow. In 1727, two years before his death, he became the first occupant of the celebrated chair of Moral Philosophy at Glasgow, subsequently adorned by his pupil, Francis Hutcheson, and later by Adam Smith. Carmichael's publications, all in Latin, comprised his *Introductio ad logicam* (1720), and the *Synopsis theologiae naturalis* (1729), but probably his most important achievement was his edition with notes of Pufendorf's *De officio hominis et civis* (1718, revised ed. 1724). Frances Hutcheson referred to this work by Pufendorf, 'which that worthy and ingenious man, the late Professor Gershom Carmichael of Glasgow, by far the best commentator on that book, has so supplied and corrected that the notes are of much more value than the text' (1747, v).

The persistence of Carmichael's influence was emphasized by W. R. Scott who, having noted that Adam Smith was reading Grotius (in Latin, of course) at fifteen, added: 'At that time his teacher, Francis Hutcheson was using as one of his textbooks, the edition of Gershom Carmichael, his predecessor, of Pufendorf's *De officio hominis et civis*' (1937, 112). Scott further observed how Adam Smith himself, in his final course of lectures in Edinburgh (1751) 'returned to Carmichael's treatment of Pufendorf, making his course one of Jurisprudence (as it was continued in the *Glasgow Lectures*) within which there were large ethical and economic parts' (112). Thus, the general framework of Hutcheson's and Smith's conception and treatment of moral philosophy, political economy, and jurisprudence came from Pufendorf, via Carmichael. So also did their first treatments of the fundamental concepts of value and price.

In Pufendorf's manual, *De officio*, the important contribution, as regards basic economic theory, comes in chapter XIV 'De pretio'. To its nine brief pages Carmichael added ten brief notes, of which the longest summarizes his analysis of price and value. Closely following Pufendorf, Carmichael noted that, in the first place, for a good or service to have a price it must possess a certain usefulness, or 'aptitude', either actual *or imagined*: 'Generally, the price of things depends on these two elements: *scarcity* and *the difficulty of acquiring* them. Moreover, scarcity can be derived from two things, the number of those demanding the good or service, and the 'aptitude', or usefulness, *which they think it contains* and which can have use for human life, or confer some pleasure' (1724, 247n., some italics added).

Thus Carmichael, like Pufendorf, explicitly recognized as fundamental the subjective element in price and value, and he was followed on this point by Francis Hutcheson. Neither Pufendorf, Carmichael nor Hutcheson sought to employ the concept of 'real', objective usefulness which was to be introduced in *The Wealth of Nations*.

Carmichael also left unpublished manuscripts in Glasgow, and until these become available the full scope and details of his ideas cannot precisely be assessed. However, the examination of these documents, in the first instance by Professor Hans Medick (1973), has revealed another important feature of Carmichael's contribution, that is, his exposition of the ideas of John Locke, in particular regarding the labour theory of property, from the second of the *Two Treatises of Government* (1690, ch. v). This theory sought to explain and justify the private occupation of land and the original acquisition of property in a previously unoccupied world: every man's labour is his own property, and so are also the things to which he has applied his labour, or worked on, notably the land which a man has occupied and cultivated (see Moore and Silverthorne, 1983, 82). But although Locke combined, in the second of his treatises of government, a labour theory of property with a labour theory of value, neither theory logically entails the other. Obviously one can hold a labour theory of value and reject a labour theory of property (as Marxists presumably do) and vice versa. So it would seem at least premature to suggest that Carmichael upheld a labour theory *of value*, or that the labour element, or emphasis, in Adam Smith's theorizing on value and price should be traced back to Carmichael's exposition of Locke, important though this was. In fact, if Hutcheson faithfully followed his teacher Carmichael, then Carmichael expounded a labour theory of property, based on Locke's theory, but not a labour theory of value.[2]

II

On Carmichael's death in 1729 he was succeeded in the chair of moral philosophy at Glasgow by his pupil Francis Hutcheson (1694–1746), of whom it has been said that, by general agreement, he was 'the personality most responsible for the new spirit of enlightenment in the Scottish universities' (Bryson, 1945, 8). Hutcheson was born in Northern Ireland, of Scottish descent, and had studied the classics, philosophy and theology at Glasgow. He had then opened his own school in Dublin, before returning to Glasgow to succeed his old teacher. 'The never-to-be-forgotten' Hutcheson, as his pupil Adam Smith described him, was evidently a most impressive teacher and lecturer. In the general coverage and conception of his courses he followed the lines laid down by Pufendorf and Carmichael, though introducing his own new directions at some points. Among his earlier writings was a severe criticism of Mandeville. Hutcheson's main doctrines were presented in two works, both published posthumously, more briefly in *A Short Introduction to Moral Philosophy* (1747) (an English translation of an earlier Latin version), and, in comprehensive form, in his three-volume *System of Moral Philosophy* (1755).

Each of these works has a chapter on 'value and price' which follow Pufendorf's corresponding chapters fairly closely, indeed almost word for word at some points. But Hutcheson covered several economic topics, such as taxation and foreign trade, not discussed by the earlier writers of the natural-law school. His re-statement of the analysis of value and price may be taken from his *Short Introduction*:

> The ground of all price must be some *fitness* in the things to yield some use or pleasure in life; *without this they can be of no value*. But this being presupposed, the price of things will be in a composed proportion of the *demand* for them, and the *difficulty* in acquiring them. The demand will be in proportion to the numbers who are wanting them, or their necessity of life. The *difficulty* may be occasioned many ways; if the quantities of them in the world be small; if any accidents make the quantity less than ordinary; if much toil is required in producing them, or much ingenuity, or a more elegant genius in the artists; if the persons employed about them according to the custom of the country are men in high account, and live in a more splendid manner; for the expense of this must be defrayed by the higher profits of their labours and few can be thus maintained.
>
> (1747, 199, italics added)

Perhaps even more clearly than Pufendorf, Hutcheson was presenting a demand-and-supply theory of value and price. Like both Pufendorf and Carmichael, and unlike Adam Smith in a crucial passage in *The Wealth of Nations*, Hutcheson explicitly emphasized not only that without providing some use or pleasure a thing could not have value, but also that value was subjective:

> By the use causing a demand we mean not only a natural subserviency to our support, or to some natural pleasure, but any tendency to give satisfaction, by prevailing custom or fancy, as a matter of ornament or distinction, in the more eminent status; for this will cause a demand as well as the natural use. In like manner, by difficulty of acquiring, we do not only mean great labour or toil, but all other circumstances which prevent a great plenty of the goods or performances demanded. Thus the price is increased by the rarity or scarcity of the materials in nature.
>
> (1755, vol. II, 54–5)

The word 'rarity' is of some significance in view of its subsequent use in French by Auguste and Léon Walras. On value, Hutcheson concluded: 'When there is no demand there is no price were the difficulty never so great; and were there no difficulty or labour requisite to acquire, the most universal demand will not cause a price; as we see in fresh water in these climates' (II, 54; see also Taylor, 1965, 66).

Hutcheson thus followed very closely the natural-law theory of value and price as developed by Pufendorf and Gershom Carmichael, in terms of scarcity, demand and supply, rather than a labour theory. But he supported the Lockean labour theory *of property*, as expounded in Glasgow by Carmichael. Hutcheson insisted on

> . . . the right of property each one has in the fruits of his own labour; that is, we must approve the securing to him, where no public interest requires the contrary, and must condemn as cruel, unsociable, and oppressive, all depriving men of the use and free disposal of what they have thus occupied and cultivated, according to any innocent inclination of their hearts.
>
> (II, 320)

Hutcheson argued strongly that this occupancy-cum-labour principle of property was profoundly beneficial to society. For the great motive force of an economy must be the individual's hopes of future wealth from his labours, for himself or his family:

> Nay the most extensive affections could scarce engage a wise man to industry, if no property ensued upon it. He must see that universal diligence is necessary. Diligence will never be universal, unless men's own necessities, and the love of families and friends, excite them. Such as are capable of labour and yet decline it, should find no support in the labours of others. If the goods procured, or improved, by the industrious lie in common for the use of all, the worst of men have the generous and industrious for their slaves.
>
> (II, 321)

Of course, if some constitution could be devised which could *compel* all men to labour, and then ensure the distribution of the product in accordance with need or merit, then the right of the individual to property in the fruits of his labour would not be necessary. But this was politically Utopian:

> Such constant vigilance ... of magistrates, and such nice discernment of merit, as could ensure both an universal diligence, and a just and humane distribution, is not to be expected. Nay, no confidence of a wise distribution by magistrates can ever make any given quantity of labour be endured with such pleasure and hearty good-will, as when each man is the distributer of what he has acquired among those he loves ... And what plan of polity will ever satisfy men sufficiently as to the just treatment to be given themselves, and all who are peculiarly dear to them, out of the common stock, if all is to depend on the pleasure of magistrates, and no private person allowed any exercise of his own wisdom or discretion in some of the most honourable and delightful offices of life? Must all men in private stations ever be treated as children or fools?
>
> (II, 323)

Hutcheson recognized some limitations to the occupany-and-labour principle of property. Occupancy of land did not bestow property rights if the land was not, or could not be, worked by the occupier. But he rejected fundamentally and explicitly the socialist, Utopian notions of Plato and Sir Thomas More. He described the former's ideas as 'too arrogant', and presented the occupation-and-labour principle of property as a justification for economic individualism and free enterprise.

Hutcheson then passed from the subject of the values and prices of goods and services to that of the means, or medium, of exchange, and the qualities of an effective medium:

> In setting the values of goods for commerce they must be reduced to some common measure on both sides ... The qualities requisite to the most perfect standard are these; it must be something generally desired so that men are willing to take it in exchange. The very making any goods the standard will of itself give them this quality. It must be portable; which will often be the case if it is rare, so that small quantities are of great value. It must be divisible without loss into small parts, so as to be suited to the values of all sorts of goods; and it must be durable, not easily wearing by use, or perishing in its nature.
>
> (11, 55–6; Taylor, 1965, 73–4)

Hutcheson emphasized that nominal changes in coins cannot affect 'real' values: 'If the legal names of our crown pieces were doubled so that the ounce of silver were called 10 shillings, the nominal prices of all goods would rise as much ... 'Tis a fundamental maxim about coin, that "its value in commerce cannot be varied by names"' (II, 59–60).

On a number of other important points Hutcheson anticipated the views of Adam Smith. For example, he emphasized the advantages of large scale and specialization, and of the division of labour:

> Nay 'tis well known that the produce of the labours of any given number, twenty, for instance, in providing the necessaries or conveniences of life, shall be much greater by assigning to one, a certain sort of work of one kind, in which he will soon acquire skill and dexterity, and to another assigning work of a different kind, than if each of the twenty were obliged to employ himself, by turns, in all the different sorts of labour requisite for

> his subsistence, without sufficient dexterity in any . . .
>
> Larger associations may further enlarge our means of enjoyment, and give more extensive and delightful exercise to our powers of every kind. The inventions, experience, and arts of multitudes are communicated; knowledge is increased, and social affections more diffused.
>
> (II, 288–9; Taylor, 1965, 58)

Today, of course, 'small is beautiful' may seem to be a more attractive maxim. Indeed, Adam Smith was to emphasize the stultifying and alienating effects of intense specialization and division of labour associated with large-scale production. But size and scale are relative and must be understood in relation to the conditions of the day.

Also in Hutcheson's remarks on taxation there may appear to be a suggestion of Smith's maxims when he emphasized proportionality: 'Above all a just proportion to the wealth of the people should be observed in whatever is raised from them' (II, 341).

He championed strongly the 'natural' freedom of the individual, as a prerequisite for his happiness,[3] but, regarding the major policy principle of freedom of trade his views were markedly opposed to those of Smith. For Hutcheson was something of a mercantilist in maintaining that a surplus of exports over imports would bring a country an increase in wealth: 'Industry is the natural mine of wealth, the fund of all stores for exportation, by the surplus of which, beyond the value of what a nation imports, it must increase in wealth and power' (II, 318). In fact, in the field of foreign trade, Hutcheson supported an active role for government and most of the usual mercantilist measures:

> Foreign materials should be imported and even premiums given, when necessary, that all our hands may be employed; and that by exporting them again manufactured, we may obtain from abroad the price of our labours . . .
>
> Foreign manufactures and products ready for consumption, should be made dear to the consumer by high duties, if we cannot altogether prohibit the consumption; that they may never be used by the lower and more numerous orders of the people, whose consumption would be far greater than those of the few who are wealthy.
>
> (II, 318–19; and Taylor, 1965, 119–21)

Moreover, industrious foreigners should be welcomed to settle, and the shipping industry should be assisted. Hutcheson also supported the doctrine of low real wages to maintain the supply of labour (in contrast to Adam Smith): 'If a people have not acquired an habit of industry, the cheapness of all necessaries of life rather encourages sloth' (II, 318).

We have noticed above the fundamental point regarding the subjectivity of utility, or use, on which Hutcheson and Smith (at one crucial point in *The Wealth of Nations*) diverged. But there was another argument, fundamental to what subsequently came to be called 'macroeconomics', on which Hutcheson pointed the way, and which Smith, following his teacher, eventually made a cornerstone of the classical model. The original point arose out of Hutcheson's opposition to Mandeville's doctrines on luxury.

Hutcheson's criticism of Mandeville was one of the earliest and perhaps the most important, since it was based not only on forthright moral opposition (as was Berkeley's), but also on fundamentally diverging economic assumptions. In opposition to Hobbes and Mandeville, Hutcheson believed that man was not exclusively selfish and incapable of genuinely altruistic choices. He therefore also believed that expenditure on necessities and serious conveniences, and on helping the poor, not only should, but *would* come before frivolous luxuries, going on to maintain, in a vital leap from normative moral principles to a positive economic assumption that income not spent in one way *would*, if not squandered on luxuries, get spent in another way, either on prudent, useful conveniences, or on necessities for the poor. Until everyone in the world had been supplied with all the necessities of life, demand could be, and, it was assumed, would tend to be, maintained at an adequate level, without luxury expenditure. Hutcheson did not emphasize the beneficial possibilities of investment expenditure, which saving would make room for, but his prudent propositions led on, in the work of his great pupil, to what Schumpeter called 'the Turgot–Smith theory' of saving and investing, to the effect that all savings passed smoothly – and even 'immediately' – into investment.

Hutcheson's criticism of Mandeville came first in his *Remarks upon the Fable of the Bees* (1725–7), before he took up the Glasgow chair. His argument was: 'Unless therefore all mankind are fully provided not only with all necessaries, but all innocent conveniences and pleasures of life, it is still possible, without any vice, by an honest care of families, relations, or some worthy persons in distress, to make the greatest consumption' (1727, 63).

Hutcheson then turned this possibility into an actuality, when he seized upon Mandeville's far-fetched example which purported to show that thieves were good for trade and the economy, because they stimulated the production and employment of locksmiths:

> Who needs be surprised that luxury or pride are made necessary to public good, when even theft and robbery are supposed by the same author to be subservient to it, by employing locksmiths? Were there no occasion for locks, had all children and servants discretion never to go into chambers unseasonably, this would make no diminution of manufactures; the money saved to the housekeeper would afford either better dress, or other conveniences to a family, which would equally support artificers.
>
> (64–5)

Here Hutcheson was adumbrating what Keynes was to call the 'classical' assumption that all income not spent in one way would be spent in another. He made no suggestion that government spending, income redistribution, or even monetary policy, might ever be necessary to maintain expenditure and demand. Hutcheson, therefore, made an important contribution to the process by which Becher's 'Principle', that one man's spending was another man's income, was transformed into Smith's 'Principle' that one man's *saving* was also another man's income.[4] On this point, though he shared his moral condemnation of Mandeville, Hutcheson differed from Berkeley, who supported government expenditure, income redistribution, and monetary and banking reform, to maintain demand. There was also, as we shall discuss below, some divergence, on this fundamental issue, between Hutcheson (and Smith), on the one hand, and David Hume, on the other.

Francis Hutcheson had been described as the 'father' of the Scottish enlightenment, since he was 'a major and often very personal influence on the two most important eighteenth-century Scottish philosophers' (see Campbell, 1982, 167). This is not to be denied regarding some central and fundamental principles of moral philosophy. But regarding economic ideas, there are important divergences between this great triumvirate. David Hume developed vital theories of money, interest and the balance of payments which were new, as far as Scotland was concerned, and not shared by Hutcheson or Smith, and which certainly ran basically counter to Hutcheson's mercantilistic tendencies. Adam Smith started from, and retained *some* of his heritage from Pufendorf, Carmichael and Hutcheson, but later went in for certain new departures, derived more from Petty and Locke.

III

The University of Glasgow was one of the first and most important of the founts and origins of the Scottish Philosophical Enlightenment, and especially of its contribution to political economy. But, in this great, meteoric intellectual movement, outstandingly the most brilliant and original thinker and writer – or 'by far the most illustrious philosopher *and historian* of the present age', as Adam Smith called him (1976, vol. III, 790, italics added) was neither a Glaswegian nor an academic. Though, as a boy, he studied for a time at Edinburgh University, David Hume never obtained a degree. Subsequently, hardly to the credit of those celebrated institutions, he failed to obtain either of the chairs he sought, one at Edinburgh in 1744–5, and one at Glasgow in 1751.[5]

Though Hume proclaimed himself, in his autobiography, as 'of a good family both by father and mother' (see Mossner, 1980, 6), the Humes were not at all wealthy. David Hume, following family tradition, made an early attempt to enter the legal profession, and then tried commerce in Bristol. Both were swiftly abandoned, though subsequently he performed highly successfully on various diplomatic missions, notably in Paris in 1763, when he was fêted by French intellectual society. He later vigorously contested what he described as 'the ancient prejudice' that 'a man of genius is unfit for business'. But, as a young man, Hume saved himself – as his first biographer put it – from 'falling into that gulf in which many of the world's greatest geniuses lie buried – professional eminence' (Burton, 1895, vol. 1, 28).

For Hume started life with a consuming passion for learning and philosophy. With no settled career prospects in front of him, at the age of twenty-three he showed what he was made of:

> I went over to France, with a view to prosecuting my studies in a country retreat: and there I laid that plan of life which I have steadily and successfully pursued. I resolved to make a very rigid frugality supply my deficiency of fortune, to maintain unimpaired my independency and to regard every object as contemptible except the improvement of my talents in literature.

Surely no one among the great thinkers was more thoroughly his own man. He settled near Rheims for about three years and wrote *A Treatise of Human Nature*, which he later described as having been 'planned before I was one and twenty, and composed before twenty five' (Hume, 1932, vol. II, 158). He called this great work a failure which 'fell dead born from the press'. But it was the presentation only, not the substance, that he recast in subsequent writings. In the twentieth century his *Treatise* came to be 'recognized as Hume's supreme philosophical effort' (Mossner, 1980, 117).

He proceeded in the 1740s and 1750s to redevelop and extend his ideas in volumes of essays, inquiries, and discourses. His work on political economy was concentrated in some nine essays which appeared in *Political Discourses* (1752). Together these pieces would add up to a single short volume, but were collected with many others on philosophical, political and literary topics. His aim was to discuss the main, broad policy issues of the day, and to correct what he regarded as prevailing fallacies. He made no attempt at a systematic view of an independent subject. He wrote almost nothing on value and price, for example. Hume's group of essays did, however, make some contribution to the identification of a separate field of study, and, though he does not appear to have used the term 'political economy', there was an element of systematization in the method he applied.

Hume's economic essays fall into two or three groups. First came those 'Of Commerce' and 'Of Refinement in the Arts', which were concerned with the longer-run effects, highly beneficent as Hume saw them, of the commercial and economic progress which he was convinced was going forward. This kind of longer-run historical process was always one of his main interests: What were its social effects? Would it last? Would, or could, poorer countries catch up and surpass the richer or more advanced? These were the historical and developmental questions to which Hume sought answers, and he broached them in the first two of his economic essays.

Then came the four essays best known to economists: 'On Money', 'On Interest', 'On the Balance of Trade', and 'On the Jealousy of Trade' – this last piece added in 1758. There were also two essays on public finance ('Of Taxes' and 'Of Public Credit') *plus*, finally, the longer work, 'Of the Populousness of Ancient Nations', which is of particular interest in relation to classical political economy.

The sub-title of Hume's great *Treatise* had been 'an attempt to introduce the experimental method of reasoning into moral subjects'. In his Introduction, Hume wrote:

> . . . as the science of man is the only solid foundation for the other sciences, so, the only solid foundation we can give to this science itself must be laid on experience and observation . . .
>
> . . . None of them [these sciences] can go beyond experience or establish any principles which are not founded on that authority.
>
> (1739 [1911], vol. I, 5–7)

The interpretation of just 'what Hume really meant' by this 'attempt', has so far taken up many shelves of literature, comment and interpretation. We may, however, begin here with what Hume said in his brief methodological introduction to the first of his economic essays, that 'Of Commerce'. Here he was concerned with the respective roles in the study of mankind, of, on the one hand, general principles, or 'reasonings', and on the other hand, of particular historical considerations, or circumstances. He first asserted that 'it is certain, that general principles, if just and sound, must always prevail in the general course of things, though they may fail in particular cases; and it is the chief business of philosophers to regard the general course of things' (1955, 4). Indeed, in his claims for the method of deduction from general principles, Hume was, at some points, highly enthusiastic about the possibility of reaching 'consequences almost as general and certain as any which the mathematical sciences afford us'. He soon, however, restored the balance by emphasizing on the next page, the variability of human opinions, manners and conduct, which would render attempts to establish generalizations either dangerous or impossible: 'Man is a very variable being, and susceptible of many different opinions, principles, and rules of conduct. What may be true, while he adheres to one way of thinking, will be found false, when he has embraced an opposite set of manners and opinions' (1955, 5).

In his essay 'Of Civil Liberty' Hume began by conceding:

> I am apt, however, to entertain a suspicion, that the world is still too young to fix many general truths in politics, which will remain true to the latest posterity. We have not as yet had experience of three thousand years; so that not only the art of reasoning is still imperfect in this science, as in all others, but we even want sufficient materials upon which we can reason. It is not fully known what degree of refinement, either in virtue or vice, human nature is susceptible of, nor what may be expected of mankind from any great revolution in their education, customs, or principles.
>
> (1752, [1800], vol. 1, 62)

Hume always sought to maintain an intellectual balance, and may be found inclining first one way and then the other, between an optimistic confidence in general principles and in the conclusions they yield, and, on the other hand, a sceptical caution, based on historical relativism and a recognition of human variety and variability. In his essays, he repeatedly demonstrated his concern to balance reliance on general principles with a rich supply of historical evidence, illustrations, and qualifications; so that he might well be regarded as a pioneer of the historical method in political economy.[6] In his essay 'Of the Study of History', Hume emphasized how history was,

> not only a valuable part of knowledge, but opens the door to many other parts, and affords materials to most of the sciences ... we should be for ever children in understanding, were it not for this invention, which extends our experience to all past ages, and to the most distant nations; making them contribute as much to our improvement in wisdom, as if they had actually lain under observation.
>
> (398)

IV

The general principle which Hume sought to establish in his essay 'Of Commerce' was that of the beneficence of economic progress and its complementarity with the increase of happiness and freedom, regarding which he was highly confident (much more so than Adam Smith). Moreover, the interests of government and people (or 'state') were complementary: 'Thus the greatness of the sovereign and the happiness of the state are, in great measure, united with regard to trade and manufacturers' (1955, 12).

Hume optimistically maintained that, in his day, a régime such as that of ancient Sparta, where the standard of living of the people was kept down and all luxury suppressed so as to enhance the military power of the government, 'appears to me almost impossible' (8). He supported the development of manufactures and 'mechanic arts', both for the employment they afforded, and for the stimulus they gave to agricultural production by providing commodities and luxuries to be worked for by the agricultural sector. The development of foreign commerce also encouraged new tastes, new manufactures, and technical progress: 'Thus men become acquainted with the pleasures of luxury and the profits of commerce; and their delicacy and industry, being once awakened, carry them on to farther improvements, in every branch of domestic as well as foreign trade' (14).

Hume wanted growing wealth to be widely distributed, and introduced the argument from diminishing utility:

> Every person, if possible, ought to enjoy the fruits of his labour, in a full possession of all the necessaries, and many of the conveniences of life. No one can doubt but such an equality is most suitable to human nature, *and diminishes much less from the happiness of the rich man than it adds to that of the poor.* It also augments the power of the state, and makes any extraordinary taxes or impositions be paid with more cheerfulness.
>
> (15, italics added)

He recognized the disadvantage of high wages in foreign trade, though he rejected the low-wage doctrine of many 'mercantilists', and maintained that there was a strong complementary relationship between wealth, widely diffused among 'the common people', and political liberty.

The essay 'Of Refinement in the Arts' developed further the arguments of the preceding essay in examining the effects of luxury. Hume was here concerned with the issue raised so provocatively by Mandeville, and so warmly debated, from the other side, by Hutcheson, and Berkeley. Here, as so often, he is to be found taking up a balanced, middle position, protesting against 'those preposterous opinions' entertained on the subject of luxury, at the one extreme by 'men of libertine principles', and, at the other, by 'men of severe morals' (20). Hume rejected both these extremes and maintained that 'ages of refinement are both the happiest and the most virtuous'. Moreover, he believed that activity and employment were beneficial for their own sake.

> In times when industry and the arts flourish, men are kept in perpetual occupation, and enjoy, as their reward, the occupation itself, as well as those pleasures which are the fruit of their labour. The mind acquires new vigour; enlarges its powers and faculties; and by an assiduity in honest industry, both satisfies its natural appetites, and prevents the growth of unnatural ones, which commonly spring up, when nourished by ease or idleness.
>
> (21)

Industry and knowledge developed in a complementary relationship. Hume rejected the example of Ancient Rome, the decline of which had been so often attributed to the growth of luxury. For this fall had been brought about, not by luxury, but by 'an ill-modelled government, and the unlimited extent of conquests'. Luxury stimulated industry.

Finally, and most important, progress in the arts was favourable to liberty and 'has a natural tendency to pressure, if not produce a free government' (28). This was because such progress fostered the emergence of 'that middling rank of men, who are the best and firmest basis of public liberty' (28).

Certainly Hume to *some* extent agreed with Francis Hutcheson that unemployment was not *inevitably* the alternative to luxury. But he was more inclined to share Mandeville's sceptical view of human nature:

> To say, that, without a vicious luxury, the labour would not have been employed at all, is only to say, that there is some other defect in human nature, such as indolence, selfishness, inattention to others, for which luxury, in some measure, provides a remedy; as one poison may be an antidote to another ... By banishing vicious luxury, without curing sloth and an indifference to others, you only diminish industry in the state, and add nothing to men's charity or their generosity.
>
> (30–1)

Hume's conclusion was: 'Luxury, when excessive, is the source of many ills; but is in general preferable to sloth and idleness, which would commonly succeed in its place' (32). Thus, his contribution to the luxury debate provided an excellent example of a Humean balancing act. Having begun by taking up the anti-Mandeville line of argument of Francis

Hutcheson, Hume then went on to accept what amounted to a moderately pro-Mandeville conclusion.

V

Much the best-known to economists of Hume's essays are those 'Of Money', 'Of Interest', and 'Of the Balance of Trade'. In each he was concerned with refuting a major current fallacy: (a) that it was important for a country to possess a large quantity of money; (b) that a large quantity of money made for a low rate of interest; and (c) that a deficit on the balance of trade was most damaging to a country, and must be actively prevented at almost any cost.

Hume was far from being the first critic of so-called 'mercantilist' doctrines on money. But he stated with great clarity and cogency what came to be regarded as the classical refutation of excessive concern with an increasing money supply. Money was 'only the instrument which men have agreed upon to facilitate the exchange of one commodity for another' (33). In fact, a greater quantity of money may be disadvantageous, as contrasted with a greater quantity of the real factors: 'The greater number of people and their greater industry are serviceable in all cases; at home and abroad, in private and in public. But the greater plenty of money, is very limited in its use, and may even sometimes be a loss to a nation in its commerce with foreigners' (34). For there were corrective processes at work which would remedy the situation: 'There seems to be a happy concurrence of causes in human affairs, which checks the growth of trade and riches, and hinders them from being confined entirely to one people; as might naturally at first be dreaded from the advantages of an established commerce' (34). For in the rich, established countries, the greater quantity of money would keep prices and costs high: 'And, in general, we may observe, that the dearness of everything, from plenty of money, is a disadvantage, which attends an established commerce, and sets bounds to it in every country, by enabling the poorer states to undersell the richer in all foreign markets' (35). Hence, Hume's doubts, about the advantages of paper credit and schemes such as John Law's, which would tend to raise prices.

Hume sought to establish two 'observations'. The first was that the absolute quantity of money was of no significance, but that an increasing quantity should be a most important objective of policy. Thus Hume was seeking to show that the frequently posed question as to what was the 'right' quantity of money for a country was, in the long run, meaningless (but only in the very abstract case of the long run):

> It is indeed evident, that money is nothing but the representation of labour and commodities, and serves only as a method of rating or estimating them. Where coin is in greater plenty; as a greater quantity of it is required to represent the same quantity of goods; it can have no effect, either good or bad, taking a nation within itself; any more than it would make an alteration on a merchant's books, if, instead of the Arabian method of notation, which

> requires a few characters, he should make use of the Roman, which requires a great many.
>
> (37)

But Hume then passed at once from this static proposition to emphasize the highly stimulating immediate effects of an increasing quantity of money, clearly assuming the existence of unemployed resources:

> ... it is certain that, since the discovery of the mines in America, industry has increased in all the nations of Europe, except in the possessors of those mines; and this may justly be ascribed, amongst other reasons, to the increase of gold and silver. Accordingly we find, that, in *every* kingdom, into which money begins to flow in greater abundance than formerly, everything takes a new face: labour and industry gain life; the merchant becomes more enterprising, the manufacturer becomes more diligent and skilful, and even the farmer follows his plough with greater alacrity and attention.
>
> (37, italics added)

Hume then traced out the channels and the dynamic process, through which the increase in the money supply took effect. Certainly the initial effects seemed highly beneficent. For prices did not rise immediately. But he warned: 'In my opinion, it is only in this interval or intermediate situation, between the acquisition of money and rise of prices, that the increasing quantity of gold and silver is favourable to industry' (38).

In his conclusion, however, in spite of all his previous proto-classical views Hume came out with a statement of what might be regarded as the essence of the mercantilist position on monetary policy:

> ... it is of no consequence, with regard to the domestic happiness of a state, whether money be in a greater or less quantity. *The good policy of the magistrate consists only in keeping it, if possible, still increasing; because, by that means, he keeps alive a spirit of industry in the nation, and increases the stock of labour, in which consists all real power and riches.*
>
> (39, italics added)

Hume certainly seemed to be describing solid, lasting gains, and not simply some fleeting, temporary advantages. It may be noticed also that he stated that 'the magistrate' should 'keep' ('if possible') the money supply 'still increasing', not merely temporarily raise it in conditions of unemployment. Of course, he was assuming growth potential in the economy, but he said nothing of possible inflationary dangers, or of the limits set by full employment. As many mercantilists would have enthusiastically agreed, Hume then followed up by emphasizing the disadvantages of a *decreasing* money supply, 'A nation, whose money decreases, is actually, at that time, weaker and more miserable than another nation, which possesses no more money but is on the increasing hand' (40).

The transitional maladjustments could be very damaging and quite long-lasting: 'The workman has not the same employment from the manufacturer and merchant; though he pays the same price for everything in the market. The farmer cannot dispose of his corn and cattle; though he must pay the same rent to his landlord. The poverty, and beggary, and sloth, which must ensue, are easily foreseen' (40).

The second 'observation' which Hume sought to establish was a counterpart of the first, in that he denied the significance, or ill effects, of a 'scarcity of money'. For he insisted that a depression should be described as flowing from a 'decrease' of money, and not from a 'scarcity', and that the real cause of the difficulties was 'the manners and customs of the people' – who should (apparently) be expected to adjust more flexibly to vagaries in the money supply.

Hume then put forward a broad, if not very precise, restatement of the quantity theory: 'It seems a maxim almost self-evident, that the prices of every thing depend on the proportion between commodities and money, and that any considerable alteration on either has the same effect, either of heightening or lowering the price. Increase the commodities, they become cheaper; increase the money they rise in their value' (41). He asserted that with economic progress and an unchanging quantity of money prices would fall (43), but did not envisage possible maladjustments. He concluded, once again, that 'the want of money can never injure any state within itself', but that a 'general increase' in the money supply was important. There was not necessarily a definite contradiction here, but there does appear to be some contrast, which could usefully have been clarified by some explanation and reconciliation.[7]

The fallacy which Hume was concerned to refute in his essay 'Of Interest' was that interest could be lowered by expanding the money supply; that is, he was rejecting what Heckscher described as the mercantilist idea of money as a kind of factor of production (1955, vol. II, 200). Hume sought to relate interest to the rate of profit, and to the 'real' return on investment, or the productivity of capital – as Joseph Massie had recently done in his *Natural Rate of Interest* of 1750 (see chapter 13, V). It was emphasized by Hume that it was not a scarcity of money, but 'real' factors, three in particular, which made for a high rate of interest: 'a great demand for borrowing; little riches to supply that demand; and great profits arising from commerce' (49). He thus put forward a supply and demand theory. He added that interest fell with economic progress, which he saw as encouraging frugality, while the competition of capitals (as Smith was to argue) depressed the rate of profit in the longer term.

In the essay 'Of the Balance of Trade'. Hume was concerned to deny 'this apprehension of the wrong balance of trade'. Here he introduced his well-known assumption of four-fifths of all the money in Great Britain being annihilated in one night (or, alternatively, of all the money being multiplied five-fold in one night). No difficulties of adjustment were discussed. In fact, it was suggested that the transition, and any problems it might bring, would be of the briefest. If four-fifths of the money was lost, 'must not the price of all labour and commodities sink in proportion?' (1955, 63). No nation could then compete with Britain in foreign markets: '*In how little time*, therefore, must this bring back the money which we had lost, and raise us to the level of all neighbouring nations? (63, italics added)

Hume certainly seems to have been referring here not to a longer-term, secular process of the rise or decline of rich and poor countries, but to a comparatively much shorter process of adjustment between countries, usually, of a similar level of wealth and development. He then proceeded to introduce the subsequently familiar comparison with how the force of gravity equalized out water levels: 'Now it is evident that the same causes, which would correct these exorbitant inequalities, were they to happen miraculously, must prevent their happening in the common course of nature, and must for ever, in all neighbouring nations preserve money nearly proportionable to the art and industry in each nation. All water, wherever it communicates, remains always at a level' (63).

Hume compared international imbalances in trade with inter-regional imbalances, as, for example, between London and Yorkshire, which gave rise to no 'gloomy reflections'. He reasserted his old suspicions about paper money, and suggested – in direct opposition to Benjamin Franklin – that paper money was quite unnecessary in the colonies, and that, if the paper were abolished, sufficient gold and silver would return – as had been available before the introduction of paper.

He reasserted, rather than denied, however, the common mercantilist doctrine of the destructiveness of hoarding, especially (as Petty had observed) by the government, and the beneficence and importance of 'circulation'. Hoarding, which Hume presumably regarded as attaining significant dimensions, was 'a practice which we should all exclaim against as destructive, namely, the gathering of large sums into a public treasure, locking them up, and absolutely preventing their circulation' (72). But he then soon proceeded to balance this proposition by asserting, on the next page, that, in the case of the massive hoarding by Henry VII, it was not 'probable that the diminution of circulating money was ever sensibly felt by the people, or ever did them any prejudice. The sinking of the prices of all commodities would *immediately* replace it, by giving England the advantage in its commerce with the neighbouring kingdoms' (73, italics added). Hume went on to make a considerable concession to 'mercantilist' doctrines regarding import duties. He did not support the wholesale removal of tariffs: 'All taxes, however, upon foreign commodities are not to be regarded as prejudicial or useless ... A tax on German linen encourages home manufactures, and thereby multiplies our people and industry. A tax on brandy increases the sale of rum, and supports our southern colonies' (76).

Hume's conclusion, however, *seemed* to be emphatic and unqualified: 'In short, a government has great reason to preserve with care its people and its manufactures. Its money it may safely trust to the course of human affairs, without fear or jealousy'. This statement, if left unqualified, might have appeared to justify an attitude of 'money doesn't matter', or of monetarist *laissez-faire*, implying that the economy should be expected to adjust rapidly to *any* vagaries of the money supply. Such suggestions were to appear, at some points, in *The Wealth of Nations*. However, Hume added a further final sentence as to the duty of government: 'if it ever give attention to this latter circumstance [sc. the money supply], it ought only to be so far as it affects the former [i.e. people and manufactures]' (77). But if the money supply, or alterations thereof, might often and seriously affect 'people and manufactures' – and therefore require governmental attention – how much was left of the pronouncement that government might safely trust its money 'to the course of human affairs'?

VI

The essay 'Of the Jealousy of Trade', added in 1758, expressed more thorough-going free-trade views, based on an international harmony of interests. Hume was here concerned to demolish the mercantilist conception of international trade as a zero-sum, your-win-my-loss game, and had been anticipated, in these views, by Carl, Gervaise and Vanderlint:

> I will venture to assert, that the increase of riches and commerce in any one nation, instead of hurting, commonly promotes the riches and commerce of all its neighbours; and that a state can scarcely carry its trade and industry very far, where all the surrounding states are buried in ignorance, sloth, and barbarism . . . I go farther, and observe, that where an open communication is preserved among nations, it is impossible but the domestic industry of every one must receive an increase from the improvements of the others. (78)

These were sweeping statements. Hume continued by maintaining that foreign trade, as in the case of Britain, gave an impetus to technical advance. Moreover: 'Nature, by giving a diversity of geniuses, climates, and soils, to different nations, has secured their mutual intercourse and commerce, as long as they all remain industrious and civilized' (79). The increase of industry among a country's neighbours, increased the consumption of that country's goods. With diversification and adaptability no country need fear the consequences of losing a market for one or other of its products. These optimistic views culminated in Hume's famous proclamation: 'not only as a man, but as a British subject. I pray for the flourishing commerce of Germany, Spain, Italy, and even France itself' (82).

When discussing adjustments in international trade, Hume seems sometimes to have been referring to relations between rich and poor countries in terms of longer-run development and progress, and sometimes to relations between countries, at a similar level of wealth, in terms of shorter-run processes. In fact, in Hume's writings, and in interpretations of them, the distinctions were not always clear as between shorter-term disequilibria, and the much longer-run secular, historical processes of the economic rise, or relative decline, of nations, such as Spain in the seventeenth (and Britain in the twentieth) century. As with George Berkeley, Richard Cantillon, and other writers of this period, the familiar modern distinction was seldom to be found between longer-term processes of growth (or decline), and shorter-run, or cyclical, increases or decreases in employment and production. Hume seems to have seen the process of adjustment to balance-of-payments disturbances as taking place in 'little time', and he actually used the word 'immediately'. But the decline of 'old' industries, and of whole economies, surely had to be envisaged as much longer-run processes. However, as in Cantillon's account of balance-of-trade adjustments, these distinctions were not always clearly observed in the writings of Hume.

These distinctions, or, at some points, the disregard of them, are significant in interpreting the exchanges between Hume and Josiah Tucker, or what has come to be called 'the rich country–poor country' debate.[8] As we have seen, Hume had expressed considerable optimism regarding economic progress, which, however, he soon qualified, or, as so often, balanced. For he had also suggested that all human things have the seeds of decay. On the other hand, the more unreservedly optimistic Dean Tucker contended that economic progress generally, for an advanced country, had no limits, or no *ne plus ultra*. The debate between the two (for some reason transacted through Lord Kames)[9] was begun by Hume's letter of 4 March 1758, with some warm compliments on Tucker's 'profound knowledge of the theory of commerce, joined to an enlarged acquaintance with its practice'. In fact, each of the participants had been fully prepared in advance to accept most of the other's arguments. As Hume stated: 'All the advantages which the author insists upon as belonging to a nation of extensive commerce are undoubtedly real: great capital, extensive correspondence, skilful expedients of facilitating labour, dexterity, industry, etc., these circumstances give them an undisputed superiority over poor nations, who are ignorant and inexperienced' (200). He proceeded to formulate the issue as follows:

> The question is, whether these advantages can go on, increasing trade *in infinitum*, or whether they do not at least come to a *ne plus ultra*, and check themselves, by begetting disadvantages, which at first retard, and at last finally stop their progress. Among these disadvantages, we may reckon the dear price of provisions and labour, which enables the poorer country to rival them, first in the coarser manufactures, and then in those which are more elaborate. Were it otherwise, commerce, if not dissipated by violent conquests, would go on perpetually increasing, and one spot of the globe would engross the art of industry of the whole.
>
> (200)

Hume would probably have accepted Tucker's point, but he countered the Dean's optimism, which was supported by 'the goodness of Providence', as follows: 'It was never surely the intention of Providence that any one nation should be a monopolizer of wealth: and the growth of all bodies, artificial as well as natural, is stopped by internal causes, derived from their enormous size and greatness. Great empires, great cities, great commerce, all of them receive a check, not from accidental events, but necessary principles' (201).

Tucker, of course, protested that he did not envisage any inevitable tendency to a national monopoly, and claimed subsequently to have influenced Hume towards his own line of thinking. But though Hume's later essay 'Of the Jealousy of Trade', showed, as we have noted, some move towards rather more unqualified free-trade sentiments, as compared with his previous essays, this may not have been due to his debate with Tucker. Anyhow, Hume concluded his letter by proclaiming his intention to launch a further attack on 'the narrow malignity and envy of nations' and he emphasized his pleasure in having the Dean as an ally (202).

VII

Two of Hume's economic essays are concerned with public finance, those 'Of Taxes' and 'Of Public Credit'.

On taxes, Hume began with an attack on the 'prevailing maxim' that each increase in taxation 'increases proportionably the industry of the people' (83). He recognized the great dangers of this notion, but maintained that it had a considerable element of truth, and he proceeded to bring to bear much historical evidence and analysis. But then – not untypically – he went on promptly to reassert the proposition in more qualified and precise terms. It depended on historical circumstances:

> When a tax is laid upon commodities, which are consumed by the common people, the necessary consequence may seem to be, either that the poor must retrench something from their way of living, or raise their wages, so as to make the burden of the tax fall entirely upon the rich. But there is a third consequence, which often follows upon taxes, namely that the poor increase their industry, perform more work, without demanding more for their labour. Where taxes are moderate, are laid on gradually, and affect not the necessaries of life, this consequence naturally follows; and it is certain, that such difficulties often serve to excite the industry of a people, and render them more opulent and laborious, than others, who enjoy the greatest advantages.
>
> (83)

It may be noted that Hume was referring to what 'often' happens, not to what always, or even generally happens. But what is most obvious is that, with regard to the vital subject of wages, Hume certainly entertained no such general theory as that of the 'natural' wage, as defined in the more hard-line versions of the Malthusian doctrine. In fact, Hume could almost be said to out-Giffen Giffen: in times of scarcity and high prices, not only did the poor apparently consume more of the basic foodstuffs, but they lived better into the bargain: ''Tis *always* observed in years of scarcity, if it be not extreme, that the poor labour more, and really live better, than in years of great plenty, when they indulge themselves in idleness and riot' (83n.).

In conclusion, Hume denied the physiocratic doctrine that all taxes fall ultimately on land, and maintained that the best taxes are those on luxury consumption goods.

In his discussion of public credit, Hume was concerned to emphasize the great disadvantages and dangers of large and mounting public debts. He refuted the idea that because they only involved a transfer, from a right pocket to a left pocket, public debts were no burden. Listing the kinds of damage and burdens such debts could bring, Hume mentioned first how London had 'already arrived at such an enormus size, and seems still increasing' (95). He emphasized that, as a form of paper credit, public debts had 'all the disadvantages attending that species of money'. Furthermore, the taxes necessary to service the debt would oppress the poor, or raise the price of labour. It could also be damaging if the debt passed, as it often did, into foreign hands, or into the hands of the idle. He warned that Great Britain was already some way down this perilous road. But, Hume explained, 'so great dupes are the generality of mankind', that the same disastrous course was followed over and over again: 'Mankind are, in all ages, caught by the same baits. The same tricks, played over and over again, still trepan them. The heights of popularity and patriotism are still the beaten road to power and tyranny' (104).[10]

In his main philosophical works, other important insights of Hume are to be found concerning the principles of economic policy. In discussing the origin of civil government he gave an excellent explanation of the role of government in providing public goods:

> Two neighbours may agree to drain a meadow, which they possess in common: because it is easy for them to know each other's mind; and each must perceive that the immediate consequence of his failing in this part, is the abandoning the whole project. But it is very difficult, and indeed impossible, that a thousand persons should agree in any such action; it being difficult for them to concert so complicated a design, and sill more difficult for them to execute it, while each seeks a pretext to free himself of the trouble and expense, and would lay the whole burden on others. Political society easily remedies both these inconveniences . . . Thus, bridges are built, harbours opened, ramparts raised, canals formed, fleets equipped, and armies disciplined, everywhere, by the care of government; . . . though composed of men subject to all human infirmities.
>
> (1739 [1911], vol. II, 239)

Significant, also, for the political principles underlying Hume's attitude to economic policy, was his theory of property. He had little place for labour in explaining property, which he regarded as derived, fundamentally, from the prevalence of scarcity (see section III, 'Of Justice', in his *Inquiry Concerning the Principles of Morals*).[11] He began with the proposition 'that public utility is the *sole* origin of justice' (1751 [1800], vol. II, 231), and went on to explain how, with scarcity lifted, in a Utopian condition of 'profuse abundance of all external conveniences', there would be no need for private property, or for government protection for it. Again, in another kind of Utopia, where everyone was so perfectly generous and altruistic, 'the whole human race would form only one family where all would lie in common, and be used freely, without regard to property' (233).

On the other hand, at the opposite extreme, in situations such as those of a shipwreck, or a besieged city, 'the strict laws of justice', and of property rights, might be suspended (234).

The usual condition of mankind, however, was very different:

> The common situation of society is a medium amidst all these extremes. We are naturally partial to ourselves, and to our friends; but are capable of learning the advantage resulting from a more equitable conduct. Few enjoyments are given us from the open and liberal hand of nature; but by art, labour, and industry, we can extract them in great abundance. Hence the ideas of property become necessary in all civil society: hence justice derives its usefulness to the public: and hence alone arises its merit and moral obligation.
>
> (236–7)

The question arose of the distribution of property. 'In a perfect theocracy, where a being, infinitely intelligent, governs by particular volitions', the principle of distribution would be, 'to assign the largest possession to the most extensive virtue, and give everyone the power of doing good, proportioned to his inclination' (241). But Hume dismissed such Utopian speculations with scathing indignation, insisting, 'that a rule which, in speculation, may seem the most advantageous to society, may yet be found, in practice, totally pernicious and destructive' (241). Though he supported the reduction of some inequalities, he went on to a comprehensive attack on egalitarianism:

> . . . however specious these ideas of *perfect* equality may seem, they are really, at bottom, *impracticable*; and were they not so, would be extremely pernicious to human society. Render possessions ever so equal, men's different degrees of art, care, and industry will immediately break that equality. Or if you check these virtues, you reduce society to the most extreme indigence; and, instead of preventing want and beggary in a few, render it unavoidable to the whole community. The most rigorous inquisition too is requisite to watch every inequality on its first appearance; and the most severe jurisdiction, to punish and redress it. But besides, that so much authority must soon degenerate into tyranny, and be exerted with great partialities . . .
>
> Who sees not, for instance, that whatever is produced or improved by a man's art or industry ought, for ever, to be secured to him, in order to give encouragement to such useful habits and accomplishments?
>
> (243)

Mention should also be made of the essay 'Of the Populousness of Ancient Nations', an historical study very learned with regard to the ancient world, but rather more concerned with politics than economics. Hume opposed the thesis, put forward by Montesquieu (in his *Esprit des lois*, book XXIII) that population had declined from the level attained by 'the ancient nations'. This question was, at the time, strange as it may seem today, one of considerable ideological importance. It bore on the question of the advance and progress represented by the contemporary, mid-eighteenth-century world, and Hume described it as 'the most curious and important of all questions of erudition' (see Mossner, 1980, 264).[12]

He suggested that the advances of the modern over the ancient world must have encouraged population increase:

> All our later improvements and refinements, have they done nothing towards the easy subsistence of men, and consequently towards their propagation and increase? Our superior skill in mechanics; the discovery of new worlds, by which commerce has been so much enlarged; the establishment of posts; and the use of bills of exchange: these seem all extremely useful to the encouragement of art, industry, and populousness. Were we to strike off these, what a check should we give to every kind of business and labour, and what multitudes of families would immediately perish from want and hunger?
>
> (1955, xc and 146)

North-western Europe was, perhaps naturally enough, the centre of the world for Hume:

> Choose Dover or Calais for a center: draw a circle of two hundred miles radius: you comprehend London, Paris, the Netherlands, the United Provinces, and some of the best cultivated parts of France and England. It may safely, I think, be affirmed, that no spot of ground can be found, in antiquity, of equal extent, which contained nearly so many great and populous cities, and was so stocked with riches and inhabitants.
>
> (170)

On the other hand, he threw out a number of somewhat Malthusian observations:

> How fast do mankind multiply in every colony or new settlement; where it is an easy matter to provide for a family; and where men are nowise straitened or confined, as in long established governments?
>
> (111)

> The prolific virtue of men, were it to act in its full extent, without that restraint which poverty and necessity imposes on it, would double the number every generation.
>
> (128)

But Hume, as we have seen from his treatment of wages, was some way from believing either in what became the classical population doctrine, or in hard-line Malthusianism, as a general theory.

VIII

We have several times noted the element of balance in Hume's views and theories. His intellectual optimism about the study of what he called 'moral subjects' was balanced by an underlying element of scepticism and agnosticism. His search for general principles was balanced by an emphasis on human variety and the diversity of particular historical cases and conditions. In fact, Hume's methodological balance was struck at a point distinctly more inclined towards the historical view than it was by his successors, even more so than by Adam Smith – who, for his part was *far* more concerned with the historical dimension than were most of his fellow classicals. Again, in his discussion of luxury, Hume's criticism of Mandeville was balanced by qualifications which conceded a large part of the Mandevillian argument. In fact, in much of his economic writing Hume was concerned to restate recent and contemporary ideas with suitable qualifications and improved elegance and precision.

Sometimes Hume has been listed with the English classical economists, and certainly the inclusion of such a brilliant and outstanding philosopher would enhance the prestige of the classical school. Doubtless he was an early exponent of classical ideas on several important topics, though his were hardly the first statements of the new theories. As regards money and international trade, he was anticipated by Gervaise, Vanderlint and Cantillon, and to some extent by Carl. Nor was he by any means the first to attack 'mercantilist' doctrines on money. Moreover, Hume rejected other classical doctrines, as we have seen with regard to population and wages, and also regarding the unconditional beneficence of frugality. Nevertheless, the force and cogency of his arguments and his great philosophical reputation gave an important impetus to some of the doctrines subsequently incorporated into the classical system.

On the other hand, to describe Hume as 'transitional' might be taken as implying a failure on his part to push his ideas to their logical or valid conclusions. But Hume, quite deliberately, did not go the whole way, and usually insisted, in the last analysis, on a qualified balance. He was too deeply committed to historical relativism and empiricism to accept a single model, without very serious qualifications.[13] Having described Locke as having one foot in the classical world, Keynes described Hume as having 'a foot and a half in the classical world. For Hume began the practice among economists of stressing the importance of the equilibrium position as compared with the ever-shifting transition toward it, though he was still enough of a mercantilist not to overlook the fact that it is in the transition that we actually have our being' (1936, 343n.). Apart from the inadequacy and ambiguity of the 'mercantilist' category – and of the 'classical' concept too – this description of Hume as three-quarters 'classical' goes too far.[14] For Hume brought to bear on controversial issues a philosophical balance and perspective. He was the archetypal two-handed economist, and none the worse for that. For surely it is perfectly valid and intellectually respectable for a philosopher to have two hands, insofar as 'two-handedness' is the attribute of one who is appropriately cautious in his generalizations because of the breadth of his views and his awareness of historical and institutional variety and variability. It is not for philosophers to make up politicians' minds for them: they have other, in the long run, more valuable, intellectual objectives to pursue.

IX

The contribution of the Scottish Enlightenment to the development of political economy was obviously one of its most important aspects and achievements. If, in our period, this contribution is taken as lasting from Carmichael's edition of Pufendorf (1718) down to *The Wealth of Nations*, it covered fifty-eight years. David Hume's *Essays* came just past half-way, fifteen years before Sir James Steuart's *Principles*, and just on a quarter of a century before the culminating achievement of Adam Smith. In 1737, at about the time that Hume was completing his masterpiece, *A Treatise of Human Nature*, the fourteen-year-old Smith was entering the Moral Philosophy class of Francis Hutcheson, who was then in the middle of his Glasgow career. According to W. R. Scott, fourteen was, at that period, late, not early, for a boy to enter Glasgow University, eleven or twelve being the usual age (1937, 28). One can only speculate as to how far Smith's late entry was connected with his being an only son, in delicate health, whose father had died before he was born. Nevertheless, he was already well advanced in Latin, which must have helped considerably his progress at the university, where he obtained as sound an educational foundation for what was to be his lifework as could have been obtained anywhere else in the world at that time, as he himself was later to maintain (in his letter to William Cullen on 20 September 1774):

> In the present state of the Scotch universities, I do most sincerely look upon them as, in spite of all their faults, without exception the best seminaries of learning that are to be found anywhere in Europe. They are, perhaps, upon the whole, as unexceptionable as any public institutions of that kind, which all contain in their very nature the seeds and causes of negligence and corruption, have ever been, or are ever likely to be.
>
> (Thomson, 1859, vol. I, 473)

Grotius, together with Carmichael's edition of Pufendorf, supplemented by ideas from John Locke on the labour theory of property (but not of value), the whole elaborated so eloquently by 'the never-to-be-forgotten' professor: this was the basis of the course of studies out of which Smith's great work was eventually to emerge.[15]

After less than three years at Glasgow, Smith, in July 1740, went on to Oxford, where, between the ages of seventeen and twenty-three, he spent six years at Balliol College. W. R. Scott patriotically asserted that 'the Oxford of his time gave little, if any, help towards what was to be his lifework' (1937, 40). Certainly Smith's denunciation of the teaching – or, rather, non-teaching – of the Oxford of his day is well known. Probably, also, he found the Jacobite sympathies current in Oxford, and in his own college, in particular, at least distasteful. Nevertheless, Oxford perhaps provided Smith, given his own remarkable original talents and dedication, with what he may then have needed most (even though he was unaware of this): that was, good libraries and leisure – (or σχολὴ, the means to scholarship) – plus the freedom to read and think his own thoughts. Anyhow, Sir George Clark has mentioned: 'the remarkable coincidence between the books referred to in the footnotes to *The Wealth of Nations* and the books which are known to have been in the college library when its future author was in residence' (1932, 73).

Moreover, the young Smith's six years in England may have been invaluable, from the point of view of his future interests in the wealth of nations, as providing first-hand acquaintance with English social, political and economic institutions, to which he was to pay significant tributes in his masterpiece. For though England was, at this juncture, philosophically somewhat in the shade compared with Scotland and France, she was approaching a supremely significant phase in her, and the world's, economic history. The observant Smith might well have found stimulating comparisons between the economic life and institutions of an economically rather more advanced country, as contrasted with his native land; and *The Wealth of Nations* may, eventually, have been enriched by its author's first-hand experience and impressions of English life and society at that juncture.

Smith returned to Scotland from Oxford in August 1746, and early in 1751 he got a chair at Glasgow. It hardly seems that he could have seriously wasted his time at Oxford, from the point of view of his subsequent work and interests, if, within less than five years of his return north, he was equipped to soar to such eminence. If the vast ignorance as to how Smith spent his six years at Oxford is highly regrettable, the scraps of rather haphazard and, apparently, not entirely reliable information about his subsequent four years or so, after his return, are tantalizing in the extreme. One fact, however, that seems certainly, though not precisely, to be established, is that sometime in these years came his first meeting, and the beginning of his friendship, with his fellow-bachelor David Hume.

Smith was well connected through his mother and through his friends, and it was apparently thanks to Lord Kames that he obtained the job – unconnected with the university – of delivering public lectures in Edinburgh, then apparently a fashionable medium of enlightenment. These lectures seem to have dealt with a wide range of subjects, including rhetoric, languages and *belles lettres*. But the final course, in 1748–9, was apparently devoted to civil law and jurisprudence, and included some discussion of what was to be a main theme of *The Wealth of Nations*. In his memoir of Smith, Dugald Stewart quoted, as apparently extracted from these lectures, the now well-known anticipation of what was to be called 'the simple system of natural liberty':

> Man is generally considered by statesmen and projectors as the materials of a sort of political mechanics. Projectors disturb nature in the course of her operations in human affairs; and it requires no more than to let her alone and give her fair play in the pursuit of her ends that she may establish her own designs . . .
>
> Little else is requisite to carry a state to the highest degree of opulence from the lowest barbarism, but peace, easy taxes and a tolerable administration of justice; all the rest being brought about by the natural course of things. All governments which thwart this natural course, which force things into another channel, or which endeavour to arrest the progress of society at a particular point are unnatural and to support themselves are obliged to be oppressive and tyrannical.
>
> (Stewart, 1811, 100; also Scott, 1973, 54)

Furthermore, according to Scott, it 'can be stated with a fair degree of certainty' that book III of *The Wealth of Nations*, on 'the different progress of opulence in different nations' can be traced back to the Edinburgh period (1937, 56). But, more recently, it has been denied, with reference to other claims regarding manuscripts in which the division of labour is discussed, that they date back as far as this (see Meek and Skinner, 1973, 1094 ff). It certainly seems, however, very probable that Smith had arrived at the basic notions of his 'simple system' in these Edinburgh years. But just how far he had got, and how his ideas compared with those already published in England by, among others, North, Martyn, Gervaise, Vanderlint and Tucker, must remain debatable.

These vital years in the young Smith's career coincided with what we have called the 'mid-century efflorescence', which extended, as we have seen, both over most of Western Europe, as well as over a full range of philosophical and 'scientific' interests, and of which developments in what was to be called 'political economy' were only a small part. As regards works devoted in part (in some cases, in small part) to political economy there may be noted those of Montesquieu (1748), Tucker (1749 and 1751–2), Postelthwayt (1749 and 1751), and Galiani (1751) – this latter probably for some time unknown in Britain. Finally, of course, there was David Hume's *Political Discourses* (1752). This was part of the background of intellectual efflorescence against which the young Smith's ideas were developing at this important stage of his life and work.

Two vacancies, in November 1750, and in 1751, opened the way for Smith's occupancy at Glasgow, first, briefly of the chair of Logic, and then, on the death of Professor Craigie, of the celebrated chair of Moral Philosophy, of which Carmichael and Hutcheson had been the first and second holders respectively, and of which the young Smith became the fourth. He was to remain in this chair in Glasgow twelve-and-a-quarter years, until in January 1764 he departed for London and France as tutor to the Duke of Buccleuch.

Just when Smith's plans for his lifework began to take shape cannot be known. Doubtless they grew and changed. But it was on settling into the chair of Moral Philosophy at Glasgow that he was able to launch effectively whatever plans he had by then formed, and through his lecture courses he was able to build up his grasp of the fields which he had set out to master. As he himself later put it:

> To impose on any man the necessity of teaching, year after year, any particular branch of science, seems in reality, to be the most effectual method of rendering him completely master of it himself. On being obliged to go every year over the same ground, if he is good for anything, he necessarily becomes, in a few years, well acquainted with every part of it. If upon any particular point he should form too hasty an opinion one year, when he comes in the course of his lectures to reconsider the same subject the year thereafter, he is very likely to correct it.
>
> (1976, 812; see Hutchison, 1978, 4).

'The particular branch of science' with which Smith was concerned comprised a very large area of moral philosophy, in fact, in modern terminology, a kind of comprehensive theory of society, covering how ethical views, attitudes, or sentiments, were formed, as well as the economic life of society, the principles of economic policy, and the principles of law and jurisprudence.

It is of interest to speculate as to what might have happened to Smith's career and achievements as a moral philosopher and political economist, if his immediate predecessor Craigie had lived ten years longer, and Smith had missed the decade or more of learning by teaching in respect of this great subject area. Would his *magnum opus* have been, perhaps, in another field, possibly in one of those broached in his essays? Anyhow, before we break off, one feature of his Glasgow environment may be noted which must have considerably stimulated and fed an interest in political economy. This was the contact Smith had with the merchants of the city – which was particularly important in imbuing *The Wealth of Nations* with its vitally realistic, practical, concrete power. For, as John Rae remarked: 'It was amid the thickening problems of the rising trade of the Clyde, and the daily discussions they occasioned among the enterprising and intelligent merchants of the town, that he grew into a great economist' (1895, 87).[16]

In these years of the early 1750s, however, important new departures were on the way in most or all of the leading countries, not only (though pre-eminently) in Scotland. Even in England, further down the west coast of Britain, in another rapidly rising port, a Welsh-born clergyman was vigorously expounding the practical principles of economic freedom. So at this point we must leave the young Smith, and the Scottish Enlightenment, to keep abreast of developments further south, before returning north again in chapters 19 and 20. First to be considered is the development of economic ideas in France, which was soon to become the pre-eminent country in the field.

12
Between Boisguilbert and Quesnay

I

The main economic writings of Pierre de Boisguilbert were published between 1695 and 1714, and we noted in chapter 7 how they have been authoritatively described as marking the 'birth' of political economy in France. They had appeared towards the close of a remarkable decade or two, in the late seventeenth century, when English writers, almost alone, had led a major advance in the subject. It was observed that the appearance of Boisguilbert's writings might, with hindsight, be regarded as a sign that, eventually, later in the eighteenth century, pre-eminence in the emerging subject of political economy would pass, for a time, to France.

The rise, however, to a much more important role for French writers took some decades to come about, in fact until more than halfway through the century – partly, presumably, because of censorship. The first half of the eighteenth century was not a fruitful one with regard to important French contributions to the literature of commerce and political economy – assuming, of course, that Richard Cantillon and Ernst Ludwig Carl are not included as Frenchmen. There were, however, certain French writers from this period who should be mentioned.

First of these was Jean François Melon (16??–1738), who had been secretary to John Law, and who published his *Essai politique sur le commerce* in 1734. Though the book has been described as 'overrated' by Henry Higgs (1897, 14), it went through several editions and an English translation was published in 1738.

One of the main features of Melon's *Essai* is his eloquent defence of luxury, in which presumably he was influenced by Mandeville, though no explicit reference appears. Luxury was 'the destroyer of sloth and idleness' (1738, 177), and had been the stimulus behind a great rise in material living standards: 'What was luxury in the days of our fathers, is now very common; and what is luxury among us, will not be so to our posterity' (175).[1] He followed Petty in favouring 'luxurious' public spending: 'Public shows cannot be too great, too magnificent or too frequent' (195). Sumptuary laws were condemned: 'Is it the business of the legislature to stop industry by such a law, to put a restraint upon liberty, reduce workmen to dangerous idleness, and take away a new motive to labour?'

Certainly Melon acknowledged that spending motivated by charity – 'the greatest of all virtues' – was incomparably worthier. But 'men are rarely guided by the rules of religion' (193). He was highly optimistic regarding the possibilities for economic progress, believing that 'the progress of industry has no bounds' (145). He has usually been classified as a 'mercantilist', though he put liberty above 'protection', or defence, which he apparently even suggested could be 'privatized': 'In the alternative between liberty and protection, it would do less hurt to take away protection than liberty. For with liberty, the power of commerce alone, can hold the place of protection. In the last war, the traders of Bordeaux fitted out a frigate' (39).

On the other hand, on the vital issue of the grain market, Melon emphasized as the 'first care of government, the certainty of having bread' (17).[2]

II

Outstandingly the most important French work for the history of economic thought between Boisguilbert and Quesnay, was Montesquieu's *L'Esprit des lois* (1748). Not that Montesquieu's *direct* contribution to economic theory, or political economy, was of major significance. It was surely one of Keynes's more fanciful claims to have described Montesquieu as the greatest of French economists – 'the real equivalent of Adam Smith ... head and shoulders above the physiocrats'. This eulogy was forthcoming apparently because, like numerous others in the seventeenth and eighteenth centuries (mostly disregarded by Keynes) Montesquieu supported luxury spending for its contribution to the maintenance of effective demand (1973, xxiv).

What was so broadly and powerfully important and consequential for political economy, and for the social sciences, or social studies, in Montesquieu's work, was his fundamental methodological emphasis on cause and effect, and on regularities in the politico-economic world, together with, more specifically, his insistence on historical-institutional relativity, and on the importance of varying, particular, historical, geographical and climatic factors, together with other differing particular circumstances, in explaining the politics and economics of different nations.

Charles Secondat, Baron de Montesquieu (1689–1755), came from a noble family in the Bordeaux region, and, at an early age, decided to devote his life to philosophic and scientific studies. In 1721 he published anonymously, his *Lettres Persanes*, which purported to be the correspondence exchanged between two Persian princes and their friends during a visit to Europe. This fiction provided the author with the means of expressing, obliquely but pointedly, some telling criticisms of French society, institutions, culture and politics. Much of the ensuing decade was spent by Montesquieu in foreign travel and in the study of the institutions of the countries he visited, which included Austria, Italy, Germany, Holland, and from 1729–31, England.

Early intimations of Montesquieu's fundamental methodological interests and principles, with his emphasis on the search for the causes and effects of political and economic change, appeared in his *Considérations sur les causes de la grandeur des Romains et de leur décadence* (1734), which was an important forerunner both of Edward Gibbon's masterpiece (to be published in the same year, 1776, as *The Wealth of Nations*) and of *The History and Termination of the Roman Republic* by Adam Ferguson of Edinburgh (1783).[3]

Montesquieu took the title of his epoch-making *L'Esprit des lois* from a chapter in Jean Domat's *Traité des lois* (see chapter 6). Montesquieu's work appeared in 1748, at a vital moment, in the same year as the Peace of Aix-la-Chapelle, and at once gave a tremendous impetus, right across Western Europe, to what we have called the great mid-century efflorescence. The influence of this book was felt significantly by most of the leading writers on political economy of the last thirty years of our period, that is, by Justi in Germany, Galiani, Beccaria, and Verri in Italy, and by the physiocrats and Turgot in France, and, most significantly, in Scotland by Hume, Sir James Steuart, Ferguson, Smith and Millar.

Montesquieu was profoundly sceptical of claims of universal validity, or universal applicability to politico-economic policies, on behalf of theories or principles; and he was also highly critical of principles which did not take account of the history, geography, climate, and traditions of particular nations or countries. He insisted, also, that political and economic principles and policies could not be ideal or permanent. The laws of each nation,

> . . . should be adapted in such a manner to the people for whom they are framed that it should be a great chance if those of one nation suit another.
>
> They should be in relation to the nature and principle of each government: whether they form it, as may be said of politic law; or whether they support it, as in the case of civil institutions.
>
> They should be in relation to the climate of each country, to the quality of its soil, to its situation and extent, to the principal occupation of the natives, whether husbandmen, huntsmen, or shepherds: they should have relation to the degree of liberty which the constitution will bear; to the religion of the inhabitants, to their inclinations, riches, numbers, commerce, manners, and customs.
>
> (1748 [1949], 6–7)

Though it seems that he knew the remarkable, revolutionary writings of Vico, Montesquieu was less radical than the Neapolitan in his historical relativism, and in distinguishing between the natural and the politico-economic worlds and the appropriate methods for studying them. But Montesquieu was certainly the great pioneer in our period of the historical and comparative method and approach in political economy, and in social studies generally, and one of the precursors of modern sociology.

Montesquieu's central concern was political philosophy, or 'political science'. But *L'Esprit des lois* had a considerable economic component, comprising some four or five chapters out of thirty-one. Regarding the development of commerce, he insisted, as Hume was to do, on its general beneficence as a softener or sweetener of manners: 'Commerce is a cure for the most destructive prejudices; for it is almost a general rule that wherever we find agreeable manners, there commerce flourishes; and that wherever there is commerce, there we meet with agreeable manners. Let us not be astonished, then, if our manners are now less savage than formerly' (316). (Presumably Montesquieu would have conceded to someone looking round the world two centuries later, that such an optimistic generalization, based mainly on West-European experience in the middle of the eighteenth century, might appear subject to serious historical and geographical limitations.)

Anyhow, Montesquieu went on to remark that 'peace is the natural effect of trade', and that commerce usually produced or flourished most under republican forms of government, rather than under monarchies, since republics provided more of the security of property necessary for greater enterprise: 'In short, an opinion of greater certainty as to the possession of property in these states [republics], makes them undertake everything. They flatter themselves with the hopes of receiving great advantages from the smiles of fortune; and thinking themselves sure of what they have already acquired, they boldly expose it in order to acquire more' (319).

Of course, Montesquieu was much concerned with what he regarded as the special case of England, and conceded that he would not 'say that any monarchy is entirely excluded from an economical commerce' (319). In fact, as for a number of other great French writers of the eighteenth century, the example of England was always of special interest to Montesquieu. He proclaimed, with almost excessive admiration: 'Other nations have made the interests of commerce yield to those of politics; the English, on the contrary, have ever made their political interests give way to those of commerce. They know better than any other people on earth how to value, at the same time, those three great advantages – religion, commerce, and liberty' (321).

Montesquieu also discussed the Japanese, remarking on a characteristic of that nation, in the middle of the eighteenth century, which , like that which he had noticed at the same period with regard to the English, seems in some contrast with anything discernible 200 years later. He laid it down that a nation 'should never exclude another from trading with it, except for very great reasons'. But he then observed: 'The Japanese trade only with two nations, the Chinese and the Dutch. The Chinese gain a thousand per cent upon sugar . . . The Dutch make nearly the same profits. Every nation that acts upon Japanese principles must necessarily be deceived.' This led to the important conclusion: 'for it is competition which sets a just value on merchandise, and establishes the relation between them' (322).[4]

Montesquieu cited approvingly England's mercantilistic restrictions:

'England prohibits the exportation of her wool; coals must be brought by sea to the capital; no horses, except geldings, are allowed to be exported; and the vessels of her colonies trading to Europe must take in water in England. The English constrain the merchant, but it is in favour of commerce' (323). He also stressed the dangers of an unfavourable balance of trade: 'A country that constantly exports fewer manufactures or commodities than it receives will soon find the balance sinking; it will receive less and less, until, falling into extreme poverty, it will receive nothing at all' (329).

He then considered processes of economic and commercial change, and started by emphasizing certain constant and regular determinants: 'Though commerce be subject to great revolutions, yet it is possible that certain physical causes, as the quality of the soil, or the climate, may fix its nature forever' (331).

Like several other leading French writers in the first half of the eighteenth century, Montesquieu generally approved of luxury spending. Commerce led to riches, riches to luxury, and luxury to 'the perfection of the arts' (334).

On the subject of money, Montesquieu remarked on the characteristics of the precious metals which rendered them serviceable as means of exchange, but he insisted on stability in value as the prime *desideratum*: 'No thing ought to be so exempt from variation as that which is the common measure of all. Trade is in its own nature extremely uncertain; and it is a great evil to add a new uncertainty to that which is founded on the nature of the thing' (377). He expounded a version of the quantity theory to explain the effects of the influx of the precious metals into Europe:

> If, since the discovery of the Indies, gold and silver have increased in Europe in the proportion of 1 to 20, the price of provisions and merchandise must have been enhanced in the proportion of 1 to 20. But if, on the other hand, the quantity of merchandise has increased as 1 to 2 – it necessarily follows that the price of this merchandise and provisions, having been raised in proportion of 1 to 20, and fallen in proportion of 1 to 2 – it necessarily follows, I say, that the proportion is only as 1 to 10'.
>
> (380)

Montesquieu insisted strongly that values and prices could not be fixed by governments without disaster: 'Thus the prince or the magistrate can no more ascertain the value of merchandise than he can establish by a decree that the relation 1 to 10 is equal to that of 1 to 20. Julian's lowering the price of provisions at Antioch was the cause of a most terrible famine' (379).

Earlier, Montesquieu had treated the subject of taxation (see chapter XIII) under the title 'Of the Relation which the Levying of Taxes and the Greatness of the Public Revenues Bear to Liberty'. He emphasized his suspicions of governments:

> The real wants of the people ought never to give way to the imaginary wants of the state.
>
> Imaginary wants are those which flow from the passions and weaknesses of the governors, from the vain conceit of some extraordinary project, from the inordinate desire of glory, and from a certain impotence of mind incapable of withstanding the impulse of fancy. Often have ministers of a restless disposition imagined that the wants of their own mean and ignoble souls were those of the state.
>
> Nothing requires more wisdom and prudence than the regulation of that portion of which the subject is deprived, and that which he is suffered to retain.
>
> The public revenues should not be measured by the people's ability to give, but by what they ought to give ...
>
> (207)

One branch of expenditure which Montesquieu specially warned about was defence:

> A new distemper has spread itself over Europe, infecting our princes, and inducing them to keep up an exorbitant number of troops. It has its redoublings, and of necessity becomes contagious. For as soon as one prince augments his forces, the rest, of course, do the same; so that nothing is gained thereby but the public ruin.
>
> (217)

Montesquieu's views on taxation have much in common with the four principles subsequently enunciated by Adam Smith.

Let us, however, in conclusion re-emphasize that the great significance of *L'Esprit des lois* for the development of political economy in the eighteenth century, and after, lay in its fundamental, methodological approach, which was especially important in Scotland, as is discussed in chapter 19.

III

Vincent de Gournay (1712–59) wrote very little but seems to have contributed immensely to the advancement of economic studies in France in the early 1750s.

After a broad Western-European experience, derived from a fifteen-year sojourn as a merchant in Spain, and from his travels in England, Holland and Germany, Gournay occupied the post of Intendant (or Commissioner) for Trade from 1751 until his death in 1759. He gathered around him a group of very able young writers, whom he encouraged and assisted in publishing a series of translations and other works. This group was far from being a closely-knit school, or sect, and included authors of such very differing views as Turgot and Forbonnais. The publications of the group included an annotated translation, by Gournay himself, of Josiah Child's *New Discourse on Trade* (together with a tract by Culpeper), which appeared as *Traité sur le commerce* (1754); the *Éléments du commerce* of

Forbonnais (1754), who had also translated from the Spanish the *Theory and Practice of Maritime Trade* by Ustariz;[5] and Turgot's translation of Josiah Tucker's *Reflections on the Expediency of a Law for the Naturalisation of Foreign Protestants* (with its anticipation of the classical doctrine of the impossibility of general overproduction), under the title of *Questions importantes sur le commerce* (1756). But, most important of all, as Mr Antoine Murphy has shown, it seems that it may have been Gournay who brought about the publication, and possibly the translation into French, in 1755, of Richard Cantillon's *Essai* (see Murphy, 1986, chapter 15, and Higgs, 1897, 67).[6]

Gournay is perhaps best known for his propagation of the slogan '*laissez faire et laissez passer*', though this, or a similar phrase, had been used previously by Boisguilbert and the Marquis d'Argenson.[7] He certainly attacked monopolies and was an advocate of competition, free markets and internal free trade. But he did not believe that foreign trade should be completely unrestricted. Though Gournay's efforts powerfully roused public interest in economic problems and policies, from which, in turn, the physiocrats, who recognized him as an ally, were to benefit, he rejected the physiocratic doctrine of the 'sterility' of manufacturing, and was by no means so unqualified or dogmatic regarding economic policy. His death came just when the ideas and school of Quesnay were coming into full bloom.

IV

Much of the work of François Louis Véron-Duverger de Forbonnais (1722–1800) appeared some time after the early 1750s, the phase with which we are now concerned. But having mentioned him as a translator and member of the Gournay group, which played such an important role at this juncture, we may note some characteristics of his *Éléments du commerce* (1754).

Forbonnais came of a rich manufacturing family and later served the régime as Inspector-General of the Mint (see Weulersse, 1910, 122). He opened his *Éléments* with a long historical survey of the origins of commerce, which he described as arising out of 'reciprocal communication', or 'reciprocal dependence'. He then proceeded to bestow high praise on the economic policies and achievements of Louis XIV and Colbert, in total contradiction, of course, to the assertions of Boisguilbert, Vauban, and Quesnay, whose work started from a diametrically opposite historical view. Commercial policy, Forbonnais maintained, should be based on the kind of principles by which the English ('the wisest people in the field of commerce') had guided their operations. These were that imports and exports must be regulated so that only raw materials, or goods for re-export, were imported, and certainly not luxuries or anything prejudicial to domestic production, while superfluities and manufactures were to provide exports (1754, 50–1).

Forbonnais, however, put the greatest stress on competition as 'one of the most important principles of commerce and a considerable element in its freedom' (63). For competition 'produces abundance', and cheapness too: 'It is the soul and spur of industry and it is dangerous to restrain it' (88). The use of money did not alter the 'real' nature of exchange, as goods against goods. Money only had value insofar as it always carried the assurance of being exchangeable for goods (89). (Here Forbonnais gave an anticipatory hint of certain basic classical doctrines.) He may also have been making the same fundamental point about the quantity of money, as David Hume had made in his famous example of the money of a country being multiplied (or annihilated) five-fold overnight. Forbonnais, for his part, compared two similar, completely self-sufficient countries, with no external economic relations, and with the same quantities of goods to be circulated, but with one country possessing, as money, 100 units of a precious metal, while the other possessed 200 units. Then, Forbonnais concluded, goods which cost one ounce of metal in the first country would cost two ounces in the other (90).

In a chapter on luxury, Forbonnais maintained that luxury was impossible to define other than as any wealth over and above the physical necessities of food, clothing, etc. (225). He opposed attacks on luxury and attempts to curb it. For luxury provided employment and roused the spirit of emulation. Moreover: 'Luxury humanises people, polishes their manners, softens their passions, sharpens their imaginations, perfects their knowledge' (238). On this subject, Forbonnais claimed the support of Hume. But he emphasized that luxury should be based on production and commerce and not on a class of idle-rich consumers of imports.

The final chapter of his *Éléments* was devoted to the balance of commerce (or trade), that is, the difference between a country's purchases and sales. This difference had to be paid in money, which alone could be offered if there was no 'natural' exchange of goods: 'The efforts of all trading nations are directed at achieving this balance, which alone can augment, positively and relatively, their sum of metals, and impart to circulation the activity which spreads comfort among all classes of people, the principle of utility and luxury' (244–5).

The general balance was the result of particular balances with different countries, which (as Thomas Mun had long before argued) did not all need to be positive, provided the general balance was 'lucrative' (245). Forbonnais claimed the support of Josiah Child for what he maintained were the basic principles or methods by which a nation should seek to achieve a balance: that is, by regarding its trade as its primary concern; by seeking to increase the number of its workers and its 'real' capital goods; and by making the most of the interest of foreigners in trading with it (249).

Thus the lessons which Forbonnais, in his *Éléments*, derived from English writers, such as Petty, Child and Locke, followed mainly the 'mercantilist' lines of an earlier period. But Forbonnais was an eclectic and empirical moderate, who, in supporting protection, wanted to limit tariffs to 15 per cent. At the same time, he was, as we have seen, an eloquent advocate of competition, as the basis of a free economy (see Morrisson and Goffin,

1967, 61–3). He later became one of the main opponents of the physiocrats, both in defending the productivity of manufacturing – in his *Principes et observations économiques*, 1767 – and in his opposition to unrestricted freedom of trade. In fact, as one associated with the Gournay group in the early 1750s, Forbonnais illustrated the degree of continuity between the more liberal forms of mercantilism, and the qualified liberalism of Gournay himself; and, moving further along the spectrum, with the much less qualified free-market principles of Tucker, Turgot, the physiocrats, and Adam Smith.

13
Josiah Tucker and the English Contribution

I

Josiah Tucker (1713–99) was the son of a Welsh farmer who got to Oxford by walking there, which he did, carrying his baggage, at the beginning and end of each term at St John's College. After Oxford he entered the Anglican church as a curate, subsequently rector, in Bristol, then Britain's second-largest city and commercial centre. His formidable abilities as a controversialist and publicist were first directed at theological issues, in particular those raised by the rise of Methodism, then flourishing in Bristol. But it was soon that city's commercial importance that was stimulating his interest in questions of trade – just as, a decade or two later, Adam Smith was stimulated by the businessmen and merchants of another major west-coast port. Indeed, so keen became his interest in the subject that his Bishop at Gloucester, whence Tucker was promoted Dean in 1758, is reported as remarking of him that 'religion was his trade and trade was his religion' – an epigram justifiably resented by Tucker. In a not necessarily derogatory sense the Bishop's observation about his Dean had some truth in it. For later in life Tucker wrote:

> How are the ends both of religion and government to be answered, but by the system of universal commerce? Commerce, I mean, in the large and extensive signification of that word; commerce as it implies a general system for the useful employment of our time; as it exercises the particular genius and abilities of mankind in some way or other, either of body or mind, in mental or corporeal labour, and so as to make self-interest and social coincide. And in pursuing this plan, it answers all the great ends both of religion and government; it creates social relations, and it serves as a cement to connect together the religious and civil interests of mankind. It is a friend to both, when rightly understood, and is befriended by them.
>
> (*17 Sermons*, 1776a, 137, quoted in Shelton, 1981, 181)

It is interesting to compare the Dean's enthusiastic eulogy of the beneficence of commerce with Mandeville's panegyric on money towards the end of his *Fable* (see chapter 7). Tucker, of course, denounced Mandeville for the 'absurdity' of his doctrine that 'private vices are public benefits'. According to Tucker: 'It is virtue alone that can make a nation flourish. And vice of every kind is either immediately, or in its consequences, injurious to commerce' (1753, 130n.). But, if the moralizing and ethical adjectives are stripped away, Mandeville and Tucker were making more or less the same fundamental statement that, for a free society, a way must be found of harnessing the most powerful human motives for socially beneficent, or, at least harmless, ends, and that free 'commerce', 'trade', and markets, more or less achieved this.

Tucker was in his thirties when he came to the subject of trade and commerce, and the first of his writings on this subject was his *Essay on Trade* (1749), or, in full, *A Brief Essay on the Advantages and Disadvantages which Respectively Attend France and Great Britain with regard to Trade*. The *Essay* announced some of Tucker's main themes as to the encouragement of immigration and naturalization, as well as his strong opposition to monopolies and restrictive practices. But on a number of points he was to develop his views in a more definitely libertarian direction, for example, with regard to the worthlessness of colonial trade, and as to government regulation of manufactures.

What Tucker had intended as his main work, and a major treatise, was his *Elements of Commerce* (1755). This work – though, as far as it went, far superior to the earlier *Essay on Trade* – was unfortunately never completed. For Tucker was not a treatise writer or theoretical system-builder. It may, however, be noted that if, in the 1690s, 'trade' was the name of the subject which writers placed on their title pages, by the 1750s the term 'commerce' figured more often (as with Cantillon's '*Essay*', published in the same year as Tucker's *Elements*, and also in Massie's plea for the subject in 1760).

Tucker's *Elements*, however, constituted his most important contribution to economic theorizing. He began with confident claims, which may be compared with Cantillon's treatment of 'Commerce in General' (though Tucker did not make explicit abstractions, like Cantillon's): 'That the principles laid down in the ensuing treatise, are, for the most part, general and universal; *viz.* such as would suit (with very little alteration) any kingdom, state, or climate whatever; and are therefore called *The Elements of Commerce*' (53).

Whether, in fact, Tucker sustained such a high level of generality is questionable. He was much too practically and policy oriented. Elsewhere, indeed, he rejected conclusions based on 'immutable truths' and abstract reasoning. Perhaps, however, his claim that his 'manner of treating this subject is entirely new', may have some validity. For though, at various points in his writings, Tucker cited Petty, Child, Mandeville, Berkeley and Montesquieu, there was much that was novel and forceful in Tucker's approach.

He began with the proposition – resembling that of Adam Smith regarding the alleged human propensity to truck, barter and exchange – that mankind had a 'natural disposition, or instinctive inclination towards commerce', which originated with human wants, natural or artificial, real or imaginary. To meet these wants, specialization and the division of labour were required:

> When human creatures are once brought together, they find a vast number of advantages in each other by mutual assistances to which they must have been strangers in their separate and independent state. Consequently then it is, that the common labour of the society is branched out into separate and distinct parts; then it is that each individual chooses a particular course of life, according as his circumstances or genius shall determine his pursuits ... Thus are the first wants of mankind, *viz*. food, raiment and dwelling, much better supplied by dividing the general labour into different branches than if each individual depended on himself alone for the supply of them. And these different parts of the common labour are nothing else, in other words, but distinct trades and manufactures ...
>
> (57)[1]

In his *Instructions for Travellers* (1758), Tucker recommended as a vital question about an economy: 'Is that labour, which is still to be performed by the human kind, so judiciously divided that men, women, and children have their respective shares in proportion to their strength, sex, and abilities?' He noted an example from Birmingham:

> When a man stamps a metal button by means of an engine, a child stands by him to place the button in readiness to receive the stamp, and to remove it when received, and then to place another. By these means the operator can stamp at least double the number, which he could otherwise have done ... And hence it is that the *Bijoux d'Angleterre*, or the Birmingham toys, are rendered so exceedingly cheap as to astonish all Europe.
>
> (242–3)

Though introducing the division of labour at such an early point, as Adam Smith was to do, Tucker then took a somewhat different path. He next emphasized the fundamental motive of 'that watchful dragon self-interest', which was, however, often directed at attempts to monopolize, or exclude competitors, though 'benevolence is some check upon this principle'. As regards the framework for commerce: 'The main point to be aimed at, is neither to extinguish nor enfeeble self-love, but to give it such a direction, that it may promote the public interest by pursuing its own' (59).

Thus Tucker did not believe in a complete harmony of interests, perhaps even less than Mandeville. For the need for government to guide and direct individual self-interest is emphasized again and again in the *Elements* and in Tucker's other writings: 'The passion of self-love therefore must be taken hold of by some method or other; and so trained or guided in its operations that its activity may never be mischievous but always productive of the public welfare' (1755, 61).

Tucker contrasted the control of self-love by penal laws, on the one hand, with the use of 'judicious policy', on the other, the method of which 'is to incline and encourage', leading people 'by their own free choice to virtuous industry'; and this should be the method 'especially in a free country'. Repeatedly Tucker stated his aim of showing how 'the universal mover in human nature, self-love, may receive such a direction in this case (as in all others) as to promote the public interest by those efforts it shall make towards pursuing its own' (92).

As Tucker insisted, 'we must take human nature as we find it; and make the best uses of it we can' (122). He also introduced a medical metaphor, similar to that used by Petty:

> For if self-love is restrained from doing mischief, it will do good. Hence therefore the physician to the body politic may learn to imitate the conduct of the physician to the body natural, in removing those disorders which a bad habit, or a wrong treatment hath brought upon the constitution; and then to leave the rest to nature, who best can do her own work. For after the constitution is restored to the use and exercise of its proper faculties and natural powers, it would be wrong to multiply laws relating to commerce, as it would be to be for ever prescribing physic.
>
> (126)

II

Like many mercantilist writers, in all countries, Tucker wanted to promote the increase of population. Indeed, after his exposition of the elementary principles, this was Tucker's first main theme, expounded at considerable length: 'Where a country is thinly peopled, it is impossible to promote a brisk and general circulation of industry and labour' (63).

Numerous and even extreme measures were set out for encouraging marriage through taxation and other inducements or penalties. Tucker certainly entertained no such fears as those so emphasized by Malthus less than half a century later; though he did consider that big cities were morally and socially dangerous. Policies were also recommended for 'the admission of wealthy and industrious foreigners' (80). In fact, Tucker gave his support to an Act for the naturalization of foreign-born Jews (and was burnt in effigy for his pains by a Bristol mob, and described as Josiah ben Tucker, ben Judas Iscariot). His main arguments, however, had been set out in his two-part tract, *Reflections on the Expediency of a Law for the Naturalization of Foreign Protestants* (1751–2). As regards the economic aspects, Tucker was concerned to oppose the notion that immigration would increase unemployment. Here his arguments anticipated the doctrine of James Mill and Say regarding the impossibility of general over-production and unemployment. He raised some questions in the manner of Berkeley's *Querist*:

> Whether the true method of finding out the causes of the want of employment is not, first to enquire, what are the *impediments* to the circulation of labour?
>
> Whether monopolies, exclusive privileges, and combinations, are not so many clogs upon the circulation of labour?

> If a particular trade is at any time overstocked, will not the disease cure itself? That is, will not some persons take to other trades, and fewer young people be bred up to that which is least profitable?
>
> (1751–2, 9–13)

In the *Elements*, Tucker, rather blithely, suggested that when a trade was 'accidentally overstocked', then 'the best and safest way is to let the evil alone, and then it will infallibly cure itself' (1755, 134).

On the other hand, Tucker, like many of his predecessors and contemporaries, believed in the 'perverse' supply curve of labour: 'For alas and this is the ruin of all our trade, too many there are who will not accept of work one part of the week, but on such terms only as may enable them to live in vice and idleness the rest' (1772, 89).[2]

Tucker wanted a strong role for government both positively and negatively, which should include enclosing common land and afforestation. Regarding the supply of timber, he explained that the case was different from that of the 'raising of corn or cattle, or engaging in merchandise or manufacture . . . For certainly there is no need of any inducement but self-interest, where self-interest can properly take place. But in the case before us, the misfortune is, that he who plants, unless he begins very young, cannot expect to reap much benefit in his own person' (1755, 121).

Tucker proposed that all landowners owning more than 400 acres should be obliged by law to allot twenty acres for timber, under daunting penalties. As regards industry, Tucker supported protection for 'infant' industries: 'As for the encouraging of new trade, it ought to be considered, that every trade at its first commencement, is properly in its infant state; which therefore during that period must be nursed; and all nursing is attended with expense' (132). Subsequently, Tucker added: 'But it doth by no means so clearly appear, that this nursing and supporting should be continued for ever . . . that particular trade is not worth having, which never can be brought to support itself' (1758, 252).

He defended patents for inventors, but his severest condemnation was directed against restrictive practices and such bodies as chartered companies, monopolizing corporations, guild restrictions, apprenticeships, etc.: 'Surely nothing can be plainer than that every man hath a right *by nature* to subsist himself, by his own labour and industry, *in any way that is compatible with the good of the whole*' (1755, 129). He protested:

> An Englishman, notwithstanding his boasted liberty, is, in regard to commerce, still not free: for he is still in bondage, not to the crown indeed, as formerly, but to his fellow-subjects; and we still want the glorious revolution in our commercial system, which we have happily obtained in the political. Then indeed, and not till then, may we be said to have abolished all the remains of ancient despotic power, and gothic barbarity. For as long as these charters and exclusions continue, so long we bear about us the marks of our former slavery.
>
> (136)

Tucker allowed some exceptions to complete freedom of occupation or trade, on grounds of morals (licensing of ale-houses), or the importance of reliability or qualifications (medicines, doctors, lawyers, etc.). In two cases he opposed government regulations which Adam Smith was prepared to support. First, Tucker condemned the Navigation Laws as 'a monopoly against the whole trade and manufactures of this country' (see Tucker, 1779, quoted by Clark, 1903, 152). Secondly, he condemned usury laws as 'foolish, absurd' (1751–2, 36–9). Foreign trading companies, such as the East India, Turkey, and Hudson's Bay companies, should also be stripped of monopolistic privileges, which were supported by 'popular errors concerning the balance of trade, and the nature of money' (140). Tucker then proceeded to denounce, most emphatically, the bullionist fallacies. He opposed prohibitions on exports of the precious metals as an 'absurdity and tyrannical imposition' (166). He also described money as a 'ticket', as had the paper-monetarist George Berkeley twenty years previously: 'Industry and labour are the only real riches; money being merely the ticket or sign belonging to them; and the use of money is to certify that the person possessing that piece of coin, hath likewise been in possession of a *certain quantity of labour*, which he hath transferred into other hands, and now retains the sign of it' (146).

A further step in Tucker's argument seems more questionable:

> Money therefore being nothing more than a certificate of labour, it necessarily follows that national industry will always command as many of these certificates, i.e. as much gold and silver as are wanted for these purposes . . .
>
> This being the case, let us now proceed to suppose, that all the gold and silver in that country was lost and annihilated in one night; and what would be the consequence, but plainly this, that the inhabitants would then devise some other ticket, or counter, for the exchange of mutual industry, and the circulation of labour among one another?
>
> (146)

Here Tucker seems to be reacting too far and too strongly against the bullionist fallacy regarding the accumulation of gold and silver, in the direction of the view, at some points suggested by Adam Smith, that money doesn't matter, for the system of natural liberty can smoothly, rapidly, and easily adjust to *any* vagaries in the money supply, even the disappearance overnight of four-fifths of it.

What, however, is most impressive in Tucker's statement of the case is the way in which he linked economic freedom with freedom of thought and debate, and indicated how it undermined the powers of despotic rulers:

> Moreover, freedom of trade brings likewise with it freedom of debate, as well as freedom of thinking. Add to all this that though the revenue increases by means of a free trade, the greatness of the prince is comparatively diminished.
>
> It is morally impossible, that an arbitrary prince should wish the generality of his subjects to be rich: for he cannot promote their riches, without diminishing at the same time his own comparative greatness.
>
> (197–8)

(This perception of Tucker's may be relevant not only to the arbitrary princes of earlier centuries, but to modern dictatorships, which, for all their great economic plans, cannot really want their subjects to be well-off to the extent of acquiring a significant measure of freedom of choice.)

Tucker concluded enthusiastically: 'As we are now blessed with liberty of conscience, and a free government, we want nothing to complete our happiness under a race of excellent princes, but that liberty of commerce, to which every man is entitled both by the right of nature, and the general tenor of the laws of this country' (1755, 212). On this high note, Tucker's *Elements* broke off. Some of the outlines or headings of the subsequent chapters which he had planned, have some interest. 'Coin and Credit as the Mediums of Commerce' is the title of one chapter, with a section devoted to changing a part of the national debt into 'circulating certificates or paper money'. A 'dissertation' was planned 'on the connection, and entire harmony between national commerce, good morals, and good government'. Indeed, as well as promoting industry and wealth, a system of taxes was to be propounded which would be 'preventive of idleness, extravagance, etc.', and 'promotive of good morals' (215–17).

III

Some of the topics planned for the *Elements* were developed by Tucker in his pamphlet, *Instructions for Travellers* (1758), in which he expressed his strong belief in comparative studies of economic history and institutions, and in using the Grand Tour, for this purpose. He was certainly proud to observe that Britain was then well ahead of her neighbours in labour-saving technology – a subject in which Tucker took much more interest than did the author of *The Wealth of Nations*, twenty years later. He vigorously attacked opposition to labour-saving innovations:

> The price of goods is thereby prodigiously lowered from what otherwise it must have been; and ... a much greater number of hands are employed ... that system of machines, which so greatly reduces the price of labour, as to enable the generality of a people to become purchasers of the goods, will in the end, though not immediately, employ more hands in the manufacture, than could possibly have found employment, had no such machines been invented.
>
> (241–2)

In some contrast, perhaps, with his enthusiasm for technical advance and the division of labour, is Tucker's opposition to the factory system and his preference for the independent journeyman, based on interesting, prophetic sociological grounds. Tucker observed with foreboding, as Marx, on the contrary, was so approvingly to perceive a century later, that massing workers in large factories would sap their independence and breed class antagonism. When working on their own,

> they are all rivals, all animated with the same desire of bringing their goods to market upon the cheapest terms, and of excelling one another . . . and likely to set up for themselves by the industry and frugality of a few years, have no conception that they are embarked in an interest opposite to that of their masters, or that they are called upon to enter into clubs or combinations against them. Thus it is, that the working people are generally moral, sober, and industrious; that the goods are well made, and exceedingly cheap; and that a riot or a mob is a thing hardly known among them.
>
> (244)

The contrasting system, which Tucker saw exemplified in the wool industry of his time, had 'one person, with a great stock and large credit', who 'perhaps employs a thousand persons under him'. Tucker perceived this as a recipe for class war: 'The master, for example, however well-disposed in himself, is naturally tempted by his situation to be proud and over-bearing, to consider his people as the scum of the earth, whom he has a right to squeeze whenever he can' (244–5). The reaction from the workmen was inevitable. They

> are equally tempted by their situation, to envy the high station, and superior fortunes of their masters; and to envy them the more, in proportion as they find themselves deprived of the hopes of advancing themselves to the same degree by any stretch of industry, or superior skill. Hence their self-love takes a wrong turn, destructive to themselves and others. They think it no crime to get as much wages, and to do as little for it as they possibly can, to lie and cheat, and do any other bad thing; provided it is only against their master, whom they look upon as their common enemy, with whom no faith is to be kept. The motives to industry, frugality, and sobriety are all subverted by this one consideration, *viz.* that they shall always be chained to the same oar.
>
> (245)

Had he lived a century or two later, Tucker might, of course, often have had to face the choice between the much greater productivity of large-scale factories and the social values of 'small is beautiful'. He would certainly have continued to place much value on smallness and individual independence, but would have had to face the costs.

In *Instructions for Travellers*, Tucker expressed a rather more passive *laissez-faire* attitude, very close to that of Adam Smith, at some points:

> Let the legislature but take care not to make bad laws, and then as to good ones, they will make themselves: that is, the self-love and self-interest of each individual will prompt him to seek such ways of gain, trades and occupations of life, as by serving himself, will promote the public welfare at the same time. The only thing necessary to be done by positive institutions is to enforce the observance of voluntary contracts by legal penalties speedily levied.
>
> (251)

Tucker then proceeded again briefly to review the 'prodigious number' of bad laws relating to trade and manufactures, most types of which had been castigated in the *Elements*.

Turning to taxation, however, Tucker became much more positive, and much more 'mercantilistic', in supporting taxes on exports of raw materials, and on imports of finished manufactures. Though, on the whole, favouring taxes on luxuries rather than on goods consumed by the poor, he advocated taxing a wide range of recreations, sports, etc., including taxes on dogs, horse-racing, play-houses, ballad singers, etc., as well as (surely quite lamentably) on cricket matches. He rightly noted, however, that England 'hath a great advantage over most other countries' in that 'tolls, and town duties, and other contrivances for stopping the circulation of mutual industry and labour, are deservedly exploded' (256).

Tucker was enthusiastic about English mechanical proficiency, holding that the Englishman had 'scarcely his equal in the construction of machinery for the various purposes of different manufactures' (1781, 64). He also praised English social mobility:

> Certain it is, that though the low bred mechanic may not always meet with respect equal to his large and acquired fortune; yet, if he gives his son a liberal and accomplished education, the birth and calling of the father are sunk in the son; and the son is reputed, if his carriage is suitable, a gentleman in all companies ... In one word, trade begets wealth, and wealth independence: but the assistance of learning and education must be called in, in order to set off, and embellish them both.
>
> (1755, 264)

Later, Tucker called for a far-reaching enquiry, on similar lines to those attempted, or suggested, by Postelthwayt and Massie into the state of the nation, covering agriculture, manufactures, transport, taxation, the national debt, etc. (see Clark, 1903, 191). In particular, he held that progress in the preceding decades should be estimated. In general, Tucker seems to have been highly optimistic regarding the prospects for continuing economic progress, as we have mentioned above when he was rejecting what he thought to be the unduly pessimistic views of David Hume (see chapter 11).[3]

One subject on which Tucker clearly and powerfully anticipated Adam Smith was in his criticism of British colonial policies. Here his views changed and advanced considerably from those expressed in his earlier work, the *Essay on Trade* of 1749. In its later form, the Dean's opposition was considerably more radical and extreme than that of the Scottish master. Here are some of Tucker's sentiments: 'As to the planting of colonies for the sake of a monopolising or exclusive trade, it is the arrantist cheat and self-deception which poor, short-sighted mortals ever put upon themselves' (1931, 35).

In 1774 Tucker predicted the independence of the American colonies:

> Colonies of every sort or kind are, and ever were, a drain to, and an encumbrance on the mother-country, requiring perpetual and expensive nursing in their infancy; and becoming headstrong and ungovernable, in proportion as they grow up, and never failing to revolt, as soon as they shall find that they do not want our assistance.
>
> (1781 [1931],533)

In particular, America 'ever was a millstone hanging about the neck of this country, to weigh it down; and as we ourselves had not the wisdom to cut the rope and to let the burden off, the Americans have kindly done it for us.' Not that Tucker was uncritically well-disposed to white Americans: 'They claim the rights of life, liberty and property by the "immutable" laws of nations, but permit me to ask, why are not the poor Negroes and Indians entitled to like benefits?' (1770, quoted in Shelton, 1981, 191).

In emphasizing how difficult it has often seemed for colonial powers to divest themselves of their acquisitions, Tucker anticipated Smith, almost word for word, when he argued that there was not, he believed, 'a single instance in all history of any nation surrendering a distant province voluntarily and of free choice, notwithstanding it was greatly their interest to have done it' (1775, 69, quoted in Tucker 1781 [1931], 37).[4]

Tucker was confident that the people of India, also, would recover their 'original and native independence'. Moreover, Tucker who rightly predicted, in advance, the separation of the American states from Britain, also correctly predicted that, through her natural advantages, and through, also, 'a spirit of industry, a thirst for gain and an ardent desire of that very independence which has at length been set up', America would, when Europe was in relative decline, 'make a most distinguished figure among the nations of the earth and in the history of the world' (1780, 26–7).

The Dean, in fact, frequently expressed radical opposition to his country's policies in the Seven Years' War, as in a letter to Lord Kames of 1761: 'War, conquests and colonies are our present system and mine is just the opposite' (see Clark, 1903, 65).

In his somewhat Cobdenite exhortations in favour of trade and peace, Tucker was following Jacob Vanderlint: 'Is this spell, this witchcraft of the jealousy of trade never to be dissolved? And are there no hopes that mankind will recover their senses as to these things? For of all absurdities that of going to war for the sake of getting trade is the most absurd; and nothing in nature can be so extravagantly foolish' (1763, Schuyler ed., 1931, 295). Tucker was fundamentally critical of the kind of patriotism on which 'mercantilist' policies claimed to be based:

> The love of country hath no place in the catalogue of Christian virtues. The love of country is, in fact, a local affection and a partial attachment; but the Christian covenant is general, comprehending all mankind within its embraces ... as to the ideas of honour, and glory, and conquest, and dominion, and other fine things usually implied in the love of country, they are so foreign to the Christian plan that in this sense the love of country neither is, nor ought to be, a part of the Christian scheme of universal love and benevolence.
> (1776a, 285–6, quoted in Clark, 1903, 169)

Sound economic principles, according to Tucker, pointed the same way as the Christian duty of benevolence towards one's enemies. Echoing Hume, he urged Britain 'to promote the prosperity of France by all just and honourable means . . . If France should grow poorer, she must be so much the worse customer of England' (1781, 46).

At the same time, Tucker condemned slavery: 'We make slaves of these poor wretches contrary to every principle, not only of humanity and justice, but also of national profit and advantage' (1776b, 21).

In his political attitudes, Tucker combined these radical anti-war, anti-colonialist and anti-slavery views with a strongly anti-populist, and even anti-democratic, position. It was popular agitators who appealed, all too successfully, to British xenophobia, to war sentiments, and to colonial adventurism. It was a political maxim of Tucker that all popular measures were, more often than not, wrong, while most unpopular measures might well have something right about them. There was no more ludicrous and blasphemous slogan than '*Vox populi, Vox Dei*'. Tucker was highly critical even of the liberal political ideas of John Locke.

IV

Dean Tucker's writings won some renown in his own day, but, among economists, his reputation has not survived at as nearly a high level as it should have. In his own day his works were highly regarded in France. Already in 1754 a French paraphrase had appeared of his *Essay on Trade*, which was approvingly cited by Quesnay. The great Turgot translated two of Tucker's works: part II of the *Reflections on Naturalization* (1751–2) – with its anticipation of the classical doctrine of the impossibility of general overproduction and unemployment – and secondly *The Case of Going to War for the Sake of Trade* (a tract of 1763, see 1931). In highly complimentary letters to him, Turgot extolled Tucker as 'the only author who perceived the advantage of free trade', and he sent him a copy of his *Réfléxions* in 1766 (Oeuvres, 1808–11, vol. IX, 366–75).

Though Adam Smith had some of Tucker's writings in his library, there is no reference to him in *The Wealth of Nations*. But Professor Bernard Semmel has cogently argued that Tucker probably exercised as much influence as Hume and Smith on the attempts by Pitt and Shelburne to liberalize British trade policy towards France and Ireland – and, in particular, with regard to Ireland in 1778 and 1785.

In the nineteenth century, Tucker's reputation among economists seems to have fallen away, except that Karl Marx, having described him as 'a parson and a Tory', nevertheless concluded that he was 'for the rest, an honourable man and a competent political economist' (n.d., 760n.). More recently, Jacob Viner dismissed Tucker as a 'mercantilist', perhaps a kind of *reductio ad absurdum* of that problematic term, the ultimate extremity of which would be to call Adam Smith a 'mercantilist' because he supported retaliatory import restrictions, Navigation Laws, and the regulation of interest rates. In fact, Tucker was an important pioneer, who, in mid-century, helped more than almost anyone else to prepare the way for a great swing in politico-economic thinking and opinion.

V

Joseph Massie (d. 1784) is an interesting figure not so much because of the originality and importance of his theoretical work, but for his methodological and bibliographical contributions to the consolidation of the subject in England. He was the author of a stream of pamphlets and tracts in the 1750s and early 1760s, of which the earliest, and one of the most important, was *An Essay on the Governing Causes of the Natural Rate of Interest* (1750), which anticipates some of the arguments of Hume's essay on the subject.[5] This pamphlet begins with seven pages of quotations from Locke, while Petty, and subsequently William Fleetwood's *Chronicon Preciosum* are cited. Massie was primarily concerned to deny Locke's proposition that the rate of interest was determined by the quantity of money in circulation, together with the volume of indebtedness, and that an abundance of money would reduce interest. Though he made some use of the quantity theory of money, Massie's attempt at refutation was based mainly on statistical and historical evidence. Somewhat rough and ready by modern standards, Massie's approach was surely methodologically commendable.

Two other points in Massie's *Essay* may be noted. First, there was his emphasis on the risk factor, and his separation of risk premia, which varied widely, from the 'natural' rate of interest. High nominal rates of interest were often high risk premia (23). But these premia could be expected to fall, and had fallen in Holland and Britain with the growth of security and confidence which had come from improved government. Second, Massie explained the rate of interest and its movements in terms of the profits on capital investment: 'The natural rate of interest is governed by the profits of trade' (48).

Rates of profit could be expected to decline, and had been declining, mainly through increasing competition, domestically and internationally (as Smith was to argue).

As a pioneer bibliographer, Massie compiled his *Catalogue of Commercial Books*, in which nearly 2400 works were listed, dating from 1557 to 1763. Some fairly well-known items seem to be absent, and in some cases authors, now well-known, are listed as anonymous. Massie claimed to have himself collected 1500 books and pamphlets, presumably the first major collection on the subject in England.

Perhaps Massie's most interesting work, however, was his *Representation Concerning the Knowledge of Commerce as a National Concern, pointing out the proper means of promoting such knowledge in this kingdom* (1760), which he dedicated to the Prime Minister, the Duke of Newcastle.

He began with some methodological comments on the state of the subject, somewhat severely critical in tone: this branch of knowledge 'still continues at a very low ebb in this kingdom'. Repetition, confusion and contradiction are rife in the literature. The somewhat restrictive proposition was laid down (perhaps incontrovertible at all times and places) that: 'It must appear that commercial writers fully understand the subject before commercial readers can fully understand it.'

Massie must be one of the first economists explicitly to distinguish the deductive and historical approaches:

> Some writers have considered commerce as a *science*, and endeavoured to deduce the knowledge of it from axioms, maxims, etc., while many others have treated it as a branch of *history*, and given narratives of transactions, occurrences, etc. but the former have made only light essays on the elementary part of commercial knowledge, and the latter have given only scraps of a commercial history, or at most have compiled only a small part of it.

As regards the deductive, or axiomatic method, only three or four English writers, notably Locke, had established their conclusions on self-evident principles. As regards the historical approach, it seems that only 'heaps of rubbish' had resulted. However, Temple, Petty, Child, Locke and Davenant are explicitly exempted from such strictures.

Commercial knowledge had been unduly neglected because: 'It is generally thought that the nature of trade as a national concern cannot be understood without practising some branch, therefore such knowledge is illiberal' (2).[6]

Merchants and practical men constantly disagree and contradict one another in Parliament. It is, however, in the national interest that trade should be studied as 'a liberal exercise of sound and extensive judgement' (3). Principles cannot, however, be established by studying one particular, small branch, for maxims based thereon cannot provide foundations for general conclusions. Trade must be studied as 'a national concern', and empirical and deductive work must be combined as in the natural sciences (or 'philosophy'): 'Experiments, or facts, and reason going hand in hand, they help each other in philosophy, as well as in other branches of knowledge' (9).

Indeed Massie seems, rather over-optimistically, to have suggested that eventually the study of commerce might achieve greater success even than 'philosophy' (i.e. the natural sciences): 'When proper facts have been as closely pursued in commerce as experiments have been in philosophy, I am persuaded that such pursuit will be attended with much greater success; for in the former, both causes and effects are discoverable to the mind; but in the latter, there are many things quite above human comprehension' (9).

Here Massie seems to have anticipated the rather optimistic claims of Cairnes, Wieser and Robbins regarding the greater reliability of the foundations of the human sciences (or studies) as compared with the natural sciences. In fact, Massie put forward the most confident claims regarding 'commercial knowledge', which 'may be established upon a firm foundation'. It would be mistaken, he asserted, to conclude that historical relativities seriously threatened the fundamentals of 'commercial studies'. Other sciences were similarly situated:

> The various migrations of commerce do indeed give some reason for thinking that the knowledge of it cannot be reduced to fixed principles: but the force of that reason will disappear, when it is considered that neither the productive laws of nature nor the principles of arts and sciences are at all affected by the removal or decay of those things to which they give being or form.
>
> (9)

Massie went on to claim the existence of 'laws' in the 'commercial', or economic field: 'The same commercial laws which brought wealth and naval power to Egypt, Greece, and Carthage, two or three thousand years ago, would under like circumstances bring wealth and naval power to the present inhabitants of those countries' (9).

After some waverings, Massie concluded that just as the physical laws of nature, involved in production, apply at all times and places, so 'by parity of reasoning, the principles of commercial knowledge, whatever they are, must retain their nature and efficacy in all changes of application' (11).

In fact, Massie maintained that 'the fundamental maxims' were already settled. But to bring about this further advance, public support from government funds was necessary. (He may have been the first English economist to ask for a government research grant.) Certainly his intellectual objectives were strictly realistic and policy-oriented. He seems to have been concerned, in particular, with commercial history and statistical surveys of trends in trade and industry, with regard to which improved knowledge would, in the first place, help to bring about increases in the public revenues; while, secondly, such studies, rightly conceived and executed, should be regarded as 'a branch of liberal knowledge'.

VI

Malachi Postelthwayt (1707–67), though known as 'a scribbler' (Redlich, 1970, 199), may also be regarded as another interesting contributor to the consolidation of economic knowledge in England in the 1750s. He was best known for his *Universal Dictionary of Trade and Commerce* (1751) in two big folio volumes, having two years previously produced, by way of advance advertisement, *A Dissertation on the Plan, Use and Importance* of such a work (1749).[7]

Postelthwayt showed a great respect for French economic and commercial institutions and policies, and claimed that France's merchants and traders had better sources of information than their British counterparts. This was due originally to Colbert, who had encouraged the collection and dissemination of commercial and economic intelligence, which had been further advanced by the compilation of a *Dictionary of Commerce* by J. Savary des Brulons. Translations from this French dictionary make up a large part of Postelthwayt's work, which was designed primarily as a compendium of geographical and commercial information for businessmen. Claiming that his *Dictionary* was the first of its kind to be published in

Britain, Postelthwayt maintained that 'a dictionary is presumed to contain matters of fact only'. He hoped, moreover, that the statistical information he provided would serve as a basis for 'political arithmetic'. However, in articles on such topics as the balance of trade, coin, credit, exchange, interest and money, some theoretical and conceptual ideas were introduced. Postelthwayt's *Dictionary* had reached a fourth edition by 1774. So presumably it was something of a success.

Postlethwayt has also been regarded as having produced the first plan for an academic education for business. It seems, however, to have been shown that he took over the idea from a merchant, James Royston, who was the true originator of the project, with whom Postelthwayt collaborated. Anyhow, these two produced their proposals in *The British Mercantile Academy: or the Accomplished Merchant* (1750). This pamphlet emphasized 'the necessity of young merchants being bred to trade with greater advantages than they usually are', and stressed the need for an academy, and the usefulness of this institution to 'the young *nobility* and *gentry*, and such who are intended for the study of the law'. The curriculum was to include mathematics, the foreign exchanges, double-entry accounting and languages.[8] Professor Redlich has concluded that the college or institution may briefly have existed (near Hempsted, Hertfordshire) but soon failed. How much of the credit is due to Postelthwayt and how much to Royston remains obscure.

Postelthwayt's preliminary *Dissertation* of 1749, announcing his forthcoming *Dictionary*, contained his most distinguished piece of plagiarism. As Professor Hayek first observed, this pamphlet included considerable borrowings, of some 6000 words, from the English version of Cantillon's *Essay on the Nature of Commerce in General*, which was not to be published for another six years, and then in French, '*traduit de l'Anglais*'. In the *Universal Dictionary* itself, 'Postelthwayt embodies almost the whole substance of the *Essai*' (see Cantillon, ed. Higgs, 1931, 384), especially in the articles on the foreign exchange, balance of trade, banking, barter, cash, coins, interest, labour, money and several others. Though Postelthwayt frequently cited, with acknowledgements, John Locke, and mentioned by name the works of Petty, Child, Law, King, Hume and others, no inverted commas, or any other kind of indication, were provided of his borrowings from Cantillon. But this major act of plagiarism will always guarantee to Postelthwayt an intriguing place in the history of economic thought as the first publisher, possibly in its original language, of one of the greatest of all economic writings.[9]

Among Postlethwayt's other works was *Great Britain's True System* (1757) which was mainly concerned with the country's policy problems in the Seven Years' War with France. In his introduction, Postelthwayt returned to the theme of the raising of the level of commercial knowledge in Britain by the founding of a business school, or 'mercantile college', together with the encouragement of the study of commerce in institutions of learning – 'even at the University of Cambridge'. But Postelthwayt was primarily concerned with the threatening problems of mounting public debt, high interest rates, the prospect of tax increases, and with 'the injurious and fatal consequences' which he predicted would follow. For he feared that retrenchment to reduce debt was much more difficult for governments even than for private individuals, 'because it is always in a forced situation with regard to its foreign safety' (77) – a point which has remained of some relevance more than 200 years later.

VII

Joseph Harris (1702–64) was born in Breconshire, and is said to have started life as a blacksmith, and also to have worked at the Mint. He was another of those who contributed to the consolidation, rather than the advance of the subject in England, in his *Essay upon Money and Coins* (two vols, 1757–8). Much of the work was devoted to monetary issues, but it started with a treatment, in the first chapter, of basic general questions of wealth and exchange and clearly owed much to Cantillon. For Harris followed the Petty–Cantillon approach to wealth and value, as being based on land and labour, mainly the latter, without, however, tackling the difficulties involved in such an approach. He started with the debatable statement that: 'Things in general are valued, not according to their real uses in supplying the necessities of men; but rather in proportion to the land, labour and skill that are requisite to produce them' (5). Water and diamonds were then introduced as illustrations, and it was remarked that diamonds, though having 'little use', 'being very scarce, have upon that account a great value' (5). Harris then continued: 'A quicker or slower demand for a particular commodity, will frequently raise or lower its price, with no alteration in its intrinsic values or prime cost' (5).

It is not too clear just how the explanation of value in terms of scarcity, and of price changes in terms of demand and supply, fitted together with the land-and-labour theory of value. There seemed to be some indebtedness to Cantillon's concept of 'intrinsic' value, as well as some anticipation of Adam Smith's treatment in *The Wealth of Nations*. Harris went on to reaffirm that, 'the price of labour' – not scarcity – was 'the chief standard that regulates the values of all things' (8) – though differences in the skills and rewards of labour were emphasized. On the question of what Petty called 'the par' between land and labour, Harris estimated that a labourer ought to earn at least twice his 'ordinary' food and clothing (9). Hence, the conclusion was reached that 'the quantity of land that goes to maintain a labourer, becomes his hire; and this hire again becomes the value of the land' (10).

However, Harris usefully distinguished the labour cost of goods from the earnings of the labour employed, arguing that it was England's low labour costs that were lifting her export trade. Harris also emphasized the importance of the division of labour: 'The advantages accruing to mankind from their betaking themselves severally to different occupations, are very great and obvious . . . each becoming expert and skilful in his own particular art' (17). On foreign trade, however, Harris remained mercantilistically inclined, warning that: 'Every nation should have a watchful eye over its foreign commerce; for it might so happen that a trade which enriches the merchant, might impoverish the public' (23).

As regards luxury and sumptuary laws, Harris was cautious and balanced. If luxury resulted in too many 'costly trifles from abroad', it should be curbed. On the other hand: 'So far as it encourages the arts, whets the inventions of men, and finds employments for more of our own people, its influence is benign' (30).

The rest of Harris's two volumes were devoted to his main topic, money and coin, most of the treatment being historical and comparative. When pointing out the awkwardness of barter and the advantages of money, he quoted from John Law's 'ingenious piece', though finding it 'not free from grievous mistakes'. Harris particularly emphasized the vital importance of not merely a stable, but an inviolable, standard, commending Locke's stance in the great controversy of the 1690s – though also finding Locke's tracts 'very deficient and imperfect' (II, viii). At one point Harris laid it down: 'The established standard of money should not be violated or altered, under any pretence whatsoever' (II, 27). On grounds of what he held to be its greater stability, he favoured a silver standard rather than gold.

Harris described the effects of inflows and outflows of money in terms somewhat similar to those of Cantillon: there were self-adjusting processes at work, but they might well not be rapid, effective and painless. Inflows of money enrich some at the expense of others, and such processes may for a time cause distress, especially outflows which may bring stagnant trade, while 'many hands will be unemployed': 'These distresses will continue till by an abatement of taxes, lowering of rents, of wages, of stipends etc., a due equilibrium among the different ranks of people is restored' (II, 85).

According to Harris, the system did not adjust easily to fluctuations in the money supply: 'It is manifest that a sudden fluctuation of money, would be pernicious whilst it lasted, *and for some time afterwards*; and that whether the tide be flowing in or going out' (II, 86, italics added). If (according to the famous supposition of David Hume) the stock of cash circulating in England were suddenly halved, 'this would strike a great consternation in all, and be a matter of real calamity to many; as the price of things would not at once abate, in proportion to this great love of money. But those distresses would not last long' (II, 90).

Thus, even though Harris's account of the effects of expansions and contractions of the money supply hardly represented any advance on that of Cantillon, written, perhaps, a quarter of a century before, he did place rather more emphasis on the intervening process of disequilibrium and on the distress it brought.

VIII

It may be clear, by now, that when the title of this chapter refers to 'the English contribution', it is signifying not the comparatively very small contribution from English-born writers, but the non-Scottish contribution *in the English language*, irrespective of the birth place of the author. Of the five writers discussed in this chapter, two were born in Wales and one in America. We have already discussed (chapter 8, II) Benjamin Franklin's remarkable early pamphlet on paper money. All through his long life he kept up his stream of pamphlets, leaflets, articles and letters on economic subjects, based on his acute observation and cosmopolitan experience in America, England, Scotland and France.[10] He also maintained close contacts with economists and philosophers in these countries.

Franklin's second work of major importance on an economic subject was his *Observations Concerning the Increase of Mankind and the Peopling of Countries* (1751), in which he emphasized the tendency for population to increase when subsistence was available, but with none of the menace proclaimed nearly half a century later in Malthus' first essay. Franklin, of course, was writing on the edge of a vast undeveloped continent, while Malthus was concerned with a favourably endowed, but comparatively small island. Franklin hardly envisaged the possibility of population decline, when he wrote: 'People increase in proportion to the number of marriages, and that is greater in proportion to the ease and convenience of supporting a family. When families can easily be supported, more persons marry, and earlier in life' (1844, vol. II, 312).

He did maintain, however, that Europe was fully settled, but in America, with land plentiful, and where 'labour will never be cheap', a labouring man could soon save enough to buy a new plot on which he could subsist with a family. Franklin was the first to put forward the estimate that, in America, population would double in twenty-five years – a formula later adopted by Malthus, as the potential rate of increase under favourable conditions. Franklin estimated that of the British population of America of over one million, only 80,000 had crossed the Atlantic.

In 1767–8, when in England, Franklin turned his attention to the question of the treatment of the poor, in *On the Price of Corn and the Management of the Poor* (1766), and *On the Labouring Poor* (1768). His approach was one of austere realism: 'I observed in different countries, that the more public provisions were made for the poor, the less they provided for themselves, and of course became poorer' (II, 358). In fact, according to Franklin, more was given in relief to the poor in England than in any other country, and the results were to be deplored: 'I fear the giving mankind a dependence on any thing for support, in age or sickness, besides industry and frugality during youth and health, tends to flatter our natural indolence, to encourage idleness and prodigality, and thereby to promote and increase poverty, the very evil it was intended to cure, thus multiplying beggars instead of diminishing them' (368).

On wages, however, Franklin, though generally holding that they depended on supply and demand (655), expressed contrasting views. In the *Principles of Trade* – 1774, a joint work with G. Whatley – he maintained a view, common in the eighteenth century, about high real wages: 'The common people do not work for pleasure generally, but from necessity. Cheapness of provisions makes them more idle; less work is then done'

(393). But later, in a pamphlet of the late 1770s – *Reflections on the Augmentation of Wages which will be Occasioned by the American Revolution* – he condemned as 'cruel' and 'ill-informed' the doctrine that 'the people should be poor for the supposed interests of commerce' (436), and he deplored low wages in Europe, distinguishing between low labour costs and low wages.

In the late 1760s Franklin was twice in Paris, where he met leading physiocrats. To some extent he was a natural romantic physiocrat, in holding that agriculture was 'the noblest of employments', and 'the only honest way to acquire wealth' (375–6). But in his *Positions to be Examined concerning National Wealth* (1769) he showed the influence of the school's doctrines in maintaining that all food and necessities came from the land, including those consumed in producing conveniences rather than necessities, and also what was consumed by those working on manufactures, who lived on subsistence advanced by their employers. Manufactures were only 'another shape into which so much provisions and subsistence are turned' (374). Indeed, the production of manufactures was advantageous only because the products were more easily transportable to foreign markets (375–6). Regarding luxuries, however, Franklin was quite tolerant, arguing that they were only damaging if produced, or traded, at the cost of necessities.

In the *Principles of Trade* Franklin gave vent to his vigorous liberal individualism. There was 'no greater enemy to trade than constraint' (386). Rather puzzlingly, he supported bounties on exports of corn, but held that free trade was the best guarantee against shortages, opposing all prohibitions on exports and imports.[11] Governments did not have the foresight to regulate economic actions, which must be left to the free play of markets: 'Plenty and scarcity must govern the course of exchange' (399), and '*pas trop gouverner*', were Franklin's watchwords:

> Perhaps, in general, it would be better if government meddled no farther with trade, than to protect it, and let it take its course. Most of the statutes, or acts, edicts, *arrêts* . . . of parliament, princes, and states, for regulating, directing, or restraining trade, have, we think, been either political blunders, or jobs obtained by artful men for private advantage, under pretence of public good.
>
> (401)

The sole duties for government were to provide protection and security.

Franklin pursued an extraordinarily wide-ranging correspondence with eminent philosophers, economists and writers of his day, including, incidentally, the other major figure discussed in this chapter, Josiah Tucker, Dean of Gloucester, the dates of whose life, covering almost the entire span of the eighteenth century, approximated so closely to Franklin's own. Unfortunately, the exchange, though defensive and polite on Franklin's part, was rather aggressive on that of the Dean.[12] Entirely different in tone were the letters to and from David Hume, in correspondence with whom Franklin praised warmly his essay 'On The Jealousy of Trade'; while Hume wrote to Franklin that he was 'the first philosopher and indeed the first great man of letters for whom we are beholden' to America (10 May 1762). In Turgot's celebrated epigram, which hailed Franklin for 'seizing lightening from the sky and the sceptre from tyrants' (*eripuit coelo fulmen, sceptumque tyrannis*) there was hardly room to mention his contributions to political economy. Just as this still-emerging subject had only a minor part – but, surely, a highly important one – in the great movement of intellectual enlightenment, so, among the wide-ranging interests and achievements of one of its greatest and most typical figures, the place of political economy was not a major one. Nevertheless, Franklin's numerous occasional contributions, spread over more than forty years, on paper money, labour and value, population, wages, poor relief, and agriculture, were, in outline, representative of some of the most important and fundamental ideas of his time, and, in one or two cases, anticipated those of the English classical period.

14
Demography and Cameralism in Germany and Austria

I

Johann Peter Süssmilch (1708–67), a Prussian army chaplain, was responsible for one of the greatest of pioneer contributions to demography in his work *Die Göttliche Ordnung*, first published in 1742. The full title was *The Divine Order in the Changes in the Human Race, through Birth, Death and Procreation of the Same*. Süssmilch claimed that a divine, natural order, with regard to human population, could be discovered, not by the light of *a priori* reasoning, but by collecting together a sufficiently large quantity of data, which would reveal regularities and laws. He began by announcing 'that in births, increase, procreation, life, deaths and in the causes of death, a general, great, complete and beautiful order reigns' (1775, 49).[1]

Süssmilch started from a law of large numbers:

> The order arises out of the similarity and uniformity of different things which are to be found together, or to follow one another. When there is no similarity in the position or sequence to be discerned, then disorder reigns. But it will be shown here that, of a certain number of people, so many die in one year as in another; that the same number die of the children, youths, grown-ups, and old people at one time as at another; that the common, perpetual diseases have the same effects at most times, and that the two sexes are reproduced in a constant proportion, etc.: so it must be concluded that in all these things not only is there an order, but an altogether great, beautiful and complete order.
>
> (50)

Large quantities of material must, however, be collected if this order was to be discerned: 'In small societies and villages it is not easy to perceive anything orderly. In one year 2 or 3 die, in another 6, and then 12 or more. Who can think then in terms of regularities or order?' (56).

Süssmilch then observed that church registers were of the greatest assistance in discerning regularities. But large numbers must be studied: 'A quantity of individual cases must be collected over many years, to bring together the material for whole provinces, in order to bring to light the hidden regularities. Only then can one discern the conformity of these regularities with order' (64).

In the original development of demography, Anglo-German co-operation was of vital importance. We have seen (chapter 4) how Halley had based his pioneering work on statistics from Breslau. Half a century later Süssmilch was much indebted to the English originators of population statistics of the seventeenth century, and also to the Rev. William Derham FRS regarding the beneficent regularities of the Divine Order. Süssmilch observed that 'a Columbus' had been needed to discover the divine truths, and that he had been forthcoming in John Graunt. He also mentioned Petty and King.

Süssmilch went on to measure fertility by comparing the number of children christened with the number of married people. Like his cameralist and mercantilist contemporaries, he considered that the objective of policy should be a large population, with cheap food and a growing economy; and he trusted in the Biblical message to 'be fruitful and multiply' – in sharp contrast, of course, with the austere doctrine of his fellow-clergyman Malthus, fifty years later. Süssmilch was opposed to luxury and believed that urbanization would reduce numbers. He predicted that population would double every century, and, highly speculatively, that world population capacity would prove to be 14,000 million. His statistics were used by German insurance companies well into the nineteenth century.

II

The cameralist tradition in Germany and Austria persisted right through our period and continued to leave its mark through the nineteenth century. The most important representative of this tradition in the eighteenth century was Johann Heinrich Gottlob von Justi (1717–71), who resembled, in several respects, his major seventeenth-century predecessor, Johann Joachim Becher. Justi, also, was something of an itinerant, polymath adventurer, more of a writer and journalist, and less of a natural scientist, than Becher, though likewise possessing an almost universal range of interests. Like Becher, Hörnigk and Schröder, though not born an Austrian, Justi spent some of his most important years in Vienna, where he taught at the Theresianum. He was also a journalist in Göttingen (1754–7), and, after a year in Denmark, entered the service of Frederick the Great as director of the mining industry in Berlin. Of his numerous voluminous writings, his *Staatswirtschaft* (1755) and his *System des Finanzwesens* (1766) were the most important. Also like Becher, he was a somewhat tempestuous character and towards the end of his life spent some time in prison for debts and financial misdemeanours.[2]

Justi was not an original writer, but a lucid systematizer and exponent of cameralist principles. He drew freely on his German predecessors and also on French writers, including, notably, Montesquieu. He shared the political principles of most cameralists; that is, he stood for a considerable measure of paternalism, but combined this with more liberal ideas. He maintained that the interests of ruler and subjects were always identical, but also insisted that 'the supreme authority can be established only by the free consent of all individual members of society' (Monroe, 1924, 383).[3] Justi shared, also, the broad economic priorities of Becher with regard to population and consumption: 'The more people, the more consumption; the more goods and products, the more duties and other contributions to the state' (1766, 37).

Money, or its circulation, must be increased by every means: 'A state from which more money flows out than comes in must naturally, bit by bit, become poorer' (37).

On the other hand, for Justi, money was not wealth, but only a measure of value for facilitating people's commercial activities. His ideas regarding tariff policies were mostly on the usual mercantilist lines. There should be no taxes on raw materials, none of which should be exported. Inessential imports should be severely taxed; essentials, and goods in transit, should be let off lightly (163–72).

Justi was probably at his best on public finance. He justified progressive, rather than mathematically proportional taxation, in volume IV of his *System des Finanzwesens*; and he was an opponent of luxury, especially with regard to the expenditure of monarchs and rulers, who were enjoined 'to make nothing but necessary expenditures for the support of the state'. Government expenses 'should not be increased by merely imagining wants' (Monroe, 1924, 381).

Justi had some notion of the public-goods concept, though his examples may not have been entirely apposite:

> There are always things which are not suitable for private property, either because their use must remain common to all citizens, and no one can be excluded from them, which is an essential characteristic of property, or because their extent is too great to enable them to be in the exclusive use and custody of an individual. In this class are rivers, lakes and seas, highways, great forests, and the metals under the earth whose lodes and veins extend too far to enable them to be included in the division of property on the surface, and which require to be worked as a unit; which would be difficult to manage without much contention among the neighbours owning the surface. All such things, therefore, are best left as a direct and special property of the state.
>
> (383–4)

Justi maintained that it would have been highly advantageous if governments had raised what was necessary for their expenditures simply from charges levied for such public goods and properties, and 'had never opened up the . . . source of taxes and contributions' (385). He saw ever-increasing taxation as an appalling danger, to which he ascribed the decline and fall of the Roman Empire. He launched, in fact, a remarkable tirade against management by government officials, and the high taxation that went with it. 'Nothing', he maintained, was 'so subject to abuse, and can so weaken the state . . . it is also human nature to abuse it.' Justi continued:

> Men are seldom prudent managers of their own property . . . How can we feel assured, therefore, that they will be good and prudent managers of property not their own, namely, the property of the state? How can we expect that they will restrain their natural tendencies to extravagance or avarice when managing the property of a stranger, when they never hold these tendencies within bounds in the case of their own property . . . ? Once taxes have been resorted to, they have not the slightest compunction about abusing them. It costs them nothing, they can simply take it out of some other man's property; and one would have to have no knowledge of men whatever, not to admit that when a man only has to take what he needs out of the property of others, his needs will always soon multiply enormously. Men are very ingenious in thinking up new needs, when they have such an easy prospect of obtaining what they want. The natural result of once resorting to contributions is therefore bound to be that these taxes are steadily increased, and finally become an intolerable burden to the subjects, resulting in the ruin of both the subjects and the state itself.
>
> (384–5)

So much of what was raised by princes in taxation was wasted, in one way or another: 'The inclination towards splendour wastes the property of the subjects; avarice gathers it into large treasures, which is just as bad for the subjects, and in some ways even worse. Ambition for honour and fame dissipates it in unnecessary wars; and great benevolence on the part of the sovereign exposes it to the plundering of favourites' (385).

Justi held that what then seemed to be the widely prevailing level for taxation of 25 per cent of incomes was seriously excessive (388). He laid down six principles of taxation, the *first* of which was that taxes must never be so high as to deprive those who paid them of necessities, or encroach upon their savings.

Justi's *second* principle was 'that contributions must be levied upon the subjects with complete equality and just proportions' (390). He interpreted this principle as requiring progression, for what he called 'just proportions' were neither equal sums, nor equal proportions, but greater proportions on higher incomes (391).[4] He denounced great inequalities in the distribution of property, but regarded it as quite impossible to bring about equality:

> Even if a state wished to undertake a new and completely equal distribution of immovable wealth among all the citizens and inhabitants, this complete equality would not last long under a money régime, and where everyone is free to dispose of his property. Since families neither have the same diligence and skill, nor make the same expenditures, there would always be families who accumulated money, and others in need who would have to sell their property.
>
> (395)

Justi, like Henry Lloyd, expressed profound misgivings about the monetary economy as promoting inequality and injustice. His attitude may be contrasted with that of Mandeville and Tucker in England, who had hailed the development of the monetary economy as a great, benevolent, liberating force, promoting the freedom of individuals. Justi seemed to hold rather to the idea of money as the root of all evil, and referred to 'the plague of money' (395–6).

A further, *third*, principle of taxation laid down by Justi was that taxes must not conflict with civil liberties. Holding that 'the general welfare of the state and of the subjects is the great purpose of all civil societies', Justi maintained that the civil liberty of subjects,

> deserves to be given just as great consideration. This freedom is certainly included in the welfare and happiness of the citizens: and without it we cannot imagine them happy. To disregard this liberty is likewise prejudicial to the welfare of the state. A state which impairs this freedom by its tax system has slight chance of developing a flourishing working class ... (396)

Justi's *fourth* principle was that 'taxes should be organised according to the nature of the state and of the form of government'. This precept was apparently directed mainly against the farming out of taxes, as had been practised by the monarchy in France and Holland. Justi held that such arrangements were 'quite unsuitable for aristocracies and democratic republics' (397).

Fifth, taxes must be clear and definite. Everyone must know the reason for a tax and how much they might be required to pay. Likewise the government must be able to estimate, not too uncertainly, how much revenue a tax would bring in.

Finally, and *sixth*, taxes must be easy and convenient to collect and to pay, with the minimum of expense to state and subjects.

Justi's principles of taxation, and his treatment of public finance, with his warnings against high taxation and high government expenditure, together with his reasonable broaching of the case for progression, set high standards in Germany for the treatment of this branch of political economy. His work also showed up some of the main contrasts between the ideas of the German cameralists and those of the more enthusiastic and unqualified supporters of liberal ideas, and of the individualist, monetary economy which was emerging in England and France. At the same time, Justi's very strong opposition to taxation and government expenditure must be borne in mind when it is suggested that German cameralism bequeathed a legacy of excessive state activity.

III

The other leading cameralist of the third quarter of the eighteenth century was Joseph von Sonnenfels, who in 1763 became the first professor of 'Cameral Science' in Vienna. He served as adviser to the Empress Maria Theresa and published his *Grundsätze der Polizei, Handlung und Finanzwissenschaft* in 1763, in which he covered the usual wide range of administrative, political, social and economic subjects embraced in cameralist treatises.[5] The *Grundsätze* remained a – or *the* – leading textbook until the middle of the nineteenth century. On some points his views on policy followed the mercantilist pattern. He advocated a large population as an objective of policy; he favoured the encouragement of exports and restrictions on imports; and he held that it was the duty of government to provide employment. But his policy proposals also showed some liberal tendencies. He supported the freeing of the internal corn trade and of exports of corn, and opposed prohibitions on the export of money as either unnecessary or useless. He opposed monopolies and guilds for restricting employment (II, 160–1).

His chapters on money and its circulation are today perhaps the most interesting (II, chapters IX and X). The effects of inflating or debasing the coinage, and the process by which 'the equilibrium' ('*Gleichgewicht*') between money and goods was restored, were analysed (II, 293). A quantity relationship between the total of exchangeable goods and the total of money was suggested. It was held, however, to be impossible to determine how large a sum was needed for the monetary circulation of a country. This depended on many factors, which included the state of credit, the habits of the people, the extent of the public debt, and even political conditions in the country. Sonnenfels noted that too great an influx of money could be dangerous in raising prices, but did not go on to suggest that any self-adjusting mechanism operated as regards the balance of payments.

The cameralist tradition, with its influence in favour of paternalist, nationalist, and public 'welfare' policies, persisted into, and through, the nineteenth century in Germany, which then was never thoroughly permeated by the liberal and free-market ideas widely prevalent in England and France. In one form, the cameralist ideas can be discerned in the nineteenth century in the doctrines of Friedrich List, and later, in another form, in those of the *Verein für Sozialpolitik*, and even, perhaps, eventually, in the second half of the twentieth century, in the 'social' emphasis of the *Soziale Marktwirtschaft*, after World War II.

15
Italian Illumination: Subjective Utility, Money, and the Mathematical Method

I

As already observed, during the century and a half before our period opened (*c.*1500–1650) probably more outstanding works on political economy came from Italian writers than from those of any other country. Especially illuminating was the Italian treatment of value and money – in particular by Davanzati – which followed, in its fundamentals, the approach of the scholastics and natural-law philosophers. Most notably the writings of St Bernardino of Siena (1380–1444) and St Antoninus of Florence (1389–1459) were influential, (though both of these were heavily indebted to Pier Olivi of Languedoc, *c.*1248–98).[1] The Italian approach, therefore, to problems of value and price, during our period, was from the side of utility, demand and scarcity, and ran closely parallel to the doctrines of the natural-law writers, such as Pufendorf – though the leading Italians formulated their theory of value as an introduction to the subject of money and currency.

Geminiano Montanari (1633–87) followed in this tradition. He was a typical seventeenth-century polymath. Born in Modena, he studied law at Bologna, where he subsequently became Professor of Mathematics, before moving to Padua as Professor of Astronomy and Meteorology. His two works on money were written near the end of his life. These were his *Breve trattato del valore delle monete in tutti gli stati* (written in 1680), and his main work *Della moneta: trattato mercantile* (1683–4). Among previous writers on the subject, Montanari cited Bodin and Davanzati, and followed quite closely the approach of the latter, though he was more of an economic historian, who filled his writings with copious historical information and illustrations.

'*Maravigligosa invenzione!*' exclaimed Montanari on the subject of money, and he actually described the use of money as the most marvellous of all human inventions (1683–4, 40). Money served as a measure of desires, in that the values of all goods which met human desires were, for purposes of exchange, measured in money. The values of goods were raised by scarcity and lowered by abundance, though not by scarcity or abundance in absolute terms, but relative to human needs, desires, and valuations. Water, for example, was usually valueless. The value of a good could only be expressed as relative to that of some other good: ten pounds of gold had the value of 14.75 pounds of silver. These relative values could not be fixed and stable, but were inevitably uncertain and changing (83). As Montanari rhetorically inquired: 'Where is, or what can have, a fixed, certain, and immutable value? I have not found such a thing in the whole world' (84).

Gold and silver were not stable in value: 'An abundance of gold caused prices to rise in Rome after the Macedonian war, and the same factor has raised prices throughout Europe after the discovery of America' (84). 'How mutable are human desires!', Montanari observed – though they were the basis of value. Any new fashion could raise the value of one good, or reduce that of another. In fact, he hardly distinguished between value and price. He concluded: 'The real price and value of a good consists, according to our theory, of nothing but a parity of valuation with a certain quantity of gold, as estimated by men' (119).

The emphasis on the relativity and subjectivity of values and prices could hardly have been asserted more decisively than it was by Montanari, while his stress on change and uncertainty was also of fundamental significance. It is also important to emphasize the continuity of the tradition, coming down from the scholastic writers, via Davanzati, which was transmitted by Montanari. Langholm writes of 'the value analysis of the Italian monetary theorists', founded on Davanzati's concepts of wants and needs, 'initiating, some would say, modern economics'. Langholm, observing how Montanari, almost a century after Davanzati, based his doctrine on the authority of Aristotle, concludes:

> The success of the value theory which was to be developed in the line extending from Montanari through Galiani to the Italian and French economists of the eighteenth and early nineteenth centuries is in no small part explained by its emphasis on utility as a psychological experience, playing down considerations of the properties in goods which cause men to desire them.
>
> (1979, 144)

II

Ferdinando Galiani (1728–87) was born at Chieti, the son of the Marchese Matteo Galiani, the magistrate of the region.[2] At the age of seven he was sent to Naples to his uncle, Archbishop of Tarento, who later on introduced his amazingly gifted and precocious nephew to such leading Neapolitan intellectual figures as Antonio Genovesi and Giambattista Vico.[3] The young Galiani's education included philosophy and mathematics, but he soon began to include political economy in his wide range of interests when, aged fifteen, he translated into Italian Locke's *Some Considerations of the Consequences of the Lowering of Interest and Raising the Value of Money*.

At the age of twenty-two, Galiani published anonymously the first of his two major works on political economy. This was his treatise, *Della moneta* (1751), one of the outstanding works of economic theory of the eighteenth century. In 1759 he was sent to Paris as Secretary of the Neapolitan Embassy, where he stayed for ten years. His friends included many of the leading figures of Parisian intellectual society, most importantly Diderot, Grimm, and Mme d'Épinay. He won great renown as a wit and satirist, at a period when Parisian brilliance was at its most scintillating. Moreover, it was in the 1760s, the decade of Galiani's stay in Paris, that political economy became the great fashionable interest of the day, thanks, mainly, to the challenging, dogmatic crusade of the physiocratic school, led by Quesnay. Policy towards the grain trade, long the most vital branch of domestic economic affairs, became more than ever the dominant issue, with the lifting of the ban on exports in 1764. The debate came to a head just before Galiani was brusquely summoned back to Naples (1769). With the aid of his friends, however, he managed to complete his second major work on political economy, his *Dialogues sur le commerce des blés* (1770), a scathing attack on the physiocrats and their policies, and surely one of the most brilliant and profound policy tracts ever written.

In the last phase of his life, back in Naples (1769–87), Galiani received many honours, was appointed to many offices, and wrote on many subjects, including the poetry of Horace, the Neapolitan dialect, and the public law of neutrality and belligerency. But he always longed for Paris, although intellectually he was a follower of the Neapolitan master Vico, and was fundamentally opposed to many of the philosophical and political ideas that dominated the French enlightenment.

Galiani's *Della moneta* covered a great deal more than the subject of money. In the Italian manner of Davanzati and Montanari, he approached the subject of money by way of the fundamentals of value theory. He confidently criticized his predecessors, though, probably, considerably indebted to some of them, specially Montanari, whom he failed to mention. But Aristotle, the Salamancan scholastic Covarruvias, as well as Davanzati, Locke and Melon are all cited, and Petty is sharply attacked.

The exuberant twenty-two-year-old, with somewhat optimistic intellectual pretensions (which contrasted, in some respects, with the conservative scepticism which was to dominate his *Dialogues*, twenty years later) proclaimed:

> . . . I shall make every effort, first of all to demonstrate what I have long believed, that not only the metals of which money is made, but everything else in the world, without exception, has its natural value, derived from definite, general, and constant principles; that neither caprice, nor law, nor the prince, nor anything else, can violate these principles and their effects.
> (1924, 282; and 1751[1963], 38)[4]

Galiani then proceeded to set out the foundations of his value theory, which, as a presentation of utility and scarcity analysis, was hardly surpassed until after 1870 – and perhaps not in a major, significant respect even then). In particular, he emphasized the subjective element more cogently than any writer, except Condillac, before the twentieth century:

> Esteem, or value, is an idea of proportion between the possession of one thing and that of another in the mind of a man ...
> From what I have said, it is evident that since the dispositions of human minds are varied, and needs are varied, the value of things varies ...
> Value, then, is a ratio: and this is compounded of the two ratios, expressed by the names Utility and Scarcity. It is evident that air and water, which are elements very useful for human life, have no value, because they lack scarcity; and, on the other hand, a bag of sand from Japan would be a rare thing, but assuming that it had no special utility, it would have no value ... By utility I mean a thing's capacity to bring happiness.
>
> (283–4; 39)

Human desires were unlimited: 'For man is so constituted that he has scarcely satisfied one desire, when another shows itself, which is always as powerful a stimulus as the first; and so he is kept perpetually active, and never manages to satisfy himself entirely' (285; 40). In particular, there was an unlimited desire for superiority and distinction, than which no desire 'has more power to move man' (285; 41).

Galiani explained the logic of the utility-and-scarcity theory with a masterly example for which he was indebted to Davanzati, whom, however, he proceeded, rather unfairly, to criticize (see chapter 2):

> But most men, including Bernardo Davanzati, reason thus: A natural calf is nobler than a golden calf, but how much less its value is. I answer that if a natural calf were as rare as one of gold, its price would be as much more than that of the golden calf as the utility and need of the one exceeds that of the other. These people imagine that value depends on a single factor, rather than on many which unite to form a compound ratio. Others, I believe, say that a pound of bread is more useful than a pound of gold. I answer that this is a shameful fallacy, due to not knowing that 'more useful' and 'less useful' are relative terms, which are measured according to the varying condition of individuals.
>
> (288; 43)

Though without explicitly introducing such terms as 'diminishing' and 'marginal' utility – Bernoulli had not done that either – Galiani was here recognizing the significance of what was much later to be described in that way:

> ... If we are speaking of one who lacks bread and gold, the bread is certainly more useful; for no one will be found who would leave the bread and die of hunger, taking gold instead. People who mine gold do not forget to eat and to sleep. But to a man who is satisfied, is anything more useless than bread? Hence it is well if he then satisfies other passions.
>
> (288; 43–4)

Galiani then went on to describe labour as 'the sole *source* of value', subject, of course, to scarcity, utility, and demand. Of the various dimensions of labour, such as time, the most significant was that of the widely differing talents of human beings. So the fundamental unity of his value theory – as later that of the neoclassicals – was maintained by applying the same principles to the valuation of human labour, talents and services, as had been applied to 'inanimate things', or goods: 'I believe that the value of human talents is determined in the very same way as that of inanimate things, and that it is regulated by the same principles of scarcity and utility combined. Men are born endowed by Providence with aptitudes for different trades, but in different degrees of scarcity' (292; 49).

Galiani then observed, perhaps with some self-satisfaction, and not quite realistically, that the values of talents were not determined by utility alone:

> It is not utility alone, therefore, which governs prices: for God causes the men who carry on the trades of greatest utility to be born in large numbers, and so their value cannot be great, these being, so to speak, the bread and wine of men; but scholars and philosophers, who may be called the gems among talents, deservedly bear a very high price.
>
> (292; 49)

Galiani emphasized the element of chance and fortune in the rewards earned by different individuals and different services. Regarding the scarcity of different services this

> ... is not to be reckoned according to the proportion in which talents are produced, but according to the numbers that reach maturity; hence the greater the difficulty of developing a talent to a high degree worthy of it, the greater is its price... Nature acts in this as in the seeds of plants, where, as if foreseeing the great losses, she produces and drops a good many more upon the ground then there come plants eventually; hence a plant is worth more than a seed.
>
> (292; 50)

Just as Galiani assembled the main elements of marginal-utility analysis, though without precise modern terminology or mathematics, so he brought together the main principles of marginal productivity analysis: 'It will be found that everything is valued by a standard. It will be realized that the only way riches come to a person is in payment for the just value of his work; although he can give these riches to someone who does not deserve to acquire them' (293; 50).

Perhaps somewhat over-generously, in moral terms, Galiani claimed that through inheritance, or gifts, 'if we trace back the riches someone possesses undeservedly, it will always be found that they were originally acquired through merit from the whole body of men' (293; 50).

Galiani went on to note the importance of fashion in determining prices, which he found somewhat difficult to define:

> After lengthy consideration, I have not been able to devise any definition of this work except the following: an affection of the brain, peculiar to the European nations, as a result of which many things become of small value,

> simply because they are not new. This is a disease of the mind which has control over not a few things; and if we wish to find something reasonable about it, we must say that this diversity of taste is due to a large extent to imitating the customs of the more dominant nations.
>
> (294–5; 51–2)

He went on to relate 'consumption', or demand, to value and price: 'for it is to be noted as a fact that, just as scarcity and value depend on consumption, so consumption varies in conformity with value' (296; 53).

Though he called it 'indeterminate', Galiani was describing interdependence, when he continued:

> ... whatever is cheaper is more readily taken for consumption; and thus price, which arises from scarcity, regulates consumption.
>
> On the other hand, prices are regulated by consumption: for if fifty thousand casks of wine, for example, are consumed in a country, and the same amount is produced, the unexpected arrival of an army in that country will raise the price of wine, because more is drunk.
>
> (296; 53)

Incidentally, Galiani's example of how the presence of an army raised the price of food and drink followed Petty (chapter 3). He then introduced the income factor: 'just as men possess unequal wealth, so the purchase of certain commodities corresponds to a certain degree of wealth. If these become cheaper, men of less wealth buy them; if they become dearer, those who formerly used them begin to do without them' (297; 54).

In a passage influenced, presumably, by Nicole, Domat, or perhaps Mandeville, Galiani explained how Providence enabled sinful, selfish men to enjoy the benefits of an orderly and efficient economy by means of a pricing system. The 'interrelationship' of economic quantities

> ... produces the great and very useful effect of the equilibrium of the whole. And this equilibrium fits in wonderfully with the just abundance of the conveniences of life and earthly happiness, although it results, not from human prudence or virtue, but from the base incentive of sordid gain: Providence out of infinite love for men having so ordered the relations of things that even our base passions, as if in spite of us, are often arranged for the good of the whole.
>
> (298, 54–5)

It should be noted that Galiani claimed only that this kind of beneficent harmony of interests came about 'often' – *not always*. He continued his analysis of value and price by fixing attention on long-run equilibrium, developing a somewhat pretentious comparison with the laws of gravity, based on the subsequently often-used example of water in a tank:

> ... it is not necessary to consider the first developments in a case, but the permanent and fixed conditions, and in this there is always order and equality; just as water in a vessel, if disturbed, returns to the due level after a confused and irregular fluctuation. Second, that no accident can occur in nature which will carry things to infinite extremity; but a certain moral

> gravity, existing in everything, always draws them back from the straight line of infinity ... Nothing corresponds more closely to the laws of commerce. What gravity is in physics, the desire for gain or for happiness is in man; and, this being assumed, all the physical laws of bodies can be verified perfectly in the morality of our life ...
>
> (298–9; 55–6)

Ten years later, however, as we shall see, when the great issue of the day in Paris was whether market mechanisms should be left free to settle the price of grain, Galiani seemed to have lost some of his youthful, Ricardian enthusiasm for long-run equilibria, and for the operations of 'laws' in the economic world which were validly comparable with the laws of gravity. He later objected that equilibrium was apt to take too long to come about.

III

Galiani began the second book of his *Della moneta* by demonstrating the basic functions of, and need for, money and a pricing system. He proceeded by decreasing abstraction, taking first a small community, like that of a religious order, guided by the socialist principle of 'from each according to his abilities, and to each according to his needs'. Everybody worked, and contributed whatever he produced to the common pool, all drawing from it according to their broadly equal needs and wants (87–9). In a small, dedicated community, dominated by altruism, such a system could survive, without any form of money. But in a larger community of less dedicated individuals, it was most unlikely to work successfully. For the lazy would tend to live off the efforts of the industrious, and there would be insufficient incentives for hard work. A remedy might be sought by giving each member of the community, on his delivering his products to the common pool, a receipt, or certificate, stating how much and what sort of goods he had contributed, which would entitle him to draw from the pool goods to the same value. But, at this point, a set of prices would be necessary to indicate how much of the various goods each individual could draw in return for his own contribution. The prince could also levy a certain percentage of each member's certificates, or receipts, to provide for government employees, who would not be contributing to the common pool.

Galiani claimed that such a set of institutions would be workable, but he then observed – 'as if a veil had fallen from before my eyes' – that what he had just described had very close similarities with the world around him (90). The dangers from public mismanagement and corruption would have to be countered by handing over the public pool, or stocks, to individual store-keepers, with the fixing of prices by a central authority being transferred to markets. The virtues required in public store-keepers and in the prince would then be unnecessary. The introduction of money and a price system would produce an economy where,

> everybody looks after his own business, with store-keepers paying out coin to build up their stocks of goods, and receiving it back again when they sell them. In this way there is no need for virtue or trust in the store-keepers, nor vigilance by the prince to prevent certificates being wasted. Everybody would be careful in spending because he would be disposing of his own money, obtained from the produce of his own effort.
>
> (90)

Galiani concluded:

> I saw, and anyone can now see, that trade and money, its main motive force, have delivered us from a miserable state of nature to a prosperous life together, in which each is concerned, and works, for all. We maintain ourselves in this latter state, not simply by virtue and piety (which are insufficient in relation to entire nations) but by the self-interest and convenience of each individual.
>
> (90)

Like Cantillon, Galiani was a 'realist' regarding money, his prime theme being that it must possess 'real', intrinsic value: 'The precious metals are used for money because they are valuable. They are not valuable because they are used for money' (58–9).

Possessing its own intrinsic value was the first of the qualities necessary for a good serving as money. The other required qualities were uniformity and divisibility, proof against fraudulence and counterfeiting, and durability. (Galiani omitted portability.) He ridiculed, perhaps excessively, the idea of money being based on convention, asking when the various nations who used gold and silver had got together to agree on such an arrangement (67). He described the two main functions of money as serving as a measure of value and as a means of payment. The value of money was determined by the same principles as the value of all other things. Galiani implied, rather than formally stated, a quantity theory, but emphasized that it was 'finally the velocity of circulation, not the quantity of metals, which makes it appear that there is a large or small quantity of money' (60).

He strongly attacked the mercantilist objective of accumulating large stocks of the precious metals, and of imposing prohibitions on their export. Keeping the economy prosperous was the best protection against the loss of money: 'Those who maintain that to avoid the loss of money one must institute good laws, build hospitals, set up a courageous militia and prudent magistrates, and cultivate the earth energetically, are proclaiming the true remedies for the outflow. For wherever there is peace, health, true virtue, and liberty, one cannot fail to have wealth and happiness' (260).

What has been recognized, by Einaudi and others, as one of Galiani's most brilliant chapters is that in which he analyses the effects of an *Alzamento* – i.e. devaluation, depreciation, or debasement – of the currency (vol. III, chapter 3).[5] Such an operation consisted in raising the nominal value of money without increasing its real value, by means of a government decree that the same weight of silver or gold represented more units of money. Galiani's treatment of a depreciation of the currency had a number of points of resemblance with Cantillon's analysis of an increase in the money supply. Galiani defined such an 'alzamento' as 'a profit which the prince, or the state extracts through the slowness with which most of the people recognize the changed relationship between the prices of goods and the monetary unit' (188). It was as though the King of Prussia, wanting, in vain, to have all his soldiers six feet tall, achieved his desire by decreeing a change in the definition of a 'foot' from twelve to eleven inches. But a prince who abused the process of devaluation by resorting to it every month would destroy 'the connection of ideas' between prices and goods – i.e. money illusion – and would thus render the policy ineffective, and be forced to use some other process to achieve his ends (188–90). Such depreciations might be, and sometimes were, harmless, or even relatively beneficial, compared with the alternatives: 'Human actions are mostly a mixture of good and bad in their effects, and one does not know, subtracting the lesser from the greater, how the balance comes out and by how much' (192). Bread was useful, but not an excessive quantity of it; water was necessary, but fatal to a man afflicted with dropsy. Utility depended on circumstances. So with the policy of devaluation (192).

The real effect of devaluation was to relieve debtors: 'When there is a devaluation the prices of goods do not change immediately, adapting to the new value of money, but change slowly, for human nature tends to adapt to events bit by bit. The whole effect of devaluation resides in this delay' (197). The first to suffer harmful effects were those employed by the prince who were paid at the former rates (197). Galiani, however, concluded: 'Given that it is only effected in cases of extreme gravity, it is a salutary remedy, because the damage only results later' (198).

Devaluation had the effect of a tax, but was not necessarily to be condemned for that reason. In some sudden crisis of war or disaster it might be justified; though it was added that the effects of such a manoeuvre should not be explained publicly, or the army and government employees would be discontented (208). But it was not inevitably tyrannical or unjust. It all depended on circumstances: 'A doctor using the therapeutic properties of medicines does not start from the hypothesis that they are being applied to the healthy' (202).

Galiani then introduced the possible expansive effects of an increase in the money supply. When a river is not navigable because there is too little water, then an increase in the water supply can increase navigation and commerce. Einaudi has doubted whether anyone, apart from Galiani, had, until much more recently, emphasized the stimulating effects of a gradual, long-run fall in the value of money – though certainly countless writers in the seventeenth and eighteenth centuries had advocated a regularly increasing money supply.

Galiani, in conclusion, enquired as to who would and should bear the main burden of such a measure: 'A tax which hit the strongest, and not everyone equally, is just.' It might be that it was the rich and idle who would bear most of the burden of devaluation: 'Those who receive rent are not only well off but are idle and slothful, and should pay more, because without adding to the wealth of the state they consume not only their own but also foreign goods' (211; see Cesarano, 1976, 396).

The really poor, who were the most numerous of those affected, were the industrious farmer, the artisan, the sailor and the merchant. It was these who deserved sympathy, and, because they were engaged in dealing and hiring, they gained from devaluation.

IV

Galiani's theory of interest came in volume V. He began by observing that it was the complaints of borrowers that had dominated down the ages, while little had been heard from the side of the lenders: 'those who have so much to say about the sin of usury have not ordinarily been endowed by Providence with the means for committing it; while those who might do so have not been placed, through defects in their education, in a position to understand the controversy' (1924, 301; and 1751[1963], 289).

He proceeded to link the question of interest with the subject of probability and chance, claiming that 'the light of the true sciences finally revealed that nothing is less fortuitous than chance, that its vicissitudes have a constant order and a regular cause, and that a proportion can be found between the certain present and the uncertain future' (301; 290). Galiani seemed to mention the work of Daniel Bernoulli. Though he did not specify to which particular member of that extraordinary family he was referring, this was possibly, or probably, the only reference, by an economist to Bernoulli's remarkable work for about a century and a half: 'Discussion of justice was heard for the first time in connection with games of pure chance; and the art of divination, so much despised, became the daughter of pure mathematics and truth in the hands of Bernoulli. From games it went to more serious things' (301; 290).

He went on to refer to insurance and then explained:

> It was then realised that the intrinsic value was always variable according to the degree of probability which existed that one could or could not count on enjoying a certain thing; and it was recognised that a hundred ducats, a long way from a man's hand, when there are ninety chances of not losing them and ten of losing them, become ninety *present* ducats, and are to be valued at ninety in any contract, whether of games or exchange, if there is a probability of ninety that they will not be lost, and of ten that they *will* be lost.
>
> (302; 290)
>
> ... Hence arose exchange and interest which are brothers. One is the equalising of present money and money distant in *space*, made by an apparent premium which is sometimes added to the present money, and sometimes to the distant money, to make the intrinsic value of the two equal, one being diminished by the less convenience of greater risk. *Interest* is the same thing as between present money and money that is distant in *time*, time having the same effect as space; and the basis of one contract, as of the other, is the equality of the true intrinsic value. This is so true that sometimes present money exchanges for less than distant money, which is known as

> *exchange below par*. The bills of exchange which represent money, and which are really nothing but future money, often have more value than cash, the excess being known as *agio*.
>
> (302; 290–1)

Galiani then maintained that the condemnation of usury arose from false ideas and the wrong use of words:

> It was an error to call a thing *gain*, and a return for *money*, when it is the restitution of what is missing, included in order to arrive at equality ...
>
> Where there is equality there is no gain, or profit; and where the intrinsic price is reduced and lessened by risk and inconvenience, the restoration of it cannot be called a profit.
>
> (302–3; 291)

Galiani agreed with the theological definition of to lend as 'to hand over something with an agreement to have the equivalent back and no more'. But he insisted, returning to his subjective value theory, that:

> ... we need a clearer idea of the equivalent ... Value is the proportion which things bear to our needs. Those things are equal which afford equal satisfaction to the one with respect to whom they are said to be equivalent. Anyone who seeks equality in some other way, following other principles, and expecting to find it in weight or similarity of appearance, will show little understanding of the facts of life ... Finally, it is certain that nothing has a price among men except pleasure, and that only satisfactions are purchased; and just as one cannot obtain pleasure without inconvenience and vexation on the part of somebody else, nothing is paid for but the loss and deprivation of pleasure brought upon another. Keeping someone in anxiety – [or with 'palpitations of the heart'] – is pain: hence it must be paid for. What is called *the product of money*, when it is legitimate, is simply the price of anxiety: and whoever thinks it is something different is mistaken.
>
> (304; 292)

Thus Galiani left out from his explanation any element of the productivity of investment. He continued:

> In any country where restitution of the equivalent was always effected by returning an equal weight of metal, without other consideration, it is certain that loans would be difficult to obtain and infrequent. Now if, to encourage men to lend, a company of merchants should undertake to insure lenders, for a certain percentage paid by the borrower, would such an insurance be lawful or not? After answering this, there is another question. If the lender, not desiring outside security, should himself collect the price of insurance, would the contract change its nature and become sinful?
>
> (305–6; 293–4)

Certainly the state should seek to prevent extortionate rates of interest being inflicted on poor borrowers. But this was not to be achieved by legal regulation of the interest rates:

> ... it will be ridiculous and foolish for statesmen to rely entirely upon piety. Morality guides men after having improved them and made them virtuous; politics has to deal with them as still foul and wrapped in their ordinary

> passions. Therefore, the prince should make such arrangements that even the wicked usurer, should he desire it, will be unable to lend at high usury . . .
>
> (306; 294)

Galiani, rather optimistically, suggested that this was no very difficult task:

> To make interest low, . . . it suffices to prevent a monopoly of money and to insure repayment. Hence it has not been merely the abundance of precious metals which has lowered and almost wiped out usury during the last two centuries, but chiefly the excellent government enjoyed in almost all kingdoms. Let law-suits be brief, justice certain, industry and economy widespread among the people, and all rich people will be disposed to lend. Where there is a crowd of offerers, the conditions of offering cannot be hard. Thus the poor will be treated without cruelty.
>
> (306; 294)

Easier said than done perhaps. But Galiani added: 'the best way to lower interest is to make the return on state debts as low as possible' (307; 295). He firmly concluded:

> Finally it appears that the rate of interest cannot be varied at will by law; but this must be done by nature itself . . . And, just as the law is broken in the case of contracts, when it is opposed to nature, so the restoration and safety of a country cannot be expected from an ill-timed law to regulate interest.
>
> (307; 295)

V

Galiani's second book on political economy, published twenty years after his first, was his *Dialogues sur le commerce des blés* (*Dialogues on the Grain Trade*). The *Della moneta* and the *Dialogues* present a considerable contrast, and a few apparent inconsistencies and even contradictions are discernible on some points. But, in important respects, the two books are complementary. The first was primarily an analytical and theoretical treatise, the later book was an essay in what is sometimes called 'applied economics', and was a sparkling, polemical contribution to a current policy issue – though much more than that. The form of the *Dialogues* was a discussion between a French Marquis and an Italian Chevalier. The Marquis – though given many good lines – embodied conventional wisdom, while the Chevalier, may be taken to represent Galiani himself.

As already noted, thanks largely to the dogmatic, challenging, and somewhat pretentious doctrines of the physiocrats, or 'economists', political economy had become, in the 1760s, the great focus of fashionable intellectual interest in Paris. Later in this decade a fundamental and dangerous issue of economic policy came to a head, which involved the most basic general questions of economic theory, as well as of physiocratic doctrine. Influenced by the theoretical doctrines of Dr Quesnay and his enthusiastic disciples, in favour of the utmost economic freedom, the government had, in 1764, abolished at a stroke the longstanding absolute prohibition on the export of corn from France. As it happened, this drastic move was followed by a decade of almost uninterrupted bad harvests, so that the price of the basic foodstuffs soared to very high levels, with considerable public disturbances resulting. For although the export of corn was now virtually unrestricted, and corn was being sold comparatively cheaply from some of the most productive provinces round the periphery of the country, a massive complex of internal barriers remained in place, which seriously hampered, or prevented, the movement of, or trade in, corn within France. Some of those internal duties yielded important revenues, and were so deeply entrenched that they were not removed until after the Revolution. So the highly provocative situation resulted that, though in some parts of the country supplies were adequate, in spite of significant food exports, in other centres there were serious shortages and very high prices.

It was Galiani who launched the first major attack, by an intellectual, on the physiocratically inspired policy of free exports. As he later wrote in a typical outburst, to his closest friend, Mme d'Épinay: 'It is strange that I was the first man of some intelligence who dared to tear the mask from the economists and to show them up for what they are, a fanatical mob whose purpose is sedition' (1881, I, 196).

It appears that earlier Galiani had been on the side of free trade – and he always continued to proclaim himself, as, in general terms, on the side of economic freedom. But, what seemed to him the obstinate dogmatism of the physiocrats, in the face of the disastrous experience of persisting high prices, distress, and disorder, turned him into a bitter opponent. It seems also to have been the case that a visit to England, which he paid in November and December 1767, considerably influenced his views.[6] England was used as an example by the physiocrats of the benefits of a large measure of freedom for the grain trade. But it seems to have been England's growing industrialization which impressed the Neapolitan, during his visit, and may have turned him against the physiocrats' exclusive emphasis on agriculture. According to Philip Koch, Galiani in a dispatch to Naples from London 'was very much impressed, he said, with the youthful vitality of the country and predicted it would progress much further than France economically and politically, although handicapped by geographic and climatic limitations' (1770 [1968], 18).[7]

It was the edict of 1764, freeing exports of corn, and the persistence in maintaining this policy, which Galiani came to see as the cause of the distress and dangers in France. It was too sudden and drastic a measure. The timing and the circumstances had been wrong. The citing by the physiocrats of the English case was totally irrelevant, a crass example of the greatest and most common of all intellectual mistakes, that of trying to use a theory, and an example, which was inapplicable to the case in hand, because insufficient attention had been paid to the particular circumstances of time and place: 'The one fault of men is to guide their reasoning by examples which do not apply to their circumstances' (57).

England was an entirely different kind of country – a nation, incidentally, 'so strange that it drew revenue from Bengal to indulge in the sport of racing at Nue Market' (*sic*, 96). For Holland, too, the unrestricted export of corn might well be the best policy. But this was certainly not the case for France in the 1760s, because freedom of export had suddenly been introduced *while formidable restrictions on the internal trade were still maintained.* The dangers from monopolies were acute, and only government could curb these.

Moreover, the real world was a much more complex and changing place than the economists assumed. To attempt, as they did, to lay down sweeping general policy doctrines, which were applicable at all times and all places, was very dangerous and wrong-headed. Universalist abstractions and oversimplifications could be utterly disastrous when applied to policy. Galiani would not have had much practical use for *Pareto optima*:

> All the problems of political economy may be reduced to doing good to human beings. But there is no good which is not linked with some bad, which often tips the balance ...
>
> Nothing in policy matters can be pushed to the extreme. There is a line or margin up to which the good is greater than the bad: if you cross it the bad outweighs the good.
>
> (220–1)

Above all, sudden, rapid, and drastic changes of policy were always dangerous: *rien tout à coup*: 'It's not enough to know the end to which one wants to direct things; one must know how to guide them there, and this guidance is difficult because too rapid movements must always be avoided ... Nothing sudden. Avoid great shocks; soften changes ... if you do not want to have them reversed' (224–5).

Sudden shifts in the price of corn could be more disastrous than inflation. The law was 'an equilibrium of utilities', as Galiani put it (1881, I, 355). But it was a delicately balanced equilibrium, which, if seriously upset, might be impossible to restore. In fact, he warned against trusting nature too far, for she operated on a much larger, longer-term scale, than that on which human affairs were conducted:

> ... nature [is] something immense, indefinite ... We are insects, atoms, nothing ...
>
> Do not make an alliance with nature. She is too out of proportion. Our task is to combat nature ...
>
> Undoubtedly she brings everything into equilibrium ... but we cannot wait ...
>
> That nature tends to equilibrium is an illuminating truth in the head of a metaphysician ... It is true because one can see the causes and the effects, but one does not take account of the long duration it takes to arrive ...
>
> Nothing is so true as that the price of wheat, if left free, comes to an equilibrium. Nothing is so true as that free commerce in wheat will distribute

> it everywhere where there are money and consumers. Nothing is so true in theory because all men seek profit.
>
> (225–7)

Then Galiani proceeded to put his finger on the vital factors of time and ignorance which had been simplified out of the physiocrat's model – as they were so often to be in economic theorizing in the ensuing two centuries. He continued:

> But take care in practice. Time is necessary to send the letters with the news of a shortage of wheat in a town, and more time is necessary for wheat to arrive there. If this length of time is fifteen days and you only have supplies for a week, the town is without bread for a week, and this insect called man can die in a week ... Thus the theorem works out perfectly, but the practical problem works out very badly
>
> (227)

Galiani's fundamental opposition to the policy of the government, and the economists, was, however, also based on profound political considerations. For him, indeed, the issue was primarily political. To maintain the supply of basic foodstuffs for the people was a first duty of government. Like security and defence, it could be a matter of life and death. The supply of subsistence was a constant, pressing, day-to-day need of the people (for which, in modern terminology, demand was extremely inelastic). The government had abandoned this fundamental duty of securing the people's food supplies, and, much too suddenly, had handed over to them the duty of securing their own supplies in an unrestricted market. Such a fundamental change in the way in which the nation's supplies of subsistence were managed could amount to, or would soon promote, a fundamental change in the nature of the political régime. However steadfastly loyal to the monarchy, Quesnay and his followers might claim, or imagine, themselves to be, their economic policies would undermine its foundations – a verdict echoed more than eighty years later by Tocqueville. Galiani was as well aware as anyone of the corruption and inefficiency to which political processes were so heavily liable. In one of his letters he frankly, even cynically, proclaimed himself a supporter of the *ancien régime*:

> The king plays his game, the parliamentarians their game. The monarchy is based essentially on the inequality of conditions, with low prices of supplies ... Complete freedom will lead to a high cost of living and to wealth for the peasants ... This leads to republicanism and finally to equality of conditions ...
>
> But, I may be asked, which of the two forms do *you* like better? I like monarchy ... I have 15,000 *livres* of revenue which I would lose for the enrichment of the peasants. If everyone would behave like me and speak out according to his interests, there would be nothing more to argue about in this world.
>
> (1881, II, 154–5)

However attractive or otherwise one may find Galiani's political philosophy, it must be agreed that he saw deeply into the interconnections of economics and politics, and that he was justified, both in giving full weight to political considerations in his policy judgements, and also, to a large extent, in charging the economists with a lack of political maturity and experience. Galiani denounced with a special ferocity the reformist enthusiasms of 'do-gooders':

> Let me frankly tell you that with all their virtue, their goodness of soul, the purity of their intentions, men like that seem to be pernicious, and are to be condemned. On an issue so delicate, to calculate wrongly, to deceive oneself about human knowledge, and to write, chatter, spread proposals, excite wrong desires, must all have consequences. It is very evil on their part. Where does this rage come from to talk about things they do not understand, and to interfere where they have no business? What do they want? . . .
>
> Believe me, don't be afraid of the rascals or the wicked: sooner or later they will be unmasked. But beware of the honest man who is mistaken. He is of good faith, believes in himself, and wants the good of the whole world. But unfortunately he is wrong about the means of procuring it . . .
>
> Enthusiasm and administration are two contradictory terms.
>
> (1770 [1968], 189, 222, and 224)

VI

Ultimately, what was most important in the *Dialogues* was their methodological significance, with regard to the complex relationships between economic theory and policy, and the importance of the historical-institutional dimension. Galiani provided the first profound criticism of deductive theorizing in economics from an historical standpoint. As Schumpeter said of him:

> One point about his thought must be emphasized . . . he was the one eighteenth-century economist who always insisted on the variability of man and on the relativity to time and place, of all policies; the one who was completely free from the paralyzing belief, that crept over the intellectual life of Europe, in practical principles that claim universal validity; who saw that a policy that was rational in France at a given time might be quite irrational, at the same time in Naples; who had the courage to say: '*Je ne suis pour rien. Je suis pour qu'on ne déraisonne pas*' (*Dialogue* I); and who properly despised all types of political doctrinaires, including the physiocrats.
>
> (1954, 292–3)

Galiani was a truly historical economist, who insisted on the differences between the material of the natural sciences, which yield general laws, and the more complex social studies, which yield only trends, and in which the historical dimension is vital. He was not the falsely historical 'historicist', who imagined that he could treat the material of human history as though it were that of the natural sciences, and proclaim 'iron' laws. In a remarkable, though somewhat telegraphic, statement to

Mme d'Épinay he wrote (6 November 1773) of the emptiness of 'some general theories which have remained the same when everything has changed, and the details are different. Now general theories and nothing are almost the same thing' (1881, II, 274). Presumably, however, Galiani would have been prepared to defend his theory of value and price as possessing *some* general validity.

Galiani was probably much influenced by Montesquieu, but he criticized even him for trying to carry generalization too far (*Dialogue* V). Galiani's true master was his fellow-Neapolitan, Vico. There are signs of Vico's influence in *Della moneta*, though, at some points, Galiani's claims for universal principles are hardly in accord with Vician doctrines. The full influence of Vico emerged, however, in the *Dialogues*.[8] Concerning policy, Galiani concluded: 'Policy is a matter of detail. It must always be concerned with particular cases. If it is made universal, it makes for confusion; in particular circumstances it produces good' (289).

Luigi Einaudi considered Galiani to be one of the two 'truly great' Italian economists between 1750 and 1850 – the other was Ferrara. But even in Italy Galiani's achievement has, at times, been neglected, while in English-speaking countries it has gone almost unrecognized. In Russia, however, the pioneer mathematical economist, V. K. Dmitriev, in a paper of 1902, paid a glowing tribute to Galiani's work on utility and value: 'We find all the information needed for the construction of a finished theory of marginal utility in the work of such an 'old' economist as Galiani – the first "positivist" in political economy who hitherto has not been properly appreciated in the literature' (1902 [1974], 182). Dmitriev went on to remark that Galiani left little of importance for the Austrians to add, apart from terminology.

Trying to rank the great economists almost always seems unwise and presumptuous. But it may be defensible, in extreme cases, when it is desirable to emphasize the merits of someone who has been unduly disregarded in the history of the subject. So we may - perhaps, venture the suggestion that, taking together his two major complementary works on theory, policy and method, Galiani, for sheer originality and penetration, is unsurpassed among the writers on our subject during our period, while, in the weight of his contribution, only Petty, Cantillon, Smith, and possibly Quesnay and Turgot, rank higher.

Galiani's *Dialogues* are mentioned further when we come, in the next chapter, to the supreme French policy issue of freedom of the grain trade, and to the French writers concerned with it on either side of the debate.

PART V

The Thirty-year Boom, Phase II: French Pre-eminence, Milanese Enlightenment and Scottish Ascendancy (*c.* 1756–1776)

16
François Quesnay and the Rise and Fall of the Physiocratic School

I

Quesnay published his first two contributions to political economy – as he conceived the subject – in 1756–7. These articles appeared under the titles 'Farmers' and 'Grain' (or 'Corn') in the *Encyclopédie* edited by Diderot and d'Alembert. Two other pieces written by Quesnay at about this time, on 'Men' and on 'Taxes', remained unpublished. In 1756 Quesnay was 62, after a career of remarkable success and 'upward mobility', in which political economy had, till then, played virtually no part. This subject was to hold his enthusiastic interest for about twelve years – from the age of about sixty-two to seventy-four – after which, near the end of his life, he switched his attention to geometry and mathematics.

Quesnay had been born in a country village, not far from Paris, and came from a modest farming family.[1] Aged seventeen he moved to the capital as an apprentice engraver. But his ambition was to devote himself to surgery, which he studied in his spare time, and in which he duly became qualified, eventually achieving a professorship in the college of surgeons. At that period, however, surgeons by no means enjoyed the kind of status which they subsequently acquired – apparently then being ranked, sometimes, roughly on a par with barbers. Doctors then possessed a considerably higher status and Quesnay concerned himself with a campaign to improve the position of his fellow surgeons. He himself (at about the age of 50) proceeded to qualify as a doctor and take the degree of Doctor of Medicine. His professional success rose with the social level of the patients he treated, until he achieved the crowning eminence of his career when he was appointed physician to the royal mistress, Mme de Pompadour, and moved, in 1749, into a small apartment in the palace of Versailles.

Quesnay must have proved himself a successful, though probably not very polished courtier, who won the confidence of the King and the royal family, and used cautiously such influence as he acquired. Aided by his prestige as an 'insider' at Versailles, he went on to demonstrate that he also possessed great qualities of intellectual leadership and persuasiveness. Over the preceding decades he had published a number of medical papers, including one or two of some importance, but none of these brought him the kind of following and fame which his economic writings were to achieve. He had turned to political economy in the early or middle 1750s, when the subject was becoming intensely fashionable with French intellectuals. He approached this new interest from the same medical direction as had the similarly 'upwardly mobile' William Petty, in that he took a basically physical view of human beings, and applied medical metaphors, and parallels, to the body politico-economic, and to its natural functions, circulation, and self-curative properties. As Gide and Rist put it, 'from Physiology to Physiocracy was not a very great step' (1948, 27); nor was that from the circulation of the blood to the circulation of payments in an economy (see Foley, 1973). Quesnay seems to have known well the writings of Petty and Locke, and to have been acquainted also with those of Davenant, Law, Hume, Melon, Dutot and Forbonnais. Undoubtedly the two economists whose works influenced him most, and who provided him with vital points of departure, were Boisguilbert and Cantillon. Boisguilbert had raised forcefully the problem, and 'vision', to which he responded: that of France's supposedly appalling economic decline and agricultural distress. As regards Cantillon, though it would be misleading to describe him as the first physiocrat (because he was so much more than a physiocrat), he certainly provided, as we have seen, the two main pillars on which Quesnay built his system, the primacy of agriculture, and the circular flow of payments.

Boisguilbert's vision, sixty years earlier, of the economic maladies of France, and especially of her agriculture, as well as that of Quesnay himself, may have been somewhat exaggerated.[2] Nevertheless, behind all the abstractions to which he was to resort, Quesnay's work was primarily concerned with the mounting politico-economic crisis of his country, and with constructing policies for the revival and expansion of her economy and for the stability of her political régime. In fact, though the physiocrats, later on, were to become markedly internationalist in their policies and sentiments, in Quesnay's first articles, traces are to be found of rather mercantilist conceptions as to the objectives of economic policy, which he then formulated in somewhat nationalist and *étatist* terms. For example, the first and last sentences both of his first economic article, and of his early papers on 'Men', and on 'Taxes', all relate their subjects to the support, or well-being, of the state, the government, or the nation (see Fox-Genovese, 1976, 11ff). Later Quesnay expressed more markedly internationalist, or cosmopolitan views.

Quesnay began his article on 'Farmers' by distinguishing between two methods of agricultural production: the first, which was mainly prevalent in France at the time, was small-scale, almost hand-to-mouth, and highly labour intensive; while the other, then less well represented in France, but according to Quesnay, more frequent in England, was based on production on a larger scale, for the market, using much more equipment and capital outlay, or 'advances'. For Quesnay, the use of horses for ploughing, rather than oxen, was the feature which distinguished between the '*petite culture*' and the '*grande culture*'. He proceeded to emphasize that much larger 'advances' of subsistence, seeds and materials, over a comparatively much longer period of time, were required for larger-scale production, which he elaborately, but rather hypothetically, calculated was vastly more lucrative and profitable than small-scale production:

> Only rich farmers can use horses for working on the land. A farmer with a cart and four horses has to make a considerable outlay before obtaining his first harvest. He cultivates the land for a year, and sows it with wheat, and after he has sowed he gets no harvest until the August of the following year. So he waits for almost two years for the fruits of his labour and his outlays.
>
> (1958, 428; see Eltis, 1984, 5)[3]

On the other hand, Quesnay calculated that the poor peasant, without wealth or capital, who worked, so to speak, 'with his bare hands', failed to cover his costs (447). Moreover, the farmer, unlike the merchant, was unable to obtain credit, because the return on his capital outlay took too long and was too uncertain (447–8). So he had to accumulate resources himself, since he could not offer sufficient security to lenders.

Of course, suggestions of these ideas about capital, and 'advances', can be found in earlier writers, but no-one before Quesnay, in the opening paragraphs of this first article, had pointed out so clearly and emphatically the vital role of 'advances', 'waiting' and time, in larger-scale and more lucrative methods of production. These fundamental ideas were to play an important role in *The Wealth of Nations* and in English classical theory, as well as in subsequent theories of capital. As Schumpeter observed, these concepts of Quesnay provided 'an interesting illustration of the way in which, in the mind of the born theorist, *analytic generalization may grow out of observation induced by preoccupation with practical problems*' (1954, 235).

Quesnay first distinguished two main types of advances, or capital, in agriculture: the *avances annuelles* on seeds, manure, and on the subsistence of labour (or circulating capital); and the *avances primitives* on tools, equipment, and horses, or oxen, (or 'fixed' capital, invested for longer periods). The *avances foncières*, or initial outlay on clearing and draining the land (which were non-recurring, or fixed for very long periods), were introduced subsequently.

Quesnay then turned to a second handicap under which farmers laboured: this was that they were not free to sell their produce abroad. He supported his case for free exports of grain, a further fundamental principle of physiocratic policy, by the example of England: 'The policy of England, in this respect, proves that there is no surer method of supporting agriculture, maintaining abundance, and preventing famines, than that of selling a part of the harvests abroad. This country, since it has favoured and encouraged exports, has suffered from neither extraordinarily high, nor from very low prices' (1958, 448).

Galiani, as noted earlier, was to deny the relevance of the English example for France. Quesnay, however, envisaged that these two key policies, outlined in his first papers on economics, namely, a switch to larger scale, and freedom of exports, were – together with a fundamental reform of tax policy, to be discussed shortly – essential for reversing the decline in agricultural productivity, and the drift of population to the cities with its accompanying decadence. (Here Quesnay introduced a touch of Rousseau-like romanticism.) He complained that the manufacture of, and trade in, luxuries had been supported at the expense of the cultivation of the land. Such ideas led on to the heart of the physiocratic matter, the principle, or assumption, of the 'sterility' of manufacturing and commerce, and of the unique 'productivity' of agriculture. As he put it in his essays on 'Grain' and on 'Men':

> ... the artisan destroys in the form of subsistence as much as he produces by his labour.
>
> (1962, 73)

> Those who make manufactured commodities do not produce wealth, because their labour increases the value of these commodities only by an amount equal to the wages which are paid to them and which are drawn from the product of landed property.
>
> (96)

Not that manufacturing did not produce something *useful*. It did. But it did not produce a net product or surplus. Only agriculture did that. Repeatedly Quesnay insisted on contrasting the productivity of agriculture with the sterility of manufacturing and commerce. On the one hand:

> The profit or revenue which the proprietors draw from their landed property, then constitutes the true wealth of the nation, the wealth of the sovereign, the wealth of his subjects, the wealth which provides for the state's needs, and consequently the wealth which pays the taxes levied to meet the expenditure which is necessary for the government and defence of the state.
>
> (104)

On the other hand: 'Manufactured goods demand on the part of those who make them expenses and costs which are equal to the value of these goods' (104).

This equality of cost and value in manufacturing, and hence its 'sterility', was explained by 'the competition of workers', which 'restricted' the price of manufactured goods, (though there was also competition in the agricultural sector). Of course, with suitable definitions of 'productive', and with the necessary assumptions regarding competition in manufacturing, this highly paradoxical doctrine can be explained. Nevertheless, there were important ideas underlying this proposition, however paradoxically it was expressed. Quesnay was emphasizing, that, under competitive conditions, the incomes of entrepreneurs and labour would be at the level necessary for maintaining them in business, or in health, and could not be squeezed without reductions either in the labour force, or in vital investment, or in the 'advances' required for maintaining production. In the return to land, on the other hand, there was a pure net surplus over costs.

This concept of net product was a further fundamental analytical contribution by Quesnay, and his doctrine of the single tax followed directly from it. The net product or surplus, produced by nature alone, which accrued entirely to the landowners, was the only 'dispensable' income, or source, which could be tapped for taxation, without damaging production.

II

While completing these early papers Quesnay was developing his *Tableau Économique*, the first version of which was published in 1758. This diagram was intended to portray the circular flow of payments between the three classes, or sectors, in the economy. First, there was the 'productive' class, of farmers (who were alone 'productive' of a net product). Secondly, there was the manufacturing, or 'sterile', class. Thirdly, there was the landowning class of proprietors, who (or whose ancestors) had been responsible for the original enclosing and clearing of the land, or for the '*avances foncières*'. This class, as the recipients of the net product, alone had to pay taxes. This burden may provide some justification, or explanation, of the deferential treatment which the landowning class received from the physiocrats. For, as the current, mainly passive, consumers of a large slice of the national income, they might well have been regarded as deserving the epithet 'sterile', rather than the manufacturers who produced useful goods under competitive conditions. On the other hand, insofar as it was maintained that the incomes of landowners were in return for their original clearing of the land – i.e. in return for their *avances foncières* – then, to that extent, their incomes represented a cost, rather than a pure surplus from the bounty of nature (see Gide and Rist, 1948, 40ff). Anyhow, apart from paying all the taxes, a main duty of landowners was the not very onerous one of spending all their incomes – and not hoarding any – on the right kinds of goods, namely agricultural products rather than manufactured 'luxuries'.

Doubtless their profound respect for the rights of property, a cornerstone of the physiocratic order, underlay the unquestioning attitude of Quesnay and his followers to the incomes of landowners and their monopoly of ownership. Otherwise, in both the agricultural and the manufacturing sectors, the entrepreneurs simply recovered their advances and received the wages of management necessary to keep them in their employment, while the workers received subsistence wages.

Quesnay's *Tableau* depicted the circular flow, in a single year, or period, from harvest to harvest, of the payments and receipts between the three classes, or sectors, and was drawn up originally on the basis of a long list of highly simplificatory, or ideal, or even optimal, assumptions, (twenty-two such assumptions in the first edition, increased subsequently to twenty-four). Among these assumptions were the exclusion of foreign trade and taxation, the ubiquity of free competition, and the absence of any hoarding or 'sterile saving'. Furthermore, it was assumed that investment in agriculture yielded a 100 per cent net revenue on the annual advances, and that the three classes each spent 50 per cent of their incomes on agricultural products and 50 per cent on manufactures.

The circulatory process started with the farmers in possession of all the money in the economy (say 2000 units) and with their paying it, as their annual rent, to the landowners, who then paid half of this (1000) back to the farmers for agricultural produce, and paid the other half (1000) to the sterile class for manufactures. These two classes then proceeded, in turn, to pay out these receipts according to the same pattern (i.e. 500 for agricultural produce and 500 for manufactures). The annual round of payments continued until each class was back where it started, with the agricultural class holding all the money, so that another identical year, or period, commenced. The farmers had available precisely the same sum for advances, to produce the next harvest, while the receipts of the manufacturers had precisely covered their costs of production.

Though Quesnay used his *Tableau* in the first instance, to depict the flow of payments in a stationary economy, in which, under ideal conditions, each annual period was a precise repetition of the previous one, he also sought to apply it to 'real-world' processes and to government policy, indicating the possibilities for growth, on the one hand, with more investment in agricultural 'advances', while, on the other hand, emphasizing the harmful effects which would follow from the erroneous policies of governments, such as damaging taxation – then crippling the French economy – or from reductions in the vital agricultural advances such as had followed from the excessive consumption of manufactured luxuries, or from the obstructions to the free sale of agricultural produce, internally and externally.

The *Tableau* went through a number of editions, some of them very difficult to track down, but which have recently been fixed at three, as to the precise details and sequence of which much confusion has long obtained, while further discoveries may continue to be possible. In fact, Ronald Meek wrote of 'a hoodoo on research in this field' (Quesnay, 1972, x). Moreover, on top of the bewildering problems of the various 'editions', there are even more baffling conundrums regarding the interpretation and precise figuring of the diagrams. Problems, puzzles and ambiguities are numerous – beginning with the paradoxical definitions of 'productive' and 'sterile'. Many times more numerous are the various interpretations, or answers, which have been put forward. Interpreting the *Tableau* has become a highly refined academic pursuit, and, in recent years, a considerable growth industry. For, as Elizabeth Fox-Genovese has put it, 'many scholars have explained it to their own satisfaction, but not to that of others' (1976, 268). For the history of economic thought, the precise details as to the correct interpretation, or assumptions, are of lesser significance, compared with the pioneering development by Quesnay of the idea of social accounting. He actually described his *Tableau* at one point as a 'Little Book of Household Accounts' (see Quesnay, 1972, xxvii). As Schumpeter said: 'What we are now interested in is the *tableau* method itself' (1954, 241). For 'the *tableau* method' was a prototype of macro-economic analysis, and it brought with it such fundamental concepts as the circular flow of payments, and both aggregate equilibrium and general interdependence, together with, emerging from these ideas, the analysis of disequilibrium, growth and decline. If it was nearing the confines of absurdity to rank the *Tableau*, as Mirabeau did, with the discoveries of writing and money, as one of the 'three great inventions which have principally given stability to political societies', the *Tableau* certainly was an achievement of major significance in the history of economic analysis.

On what were, however, the central questions of economic theory, those of value and price, interest and money, the contributions of Quesnay and his disciples were incidental and sometimes inconsistent, and compare unfavourably with Cantillon's *Essay*. The main determinant of price, or of the *prix fondamentale*, was taken to be cost of production. Though putting forward, however, what was primarily an objective cost theory, Quesnay also included the demand side in holding that goods 'constitute wealth only insofar as they are necessary to man, and insofar as they are exchangeable'. In fact, Quesnay's treatment of value approximated to that of Adam Smith in separating, perhaps rather too emphatically, use-value and value-in-exchange (see Meek, 1962, 90).

On wages, we have noted Quesnay's strong emphasis on subsistence as the determinant, anticipating the more hard-line Malthusian and classical doctrine. On another aspect of wages, however, he took a severely realistic attitude, common among 'mercantilist' writers, but opposed by the more optimistic Adam Smith: 'it is very harmful to allow the people to get used to buying corn at too low a price. As a result they become less hard-working; they spend little on the bread they eat and become lazy and presumptuous; farmers have difficulty in finding workers and are very badly served by them in years of plenty' (86).

Regarding interest, the scholastic influence on the physiocrats was apparent, in that they supported legal limitations on the interest rate, but regarded the payment of interest as justified on productive investment in agriculture.

On the subject of money, Quesnay also held both 'mercantilist' and 'classical' attitudes. On the one hand, there were his repeated warnings of the dangers of hoarding (denied or excluded by Turgot and the English classicals). On the other hand, in the classical manner, he denounced the accumulation of money in a country, as an objective of policy, as wasteful and senseless.

A summary review of Quesnay's doctrines was provided in his thirty 'General Maxims for the Economic Government of an Agricultural Kingdom' (see Meek, 1962, 231–8). Many of the points in these 'Maxims' have already been discussed, but there are one or two more which may be noted or re-emphasized. It was stressed that second, of course, to investment in agriculture, it was public needs, and spending thereon, which are 'the *wealth of primary necessity* in a state, in order to defend subjects against scarcity and against the enemy, and to maintain the glory and power of the monarch and the prosperity of the nation' (Maxim XIII, 234).

There was something markedly 'Keynesian' about Quesnay's warnings against hoarding, together with his emphasis on public spending.[4] Marketing and transport should be facilitated by spending on roads and canals, as well as on transport by river and sea (XVII). Following Boisguilbert, Quesnay maintained that it was essential to maintain high prices for agricultural produce, which 'should never be made to fall' (XVIII); for 'it should not be believed that cheapness of produce is profitable to the lower classes' (XIX). It was suggested that the nation might lose from foreign trade because the merchants hoarded their gains (XXIV). But 'complete freedom of trade should be maintained' (XXV). Though 'the government should trouble itself less with economising than with the operations necessary for the prosperity of the kingdom' (XXVII), borrowing from financiers should be strictly avoided, to prevent the accumulation of monetary fortunes, which are 'a clandestine form of wealth which knows neither king nor country' (XXIX) – Cantillon could only have strongly disagreed.

Finally, the two overriding policy doctrines of Quesnay and the physiocrats were the single tax and *laissez-faire*. Adhering to these two principles, it was held, would ensure the achievement of that supreme objective, which Quesnay was one of the first to formulate in maximizing terms, specifically for economic policy, as that of 'the greatest possible reduction in disagreeable labour with the greatest possible enjoyment' (Meek, 1962, 212).

III

The economic ideas and theories of Quesnay and the physiocrats were part of a comprehensive corpus of political, philosophical and epistemological doctrines. Certainly the economic ideas can be discussed separately, if one is concerned with a history of economic 'analysis' (as Schumpeter was) rather than with a history of political economy or economic 'thought'. The physiocrats themselves, however, did not regard their economic doctrines, which were primarily policy doctrines, as distinct and separable from their firmly held political and philosophical principles. In fact, their economic doctrines were inevitably coloured by their political assumptions and beliefs, and by their philosophical theories and methods. Any treatment of the politico-economic thought of the physiocrats would be seriously inadequate if it regarded them simply as economic technicians, and did not present a reasonably full account of their politics and philosophy. Quesnay himself was concerned to supply this political and philosophical direction and framework for physiocracy.

One interesting philosophical statement by Quesnay appeared in 1756, in the same year as his first article on economics. This was his paper '*Evidence*', best translated (as by Ronald Meek) as 'self-evident truth': 'The term '*evidence*' means a certitude, which is so clear and manifest in itself, that the mind cannot deny it' (Meek, 1962, 40).

For Quesnay, self-evident truths of this kind may take the form of both physical laws, and of moral laws of good and evil. As the concluding sentence of Quesnay's essay stated:

> These primary self-evident truths are the basis of supernatural knowledge, and of the primary developments of natural knowledge, the fundamental truths of the sciences, the laws which direct the mind towards the progress of knowledge, the rules of conduct of all animals in actions concerned with their self-preservation, their needs, inclinations, happiness and unhappiness. (1958, 426)

Quesnay believed that such self-evident truths, and certainties of the greatest significance, were embodied, as far as political economy was concerned, in his own doctrines. Among these self-evident certainties were his doctrines of 'natural right', which he developed in an article of that title (1765), in which he defined 'justice' as: '*a natural and paramount rule, recognised through the light of reason, which self-evidently determines what belongs to oneself or to another*' (Meek, 1962, 45).

A natural right was not a legal right – though, of course, ideally it should be. Legal rights were conferred by positive human laws, which may, and do, diverge disastrously from the perfect natural laws of 'the Author of Nature', though it was the prime duty of rulers to make natural and positive laws coincide:

> In order to understand the order of time and space, and to control navigation and safeguard trade, it has been necessary to observe and calculate precisely the laws of the movement of celestial bodies. Similarly, in order to understand the extent of the natural right of men joined together in society, it is necessary to settle upon the natural laws which form the basis of the best government possible. (53)

These natural laws 'are immutable and indisputable and the best laws possible; thus they are the foundation of the most perfect government, and the fundamental rule for all positive laws . . . It is only the understanding of these supreme laws which can ensure the continuing peace and prosperity of an empire' (54).

Through reason and knowledge, however, human beings can, and must, achieve an understanding of these natural laws. There can be little or no excuse for ignorance of these laws in a cultured society: 'Ignorance is the original attribute of man in his uncultured and isolated state; in society it is man's most disastrous infirmity. In society it is even a crime, since men, being endowed with intelligence, ought to raise themselves to an order superior to the state of the beasts. In society it is a monstrous crime . . .' (55).

Finally, only madmen would refuse obedience to these laws – which, regarding the economy of a country, he himself had fully propounded: 'Man cannot reasonably refuse the obedience which he owes to these laws; otherwise his freedom would be only a freedom harmful to himself and to others. It would be nothing but the freedom of a madman, who, under a good government must be checked and cured through the authority of the positive laws of society' (56).

Psychiatric clinics were not available, of course, in eighteenth-century Paris, for dealing with such madmen, though Quesnay did not appear to regard such curative problems as very difficult. Certainly, however, the political implications of Quesnay's version of natural law and natural right seem very formidable.

Quesnay's political doctrines were summed up in the first two of his 'General Maxims'. First, with a hostile reference to Montesquieu's doctrine of the separation of powers, he proclaimed his absolutist doctrine: '*That there should be a single sovereign authority, standing above all the individuals in the society and all the unjust undertakings of private interests* . . . The view that there should be a balance of forces in the government is a disastrous one' (Meek, 1962, 231).

Second, to sustain the absolutist regime there must be a system of public education: 'That the nation should be given instruction in the general laws of the natural order, which constitute the form of government which is self-evidently the most perfect' (232).

Quesnay's philosophical and political doctrines emerged, however, in their fullest and most interesting form in his work 'The Despotism of China', published in four parts in *Éphémérides* in the first half of 1767 – a work which has not received the attention it deserves from historians of political economy. Enthusiasm for China and its culture was a curious aspect of the Enlightenment, and Quesnay's essay 'The Despotism of China' has been described, by his translator, as the high-water mark of the sinophile movement (Quesnay, 1946). It seems that Quesnay had acquired his knowledge of China, such as it was, from a ten-volume work of social geography which covered most of the non-European world.[5]

He began by explaining that there were legal despots, and arbitrary, or illegal, despots. Legal despots ruled in accordance with natural law, so that their despotism was not that of a person but of natural law itself. According to Quesnay, China was a, or rather, *the* country where natural law was fully implemented. He noted, incidentally, that few countries had so much poverty as China, but, somewhat paradoxically, this demonstrated a kind of economic success. (In fact, Adam Smith was to describe China as having attained 'a full complement of riches'.) Anyhow, Quesnay's explanation was on highly Malthusian lines: 'Population always exceeds wealth in both good and bad governments, because propagation is limited by nothing but subsistence and always tends to increase even further; there are poor people everywhere' (Quesnay, 1946, vol. II, 261).

The Chinese economic order, however, according to Quesnay, possessed, to a high degree, those characteristics which he regarded as essentially required by natural law. *First*, in China, agriculture had always been held in veneration, and farmers were ranked above merchants and artisans. *Second*, ownership and property rights were securely upheld. *Third*, between the provinces of the vast empire, free exchange ruled: 'Inasmuch as each province has its needs, and only its own particular products, all would lapse into poverty, were it not for the fact that they exchange with one another their useful products' (208).

In fact, according to Quesnay, the merits of the government of China were such that it 'gives few handholds to its detractors' (243). This was because the constitution of China was 'based upon a knowledge of the natural law, of which it is the outgrowth' (246). Natural laws were not merely beneficent, but optimal in their effects, for they 'were established forever by the author of nature for the continual reproduction and distribution of the goods that are necessary for men united into society ...' (265). Under such a régime, men were 'taught by these same laws to cooperate with the greatest success for the common good, and to assure the most beneficial distribution possible to all the different classes of men' (265).

To operate, or embody, these ideal, optimal laws, there had to be, and was, in China, a single absolute, authority (or 'despot'). Otherwise, 'authority divided among the different orders in the state would become abusive and discordant' (268). Knowledge was required to discern and understand these natural laws and their mode of operation, but such knowledge was now not very difficult to acquire:

> These laws require on the part of the legislator and of those who enforce them a very extensive knowledge and elaborate calculation, the results of which must present, with proof, the advantages to the sovereign and to the nation, especially the advantages to the sovereign for he must be induced by self-interest to do the right thing.
>
> (272)

Under natural law, harmony reigned between nation and sovereign: 'Happily, his interest when properly understood always agrees with that of the nation' (271).

It was then necessary for the administration and courts to 'be sufficiently informed as to the effects of the positive laws upon the course of the annual reproduction of the wealth of the nation, to evaluate a new law in terms of its effect upon this operation of nature' (271). This, of course, was where the *Tableau* came in, which would supply the vital, and fully adequate knowledge. But public education was necessary to disseminate the teachings of this new science, and China was the first and only country in which the government provided such public enlightenment (or '*Volksaufklärung*'): 'The first political establishment of the government then, will be the institution of schools for teaching this science. Every kingdom but China has been ignorant of the necessity for this provision, which is the basis of government' (271).

If a ministry of public enlightenment had done its job, Quesnay was confident of the stability of the government against all subversion:

> ... In a government in which all the classes of citizens have sufficient enlightenment to know clearly and to point out with certainty the order of law most advantageous to the ruler and the nation, would a despot be found who would undertake with the support of the military forces of the state manifestly to do evil for the sake of evil? To subvert the natural and constitutional laws of the society unanimously recognized and respected by the nation?
>
> (272)

Quesnay was clear as to where this supreme and certain knowledge was, and was not, to be found. History was useless – 'bunk', as it was subsequently declared by Henry Ford: 'Let us not seek into the history of nations or into the mistakes of men, for that only presents an abyss of confusion. Historians have only endeavoured to satisfy the curiosity of their readers, and their too literal erudition does not serve to throw a light which can illuminate this darkness' (273). As Tocqueville was to remark, 'our economists had a vast contempt for the past' – though it might be unfair to press this charge against Mirabeau. In fact, so 'vast' was this contempt that it included empirical methods generally. Natural laws could not, of course, be discovered by 'looking and seeing' – as Richard Jones was to recommend. They were to be discerned by the inner light of reason: 'They print themselves into the hearts of men. They are the light that guides and directs their consciences' (276). Moreover, once discovered, these laws remained in force always and everywhere, since they 'are immutable and perpetual, and they induce observance that is voluntary and made with discernment, by aid of selfish incentives which themselves point out the advantages of observance. The natural laws assure rewards; the positive laws rest upon punishment' (275).

The method of economic science was based on reasoning from the self-evident revelations of natural law: 'It is *only* by this free exercise of reason that men may make progress in economic science . . .' (277). Pursued along these lines, economic knowledge was revealed to possess a superbly easy accessibility and certainty. The physiocrats did not, however, produce any children's textbooks: these were to come with Ricardianism, half a century later. But with regard to the subject of taxation, for example – still, apparently, highly contentious two centuries later:

> . . . that source of dissension and opposition arising out of ignorance, unrest and avidity, is essentially determined by immutable laws and rules . . . These laws and these rules, as we shall later see, show themselves with a rigorous exactitude which excludes all injustice, all arbitrary acts, and all malversation. Banish ignorance and recognize the essential, and you will worship the divine providence which has placed the torch in your hand, to enable you to proceed with sure steps in this labyrinth.
>
> (278)

The close, mutually reinforcing, interconnections are obvious between political absolutism, and the epistemological absolutism, or infallibilism, of fully available, exact, and certain knowledge. The absolute political authority (or party) has access to absolutely, or 'apodictically', certain politico-economic knowledge, which, in turn confirms and justifies the policies and authority of the absolute, infallible political leadership (or party).

Finally, Quesnay insisted that a state based on natural laws would be inherently stable and lasting, as the Chinese empire had proved itself to be. It was 'absurd fatalism' to believe 'that governments can take only transitory forms, that everything here below is subject to continual vicissitudes, that empires have their beginning, their progress, their decadence and their end' (303).

In fact, according to Quesnay, if the methods which he recommended, as put into practice in China, were followed, what would emerge would be something like 'a Thousand-Year Empire' – as a twentieth-century claim was to put it.[6]

IV

The physiocratic school was launched on its meteoric career at the meeting at Versailles of Quesnay and Mirabeau in July 1757. It was the first school of economists in the history of the subject, and probably the most closely knit of all such groups, much more so than the Ricardians, or the Keynesians, or the Austrians, though perhaps rather less dictatorially directed than the Marxians. Something between a scientific research group, a political party, and a religious sect, the physiocrats gathered behind their leader and his texts, to propagate their common creed and doctrines, and to find mutual support and encouragement. They held regular meetings, on Tuesdays, at Mirabeau's Paris *hôtel*. During the peak years of the school they published their journal, the *Éphémérides du Citoyen*.

'A feudal character invaded by democratic ideas', was how Tocqueville was to describe Mirabeau; or, as Victor Hugo put it, he was a man 'at once in advance and behind his age' (Higgs, 1897, 52). 'Let us go forward to the good old days' might seem to be the rallying-cry with which the Marquis summoned his fellow-countrymen to battle with their problems.

Victor Riquetti, Marquis de Mirabeau (1715–89), was born in Provence, and, after service in the army, devoted himself to his estates and to agriculture. The rural scene confronting him stirred his fervent, reformist spirit. His interests veered towards political economy, and, for some years, he apparently had in his possession a manuscript of Cantillon's *Essay*. (As noted above, in chapter 9, how he acquired this vital document and what he did with it, remains largely a mystery.) Mirabeau, however, must have been deeply indebted to Cantillon for some of his main ideas, as to the primacy of agriculture, and regarding population. But Cantillon, the great pioneer of positive economics, and Mirabeau, the enthusiastic, moralistic reformer, were not concerned with the same kind of enquiry (see Brocard, 1902, 49).

The Marquis poured out his ideas in his first major work, *L'Ami des hommes* (dated 1756, but probably not published until 1757). Few writers have found for their *magnum opus* so striking a title, which became the nickname under which they themselves became famous. *L'Ami* was an immediate, triumphant success, and went through numerous editions, some of which were revised under Quesnay's supervision. The book's rather bewilderingly discursive composition was evidently no barrier to its popularity, nor did it put off the much more concise and laconic Doctor, who perhaps perceived a fruitful complementarity of intellectual styles. There was, of course, an important measure of basic agreement on fundamental principles between the Doctor and the Marquis, though there were deep divergencies in their underlying political outlooks, which were never bridged or explicitly formulated. The two men first met very shortly after the appearance of *L'Ami*, when the Doctor was working out his *Tableau*. They were soon cooperating on several works, in close intellectual partnership. Though he claimed that 'population and agriculture are intimately and necessarily related', Mirabeau did not seem to decide which way the relationship worked. Anyhow, the prevailing mood of the book was one of expansive optimism – in wide contrast with the 1798 *Essay* of Malthus. The government was summoned to promote agriculture and remove obstacles to population growth. The economy, or the state, was, Mirabeau maintained, like a tree, the roots of which were agriculture, the trunk was population, and the branches were industry and commerce: 'It is from the roots that the tree derives its nourishment' (1756, vol. II, 15).

Mirabeau passionately condemned luxury as 'the greatest evil of society' (II, 367), and maintained a strongly pro-saving attitude, though not to the extent of disagreeing with Quesnay's denial of the unconditional beneficence of frugality and saving, as when hoarding was allowed to obstruct or disrupt, the circulation of payments.

In 1760 Mirabeau produced (under Quesnay's guidance) the main physiocratic monograph on taxation, *Théorie de l'impôt*, in which, while expounding the basic doctrine, which insisted on a single tax on the agricultural surplus, he included some pointed remarks on the inefficiency and injustice of prevailing tax burdens. This outspokenness earned the Marquis a brief spell in gaol, which however, lasted only eight days, thanks to his friends at court. The episode illustrated the constraints under which French economists wrote with regard to economic policy and public finance.

In 1763 the *Philosophie rurale* appeared, written in cooperation with, or under the supervision of, Quesnay. The sub-title was, '*the general economics and politics of agriculture reduced to immutable physical and moral laws, which ensure the prosperity of empires*'. It seems that Mirabeau was originally responsible for the passage, endorsed by Quesnay, which outlined a kind of economic, or materialist interpretation of society in terms of subsistence (see Meek, 1962, 37n.):

> It is upon subsistence, upon the means of subsistence, that all the branches of the political order depend.
>
> ... This is the fundamental force to which is due everything which men cultivate, navigate and build ...
>
> ... All the moral and physical parts of which society is constituted derive from this and are subordinate to it.
>
> (Meek, 1962, 57)

Religion, virtues, vices, civil law, government, the sciences, the liberal and mechanical arts, agriculture, trade, industry – 'all are subordinate to the means of subsistence'; or 'all politics starts with a grain of wheat', as Mirabeau once observed (quoted in Fox-Genovese, 1976, 47). The congruence, *mutatis mutandis* with subsequent Marxian doctrines – such as '*erst kommt das fressen*' as Brecht put it – is obvious. Mirabeau reversed Montesquieu's order of precedence, which had given primacy to the political order. The Marquis continued: 'If the moralists and politicians do not base their sciences on the economic order, on agriculture, their speculations will be useless and illusory: they will be doctors who perceive only symptoms and ignore the disease' (69).

Finally, Mirabeau endorsed, in glowing, theological terms, the 'magic' harmony of interests which obtained in an economy based on natural law:

> The whole magic of well-ordered society is that each man works for others, while believing that he is working for himself. This magic, the general character and effects of which are revealed by the subject we are studying, shows us that the Supreme Being bestowed upon us as a Father the principles of economic harmony, when he condescended to announce and prescribe them to us, as God, in the form of religious laws.
>
> (70)

Having noted, however, certain similarities, one should observe how profoundly the theological presuppositions of the physiocrats distinguished their philosophy from that of the Marxians.

Mirabeau and Quesnay also cooperated in a political work, *Traité de la monarchie*, drafted in 1758, but never published, because, presumably, of the censorship, and possibly also because the two authors were unable to formulate a really consistent political doctrine (see Fox-Genovese, 1976, 170ff). Their political views, or 'visions' diverged too widely. They agreed that natural laws had to be implemented by an absolute political authority. But Mirabeau was not enthusiastic on behalf of modernization and largeness of scale in agriculture, and was, apparently, prepared to pay a price in terms of economic growth. He favoured something more like a restoration of feudal relationships. On the other hand, Quesnay wanted a fundamental revolution in agriculture and rural life, which – (though he seems not to have perceived this) – would hardly have been consistent with the retention of the monarchy and social order such as existed under the *ancien régime* (Fox-Genovese, 1976).

V

The work of Quesnay and Mirabeau had aroused great interest. If, however, the school was to live up to its claims, the somewhat condensed pronouncements of the Doctor, and the enthusiastic, but sometimes rather unstructured effusions of the Marquis, needed to be supplemented by a systematic treatise of principles. The man who met this need was Paul-Pierre Le Mercier de la Rivière (1720–93), who got to know Quesnay, and became a disciple, shortly after the historic encounter between Doctor and Marquis in 1757.[7]

Mercier came of a family of high officials in Saumur, and, following legal studies, devoted himself particularly to constitutional law. In 1759 he was sent to Martinique as *Intendant*, where he won high praise for the measures he took to sustain the economy of the island when it was blockaded by the British navy during the Seven Years' War. When the war ended (1763), Martinique was one of the few colonies left to France, and Mercier boldly introduced a policy of economic freedom, and of curbing the powers of the entrenched monopolists in the colonial trade. As, however, Turgot was to be, a dozen years later, Mercier was defeated by the strength of the vested interests in Paris opposed to free-market policies.

On returning from the West Indies, Mercier took up the composition of his major work, *L'Ordre naturel et essentiel des sociétés politiques*, which was published in 1767. In the same year he accepted an invitation to Russia to explain in person the principles of physiocracy to the Empress Catherine the Great, who was eager to apply the latest and most enlightened Parisian notions to the government of her empire. Mercier's journey to Russia was long and strenuous but his meeting with the Empress was brief and almost farcical.[8]

Meanwhile, however, in Paris, Mercier's *L'Ordre naturel* had won much acclaim and was performing a considerable service for the physiocratic school. The book was written under the supervision of Quesnay, and Mercier's political and philosophical doctrines follow very faithfully those of the master, as expounded in *Le Despotisme de la Chine*, and elsewhere. Indeed one of Quesnay's closest friends, Mme du Hausset, described Mercier as 'the man he estimated most' (see Richner, 1931, 14). Moreover, Adam Smith later maintained that *L'Ordre naturel* was 'the most distinct and best connected account of the doctrines of physiocracy' (1776, 679).

Whereas Quesnay and Mirabeau had started from basic economic and agricultural principles, Mercier began with the fundamentals of ethics, politics and law. His approach, however, was not in conflict with the kind of qualified economic determinism adumbrated by the Marquis in *Philosophie rurale*. For Mercier was simply concerned with the order in which he expounded the principles of physiocracy, and was not challenging the primary role of economic and agricultural factors in shaping a society.

Mercier maintained that natural laws were basically physical, and, somehow, because of their divine origin, were both positive and normative. He had, therefore, no difficulty in including both the Newtonian laws of the physical universe, and beneficent moral and social laws, in the same comprehensive category of natural laws. At one point he compared, as essentially similar, the work of a magistrate, and the work of a doctor, for both were concerned with implementing natural laws, on the one hand those of politico-economic well-being, and, on the other, the natural laws of physical health. Nor was there any serious difficulty in discerning and establishing what these God-given natural laws were. For God had equipped man with the power to perceive and understand these laws as self-evident certainties, which were revealed, as described in St John's Gospel (I.9), quoted by Mercier, by 'the light that lighteth every man that cometh into the world'.

Obviously, however, though enlightenment was available to all, some were assumed to be more enlightened than others, otherwise it was difficult to see why such a concentration of political power was essential. Mercier's attitude to freedom of the press was typical: of course he was all in favour of 'freedom' – but not for those who attacked the truth. (In other words, freedom was only for the enlightened, or for those whom the state regarded as enlightened.) He set out the relation between the possession of self-evident, certain knowledge, on the one hand, and political authoritarianism on the other hand, as follows:

> It is, then, a constant truth that everywhere where self-evident, public knowledge reigns of the natural and essential order of each society, and everywhere where despotism is legal, the authority, far from being liable to abuses in relation to public revenue, finds itelf necessarily providing the strongest support for the natural order, and this for the sole reason that it is the unique means by which the sovereign can assure the greatest possible revenue.
>
> (1767, II, 88–9)

The foundations of the natural order consisted of property, security and freedom. Resorting to both capital letters and italics, Mercier proclaimed: 'PROPERTY, SECURITY, FREEDOM: that is the entire social order. It is from this, from the right of property, *maintained to its full natural and primitive extent*, that there *necessarily* results all the institutions which constitute the essential form of society' (II, 441). Above all, secure private property was the basis of liberty. It was within such a framework that society could reach its maximum potential:

> Do you want society to attain to the highest possible degree of wealth, of population, and consequently of power? Then entrust its interests to liberty; make this the general rule. By means of liberty, which is the true basis of industry, the desire for pleasure, stimulated by competition, and enlightened by experience and example, will guarantee you that each acts always for his own greatest possible advantage, and consequently cooperates, with all his power, to the greatest possible growth of the total of particular interests, which together can be called the general interest of the body social, or the common interest both of the head, and of each of the members of which the body is composed.
>
> (I, 57–8)

The '*best possible*' state, or condition, was repeatedly italicized by Mercier, as that which natural law '*necessarily* brought about' (II, 84–90). The administration 'had nothing to do, it only had to refrain from hindering' the maximizing and optimizing operations of natural laws, under which: '*Le monde va de lui-même*'.

On several points Mercier added a useful contribution to the economic analysis of the physiocrats. In cost of production – or the 'necessary price', as Mercier called it – of manufactured goods, he included the interest on advances together with rewards for personal effort and risk, observing that the risk element was far from equal in different trades (II, 412–15). As regards the farmer-entrepreneur, Mercier emphasized that the return on his capital must at least equal what could be obtained elsewhere (see Meek, 1962, 309).

On a crucial point of macroeconomic analysis, however, where Quesnay had stressed the possibility and danger of hoarding – which the classicals were to rule out – Mercier introduced some phrases highly suggestive of what subsequently came to be known as 'Say's Law', together with the Turgot–Smith analysis of saving and investing (or saving *is* investing): 'No one has money except insofar as he buys it by giving other values in exchange' (II, 119).

The strongly Utopian elements in Mercier's work, which fundamentally underlay so much of the physiocratic system, emerged very explicitly, decades later, in his last work, which was couched in outright Utopian terms, and entitled *L'Heureuse nation ou relations du gouvernement des féliciens; peuple souverainement libre et heureux sous l'empire absolu des lois*. This work appears to confirm the observation of Tocqueville that socialism had some roots in physiocracy. Mercier's last work has also been described by his careful and scholarly expositor as demonstrating certain 'fascist' tendencies (Richner, 1931, 209–10). But this book lies, chronologically, some way outside our period. We shall, however, be returning briefly to Mercier when discussing his answer to Galiani's attack on physiocracy in his *Dialogues* (1770), an attack which played an important initial role in the decline of the physiocratic school.

VI

Pierre Samuel Dupont de Nemours (1739–1817), like Mirabeau and Mercier, had probably come some way towards the main physiocratic ideas under his own steam, before meeting Quesnay. Indeed, the idea of the prime, fundamental importance of agriculture had certainly become highly fashionable in France in the 1750s. Anyhow, Dupont, born in Paris, the son of a watchmaker, a precocious schoolboy and student, and a voracious reader, published his first work at the age of twenty-three, in which he brought together the two main physiocratic themes of agriculture and taxation. His pamphlet was a reply to a work supporting the reform of taxation in accordance with Vauban's *Royal Tithe*, which Dupont criticized as damaging to agriculture (see McLain, 1977, 52ff). Dupont's pamphlet (1763) attracted the attention of Mirabeau who introduced the young enthusiast to Quesnay, who, in turn, enrolled him as a research assistant and publicist for the school. In meeting the Doctor, Dupont found his destiny: 'From then on I stuck to him, as to a master, a teacher, a father' (McLain, 1977, 69).[9]

Dupont also met and assisted Turgot and became the editor first, in 1765–6, of the *Journal de l'Agriculture*, and then in the crucial years 1768–72, of the *Éphémérides du Citoyen*, which he took over from the Abbé Baudeau, its founder.[10] The physiocratic magazine was a lively publication, not confined to contributions from adherents of the school, though a loyal member usually promptly counter-attacked any critics.

Dupont was a man of articles and pamphlets rather than of the full-scale treatise. In fact, Schumpeter described his talents as 'those of the pianist and not the composer' (1954, 226). But he produced one or two lucidly and forcefully argued statements of physiocratic principles; and he is often credited with the invention of the term 'physiocracy' – though this may have originated with Quesnay.

Dupont's most accomplished and valuable work was probably his *De l'origine et des progrès d'une science nouvelle* (1768). Certainly his claims for the 'new science' – half a century later, of course, the Ricardians were also to describe themselves as the exponents of a 'new science' – were no less grandiose than those of Mercier. He began by asking whether, in that enlightened age, there could be room for any new branch of knowledge. Had not such giants as Confucius, Pythagoras, Socrates, Galileo, Descartes, and others he listed, provided us with a knowledge of just about all that human beings could, would, or needed to, know? Not quite, Dupont claimed. 'Thirteen years ago, a man of the most vigorous genius' had produced a whole new department of knowledge, which gave the new and certain answer to the vital question: 'how must one act for a political society to be flourishing, rich and powerful, so that the families and individuals of which it is composed are as happy as possible?' (1768, 5).

How one must act to achieve this great end was summed up in the *Tableau Économique*, which was described as 'this astonishing formula which depicts the distribution and production of wealth, and which serves to calculate, with so much reliability, promptitude, and precision, the effects of all processes concerned with wealth' (11).

It was the duty of the magistrates, under the supreme hereditary ruler, to implement and uphold natural laws. Ignorance was no excuse; in fact, as Quesnay himself had insisted, 'ignorance itself is a crime' (35). Perfect, or adequate knowledge, therefore, should, or must, be assumed, based on the self-evident character of the natural laws themselves – an assumption which seems to have been the precursor of the perfect-knowledge postulate, which came, of course, after Ricardo, to permeate a great deal of orthodox, economic theorizing.

When, around 1770, the crisis came for physiocracy, Dupont counter-attacked the critics in the *Éphémérides*, and then, with the waning of the movement in France, he sought to spread the gospel abroad. He visited the Grand Duke, Carl Friedrich of Baden, an important supporter, with whom he had a long exchange of letters, essays, and memoranda between 1769 and 1787 (see Knies, 1892, vol. II). In his advice to the Grand Duke, Dupont seemed to broaden somewhat the physiocratic conception of the role of government with regard to the treatment of poverty. In an article of 1773, he deplored the large numbers of poor in France and the lack of provision for them. He proposed that they be employed on the construction of much-needed roads. (Like Cantillon, the physiocrats were much concerned with the improvement of transport facilities.) Dupont even maintained that 'society needs to have as many public works carried out as possible, at the least expense' (see Knies, 1892, 102; and McLain, 1977, 129).

One of the essays which Dupont sent to the Grand Duke was that *On Economic Curves* (1774), in which he advocated the use of mathematics and made one of the first uses of curves in political economy. He claimed that, as regards the applicability of mathematics, there was no difference between political economy and mechanics: 'The objection that higher mathematics is not applicable to political economy is an absurd proposition, as absurd as if a person were to insist that one could not apply higher mathematics to mechanics or hydraulics' (1774 [1955], 2).

Dupont was concerned in this paper with the effects of taxation on prices and incomes. He started by stressing the obnoxious effects of any tolls or taxes on trade, and asserted, regarding prices, that 'they are all mutually interrelated' (4). He observed that the effects of imposing or removing taxes were felt only gradually, and he sought to demonstrate dynamically the path such effects would take by means of 'economic curves'. But he admitted that he had not fully developed his idea – which is certainly difficult to follow – though he described it as 'part of a general theory of prices'.

When Turgot became Minister of Finance, in 1774, and hopes for economic freedom and reform flared up again, all too briefly, Dupont returned from teaching in Poland to assist. Later he was to produce the first edition of Turgot's writings (nine vols, 1811). During the Revolution, Dupont continued to supply advice to the government and warned of the inflationary dangers arising from the issue of the *Assignats* (1790 [1950]).[11] Contrary to his strongly held position of twenty years previously, he recommended the imposition of restrictions on the export of grain, during the emergency, and supported some government regulation of the grain market (see McLain, 1977, 144–58).

Dupont spent the last two years of his life in America (1815–17), which he had visited earlier (1799–1802), and where he founded a great dynasty. Living well on into the classical era, he published his last writings, critiques of Malthus and Say, in the year of his death. He persisted to the end staunchly loyal to the basic physiocratic doctrines, which he had embraced so enthusiastically, as universal truths, half a century previously. Dupont may thus provide an illustration of the tendency for change and development in economic theory and doctrine to come about rather as a result of human mortality than because individuals change their views as a consequence of argument, discussion and testing.

VII

In the mid-1760s, following the edict freeing the export of grain, the physiocratic school reached the peak of its influence and prestige. After that, its decline was even more rapid than its rise had been. For the physiocrats were unlucky in their timing, in that the freeing of exports (1764) was almost immediately followed by a series of bad harvests. When food prices doubled and trebled, the physiocratic doctrine, which followed that of Boisguilbert in proclaiming the beneficence of high grain prices for producers, made it no easier to counter the inevitable popular protests. Together with the generally soaring prices there were sharp variations from region to region, while, with money incomes lagging far behind, and with unemployment increasing, rioting and violence ensued. Of course, the economists blamed the government for not having been sufficiently persistent and uncompromising.[12] Criticisms, moreover, were being launched by several able writers, including Forbonnais and Graslin.[13] By far the most damaging attack came from Galiani in 1770 (the same year in which the edict freeing grain exports was annulled). In the previous chapter, Galiani and his *Dialogues* were discussed at some length. It was observed that he was never fundamentally opposed to policies of economic freedom. He considered that the decree of 1764 was disastrous for France at that particular juncture, and he denied the relevance of the English example, put forward by Quesnay. Later in the year, Galiani was answered from the physiocratic side by Mercier in his work entitled, and subtitled: *The General Interest of the State, or the liberty of the grain trade demonstrated as being in conformity with natural law; with the public law of France; with the fundamental laws of the kingdom; with the common interest of the Sovereign and of his subjects at all times; and the refutation of a new system published in the form of Dialogues on the Grain Trade.*[14]

In his reply, Mercier did not get very closely to grips with Galiani's arguments, relying to a large extent on the reiteration of comprehensive, general propositions, such as that: '(1) Freedom of commerce must always be advantageous; (2) it always has been advantageous, and (3) great evils have always resulted from the suppression of this freedom' (1770, 15). The double object of policy must 'self-evidently' always be to produce the greatest abundance of useful things, and 'the most rigorous justice in their distribution' (29–30). Complete freedom of trade was essential for obtaining these objectives, for it derived from the right of property, which was established by 'physical necessity', and 'by the unchangeable will of the creator' (78).

Mercier then proclaimed the kind of methodological universalism so sharply opposed by Galiani:

> I do not cast my eye on any particular nation or sect. I seek to describe things as they must *essentially* be, without considering what they have been, or in what country they may have been. As the truth exists by, or of, itself, it is the truth in all places and at all times . . . by examining and reasoning we arrive at knowing the truth self-evidently, and with all the practical consequences which result from it; examples which appear to contrast with these consequences prove nothing . . .
>
> (1767, vol. I, 194)

Mercier sought, however, to support his arguments by citing examples and facts from English and French economic history, and maintained that, in England, freedom of export and import had raised prices in years of abundance and lowered them in years of dearth. He argued effectively that freedom was necessary against the 'scourge' of monopoly: 'In a nation where competition from outside is not admitted for the sale of goods of basic necessity, nobody can say at what level dearness may be halted' (274). He sought to justify higher prices as necessary for maintaining and expanding cultivation, and accused 'the Neapolitan' of neglecting the costs of producers, who needed assured prices.

Galiani composed a savage parody, *La Bagarre* – not published until 1979 – in which passages from Mercier's *General Interest* were printed side by side with satirical comments, or parodies, by Galiani. In effect, he accused the supporters of free grain exports of being responsible for riots and disorders, and denounced the physiocrats for 'constantly proclaiming vague general ideas, without ever being willing to examine rigorously either the application of theories, or the exceptions to the rules, or the circumstances' (Galiani, 1979, 75).

Galiani's *Dialogues*, and the economic facts of the crisis, helped very much to turn the tide of 'philosophic' opinion against physiocracy. It was not necessary to go as far as Galiani did in his comprehensive denunciation of the policy of free exports as the main cause of the crisis. It would have been enough to conclude, as the major modern study concludes, that, 'liberalization did not cause the dearth, but [that] it helped, directly and indirectly, to transform it into a crisis' (Kaplan, 1976, vol. II, 693). As an example of the swing against physiocracy in philosophical opinion, the change in Diderot's allegiance is notable. Ten years before, in the early, heady days of the movement, Diderot had been an enthusiastic fellow-traveller. But when the implementation of the free-market policy was followed by a deepening crisis, he was not prepared to go along with what had turned out to be the consequences of such a revolutionary step. In fact, this most radical of the leading '*philosophes*' came out on the side of Galiani (see Kaplan, 1976, vol. II, 687).

A further step in the decline was the closing down of the *Éphémérides du Citoyen* in 1772 (though it was restarted briefly while Turgot was Minister). Certainly in 1774 hopes for freer economic policies, including the freedom of grain exports, were very briefly revived again, when the new king, Louis XVI, sent for Turgot to be Controller-General of Finance, who then called on Dupont to be his assistant. Admirable as Turgot's struggle was, hopes for lasting success were even more short-lived than had been those of the 1760s. At the end of 1774 Quesnay died, having, in his last years, turned away from political economy, which less than a decade before he had proclaimed to be of the greatest interest and importance. Just over a year later, in February 1776, came the publication of *The Wealth of Nations*, with its rather cool treatment of physiocracy. The rapid, sweeping, and lasting predominance of Adam Smith's work brought the eclipse of Quesnay's school. In May 1776 Turgot was dismissed.

However, had the aged Doctor survived another six to twelve months it appears that Adam Smith would have dedicated *The Wealth of Nations* to the physiocratic master, a fact which it is interesting to contrast with the exhortation of David Hume regarding the school: 'Crush them, and pound them, and reduce them to dust and ashes' (Hume, 1932, vol. II, 205).

Hume's judgement of the physiocrats as 'the most chimerical and most arrogant set of men that now exists', was very similar to that of Galiani – the other of the two supremely sharp philosophic minds of the century.

VIII

Any attempt at an assessment of the work of Quesnay and his school must start with an emphatic distinction between their technical-analytical, economic achievements, and their political-philosophical doctrines. Any valid judgement must take full account of both aspects of their work, and will turn on the relative 'weighting' applied. Peter Gay has maintained that physiocracy was science masquerading as mysticism, rather than mysticism masquerading as science (1969, 349). There was certainly much of both in their peculiar intellectual concoction. But if exaggerated 'masquerading' arouses extravagant expectations, as part of a drive for influence and power, it may surely be regarded as an intellectual misdemeanour. Anyhow, if the view is taken that in political economy, technique, *by itself*, can achieve only *very* limited advances towards the proclaimed objectives of economists, in the form of less unsuccessful policies, and that what *is* highly important is the quality of the political and philosophical understanding with which any technical analysis is applied, then the judgement of the work of Quesnay and his school may be less favourable than if technical analysis is regarded as all-important.

Certainly, Quesnay's technical and conceptual contributions were of the greatest and most fundamental value: the analysis of different types of capital, and of the role of 'advances' and of time in production; the clarification of the circular flow of payments between classes, or sectors; the pioneer attempt at social accounting, together with the concepts of aggregate stationary equilibrium, and of a growing economy: all these amounted to an outstanding technical achievement. The judgement, however, on the whole peculiar agricultural emphasis of physiocracy cannot be so favourable. Certainly the stress on agriculture must be considered in relation to the economic condition of France in the middle of the eighteenth century – though the physiocrats themselves rejected any such relativist qualifications. There may well, at that juncture, have been a good case for correcting drastically the excesses of Colbert's industrial planning. Recently, also, fashions in development policy have moved against any kind of Colbertian-Stalinist 'crash' programmes of industrial development – so optimistically supported, in many quarters, during much of the twentieth century. In fact, physiocratic doctrines may well have possessed much relevance with regard to the time and place in which they originated – just as Marxian doctrines did for the Manchester of the 1840s, where *they* were conceived, and Keynesian doctrines for England in the 1920s and 1930s. None of these systems, however, retained their relevance long enough to justify the claims made by their exponents to universal applicability and to vast and substantial general validity.

Anyhow, to have relegated industrial expansion to 'sterility', in what was almost the richest and most advanced country of the day, just at the very moment when the vast development known as 'The Industrial Revolution' was gathering momentum, hardly seems to indicate a very acute sense of historical timing – which the physiocrats, of course, regarded as of no importance. As regards more developed countries today, with their high-spending departments of agriculture piling up butter mountains and wine lakes, it might seem the physiocratic priorities are being followed all too extravagantly.

Moreover, a profound, unresolved contrast, at the very basis of the physiocratic programme, was that between Quesnay's absolutist, political support for the – or a – *ancien régime*, and, on the other hand, his demands for a competitive, free-market, large-scale agriculture, which would have required a fundamental social transformation in France, scarcely incompatible with the conservative political institutions upheld by the master and his school.

Quesnay eventually received from posterity, as represented, notably, by Marx and Schumpeter, the credit due for his technical and conceptual achievements. But the agricultural 'vision' and emphasis of physiocracy did not subsequently obtain, and perhaps did not deserve, any wide acceptance, except, in some measure, from Malthus and one or two lesser figures. On the other hand, Quesnay's methodological doctrines, detached from their theological foundation, have had important followers, such as the Ricardians, with their pretentious claims for the laws of their 'new science' – which they also compared with the laws of physics. Also von Mises and his disciples, with their assertions of 'apodictic certainty', have, methodologically, in important respects, followed the physiocrats.

We have noticed the ferocious and comprehensive denunciations of Hume and Galiani. Later, Tocqueville recognized the political and philosophical importance of the physiocrats, and launched some significant criticisms. He ascribed to the school a considerable intellectual role in shaping the ideas behind the French Revolution: 'Though the Economists figure less prominently than our philosophers in histories of the period . . . I am inclined to think that it is from their writings that we learn most of its true character (1856 [1955], 158, quoted by Ruben, 1936, 35n.).

Tocqueville also noted how the physiocrats 'carried their theories to fanatical lengths' (159), and he emphasized the rather sinister significance of the political absolutism for which they stood, reinforced by universal public education and popular enlightenment:

> According to the Economists, the function of the State was not merely one of ruling the nation, but also that of recasting it in a given mold, of shaping the mentality of the population as a whole in accordance with a predetermined model, and instilling the ideas and sentiments they thought desirable into the minds of all.
>
> (162)[15]

Surely a faint whiff may here be discernible of what might, somewhat cacophonously, be described as 'proto-totalitarianism'. In fact, more recently, Friedrich Hayek has described Quesnay and the physiocrats as 'false individualists', 'who were led from the rationalistic individualism from which they started, not only close to socialism . . . but to advocate the worst despotism' (1949, 5).

Be that as it may: a careful survey concludes that the critics of the physiocrats such as Galiani, Forbonnais and Graslin, in their own day, had much justification:

> The economists critical of physiocracy, although their contribution to theoretical economics was (with the possible exception of Galiani) less important than that of the physiocrats, showed a much keener perception of the economic problems of eighteenth century France. On the issues of the grain trade, taxation, commerce, manufacturing and population, their ideas were more firmly grounded in observation and their policies more informed by a sense of what reforms were practical and feasible of execution, as well as desirable from a theoretical point of view.
>
> (Rogers, 1971, 363–4)

Certainly there are large items on both the credit and the debit sides of the intellectual accounts of Quesnay and his school.

17
The Milanese Enlightenment: Utility, Liberty and Mathematics

I

Cesare Beccaria (1735–94) and Pietro Verri (1728–97) were the two most important figures, certainly for the history of political economy, in what has been called the Milanese Enlightenment. They were the leaders of a group of enthusiastic, liberal, *avant-garde* political, legal, penal and economic reformers, active in Milan in the 1760s, associated with their journal *Il Caffè*.

Verri, born 1728 in the same year as Galiani, came of a wealthy and noble Milanese family and spent some time as a young man in Germany and Austria, in the Austrian army and at the court in Vienna. Returning to Milan he immersed himself in journalism and public affairs, and, in 1762, met Beccaria, seven years younger and another offspring of a noble family, who had studied law at the University of Pavia, graduating in 1758. They became, for a brief period, intimate friends and very close intellectual collaborators. Perhaps no two important contributors to the history of political economy have had a more intense, personal and turbulent relationship.[1] For a few years, they pursued very similar intellectual interests, and wrote on closely similar topics. Both men included among their first works tracts on the monetary problems of Milan, and, while Verri published in 1763 his proto-utilitarian *Discorso sulla felicità*, in the following year there appeared Beccaria's celebrated *Dei delitti e delle pene*, an outstanding work in the history both of penology and utilitarianism, which set up 'the greatest happiness shared by the greatest number' as the supreme objective of legislation and policy.[2] Verri had contributed to a similar subject in his *Osservazioni sulla tortura* (not published until 1804, seven years after his death). Incidentally many of Verri's and Beccaria's writings, for obvious reasons of censorship, were first published anonymously (or posthumously).

It seems that in the production of Beccaria's epoch-making essay, Pietro Verri, as well as providing vital, original ideas and stimulus, also played a major part in preparing the work for publication.[3] In 1766 Beccaria made a brief, reluctant and very unhappy visit to Paris, the purpose of which was to receive the plaudits of French intellectual society, and, in particular, of Voltaire. He was accompanied by Verri's younger brother, Alessandro, Pietro himself being unable to make the journey, though vigorously urging on Beccaria to do so. It was on the return from this brief expedition that a bitter quarrel broke out between Beccaria and Pietro Verri. Much later some public reconciliation took place and Verri paid fulsome tribute to the work of his one-time friend and fellow-reformer, and thus assisted in the emergence of what has been called, by his translator, 'the Beccaria myth' (1963).

Cesare Beccaria's most important economic writings were his essay on the monetary disorders of Milan (*De disordine e de rimedi delle monete nello stato di Milano*, 1762), and his *Elementi di economia pubblica*, the text of a course of lectures, apparently written up in 1769, before or soon after their delivery, but not published until 1804, ten years after the author's death. Mention should also be made of his inaugural lecture (1769) and of a brief note on the mathematical theory of smuggling, *Tentativo analitico sui contrabandi*.[4]

Monetary theory in the seventeenth and eighteenth centuries was often, or primarily, concerned with problems of coinage, such as debasement, depreciation and the parities between gold or silver coins. Such were the 'disorders' of the Milan currency, with which Beccaria was concerned. Beginning with a long quotation from Locke, Beccaria went on to describe the introduction of money as emerging from general consensus, rather than by premeditated design, and he set out the well-known reasons why gold and silver came to serve the purposes of money more effectively than any other goods. Subsequently, he recognized that some measure of public authentication or regulation might serve a useful purpose in preventing fraud. The first main principle on which an effective coinage must rest, according to Beccaria, was that the nominal, or face, values of coins must correspond with the intrinsic values of the metals they embodied (and he quoted Pufendorf on this point). Otherwise, some coins would be lost from the nation's money supply. With regard to the values of coins, and, more generally, regarding economic processes, Beccaria repeatedly emphasized the uselessness of governmental attempts to decree or enforce values by positive laws, and indeed, he wrote of 'fundamental laws of nature, written in men's blood in characters more indelible than bronze or marble' (1762, 225–6n.) – the kind of methodological phraseology adopted by the physiocrats.

In 1768–9 Beccaria was appointed to a new chair of 'Cameral Science' in Milan – a rare use of the term outside Germany and Austria. In his inaugural lecture 'A Discourse on Public Economy and Commerce', of which an English translation soon appeared (1769), he described his subject as 'the principles of public economy and commerce, or those sciences which furnish the means of increasing the riches of a state, and applying them to the most useful purposes'.[5]

He then proceeded to list those who had brought the subject to what he regarded as its very high level. The most important, he suggested, were, probably, Montesquieu, Hume and Genovesi. Also mentioned were Vauban and Melon from France, and Ustariz and Ulloa from Spain.[6] Galiani, as well as Petty, Cantillon, Quesnay and Turgot were not on Beccaria's list, though the influence of physiocracy is apparent in his work. He then went on, with the rather pretentious over-optimism typical of the Enlightenment, to claim, regarding political economy, 'that nothing more seems wanting, unless the last and not least lineaments, to render it perfect, and of general and certain utility'.

On turning to governmental service in Milan, Beccaria did not continue his course of lectures, or complete the text in accordance with the ambitious plan he had set out. This had been to start with agriculture, as the fount and origin of wealth and economic life, and to continue with manufacturing and commerce (including money and foreign trade), concluding with taxation and public finance and policy. Agricultural policy is discussed with a somewhat physiocratic emphasis, though the writings of the leading physiocrats are not cited. Beccaria came down in favour of free trade in agricultural produce, together with improvements in transport and larger-scale farming. As regards manufacturing, this simply consisted of the transformation of the raw produce of nature. Countries that lived entirely from their manufacturing output were dependent on the original natural resources of others. The overriding aim of economic policy was to stimulate, or to bring into operation, the maximum possible quantity of *useful* labour.

Perhaps the most interesting analytical contribution of Beccaria's *Elements*, was on the subject of the value and price of goods (1804, 344ff.). On this subject he differed fundamentally from the physiocrats in that he offered a re-statement of the utility-cum-scarcity explanation of value, as expounded by the natural-law philosophers and by his Italian predecessors:

> Goods may be considered to have value, first, to the extent to which they contribute to satisfying needs, or adding to the conveniences, or promoting the pleasures of life; and secondly, to the extent that they are scarce and difficult to obtain. Goods which are common, and to be found everywhere, however essential, such as air, and, almost always, water, have no value. In the same way, things which are of no use or convenience, or which give no pleasure, however scarce, are of no value. But this utility and scarcity of goods is not always absolute and universal, but varies, or is relative. Many things cease entirely to have utility because other goods, which are easier to obtain, and more useful, replace them, so the value of the former ceases, or is diminished. Many goods, on the other hand, increase in value because they are discovered to have new uses and new utility. Many, too, are scarce in one country and abundant in another.
>
> (344–5)[7]

Beccaria went on to describe a model of the two-person, two-commodity barter of corn for wine. In the first, highly simplified case, he assumed that the two parties, one with corn and the other with wine, each decided that a certain quantity of what they held was superfluous to their needs, and proceeded to exchange the two superfluous quantities at a constant rate of so much corn for a litre of wine. Then it was supposed that the wine-owner might have a much greater need for corn than the corn-owner for wine, so that the exchange rate would alter. It was then concluded: 'Between only two contracting parties it is not possible to calculate the extent to which differing demands may raise the price of one good, and lower that of another, with each party seeking to give less, rather than more, and to obtain, in return, as much as possible' (347–8).

Beccaria then introduced a third party possessing hides, who needed wine and corn, just as the original pair wanted hides. The corn- and the wine-owner are assumed, before the arrival of the third party, to have agreed on a price of two measures of corn for one of wine. It was then agreed by the *three* parties that the owner of hides should give one hide for three measures of corn, and so, also, for one-and-a-half measures of wine. Thus it could come about that corn would be adopted as the measure for other goods, or as a corn standard of value. A further complication was then introduced of a second hide merchant, who offered some better quality, or better finished, hides than those of the first, and demanded a higher price for them, according to the quantity of labour devoted to improving his hides, as compared with the unimproved or unfinished hides.

In spite of some obvious missing elements, such as the idea of diminishing utility in a clear, explicit form, Beccaria provided here a notable anticipation of the neoclassical approach to value and price, starting from a subjective value concept, and a simple barter case, rather on the lines of both Menger and Walras. In fact, Beccaria's treatment of value and exchange, brief as it was, bore a marked resemblance to that of Turgot in his unpublished paper on 'Valeurs et Monnaie', written at a rather similar date. But Beccaria does not seem to have penetrated as far, and as incisively, on this subject, as Galiani had twenty years previously.

Beccaria's *Tentativo analitico sui contrabandi*, which appeared in *Il Caffè*, was only a three-page note, but it contained one or two interesting methodological pronouncements. On the one hand, Beccaria recommended the use of algebra in 'political science' as 'a precise and very rapid method of reasoning about quantities' (1765, 427). On the other hand, the considerable limitations of mathematics were emphasized: 'Because political principles depend in large part on many particular wills, and the most various passions, which cannot be determined with precision, a policy completely drawn up in figures and calculi would be ridiculous, more applicable to the inhabitants of Laputa than to us Europeans' (427).

In his analysis of smuggling, Beccaria, perhaps not very realistically, started by assuming that the alternatives for the smugglers were simply, if caught, those of either paying the duty, or having their goods confiscated. This defined the risks to the two parties: to the government that of losing the duty, and to the smugglers that of losing their goods. Beccaria claimed that an analysis on these lines might help the government in drawing up its list of duties on goods.

Beccaria's discussion of money began with the idea of one good (corn, in Beccaria's example) emerging as a measure of value, or *numéraire* (7–8).

But to serve effectively as a means of exchange a good must have the qualities of uniformity, durability, and portability, as well as divisibility. He went on to propound a quantity theory. Regarding international trade, presumably following Hume, Beccaria asserted that a country's active or passive balance would be corrected over time by self-adjusting processes, and that the balance 'is continually tending to an equilibrium' – though he did not specify at all fully or precisely how the mechanism operated (87–8).

Certainly Beccaria's *Elements* demonstrate a great mind being applied to the subject, at this important, formative, juncture in its history. But the work remained in a somewhat unfinished state. On policy, Beccaria does not seem to have been as fully and consistently on the side of economic freedom as the physiocrats and Adam Smith. Indeed he was something of a protectionist. Joseph Schumpeter, however, claimed to have discerned a number of very close similarities between Beccaria and Smith. Of course, they were both wide-ranging, philosophical thinkers, writing at the same historical juncture, and subject to a number of common influences. But Schumpeter pressed his comparison to exaggerated and misleading lengths (and its significance also seems doubtful in view of some of his highly unfavourable comments, at other points in his *History*, on Smith, and on Smith's contribution to economic theory).[8]

II

Pietro Verri's wide-ranging writings included two notable philosophical contributions to utilitarian ideas: the already-mentioned *Discorso sulla felicità* (1763), and the *Discorso sull 'indole del piacere e del dolore* (*Discourse on the Character of Pleasure and Pain*) (1773). The earlier *Discorso* included the proposition that public happiness should consist of 'the greatest possible happiness distributed with the greatest possible equality' (1763 [1964], 100) – just as Beccaria would set up 'the greatest happiness shared by the greatest number', as the supreme *desideratum*, in his great work published the following year. On political economy, Verri's most important works were his *Reflections on the Laws Restricting the Trade in Grain* (written, apparently, in 1769, but not published until 1797) and, in particular, his *Meditations on Political Economy* (1771).

Verri's *Reflections on the Grain Trade*, were devoted to the major central problem both of policy and theory, in several leading countries, throughout much of the eighteenth century. On the one hand, this was the most acute, recurring issue of public policy, on which internal peace and order might closely depend, and, on the other hand, it was the most important and controversial example in the growing, theoretical discussion of the beneficent, equilibrating properties of free markets. At the moment when Verri was writing in Milan, a fierce debate, as we have seen, was about to break out in Paris with the publication of Galiani's *Dialogues*. Verri argued emphatically for freedom of trade and competition, pointing to the example of England – rejected, of course, *for France*, by Galiani. Verri marshalled empirical and statistical evidence in support of his case, and opposed public granaries as expensive and dangerous. He cited in support Antonio Genovesi, and also, not *entirely* justifiably, Boisguilbert's *Détail*, of three-quarters of a century earlier.

This essay of Verri is of special interest as an example of the international spread of economic ideas, a wide range of French, English and Spanish writers being cited or quoted, sometimes in Italian or French translations.[9] Among French writers mentioned, in addition to Boisguilbert, were Vauban, Montesquieu, Morellet and the physiocrats Mirabeau, Baudeau and Dupont de Nemours. Verri also quoted from an Italian translation of John Cary's works, and from a French translation of Robert Wallace's *Dissertation on the Numbers of Mankind in Ancient and Modern Times* (1753).

In his *Meditazioni* (1771), Verri described political economy as 'a kind of empirical medicine' (128n.)[10] He maintained that his method differed from that usually followed by many writers who, in the tranquillity of their studies, constructed abstract ideas about commerce, finance and the various types of industry, on the basis of hypotheses and speculations, and not by starting from an empirical examination of the elements of their material. He claimed for his part, to start empirically from particular facts (128).

Verri approached his subject from the side of human needs and wants (as Carl Menger and Marshall, among others were to do), as the original stimulus to economic and commercial activity. New and growing needs brought new and growing production and industry, so that a prosperous state was, first, one with many and complex needs, and the ability to satisfy them; and, second, it was one which could and did produce more than it consumed. Growing and more complex exchanges required common ideas and stable standards of valuation; these were brought about by the introduction of money. This development of a kind of 'universal good' led, in turn, to more uniformity in, and a more common measure of, the values of all goods. *In fact, the means and media of communication were fundamental for economic development*:

> The most beneficent inventions for the human race, which have developed its genius and the human spirit, are those which bring men together, and facilitate the spread of ideas, wants, and sentiments, by turning the human race into a mass. These are the perfecting of shipping, postal services, the press, and in the first place, money.
>
> The more that transport is facilitated, the more the means of communication are extended and ideas multiplied; the more needs increase, the more commerce increases.
>
> (133)

It was this increase in commerce that promoted the growth of agricultural production. Verri had thus outlined and clarified what was to be the Smithian concept of the extent of the market, as a major factor in economic growth, by describing it as a system of inter-communication of ideas, needs, wants and knowledge.

In another Smithian passage, Verri emphasized the vital relationship between a nation's annual production and its annual consumption: 'Two main objects must be observed: annual production and annual consumption ... When the total value of production is equal to the annual value of consumption, the nation remains in the same state, all other things being equal. A nation declines when annual consumption exceeds annual production, and progresses when annual production exceeds consumption' (134; see also 137). Verri – unlike Beccaria – rejected fundamentally the physiocratic doctrine of the 'sterility' of manufactures: there was value added by human labour in manufacturing: 'there is, therefore, production of value and wealth, if earth, air, and water transform themselves into corn in the fields, or if, by human hands, the gluten of a worm is transmuted into velvet, or if pieces of metal are arranged to make a machine' (135). In fact, artisans were often paid more than agricultural workers, and rightly so: 'the industrial worker receives, as part of the price charged, not only a sum equal to what has been consumed, but an additional sum beyond this, which is a new quantity of value, and part of the annual production ... The manufacturing class cannot be described as sterile' (136). Verri thus rejected both the methodology and the fundamental axioms of the physiocrats.

On value and price, Verri – like Beccaria – offered an accomplished rendering of the Italian utility-cum-scarcity version of the natural-law theory. A good could not command a price through utility alone if it was available in abundance. Scarcity (*rarità*) was also necessary, and price would rise with increasing scarcity.

Verri then produced a more elaborate analysis of supply and demand, depending on the numbers of suppliers and demanders on either side of the market, an analysis which Luigi Einaudi (1953, 185–9) compared with that of Cournot in chapter 5 of his *Recherches*. Verri, like Cournot, examined the workings of markets with different numbers of sellers, starting with a monopolist, and going on to duopoly, and then to a further increase in the number of sellers, where any form of agreement was more difficult (144ff).

Turning to the subject of distribution, Verri asserted that both too much inequality and too-perfect equality would reduce annual production, which would be promoted by large numbers of freely competing sellers. He expressed strong opposition to monopolies and to all claims for exclusive privileges, whether by unions or guilds, or by setting up colonies, regarding the benefits of which he was doubtful. He also condemned restrictions on exports, and, as in his *Reflections on the Grain Trade*, he argued for freedom of the grain trade. He particularly forcefully rejected price regulation when 'the price becomes an arbitrary action of the legislature which wrongs the sellers and so reduces numbers' (171). Whatever the form of government, 'it is in the interest of the sovereign to leave to the citizens the greatest possible liberty' (172). Verri went on to describe a process of decline along a kind of road to serfdom:

> It seems to me that every bit of freedom removed from men amounts to a political error, because this deliberate action by the legislator is regarded by the people as a use of power. Gradually the imitation will spread. The

> people's ideas of morality will weaken, and as they cease to trust their security, they will resort to deception. Moreover, if these political errors multiply, the nation will become fatally timid; then it will become a pretence, and finally inert, and will decline in numbers, if the too habitual exercise of power becomes oppressive.
>
> (172–3)

Verri at once adds, however, a typical touch of optimism, characteristic of the Enlightenment: 'In our fortunate condition today, with the progress of philosophy in all branches of knowledge, and with the gentle humanity of present-day governments, such things cannot occur, except in speculation' (173).

Verri attempted to combine price theory with a quantity theory of money by treating the prices of commodities as dependent on the quantity of money in circulation, as well as on supply and demand and the number of sellers and buyers of particular commodities:

> Prices are in direct proportion to the buyers and inverse proportion to the sellers . . . If the quantity of money in circulation falls, other things remaining equal, price will fall. If the quantity for sale increases, everything else remaining equal, then the price will fall; that is, if the number of buyers falls, and that of sellers increases, prices will be reduced.
>
> (177)

On the theory of money Verri seems to have been influenced by his friend Henry Lloyd (see section III below). Both men described money as 'the universal merchandise', and attempted a mathematical formulation of a quantity theory.[11]

Verri maintained that it was a normal human tendency for population to increase 'prodigiously'. In fact, unless there was some special cause at work, there was something wrong in a country if population was not increasing, or only increasing less than in proportion to natural fecundity. The growth of population in a state indicated growing annual production, and the main task of economic policy was to achieve 'the maximum possible growth in production with the minimum possible labour' (201). Verri observed, however, that, as with the balance of payments, it was all too difficult to obtain reasonably accurate statistics of population and its movements, and especially so with regard to comparisons between countries (205–6).

Verri devoted much attention to taxation, anticipating the importance which Italian economists were subsequently to attach to the subject of public finance. He emphasized that the system of taxation had a major influence on production, circulation and industry, and with regard also to increasing the wealth of the state and the community and using that wealth beneficently. Taxation originated justly from the need of all citizens for defence and security, internally and externally, but if allowed to increase, or if wrongly distributed, it could bring economic decline. Verri laid down five main principles for taxation: (a) taxes should not fall immediately on the poor; (b) they should be imposed in a manner which minimized costs of collection; (c) tax legislation should be clear, precise, inviolable and impartial; (d) taxes should never raise transport costs; and (e) taxes should never penalize the growth of industry (223–32).

Verri concluded that public policy must proceed by indirect routes, in that it must *invite* and *guide* and not force or command. The Minister for the Economy must be active negatively, rather than positively. His task was

> ... to remove obstacles, abolish restrictions, open up ways of competition, or the encouragement of production; increase civil liberty, leave a wide field for industry, specially protect the producing class by good legislation, so that neither the agricultural workers nor the artisans fear the domination of the wealthy; ensure the easy, prompt and disinterested completion of contracts for sales and purchases, spreading commercial good faith by not leaving fraud unpunished; fighting for the interests of the public, rightly understood ...
>
> (259)

Verri's final word is that it is only error and opinions that hold men in chains and render entire nations unproductive. His *Meditations* contains many penetrating insights. Written very rapidly, however, its conciseness seems sometimes to lead to inconsistency.[12] Part an introduction to principles, and part a policy pamphlet, with a deep concern for reform, it is an outstanding work from the years immediately preceding the publication of *The Wealth of Nations*.

III

How on earth, it might be enquired, can a Welsh-born, itinerant army officer and military adviser have had anything to do with the economic ideas of the Milanese Enlightenment? The explanation is as follows.

Henry Lloyd (?1720–83), born Henry Humphrey Evans at Wrexham, the son of a Welsh clergyman, served at various times in a number of European armies, including the French, Austrian and Russian. He is best known as a military historian, and was interested in economics and politics insofar as they were concerned with the foundations of the military power of nations. It was while they were both serving in the Austrian army in 1759 that Lloyd met Pietro Verri, with whom he struck up a very warm friendship, renewed when Lloyd later visited Milan. Lloyd seems to have influenced and encouraged Verri in his interest in political economy and in his writing of the *Meditazioni*, and was himself the author of what Jevons, in his important bibliography of mathematical economics, described as 'the earliest work of the kind yet discovered' (1911, xlvi). This was a volume, with a rather twentieth-century title, *An Essay on the Theory of Money*, which included a rough-and-ready algebraic formulation of the quantity theory. Money was defined as 'the universal merchandise', and its introduction had played a major role in human progress. Money 'by facilitating the communication between mankind gave birth to all the arts, manufactures, sciences, and forms of government which we now see and enjoy in the different parts of the globe' (vi).

But the growth of the monetary economy had also produced dangerous inequalities and discontents.

An adequate supply of money, essential for a growing economy, was only obtainable by a relatively large paper issue. Paper money, moreover, enabled 'ready money' (i.e. metallic money) to be exported for vital imports. The necessary banking and monetary institutions were only possible in a free country, for, under a tyranny, individual fortunes were too precarious for the extension of credit.

Not much concern was expressed as to the dangers of inflation. But it was asserted that in England and Holland, 'the quantity of circulation' was 'probably too great, which enhances the price of provisions', and so reduced exports. It was maintained that the issue of paper money was not excessive if it did not exchange at a discount, and if the level of prices and provisions was not so high as to reduce exports.

The idea of the quantity theory was expressed in the proposition that 'the price of any merchandize whatsoever is in an inverse ratio of its quantity' (82). The algebra was set out as $C/M = P$, where C was 'circulation' (or MV in Fisher's terms) and M was 'merchandize' (or T). Lloyd did not include velocity, though he related 'circulation' to the size of the population. Stock and flow concepts were not distinguished. A similar algebraic formula was propounded for the rate of interest, as determined by the supply and demand of lenders and borrowers.

Lloyd's *Essay* does not seem to have had any impact or recognition in England before Jevons. In Italy, however, through his relationship with Pietro Verri, there has been considerable interest in his work. The Verri–Lloyd relationship remains a remarkable example of Italo-Welsh friendship and intellectual cooperation in the field of political economy.[13]

IV

Let us, in conclusion, re-emphasize how, in the eighteenth century, most of the main pioneering attempts at applying mathematics to the formulation of economic theories, came from Italian writers. We noted at the end of chapter 9 the highly original work of Giovanni Ceva of Modena (1711). Moreover, though Daniel Bernoulli cannot be counted as an Italian, it seems that he was probably significantly influenced by the Italian approach to utility and value, while the only recognition his work seems to have received from an economist, for about a century and a half, came from the young Galiani. In this chapter we have just seen how the two leaders of the Milanese Enlightenment, Beccaria and Verri, together with the mathematician Paolo Frisi, another member of the group around the journal *Il Caffè*, were pioneers in attempting the mathematical formulation of theories in both of the main branches of economics, 'micro' and 'macro': Beccaria with regard to import duties and smuggling, and Verri with regard to a quantity theory of money.[14]

18
French Pre-eminence: Saving and Investment: Subjective Utility and Expectations

I

Anne Robert Jacques Turgot (1727–81), born in Paris, the youngest son of a noble Normandy family, was, in his youth, destined for the church until, in 1750–1, aged twenty-three, a crisis of conscience diverted him from an ecclesiastical to an administrative career. In 1749 he had written his first work on political economy, an 'Essay on Paper Money', in which he criticized the ideas of John Law and upheld an 'intrinsic', or 'realist', view of the value of money. In 1750, while still studying theology at the Sorbonne, he produced a remarkable 'Discourse on the Successive Advances of the Human Mind', together with further plans for discourses, including one on universal history. These youthful works announced a faith in human progress and perfectibility which Turgot was to retain throughout his life.

At some point in the early 1750s Turgot got to know Vincent de Gournay, and he contributed to the series of economic writings and translations which appeared at this time, under the inspiration and initiative of that important intellectual leader. Turgot contributed comments to the French translation (1754), partly by Gournay, of Josiah Child's *New Discourse of Trade*, and in 1755 his translation appeared of Josiah Tucker's *Reflections on the Naturalization of Foreign Protestants*, (which contained a suggestion of the classical doctrine of the impossibility of general over-production). This was Turgot's first published economic work.

In 1755–6 Turgot accompanied Gournay the '*Intendant*', or Commissioner, for Trade, on tours of inspection in the provinces; and, on Gournay's death in 1759, wrote the eloquent *Éloge de Gournay*. Precisely when Turgot met Quesnay does not seem to be known. But, though accepting and supporting some physiocratic ideas, Turgot remained outside the school, and insisted on his indebtedness to Gournay as well as to Quesnay. He never accepted the profundity of the contrast drawn by the physiocrats between agriculture, on the one hand, and industry and commerce, on the other. He also generalized the emphasis on, and idea of, 'advances' to include all forms of 'moveable' capital; and he argued much more strongly than the physiocrats for the legitimacy of interest. As Schumpeter put it, Turgot 'should not be classified as a physiocrat with reservations, but as a non-physiocrat with physiocratic sympathies (1954, 244).[1]

In 1761 Turgot was appointed *Intendant* at Limoges, then a poor part of France, where he remained for thirteen years. The post gave him great independent power locally. He worked strenuously on a wide range of economic reforms, including notably the reform of taxation, and of the *corvée*, or system of forced labour on the harvest. During the grain crisis of 1769–70 he organized public works and poor relief. He also much improved the road system. In these years, on top of these labours as a devoted, over-worked administrator, Turgot wrote his most important economic works and papers. Most of these were related to the current policy problems he was facing, such as his *Paper on Lending at Interest* (1770), his *Letters on the Grain Trade* (also 1770), and his *Letter on the 'Marque des Fers'* (1773), which was concerned with duties on the iron trade. There were two very important works, on fundamental theoretical problems, which must be discussed fully. These were his *Reflections on the Production and Distribution of Riches*, and his unfinished essay, 'Value and Money'.

In 1774 Turgot was called to Paris to the top economic post in the government, there to begin a heroic phase of his life which lasted less than two years, and which we shall discuss at a later point.

II

The *Reflections on the Formation and Distribution of Riches*, Turgot's largest single work on political economy, was written in 1766 and published in three numbers of the *Éphémérides* in 1769–70. The *Reflections* were intended for the instruction of two Chinese students, brought to Paris by missionaries, who were to return home to China for the enlightenment of their fellow-countrymen. There was, thus, a contrast with Quesnay, who proclaimed, rather, that the West should learn from China, and that the Chinese had little to learn from westerners, or anyone else, since in their country an ideal régime, in accordance with natural law, had already been instituted.

Turgot led into the fundamental problems of economics by starting from the specialization and division of land. (Ten years later, in the celebrated opening chapters of *The Wealth of Nations*, Adam Smith was to introduce the problems of his subject by explaining the role of the division of labour.) Turgot opened with the observation that no trade or exchange would, or could, exist, if all land were of the same quality, and were divided equally, so that everyone possessed just sufficient to yield a bare subsistence. In the real world, however, the inequalities of land ownership, together with the diversity of soils, and the multiplicity of wants, brought into existence the exchange economy. Some would own land most suitable for one kind of product, and some for another.

Turgot then turned to the most important theme of the *Reflections*, that of the different forms of capital, and the role of capital and time in methods of production which required long preparations and processes to satisfy the final wants of consumers: 'Take, for example, the preparation of hides; what labourer could attend to all the details necessary in this operation, which lasts several months and sometimes several years?' (1769–70 [1898], 5). A man who was 'reduced to his own field and his own labour, would consume much time and trouble and be very badly equipped in every respect, and would cultivate his land very badly' (6). So a great expansion in productivity resulted from the division of labour, in the first instance between those owning different kinds of land, and then between those who worked on the land and those who worked up the raw produce of the land: 'Everyone profited by this arrangement, for each, by devoting himself to a single kind of work, succeeded much better in it . . . Each workman laboured to satisfy the workmen of all the other kinds, who, on their side, all laboured for him' (6).

Turgot then indicated his physiocratic inclinations by maintaining that it was the produce of the agricultural worker, or husbandman, that was basic, constituting a 'physical necessity':

> The husbandman, we may say in general terms, can get on without the labour of the other workmen, but no workman can labour if the husbandman does not enable him to live. In this circulation, which by the reciprocal exchange of wants, renders men necessary to one another and forms the bond of the society, it is, then, the labour of the husbandman which imparts the first impulse. What his labour causes the land to produce, beyond his personal wants, is the only fund for the wages which all the other members of the society receive in exchange for their labour.
>
> (7)

Here Turgot expounded the fundamental classical concept of the wages fund. His theory of wages, at this point, also anticipated the classical doctrine, in terms of strict subsistence, though later he was to allow for some flexibility: 'The mere workman, who has only his arms and his industry, has nothing except in so far as he succeeds in selling his toil to others' (8). As Turgot explained, in a passage cited by Marx, the employer

> . . . pays him as little as he can; as he has the choice among a great number of workmen, he prefers the one who works cheapest. The workmen are therefore obliged to lower the price, in competition with one another. In every kind of work it cannot fail to happen, and as a matter of fact it does happen, that the wages of the workman are limited to what is necessary to procure him his subsistence.
>
> (8)

Subsequently Turgot relaxed this austere doctrine – as did, subsequently, some of the English classicals – maintaining that though the cost of subsistence was the *fundamental* price of labour, the *current* price, determined by supply and demand, might vary from the subsistence level. As he put it in his *Letters on the Grain Trade*:

> It is certain that competition, by causing wages to be at a lower level, reduces those of the simple unskilled workers to what is necessary to their subsistence. It should not be thought, however, that this necessity is thus reduced to the essentials for avoiding starvation to such an extent that nothing remains outside it, which these men may have at their command either to obtain some little luxuries, or, if they are thrifty, to create a little movable fund which becomes their resort in unforeseen cases of sickness, or times of high prices, or unemployment.
>
> (Groenewegen, 1977, 168)

Anyhow, it was land alone which provided the cultivator with a surplus of produce over and above his subsistence. Turgot supposed that originally the landowner must also have been the cultivator, but the more industrious or fortunate landowners acquired larger properties, and began to employ workers, bringing about division into classes:

> By this arrangement the produce of the land is divided into two parts. The one includes the subsistence and the profits of the husbandman, which are the reward of his labour and the condition upon which he undertakes to cultivate the field of the proprietor. What remains is that independent and disposable part which the land gives as a pure gift to him who cultivates it, over and above his advances and the wages of his trouble; and this is the portion of the proprietor, or the revenue with which the latter can live without labour and which he carries where he will.
>
> (1769, 14)

Thus Turgot, at this point, distinguished three classes: the cultivators (or agricultural workers), the artisans, and the landowners. These three classes he described with rather strange-sounding adjectives: the 'productive' class, the 'stipendiary' class (i.e. paid by others); and the 'disposable' class (or those whose incomes did not represent essential costs of production).

Different agricultural methods were then reviewed by Turgot: such as using wage labour, or slaves; the adoption of the *métayer*, or share-cropping, system, prevalent in the south of France; or, finally, letting out the land, either in perpetuity for a fixed payment, or for a few years at a time. This last method, Turgot asserted, which obtained in northern France, with the cultivators responsible for the advances, was the most advantageous. Provided that a certain level of wealth had been attained, this would enable larger advances to be made of labour and manure, which would bring 'a prodigious increase' in the produce and revenue of estates.

Turgot then turned to the analysis of money, exchange, value and price. Starting with the case of two-person, two-commodity barter, he showed how different pairs of exchangers, at different times, might arrive at different exchange rates, as their supplies and needs fluctuated. It was only when small, isolated exchanges were replaced by the competition of numbers of exchangers that a common rate was arrived at. The relative values of two commodities, say corn and wine, were 'no longer debated between the two isolated individuals in relation to their relative wants and abilities; it is fixed by the balance of the wants and abilities of the whole body of the sellers of corn with those of the whole body of the sellers of wine' (30).

Turgot then foreshadowed, in outline, the Walrasian concept of the *numéraire*: 'Commerce gives to each article exchanged a current value, with respect to every other article; whence it follows that every article of commerce is the equivalent of a certain quantity of every other article, and can be regarded as a pledge which represents it' (30). Thus 'each article of commerce can serve as the scale or common measure wherewith to compare the value of others' (31). Some goods, however, are much more convenient than others for providing a scale of values, by possessing the qualities of homogeneity, stability, and divisibility. Hence the emergence of gold and silver as units of account, though these goods too, vary in value at different times and places. Here Turgot reasserted his 'intrinsic', or metallic view regarding the value of money (which he had proclaimed in his early paper on paper money). He maintained that 'all commodities are, in some respects, *money*' (36). Turgot was to develop these ideas much further in his important paper 'Value and Money'.

The development of exchange and money had greatly assisted the division of labour, and so promoted economic progress (42). The use of money had also assisted the accumulation of 'movable riches', which had immensely facilitated the necessary advances and investment: 'It is even necessary that in every trade the workmen, or the entrepreneurs who set them at work, should have a certain fund of moveable riches accumulated beforehand' (44).

Turgot described the process by which the accumulation of capital, in money form, took place: 'Whoever, either from the revenue of his land, or from the wages of his labour or of his industry receives each year more values than he needs to spend, may place this superfluity in reserve and accumulate it; these accumulated values are what is called *a capital*' (50).

Turgot then went on to analyse the different ways in which capital in money could be employed. There were always profitable investment opportunities, he implied, and he treated as pathological the hoarding of 'the timid miser, who amasses money only to quiet his imagination against the apprehension of needing the necessaries of life in an uncertain future' (50). The person with a sum of money to invest could, first, buy land, the most secure investment, and, therefore, the one with the lowest return. Secondly, he could employ his money in advances to manufacturing or industrial enterprises. For, just as in agriculture, so in industry, there were two classes: one was 'that of the undertakers, manufacturers, employers, all possessors of large capitals which they make a profit from'; and, the other was that of the 'simple artisans who have no other property but their arms' (54). Thirdly, capital could be employed in advances to agriculture. By now Turgot was pointing to the similarities between agriculture and industry, rather than emphasizing the unique or exclusive characteristics of production from the land. Fourthly, capitals might be employed in commerce, or in the intermediary processes linking original producers and final consumers. The merchants helped entrepreneurs to obtain their return as soon as possible. All merchants, whether wholesale or retail, purchased in order to sell again.

Thus capital, or 'moveable accumulated riches', were required in all forms of economic activity, and the continual advance and return of capitals constituted the 'circulation' in an economy:

> It is this advance and this continual return of capitals which constitute what *one must call the circulation of money*; that useful and fruitful circulation which gives life to all the labours of the society, which maintains movement and life in the body politic, and which is with great reason compared to the circulation of blood in the animal body.
>
> (63)

Turgot emphasized the dangers of any disruption of this circulation:

> For if, by any disorder, be it what it may, in the sequence of expenditures on the part of the different classes of society, the undertakers cease to get back their advances with the profit they have a right to expect from them, it is evident that they will be obliged to reduce their undertakings ... that poverty will take the place of wealth, and that the common workmen, ceasing to find employment, will fall into the extremest destitution.
>
> (63)

According, however, to Turgot's assumptions regarding the workings of a free economy, and, in particular, his dismissal of hoarding, such disorders simply could not, or would not, occur.

Since capital was so necessary in all undertakings, those who wished to produce anything, but had not the capital required for starting up production, would be ready to pay the 'capitalist', who would supply him with funds. These investors had to balance the risk of loss against their prospective share of the profits. Turgot then delivered a forthright attack – which the physiocrats had generally refrained from launching – on 'the errors of the schoolmen' in condemning lending at interest and endeavouring 'to make us regard it as a crime' (68). In fact, the rate of interest was (as he put it elsewhere) – 'the price of loanable funds' (153), and should be 'regulated, like that of all other merchandise, by the balance of supply and demand ... It is a current price, fixed like that of all other merchandise' (74).

The rate of interest depended on the demand of borrowers, and the supply from lenders of accumulated savings, therefore 'the spirit of economy in a nation' added to the supply of savings, and lowered interest rates. The fall in interest in Europe, in recent times, had proved that frugality had prevailed over luxury (80).

The yields from different types of investment varied, in accordance with varying risks, but were related to one another in that there was 'a sort of equilibrium' between them. Turgot likened the current rate of interest on loans to 'a kind of thermometer of the abundance or scarcity of capitals in a nation, and of the extent of the undertakings of every sort on which it may embark'. He demonstrated the international advantages of a low interest rate:

> If interest is at five per cent, all uncleared land whose produce would not bring five per cent, over and above the replacement of the advances and the recompense for the care of the cultivator, would remain uncultivated. No manufacture, no commerce will maintain itself which will not bring in five per cent, over and above the wages of the undertaker's exertions and risks. If there is a neighbouring nation in which the interest of money is only two per cent, not only will it carry on all the branches of commerce from which the nation where interest is at five per cent finds itself excluded, but, moreover, as its manufacturers and merchants can content themselves with a lower profit, they will place their commodities on all the markets at a much lower price . . .
>
> (85–6)

'The price of interest', Turgot concluded, 'may be looked upon as a kind of level beneath which all labour, all agriculture, all industry, all commerce come to an end' (86). He went on to emphasize that the interest on money, whether lent to agriculture or to industry, was not 'disposable', and that the state could not tax it without reducing the supply:

> This return ought, then, to be inviolable, and enjoy an entire immunity, because it is the price of an advance made to an undertaking, without which the undertaking could not go on. To touch it, would be to augment the price of advances in all undertakings, and consequently to lessen the undertakings themselves, that is to say, agriculture, industry and commerce.
>
> (93)

Thus Turgot returned to the physiocratic principle that the only 'disposable', or taxable income was the net product of land.

Finally, in the last paragraph of his *Reflections*, Turgot spelt out the theory of saving, investment and the rate of interest, which Schumpeter called 'the Turgot–Smith theory', to the effect that all savings were 'immediately' invested:

> In fact, almost all savings are made in nothing but money; it is in money that the revenues come to the proprietors, that the advances and the profits return to undertakers of every kind; it is, therefore, from money that they save, and the annual increase of capitals takes place in money; but none of the undertakers make any other use of it than to convert it immediately ['*sur le champ*'] into the different kinds of effects upon which their undertaking depends; and thus this money returns to circulation . . .
>
> (98–9)

Adam Smith, in vol. II, chapter 3 of *The Wealth of Nations*, was to elaborate this theory, from which he derived his doctrine of the unconditional beneficence of parsimony and frugality. But the Turgot–Smith theory ran counter to the views of Quesnay, who, like many other writers in the seventeenth and eighteenth centuries, regarded hoarding as a serious danger.

III

In his *Reflections* Turgot touched only rather fleetingly on the question of value and price. His earlier approach to this central and fundamental subject was well summarized in a footnote in his *Observations on a Paper by Saint-Peravy* (1767):

> Two types of value may be distinguished: fundamental value and exchange value. The fundamental value is what the thing costs to him who sells it, that is, the raw material cost, the interest of the advances, the wages of labour and industry. The exchange value is the price which the buyer agrees upon with the seller . . . The latter is ruled by supply and demand, it varies with needs, and often a single event suffices to produce very considerable and very sudden fluctuations. It is not in any essential proportion to the fundamental value, but it has a tendency to approach it continually, and can never move far from it permanently.
>
> (Groenewegen, 1977, 120)

Here Turgot's treatment of the theory of value anticipated somewhat that of Adam Smith, with his distinction between 'natural' and 'market' price. But Turgot's term 'fundamental' does not give quite the same emphasis on value as determined, *ex post*, by cost, as does Smith's persuasive adjective 'natural'.

Subsequently, however, in his important paper 'Value and Money' Turgot went much further in exploring, more penetratingly, the subjective elements behind the demand determinants of exchange value, or 'market price'. His analysis here foreshadowed the treatment of the neoclassicals, a century later. The influence of Galiani (who is quoted by Turgot) and, directly or indirectly, of the Italian subjective approach of, for example, Montanari and Verri, is apparent. In fact, Turgot seems to have been approaching the subject of money in the manner of Davanzati and Galiani, via an analysis of value based on subjective utility and scarcity.

Turgot began by describing value as dependent on 'the suitability of an object for our enjoyment', which 'is always relative to ourselves' (137). Value, in this sense, should be analysed initially in terms of 'a man in isolation'. He was thus approaching the value problem, as some of the leading neoclassicals were to approach it, by considering the individual, 'micro-economically', by means of a Robinson Crusoe example. He showed how such an individual's relative valuations changed with his circumstances, or his supplies: 'When the savage is hungry, he values a piece of game more than the best bearskin; but let his appetite be satisfied and let him be cold, and it will be bearskin that becomes valuable to him' (138).

In forming his valuations, the individual considered, as well as the scarcity of goods, both his present and his future needs, especially with regard to goods that were storable. He called this pre-exchange valuation, or scale of preference, 'esteem value' (*valeur estimative*), because it was 'the expression of the degree of esteem which a man attaches to the different objects of his desire'. It was represented by 'precisely that portion of his total resources which corresponds to the desire he has for this object, or what he is willing to use to satisfy this desire' (139–40, quoted by Menger, 1871, 108n.). Such basic neoclassical concepts as diminishing utility, or rate of substitution, and opportunity cost were foreshadowed in these passages from Turgot's 'Value and Money'.

The idea of an absolute measure of value, of which some of the English classicals were subsequently to make such heavy weather, had, as we have seen, been dismissed nearly a century previously, by Montanari, and, as a follower of the Italian tradition, it was dismissed by Turgot: 'if values are measured by comparison with other values, as length is measured by comparison with other lengths, then, in both means of comparison, there is no *fundamental unit*, given by nature, there is only an arbitrary unit given by convention' (145).

He then took the case of barter between two isolated individuals, as he had in the *Reflections*. In 'Value and Money', assuming two parties on a desert island exchanging corn for wood, Turgot emphasized (as Condillac was to do) the different 'esteem value' which the two exchangers would have had for various quantities of corn and wood, so that the exchanges were not of equalities:

> At the moment of exchange the one who, for example, gives four measures of corn for five armfuls of wood, without doubt prefers these five armfuls of wood to the four measures of corn; he will give them a higher esteem value. But for his part, the one who receives the four measures of corn prefers them to the five armfuls of wood. This superiority of the esteem value attributed by the acquirer to the thing he acquires over the thing he gives up is essential to the exchange, for it is the sole motive for it.
>
> (142)
>
> . . . the introduction of exchange between our two men increases the wealth of both of them, that is, it gives them both a greater quantity of satisfaction in return for the same resources.
>
> (144)

Turgot was proceeding to introduce more exchangers, four, in fact, and to analyse the effects of competition, when the paper broke off unfinished.[2] His treatment, however, of value and exchange, here, and, briefly, in the *Reflections*, foreshadowed that of such leading neoclassicals as Menger, Böhm-Bawerk, Walras and Marshall. As Professor Groenewegen has concluded: 'He has no peer in the eighteenth century in the elegance with which the exchange models are developed. They resemble contributions of the neoclassical school much more than those offered by Turgot's contemporaries' (1970, 196). Only Beccaria, of Turgot's contemporaries, might be said to have developed an analysis of models of exchange approximating that of Turgot, though Condillac was certainly to take the subjective theory of value further in some important directions.

Turgot's essays and papers, though mostly concerned, in the first instance, with current policy problems, contained some other fundamental ideas of the greatest importance, such as, notably, his statement of the principle of eventually diminishing returns. In his 'Observations on a Paper by Saint-Peravy', Turgot wrote:

> The earth certainly has a limited fertility, and assuming it to have been ploughed, manured ... watered, weeded, as far as it can be, it is obvious that all further expenditure would be useless, and that such increases could even become detrimental.
>
> While it may be granted to the author that, in the case of ordinary good cultivation, the annual advances return 250 for 100, it is more than likely that as the advances are increased gradually past this point up to the point where they return nothing, each increase would be less and less productive ... Seed thrown on a soil which is naturally fertile, but has not been prepared at all, would be virtually a waste of expenditure. If the soil were tilled once, the produce would be greater; tilling it a second or third time would not just double or triple, but quadruple or decuple the produce, which will thus increase in a much larger proportion than the expenditure, and this would be the case up to a certain point, at which the produce would be as large as possible relative to the advances.
>
> Past this point, if the advances are still further increased, the product will still increase, but less so, and continuously less and less until an addition to the advances would add nothing further to the produce ...
>
> I will mention that it would be mistaken to imagine that the point at which the advances yield the most is the most advantageous one which the cultivator can attain, for, although further increments in advances do not yield as much as the preceding increments, if they yield enough to increase the *net product* of the soil, there is an advantage in making them, and it will still be a good investment.
>
> (Groenewegen, 1977, 111–12)

So, in addition to anticipating the neoclassical theory of value, Turgot here went a long way towards the development of an incremental, or marginal productivity analysis.

Two further fundamentally significant ideas of Turgot may be mentioned: first, though not then highly original, was his statement of the important self-adjusting, specie-flow mechanism in international trade (198, also in the 'Observations on a Paper by Saint-Peravy'); and second his concept of general interdependence and equilibrium: 'the exchange value of the produce, the revenue, the wage rate, the population, are things related to each other by a mutual dependence, which spontaneously reach their equilibrium according to a natural proportion; and this proportion is always maintained when commerce and competition are completely free' (127).

Turgot's pronouncements on the principles of policy had a forthright sweep and confidence which derived much from the fundamentally individualist and subjectivist nature of his value theory as presented in 'Value and Money', in which he emphasized especially the question of knowledge. He denounced government intervention, inspired by what he called 'the mania of directing all, regulating all, and of never relying on the self-interest of man' (16). For it was individuals, not governments, who generally possessed more of the vital knowledge on which any beneficent economic policies, or plans, had to be based:

> ... in general every man knows his own interest better than another to whom it is of no concern.
>
> (26)

> He alone has the particular knowledge without which the most enlightened man could only argue blindly. He alone has the experience, which is all the more reliable since it is limited to a single object. He learns by repeated trials, by his successes, by his losses, and he acquires a feeling for it which is much more ingenious than the theoretical knowledge of the indifferent observer because it is stimulated by want.
>
> (28)

Again, in a later paper, he argued (*contra* Galiani in his *Dialogues*) that the government simply did not possess the necessary knowledge to guide or control the market:

> For, in order to guide it without disturbing it, and without injuring ourselves, it would be necessary for us to be able to follow all the changes in the needs, the interests, and the industry of mankind. It would be necessary to know these in such detail as would be physically impossible to obtain, and in which even the most skilful, the most active and the most painstaking government will risk always to be wrong in half the cases ...
>
> ... I add that, even if we had for all these particulars the mass of knowledge which is impossible to gather, the result would only be to let things go precisely as they would have gone by themselves, by the simple action of the self-interest of man, enlivened and held in check by free competition.
>
> (187)

Incidentally, though one may completely agree with Turgot's judgement regarding the comprehensive ignorance of governments, one may question the assumption on which he seems to be insisting – as some over-enthusiastic defenders of market processes were to do in the nineteenth and twentieth centuries – that an *individual's* market decisions are, or can be, taken on the basis of omniscience. So, while contributing valuably by following Galiani in his emphasis on subjective utility, Turgot rather excluded a further advance in subjectivist analysis by failing to recognize the ubiquity of human ignorance and the inevitable subjectivity this necessitates regarding risk preference and risk avoidance in a world of uncertainty. (This further advance was to be made shortly after by Condillac.)

Regarding price-fixing, Turgot concluded: 'There is no commodity for which the most enlightened, the most meticulously careful, and the most accurate administration can take the responsibility of balancing all the cirucmstances which must influence the determination of the price, and of setting one which is disadvantageous to neither the seller nor the buyer' (161).

Turgot did, however, see at least one role for government in encouraging industry, and that was by supporting education and research:

> If, after complete liberty has been obtained by the relief from all taxes on the manufacturing, transportation, sale and consumption of commodities, anything remains to be done by the government to encourage a branch of

trade, it can only be by means of education, that is, by encouraging the research of men of science and craftsmen, who tend to perfect the craft, and, above all, by extending the knowledge of the practical processes which greed seeks to keep as so many secrets. It would be useful for the government to incur some expenses in sending young men to foreign countries in order to learn processes of manufacture unknown in France, and to publish the results of these researches.

(183)

IV

Soon after the accession of the young Louis XVI Turgot was called to Paris, first to be Secretary of the Navy for five weeks, and then to take over the vital post of Controller-General of Finance, a position in which he battled heroically for some twenty months (24 August 1774–12 May 1776), during much of which time he was seriously ill. As had hardly been necessary for him during his thirteen years in Limoges, he now had to cope with the treacherous high politics of the capital. His policies included the abolition of the *corvée*, or forced labour on the harvest, and the removal of many taxes. But his cuts in public expenditure, and his curbs on the privileges of guilds and trade corporations, stirred up powerful opposition, while his attempt to free the corn trade happened to coincide with another bad harvest. The continuing support of the monarch was vital for one who believed in enlightened absolutism, but the drastic forthright boldness of Turgot's measures were too much for Louis. In an atmosphere of obscure intrigues, Turgot was ordered to resign, and he departed to spend the last five years of his life in literary and intellectual pursuits, though no further important economic writings were forthcoming.

A recent study has concluded:

It is not surprising that the euphoria in which Turgot came to office was soon dissipated and the hopes of the enlightened disappointed. His fall must have been as inevitable as anything in politics, for which, in the partisan sense, Turgot turned out to be ill-suited. Only rarely can the intelligence to understand the economic and technical factors required to redeem a polity have been coupled with the political address and dexterity to carry them into effect. The Limousin might be administered, but France had to be governed, and Turgot's genius was of an administrative and scientific rather than a governmental order.

(Gillespie, 1980, 19)

In fact, though Schumpeter described him as 'first and last a great civil servant' (1954, 246), Turgot maintained, for a seasoned, practical administrator, a remarkably confident, euphoric intellectual optimism as to the rapid and comprehensively beneficent effectiveness of the very radical policies he sought to implement. In the first place, such optimism derived from his faith in human progress and perfectibility, proclaimed initially in his early twenties, when still a theological student at the Sorbonne. Turgot, however, also observed very few qualifications, or exceptions, to his economic policy principles, which he regarded as the way forward towards human progress and perfectibility, and which he retained, scarcely qualified, through all the repeated discouragements of bad harvests, soaring prices, and the machinations of vested interests.

More broadly, though he discerned, regarding the possibilities of, or limitations on, economic progress, the principle of diminishing returns, together with the fall in the rate of interest as economies progressed, and while hardly envisaging the continuation of technical progress – any more than did the earlier English classicals – Turgot entertained few or none of the doubts about the future which worried even the comparatively optimistic Adam Smith. In fact, it is of interest to notice how much more confidently optimistic and unqualified in his liberal, progressive views, the French civil servant was compared with the markedly more cautious Scottish academic. For Turgot, unlike Smith, there seem to have been no looming threats from the possible onset of a stationary state (as already realized in China with its widespread infanticide and 'garbage' subsistence for the masses).[3] Nor were any dangers foreseen from the culturally stultifying effects of heightened specialization and the division of labour. In other words, Turgot belonged to the French Enlightenment and Smith did not.

In the previous chapter, attention was called to the charge of 'false individualism' which Friedrich Hayek, quite validly, it would seem, brought against Quesnay and the physiocrats, in that their 'rationalistic individualism' led them 'not only close to socialism' but 'to advocate the worst despotism' (1949, 5n.). This charge cannot be brought with the same force against Turgot, though he, also, like the physiocrats, rejected the scepticism and historical relativism of Galiani, and certainly contributed ideas to the nineteenth-century scientism of Comte and others.[4] Nor did Turgot advance the principle of subjectivism as far as he might, with regard to the ubiquity and inevitability of ignorance, governmental and individual, though certainly his emphasis on subjective utility, following Galiani, provided a vital foundation for libertarian economic policies, not recognized in *The Wealth of Nations*.

Schumpeter described Turgot as 'one of the greatest scientific economists of all time' (1954, 247) – at any rate as far as this was possible, given the administrative duties, to which his life was 'first and last' devoted. It is clear enough that Turgot could have produced, had he been able to take a few years sabbatical leave from his administrative labours, a comprehensive treatise of economic principles perhaps hardly surpassed in the eighteenth century. Starting from the masterly outline in his *Reflections*, he could have incorporated the various fundamental insights developed in his other writings: such as his observations about the principle of diminishing returns, and about general interdependence and equilibrium, and, especially, his fundamental analysis of subjective value, where, on the one hand, he had carried forward the Italian tradition of Montanari and Galiani, while, on the other hand, anticipating the neoclassical analysis developed a century later by Menger and Walras. His great contributions must also be recognized to both the English classical and the Böhm–Bawerkian analysis of capital, advances, and waiting. As to the significance of his pioneer work on the Turgot–Smith theory of saving and investing, (the original cornerstone of 'classical' economics in the Keynesian sense), differing views may be held today.

Turgot (1727–81) and Galiani (1728–87) were great contemporaries, among the greatest men of their century, with much respect for one another. Turgot seems to have learnt from Galiani on value and utility. But on the great, fiercely contested policy issue of their day they were on opposite sides. It is of interest to note what they thought of one another. In 1770, Turgot wrote regarding Galiani's *Dialogues*:

> Neither do I particularly like to see him always so prudent, so much the enemy of enthusiasm, so much in agreement with all the *ne quid nimis* and with all the men who are comfortable in the present and perfectly happy to let the world go as it will, because it goes well for them, and who, as M. de Gournay used to say, having their bed well made do not want anyone to disturb it.
>
> (Letter of 26 January 1770, quoted by Rogers, 1971, 267)

In 1774, when Turgot had come to power, Galiani predicted:

> Turgot is Controller-General. He will not remain in office long enough to put his system (systèmes) into practice ... He will punish a few rascals; he will curse, get mad, wish to do good, and meet everywhere thorns, difficulties, rogues. His credit will fall, he will be detested, it will be said that he is not the man who is needed, enthusiasm will dwindle, he will retire or be dismissed, and everyone will recognize the error of having given an office like his in a monarchy like yours to a man who is virtuous and *très philosophe*.
>
> (Quoted and translated by Rogers, 1971, 272)

Anyhow, whatever may be one's appraisal of Turgot's politics and policies, he contributed outstandingly to economic theory, both as regards utility and value, and to the analysis of saving, investment and capital formation.

V

We conclude our review of this great phase of French pre-eminence in the emerging subject of political economy, with a discussion of two writers, whose works appeared (one of them posthumously) right at the end of our period, and who, in contrast to the physiocrats, stood for a subjective approach to the central and fundamental problem of value and price. While Jean Jacques Burlamaqui (1694–1748) did no more than usefully restate the analysis of Pufendorf, Etienne Bonnot de Condillac (1715–80) was responsible for a remarkable advance in the subjectivist approach, in some respects not surpassed until the twentieth century.[5]

In chapter 6, following the discussion of Samuel Pufendorf's doctrine of value and price, it was observed that his 'natural-law' theory was transmitted down along two major, separate lines of descent: one in Glasgow, which led via Gershom Carmichael and Frances Hutcheson to Adam Smith; while the other led via Jean Jacques Burlamaqui to Auguste and Léon Walras. Chronologically, and in other other respects, Burlamaqui's role corresponded very closely with that of Hutcheson. Their vital dates coincided almost exactly, while some of the main works of both philosophers were published posthumously. On the subject of political economy, however, while at some interesting points Hutcheson went further than Pufendorf, Burlamaqui, though accurately restating the master's doctrines, hardly went as far in some directions.

Burlamaqui, who came of an Italian Protestant family which had settled in Geneva, was a teacher of law at the university there. His travels in France, England and Holland, included visits to Oxford, and to Groningen, where he met the great editor and translator of Pufendorf, Jean Barbeyrac (1674–1744).[6] Burlamaqui's two works, *Principes du droit naturel* (1747) and *Principes du droit politique* (1751) became very well known textbooks in the eighteenth and nineteenth centuries and were published in numerous editions and translations in France, England and America. But these books do not contain any discussion of value and price. Burlamaqui's treatment of this subject came in his *Élémens du droit naturel*, a much rarer work, never translated into English, which was printed first in French, in 1773, from the text of his lectures.[7]

The economic analysis occurred in chapter 11 of his *Élémens* (1773, 204ff.), entitled *Du prix des choses et des actions.* He found that the fundamental basis of value, and of 'the right and intrinsic price' ('*du prix propre et intrinsèque*') consists of, 'first, the aptitude which things have to serve the needs, conveniences or pleasure of life; in a word, their *utility* and their *scarcity*' (225).

Burlamaqui went on to emphasize subjectivity and human error:

> I put first utility by which I understand not only a real utility, but also that which is only arbitrary, or imagined, like that of precious stones; and from that it follows that one commonly speaks of a thing that has no use is said to have a nil price.
>
> But utility alone, however real it may be, is not sufficient to put a price on things, one must also consider their scarcity (*rareté*), that is the difficulty one has in obtaining things which brings it about that no one can easily obtain all he wants.
>
> (225)

Of course, the extent to which something is needed is far from deciding its price, for the most necessary things may be the cheapest – as with water. On the other hand, its scarcity alone cannot give something a price. The utility and scarcity of goods are often changing:

> If the fashion for something passes . . . it becomes cheap, however expensive it may previously have been. On the other hand, if something common, which cost little or nothing, becomes rather scarce it at once has a price, sometimes quite high, as, for example, with water in desert places or some times during a siege, or a sea voyage.
>
> (226)

All the particular circumstances which combined to raise the price of a good could be included under the heading of its scarcity. This comprised such factors as the skill, delicacy, difficulty, and 'utility,' which raised the price of the labour involved. As regards everyday things, it was need or necessity, joined with rarity, which raised price.

Burlamaqui then observed (208–9) that in civil society prices might be fixed by law, or be arrived at by 'common estimation' and the agreement of the contracting parties. His treatment of the factors shaping market prices became very sketchy at this point, as was his treatment of money, though he indicated why the precious metals performed the monetary functions most conveniently (211).

Burlamaqui's analysis of value and price should have helped to keep alive in France the Pufendorfian, natural-law tradition on the subject. It was an analysis which was easily reconcilable with the theories of Galiani, Turgot and Verri, though surpassed, or refined, by them on a number of points. The natural-law theory contained important subjective elements, without, as we shall see, being as fully and consequentially subjective as that of Galiani, Turgot and Condillac. More than half a century later, however, Auguste Walras was to complain, in his *De la nature de la richesse et de l'origine de la valeur* (1831), of the eclipse of the natural-law theory of Pufendorf and Burlamaqui.

Perhaps we may, at this point, trespass briefly outside the limits of our period. Walras (senior) proceeded to explain:

> The doctrine, which I am about to present to my readers on the nature of wealth and the origin of value, is so little new or modern, that it has been set out a long time ago in a work on public law, written in French and published on the frontiers of France. I wish to mention the *Élémens du droit naturel*, by Burlamaqui.
>
> (1831, 209)

Auguste Walras then went on to give a more than two-page quotation, much of which we have just reproduced. He then concluded with the claim that this passage from Burlamaqui 'is irrefutable. The reflections it contains are strikingly correct'. It provided a triumphant answer to J. B. Say:

> After having read this passage, there is only one question to ask. How did such a doctrine remain buried in a treatise of natural law? Why has it not already passed into the writings of economists? It would have produced the most valuable fruit.
>
> But I am saying that the doctrine of Burlamaqui is mine . . .
>
> (212)

Subsequently, Auguste's son Léon was to complain that, while the English classical solution of Smith, Ricardo and McCulloch, which traced the origin of value to labour was 'too narrow', the solution of Condillac and J. B. Say, in terms of *utility*, was too broad. The correct solution was 'that of Burlamaqui and my father' – and he might, of course, have added, of Pufendorf and Francis Hutcheson (though hardly, in *The Wealth of Nations*, of Adam Smith). Léon then proceeded to re-quote from his father's quotation of Burlamaqui's chapter 11 (see 1954, 203–4).

VI

Etienne Bonnot, Abbé de Condillac (1715–80) was born at Grenoble of a distinguished family, his father being the Secretary to the Parliament of Grenoble, while his elder brother was the socialist philosopher, the Abbé de Mably. Educated at a theological seminary in Paris, Condillac left it to study philosophy independently. A follower of Locke, he developed a 'sensationalist' epistemological theory, according to which human knowledge was built up from the sense data of individuals. In his thirties, he produced a number of important philosophical works, notably *Essai sur l'origine des connaissances humaines* (1746); *Traité des systèmes* (1749); and later his *Traité des sensations* (1754).[8]

In 1758 Condillac went to Italy as tutor to the son of Duke Ferdinand of Parma. It was there that his interest in political economy was stimulated by contact with the Duke's state secretary, Tillot, who was responsible for economic policy, and who, while supporting industrial development, also carried through a free-trade policy. At this time he got to know the work of Galiani, and very probably that of Montanari, while subsequently he met Beccaria in Milan (see Meyer, 1944, 8–11). He would have found that the Italian subjective approach to the theory of value fitted congenially alongside his 'sensationalist' epistemology. After a decade as tutor he wrote up the *Course of Studies* which he had devised for his pupil, in which history had a major part, and which was later published in sixteen volumes.

When Condillac returned to Paris in the late 1760s, interest in political economy and in the *économistes* was at its most intense, especially because of the crisis in the grain trade. He had always been a supporter of the principle of economic freedom, but on his own grounds, which were not quite the same as those of Gournay, and were very different from those of Quesnay. In 1771 he settled in the country and devoted himself to the fundamental problems of political economy and to writing his last work, *Le commerce et le gouvernement considérés relativement l'un à l'autre*, which he must have been working on during Turgot's great, final, eighteen-month effort to achieve some measure of freedom for the French economy, an effort which Condillac would have strongly supported. His book appeared in February 1776, about one month before *The Wealth of Nations*.

Condillac's economic theory followed closely from his fundamental epistemological principles. It was a comparatively short step from the theory that knowledge was derived from sensations, or sense data, to a subjective economic theory which derived value from the utility of goods for individuals. He rejected categorically the idea of objective value advanced by the physiocrats.[9] He had written about abstract deductive systems in his *Traité des systèmes* (1749):

> There are such works which force us to admire them. They resemble palaces, where the taste, the convenience, the grandeur and magnificence, combine to form a masterpiece of art, but which are supported by foundations of so little solidity, that they seem to support themselves by magic. One doubtless bestows praise on the architect, but praise balanced by criticism of his imprudence. One regards as the most downright folly the construction of such a superb edifice on such feeble foundations. While it is clear that this is the work of a superior intelligence, and that the pieces have been put together in an admirable order, no one would be so unwise as to want to inhabit the building.
>
> (1776 [1821–2], vol. II, 286; quoted by Meyer, 1944, 26–7)

Probably the most important of the fundamental principles of the physiocrats – and of many subsequent economists – on which they had built their ambitious theoretical constructions, and which Condillac rejected as fundamentally unsound, were those which postulated a kind of rationalistic, full knowledge, and even certainty, together with *objective* values. Condillac started from the subjectivity of value and utility, and from the prevalence of uncertainties, errors, passions and habits in human decisions and actions. His theory of knowledge was fundamentally fallibilist, and he rejected the kind of dogmatic infallibilism proclaimed by physiocracy – and subsequently by other schools of economists.[10] As Isabel Knight puts it, Condillac always stressed 'the relative, the subjective, the historical, and the empirical' (1968, 259). His methodology can be summarized in terms of conjectures and refutations: 'The history of the human spirit proves that conjectures are often the road to truth. We shall be obliged to make conjectures ... That is, in general, the method of the human spirit ... It receives observations, it makes hypotheses, as these observations suggest, and finishes with experiments which confirm or correct these hypotheses' (quoted by Meyer, 1944, 33).[11]

Condillac's book, *Le commerce et le gouvernement*, is divided into two parts, theoretical and practical. But the foundation and centrepiece of the entire work is his subjective theory of value, which is presented in the first chapter. Values were derived from needs, and depended on the utility or capacity which things have for satisfying needs: 'We say that something is useful when it serves some of our needs, and that it is useless when it does not serve them. Its utility is founded on the need we have for it' (1776 [1821–2], 8–9).

The value of a thing increased with its scarcity and fell with its abundance: 'It can diminish to nothing with abundance. A super-abundant good, for example, will be without value whenever no use can be made of it ...' (9). But scarcity and abundance were not objectively known, but had to be subjectively estimated, from a position of uncertainty and ignorance with regard to both present and future needs:

> There might be an abundance of grain if it was considered in relation to the quantity needed for consumption in that year. But considered in relation to the following years, when the harvest might be insufficient, the grain would have a value, because it might be judged to form part of the quantity necessary for meeting needs. These needs are distant. For that reason they do not give a good the same value as a present need.
>
> (9)
>
> The utility being the same, the value would be greater or less depending only on the degree of scarcity or abundance, if this degree was known with precision . . .
>
> But this degree will not ever be known. It is, therefore, principally on opinion that the greater or less value [of goods] is founded.
>
> (10)

With fluctuating grain harvests and stocks, opinion, or expectations, were key determinants of values and prices. Ignorance could produce panic and panic a huge swing in prices: 'It is clear that the value of grain may increase in proportion to the extent that opinion exaggerates the dearth' (11)

Condillac rejected an *ex-post*, pseudo-objective theory of value based on costs, because 'a thing does not have value because it costs something, but it costs something because it has value' (12) – and value rested on subjective opinion. As Professor Isabel Knight puts it,

> . . . a governing principle of Condillac's entire economic theory is that it is opinion, not fact, which determines everything . . .
>
> . . . Thus, at the most elementary level of economic organization, what matters is not the actual relationship of the supply of a given community's need . . . but the community's opinion of that relationship. This principle remains valid as the society grows more complex. Every man's economic actions arise from his judgment: of his own needs, of the relative value of commodities, of the likelihood of stability or change in the market, of the advantage he may gain by selling or withholding his goods, and so on. His judgment may indeed turn out to have been mistaken, but that is irrelevant, except as a corrective factor that will govern his future actions.
>
> (1968, 236–7)
>
> Thus everything important in economics – including, as we shall see, productivity, labor, money – rests on value, defined as a subjective opinion, which varies relative to the same object not only according to general circumstances but according to the person who has the opinion.
>
> (248)

Passing to the subject of exchange, Condillac emphasized how exchanges benefited both parties, in that each gave (subjectively) less for (subjectively) more. He started with the case of two people bartering grain for wine, putting forward prices of one in terms of the other, and adjusting them until a deal was completed. He then demonstrated the effect of numbers on market exchanges by supposing that the single wine-seller was replaced by twelve, while the single grain-seller remained, who was thus able to get a better price for his grain in terms of wine, because of the greater quantity of wine being offered (1776, 25ff.)

Condillac regarded markets as, primarily, places where information and experience could be obtained, or exchanged, as to the state of the demand and supply of different goods. Enlightened by such observation and experience, demanders and suppliers were led to modify their consumption or production, and so reduced variations and discrepancies in prices:

> Here again is a matter on which experience will shed light. By observing prices at a succession of markets and the causes of their variations, one will learn the kind of good, and the quantity, which can be supplied and exchanged with advantage, or the least possible disadvantage . . .
>
> Prices will vary less as experience teaches the peasants what is consumed of each good . . . and they will only bring to market as much, or approximately, as they expect to exchange.
>
> (30–1)

Condillac concluded by praising markets as the places where vital information could be sought:

> One sees again that prices can only be settled in markets because it is only when people can assemble and compare the interests they have in exchanging, that they can judge the relative values of things in accordance with their needs. Prices can only be settled there, because it is only in markets that all the things to be exchanged are in evidence: it is only in markets that one can judge the extent of the abundance or scarcity of goods, relatively to one another, which determine the respective prices . . .
>
> (31)
>
> We see that the government strikes a blow at agriculture and commerce every time it undertakes to fix the price of goods.
>
> (29)

For Condillac, competition produced 'the true price' (surely a term or concept which represented a slight lapse from strict subjectivism). Unlike Smith and the classicals, however, Condillac did not assume that competition *usually* regulated markets. For him, monopoly generally ruled: 'Today all the trade of Europe is done by monopolists' (165). With monopolists he included any 'small number' of suppliers. It was governments who often encouraged the growth of monopoly by restricting imports and foreign competition, and thus brought about further restrictions in other countries.

Just as Condillac's theory of value followed from his theory of knowledge, so his theory of distribution followed from his theory of value (or even more closely). People could expect to receive in income whatever they could expect to receive from the sale of such productive agents as they commanded. He rejected the idea of a general subsistence wage. Pay was regulated in markets by sellers and buyers, and depended on productivity and the expected utility of what was produced. Superior intelligence and skills, which might take time to develop, could command higher prices because less would be supplied (52–3). The physiocratic doctrine of the unique productivity of agriculture was rejected. Artisans and industrial workers transformed otherwise useless raw materials into goods which had utility; agricultural workers did the same. Land was 'sterile' unless worked on by labour and equipment (59).

Condillac distinguished three classes in production, whether industrial or agricultural: the capitalist or landowner who advanced the capital, the entrepreneur who both managed the business and bore the uncertainty, and the workers who worked under his direction. The capitalist, or landowner, drew an income based on the rights of property and the productivity of what he was leasing, and, in the case of land, on account of whatever drainage and improvements he had made (72–5).

Condillac's theory of interest formed simply a sub-section of his theory of value and price:

> Interest rises and falls in proportion to the quantity of money which is offered for lending and the quantity demanded for borrowing. This proportion can constantly change . . .
>
> Just as prices are regulated on the market according to the negotiations of buyers and sellers, so interest, or the price of money, is regulated in commercial markets according to the negotiations of borrowers and lenders. The government recognises that it is not its duty to regulate the price of things sold on the market, so why does it believe that it ought to fix interest, or the price of money?
>
> (134–6)

As regards the profits of the entrepreneur, Condillac emphasized the element of uncertainty. He took the example of an entrepreneur-farmer and indicated all the uncertainties with which he was confronted. When leasing some land he had to predict the average crop it would produce, and the prices this crop would fetch in the market. He had to estimate what crops his neighbours would be producing and marketing. He might consider an innovation, or new method of cultivation, which he would be the first to attempt, so that 'his speculations were still more uncertain' (384). Artisan-entrepreneurs also had to speculate, with regard to the current price of raw materials, and the wages which were asked of them, as well as with regard to public taste, and the number of their competitors working at the same product (385). Fashion and luxury tastes introduced further uncertainties. The entrepreneurs' incomes, whether in industry or agriculture, represented their return for covering the costs of meeting such uncertainties, together with wages of management.

Condillac logically derived his theory of the value of money from human needs, and the utility which money provided by meeting them. Like Cantillon, he denied any conventional, or arbitrary, source of value for money. Metals acquired certain values which rose or fell according to their subjectively perceived scarcities or abundance. Moreover, people had to know, or discover, the utility of metals and how they could be used:

> If people were ignorant of their suitable uses, metals would be quite useless, and not searched after. They would be left like stones or earth without value.
>
> But when their utility is known they are searched for and sought after so much the more because they are scarce and objects of interest. So they

> acquire a new value and this value is in proportion to the number of those interested.
>
> (81)

Condillac ascribed much importance to the velocity of circulation of money and described the motives for holding a store of money: 'There is always a certain quantity which does not circulate; such as is put in reserve as a resource in case of an accident, or for one day improving one's condition, including, also, the savings of misers . . .' (99). He showed how velocity depended on habitual methods of making payments, whether annually, semi-annually, or daily. He cited Cantillon when observing that it was impossible to establish precisely what was the quantity of money in circulation (105).

On the foreign exchanges, on which subject he was also probably indebted to Cantillon, Condillac emphasized how ignorance and 'psychological' factors had an important influence. Finally, his suggestion may be noted of the existence of a self-adjusting mechanism, and equilibrating tendency, in the balance of payments:

> If one province believed that it could enrich itself by attracting and retaining gold and silver from all the others, this would be an error as fatal as it was gross. Everything would become dearer for it; population would depart, and sooner or later it would be forced to shed its gold and silver; and it would not know how to get them back, because, with everything higher in price, it would have lost its manufactures, and would need much time to reestablish them.
>
> (270)

As regards policy, Condillac was fundamentally opposed to restrictions on trade. His analysis of exchange constituted a basic denial of the conception of trade as a zero-sum game, and of the principle enunciated by Montaigne that '*le profit de l'un est dommage de l'autre*'. On the principles of policy, Condillac seems to have been influenced from across the Channel by Josiah Tucker, whom he quotes. He was particularly opposed to what he regarded as the political objectives of mercantilism, identifying them with preparing for, and making war. He condemned the appalling damage that resulted, together with, 'that glory which peoples, in their stupidity, attach to conquests, and which still more stupid historians love to celebrate, to the extent of boring their readers' (278). 'What advantage do they bring?' he asked. He then set out the many reasons for, and benefits from, freedom of trade. It yielded advantages from differences in climate (361), and, with regard to grain, brought greater price stability. Protection, on the other hand, encouraged monopoly:

> When France forbids the importing of English goods we reduce the number of merchants who are selling to us, and consequently our own national merchants become monopolists, selling at a higher price than they would if they had been selling in competition with English merchants . . .
>
> It is only the competition of as large a number as possible of sellers and buyers which can put the true price on goods, that is, the price which is equally advantageous for all nations . . .
>
> (165–6)

Government policies were constantly shifting in response to the clamour of vested interests. Government 'obeys the demand which appears the strongest, in turn permitting and then prohibiting exports' (378). Such shifts increased uncertainty. Moreover, once free trade had been broken off for a period, it took time to benefit from its restoration, for it was necessary to rebuild contacts and knowledge: 'To succeed in any kind of commerce, it is not enough to have the freedom to do so, it is necessary, as we have observed, to acquire the knowledge, and such knowledge is the fruit of experience, which is always slow in developing' (344, italics added).

Similarly, it took time for the gains from freedom of trade to accrue. (Perhaps Condillac was here calling for patience in awaiting the fruits of Turgot's free-trade policies, which had been launched at about the time he was writing.)

Finally, we may note his view of the kind of near-omniscience required by those in government who took on the comprehensive, central direction of an economy. Nothing less would be required than

> . . . a vast genius, who knew everything, who estimated everything, and who, directing all the resources of government, kept them in perfect harmony. It would be difficult, or impossible, to find such a genius. The best-intentioned and most skilful statesmen have made mistakes through ignorance or impatience, since it is difficult to see and combine everything, without sometimes falling into errors . . .
>
> Statesmen never do more harm than when they try to concern themselves with everything. It would be wiser for them to limit themselves to preventing abuses, and otherwise resort to *laisser-faire*. Doubtless they would all adopt such conduct, if they wished always to do good, and if their knowledge of public resources was better than it is.
>
> (*Œuvres*, 1822, vol. XIV, 554; see Meyer, 1944, 234)

We would re-emphasize, in conclusion, that Condillac's work, theoretical and practical, depended on his fundamentally subjectivist analysis of utility and value and of their relationship. He followed this up with an account of both individual and government behaviour based not on the assumption of certainty and full knowledge, as maintained by the physiocrats and so many later economists (notably Ricardo), but on an assumption of widespread ignorance and uncertainty, on the part of both individuals and governments. Condillac may, therefore, be said to have provided, on the one hand with his subjectivist approach, and, on the other, with his fallibilist methodology, a much more valid and realistic foundation for libertarian economic policies than did the physiocrats, or, it might be argued than any other writer of his time, or for quite a long period after, either in France or elsewhere.

Condillac's work might be described as, so to speak, the last word from France before the publication of *The Wealth of Nations*. In France, *Le commerce et le gouvernement* was treated rather unfavourably by J. B. Say, but it was praised by Auguste Walras, though unmentioned by his son Léon. In England, only the maverick H. D. McLeod recognized Condillac's significance until Jevons did so in his masterly historical introduction of 1879.

Carl Menger has come to be regarded by many as a kind of patron saint of subjectivism in economic theory, and he duly cited Condillac's work. But, as Dr Paul Meyer maintained, none of the leading early neo-classicals was as consistently and consequentially subjectivist as Condillac – not even Menger himself.[12] Condillac's work represented the crowning achievement in the long and distinguished line of Italian and French theorists of utility and subjective value, which, coming down from the scholastic writers, then proceeded, via Montanari, Bernoulli and Galiani, to Turgot and Condillac himself. It is Condillac, with his emphasis on ignorance, uncertainty and erroneous expectations, who has stronger claims than anyone else to be regarded as the founding father of subjectivist analysis in economic theory. Condillac's emphasis on the subjectivity of value and price included not only the subjectivity of utility but also that of expectations and errors.

19
History and Political Economy in Scotland: Alternative 'Inquiries' and Scottish Ascendancy

I

David Hume, in his own day more famous as an historian than as a philosopher, is reported to have stated: 'I believe this to be the historical age and this the historical nation' (see Bryson, 1945, 78). Certainly, in the middle decades of the eighteenth century, in much of western Europe, a remarkable surge of interest in history and historical inquiry took place. Vico and Montesquieu were the inspiring pioneers, with Montesquieu's work much the better known. The *Esprit des lois* was translated into English in 1750 and had probably its most powerful effect in Scotland. Earlier, the natural-law system of moral philosophy, as developed in Glasgow by Carmichael and Hutcheson, had not provided much scope for the historical method, though Adam Smith, from an early stage of his work, had shown an interest in an historical approach (see Skinner, 1965, 3). In the second half of the century Hume's claim that Scotland was 'the historical nation' acquired much justification, and it was pre-eminently Hume himself who led the way by providing the philosophical foundations, and by demonstrating the possibilities in moral philosophy, or in the moral or social sciences, of the historical method, a method and approach closely linked with his empirical principles. Indeed, Albert Schatz went so far as to claim that Wilhelm Roscher's manifesto of the German Historical school, in 1843, had been fully anticipated in Scotland a century previously insofar as David Hume 'had done more than formulate it, he had applied it' (1902, 61). Certainly, as regards political economy, one of the first and most important, if small-scale, applications of an historical method and approach is to be found in Hume's economic and political essays. The full-scale application, however, of history to political economy, came with the two great, contrasting Scottish *Inquiries*, that of Sir James Steuart into the principles of political economy, and that of Adam Smith into the nature and causes of the wealth of nations.

Before we turn to these major applications of an historical approach, a few brief remarks about the historical method, and about two lesser, but highly interesting Scottish exponents, may be appropriate. Together with its interest in historical records and research, the Scottish concern with history focused on two sets of questions, or processes: on the one hand on origins, and, on the other hand, on empirically observed processes of the development and progress of nations and peoples, the historical treatment of which included their economics, politics, law and sociology, in a comprehensive theory of society. As Professor Lehmann, in his distinguished study of the Scottish Enlightenment, writes regarding the 'historical-mindedness' of Scottish thought at this juncture:

> We use this term with a threefold implication: first, there is the more obvious meaning of an interest in recorded history, historical research and historical interpretation; next is implied an interest in origins, in continuities through time in the development of social and political institutions, present, of course, also in the first meaning but viewed now on certain theoretical assumptions that can best be indicated by such terms as 'natural history,' 'evolution,' the 'idea of progress'; and finally there is implied an empirical approach to socio-historical reality that attempts to see any subject under study – be it political, economic, literary, any particular custom, institution or what not – in the concreteness of a particular time and place, in an organic relation to other phenomena whether past or present.
>
> (1960, 98)[1]

Two interesting Scottish exponents of the historical method, who have both been described as pioneers of sociology, and who were both very well known to Adam Smith, were Adam Ferguson (1723–1816) and John Millar (1735–1801). Ferguson, before becoming, in 1759, a professor at Edinburgh, where he occupied a succession of chairs, had been an army chaplain with the Black Watch regiment (thus providing a parallel with Süssmilch, the Prussian army chaplain and great pioneer of demography). Ferguson began his *History of Civil Society* (1767), his most important work, with a strongly social or sociological – rather than individualist – methodological emphasis: 'Mankind are to be taken in groups, as they have always subsisted. The history of the individual is but a detail of the sentiments and thoughts he has entertained in the view of his species: and every experiment relative to this subject should be made with entire societies, not with single men' (1767, 6). Ferguson continued with a quotation from Montesquieu: 'Man is born in society, and there he remains' (24). Ferguson subsequently went on to stress the beneficence of spontaneous, unplanned processes, as contrasted with the effects of deliberate governmental regulations (and has been approvingly quoted by Hayek on this point). Ferguson described how,

> ... nations stumble upon establishments which are indeed the result of human action but not the result of human design. (187)

> The forms of society are derived from an obscure and distant origin; they arise, long before the date of philosophy, from the instincts, not from the speculations of man ... We ascribe to a previous design, what came to be known only by experience, what no human wisdom could foresee, and what, without the concurring humour and disposition of his age, no authority could enable an individual to execute.
>
> (188, quoted by Hayek, 1949, 7)

The anti-governmental implications of these ideas, and how little government regulations and planning could achieve, were emphasized by Ferguson:

> A people intent on freedom, find for themselves a condition in which they may follow the propensities of nature with a more signal effect than any which the councils of state could devise. When sovereigns, or projectors, are the supposed masters of this subject, the best they can do is to be cautious of hurting any interest they cannot greatly promote, and of making breaches they cannot repair.
>
> (215)

Ferguson summarized his individualist and libertarian economic philosophy as follows: 'Secure to the workman the fruit of his labour, give him the prospects of independence or freedom, and the public has found a faithful steward in hoarding what he has gained ... Commerce ... is the branch in which men committed to the effects of their own experience, are least apt to go wrong' (219). With regard to national wealth:

> The great object of policy ... is to secure to the family its subsistence and settlement; to protect the industrious in the pursuit of his occupation; to reconcile the restrictions of police and the social affections of mankind, with their separate and interested pursuits ... When the refined politician would lend an active hand, he only multiplies interruptions and grounds of complaints.
>
> (220)

Ferguson described the advantages of the divisions of labour, and how 'the subdivision of arts and professions tends to improve the practice of them, and to promote their ends' (353). But, as noted by Marx, he emphasized the damaging and stultifying effects of the specialization of labour even more forcefully than Adam Smith:

> Many mechanical arts indeed, require no capacity; they succeed best under a total suppression of sentiment and reason; and ignorance is the mother of industry as well as superstition. Reflection and fancy are subject to err; but a habit of moving the hand or foot, is independent of either. Manufactures, accordingly, prosper most where the mind is least consulted and where the workshop may, without any great effort of the imagination, be considered as an engine, the parts of which are men.
>
> (280, quoted and discussed by Skinner, 1965, 17)

By including a mention at this point, of John Millar and his work, we are jumping a little ahead chronologically. For Millar was a pupil, perhaps the most distinguished, of Adam Smith, who had attended Smith's Edinburgh lectures and his first classes at Glasgow. Subsequently Millar was Professor of Civil Law at Glasgow from 1761 until 1801. He was described by Adam Smith's biographer, John Rae, as 'the most effective and influential apostle of Liberalism in Scotland in that age' (1895, 53–4). Rae's judgement, while apparently, in one important respect, putting the pupil above the master, should be compared and contrasted with Millar's criticisms of Smith's forthright views on the freedom of markets.[2]

Millar summed up his historical approach in the Introduction to his most important work, *Observations concerning the Origin of the Distinction of Ranks in Society* (1771). According to Millar, in order to know what is the best form of government, we have to study the past. But really to understand the past we must know the circumstances which produce certain social forms.[3] Millar has been interpreted as an anticipator of the historical materialism of Marx, though it seems unlikely that Millar's writing exercised any influence, directly or indirectly, on German thought. But the Scottish historical school of the eighteenth century were certainly, on some important points, anticipators: Ferguson of Carl Menger and Hayek, and Millar of Marx. In some of its manifestations, however, the Scottish historical movement took on some objectionable and pretentious historicist features, most notably in James Mills' *History of India* (1818) – which was so enthusiastically received by Ricardo. As Roy Pascal noted in his seminal article: 'It is very remarkable how this whole historical school becomes lost in the nineteenth century' (1938, 177). According to Professor D. C. Coleman, most of the blame for the distortion and 'bowdlerization' of the role of history in political economy should be ascribed to the 'two southbound Scots', James Mill and McCulloch (1987, 20).[4]

It remains immensely regrettable that in nineteenth-century political economy in England, dominated by the abstract deductivism of Ricardo and Senior, the historical dimension of the subject was so long and so thoroughly neglected. Apart from the efforts of a few such isolated figures as Richard Jones, historical economics was largely abandoned to the Germans, though it was to Scotland that its origins and two of its earliest outstanding achievements were due. The title, proudly but justifiably claimed by Hume, of being 'the historical nation', passed, in the nineteenth century, from Scotland to Germany. Only after the decline and fall of the English classical school, around 1870, was the historical method of Hume, Steuart and Smith cultivated widely again in Britain.

II

Sir James Steuart (1713–80) came of a family eminent in law and politics, with its country seat near Edinburgh, where, at the university, he studied history and law, the former subject under the first professor of history to be appointed at that ancient institution. He took his bar examination in 1735, but never practised law. Most of the next five years were spent in travelling in Western Europe, first in Holland, then in Spain, where a famine in Andalusia may first have aroused his interest in political economy. Later he was in the south of France and Rome. By this time

Steuart was committing himself to the Jacobite cause, in support of the claims to the English throne of 'the Old Pretender', the would-be James III, whom Steuart met in Rome.[5]

In 1745, on the outbreak of the rebellion, Steuart was sent to Paris to become Prince Charles' ambassador and to seek French support. But after the battle of Culloden (1746), when the Jacobites were routed, Steuart faced a long exile as a rebel, spending the next seventeen years in various parts of Western Europe.

Just when Steuart first developed his interest in political economy is not clear. But according to the closing words of his great *Inquiry*, he began its composition in 1749, eighteen years before its publication. As we discuss later, both his political allegiance, and his long residence abroad in diverse countries, may have helped to shape his approach to economic problems. In 1754 he was in Paris, where he probably met Montesquieu and perhaps Mirabeau. Then he spent four years (1757–61) in the small, but delightful university town of Tübingen in Württemberg, where he made much progress with the composition of the *Inquiry*. At this time he also wrote his *Dissertation upon the Doctrine and Principles of Money applied to the German Coin* (1761). Subsequently, at the end of 1762, he was at last allowed by the English government to return home to Scotland, though he was not finally pardoned by King George III until 1771 (see Skinner, 1966, xliii).

In the meantime, Steuart had completed and published his *magnum opus*, his *Inquiry into the Principles of Political Economy: being an Essay on the Science of Domestic Policy in Free Nations, in which are particularly considered, Population, Agriculture, Trade, Industry, Money, Coin, Interest, Circulation, Banks, Exchange, Public Credit, and Taxes* (1767). These subjects, in the order given, were dealt with in five books. For some years the *Inquiry* met with modest, if qualified, approval. David Hume, who had helped Steuart obtain his royal pardon, was pleased with the work, though critical of its style. In 1772, Steuart's advice was sought by the East India Company, and he produced a report on the *Principles of Money Applied to the State of the Coin in Bengal*. In 1776, however, with the appearance of *The Wealth of Nations*, Steuart's work suffered, in Britain, an almost total eclipse. What Professor Andrew Skinner describes as Smith's 'curious omission', of any reference whatsoever to Steuart in *The Wealth of Nations*, on any subject, not even that of money and banking, proved to be a thoroughly successful controversial tactic.

Of the roughly twenty-eight years, from when (aet. 22) Steuart had departed on his five-year grand tour until, in 1763 (aet. 50), he returned home from exile, he had spent about twenty-two years in various European countries. His material, ideas and 'vision' were thus derived from a very wide and varied range of economic, social and political conditions, and, to a large extent from economies not then as advanced in economic and industrial development as Britain. In particular, Steuart may have been specially apprehensive regarding the dangerous and disadvantageous possibilities for his countrymen, of the merger of their smaller, weaker, and more remote, economy, with that of their much larger, more powerful, and rapidly growing, southern neighbour.[6]

Certainly, Steuart's wide and varied experiences were intellectually reinforced by the influence on him of Montesquieu's *L'Esprit des Lois* (1748), with its message of historical-institutional relativism. Professor Skinner suggests that, in view of his knowledge of Italian, Steuart may also have been acquainted with the even more radical historical relativism of Vico. It also seems probable that, in his years in Tübingen, when writing his *Inquiry*, Steuart might have got to know the ideas of the cameralists, such as Becher or Justi, though he made no explicit references to German writers. Among works referred to, always politely, by Steuart, were those of Cantillon, Child, Davenant, Law, Locke, Melon, Mirabeau and Petty. Finally, there was the important influence of David Hume, who had deployed a historical-relativist approach to problems of political economy, though on a much smaller scale, in his *Essays*. Steuart was concerned with a much larger and more systematic treatise, for the title of which he very appropriately reintroduced from the French, the term 'political economy' – first used by Montchrétien, with not much significance, in 1615. This proved a timely stroke of nomenclature, as the subject moved towards its independence, for 'The Principles of Political Economy' remained a title very much in use during the next century. Moreover, Steuart was attempting a comprehensive treatment, similar to that of Ernst Ludwig Carl nearly half a century previously, but by no one else since then, not even Cantillon, with regard to historical, political, and social factors.

III

The first sentence of the *Inquiry* proclaimed 'the greatest diffidence' with which Steuart put forward his theories and doctrines. Throughout, he set an example of caution and modesty. There could be no more extreme contrast – or, to some intellectual tastes, a more welcome one – with the dogmatic claims to self-evident certainty of the physiocrats. Such an example as that of Steuart carries a highly important and salutary message – though usually one that is unpopular and often disregarded. At the end of his preface, Steuart warned of the dangers of political disillusionment ensuing from overconfident, or pretentious, economic policy doctrines, based on economic theories of apodictic certainty: 'A people taught to expect from a statesman the execution of plans big with impossibility and contradiction, will remain discontented under the government of the best of Kings' (1966, 13).[7]

Together with this general caution, Steuart committed himself to the pursuit of impartiality, though he was well aware of the impossibility of achieving perfection in this respect:

> Every writer values himself upon his impartiality; because he is not sensible of his fetters. The wandering and independent life I have led may naturally

> have set me free, in some measure, from strong attachments to popular opinions. This may be called impartiality. But as no man can be deemed impartial, who leans to any side whatever, I have been particularly on my guard against the consequences of this sort of negative impartiality . . .
>
> (10)
>
> . . . The speculative person who, removed from the practice, extracts the principles of this science from *observation* and *reflection*, should divest himself, as far as possible, of every prejudice in favour of established opinions, however reasonable, when examined relatively to particular nations: he must do his utmost to become a citizen of the world, comparing customs, examining minutely institutions which appear alike, when in different countries they are found to produce different effects . . .
>
> (17)

Steuart was constantly concerned with the dangers of oversimplification – a concern which may have inclined him towards the excessive prolixity and ambiguity with which he has been charged. His warnings against a narrow systematization, or 'conceits', as he called them, ran along similar lines to those of Condillac's castigation of *a priorist*, deductive systems:

> The great danger of running into error upon particular points relating to this subject, proceeds from our viewing them in a light too confined, and to our not attending to the influence of concomitant circumstances, which render general rules of little use. Men of parts and knowledge seldom fail to reason consequentially on every subject; but when inquiries are made concerning the complicated interests of society, the vivacity of an author's genius is apt to prevent him from attending to the variety of circumstances which render uncertain every consequence, almost, which he can draw from his reasoning. To this I ascribe the habit of running into what the French call *Systèmes*. These are no more than a chain of contingent consequences, drawn from a few fundamental maxims, adopted, perhaps, rashly. Such systems are mere conceits; they mislead the understanding, and efface the path to truth.
>
> (8)

In fact, in a version of his preface, written for his friend Lady Mary Wortley Montague, Steuart characterized, not unfairly, some aspects of the age of the Enlightenment as follows: 'The vice of our age seems to be a propensity to run into such conceits with an appearance of reason' (quoted in Chamley, 1965, 134).

Subsequently, Steuart confessed:

> I am not fond of condemning opinions; but I am very much for limiting general propositions. I have hardly ever escaped being led into error by every one I have laid down. Nothing is so systematical, nothing so pretty in a treatise as general maxims; they facilitate the distribution of our ideas, and I have never been able to dash them out but with a certain regret.
>
> (Steuart, 1966, 67–8)

The quantity theory of money was, for Steuart, a major example of the danger of trying to lay down 'general propositions'. The limitations of such generalities had constantly to be kept in view, for they were 'only true or false as they are understood to be accompanied with certain restrictions, applications and limitations' (358).

If economic theories should be stated with such careful qualifications and restrictions, then, *a fortiori*, policy statements needed to be even more qualified, with regard to the political, social and institutional conditions of the people, or country, to which the policies were being applied. For Steuart, political economy was essentially a policy subject, both 'science' and 'art': 'The great art therefore of political economy is, first, to adapt the different operations of it to the spirit, manners, habits, and customs of the people; and afterwards to model those circumstances so, as to be able to introduce a set of new and more useful institutions' (16).

The variety of conditions and institutions, at different times and places, with which the economist was confronted, was immense:

> If one considers the variety which is found in different countries, in the distribution of property, subordination of classes, genius of people, proceeding from the variety of forms of government, laws, climate, and manners, one may conclude, that the political economy in each must necessarily be different, and that principles, however universally true, may become quite ineffectual in practice, without a sufficient preparation of the spirit of a people.
>
> (17)

Steuart put much emphasis on what he called 'The Spirit of a People' – the title of his second chapter. He thus provided an intellectual link between Montesquieu before him, and – as Professor Paul Chamley has shown – Hegel subsequently, with his concept of the '*Volksgeist*': 'there is no treating any point which regards the political economy of a nation, without accompanying the example with some supposition relative to the spirit of the people' (23).

'Theorists' had to be especially careful when they descended into the policy arena to discuss particular proposals:

> Let theorists, therefore, beware of trusting to their science when in matters of administration, they either advise those who are disposed blindly to follow them, or when they undertake to meddle in it themselves. An old practitioner feels difficulties which he cannot reduce to principles, nor render intelligible to every body; and the theorist who boldly undertakes to remedy every evil, and who foresees none on the opposite side, will most probably miscarry, and then give a very rational account for his ill success. A good theorist, therefore, may be excellent in deliberation, but without a long and confirmed practice, he will ever make a blundering statesman in practice.
>
> (1767 [1770], vol. II, 73)

IV

Steuart opened volume I of his *Inquiry* with the subjects of population and agriculture, starting with a three-stage theory of economic development

– as contrasted with the four-stage theory of Smith and Turgot. Steuart's theory involved the interaction of population growth and food supply. The first and most primitive stage was that of nomads, or savages, living off the fruit and meat supplied by nature – or from beaver and deer in Smith's 'early and rude state of society'. The second stage was that of agriculture, with the regular application of labour to land, which made possible a great increase in food supply and population. The agricultural surplus had a vital role. For, with the third stage there was a surplus of food which could be used to meet other than basic, subsistence needs, so that manufactures could develop; and with the greater variety of goods, and expansion of trade, there came the emergence of money and an exchange economy. At each of the three stages of the growth process it was vital to raise the aspirations of the population for a higher material standard of living, by developing additional wants for new and superior-quality goods. Such aspirations were a main motive force towards higher productivity and production (see Eagly, 1961). It was the denial of the existence, or possibility of thus raising aspirations, or the belief that the labouring classes were wedded to traditional, static living standards, that was behind the doctrine of low wages, and the belief that higher wages would simply be taken out in more leisure. Steuart perceived the great importance of inducing higher levels of agricultural production by encouraging higher material aspirations in agricultural and manufacturing workers alike: 'We may lay it down as a principle, that a farmer will not labour to produce a superfluity of grain relative to his own consumption, unless he finds some want which may be supplied by the means of that superfluity' (Steuart, 1966, 40). Conversely 'other industrious persons' will not work to supply the wants of the farmer except to procure subsistence. These, Steuart continued, were 'the reciprocal wants which the statesman must create, in order to bind society together' (40) – assuming that the society consists of free men and not of slaves.

Not much was made, in Steuart's *Inquiry*, of the division of labour as a prime mover in promoting growth. In Steuart's account, two major principles, or drives, were at work: one was what he called 'the generative faculty', which operated as in Malthus' theory, in that it 'resembles a spring loaded with a weight, which always exerts itself in proportion to the diminution of resistance: when food has remained some time without augmentation or diminution, generation will carry numbers as high as possible; if then, food comes to be diminished, the spring is overpowered . . . Inhabitants will diminish, at least, in proportion to the overcharge' (32).

The second principle at work was that of 'self-love, or a desire of ease and happiness', which, fortified by the aspiration effect, promoted the growth of production, the striving after luxury, and the expansion of the market economy.

According to Steuart:

> The principle object of this science is to secure a certain fund of subsistence for all the inhabitants, to obviate every circumstances which may render it precarious; to provide everything necessary for supplying the wants of the

society, and to employ the inhabitants (supposing them to be free-men) ... so as to make their several interests lead them to supply one another with their reciprocal wants.

(17)

Economic growth did not figure prominently in Steuart's statements of the aims of policy. In fact, security was given a more prominent place. But it is rather anachronistic, and not very profitable, to argue over whether he took a shorter- or a longer-term view of policy objectives – that is, more in terms of short-term employment or long-term growth. Such distinctions have been developed much more recently and were by no means so clear-cut in the eighteenth century when the fundamental concepts of modern 'growth' theory, such as productive capital investment, and technological progress, were only just beginning to emerge explicitly; and while even the possibilities of the division of labour were not stressed by most writers. As Professor Skinner states, Steuart 'did not emphasise the importance of capital' (lxx); nor, as we have noted, did he make very much, explicitly, of the division of labour as part of economic development; while the idea of technological progress, so central in the twentieth century, was omitted even from some of the leading classical models, – not to mention those of the pre-classicals, and mercantilists. Economic growth, for Steuart, as for most eighteenth-century writers, was seen mainly in terms of increasing the output of the economy by raising the level of employment, and by providing the stimulus of suitably expansive monetary conditions, within a competitive framework.[8]

V

Steuart repeatedly emphasized the objective of a high level of employment:

> A statesman should make it his endeavour to employ as many of every class as possible, and when employment fails in the common run of affairs, to contrive new outlets for young people of every denomination ... Such members of the society as remain unemployed, either from natural infirmities or misfortunes, and who thereby become a load upon others, are really a load upon the state ... A state should provide retreats of all sorts, for the different conditions of her decayed inhabitants: humanity, good policy, and Christianity, require it.
>
> (73)

These problems were, of course, not much discussed by Adam Smith; nor was the following question, which Steuart considered to be of major importance for the statesman: 'How he keep the whole of his people constantly employed, and by what means he may promote an equable circulation of domestic wealth?' (276). For, as Steuart noted when discussing government revenues: 'The number of people, well employed, makes the prosperity of a state' (1767 [1770], vol. II, 336). Moreover, he recognized as part of 'the contract of society,' a 'right to work,' and insisted that it was a duty of government to provide employment for those returning from war service (1966, 122).

For Smith, most or all of these problems of unemployment would have been regarded as soluble by the spontaneous, self-adjusting processes of 'the simple system of natural liberty'. But Steuart did not discern any such mechanisms at work as would automatically bring about high and stable employment and growth, while leaving the human pilot, or statesman, with comparatively little to do.

Again and again Steuart emphasized the importance of maintaining what he called 'the balance of work and demand', more often, apparently, employing the concept of 'balance' in an aggregate sense, though sometimes with reference to particular goods or industries. He explained that he preferred 'the word "work" to that of supply, because it is the interests of the workman which chiefly come under our consideration' (1767 [1770], vol. II, 65). Steuart insisted: 'The greatest care must be taken, to support a perfect balance between the hands in work and the demand for their labour' (195).

This balance was important, 'not with a view to enrich the state, but in order to preserve every member of it in health and vigour' (236). Steuart described four harmful consequences of an imbalance: 'Every subversion, therefore of this balance, implies one of four inconveniences, either the industrious starve one another; or a part of their work provided lies upon hand; or their profits rise and consolidate; or a part of the demand made is not answered by them' (1767 [1770], vol. II, 65).

Like many writers in the seventeenth and eighteenth centuries, Steuart was much concerned with maintaining 'circulation', and with emphasizing the harm done by unused savings, hoarding, and stagnation. Like Boisguilbert, Steuart stressed the greater propensity of the rich to hoard: 'When large sums are locked up, they produce nothing; they are therefore locked up not to be useful while they remain secreted, but that they may be useful when brought out in order to be alienated. In a state, therefore, where there are a few very rich and many very poor, there must be much money locked up' (II, 28).

Fiscal policy could be used to counter stagnation:

> Every application of public money implies a want in the state; and every want supplied, implies an encouragement given to industry. In proportion, therefore, as taxes draw money into circulation, which otherwise would not have entered into it at that time, they encourage industry; not by taking the money from individuals, but by throwing it into the hands of the state, which spends it; and which thereby throws it directly into the hands of the industrious, or of the luxurious who employ them.
>
> (725)

Together with fiscal policy, monetary and debt policy should be applied. The statesman:

> ... ought all times to maintain a just proportion between the produce of industry, and the quantity of circulating equivalent, in the hands of his subjects for the purchase of it; that by a steady and judicious administration, he may have it in his power at all time, either to check prodigality and hurtful luxury, or to extend industry and domestic consumption ... For this

> purpose, he must examine the situation of his country, relatively to three objects, *viz.* the propensity of the rich to consume; the disposition of the poor to be industrious; and the proportion of circulating money, with respect to the one and the other.
>
> (323–4)

It may be desirable to introduce paper or other 'symbolical' money:

> It is, therefore, the business of a statesman, who intends to promote circulation, to be upon his guard against every cause of stagnation; and when he has it not in his power to remove these political obstructions, as I may call them, by drawing the coin of the country out of its repositories, he ought . . . to facilitate the introduction of symbolical money to supply its place . . . he must facilitate circulation, by drawing into the hands of the public what coin there is in the country, in case he finds any part of it locked up; and he must supply the actual deficiency of the metals, by such a proportion of paper-credit, as may abundantly supply the deficiency.
>
> (325–6)

But the 'balance' must not be upset in the opposite direction: 'A statesman who allows himself to be entirely taken up in promoting circulation, and the advancement of every species of luxurious consumption, may carry matters too far and destroy the industry he wishes to promote. This is the case when the consequence of domestic consumption raises prices, and thereby hurts exportation' (326).

VI

We discussed earlier Steuart's emphatic warnings against attempts to lay down general rules, or theories, in political economy, and we noticed that the quantity theory of money was, for him, a major example of such an oversimplification. Of the quantity theories of Montesquieu and Hume, Steuart remarked: 'The ideas they have broached are so pretty, and the theory they laid down for determining the rise and fall of prices so simple, and so extensive, that it is no wonder to see it adopted by almost every one who has written after them . . .' However: 'I think I have discovered, that in this, as in every other part of the science of political economy, there is hardly such a thing as a general rule to be laid down' (339).

Steuart stated his case against a quantity theory as follows:

> Let the specie of a country, therefore, be augmented or diminished, in ever so great a proportion, commodities will still rise and fall according to the principles of demand and competition; and these will constantly depend upon the inclinations of those who have *property* or any kind of *equivalent* whatsoever to give; but never upon the quantity of coin they are possessed of.
>
> Let the quantity of coin be ever so much increased, it is the desire of spending it alone which will raise prices. Let it be diminished ever so low, while there is real property of any denomination in the country, and a

> competition to consume in those who possess it, prices will be high by the means of barter, symbolical money, mutual prestations, and a thousand other inventions. (345)
>
> ... if the specie be found above the proportion of the industry, it will have no effect in raising prices, nor will it enter into circulation: it will be hoarded up in treasures ... The value of each particular species of ... consumption is determined by a complication of circumstances at home and abroad; consequently, the proportion is not determined by the *quantity* of money actually in the country. (350)
>
> Suppose the specie of Europe to continue increasing in quantity every year, until it amounts to ten times the present quantity, will prices rise in proportion? I answer, that such an augmentation might happen, without the smallest alteration upon prices, or that it might occasion a very great one, according to circumstances.
>
> (355)

Steuart put great stress on the velocity of circulation as an element of effective demand. The quantity of metallic money was a largely passive element:

> ... The money of a country ... bears no determinate proportion to circulation; it is the money circulating, multiplied by the number of transitions from hand to hand. Again, we have said that the prices of all things are determined by demand and competition. The meaning of this, as it concerns the present question, is, that in the proportion to the competition of those who appear with money, in order to acquire what comes to market, a larger or a smaller sum is brought to circulation.
>
> (715)

Certainly Lionel Robbins was well justified in his observation, or complaint, that Steuart provided 'a sort of compendium of all subsequent anti-quantitative theories of money' (1963, 209).

On the subject of interest, Steuart showed how the rate of interest would be settled in a market by lenders and borrowers. He therefore criticized Sir Josiah Child, because, believing that a low rate of interest is good for trade, 'he seems to think, that it is the power of a legislature, by statute, to bring interest down to that level which is most advantageous to trade' (455).

The intervention of government was, however, needed for what Steuart called 'striking out as much as possible, the competition of spendthrifts at the money-market', who drove up the interest rate. But the rate should not be fixed by statute, but rather by the government influencing 'the extent of credit and paper money in circulation' (462). It could hardly be said that on the question of the regulation of the rate of interest Steuart was less liberal than Adam Smith.

VII

Turning to the problem of value and price, Steuart rejected the notion of absolute value, and emphasized subjective estimation:

> Value is a relative term; there is no such thing as absolute value; that is to say, there are no two substances in the universe different in themselves which can be so proportioned in their parts, as to be permanently of the same value at all times . . . Value is the estimation mankind put upon things; and this estimation, depending upon a combination of their own wants, fancies, and even caprices, it is impossible it should be permanent. The measure of value, then, must be that which measures not the positive worth of any thing; but the relative worth of all things compared with one another.
>
> (*Works*, 1805, vol. V, 175)

In his *Inquiry*, however, Steuart defined the 'real value' of a good as its cost of production, any excess over which, in the price received, represented profit (159). The level of demand determined how far price exceeded cost of production. Emphasizing the importance of ignorance, he explained that demand and supply can only be estimated imprecisely and uncertainly, since it was 'next to impossible to discover it exactly', so that merchants 'can only regulate the prices they offer, by what they may reasonably expect to sell for again' (175). Steuart also understood demand in terms of a schedule, relative to prices: 'What I mean by *relative* is, that . . . demand is *great* or *small*, according to prices: there may be a great demand for grain at 35 shillings per quarter, and no demand at all for it at 40 shillings' (176).

Moreover, Steuart discerned the idea of elasticity of demand: 'Demand has not always the same effect in raising prices: we must therefore carefully attend to the difference between a demand for things for the first necessity for life, and for things indifferent' (153).

He defined the equilibrium price as follows:

> . . . When we say that the balance between work and demand is to be sustained *in equilibrio*, as far as possible, we mean, that the quantity supplied should be in proportion to the quantity *demanded*, that is, *wanted*. While the balance stands justly poised, prices are found in the adequate proportion of the real expense of making the goods, with a small addition for profit to the manufacturer and merchant.
>
> (189)

This justly poised balance came about in conditions of what Steuart called 'double competition', that is, with numerous competitors, buying and selling on both sides of the market. He regarded double competition as bringing about a beneficent equilibrium, or balance, by preventing the excessive rise or fall of prices: '*Double competition* is what is understood to take place in almost every operation of trade; it is this which prevents the excessive rise of prices; it is this which prevents their excessive fall. While *double competition* prevails, the balance is perfect, trade and industry flourish' (173).

But, unfortunately, beneficent double competition was liable to be eroded by barriers or privileges, or superseded by monopolies. In particular, it was not effective enough in the most important market of all, that for the people's basic foodstuff. In the eighteenth century, a vital test of an economist's stance regarding economic policy turned on his attitude regarding the market for grain. According to Steuart, the market for the people's subsistence did not operate sufficiently smoothly and beneficently to be left free:

> A statesman therefore, should be very attentive to put the inland trade in grain upon the best footing possible, to prevent the frauds of merchants, and to promote an equal distribution of food in all corners of the country: and by means of importation and exportation, according to plenty and scarcity, to regulate a just proportion between the general plenty of the year in Europe, and the price of subsistence; always observing to keep it somewhat lower at home, than it can be found in any nation rival in trade.
>
> (255)

In his *Dissertation on the Policy of Grain*, Steuart warned against the effects in lean years of panic buying by an ignorant public:

> Natural subsistence must be kept, as to its value, in as exact a proportion as may be to the plenty of the year. And in times of scarcity, all a statesman can do, is to prevent the fears and prejudices of mankind arising from their inadequate notions concerning the degrees of scarcity, from destroying this proportion.
>
> (From *A Dissertation on The Policy of Grain*, *Works*, 1805, vol. V, 353)

Steuart put forward a rather elaborate scheme for a public granary. In the debate over government intervention in the grain market, there were also at various times in the eighteenth century, on the same side as Steuart, such important and not illiberal writers as Boisguilbert, Galiani and Jeremy Bentham.

Steuart also applied his analysis of demand and supply (or 'work') to the prices of labour of different types. He denied that the price of labour was generally determined by the price of subsistence, and insisted that the price of the products was the main determinant: 'Now the price of a manufacturer's wages is not regulated by the price of his subsistence, but by the price at which his manufacture sells in the market . . . It is therefore the rate of the market for labour and manufactures, and not the price of subsistence, which determines the standard of wages' (691).

Steuart described the movement of wages as follows:

> When workers can insist upon an augmentation of their wages, the demand of the market must be greater than the supply from their work . . . Let the demand of the market fall, the prices of labour will fall . . . The workmen will then enter into hurtful competition, and starve one another, as has often been observed . . . Let the demand of the market rise, manufacturers may raise their wages in proportion to the rise of the market; they may, in the cheapest years, enjoy the highest wages; drink one half of the week, and laugh at their employer, when he expects they should work for less, in order to swell his profits in the rising market.
>
> (694)

The conclusion was: 'The price of subsistence, whether it be influenced or not by the imposition of taxes, does not determine the price of labour. This is regulated by the demand for the work, and the competition among the workmen to be employed in producing it' (695).

The basic framework, therefore, of Steuart's analysis of value, price and distribution was on rather different lines, and had a rather different emphasis, from that which was to underlie much of English classical theorizing. With his rejection of absolute standards of value, or of objective value, with his emphasis on relativity and subjective estimates, with the refinements which he added to the concept of demand, with his denial of a link between subsistence and a general wage, and his insistence on relating wages to products, Steuart's theoretical framework approached more closely that of the Italian and French theories, and the subsequent neoclassical framework of value and distribution analysis, than the system which was to prevail among the English classicals.

VIII

Regarding, finally, Steuart's policy views, he certainly tended to approach policy issues from the viewpoint of an ever-active 'statesman'. He supported government intervention in the vital market for grain; in less advanced economies he supported protection for manufacturing; in more advanced economies he considered that policies to raise employment would be necessary. But it would be misleading to describe Steuart as a thoroughgoing totalitarian *dirigiste* or 'planner', just because he took seriously the problem of involuntary unemployment. Certainly, at one point he stated that 'a government must be continually in action' (21). Nor did he recognize the workings of far-reaching, self-adjusting mechanisms as operating very widely and effectively in the various economies he had observed at first hand – which hardly included the English economy. So with regard to important sectors, at any rate, he did not consider that such mechanisms could generally be left without governmental attention. But Steuart again and again declared himself, in the most emphatic terms, on the side of liberty. In particular, he stressed the need for the statesman, or policy maker, to work with, and not against, the grain of individual self-interest, in that he should,

> ... by direct motives of self-interest, gently conduct free and independent men to concur in certain schemes ultimately calculated for their own proper benefit.
>
> (1767 [1770], vol. I, 149)

> The principle of self-interest will serve as a general key to this inquiry; and it may, in one sense, be considered as the ruling principle of my subject, and may therefore be traced throughout the whole. This is the main spring, and only motive which a statesman should make use of, to engage a free people to concur in the plans which he lays down for their government ... Were public spirit, instead of private utility, to become the spring of action in the individuals of a well-governed state, I apprehend, it would spoil all.
>
> (42–3)

Steuart could hardly have insisted more strongly than he did on the libertarian principles underlying his approach to economic policy: 'any free people who invest a statesman with a power to control their most trivial actions, must be out of their wits and considered as submitting to a voluntary slavery of the worst nature, as it must be the most difficult to be shaken off' (278).

Such a statement is hardly that of a totalitarian planner. Steuart emphasized regarding the kind of policies he advocated, that when,

> ... the legislative power is exerted in acquiring an influence only over the actions of individuals, in order to promote a scheme of political economy, uniform and consistent in all its parts, the consequence will be so far from introducing slavery among the people, that the execution of the plan will prove absolutely inconsistent with every arbitrary or irregular measure.
> (278)

Steuart indicated what he meant by liberty:

> By a people's being free, I understand no more than their being governed by general laws, well known, not depending upon the ambulatory will of any man, or any set of men, and established so as not to be changed, but in a regular and uniform way; for reasons which regard the body of society, and not through favour or particular classes.
> (206)

Free exchange of goods and services was the vital constituent of freedom: 'This communicates the idea of a free society; because it implies the circulation of a real equivalent for everything transferred, and for every service performed' (261). Steuart, moreover, saw 'the public good' as formed by 'the combination of every private interest' (143). Certainly he entertained no notions of democracy – nor, of course, did Adam Smith.

It is worth re-emphasizing, at this point, Steuart's mistrust of general policy judgements, and his insistence that policies must be related to the particular stage of development of an economy, as well as to the traditions, institutions and circumstances of different countries and peoples. As Professor Skinner has observed regarding Steuart's views on trade policy; he 'cannot be linked with any particular policy recommendations. Policies such as freedom of trade or protection are to be applied wherever they are relevant; whether or not they are relevant depends in turn on the conditions of the particular case' (1966, lxxix).

Professor Skinner goes on to observe that Steuart was more concerned with the objective of economic welfare than with that of power. If power, or military might, was the objective, Steuart considered that the Spartan system of Lycurgus, with its agrarian egalitarianism, was 'the most perfect plan of political economy' (218) – which, however, he refused to take seriously for his own country in his own day, describing his interlude about Sparta as 'a farce between the acts of a serious opera' (227).[9]

In some respects Steuart's approach to policy questions was closer to that of the German cameralists than to that of many of the mercantilists. Furthermore, from his observation and experience, both at home and in

Scotland, and during his travels in Europe – where he had studied economic problems more closely than any other English or Scottish economist of his time – Steuart had come to view policy from the standpoint of smaller and less advanced economies, and to develop his ideas regarding policy for 'infant trades' – anticipating, to some extent, the ideas of Friedrich List some three-quarters of a century later. His main point was that the learning of skills took time, and that learners needed protection against the already adept;

> The new beginners are put among a number who are already perfect: all the instructions they get is, *do as you see others do before you*. This is an advantage which an established industry has over another newly set on foot ... What loss must be first incurred! What numbers of aspiring geniuses overpowered by unsuccessful beginnings when a statesman does not concern himself in the operation! ... The ruling principle, therefore, which ought to direct a statesman in promoting and improving the infant trade of his people is to encourage the manufacturing of every branch of natural productions by extending the home consumption of them; by excluding all competition from strangers; by permitting the rise of profits, so far as to promote dexterity and emulation in invention and improvement.'
>
> (262–3)

When, however, an economy moves into the next stage, that of foreign trade, the protection of infants should be removed:

> When a people have taken a laborious turn, when sloth is depised, and dexterity carried to perfection, then the statesman must endeavour to remove the incumbrances ... The scaffolding must be taken away when the fabric is completed. These incumbrances are high prices, at which he has been obliged to wink, while he was inspiring a taste for industry ...: but when he intends to supply foreign markets he must ... bring down the price both of subsistence and work.
>
> (1767 [1770], vol. II, 74)

There may seem, indeed, to be something over-optimistic, or even naïve, in the assumption that 'the statesman' will be willing and able to reverse his policy of supporting particular interests in the economy, just when historical changes may require such a reversal, in the interests of the people as a whole.[10]

IX

It has been the versions of the victors – the victors, at any rate, for a particular time, in particular countries – which have become the dominant, and even orthodox, versions of the history of economic thought. The versions, or viewpoints of the losers are largely disregarded, and Sir James Steuart has been one of the most consummate, outstanding losers in the history and historiography of the subject. In England in the nineteenth century, while the régime of classical orthodoxy dominated in that country,

Steuart and his work suffered almost total eclipse, punctuated by occasional expressions of contempt; and this in spite of some recognition from McCulloch that he was, indeed, the author of 'the first English work which had any pretensions to be considered as a systematic and complete view of the subject' (1845, 11). Pigeon-holed ignominiously as 'the last of the mercantilists', Steuart was relegated, by such an authoritative nineteenth-century pundit as Sir Leslie Stephen, to a position 'amongst the most tiresome individuals of the most tiresome of all literary species – the inferior political economist' (1876, vol. II, 304).[11]

To some extent, it is fair that the prolixity and lack of organization in Steuart's sprawling *Inquiry* should take the blame for its eclipse – he himself confessed to 'needless repetitions'. But in a serious subject, as the decades went by, such defects should not have proved fatal. To some extent, Steuart's stylistic faults were brought about by his intellectual virtues, and by his more persistent resistance to oversimplification than that shown by his leading rivals and critics. It is easier to write clearly and engagingly when one has a 'simple system' to expound.

More serious and more controversial are the questions about Steuart's politics, which are ambiguously stated, and might well be regarded as combining a lack of realism with a normatively unacceptable paternalism. A lack of political realism might be regarded as proved by his reliance, in economic policy, on the knowledge and benevolence of the statesman.

It should, however, be emphasized that Steuart's views on policy followed from his inability to discern, and therefore his unwillingness to rely on, the sufficiently rapid operation of self-adjusting mechanisms in the economies of his day, especially with regard to money and aggregate demand. He regarded involuntary unemployment as a very serious problem. It is, moreover, unjustifiable to accuse Steuart of assuming that governments were always omniscient. What he asserted was that, for perfectly successful policies, either through government action or by individuals in free markets, perfect knowledge would be required, and the more accurate the knowledge of the statesman the greater was his power to achieve the results he aimed at. Steuart had warned emphatically about the difficulties of arriving at reliable general theories in economics. Unlike his 'enlightened' contemporaries, he was well aware how scarce a commodity useful, well-tested economic knowledge was.

There can be no doubt that Adam Smith's politics, compared with Steuart's, seem more realistic with regard to the knowledge and benevolence of governments (though some might maintain not invariably with regard to the working of market mechanisms). Normatively, moreover, Smith's individualism was more widely acceptable among those who, in the ensuing decades, wielded most influence on economic policy and economic doctrines.

What should be respected, however, are the quality and importance of Steuart's contributions on a number of central questions of economic theory and analysis, in particular with regard to demand analysis and monetary theory. His wise methodological caution and unpretentiousness also deserve recognition and, still more, his emphasis on the historical dimension, and historical–institutional relativism – an emphasis he shared with Adam Smith. To refuse to recognize such positive contributions, because of a distaste for Steuart's political inclinations, is hardly today characteristic of a serious professional attitude. Steuart's technical contributions to economic theory and analysis were not as important as those of Quesnay, but they were substantial. As regards the political element in their economic writings, both Steuart and Quesnay may be seriously criticized. Quesnay's political and philosophical doctrines, however, contain clear suggestions of modern totalitarianism not present in Steuart's work, which inclines politically rather in the direction of a Keynesian or social-democratic concern with economic insecurity and unemployment (see Vickers, 1970).

20
Adam Smith and *The Wealth of Nations*

I

The quantity of secondary literature about the economics and political economy of Adam Smith – especially since the very weighty additions which appeared in 1776 – may well be greater than the total amount of literature devoted to the economics of perhaps even a dozen, or more, of the writers so far discussed in this book. Not aspiring to add appreciably to this vast Smithian accumulation, we shall be drawing, for the most part, on a previous minuscule contribution (Hutchison, 1978, chapter 1).[1]

The Wealth of Nations lies on the borderline of our period. In this chapter we are more interested in this supreme work as the culminating achievement, which brought to a close our formative period, than as the opening, keynote work of a new era. We shall be concerned with what Smith made of his predecessors' work, together with what he failed to make of it, either because he did not know it (e.g. the writings of Galiani and Condillac) or because he deliberately chose to ignore it (e.g. Steuart's *Inquiry*).

At the end of chapter 11 we left the twenty-eight-year-old Smith, in 1751, at a turning-point in his career when he was appointed to the chair of Logic at the University of Glasgow, from which he moved a year later to the chair of Moral Philosophy. Smith taught in Glasgow for twelve years and three months, building up his course in Moral Philosophy, while presumably, until 1759, concentrating his creative thinking on his social-psychological study of 'moral sentiments', his *Theory* of which (1759) won for him a high reputation and much applause in France.

Smith's lecture course in Glasgow was extremely wide-ranging, including ethics, law and jurisprudence, together with economic analysis and policy. The lectures possessed some characteristics very different from any to be found in college courses today. On the one hand, they covered a number of very complex subjects for the grasp of which highly mature minds might seem to be required. On the other hand, it was addressed to young teenagers, who were discouraged from taking notes, and whose textbooks were in Latin. Of the four main parts of the course, 'policé', or political economy, came last. Smith had dealt with topics in political economy in his lectures in Edinburgh in 1748–50. Presumably, however, his main creative effort in this sector of his vast field of interests did not come until the 1760s, or perhaps until some time after he had left Glasgow. Anyhow, the notes taken from this section of his lectures in 1762–3 and 1763–4 (see Smith, 1978, 331–94 and 486–554) may provide some indications of Smith's main ideas on political economy around the time of his fortieth birthday, and of his departure from Glasgow some six months later. Some tentative conclusions may be suggested as to which of the main topics eventually discussed in *The Wealth of Nations*, had been broached by Smith in his Glasgow lectures, and as to which questions he first addressed or formulated after 1764, or when he got down to writing his book in 1766–7.

In broad terms, it seems that in his lectures Smith's treatment of value and price kept more closely to the lines laid down by Francis Hutcheson (even more closely, it would appear in 1762–3 than in 1763–4). In the lectures also there was relatively much more concern with market price than with natural price, as contrasted with *The Wealth of Nations*.[2] Though the distinction between market and natural price appeared in the lectures, the notes are hardly full or clear regarding the relations between the two. What is absent from the lecture notes was the prominent emphasis on labour, either in terms of a labour-commanded theory of the absolute measure of value (in spite of a fleeting reference, see 1978, 503); or in the form of a labour-embodied theory of the determination of value in the 'early and rude state of society'. Nor, in the section devoted to jurisprudence does Smith follow up at all closely Locke's labour theory of property, though at certain points (1978, 17, 20 and 338) there seems to be a significant indebtedness – identified by the editors – to Locke's *Second Treatise of Civil Government*, the major, though not the only, fount and origin of labour theories both of property and value. Professor Bowley certainly did not exaggerate when she maintained: 'In the *Lectures* it is notable that Adam Smith has no trace of a labour theory of value, while labour as a measure of value is mentioned only in passing' (1973, 110).

Moreover, also almost entirely absent from the lecture notes is the fundamental analysis, in volume II of *The Wealth of Nations*, of saving, investing, capital and money, which was to become the central pillar of classical macro-economics.

II

In January 1764 Smith abandoned Glasgow and academic life for wider prospects; or, as Keynes put it, 'at the age of 41 (just at the right moment, neither too soon or too late)', he 'launched himself on the great world' (1938, 33). He took the plum job of private tutor to a young Duke and, for nearly three years, travelled with his pupil in France, Switzerland and Italy, ending up with about nine months in Paris in 1766. At that time interest in, and enthusiasm for physiocracy, and the 'economists', was at or near its peak, and Smith met and discussed political economy with Quesnay, Turgot and others – the most important and consequential intellectual encounters of his life outside Scotland. Early in 1767 he was back with his mother in his native Kirkcaldy, in which small coastal town, in what must have been considerable intellectual isolation, he spent some seven years producing what eventually was recognized as his masterpiece. This was surely a feat of single-minded dedication and concentration, indicative of an almost infinite capacity for taking pains. In 1773 Smith relaxed somewhat, coming south to London for three years of more convivial revision and consultation with friends and intellectual society in London.

III

No comprehensive account of, or 'reader's guide' to, *The Wealth of Nations* is provided here. We merely discuss selected topics which seem significant from our particular perspective, that of considering Smith's book as the final, culminating work of our period. Let us take first the subject of scope and method.[3]

It must be emphasized first that Smith would never, for one moment, have entertained or accepted – even in his later years, after 1776, when *The Wealth of Nations* was bringing him such resounding and rewarding success – an interpretation of his intellectual career as having been centred upon, or dominated by, political economy, even in the broadest sense of the term.

For Adam Smith was, in fact, and undoubtedly always considered himself to be, a philosopher, in a highly comprehensive sense, not as interested in epistemology as Locke, Berkeley and Hume, but penetrating much more deeply into social and legal philosophy and the psychology of ethics. Smith remained a philosopher from the beginning to the end of his life. He would never have regarded his work as a whole as primarily economic. He thought of economics, or political economy, as only one chapter, and not the most important chapter, in a broad study of society and human progress, which involved psychology and ethics (in social and individual terms), law, politics, and the developmet of the arts and sciences.[4] Smith did not merely start life with a youthful enthusiasm for philosophy, and then eventually narrow down his interests in his maturity to become an economist. Fortunately for our subject, as it turned out, he did devote a decade or so of his prime years to political economy (using up, perhaps, quite a lot more scarce time than he had originally intended in completing his work in that particular section of his vast field). But having finished *The Wealth of Nations* Smith moved on, or back, to the history and philosophy of law and to the progress of the arts and sciences. When he lamented in his last days that 'he had done so little', Smith did not, of course, mean that he had planned, but failed to complete, further volumes on political economy (as Alfred Marshall originally planned a multi-volume *Principles of Economics*, which very unfortunately for the subject in the twentieth century was never completed in the form originally intended). What Smith, with excessive modesty, was lamenting was that he had not completed more than a small part (which fortunately included the politico-economic part) of his original vast philosophical-historical plan.[5] Therefore, that *The Wealth of Nations* played such an important role in establishing political economy as an independent subject is one of those felicitous, unintended and quite unplanned outcomes to which Smith himself assigned such an important, and often beneficent, role in human affairs. In his own celebrated words Smith himself was 'led by an invisible hand to promote an end which was no part of his intention' (1976a, 456) – the end, that is, of establishing political economy as a separate autonomous discipline.

One of the most important themes of Smith's vast, uncompleted life-work, seems to have been centred around the idea of human progress, or the progress of society.[6] In fact, as Walter Bagehot, in his essay of 1876, illuminatingly observed regarding *The Wealth of Nations*:

> It was not the exclusive product of a lifelong study ... It was in the mind of its author only one of many books, or rather a single part of a great book, which he intended to write ... He spent his life accordingly, in studying the origin and progress of the sciences, the laws, the politics, and all the other aids and forces which have raised man from the savage to the civilised state ...
>
> He investigated the progress of opulence as part of the growth and progress of all things ...
>
> The last way in which he regarded Political Economy was as a separate and confined speciality; he came upon it as an inseparable part of the development of all things, and it was in that vast connection that he habitually considered it.
>
> (1881, 248–50; and 1895, 129)

But what interest, it may well be asked, for economists today, have Smith's apparently vast intellectual ambitions regarding the intended scope of his life-work, and the somewhat limited and subordinate place of *The Wealth of Nations* in that intended work? Are Smith's comprehensive intellectual ambitions and concepts more than a rather magnificent, 'period', museum specimen of eighteenth-century intellectual design, which, in any case, Smith himself came nowhere near to completing, and which have become quite obsolete and irrelevant in scale for the tasks of today?

Of course it can be validly claimed that for nearly two centuries the concentration and specialization carried through by successive generations, beginning with Ricardo and Senior, has largely paid off, in spite of objections advanced from time to time by Historical, Comteist, Marxist and Institutionalist critics. But this specialization and concentration in political economy and economics has depended, to a large extent, on the assumption of a fairly stable social and political environment which would not too seriously or irregularly interfere with economic processes, which processes, therefore, could be studied more or less in isolation. This assumption of a stable social framework – or what Pigou (1929, 21), before the world depression, was describing as a 'stable general culture' –

permitted the development of classical, neoclassical and Keynesian economics in Britain. Indeed, there may always be plenty of more narrowly and specifically economic questions which will not require the kind of comprehensive social and historical setting envisaged by Adam Smith. But to the extent that the assumption of a more or less stable social framework, and the kind of specialization in economics which it permits, *may be* becoming significantly less valid than it used to be, there may well be reasons for regarding Smith's conceptions of the scope of the subject, and its close inter-relationships and interpenetration with other fields, especially that of law, not simply as an obsolete, impracticable, intellectually unfeasible irrelevance, of no more than period interest for economists today. What, at least, might be concluded is that Adam Smith would not have neglected, or underestimated, the legal, social and social-psychological factors in our contemporary economic problems (for example, the problem of inflation) just because such factors may be outside what have more recently come to be regarded as accepted 'professional' or departmental frontiers.

IV

Conceptions of the scope of the subject are naturally related to conceptions regarding methods, and in turn are related to the kind of conclusions regarding policy which are considered intellectually feasible or justified. The combination and balance of methods employed in *The Wealth of Nations* have been as rarely followed by subsequent economists as have Smith's comprehensive conceptions of the scope, and of the wide-ranging interdependencies of social and economic enquiry. There was surely some justification for the claim of the historical economist Thorold Rogers, at the centenary celebrations in 1876, that there was 'nothing more significant than the differences of the process by which Adam Smith collected his inferences, and that by which his followers or commentators have arrived at theirs'.[7]

In fact, following what may be described as the James Mill–Ricardo methodological revolution, the comprehensiveness and balance of methods deployed in *The Wealth of Nations* has hardly ever been regained in a general work on the subject of major stature. It is a tribute to the remarkable balance which Smith achieved that he has been both acclaimed and criticized from both or all sides in subsequent methodological debates. But there is certainly a most striking contrast with the Ricardian methods which later obtained such prestige.[8] For the bulk of the text of *The Wealth of Nations* consists of descriptive and historical material. As one of Smith's recent successors at Glasgow has noted:

> He was rather a rich inductive thinker than a rigidly logical system-builder ... though he was both. He had the modesty and wisdom always to give true weight to the facts ... [He had a] genius for choosing and using factual data. He was at home in facts. He enjoyed ferreting them out, and giving them their proper weights.
>
> (Macfie, 1967, 13 and 139)

Sixty years after the appearance of *The Wealth of Nations*, Nassau Senior, in formulating the viewpoint established by the Ricardian methodological revolution, was to complain of 'the undue importance which many economists have ascribed to the collection of facts' (1836, 6).

According to Senior, the science of political economy, apart from its multifarious applications, was not, '*avide de faits*'. *Adam Smith emphatically was 'avide de faits'*, and overwhelmingly demonstrated his avidity, and the conception of the subject which this avidity implied, in *The Wealth of Nations*.

In his *Lectures on Rhetoric and Belles Lettres*, Smith is reported as referring to 'abstract and speculative reasonings, which perhaps tend very little to the bettering of our practice' (1983, 37).

In fact, in *The Wealth of Nations* 'abstract reasonings' are mostly kept on a very tight rein. Smith is certainly not one for taking off into the Ricardian stratosphere of 'strong cases' or extreme, arbitrary abstractions. Of course Smith employed a 'system', as he called it, by which he meant an abstract, deductive model. But he sharply denounced 'the man of system' who indulges in, what Viner called, 'over-attachment or an exaggeration of the applicability to concrete issues withut qualification of abstract and therefore at its best partial and incomprehensive theorizing'. Smith very much doubted that abstraction could provide either understanding of the real world or, by itself, safe guidance for the legislator or statesman' (Viner, 1965, 32; and 1968, 327).[9]

When Smith wanted to use a simple case for its illustrative value he seldom invented an abstraction. He sought to go back in history and find a factual illustration in a simpler kind of economy, such as the hand-to-mouth hunting and fishing economy which is so frequently referred to from the first page onwards in *The Wealth of Nations*. How far Smith's history, or sometimes what has beeen called his 'conjectural history', or conjectural anthropology, was always accurate, is beside the point methodologically. Smith did not consider that students of society, or of the wealth of nations, could, or should seek to compensate very far for their inability to experiment by setting up abstract models.

Smith was methodologically comprehensive. Though sharing much of the intellectual confidence of his age, he realized that significant or useful social and philosophical truth, including economic truth, was always a *very* scarce commodity, and especially so in relation to the extravagant needs for it implicitly postulated by, though often not explicitly understood to be an essential prerequisite for, the plans and projects of reformers and revolutionaries. So the student of society, or of the economy, cannot afford to overlook *any* method by which some grain or crumb of truth, however insubstantial and fragmentary, may be picked up. As John Neville Keynes said of Smith: 'He rejected no method of enquiry that could in any way assist him in investigating the phenomena of wealth' (1917, 10).[10]

In fact, Smith employed methods which recently have been powerfully denounced by some philosophers and economists. For Smith was a historical economist not only in the sense that he was empirical, but in that the theme of *progress through natural stages of development* runs all through his *Inquiry into the Nature and Cause of the Wealth of Nations*. Smith, in fact, like Hume, Ferguson and Millar, belonged to 'the historical age' and 'the historical nation'. He did not claim to have discovered 'laws' of economic development, or indeed, *any* economic laws, and so might not be describable as a 'historicist' in the fullest sense. But, especially in the often rather neglected volume III of *The Wealth of Nations*, 'Of the Natural Progress of Opulence', Smith seeks to lay down 'the natural course of things' or an 'order of things which necessity imposes in general', though he allowed that this natural course or order could be 'inverted' by misconceived government policies.

Of course, as with most methods (including, for example, quantitative methods) 'historicist' procedures, as Sir Karl Popper has demonstrated, have been grossly misused, and wildly exaggerated claims have been made on their behalf. But if one is interested in different kinds of economy, existing at different times and places, and their different actual and potential levels of development, then one cannot afford fastidiously to dismiss 'historicist' concepts, questions, and methods, however uncertain and unreliable. Though the economist should test and scrutinize results or predictions with the utmost feasible strictness, he cannot dismiss in advance *any* method which may yield some fragment of insight – and certainly not just because such a method is not employed in what are called the most 'mature' natural sciences such as physics.

Therefore, even more definitely than with regard to the scope of the subject, there may seem to be important lessons to be found in the methodological comprehensiveness and balance of Smith's *Inquiry*, which has, in this respect, virtually never been emulated in a book of general principles of major importance. Though Marshall discerned and wrestled with the problem of meshing history and analysis in an exposition of general principles, following the methodological revolution of James Mill and Ricardo, no one has really been able to put it all together again with the balance and comprehensiveness achieved in *The Wealth of Nations*.[11]

V

Adam Smith's *Inquiry*, with its abundantly marshalled empirical and institutional data, evidence, and illustrations, with its sometimes extensive historical digressions (for example, on silver, or on the corn trade, or on the Bank of Amsterdam), and with its exhaustive surveys of institutions (for example, educational institutions), is all eventually held together, securely but flexibly, by the thread provided by a single *type* of model or 'system': what Smith called 'the simple system of natural liberty', or what we might call the freely competitive, self-adjusting, market model. The conditions for 'natural' values and prices, wages, profits and rents, having been analysed the model is applied generally – but not dogmatically, universally, or exclusively – both to domestic and foreign trade as well as to the allocation of particular resources and to their accumulation and employment in the aggregate. Moreover, Smith uses his simple system of natural liberty as a historically 'dynamic' model, in that it is concerned not only with a static criterion, or ideal condition, but with the *progress* of the economy – an essential part of Smith's central theme. What Smith's *Inquiry* is primarily about is how 'the simple system', starting from individual initiative, allocates, accumulates, and reallocates resources via free markets so as to release and stimulate, more effectively than any other 'system', the economic forces which make for progress. The essential unique contribution of 'the simple system' is this vital and attractive complementarity between individual freedom and the economic progress of society.

This assertion of the simple 'system', or the free-market model, in such broad, general terms (but not universally or exclusively) provides one of the main grounds for maintaining that Smith's *Inquiry* marks an epoch in the history of economic thought, or even a revolution in the subject. For it was Adam Smith who really generalized the theory of market self-adjustment as operating effectively, by and large – though with several and, in some cases, important exceptions – throughout the economic cosmos, domestically and internationally, micro-economically and macro-economically. We have already discussed the works of many writers before Smith who had discerned self-adjusting forces at work in particular sectors, and had also sometimes urged that in some areas these forces should be allowed to work themselves out free of government intervention: for example, Gervaise and Hume for international trade, North, Mandeville, and Josiah Tucker for domestic markets, and with regard to labour or capital markets. But it was Smith who asserted the 'system', or model in general terms, as a general answer regarding most economic processes of a 'natural' or normal kind. It must also be emphasized that for Smith self-adjustment was not assumed as a hypothetical abstraction, but was asserted as an imprecise and qualified empirical theory, open, in principle, to refutation, regarding how particular market processes actually and usually worked out. Smith discerned and asserted that market processes worked out in general, given some reasonably simply specifiable, and practically feasible, conditions, in a very different way from that which had mostly been stated or implied in previous economic writings.

In *The Wealth of Nations* there are two great economic forces or processes making for economic progress, which depend, in their turn, on the psychological factor of the individual's striving to better his condition, and on a favourable legal framework (especially regarding property and land tenure). The first of these two great economic forces is the division of labour. It has been justifiably asserted that the initial and basic proposition of Smith's *Inquiry*, that the division of labour depends on the extent of the market, 'is one of the most illuminating generalizations which can be found anywhere in the whole literature of economics' (Young, 1928, 529) – though hardly new in *The Wealth of Nations*.

What might be called Smith's micro-economics and international economics are concerned with how free competitive markets allow the division of labour to contribute with its full power to economic progress. The second great force, or process, making for economic progress is individual frugality or parsimony; and Smith's 'macro-economics' shows how, under his simple system of natural liberty, individual frugality, or parsimony can be fully implemented in the progress of the economy.

Of course, as we have already emphasized, Smith does not, for the most part, assert the empirical validity of the 'simple system', or model, in dogmatic, unqualified, or universal terms. In the mass of historical evidence and illustration, which it is an essential part of Smith's method to bring to bear, and to assign its due weight, a variety of qualifications and exceptions are to be found, certainly in micro-economic and international applications of 'the simple system' or model.

In the first place Smith emphasizes the basic preconditions to be satisfied, such as a favourable legal and property framework. It was laws and customs relating to land tenure which 'have perhaps contributed more to the present grandeur of England, than all their boasted regulations of commerce taken together' (1976a, 392).

Smith is, of course, also constantly emphasizing (and denouncing) the striving after monopoly and the persistence of monopolies and restrictive practices, 'which may endure for many centuries,' or 'for ages together,' and which are based sometimes on 'particular accidents' and sometimes on 'natural causes', as well as government legislation (1976a, 76–9).

The important qualifications and exceptions, which Smith cites, to the beneficent working of his simple system are well known.[12] They include, notably, defence and shipping, justice, public works (a potentially capacious category), and building methods and standards. Smith is even prepared to allow the government to fix or limit the rate of interest (for which he was logically rebuked by Jeremy Bentham). As regards foreign trade, he was ready to support an export duty on wool and moderate import duties for the purposes of revenue and retaliation or bargaining.

VI

Smith once described his treatment of economic policy in *The Wealth of Nations* as a 'very violent attack upon the whole commercial system of Great Britain' (Scott, 1937, 283).

Moreover, when he delivered that attack it was from what was still a heretical or minority point of view. As Walter Bagehot said, a hundred years ago, 'It is difficult for a modern Englishman, to whom "Free Trade" is an accepted maxim of tedious orthodoxy, to remember sufficiently that a hundred years ago it was a heresy and a paradox. The whole commercial legislation of the world was formed on the doctrines of Protection' (1895, 128).

But if Smith could be 'violent' in denunciation, and revolutionary in policies and objectives, he tended to be moderate and gradualist regarding timing and methods. As an empirical and historical economist, and as something of a historical relativist, Smith does not resort to abstract, absolute optima and maxima in his criticisms and appraisals of economic institutions and policies – which highly abstract criteria can be and often are used by economists in such misleading and question-begging ways. In *The Theory of Moral Sentiments* Smith's approach to policy-making even bears a somewhat conservative cast, in that he urges 'the man whose public spirit is prompted altogether by humanity and benevolence' to be prepared to bear with the faults and injustices of the existing order of society:

> He will content himself with moderating, what he often cannot annihilate without violence. When he cannot conquer the rooted prejudices of the people by reason and persuasion, he will not attempt to subdue them by force . . . he will accommodate, as well as he can, his public arrangements to the confirmed habits and prejudices of the people; and will remedy, as well as he can, the inconveniences which may flow from the want of those regulations which the people are averse to submit to. When he cannot establish the right, he will not disdain to ameliorate the wrong; but like Solon, when he cannot establish the best system of laws, he will endeavour to establish the best that the people can bear.
>
> (1976b, 233)[13]

It was here that Smith's methodological approach implied an attitude to policy differing very significantly from the narrowly abstract, *a priori*, deductive, 'rigorous' *laissez-faire* of Quesnay – and Ricardo. For Smith accused Quesnay of irrelevantly and misleadingly applying the criteria of absolute or perfect optimality, in imagining that an economy and polity 'would thrive and prosper only under a certain precise regimen, the exact regimen of *perfect* liberty and *perfect* justice . . . If a nation could not prosper without the enjoyment of *perfect* liberty and *perfect* justice there is not in the world a nation which could ever have prospered' (1976a, 674). In his theory and advocacy of free markets Smith did not concern himself with the Utopian abstractions of perfect *maxima* and *optima*.[14]

One of the most powerfully persuasive aspects of *The Wealth of Nations* derived from Smith's ability, in the conditions of his day, plausibly and validly to make the complementarity of freedom and economic growth, or progress, one of his central themes, proclaiming that more of both of two great, highly valued *desiderata* were simultaneously obtainable, so that there was no need to sacrifice one of them to obtain more of the other. But there can be no doubt as to which of this happily complementary pair Smith would have chosen if he had been forced to do so.[15] Smith was doubtful and ambiguous about the value or significance of an increase in wealth as a value or objective.[16] While greater wealth for a society had a part in rendering it more civilized and more free, or was an indicator of social progress, at any rate regarding individuals he insisted: 'In ease of body and peace of mind, all the different ranks of life are nearly upon a level, and the beggar, who suns himself by the highway, possesses that security which Kings are fighting for' (1976b, 185).

This belief perhaps partly explains why Smith does not seem to show much interest in policies concerned with the distribution of wealth or income, or with problems of poverty. Anyhow, Smith would always have put freedom first, and he valued economic freedoms not mainly or simply because he believed that they promoted a more rapid growth rate of GNP per head, but for their own sake, or because they were an essential component of civil freedom.

VII

The primary economic idea, or theme, of *The Wealth of Nations* was one which had been developed bit by bit, throughout our period, by a number of different writers – from North and Martyn, Nicole and Boisguilbert, Mandeville, Carl, and others, through to Tucker and Hume. This idea, which, from the first page, provided both theoretical and policy *leitmotiv* of Smith's work, was concerned with how an economy progressed via specialization and the division of labour, with the drive of self-interest of its individual participants canalized into socially beneficent directions by competitive markets. Some writers – such as E. L. Carl – emphasized the specialization of land and machinery, as well as labour. It may, however, be noted that Adam Smith almost completely excluded one main reason for the specialization of labour which had been emphasized by most of his predecessors on the subject: that of taking advantage of human diversity, which he saw as, in the main, not so much the cause, as the effect of the division of labour. Smith's view is one that might be expected rather from a social engineer or egalitarian.[17]

With the emphasis on specialism and the division of labour as a main cause, or source, of economic progress came the policy message of freeing and opening up markets, so that this source of progress could be drawn on to the full. Of those writers who developed the analysis of the beneficent effects of the division of labour, only the German cameralist, Ernst Ludwig Carl, was generally on the side of a *dirigiste* paternalism, rather than that of the freeing of markets and the economic initiative of the individual. Widespread, beneficent, more-or-less automatic self-adjusting mechanisms were, however, more and more perceived and analysed with regard to particular markets. But what would today be called 'macro-economic' self-adjustment with regard to money, saving and investment, which would obviate the need for concern or for central regulation with regard to the money supply, was hardly discerned as a possibility. Anyhow, in expounding his central theme Smith, while largely, but not entirely following his predecessors, applied all the philosophical, psychological and political insight for which he is almost unrivalled in the history of the subject.

VIII

We focus now on two basic theoretical innovations, introduced in *The Wealth of Nations*, which owed comparatively little to previous writers. (For we consider somewhat misleading Schumpeter's statement that *The Wealth of Nations* 'does not contain a single *analytic* idea, principle, or method that was entirely new in 1776' (1954, 184).) Indeed, we would claim that, as developed by Smith, these two innovations seem sufficiently new and fundamental as to justify the adjective 'revolutionary', especially in the light of the very powerful influence which they exerted in Britain for the next century. One of these innovations was central to Smith's micro-economics and one to his macro-economics.

The first of Smith's fundamental innovations was his crucial alteration of the concept of 'value in use', or utility, at a vital point in volume I, chapter 4. He introduced his treatment of price and value by maintaining that 'utility', which 'may be called "value in use"', was *not* a necessary prerequisite for value in exchange. For goods 'which have the greatest value in exchange' may have *no* 'value in use' (1976a, 44). Smith thus confused the relations between utility, demand, and value, by maintaining that what should be meant by a good having 'value in use',was not what had, and has, been meant by the great majority of economists, before and since, that is, the quality of being expected to satisfy a want, of whatever kind, 'real' and objective, or fanciful and subjective. It has been explained that Smith must rather have been restricting the meaning of value-in-use to some kind of normative, 'real', objective usefulness (see Bowley, 1973, 110ff; and Hollander, 1973, 133ff).

Two comments may be offered regarding this explanation. First, as has been set out in earlier chapters (especially 2, 6 and 11), Smith inherited from Frances Hutcheson a long tradition which went back through Pufendorf, the Salamancan school, and a majority of the scholastics, according to which a fundamental role was played by a comprehensive, basically subjective, positive concept of utility. As we have seen, Pufendorf defined a good as possessing 'use' 'not merely' when it 'truly' helped to preserve or make pleasurable our existence, but when it did so, 'in the sole opinion of certain men' (1660 [1931], 65).[18]

Second, Smith's concept of utility was fundamentally at variance with the libertarian, individualist message of which Smith otherwise, throughout *The Wealth of Nations* was such a determined and effective champion. The case for economic freedom requires, or is crucially assisted by, a value analysis which gives a full role to *subjective* utility and *individual* choice and demand. Smith's 'real', normative, biological, or 'moralistic' concept of utility contained implications from which Smith himself would have recoiled in horror: that is, that there are real objective 'utilities', which experts, of one sort or another, are qualified to instruct us, or direct us about, which ought to control our valuations, preferences or choices. It is not too much to maintain that a subjective concept of utility is essential and fundamental to the case for, and explanation of, a pluralist and free economy and society. Seeking to explain Smith's conception of value-in-use or utility as unnecessary for exchange value, Professor Bowley (a steadfast supporter, who described his usage as 'exceedingly awkward' and 'all very tiresome' for Adam Smith's students) posed the question: 'Who does not remember the "utility" goods in the last war' (1973, 136). The parallel is all too precise. It seems, however, somewhat incongruous to have to resort to the usage of wartime, governmental rationing officials for an explanation as to how the supreme champion of individual economic freedom came to break with the tradition of such a long line of distinguished predecessors regarding utility.

Since he was excusably ignorant of their writings on this subject it would be quite unfair to blame Smith for not following the analysis of utility and demand put forward by Galiani and Turgot, which, as has been observed, left comparatively little for the neoclassicals to achieve in the field of utility and demand analysis, apart from terminological precision or the application of mathematics.[19] In breaking, however, with the treatment of Pufendorf and Hutcheson, Smith both diminished or excluded the element of subjectivity and confused the relationship between utility and demand. Alfred Marshall's judicious conclusion seems unavoidable: 'Adam Smith makes himself the judge of what is useful to other people and introduces unnecessary confusion' (1975, 125).

Nor can Smith be criticized for not having followed up Condillac's path-breaking analysis of subjectivity, uncertainty, and erroneous expectations in market decisions. Condillac's work did not appear until a month or two before *The Wealth of Nations*. Professor Hayek, however, has maintained 'that every important advance in economic theory during the last hundred years was a further step in the consistent application of subjectivism' (1952, 52). Anyone prepared to uphold the wisdom of this *aperçu*, and to extrapolate it back another hundred years, will probably have to conclude that, with regard to the utility concept, a fundamentally retrogressive step was taken in *The Wealth of Nations*.

Moreover, Smith's treatment of utility and demand was followed up by his theories of labour commanded as an absolute measure of value, and of labour embodied as a determinant of value in primitive economies, together with his general cost of production theory of value.

Labour theories of value hardly have a coherent history before *The Wealth of Nations* independently of the scarcity and utility theory. Petty – followed by the young Benjamin Franklin – had thrown out, in passing, the idea of labour embodied – or labour and land embodied – as a rough-and-ready method of assessing properties for tax purposes. Locke had leaned heavily in the direction of labour in the value analysis in his political treatise, but not in his economic writings.[20] It was *The Wealth of Nations* which opened up the divisions – regarded by some as of the most fundamental importance – between theories of value based on scarcity and utility and those based on labour and cost of production.[21] We would not, however, go so far as to say, with R. L. Meek, that Smith 'makes it perfectly clear' that 'demand has nothing directly to do with the determination of exchange value' (1973, 73). For, in spite of his fine chapter 'of the natural and market price of commodities', there are several important points with regard to demand and value on which Smith hardly offers a 'perfectly clear' analysis.

As regards labour commanded as an absolute measure of value, most value theorists had abandoned the idea of an absolute measure of value long before *The Wealth of Nations*. Montanari and Galiani had rejected the very notion, as did Steuart. As Smith's fellow-classical Nassau Senior remarked: 'Aristotle's description of value as depending on demand . . .

approaches much more nearly to perfect accuracy than Smith's who, by adopting labour as a measure of value, and talking of labour as never varying in its own value, has involved himself and his followers in inextricable confusion' (1978, vol. II, 45).

Smith made a number of valuable contributions to the theories of rent, wages and profits. His theory of distribution, however, was shaped by his treatment of utility and value, which approached the valuation of factors of production from the cost side rather than from that of their utility and scarcity, or the productive contribution rendered. Galiani, on the other hand, drawing on scholastic sources, had recognized the labour element in the value of goods and services, but had subordinated this to his general scarcity-and-utility value analysis.

It is not the case, however, that Smith clearly and categorically put forward a general labour theory of exchange value. He did not. Nor did he entirely omit either the demand side, or the subjective element – (which may be present in his concept of 'toil and trouble' in his labour-commanded measure of value). But his unhappy, tiresome, and awkward treatment of value-in-use, together with his introduction of a labour element both in the measurement of value and in the simplest case of exchange value, had confusing consequences which were very important for the subsequent history of value theory. According to Professor Bowley: 'Adam Smith is traditionally regarded as having introduced a labour theory of value into *The Wealth of Nations*' (1973, 110). This tradition may be wrong. No doubt some of his leading classical successors, together with most Marxists, have misunderstood or misrepresented Smith's views. Smith himself, however, must take his share of the blame, if he has been misunderstood or misrepresented. If Smith's treatment of value was not – as Professor Donald Winch justifiably denies that his politics were – 'an episode, however crucial, that occurred some way along a road which runs from Locke to Marx' then a less unhappy, tiresome, and awkward treatment of utility and value by Smith himself would have rendered such an interpretation impossible from the start. Smith's treatment of value, however, would have needed to remain more precisely faithful to his predecessors, Pufendorf and Hutcheson, and to have avoided such an apparently fundamental influence from Locke's political writings.

A deep-seated source of Smith's confusion may be traceable to his failure to apply, sufficiently consistently, the positive-normative distinction, which had been developed by Petty and others in the seventeenth century, and which had been explicitly and masterfully employed by Cantillon. Smith, on the other hand, not only made much play with the fundamentally ambiguous adjective 'natural', he also introduced a normative-positive ambiguity into the basic concept of value-in-use, by assigning it a normative quality, according to which goods *ought* to be valued or demanded, rather than confining himself strictly to the positive treatment of how, in fact, goods actually were valued and demanded by fallible, gullible human beings.[22]

The most accurate account of Smith on value seems to have come from Professor Denis O'Brien:

> Adam Smith laid the foundations for classical value theory. What he did, and the way he did it, were to prove extremely important because he seems deliberately and consciously to have rejected the value theory which he inherited. He inherited a subjective value theory: and instead of developing this he largely substituted for it a cost of production theory . . . The dismissal of utility as a determinant of value is justified by reference to the 'diamonds and water' paradox although, as we have seen, Smith solved this in his *Lectures.* It is interesting to see that Smith so far purges his analysis of the subjective elements as to redefine utility.
>
> (1975, 78ff.)

IX

The second of Smith's fundamental and indeed revolutionary theoretical innovations was that of his classical macro-economics, including his analysis of saving, investment and the rate of interest, together with his treatment of money. Certainly Smith had here one major anticipator, Turgot, in section 101 of his *Reflections,* which appeared ten years before *The Wealth of Nations* and propounded what Schumpeter called the Turgot–Smith theory of saving and investment – or saving *is* investment. Smith, however, built up the implications of the theory, as regards money and government policy, much further than Turgot. Apart from Turgot's paragraph only a few faint suggestions of what came to be classical macro-economics appeared before *The Wealth of Nations* – for example, very briefly in the writings of Hutcheson and Tucker.

Certainly the stress on the role of saving, investment, and capital accumulation was one of the most important, and relatively very new, features of *The Wealth of Nations.* Smith's point, however, was not merely the importance for economic progress of capital accumulation, but how, within the simple system of natural liberty, individual frugality would, in free markets, almost inevitably be fully and smoothly implemented and converted into capital accumulation and economic progress, without the intervention or activity of governments.

It was the simple system which enabled the frugal or parsimonious man, concerned simply to better his own condition, to be a public benefactor. Throughout his macro-economics, in both his analysis of saving and investment, and in his treatment of money, Smith held to the logic of his 'simple system', and its implications for government policy, in an almost completely consistent manner – apart from his incongruous approval of a maximum rate of interest. The author of *The Wealth of Nations* was the major creator of classical macro-economics. The saving and investment analysis of volume II, chapter 3 constituted the keystone, supporting the exclusion or denial of hoarding, the condemnation of luxury expenditure, and the emphasis on the unconditional beneficence of frugality, doctrines which broke fundamentally not simply with the ideas of 'mercantilists', but, at vital points, with those of Boisguilbert, Mandeville, Hume, Steuart and Quesnay. These doctrines on saving and hoarding fitted logically with Smith's treatment of money. Assuming a certain institutional framework – not very easily defined, set up, or maintained, via the political process – Smith went on to expound a policy of monetary, or macro-economic *laissez-faire*, including what came to be the Ricardo (or 'Treasury') view regarding public investment. There had, moreover, been only a few intimations previously of the new, unconditionally pro-saving model in the writings of one or two of Smith's predecessors – as for example, in Francis Hutcheson's notable denunciation of Mandeville's eulogy of luxury spending – until, of course, the statement of the saving-is-investing analysis in Turgot's *Réflexions*.[23]

We noted the flexibility and qualifications with which Smith applied his 'simple system' in the fields of micro-economics and international trade. His macro-economics, on the other hand, was the one major area where he applied this 'system' without sufficient regard to qualifications and exceptions, or to the necessary conditions, which very much needed specifying, with regard to the monetary and banking framework.

First, there was Smith's bald, unqualified assertion about saving and investing that: 'what is annually saved is as regularly consumed as what is annually spent, and nearly in the same time too.'

Consequently: 'Every prodigal appears to be a public enemy, and every frugal man a public benefactor' (1976a, 337–40).

Secondly, there was Smith's treatment of the money supply. He seemed at times to suggest that it was simply a crude fallacy of 'the mercantile system' to be concerned about the money supply any more than, say, the wine supply: *laissez-faire* applied equally to wine and money. 'We trust with perfect security that the freedom of trade, without any attention of government, will always supply us with the wine which we have occasion for; and we may trust with equal security that it will always supply us with all the gold and silver which we can afford to purchase or to employ, either in circulating our commodities, or in other uses . . .' (1976a, 435).

At some points it seems that Smith was implying that his 'simple system' of competitive freedom could and would always be so flexible as to adjust satisfactorily to any variations in the money supply. Elsewhere Smith seemed to recognize that a growing economy needed a growing money supply, while pointing out, in the 'Digression on Silver', that the world supply of precious metals, or internatonal liquidity, might be extremely uncertain and unreliable. However, Smith seemed also to assume that, internally, if the quantity of gold and silver was not maintained in a country, then paper money would automatically be created to the appropriate amount, without giving rise to any serious problems of central regulation: 'Upon every account, therefore, the attention of government never was so unnecessarily employed, as when directed to watch over the preservation or increase of the quantity of money in any country' (1976a, 437).

The foregoing statement appears to suggest that the money supply doesn't matter, and this rather cavalier treatment generated a long-persistent over-optimism, first regarding the intellectual and practical difficulties of devising and implementing, through governments, a satisfactory framework of monetary and banking rules and institutions, and secondly regarding the seriousness of defects in these rules, or in their implementation, for economic stability. With regard to money and macro-economics, Smith did not adequately develop the conditions and qualifications for his simple system which had been suggested by the less 'revolutionary' but more perceptive insights on these subjects of his greatest friend, David Hume, and of his eclipsed rival Sir James Steuart – sometimes referred to as 'the last of the mercantilists'. In an illuminating article Professor Checkland concluded:

> The banking expression of Smith's system of natural liberty was a set of institutions composed of many enterprises, none capable of monopolistic power or even leadership, each guided by prudential rules, and all trading within an environment of law provided by the state. Acting in aggregate they would, Smith implied, provide an optimal money supply or an effective approximation to it. But in the light of banking conditions in the Scotland of Adam Smith's time, not to speak of the years to follow when matters approximated even less to his assumption, his view of banking omitted important aspects of reality which, if properly attended to, might have damaged his view of economic processes.
>
> (1976, 523; quoted by Hutchison, 1978, 144n.)

The two fundamentally contrasting *Inquiries*, Steuart's of 1767 into the principles of political economy, and Smith's of 1776 into the wealth of nations, epitomized the two opposing macro-economic viewpoints and doctrines, 'classical' and 'anti-classical' (or mercantilist-Keynesian) of the ensuing two centuries. If one wishes to sum up the contrast in a single assumption or idea, one can find it in that of smooth, rapid, beneficent self-adjusting tendencies: their denial by one and their assertion by the other. It was this powerfully fascinating idea and assumption of general, beneficent self-adjustment and self-equilibration, not only micro-economic but monetary and macro-economic, which underlay the Smithian-classical orthodoxy. Regarding macro-economics Steuart had, as his editor puts it, 'no very clear model' (Steuart, 1966, vol. I, lviii). This was just what Smith seemed to offer, micro-economically *and* macro-economically.

Smith's theory of saving, investing and money broke fundamentally with the ideas, not only of Steuart, but with those of Quesnay, Hume, and most of the writers of our period from Petty onwards. Regarding the doctrines of Smith's predecessors, Professor C. H. Wilson has commented:

> Much thought and policy was devoted to ensuring that a supply of precious metal was maintained adequate for a sound and plentiful currency. The anxiety lest 'a scarcity of coin' should slow down the volume of trade and bring about an economic depression affected writers repeatedly every time a crisis threatened. To Adam Smith such anxieties were absurd. Yet his sense of historical change was not strong and his own chapter on Metallic and Paper Money contained implications which he does not fully consider. If the growth of new methods of payment had been of such significance in the century before 1776, how had Mun and his contemporaries fared without these later devices of paper money, bank credit, etc. whose effects Adam Smith found so beneficial?
>
> (1958, 17)

In other words, while for many or most of Adam Smith's predecessors the money supply, or the dangers of its inadequacy or instability, were serious and pressing problems; Smith, in *The Wealth of Nations* encouraged the idea that money and the money supply did not present any very urgent problems for policy, at any rate no more serious problems than did wine and the wine supply.

Smithian or 'classical' macro-economics were to achieve an extraordinarily long domination. As Schumpeter put it, the Smithian theory

> ... proved almost unbelievably hardy. It is doubtful whether Alfred Marshall had advanced beyond it, certain that J. S. Mill had not ...
> ... Secondly, the theory was not only swallowed by the large majority of economists: it was swallowed hook, line and sinker. As if Law – and others – had never existed, one economist after another kept on repeating that only [voluntary] saving was capital creating ... this came to mean that every decision to save coincides with a corresponding decision to invest so that saving is transformed into [real] capital practically without hitch and as a matter of course.
>
> (1954, 325)[24]

Sir John Hicks, noting the significance of the Smithian revolution in macro-economics, explains its triumph in terms of the power of the self-adjusting model, emphasizing its neglect of uncertainty:

> I believe that it is to be explained – that the whole change is to be explained – if we attribute it to the power of a model ...
> ... It was because the model paid no attention to plans and expectations that it neglected uncertainty and liquidity; so that the bridge between real theory and monetary theory, of the possibility of which Hume had had some inkling, remained unbuilt. The only monetary theory which could match the static real theory was one which concentrated upon the more mechanical aspects of the monetary system; this is just what the 'classical' Quantity Theory was. The responsibility for all this goes back to Adam Smith; it is the reverse side of his great achievement.
>
> (1965 41)[25]

X

In the preceding sections of this chapter a number of critical judgements have been suggested regarding two of Smith's most fundamental, and relatively novel contributions in *The Wealth of Nations* (so a precautionary restatement of the obvious may be prudent to the effect that Smith's book is, without question, by far the greatest ever written on its subject). Needless to say, many economists (including, almost by definition, the main body of Smith's orthodox English classical successors) over the century following 1776 upheld the main approach of these two fundamental theories, although with modifications at some points, especially in the case of the Smithian theory of value and price. Certainly, after the 1870s, support for Smith's approach to the theory of utility, value and price fell away markedly. Outside its native country, however, this branch of English classical orthodoxy – the labour and/or cost-of-production theory of value – never dominated as it did for nearly a century on its home ground.

Writing of his achievement in *The Wealth of Nations*, Jacob Viner maintained that 'Smith gave to economics for the first time a definite trend toward a logically consistent synthesis of economic relationships' (1928, 116). Such processes of logically consistent synthesizing, together with their accompanying processes of selecting, simplifying, and systematizing, sometimes also combined with changes in interest and emphasis, may bring impressive gains in the form of enhanced analytical rigour or persuasive power. Such gains, however, may have to be bought at a significant price in terms of flexibility and breadth of relevance. Furthermore, as Professor Skinner notes, '*The Wealth of Nations* succeeded', because it was 'a publication for the present time', and also 'contained a stirring message' (Smith 1976a, 47). 'A publication for the present time' which contained 'a stirring message', while representing 'a logically consistent synthesis' might certainly have had to forgo a wide institutional applicability. (Keynes's *General Theory* is another obvious example.)

Moreover, what Viner called the 'definite trend toward a logically consistent synthesis' so powerfully initiated by *The Wealth of Nations* was pushed drastically, in the half-century after 1776, to the extent of excluding or seriously diminishing some of the most important and valuable aspects of the original Smithian synthesis in *The Wealth of Nations*, notably the historical–institutional methodological approach and its rich, mature, political and psychological component.

Regarding the losses involved in what we called 'the Smithian revolution', we concluded, in 1978:

> A 'revolution' in political economy or economics usually or inevitably involves, or consists of some drastically new selection and simplification, *either* with regard to the questions given priority, *or* possibly, with regard to important elements in the answers – or both. In the case of the Smithian revolution, questions and theories, to which economists before and since Smith have attached great importance, were submerged by its triumph, mainly questions and theories regarding employment, interest and money, but, possibly also regarding utility and value. Any intellectual cost-benefit analysis will, of course, inevitably involve subjective valuations. However, in the case of the Smithian 'revolution', . . . there would appear to have been an overwhelming consensus, supported by almost all schools of economists, as to the epoch-making intellectual gains represented by *The Wealth of Nations*.
>
> (Hutchison, 1978, 25)

I do not wish to deny the existence of this overwhelming consensus regarding 'the epoch-making gains represented by *The Wealth of Nations*'. A decade later, I would maintain that the losses and exclusions which ensued after 1776, with the subsequent transformation of the subject and the rise to dominance of English classical orthodoxy, were also immense.

These losses need to be considered seriously, since they include a major part of the *gains* established in the pre-1776, pre-classical period which this book has reviewed. The following chapter is concerned with opening such an examination.

21
Postscript

I

I aspired originally simply to set out a reasonably adequate account, in approximately chronological order, of the economic thought and theories between Petty and Smith. Such an account, if it has been achieved here, seems interesting enough for its own sake, and I would have preferred to leave readers to draw their own conclusions and to elaborate their own interpretations. To forestall, however, possible charges of evasiveness, or of neglect of duty, I am attempting here to formulate one or two concluding points which have struck me rather forcibly on coming to the end of this review. Let us endeavour, therefore, to stand back and examine briefly, from a late-twentieth-century point of view, what has happened, in approximately the last two centuries since 1776, to the ideas, theories, and lines of thought, initiated or developed in the period between Petty and Smith.

Our first conclusion – perhaps barely worth drawing – is a total rejection of the view of J. B. Say, still to be met with today, that, before Smith, there was virtually no political economy. (I hope this book has not been about a non-subject.) In fact, Smith was not the founder of political economy, but the founder of English classical political economy – which some classicals considered was the same thing, because they maintained that no one had thought or written seriously about the subject before *them*. Political economy, however, was not created by one person in one country, but by many people in several countries of Western Europe. Whether or not it was fully adequate and proper for Adam Smith to make no mention whatsoever in *The Wealth of Nations* of such predecessors as, for example, Petty, Carl, Tucker, Galiani, Verri, Turgot, Condillac and Steuart – and to refer only once to Cantillon – such treatment of the economists of the seventeenth and eighteenth centuries is completely inadequate and misleading for serious, twentieth-century students of the history of political economy.

What may strike one next is that so many of the most important and central ideas, theories, or lines of thought, which have been alive and developing in the twentieth century, emerged in a clear form, or first underwent significant developments in this period. (Not, of course, that the seventeenth- or eighteenth-century writers employed the same degree of analytical sophistication or mathematical precision as late twentieth-century academics; but the main issues were clearly perceived and stated.) Some of these issues, ideas and theories can, of course, be traced back well before 1662. Other ideas and lines of thought, whether or not they were totally new in the period, were powerfully developed and clarified – for example, the idea of the quantity theory of money and the criticism thereof; or the idea of self-equilibrating market processes.

Jointly with this observation, or conclusion, what should also be remarked is the fate, or treatment, of some of the most important and fundamental of these ideas and lines of thought – still, of course, alive and widely defended more than two centuries later – in the approximately 100 years following 1776, when they were excluded, disregarded, seriously under-emphasized, or explicitly rejected as erroneous, by the classical orthodoxy which then prevailed. Adam Smith and *The Wealth of Nations* were responsible, in varying degrees, for these exclusions and rejections, bearing no responsibility whatsoever for one, being partly responsible for others, and being almost totally responsible in another major case.

II

The Wealth of Nations provided many of the fundamental ideas, theories and principles of English classical political economy, which was virtually the first major, modern body of economic doctrine to establish itself as a broad, theoretical orthodoxy in the subject. In its own day, and on its home ground, English classical political economy achieved, for some decades, a degree of prestige, influence, confidence and pretentiousness, unequalled before or since, in the history of the subject in the western world. Some elements in English classical political economy also had much influence outside Britain, though other English classical theories – notably the classical value and price theory – never exercised the same domination abroad as they did at home. Certainly, also, the English classical system never possessed the coherence and uniformity often attributed to it. In fact, the methodology and content of classical theories underwent, from Smith's successors, very important modifications, which included a considerable narrowing of scope by such later classicals as Senior and Cairnes, in the direction of the positive economics represented originally by Cantillon, and subsequently by some neoclassicals. It was Mills, Ricardo and Senior who established an orthodoxy based on a body of doctrine, which was much more deductively based, and which considerably reduced, or excluded, the historical element, so richly represented in *The Wealth of Nations*.

At the same time, the classicals developed a version of the history of the subject – just as the Marxians and Keynesians were to – which, though devoid of the theological element, followed in its pretentiousness the version of Quesnay and the physiocrats.[1] The embryo of this version may be found in Smith's own rather dismissive treatment of his predecessors in *The Wealth of Nations*. Anyhow, it was maintained by his classical successors that Smith had created or founded the subject almost single-handed – as we have noted J. B. Say claiming. McCulloch maintained that political economy was 'of very recent origin' (1824, 20), though, in the last few decades extraordinary progress had been achieved: 'The errors with which Political Economy was formerly infected have now nearly disappeared, and a very few observations will suffice to show that it really admits of as much certainty in its conclusions as any science founded on fact and experiment can possibly do' (1824, 9).[2]

Moreover, regarding the basic theories a remarkable measure of agreement had been established *among those qualified to hold an opinion* (i.e. those who accepted the classical doctrines). According to James Mill:

> Among those who have so much knowledge on the subject as to entitle their opinions to any weight, there is a wonderful agreement, greater than on any other moral or political subject. On the great points, with hardly any exception, there is general concord ... In the great doctrines concerning production, distribution, exchange and consumption, you find perfect concurrence ... There is no branch of human knowledge more entitled to respect.
>
> (1836 [1966], 382)

These claims were taken up by the younger Mill, who emphasized the almost universal intellectual darkness which had preceded the recent emergence of the new science:

> Before the appearance of those great writers whose discoveries have given to political economy its present comparatively scientific character, *the ideas universally entertained both by theorists and by practical men, on the causes of national wealth, were grounded upon certain general views, which almost all who have given any considerable attention to the subject now justly hold to be completely erroneous.*
>
> (1844, 47, italics added)

In fact, even *The Wealth of Nations* was outmoded and inadequate:

> *The Wealth of Nations* is in many parts obsolete and in all imperfect. Political Economy, properly so called, has grown up almost from infancy since the time of Adam Smith; and the philosophy of society, from which that eminent thinker never separated his more peculiar theme, though still in a very early stage of its progress, has advanced many steps beyond the point at which he left it.
>
> (1848 [1909], xxviii)

Fully in tune with these claims by Mill was his celebrated assertion that, thanks to the progress made by his fellow classicals, 'happily, there is nothing in the laws of value which remains for the present or any future writer to clear up; the theory of the subject is complete' (436). It might seem that, with J. S. Mill, the intellectual millennium had arrived.

III

In emphasizing, therefore, how many of the more important theories, or lines of thought of the pre-classical period were excluded or rejected by orthodox classical political economy, we are only repeating, in a much more moderate form, a main point in the classicals' own version of the history of the subject.

We do not accept, however, the assumption of most of the leading English classicals, according to which their debts to their predecessors, who wrote in our period, were virtually nil. Regarding one broad, central idea, or theory, English classical political economy can be seen as completing the statement, or perhaps over-statement, of a basic principle, which had been developed, piece by piece, throughout the period from 1662 to 1776, which may be said to have been suggested by Petty, clearly stated by North and Martyn, and carried further, much more systematically, through Pierre Nicole to Boisguilbert and Mandeville, and then, through the work of many others, to Hume, Galiani, Quesnay and Turgot. This was the broad idea, or theory, summarized in the title of chapter 7: 'Economic Harmonies, Equilibrating Tendencies and Freedom of Trade.' The discernment of more or less beneficent harmonies of interest and of equilibrating tendencies in unrestricted markets, was accompanied by the policy conclusion that freedom from government intervention was desirable in one sector after another, with regard to interest rates, labour markets, and international trade – while the issue remained profoundly controversial, especially in France and Italy, of extending complete freedom to the vital grain market. At the same time there was increasing recognition from Petty, Martyn, and especially E. L. Carl, of the increasing productivity forthcoming from the division of labour, which required free markets for its fuller implementation.

The Wealth of Nations can be seen as a culminating re-statement of these long-developing ideas. *Smith's* magnum opus, *however, was also something much more than a culminating re-statement, in particular, because it added the vital and indeed revolutionary assertion of – what would today be called – macro-economic self-adjustment with regard to interest and money.*

In fact, some of the main classical ideas and theories had only few, or brief, pre-classical anticipations in the earlier period. Certainly, as regards the classical population theory, there were several important precursors, from Botero to Cantillon and Wallace. Other important components, however, of the Smithian-classical corpus of doctrines, such as the analysis of the accumulation of capital, had, before *The Wealth of Nations*, only a short – but very important – previous history, confined mainly to the writings of Quesnay and Turgot.

IV

Let us now, however, focus on four of the most important and fundamental ideas, theories, or lines of thought, which were initiated, or significantly developed, between 1662 and 1776, which are still widely held, or followed, in the late twentieth century, but which were largely excluded or rejected by English classical orthodoxy. These four fundamental methods, ideas, or theories were:

1 The historical method of the Scottish school, as applied to political economy by Hume, Steuart, and Adam Smith in *The Wealth of Nations*.
2 The utility and scarcity approach to value and price theory of the natural-law school, and, in particular, the utility analysis of Galiani and Turgot.
3 The theories of money, employment, and 'macro-economics', developed in varying directions by, among others, Petty, Boisguilbert, and Quesnay, and also, on some points, by Hume; and especially by Sir James Steuart, who with most of the leading writers of this era, regarded involuntary unemployment, hoarding, and deflation as serious problems, or dangers, and who believed, like most so-called 'mercantilists', that 'money mattered'.
4 The emphasis on uncertainty, ignorance, and erroneous expectations, as initiated by Boisguilbert, and, on some important points, by Cantillon, which was especially and explicitly developed by Condillac right at the end of our period.

In fact, in the last century or more, since the decline and fall of English classical orthodoxy around 1870, the history of economic thought has, to a large extent – though not entirely – consisted of challenges, to one or other aspect of English classical political economy, for having excluded or rejected these four – and other – fundamental lines of thought. These four challenges – associated respectively with the historical critics, Jevons, Keynes, and the neo-Austrians – have sought (whether this was realized or not) to rehabilitate and reintroduce ideas, theories, and lines of thought originally initiated, or considerably developed, in the period covered in this book, but which had undergone almost a century, or more, of exclusion, diminution, or neglect, under the régime of English classical orthodoxy.

Let us examine briefly these four cases, one by one.

V

In the first case, an institutional-relativist criticism of the abstract-deductive theories of the physiocrats had been brilliantly deployed by Galiani in his *Dialogues*, while a constructive historical and institutional approach had been developed by the great pioneers of the Scottish historical school, Hume, Steuart and Smith, which they applied to political economy. This approach was, however, to a large extent discarded, or seriously neglected, when the deductive, abstract method of Ricardo and Senior came to dominate English classical orthodoxy.[3] Obviously Adam Smith had no responsibility for this rejection. The Scottish historical movement had, however, rather faded away in the earlier decades of the nineteenth century, when David Hume's title of 'the historical nation' passed from Scotland to Germany. The protests of the German historical school, as expressed by Wilhelm Roscher in 1843, revived the case for an historical approach in political economy, and were followed in England, in the 1860s and 1870s, by Cliffe Leslie and others – and, later on, by institutionalist critics. There would, of course, have been little scope for the German historical critique, or for various subsequent historical and institutionalist protests, in England and elsewhere, if the Scottish historical method of Hume, Steuart and Smith had continued to have as important a role in political economy, as it had had in *The Wealth of Nations*; or if Adam Smith's work had continued to provide the methodological model for the dominant corpus of economic doctrine.

VI

Second, there came in the 1870s the most important, and, in the long run, the most widely accepted of the various protests, rebellions, or 'revolutions', against English classical doctrines: that concerned with the fundamentals of utility, value and price. Whether, or not the neoclassical protesters against English classical value theory were fully aware of their pre-classical forerunners, they were, in fact, calling for a return to the kind of analysis of utility, scarcity, and value developed by the natural-law writers, and, especially, as regards the emphasis on utility, by Galiani and Turgot – not to mention Daniel Bernoulli.

Considerable, though not total, responsibility for the switch of emphasis towards a labour and cost-of-production analysis of value and price, as well as for the comparatively minor role assigned to value-in-use, or utility, must rest with *The Wealth of Nations* and its author, and with the 'tiresome', 'awkward' and 'unhappy' alteration which he introduced regarding the concept of value-in-use.

A historian of value theory before Adam Smith, writing when the neoclassical theories of Jevons and Marshall, Menger and Walras, were at the peak of their influence, justifiably claimed of the writers on value of the seventeenth and eighteenth centuries: 'So much was done that there is scarcely any proposition of importance in the modern discussion of value [i.e. *c*.1900] which was not either stated or suggested by the writers of this first period of economic science, and which had not been discussed before Adam Smith' (Sewall, 1901, 124).[4]

There would have been little or no need or scope for any 'Jevonian revolution' – as Maurice Dobb once called it – or even for the measure of evolutionary reform undertaken by Marshall, if the ideas on value and price of Galiani and Turgot, and of the natural-law philosophers, had been given their due weight in the dominant English classical orthodoxy of 1776–1871; or even if such contemporary English utility theorists as W. F. Lloyd had received some recognition from the authoritative classical spokesmen who were instead proclaiming that they had brought the theory of value to a state of complete perfection.

We have noticed how Auguste Walras had complained that the admirably balanced value analysis of Pufendorf, Hutcheson and Burlamaqui, had remained 'buried in a treatise of natural law'; and how Walras (senior) had pointedly enquired regarding the natural-law theory: 'Why has it not already passed into the writings of economists?' The English classicals must surely bear most of the responsibility for this burial, while the role of first – though not sole – gravedigger must surely be assigned to the author of *The Wealth of Nations*. Adam Smith and Léon Walras received an almost identical inheritance regarding value theory, the natural-law analysis descending to Smith through Pufendorf, Carmichael and Hutcheson; and to Léon Walras, through Pufendorf, Burlamaqui and Auguste Walras. It is of interest to contrast what Adam Smith, and subsequently Léon Walras, made of the same natural-law inheritance.

It may be added, in conclusion, that it is not necessary here to take sides, very dogmatically, for or against a labour and cost-of-production explanation of value and price, as against theories based on utility and scarcity. What is to be criticized is the dogmatic, over-confident rejection, or exclusion of a vital and valuable line of thought, which has, in fact, subsequently become an essential component of the modern theory of value.

VII

Third, there was the emphatic English classical rejection of the theories of employment, saving, money or 'macro-economics', which had been expounded, with varying emphasis by, among others, Petty, Boisguilbert, and Quesnay; on some points by Hume, and, most especially by Steuart; as contrasted with the unqualified assertion, almost or virtually for the first time in *The Wealth of Nations*, of the opposite doctrine of thoroughgoing, macro-economic self-adjustment. Indeed, Adam Smith, rightly or wrongly, was almost entirely responsible for the rise to dogmatic orthodoxy of the classical, macro-economic model. Certainly it may be agreed that it was well worth setting out the kind of self-adjusting model of saving and investment, which Smith and Turgot elaborated, and from which Smith proceeded to draw such vitally important consequencs for government policy. But before such important conclusions for policy were drawn, it would surely have been desirable that the necessary assumptions, the real-world conditions regarding knowledge, on the one hand, and money and banking institutions, on the other, had been more clearly envisaged and stated. It is one thing to assert that government intervention is, in practice, unlikely to reduce economic instability and unemployment; and it is quite another thing to belittle or deny the practical possibility of serious economic instabilities in the real world.

Recently, however, during and since the occurrence of 'the Keynesian revolution', in the 1930s and 1940s, stark conflicts of view have been evident, the main outlines of which were fairly clearly prefigured in the contrasts between the two great *Inquiries* by Steuart and Smith, in the closing decade of our period. The Smithian-classical doctrines, however, proceeded to deny the seriousness of involuntary unemployment, which had so profoundly concerned many of the leading writers of the seventeenth and eighteenth centuries, while also dismissing the dangers of hoarding, or of interruptions in the circulation of payments, which had been regarded so seriously by Boisguilbert, Quesnay and others. Indeed the suggestion seemed to be conveyed, at some points, that 'money didn't matter'. According to Smithian-classical orthodoxy, the business cycles of the nineteenth century, like the unemployment and depression which caused Petty and Boisguilbert so much concern – were to be regarded as frictions. J. S. Mill tended to dismiss the problem of cyclical unemployment as 'unimportant', maintaining that 'the normal state of affairs was a state of full employment' (Link, 1959, 168, 177–9; and Hutchison, 1978, 154n.).

The study of business cycles, therefore, one of the main sources out of which twentieth-century macro-economics developed, was, with one or two exceptions, initiated and advanced, until well into the twentieth century, mainly by economists outside the dominant English classical orthodoxy, and also outside the main neoclassical schools of thought. As Wesley Mitchell put it:

> It was not the orthodox economists ... who gave the problem of crises and depressions its place in economics, but sceptics who had profited by and then reacted against their teachings. From Adam Smith to Mill, and even to Alfred Marshall, the classical masters have paid but incidental attention to the rhythmic oscillations of trade in their systematic treatises.
>
> (1927, 3; quoted in Hutchison, 1953, 374)

If, on the other hand, the ideas of Petty, Boisguilbert, Steuart and others, had not been so summarily and comprehensively swept aside, the problems of instability and unemployment might have received more attention, and the eventual Keynesian protest would have been, in large measure, unnecessary. We would repeat here the conclusion of our previous section that we do not wish to take sides, at this point, for or against classical, or mercantilist-Keynesian, macro-economic theories and models, but simply to register a protest against a premature, dogmatic exclusivism.

VIII

Fourth, in the 1930s, at about the time the Keynesian 'revolution' was getting under way against Smithian-classical macro-economics, another parallel, but perhaps even more fundamental protest was being heard from several writers, including Hayek and some members of the Swedish school, and, most forthrightly, from Keynes himself. This fundamental criticism had been launched by a number of isolated protesters from the 1870s onwards, notably by the historical economist Cliffe Leslie in 1879 in his remarkable paper 'The Known and the Unknown in the Economic

World'. Keynes's formulation of this protest probably remains the best known: 'I accuse the classical economic theory of being itself one of those pretty, polite techniques which tries to deal with the present by abstractng from the fact that we know very little about the future' (1937, 192). More recently this accusation has been expressed in the penetrating critical *aperçus* of Professor George Shackle and his neo-Austrian followers. This fundamental objection focuses on the limitations of the – often tacit – classical assumption of full knowledge, and on the exclusion, from so many classical and neoclassical models, of any serious role for uncertainty, ignorance, and erroneous expectations.

Some, though certainly not all or most, of the responsibility (or credit?) for this vast simplification must be laid at the door of Adam Smith and *The Wealth of Nations*. As already noted, Sir John Hicks has observed that Smith, in his treatment of saving, investment, money and hoarding, 'neglected uncertainty and liquidity' (1965, 41). Adam Smith, however, did not go nearly so far in excluding uncertainty and ignorance as did his successors, notably Ricardo, who incorporated much more comprehensively, and, at points, explicitly, the assumption of certainty and full knowledge into the main body of orthodox economic theory – in so much of which it has so long enjoyed a vital position, with only intermittent protests regarding its inadequacy (see Hutchison, 1978, chapter 7).

The pseudo-objectivity of the classical cost-of-production approach to value may have encouraged this profound simplification. Viewed superficially, costs seem to be objective, knowable, and often fairly accurately known. Certainly, also, the full-knowledge model was well worth developing. There have always been *some* real-world conditions to which it has represented a reasonable approximation. The assumption, however, that the supply of correct knowledge was usually ample and costless was often introduced inexplicitly, and was likely to be seriously confusing in the analysis of economic fluctuations and instability.

It was mostly French writers, of our period, who had first recognized the vital role of uncertainty and erroneous expectations in real-world problems, particularly with regard to the extreme and dangerous fluctuations in the supplies and prices of grain, or the staple foodstuff of the people. Boisguilbert was the first economist to give ignorance and uncertainty their due role in economic processes. Cantillon, also, recognized the uncertainties facing the entrepreneur in his pivotal role in a market economy. It was, however, Condillac, in the opening chapters of his *Commerce and Government*, who launched his analysis of suppliers and demanders in the market with an explicit recognition of the ignorance, uncertainty, and erroneous expectations with which decisions would necessarily have to be taken.

If the ideas of Boisguilbert, Cantillon, and, especially, of Condillac, had not been so totally disregarded in the orthodox English classical system of theory, and if this orthodoxy had not concentrated as far and as long as it did on the simplification of full knowledge and correct expectations, then the subsequent protests of Cliffe Leslie, Keynes, Shackle and others, would have been unnecessary, and economic theory might have been less inadequately equipped to face the fluctuations and instabilities of the twentieth century.

IX

The historical-institutional method and critique, the neoclassical-Jevonian revolt, the Keynesian 'revolution', the expectational Keynesian-neo-Austrian protest, make up a considerable part of the history of political economy and economics over the last 100 years or so, since the decline and fall of English classical orthodoxy around 1870. All of these four ideas, theories, or lines of thought, had been initiated, or significantly developed, before 1776, and had been largely excluded from, or diminished in the English classical corpus of doctrines. One has, therefore, to go back to the seventeenth and eighteenth centuries, before English classical orthodoxy came to dominate, if one wishes to follow the history of several of the most significant theories, ideas and issues, which have been debated and developed in the twentieth century.

There is, however, one well-known system, or set, of economic doctrines which has figured rather prominently in the late-twentieth-century history of the subject, which had not emerged, to any very significant extent, before 1776; this is Marxian economic theory. For Marxian economics was, in fact, not so much a revolt against English classical political economy, as an offshoot of it, or a kind of development of some of its basic theories, with its roots in the Manchester of the 1840s.

Searching for some kind of pedigree for the labour theory of value before *The Wealth of Nations*, Marxian historians have not been able to find very much. There were *obiter dicta* – as Ronald Meek described them – from the great William Petty, which were repeated, but not developed, by Franklin and one or two comparatively little-known pamphleteers. The labour theory of value was mainly a product of the English classical period. On the other hand, for the Marxian materialist philosophy of history, a valid ancestry could be claimed in the Scottish historical writers, in particular in the work of John Millar, Smith's most distinguished pupil.

X

There was another loss, of a rather different kind, probably serious, but difficult and controversial to assess, in the transition from pre-classical political economy to that of the English classicals. This is concerned with the political element, or input, in political economy. So long as a narrower programme of positive economics, as preached and practised by Cantillon, Senior and many neoclassicals, is genuinely maintained, there is, or should be, little room for a political element. If, however, the subject is explicitly proclaimed and practised as 'political' economy, then the quality of the political input is vital for the quality of the politico-economic doctrines expounded, and probably, or often, it is the political element which is more widely and profoundly influential than the technical economics. At no time in the history of the subject has a higher quality of realistic political insight been applied to political economy than was forthcoming from Mandeville, Montesquieu, Hume, Galiani and Smith – though certainly the physiocrats, who anticipated the shape of things to come, must be excluded from this generalization.[5] It may, indeed, seem that never since 1776 has the quality of the political element in political economy surpassed the eighteenth-century level, and all too often it has fallen seriously below it.[6]

XI

The publication of *The Wealth of Nations* marked a major shift, turning-point, or 'revolution' in the history of the subject, in the course of which a new systematization, simplification and selection of interests, emphasis and attention took place. As a part of such processes, serious exclusions or omissions are very likely to occur. There was a certain shift of emphasis from trade to growth, as the central focus of interest – though this should not be exaggerated. *The Wealth of Nations* remained much concerned with trade and exchange. Questions and alternatives were, however, dropped or ignored, complications got left out, possibilities were not followed up – e.g. in the Smithian-classical synthesis, questions regarding the relation between utility and value, and regarding the effects of hoarding money, or of changes in liquidity preference, or of uncertainty and erroneous expectations.

The gains and losses of such turning-points or revolutions tend to be much exaggerated both by their supporters and by their opponents, who tend to represent the 'revolution' in question as bringing either all gains, or all losses. We are not, of course, attempting here any cost–benefit assessment of the Smithian-classical revolution – from which the benefits were certainly very considerable. Such benefits are not relevant so far as our pre-classical period is concerned. It is the losses which are relevant with regard to the conclusions of this book, for they represent a large part of the achievements of the period we have been studying. These losses, moreover, have been largely ignored, or at least very insufficiently appreciated, because of the tenacity of the classical version of the history of the subject, according to which few or no such losses could have existed, since political economy, in any intellectually serious form, hardly existed before the appearance of *The Wealth of Nations* and the establishment of the English classical orthodoxy.

A further point is concerned with the role of orthodoxies in the history of political economy and economics. Orthodoxies are sought or established for the influence and prestige which they bring to the subject, or to those practitioners of the subject who proclaim the orthodoxy. The first successfully established orthodoxy, that of the English classicals, was followed – after a brief confused interregnum in England in the 1870s – by the neoclassical academic orthodoxy led by Marshall; this was, in due course, followed by the Keynesian orthodoxy, or the Keynesian-neoclassical synthesis which, in major respects, dissolved some time around 1970.

Since about 1970, for the first time in about a century and a half or more, that is, since the establishment of the English classical orthodoxy, there have been, over a large area of the subject, fundamental divisions with no prevailing orthodoxy anything like as dominant as any of the three or four major orthodoxies of the previous century and a half. Certainly, regarding micro-economic doctrine, a considerable consensus prevails, in which, incidentally, ideas, or lines of thought, which originally emerged in the pre-classical period, play a fundamental part. This consensus, however, seems overshadowed by the division in macro-economics, regarding both theory and policies, which was prefigured by the basic contrast between the doctrines proclaimed in the great *Inquiries* of Sir James Steuart, on the one hand, and of Adam Smith, on the other (1767 and 1776).

Of course, a relevant orthodoxy, based on a reasonably well-tested consensus should be the prime objective of a disciplined subject, but not a premature orthodoxy, to a serious extent ideologically based and biased, sought for the sake of the influence and public prestige, which an established, widely accepted body of doctrine can wield.[7] Calls for a new synthesis, as the basis for a new orthodoxy, should be treated with some reserve. The establishment of a new orthodoxy might be accompanied by excessive losses and exclusions.

The outstanding qualities of *The Wealth of Nations* have always provided much justification for regarding 1776 as the most important single date in the history of political economy What needs more critical examination, however, is the narrowness of the basis on which Smith's followers established their claims to orthodoxy, and their version of the history of the subject propagated in support of those claims. For while the English classicals built on much too little of the work of the pre-classical period, they consigned to oblivion much too much of it. Too much, moreover, of the influence and durability of the English classical version of the history of the subject seems to have depended on its compact, labour-saving, Anglo-centric convenience. A less inadequate and inaccurate view of the work of the pre-classical period is necessary, both for its own sake, and for attaining to a fuller and more balanced appreciation of the subsequent development of the subject, including the contributions of the English classical, historical, neo-classical and Keynesian schools. A more accurate view and a more adequate perspective are also required for a clearer understanding as to what kinds of growth, or progress, in economic knowledge has been attained, and of what kinds can reasonably be expected in the future, which might serve as a basis for less unsuccessful policy-making.

Notes

1 In quotations from seventeenth- and eighteenth-century writers, spelling and punctuation has frequently been modernized.
2 When an already published translation is used the translator is cited. Where no previously existing translation is mentioned, the English version is by this author.

Chapter 1 The Period and its Starting-point

1 The term 'pre-classical' was introduced by Professor Douglas Vickers to cover the period of his *Studies in the Theory of Money, 1690–1776*.

2 J. B. Say declared that 'if one reads Smith as he deserves to be read one perceives that before him there was no political economy' (1841, 29). Alternatively, if the subject was allowed to have existed before 1776 its ideas were described as being recognized, virtually universally, as 'completely erroneous', as by the young J. S. Mill, who declared that before the classical writers 'the ideas universally entertained, both by theorists and practical men, on the causes of national wealth, were grounded on certain general views, which almost all who have given any considerable attention to the subject now justly hold to be completely erroneous' (1844, 47). In 1986 in Oxford, the view was proclaimed that 'economics in the modern sense was as good as invented in one country (Scotland) only 200 years ago' (Bliss, 1986, 368).

3 The inadequacy of the term 'mercantilist' when applied to this period of the history of economic thought has long been recognized by more discerning writers. As E. A. J. Johnson wrote (1937, 3): 'Worst of all, a critical tradition was established which insisted that each early writer should be judged in terms of whether he was or was not a mercantilist.' Long previously the great Wilhelm Roscher had proclaimed:

> Our widespread custom of categorizing the entire period of the development of econmic theory, before the physiocrats, under the name of the mercantile system, is highly unsatisfactory. The well-known picture, in the traditional textbooks, of a mercantilist, corresponds with some of the more insignificant writers of the 17th and 18th centuries; but the most significant are in no way described by the term. (1851, 122)

4 Bacon and Descartes have long and frequently been cited as standing for the two opposing extremes of, on the one hand, empirical, inductive fact-finding (often described as 'naive'), and, on the other hand, abstract, *a priorist* deduction; which have battled over the centuries with regard to the methodology of

political economy and economics. Newton emerged, in the eighteenth century, as the supreme exemplar of scientific method, but his principles were interpreted in different ways, either with a more empirical, Baconian emphasis, or with a more Cartesian emphasis. Thomas Hobbes, who much influenced Petty, is discussed in the next chapter.

5 More recently there have appeared the valuable editions of Cantillon (1952), and of the French masters, Quesnay (1958) and Boisguilbert (1966), from the INED; also Eugene Rotwein's collection of David Hume's economic writings (1955), and Andrew Skinner's edition (1967) of Steuart's *Principles of Political Economy*. Other important works on particular aspects of economic thought include Viner's *Studies in the Theory of International Trade* (1937) and Marian Bowley's *Studies in the History of Economic Theory before 1870* (1973). On theories of value, Hannah Sewall provided an excellent survey in *The Theory of Value before Adam Smith* (1901).

6 It should be remembered that Joseph Schumpeter did not have the chance to complete the final revision of his monumental work.

7 See Hutchison (1985) and Peach (1986), who concludes that 'much of the continuing interest in Ricardo has been stimulated by distortion and counter-distortion, acquisitiveness and the desire to justify contemporary doctrine' (125).

Chapter 2 The Century before Petty: Some Outstanding Writings

1 Copernicus emphasized stability in value as the prime requisite for whatever good served as money, which, he held, must have its own intrinsic worth while also acquiring additional value in serving as money. Copernicus was concerned with the contemporary problems of the Prussian coinage.

2 On the question of the authorship of the *Discourse*, see Mary Dewar's discussion in her edition of 1969. Apparently the attractive, but unfortunately quite unrealistic possibility has been entertained that 'W.S.' might stand for William Shakespeare (aged seventeen at the date of publication).

3 On the *Discourse of the Commonweal*, see Chalk (1951), who observes how in that work, and in the literature of the following century, the individual profit motive received more and more recognition as a basic postulate or natural law, so that it became 'an undeniable maxim that every one by the light of nature and reason will do that which makes for his greatest advantage' (Joseph Lee, 1656, quoted by Chalk, 1951, 340). Alongside this maxim of individual self-interest there developed the doctrine – expressed in the *Discourse* – of the harmony of interests between private profit and the public benefit. As Chalk concluded, what is described as 'the mercantilist literature contained much that can properly be regarded as an anticipation of *laissez-faire*'; and 'what began as opportunistic and sporadic protests against commercial controls thus emerged, almost two centuries later, in the form of a systematized philosophy of economic individualism' (332 and 347).

4 I am much indebted in this section to Professor B. E. Supple's *Commercial Crisis and Change in England 1600–1642* (1959), especially chapter 9: 'Economic Thought'.

5 Another work worthy of mention is Rice Vaughn's *A Discourse of Coin and Coinage*, published in 1675, but according to Supple (1959, 219n.), probably written much earlier. Vaughn's *Discourse* may be more noteworthy today for a remark on the determinants of value and price, than for his sensible discussion of money. He put forward a subjective basis for value and price, very much

on the lines long expounded by scholastic and natural-law writers: 'Use and delight, or the opinion of them, are the true causes why all things have a value and price set upon them, but the proportion of that value and price is wholly governed by rarity and abundance' (1675, 19). Calling attention to Vaughn's emphasis on the role of demand in creating value, Professor Joyce Appleby (1978, 179) remarks that 'little effort was made to go beyond Vaughn's expression until the flowering of economic analysis in the closing decade of the century'. This is correct regarding English writers. But a subjective approach, based on utility and demand, to the questions of value and price, had long been followed by writers of the scholastic and natural-law tradition, as well as by leading Italian writers who followed this line, like Davanzati (1588).

6 On the subject of taxation Hobbes supported equality of burdens:

> . . . it concerns the duty of the magistrate to see that the public burdens be equally born. Furthermore, since what is brought by the subjects to public use is nothing else but the price of their bought peace . . . they who equally share in the peace should also play an equal part . . .
>
> Now in this place we understand an equality, not of money, but of burden, that is to say, an equality of reason between the burdens and the benefits. For although all equally enjoy peace, yet the benefits springing from thence are not equal to all; for some get greater possessions, others less; and again some consume less, others more. (1642, 161–2)

Chapter 3 Petty on Policy, Theory and Method

1 For the life of Petty, see Strauss (1954) and Fitzmaurice (1895). Much the liveliest and pithiest account of Petty is in Aubrey's *Brief Lives,* who described Petty as 'my especial friend'.

2 See Roncaglia (1985, 78–9) on 'The Dialogue of Diamonds' in Hull (1899, vol. II, 624–30). See also Sewall (1901, 71) on Petty's distinction between 'intrinsic' and 'extrinsic' causes of value. Intrinsic causes relate to physical characteristics and extrinsic to demand and to fluctuations thereof.

3 On the foundation of the Royal Society and Petty's important role, see Strauss (1954, 113).

4 On the doctrine of low wages in the seventeenth and eighteenth centuries, see Furniss (1920, chapter 6).

5 For Petty's comparison of London with Paris, see Hull (1899, vol. II, 505ff).

6 For Petty on increasing returns, see Roncaglia (1985, 65–6).

Chapter 4 English Pioneers of Social and Economic Statistics

1 On Graunt's life and his relations with Petty, see Fitzmaurice (1895) and Sutherland (1963). See also John Aubrey's *Brief Lives* on both Graunt and Halley, as well as Petty.

2 Graunt seems to have taken a very different view regarding relief works for the unemployed from that of Petty. Graunt came nearer to holding the 'Treasury View', according to which there was a fixed quantity of work or investment:

> We have said, 'twere better the public should keep the beggars, though they earned nothing . . . But most men will laugh to hear us suppose, that any able to work . . . should be kept without earning anything. But we answer, that if there

> be but a certain proportion of work to be done, and that the same be already done by the not-beggars, then to employ the beggars about it, will but transfer the want from one hand to another . . . (34).

3 Rev. William Derham's *Physico-Theology* was originally delivered as the Boyle Lectures of 1711–12. Derham wrote:

> It appears from our best accounts of these matters, that in our European parts, and I believe the same is throughout the world, that, I say, there is a certain rate and proportion in the propagation of mankind: such a number marry, so many are born, such a number die; in proportion to the numbers of persons in every nation, country, or parish. And as to birth, two things are very considerable: one is the proportion of males and females, not in a wide proportion, not an uncertain, accidental number at all adventures, but nearly equal. Another thing is, that a few more are born than appear to die, in any certain place, which is an admirable provision for the extraordinary emergencies and occasions of the world . . . (175–6)

Derham concluded: 'And now, upon the whole matter, what is all this but admirable and plain management? What can the maintaining throughout all ages and places, these proportions of mankind, and all other creatures; this harmony in the generations of men, be, but the work of one that ruleth the world?'. Derham, regarding food supply, was much more optimistic than Malthus, some eighty-five years later: 'To consider the adjustment of the quantity of food, in proportion to the eaters. In all places there is generally enough; nay such a sufficiency as may be styled a plenty; but not such a superfluity as to waste and corrupt and thereby annoy the world' (181).

Derham also saw, as part of the Divine plan, how the variety of human qualities and inclinations promoted an efficient and effective division of labour: 'We see how naturally men betake themselves to this and that employment: some delight most in learning and books, some in divinity, some in physic . . . and some have their inclinations lie even in the servile offices of the world' (143). Derham concluded that 'all this is an admirably wise, as well as most necessary provision for the ease and sure transacting of the world's affairs, to answer every end and occasion of man' (144, quoted by Myers, 1983, 80–2). (As we shall note below, however, Adam Smith was to deny any inherited variety in human abilities and inclinations, insisting that they were an effect rather than a cause of the division of labour.) According to Basil Willey (1940, 39), Derham, 'though in no way remarkable either as a scientist or as a theologian, is a worthy representative of that class of eighteenth century country parson who pursued both vocations with confident assurance of their essential harmony'.

4 Barnett (in King, 1936) called attention to some brief calculations by King, in some unpublished notes, of a relation between the price of wheat and its scarcity. King noted that if, in England, the wheat harvest was 'but a fourth part of its ordinary produce, the price will be four times its ordinary price' (see photocopy by Evans, 1967, 486–7). King also calculated that a one-fifth fall in consumption would result from a tripling of the price. This note is far from corresponding (as far as it goes) with the statement of the law by Davenant.

5 Concerning the interpretation of the 'law' of demand I am much indebted to the valuable article by Professor John Creedy (1986).

6 Sir William Davenant is supposed to have been a natural son of William Shakespeare, according to the *Dictionary of National Biography*, vol. V. John Aubrey, in his *Brief Lives* supported the story. See also Thomas (1926, 71n.).

7 On Davenant's political views, see Waddell (1958), and Viner (1937, 116). Waddell concludes, rather severely, regarding Davenant, that 'his motives may

have affected the reliability of his judgement,' and that 'the relationship between his writings and his personal circumstances suggests that his enemies may have had some excuse for regarding him as a purely self-seeking and mercenary time-server'; and also that 'he was on the losing side in nearly every controversy he joined' (279 and 288).

8 On the quantitative methodology of Graunt, Petty and Davenant, see Endres (1985).

Chapter 5 John Locke and the 1690s

1 See Letwin (1963, 79ff).

2 See Thomas (1926, 71): 'Those were the days of brilliant pamphleteering. We can almost conjure up the conditions under which the above warfare went on. Some poor printer of Grub Street brings out a pamphlet, and that very day it forms the chief topic in the crowded coffee-houses of the day.'

3 The reasons for the economic success of the Dutch were much pondered and debated by English writers in the second half of the seventeenth century. One of the best-known works on this subject was the *Observations upon the United Provinces* (1672) by Sir William Temple, who was a successful diplomat and representative of the English government in the Low Countries in the 1660s and 1670s. In his *Observations* Temple maintained that the dense concentration of population had produced the industry and frugality of the Dutch, which were the main reasons for their prosperity: 'I conceive the true original and ground of trade, to be the great multitude of people crowded into small compass of land, whereby all things necessary to life become dear, and all men who have possessions are induced to parsimony; but those who have none, are forced to industry and labour or else to want' (1672, 211). Temple's Smithian message regarding the beneficence of frugality and the harmfulness of luxury was the exact opposite of the doctrine subsequently so eloquently expounded by the Anglo-Dutchman, Mandeville. Temple also included 'general liberty, mutual trust and confidence, and good government' as conducive to low interest rates and economic advance, with 'every man following his own way, minding his own business, and little enquiring into other men's' (218).

4 Several leading writers have been rather severely critical of Child, notably Viner and Letwin. But Schumpeter undertook a spirited defence (see Viner, 1937, 114–15; Letwin, 1963, chapter 1; and Schumpeter, 1954, 361–4).

5 On the life of Locke, I am much indebted to Cranston (1957).

6 See Letwin (1963, 176).

7 See Viner (1937, 76), and Leigh (1974, 206ff).

8 See Appleby (1978, 217ff).

9 William Lowndes was Secretary to the Treasury. Subsequently he was an MP. He helped to initiate the funding system for short-term debt.

10 John Pollexfen (vital dates unknown) was an MP and one of the Commissioners who supported Locke's proposals regarding the Irish woollen industry. He published two works both in 1697: *A Discourse of Trade, Coin, and Paper Credit*, and *England and East India: Inconsistent in their Manufactures*. Pollexfen opposed Lowndes on depreciating the currency. Regarding trade, he was opposed to imports from India as consisting of trivial luxuries, and supported the prevention of the import of manufactures, and of the export of raw materials, such as wool. Schumpeter defends Pollexfen's work (1954, 364n.) against the criticisms of Viner (1937, 18).

11 See Leigh (1974, 201).

12 See Vaughn (1980).
13 On Barbon's contribution to value theory, see Appleby (1978), Bowley (1973), and Letwin (1963). There seems to be no evidence that Barbon was acquainted with the writings of the Salamancan school or with those of his Italian contemporary, Montanari. But his emphasis on the subjectivity of utility and value is stronger than that of any English writer in our period.
14 Contrast Letwin's critical view (1963, 61–2).
15 On North and his *Discourses*, see Letwin (1963, chapter 7).
16 On Descartes and his influence on the development of 'false individualism', see Hayek (1949, 1ff and 1969, 392).
17 As Christine Macleod observes (1983, 228), another writer who envisaged technological progress at this time was John Cary (d.1720) the Bristol merchant, in his *Essay on the State of England in Relation to its Trade, its Poor and its Taxes* (1695), a work highly praised by Locke, which was translated into French (1755) and into Italian (1764). Unlike Martyn, Cary was a strong protectionist and maintained that England lost from the East India trade. Public opinion opposed the introduction of labour-saving machinery because it increased unemployment and expenditure on the poor.
18 An earlier suggestion of free-trade ideas supported by the concept of cost-effectiveness and derived from the variety of national endowments of resources and skills, was put forward in the anonymous *England's Great Happiness* (1677). The author defended the East India trade, maintaining that there was a great advantage in exporting money, and went on to point out, regarding imports of wood from Norway: 'for that kind of timber we cannot be without, and I suppose our land can be better employed than in great groves of such like' (9–11).
19 The suggestion that Henry Martyn was the author of the *Considerations* was put forward by Thomas (1926, 171–3). More recently, however, conclusive evidence has been revealed by Christine Macleod (1983), who offers a plausible explanation of Martyn's apparent change of view from his fundamentally free-trade arguments in the *Considerations* to the protectionist views put forward in his articles in *The British Merchant* (1713). Ms Macleod maintains that free-trade ideas 'were not welcomed' at this time in influential political circles, and 'were virtually ignored. Thorough-going free trade had to wait almost another century to be unashamedly appreciated' (229). Ms Macleod also discusses Martyn's *Essay towards finding the Balance of our Whole Trade annually from Christmas 1698 to Christmas 1719*, which she describes as 'a very solid, careful . . . piece of writing', which set out how the figures of exports and imports were compiled and how estimates of the balance of payments were arrived at.
   Martyn, like Davenant, was clearly much concerned with party politics when he sided with the Tories in opposition to the trade treaty with France (1713). His contributions to the *British Merchant* were countered from the Whig side by Defoe in *Mercator*. The merits of Martyn's economic analysis of trade and specialization in his work of 1701 remain undiminished.
20 On 'liberal mercantilism', see Grampp, 1965 (vol. I, 48ff). See also below (chapter 7, note 4) on the use of this term by Schatz and Caillemer (1906).

Chapter 6 Continental Alternatives: Colbertism and Cameralism: Natural Law and Moral Philosophy

1 On the life of Becher, see Hassinger (1951) and Kauder (1924).
2 There is an English translation of the most important parts of Hörnigk's work

in Monroe (1924, 222–43), which I have used here.

3 The first edition of Schröder's work appeared in 1686. The edition used here is the sixth (1737).

4 Another transmitter and expositor of Pufendorf's ideas about value and price was the great Scandinavian writer Ludvig Holberg (1684–1754) who has been described as 'the first Dano-Norwegian economist' (Saether, 1984). In his *Introduction to Natural Law and the Law of Nations* (1715–16), Holberg, according to Professor Saether, explained how 'some things are useful even if they do not have a price and that rare things can have high prices although they are not very useful'. Saether quotes Holberg: 'One thing, which in itself seems insignificant and useless, is sometimes appreciated more than another which is both useful and necessary. The cause being (1) its rarity . . . and (2) people's ambitious luxuriousness [which] has put many things at a very high price, like pearls and jewels which one could very easily be without' (Saether, 1984, 12–13). Professor Saether also shows that Holberg was a powerful expositor of Mandeville's ideas regarding the beneficence of luxury and the dangers of parsimony and saving, and quotes Holberg's assertion that 'the profusion of the rich gives life to the body politic as the circulation of the blood in the human body gives strength and vigour to the limbs'.

5 Regarding the direct line on value theory, which runs from Aristotle through the scholastics to Adam Smith, Odd Langholm has commented unfavourably on the role of Grotius and Pufendorf as transmitters, compared with earlier Italian writers:

> Placed in proper perspective, the two seventeenth century jurists can be seen to transmit something of mediaeval value theory and partly in the Aristotelian tradition, but I personally see them as somewhat out of touch with the more vigorous branches of this tradition. If they did indeed inspire Smith, this mainly goes to explain the sterility of early classical value theory as compared to the development, rooted in Italian economics, which drew on Buridan and Odonis and in the early nineteenth century provided a new inspiration for British economists as well. (1979, 105n.)

Langholm is referring to Senior and W. F. Lloyd. On Buridan (born towards the end of the thirteenth century), and Odonis (born about 1290), see Langholm, chapters 5 and 6. Buridan's ideas flourished later in Vienna, but centuries before Carl Menger and his school arrived on the scene.

6 Jansenism was a puritanical religious revival in the Catholic church in the mid-seventeenth century, named after Jansenius, Bishop of Ypres.

7 I have used an edition of Nicole's *Essais* published in 1715 in six volumes.

8 Mention may be worth making of Nicole's elucidation of a fundamental point regarding prediction and predictability, which has caused much confusion among libertarians in recent years. Three hundred years ago Nicole saw clearly, unlike some twentieth-century champions of free markets, that a libertarian who insisted on the unpredictability of human actions was destroying the intellectual foundations for a market economy. As E. D. James has observed:

> In his discussion of free will, Nicole had set out to show that free action was compatible with predictability, and he observes that the social order is based on the confidence we have that our freely-acting fellow-men will behave in a predictable way. We are confident we shall not be assaulted by passers-by, drowned by ferrymen, poisoned by suppliers of food, killed by doctors, because all these know that it is not in their interest to act in this way. (1972, 149–50)

9 Pascal, in his *Pensées*, suggested the main point regarding the harmony of self-interest and public benefits, when he referred to 'those men of the world who take a healthy view of things, and who know that the only way to succeed in

this life is to make ourselves appear honourable, faithful, judicious, and capable of useful service to a friend; because naturally men love only what may be useful to them' (1670 [1931], 57).

10 See Faccarello (1986, chapter 3).

11 On Nicole and Boisguilbert, see Faccarello (1983a, 37 and 1983b, part I, chapter 2); on Nicole and Mandeville, see Viner (1953 and 1978); and Horne (1978, 23), who writes: 'It is this aspect of Jansenism – its refusal to see virtue as the cement holding society together – which constitutes its contribution to social thought, and which is most important for the tradition out of which Mandeville emerged.' In this section on Nicole and Domat I am profoundly indebted to Professor Gilbert Faccarello for his writings and comments, though (like so many other writers), we disagree in our interpretation of Mandeville's work (see the next chapter.)

Chapter 7 Economic Harmonies, Equilibrating Tendencies and Freedom of Trade

1 I have used the INED edition mentioned in the text: *Pierre de Boisguilbert: où la naissance de l'économie politique*, two vols, (eds Hecht and Sauvy, 1966). All page references are from this edition, unless otherwise stated. The original dates of the works quoted are given. In this section on Boisguilbert I am very much indebted to the three works by Professor Gilbert Faccarello cited in the list of references and to his valuable comments on an earlier draft of this section.

2 Among Boisguilbert's earlier literary and historical writings is his *Life of Mary Stewart, Queen of Scotland and of France*, an English translation of which, by James Freebairn, was published in Edinburgh in 1725. The work is a passionate defence of Mary.

3 Professor Earl J. Hamilton (1969) has maintained that Boisguilbert committed 'an amazing mistake in estimating that France suffered a colossal decline in income from 1660 to 1695 or 1707', and that he was

> certainly wrong in proclaiming (with monotonous frequency) that since 1660 income in France had fallen by one half . . . though the French economy was probably stagnant from about 1716, and there may have been a slight decline. Yet in 1716 France was certainly the richest and probably the most powerful nation in the world. Even Boisguilbert recognized that England's wealth was less than one fourth as great as that of France. (126–37)

This question must be left to economic historians. From a theoretical standpoint, though empirical and statistical errors may be disastrous with regard to policy and policy recommendations, such inaccuracies do not necessarily detract from the value of the kind of analytical and conceptual contributions which Boisguilbert rendered. An interesting eighteenth-century writer (discussed further in chapter 18), who strongly disagreed with both Boisguilbert and the physiocrats with regard to the economic decline of France and French agriculture, was Isaac de Pinto (1715–87) in his *Essay on Circulation and Credit* (1773, English translation 1774, 156–9). Pinto maintained that Boisguilbert had much exaggerated the depression and had been 'led astray by enthusiasm'.

On the other side, there is the account of La Bruyère (1645–96), a detached observer, whose description of the French countryside and its inhabitants has been quoted by Hazel Roberts:

> Scattered over the country certain wild animals, males and females, dark, livid, and all sunburned, are seen bent over the ground which they work and which they turn with an invincible persistency. They have articulate voices and when they stand upright they disclose human faces, and, in truth, they are men. At night they retire into dens where they live on black bread, water and roots. They spare other men the pain of sowing, of cultivating, and of reaping in order to live, and thus deserve not to lack this bread they have sown. (Roberts, 1935, 3)

4 Marshall Vauban (1633–1707), the celebrated general and military engineer, hardly belongs in a chapter devoted to pioneers of ideas about economic freedom. He was a supporter of the policies of Colbert and of most of the typically mercantilist policies. He was also an important pioneer of French economic statistics. But Vauban may suitably be mentioned alongside Boisguilbert, with whom he agreed as to the dire economic condition of France, and with whom he exchanged views, while disagreeing sharply on tax reform. Vauban estimated that about one-tenth of the French people had been reduced to beggary, another half to near-beggary, while another three-tenths lived in debt and distress. Only one-tenth were comfortably off (1707, 7). At the same time, he maintained that France was the richest country in the world. Vauban expressed his concern to the king regarding the poor, and 'the little people', that they should be so miserable, although they were the most numerous class and rendered the greatest services (17). He proposed 'A Royal Tithe', or a tax on agricultural produce of 5–10 per cent, together with a levy on all forms of property, and taxes on luxuries. Vauban was a staunch supporter of the monarchy, and he was gravely shocked by the royal displeasure which his book incurred, and died later in the year of its appearance.

An interesting figure of more definitely liberal tendencies, at this time, was Charles-Paul Hurault de Belesbat (d.1706) (on whom see the important five-part article by Schatz and Caillemer, 1906; see also Faccarello, 1983b, 133 and 188–9). Belesbat was a strong critic of Colbert and his policies and wrote six memoranda to the king (1692ff). He was made something of a liberal by experience under Louis XIV, though a loyal supporter of the monarchy – like the physiocrats subsequently. He wrote: 'One must lay down as a principle that liberty is the soul of commerce, and that, without liberty, good harbours, great rivers, and great fertility are useless. When liberty is lacking, everything is lacking' (Schatz and Caillemer, 1906, 630). But Belesbat was a bullionist in his emphasis on the importance of gold and silver. The following description of Belesbat's position by Schatz and Caillemer is relevant regarding a number of other writers in our period: 'If a name must be given to this singular position, which is lacking among the generally received classifications of the history of economic doctrines, one must speak, strange as the category may appear, of mercantilist liberalism, or liberal mercantilism: an intermediate or transitional doctrine in the evolution of economic thought which seems not to have been recognised' (38). William Grampp has also made effective use of the term 'Liberal Mercantilism' (see *Economic Liberalism*, two vols, 1965).

5 De Souligné's pamphlet, *The Desolation of France Unmasked* (1697), may have been influenced by Boisguilbert's *Détail de la France*.

6 See Quesnay's note on the twenty-sixth of his 'Maximes Générales', in Meek (1962, 261–2).

7 The page references for part I of the *Fable* are to the excellent and highly accessible Pelican edition (1970) by P. Harth; and for part II to the great two-volume edition of F. B. Kaye (1924).

8 On the moral reform movement, see Horne (1978, chapter 1: 'Mandeville and the Reformation of Manners').

9 On the luxury debate in the eighteenth century, see Morize (1909). Keynes was quite wrong in supposing that Mandeville fought a lone battle in defence of luxury. He had many followers, and was especially strongly supported in France (see Keynes, 1936, chapter 23).

10 For Temple's emphasis on frugality as a factor in the economic success of the Dutch, see chapter 5, note 3.

11 Professor Landreth (1975, 193–4) has set out very fully the wide range of sharply conflicting interpretations of Mandeville's work:

> Among those who find that Mandeville influenced Adam Smith, but do not explicitly state that he was an advocate of *laissez-faire* are Bonar, Cannan, Gide and Rist, McCulloch, Schumpeter, Joan Robinson, and Smith himself in *The Theory of Moral Sentiments* ... Another group, economists and others, explicitly states that Mandeville was an advocate of *laissez-faire* and a very important predecessor of Smith on this score. Non-economists holding this position include Anderson, Kaye, Morrow, Primer and Schatz. Economists who have reached this conclusion are Bitterman, Chalk, Hayek, Fay, Palgrave, Spengler and Viner. A still smaller group – Hollander, Heckscher, O. H. Taylor, Viner and Zweig – find Mandeville a mercantilist and not a proponent of *laissez-faire* at all. Finally Chalk and Rosenberg in recent studies place Mandeville somewhere between mercantilism and classical liberalism. An index of the complexity of this issue is that Viner and Chalk have changed their interpretations of Mandeville.

Professor Landreth himself concludes 'that Mandeville was a thoroughgoing mercantilist'. The case for this conclusion looks formidable, and is to *some* extent valid. But two unnecessary assumptions are mainly responsible for this long-running argument: (a) that Mandeville, over quite a long career must be regarded as always having stuck consistently to a single point of view; and (b) that writers can and must be pigeon-holed into one or other of the two exclusive categories: 'mercantilist', or 'classical liberal and supporter of *laissez-faire*'.

12 For biographical information abut Gervaise, see Professor Letiche's introduction to his edition of 1954.

13 See Viner's foreword to the Letiche (1954) edition:

> It will facilitate appreciation of the quality of the essay as a pioneering application of the 'income' or 'macroeconomic' approach to the theory of international economic equilibrium if the reader makes allowances as he reads for Gervaise's unhappily archaic verbal usage. Thus when Gervaise writes 'labour' this should be read as either 'national production' or 'national productive resources' according to the context, and when he writes 'rich' and 'poor', this should be read as 'consumers' or 'national expenditures on consumption', and 'producers' or 'national production' respectively. This is not, I think, unduly generous to Gervaise if his terminology is examined in the context of his own text and of common verbal usage at the time he wrote. (vi)

14 Vanderlint was highly commended by Marx who maintained that Hume must have known, and been indebted to, his monetary theory. Marx also approved of Vanderlint's emphasis on profit as 'the sole end of trade', and even described him as one of the foremost 'among the defenders of the working classes' (see Marx 1867, 124 and 274n.).

15 Another immigrant from the Low Countries was Sir Matthew Decker (1679–1749), born in Amsterdam. His ideas have some similarity with those of Vanderlint, though he is not comparable with Vanderlint as a theorist, in which respect he resembled more such seventeenth-century 'mercantilists' as Mun and Child. Decker also was a director of the East India Company. His two publications were: *Serious Considerations on the Several High Duties which the Nation in general, as well as Trade in particular labour under, with a proposal*

for ... raising all the public supplies by one single tax (1743), and *An Essay on the Causes of the Decline of the Foreign Trade* (1744) ('begun in the year 1739'). The *Essay* is much the weightier work, and a French translation of it appeared in 1757.

Decker started from such mercantilist principles as that money was 'the life of trade and the sinews of war', and that a nation 'grows rich' if exports exceed imports, and *vice versa*. But he vigorously opposed such monopolies as those enjoyed by trading companies and guilds, and he supported freedom of immigration and the removal of customs and excise duties.

Like Martyn, Gervaise and Vanderlint, Decker emphasized the significance of different national endowments and how 'nature has given various products to various countries and thereby knit mankind in an intercourse to supply each other's wants' (1744, 114). Removing trade barriers and restrictions was beneficial even if other countries did not reciprocate. Decker introduced the 'snob' effect to oppose duties on foreign luxuries. Raising the duties on, and prices of luxuries *increased* their consumption: 'The dearer outlandish luxuries are, the more they are esteemed by our people of taste; it is the expense that makes the elegancy, therefore duties on them only further their sale' (25).

Decker started from the assumption that English trade was seriously depressed, which may have been erroneous, but which seems to have been held by several observers at this time. He was, however, eloquent, and perhaps prescient, regarding Britain's great natural advantages at this period of history, and as to how free trade could exploit these advantages to the full: 'our natural advantages in trade are undoubtedly superior to any nation's whatsoever; that if properly cultivated they would render us more formidable than France, consequently than any country in Europe' (185). Moreover, '... Great Britain, by disencumbering and making its trade quite free, cannot be hurt by France ... but must of necessity hold the first rank in trade' (144, quoted by Raffel, 1905, 103).

Decker's proposed fiscal reforms were highly progressive. He called for the abolition of almost all duties, and their replacement by annual licences for the consumption of luxuries, together with a tax on houses, with extensive exemptions for the poor. These proposals were criticized by Joseph Massie and Adam Smith. On two points Decker was more liberal than Adam Smith: (a) he questioned the beneficence of the Navigation Acts; and (b), as already noted, he rejected retaliatory trade measures, which Smith was prepared to support. On Decker, see Raffel (1905, 84ff), and, regarding his contacts with Richard Cantillon, see Murphy (1986, 51 and 61).

Chapter 8 Paper Money, Employment and the Increase of Wealth

1 On the life of John Law, see Hyde (1948).

2 The Bank of Amsterdam had been founded in 1609 to provide a stable currency. It developed a system of 'bank money' with the use of cheques for making payments, with the granting of credits on which cheques could be drawn. For Adam Smith's account, see Smith (1776, 480–7).

3 The Duc de Saint Simon, surely a discerning observer, wrote of Law: 'There was neither avarice nor roguery in his composition ... He was a gentle, good, respectable man whom excess of credit and fortune had not spoiled' (quoted by Hyde, 1948, 86). According to J. Shields Nicholson, a fellow Scot, whose century-old essay contains some of the best writing on Law, he possessed 'wonderful originality', and 'in power and determination was one of the

strongest men Scotland has produced' (1893, 150).

4 Professor Hayek has observed that Carl Menger cited Law as an early pioneer of the idea of money as a spontaneous, unplanned social institution (1966, 137n.; and Menger, 1871, 258n.).

5 It seems probable that Franklin took his labour-corn-and-silver analysis of value from Petty (v. Petty, 1662 et seq., vol. I, 43; and above chapter 3, II). Later, in a letter to Lord Kames, Franklin returned to this theory:

> Food is *always* necessary to *all*, and much the greatest part of the labour of mankind is employed in raising provisions for the mouth. Is not this kind of labour therefore the fittest to be the standard by which to measure the values of all other labour, and consequently of all other things whose value depends on the labour of making or procuring them? May not even gold and silver be thus valued? If the labour of the farmer in producing a bushel of wheat be equal to the labour of the miner in producing an ounce of silver, will not the bushel of wheat just measure the value of the ounce of silver? (Letter of 21 February 1769, *Papers*, 1972, vol. 6, 47)

Earlier (1762) in a letter to Hume, Franklin had proposed a supply-and-demand theory for explaining the different values of goods, that is, one in terms of 'the various proportions of the quantity to the demand' (*Papers*, vol. 7, 1964, 238). According to Marx, however, it was Franklin who first 'deliberately and clearly ... formulated the basic law of modern political economy (1859, 55).

6 In this section I have drawn on my article and comment of 1953 and 1960 (see also Ward, 1959 and 1960).

7 This appendix is taken, with permission, from the Cambridge University Press, from Hutchison (1978, 127–35).

8 Mr Roy Harrod (as he then was) strongly objected to Keynes's penultimate chapter in his *General Theory* as 'a tendentious attempt to glorify imbeciles' (1951, 460).

9 On one quite vital and fundamental factual assumption Heckscher supported the views of 'the mercantilists' rather than 'the classicals'. This relates to the existence and importance of 'hoarding', with which the former were much concerned and which the classicals largely assumed out of existence. According to Heckscher (1955, 349): 'there is every reason to suppose that far into the nineteenth century people continued to hoard great quantities of money'. Presumably these hoards fluctuated. This is just what the seventeenth- and eighteenth-century writers were anxious about, and which Smithian doctrine emphatically denied.

10 Petty, Davenant, Law, Mandeville, Berkeley, Massie and numerous lesser writers could all be cited as asserting the existence of *in*voluntary unemployment: not that any clear-cut line was, or can be, drawn in practice. As the great lawyer Sir Mathew Hale (1609–76) observed: 'It is a difficult thing to determine who shall be said an idle person; it is a reasonable answer that they are idle for want of such work as they are able to do, or for want of such ways as might give them a reasonable support' (1805, vol. I, 521). In spite of the vastly greater supply of statistical and empirical material today, there is probably not much agreement in moral attitudes regarding the 'unemployed', or as to how many should be described as 'involuntary' and how many 'voluntary'. Some writers maintain that the number of 'unemployed' is 'really' vastly above the official figure, and some that it is significantly below. The books of E. S. Furniss (1920) and B. Suviranta (1923) provided much material in support of Keynes's thesis about the 'mercantilist' writings.

11 See also Ashton (1955, 173 and 209), where 'the dearth of money of all kinds' and the extent of unemployment in manufacturing are emphasized.

12 See 'Treasure and Trade Balances' in Wilson (1967). Professor Wilson acknowledges the hint of G. N. Clark: 'The explanation of the mercantilist attitude seems to lie in the commercial conditions of the time, especially in the needs of traders for capital in a solid and ponderable form' (1947, 27).

13 Grampp (1952, 468). Professor Grampp has maintained:

> The unemployment of the sixteenth and seventeenth centuries was, in the language of today's economics, the result of (a) frequent deflations, some of them quite severe; (b) the long-run decline of particular industries . . . (c) the immobility of resources and especially labour; and (d) the wage and price rigidity caused mainly by the monopolistic practices of the guilds . . . It is interesting to note that Great Britain had a similar unemployment problem about 200 years after the close of the mercantilist period.

Grampp emphasizes how Keynesian economics 'has an affinity to mercantilist doctrine' (1965, vol. I, 92–3).

14 Professor John Wood has concluded regarding the history of monetary theory:

> Keynes was a better historian of economic thought than he has generally been given credit for. And if the great similarities between Keynes and the predecessors of Hume are not obvious to you, then we have all been wasting our time. An interest in periods of transition and a belief in the importance of money in the short run was common to Keynes and the mercantilists. (1972, 12)

15 R. W. K. Hinton has expressed the view that Suviranta's work 'remains the most useful study on this subject for the historian' (1955, 283). Certainly, together with the work of E. S. Furniss, that of Suviranta comes nearest, among pre-Keynesian writers, to anticipating the interpretation given in *The General Theory*.

16 Jacob Viner cited as an 'anticipation' of Keynes that 'from the seventeenth century on, there was an almost continuous stream of expositions of the view that unemployment and sluggish trade were the consequences of the failure of purchasing power to keep step with the expansion of productive power. Keynes found to his delight that the literature of mercantilism was saturated with this idea' (1964, 256).

Incidentally, the monetarist explanation of the great depression of 1929 and after was primarily in terms of a failure of purchasing power, or of a failure to maintain a steadily increasing money supply in a growing economy – the great *sine qua non* of 'the mercantilists'.

Chapter 9 Fundamental Ideas and Concepts: the Emergence of Systematic Theories

1 I am much indebted in this section to the writings on Carl of Anton Tautscher, his rediscoverer. The omniscient Wilhelm Roscher had given Carl a favourable mention, and there had been one or two other fleeting references. In English there had been an isolated article by Katscher in the *Journal of Political Economy* (1901). In 1965, in a work on the biography of Adam Smith, Jacob Viner briefly, and not very generously, discussed Carl's work (1965, 107–9).

2 Carl's *Traité*, seems to be a very rare book. Tautscher mentioned that he had located only four copies in German libraries in 1939 (1939, 158). The British library could trace no copy in 1985, though the Goldsmiths' library had a photocopy of the one in the Kress Library at Harvard. It seems that the only other copy in the USA is at Princeton. Tautscher announced his plans for a new edition, in German translation, in 1939, but it never appeared.

A rather lengthy work, written in French by a German, perhaps has rather small prospects of being re-edited or reprinted. But some selection, if not the entire work, ought to be published.

3 Smith might well have got the idea of the division of labour, and of the particular case of pin-making, from the *Encyclopédie* of Diderot and d'Alembert (1755). But then the encyclopedists might have got the idea from Carl.

4 For the life of Cantillon, see Fage in the INED edition (1952, XXIIIff), and Murphy (1986). Mr Murphy has produced a wealth of remarkable new material regarding Cantillon's extraordinary financial career. He also rejects the year 1697 as the date of Cantillon's birth – put forward in Hone (1944). Such a date would have meant that Cantillon was a juvenile prodigy as well as a financial and intellectual prodigy. Mr Murphy suggests, very reasonably, that Cantillon must have been born between 1680 and 1690. I am much indebted to Mr Murphy's work, though it appeared after I had completed a first draft of this section.

5 Parallels may be drawn not only between Cantillon and Law, but also between Cantillon and Ricardo (see Hyse, 1971), and between Cantillon and Keynes, as successful operators on the foreign-exchange markets. (See Sir John Hicks's Foreword to Murphy, 1986, v.)

6 Mr Murphy suggests that the *Essay* was probably written between 1628 and 1630.

7 See Tsuda's edition from the MS in Rouen. Murphy suggests very plausibly that Gournay may have been responsible for the publication of Cantillon's *Essay* in a series for which he was mainly responsible, which included a number of translations into French. See chapter 12.

8 It is not clear just when any meeting and discussion between Cantillon and Newton may have taken place.

Sir Isaac Newton spent thirty-one years at the Mint, first as Warden, and then, from the end of 1699 as Master, until his death in 1727. He retained his chair of mathematics at Cambridge to which he had been elected in 1669. As Warden, Newton served as representative of the monarch without responsibility for policy. Though he arrived at the Mint during the time of the great recoinage, the policy decisions had already been taken. Newton appears to have agreed with Locke that the silver coins should be preserved at their existing weight.

Newton's best-known report as Master was that of 1717, when the value of the gold guinea was reduced to 21s as a maximum (see Shirras and Craig, 1945, 235).

Differing views have been expressed regarding Newton's ideas and policies as Master of the Mint. The conclusion of the study undertaken at the time of the tercentenary (1943) is, however: 'It is understandable that so great a genius in the world of pure science should have been considered to have held a similar position in economics, but that view is not borne out by the facts' (Shirras and Craig, 1945, 241).

9 Jean Boizard was the author of *Traité des monnaies, de leur circonstances et dépendence*, Paris 1711–14. He died early in the eighteenth century.

10 All page references are to Higgs' edition of Cantillon's *Essai* (1931), unless otherwise indicated.

11 Pufendorf used the term 'intrinsic' price, but in a quite different sense from that of Cantillon. For Pufendorf the 'intrinsic' price depended on aptitude and the power to satisfy needs, rather than on cost of production. Schumpeter accused Cantillon (along with nineteenth-century 'classics') of never having

> asked the question *how* market price is related to normal price and precisely *how* the latter emerges – if indeed it does emerge – from the supply and demand mechanism that produces the former. Taking this relation for granted, he was led

> to treat market price as a separate phenomenon *and to restrict the supply and demand explanation to it*. Thus emerged the superficial and, as the later development of the theory of value was to show, misleading formula – normal price is determined by cost, market price is determined by supply and demand . . . (1954, 220)

12 The word 'undertaker' was only just beginning to acquire its modern meaning in the early eighteenth century, that is as 'one who makes a business of carrying out the arrangements for funerals' (OED). The word is used in the excerpts included in Postelthwayt's *Universal Dictionary* (1751) and in the advertisement or '*Dissertation*' about the *Dictionary* of 1749.

13 Regarding the idea of the circular flow of payments Schumpeter wrote:

> Cantillon was the first to make this circular flow concrete and explicit, to give us a bird's eye view of economic life. In other words, he was the first to draw a *tableau économique*. And, barring differences which hardly affect essentials, this *tableau* is the same as Quesnay's, though Cantillon did not actually condense it into a table. Cantillon's priority is thus beyond question . . . (1954, 222, quoted by Murphy, 1986, 261)

14 Viner (1937, 74n.) maintained that 'the self-regulating mechanism is clearly and ably explained' by Cantillon. Certainly *a* self-adjusting mechanism is explained, but over what kind of period, or time-scale it may be expected to operate is not clear. Nor, of course, did Cantillon draw any free-trade conclusions.

15 Murphy presents a discerning contrast between Cantillon and Law. Cantillon 'was not optimistic about the human condition'; he saw wealth as 'concentrated in the hands of the few. He believed population growth occurred at the expense of the people's standard of living . . . He perceived international trade as a zero sum game . . . Even if a country achieved growth, he believed that such growth was only part of the upswing of an economic cycle that was deterministically followed by depression and decay'. On the other hand, John Law was highly optimistic. He believed that employment and output could be expanded through monetary policy. He found nothing natural about the constraining factors to growth, the shortage of money, and the underutilization of resources in Scotland and France. Controversially, but not unjustifiably, Murphy concludes that Law's 'vision of the way in which paper money and the banking system would evolve was far more perceptive than that of Cantillon' (1986, 279).

16 Murphy makes out a case for the exciting possibility that Cantillon may not have died in the fire at his house in Albemarle Street, but had staged the blaze, with a purchased corpse, in order to disappear overseas. Cantillon may, in fact, have been a mysterious 'Chevalier de Louvigny', who landed in Surinam in December 1734. The Chevalier was never traced, but left behind him in the Dutch colony a large collection of papers belonging to Richard Cantillon.

17 For Ceva and his work see the discussion in Marco Bianchini (1982, 9–25), and R. D. Theocharis (1961, 5–9).

18 Regarding the Italian influences on Daniel Bernoulli, Kauder has maintained that, 'it is probable that his studies in Italy brought him into contact with economists who taught him the elements of value-in-use theory' (1965, 32).

19 On Bernoulli and the St Petersburg paradox, see G. J. Stigler (1965, 109ff).

20 On Bernoulli and neo-classical value theory, see A. Pringsheim (1896).

Chapter 10 Mid-century Efflorescence, the French Enlightenment and the Thirty-year Boom

1 On the growth of economic literature at this period, see Higgs (1935, Foreword).

2 Dr Daniela Parisi Acquaviva (1984, 118ff) has traced the important influences on Italian economists of foreign writers, some of whose works were translated into Italian. From France, the writings of Graslin, Turgot and Condillac were influential, as were the writings of some of the later mercantilists (e.g. Mun and Cary) from England; and those of David Hume and the historical school (e.g. Steuart) from Scotland. It was most unfortunate that there was so very little influence of the ideas of Galiani, Verri, and Beccaria on English and Scottish writers.

3 On the new journals appearing at this time, see Einaudi (1953, 52–3) and Higgs (1935, x).

4 See Tribe (1984, 263) and Higgs (1935, x).

5 For a most illuminating account of this phase of the enlightenment, see Gay (1969).

6 As Professor D. C. Coleman has recently remarked of economic history: 'Today, any sort of study which has its roots in the optimistic rationalism of the Enlightenment cannot but experience at least a modicum of disillusion' (1987, 3). This is probably even more true of economics than of economic history (or should be).

Chapter 11 Moral Philosophy and Political Economy in Scotland

1 Knowledge of Carmichael has been much extended by Hans Medick's profound study (1973), and by the essay of James Moore and Michael Silverthorne (1983). I am most grateful to Mr P. K. Escreet, Keeper of Special Collections at the Glasgow University Library for advice about the Carmichael manuscripts (which are in Latin).

2 Professor Medick has maintained that 'the labour theory of value, as well as Adam Smith's conception of property, is to be traced back via his teacher Frances Hutcheson and Hutcheson's teacher Carmichael to Locke' (1973, 301). Undoubtedly Locke's influence in the emergence of the labour theory of value was of major importance, as far as Adam Smith, and others, were concerned. But, Hutcheson and Carmichael, though maintaining a labour theory of *property*, upheld a scarcity-and-utility theory of value. It is not clear that the labour theory of *value* necessarily came down to Adam Smith via Carmichael or Hutcheson, neither of whom have been shown to have held a labour theory of value in any explicit or significant form. Locke's influence on Smith, regarding the labour theory of value could easily have come about during Smith's six years in Oxford. In the notes of his *Lectures*, however, Smith does not seem to follow, to any significant extent either Locke's labour theory of property, or his labour theory of value.

3 Hutcheson, however, expressed much scepticism as to the human capacity for judgement: 'It is certain from the indolence, and the necessary avocations of multitudes, that scarce one in a hundred will ever exercise this right of private judgement' (1755, vol. I, 311).

4 See Hutchison (1953, 71).

5 It seems that Francis Hutcheson may have been partly responsible for the failure of Hume to obtain a chair at Edinburgh (see Mossner, 1980).

6 See Bonar (1922, 106). According to Albert Schatz (1902, 61) Hume anticipated Roscher and may be regarded as a precursor of the German Historical School. See the quotation in chapter 19 (I) and the discussion of Hume, Steuart and others as pioneers of the historical method.

7 See Hume (1955, iv), and Vickers (1959, 226ff).

8 See Hont (1983) and Hume (1955, 199ff).
9 Henry Home, Lord Kames (1696–1782) was a Scottish lawyer and philosopher who wrote voluminously on those subjects including *Essays upon the Principles of Morality and Natural Religion* (1751) and *Sketches of the History of Man* (1774). He was one of the founders of what became the Royal Society of Edinburgh and sponsored the lectures there of Adam Smith in 1748 when he first declared some of his doctrines of economic freedom.
10 Hume's attitude to public debt was criticized by Isaac de Pinto (1715–87), a friend of Hume in Paris, and author of *Traité de la circulation et du credit* (1773, English translation by Rev. S. Bagges, 1774). Pinto maintained that the public debt supported 'circulation' and that England's economic advance had been promoted by her public debt and public credit.
11 See Robbins (1952, 49–55). It may be noted that Hume comprehensively rejected the labour theory of property (see 1739 [1911] vol. II, 209n.). I am indebted on this point to an unpublished paper by Professor P. L. Porta on 'The Labour Theory of Value in Adam Smith'.
12 Hume's views 'On the Populousness of Ancient Nations' were opposed by his friend Robert Wallace (1697–1771), a Presbyterian minister and author of *A Dissertation on the Numbers of Mankind in Ancient and Modern Times, in which the Superior Populousness of Antiquity is Maintained* (1753). Wallace's *Dissertation* had been written before Hume's. He also wrote *Various Prospects of Mankind, Nature and Providence* (1761) which anticipated some of the arguments of the first essay of Malthus (1798), to the effect that population would double in each generation if not checked by vice, war, etc. Wallace defended Hume in his application for a chair at Edinburgh University and had been a lecturer in mathematics at that university.
13 See Duke (1979, 585–6). E. A. J. Johnson (1937, 163–4) maintains that 'Hume's economic ideas for the most part belonged to the old régime', and that he has been placed 'much nearer to Adam Smith in economic ideas than he really was'.
14 We discuss elsewhere Hume's very unfavourable view of Quesnay and his followers, as contrasted with that of Adam Smith. For Hume the physiocrats were 'indeed the set of men the most chimerical and most arrogant that now exist . . .' (letter to Morellet, of 10 July 1769). Adam Smith, however, was apparently intending to dedicate *The Wealth of Nations* to Dr Quesnay, had the doctor not died before its publication.
15 In this section on Smith I have drawn on chapter 1 of Hutchison (1978).
16 In a letter of Sir T. Munro to Kirkman Finlay (15 August 1825) he wrote: 'I remember about the time of the appearance of *The Wealth of Nations*, that the Glasgow merchants were as proud of the work as if they had written it themselves; and some of them said it was no wonder that Adam Smith had written such a book, as he had the advantage of their society, in which the same doctrines were circulated with the punch every day' (*James Finlay and Co.*, 1951; see Hutchison, 1978, 3).

Chapter 12 Between Boisguilbert and Quesnay

1 In the second quarter of the eighteenth century, several French writers were upholding the economic and social beneficence of luxury along the lines of Mandeville (see Morize, 1909). As Voltaire wrote in 'Le Mondain' (1736):

Ainsi l'on voit en Angleterre, en France,
Par cent canaux circuler l'abondance.
Le goût du luxe entre dans tous les rangs
Le pauvre y vit des vanités des grands,
Et le travail, gagé par la mollesse
S'ouvre à pas lents la route à la richesse.

2 Alongside Melon, C. de F. Dutot is frequently mentioned. He had been an official of the Compagnie des Indes, with which John Law was associated. He was the author of *Réflexions politiques sur les financès et le commerce* (1738, two vols). Unlike Melon, but in agreement with cantillon, Dutot maintained that money should have intrinsic value. He emphasized the importance of velocity of circulation and stressed the fundamental role of agriculture. His work was translated into English as *Political Reflection upon the Finances and Commerce of France* (1739). In his introduction, the anonymous translator stressed the wisdom of recent French economic policies, from which he concluded that Britain should learn, since, he maintained 'complaints of its [Britain's] decay are coming up from all quarters'. He further maintained that Britain was buying much more French manufactures than France was of ours.

3 As Montesquieu put it: 'Since men have had the same passions in all ages, though the occasions which produce great changes are different . . . the causes are always the same' (1734 [1882], 23).

4 On the Russians Montesquieu wrote: 'Commerce itself is inconsistent with the Russian laws. The people are composed only of slaves employed in agriculture, and of slaves called ecclesiastics, or gentlemen who are the lords of those slaves; there is then nobody left for the third estate, which ought to be composed of mechanics and merchants' (393).

5 On Ustariz see chapter 17, note 8.

6 In a letter of 1755, quoted by A. Murphy (1986, 310), Baron Grimm wrote, rather optimistically of political economy: 'The subject [trade] is becoming each day more interesting; and as the public fixes its attention on it, as it seems bent on doing, we will have the double advantage of being instructed in a science which will soon become the basis for the superiority . . . of the French government.'

7 The Marquis d'Argenson (1694–1757) is not known to have published any work on political economy, but is said to have been responsible for the maxims '*pas trop gouverner*', and '*laisser-faire, laisser passer*' (though the credit for the latter phrase seems to be disputed: Murphy (1986, 308) attributes it to Gournay).

Chapter 13 Josiah Tucker and the English Contribution

1 Elsewhere Tucker observed how the division of labour depended on the level of market demand:

> In the richer country where the demands are great and constant, every manufacture that requires various processes, and is composed of different parts, is accordingly divided and sub-divided into separate and distinct branches; whereby each person becomes more expert, and also more expeditious in the particular part assigned him. Whereas in a poor country the same person is obliged by necessity, and for the sake of getting a bare subsistence, to undertake such different branches as prevent him from excelling, or being expeditious in any . . . (1774a, 25, quoted by Rashid, 1986, 294)

Tucker also (unlike Adam Smith) noted the variety of human endowments and innate abilities which made the division of labour so advantageous:

> ... Nature herself has formed certain persons for certain trades, and given them such knowledge by instinct, as no human artist could communicate by instruction; and it is very remarkable, that not only all new inventions, but almost all the improvements in arts and sciences were the discoveries of those, who had not served a regular apprenticeship in the business. (1755 [1931], 70)

2 Regarding the 'perverse' or backward-sloping supply curve of labour, see Furniss (1920, reprinted 1957, chapter VI) on 'The Doctrine of the Utility of Poverty'.

3 See Rotwein (1955, 199ff), and Semmel (1965). Tucker set out his views in the first tract (1774a), where he posed the question: 'Whether a rich country can stand a competition with a poor country (of equal natural advantages) in raising of provisions, and cheapness of manufactures?' Tucker maintained that 'the rich country is not only more *knowing*, but is also more able than the other to make improvements' (23). On the other hand, countering these disadvantages in knowledge and investment, poor countries could produce raw materials more cheaply: '... *operose* or *complicated* manufactures are cheapest in rich countries; and *raw materials* in poor ones; and therefore in proportion as any commodity approaches to one or other of these *extremes*, in that proportion it will be found to be cheaper or dearer in a rich or poor country' (see Semmel, 1965, 761). Tucker mentioned seven advantages which richer or more advanced countries had over less developed: in transport; skills; capital; higher wages (to attract better workers); more specialization; more competition to reduce monopoly profits. Tucker did not believe in the existence of any self-adjusting mechanism which would reduce differences between nations in wealth or economic development. He seems rather to have believed in the Biblical maxim: 'To him that hath shall be given'.

4 Tucker ascribed to Franklin another idea put forward in *The Wealth of Nations* (see Smith, 1776, 625–6). According to Tucker: 'The more we familiarise ourselves to the idea of separation, the less surprised and the more prepared we shall be whenever that event shall happen. For that it will happen, one day or other, is the opinion of almost everyone' except '... the celebrated Dr Franklin, who thinks the capital of government should be transferred to America' (1774a, xii).

5 Karl Marx described Massie's *Essay* as 'epoch-making' and as having anticipated Hume. Many or most of Massie's tracts are pioneer statistical or historical essays about particular trades or current policy controversies. They may represent an attempt to follow up the quantitative programme of Petty, in the belief that any reasonable attempt at quantification is better than none.

One such pamphlet set out *Calculations of the Present Taxes Yearly Paid by a Family of Each Rank, Degree, or Class* (2nd ed., 1761). In a dedication to the new monarch, George III, Massie stated his purpose as 'to calm the minds of the people of Great Britain by undeceiving them in regard to their payments for taxes'. Apparently, it was being claimed that government was costing people two-thirds of their incomes. By means of some apparently rather simple, if cavalier, calculations, Massie concluded that, at the top of the scale, a nobleman with £20,000 per annum was paying just under a third of his income in taxation, or 6/5d in the £; that the rate then rose regressively down to the gentleman with £200 per annum, who paid 7/3d in the £; but then, for those who paid no land tax, progressively fell to one-third in the £ in indirect taxes payable by the country labourer earning £13 per annum.

6 Massie would have had the support of Dr Samuel Johnson., When it was questioned whether Adam Smith, who had never 'been in trade', could be expected to write well on that subject, Johnson replied '... a man who has

never engaged in trade himself may undoubtedly write well upon trade, and there is nothing which requires more to be illustrated by philosophy than trade does ... A merchant seldom thinks but of his own particular trade. To write a good book upon it, a man must have extensive views. It is not necessary to have practised to write well upon a subject' (Boswell, 1791 [1906], vol. I, 607).

As Johnson rather mildly put it of the relations between himself and Smith: 'We did not take to each other.' Smith, for his part, is reported as having said: 'Of all the writers, ancient or modern, he that keeps off the greatest distance from common sense is Dr Samuel Johnson' (see Bryson, 1945, 212). Probably James Boswell did little to encourage good relations between the two. He disapproved of Smith's remarks about Oxford and what he called his 'decisive professorial manner' (II, 332). Boswell apparently liked to remind Johnson that once 'when Dr Adam Smith was expatiating on the beauty of Glasgow, he had cut him short by saying, "Pray, Sir, have you ever seen Brentford?"' (II, 445).

Johnson's views on unemployment, demand and wages are of some interest. Perhaps surprisingly he defended Mandeville and the benefits of luxury expenditure. He regarded *involuntary* unemployment as a serious problem (II, 284), as did most of the leading writers in our period. (A contemporary of Samuel Johnson who also explicitly recognized that much unemployment was involuntary was another compiler of a dictionary, Malachi Postelthwayt, whom we shall discuss next.) But the 'unemployed' probably always have been, and always will be, a very mixed bunch of people. There was, therefore, nothing inconsistent in Johnson also believing in a significant amount of *voluntary* idleness, which led him – like Petty and others – to oppose raising the wages of labourers, because 'it does not make them live better, but only makes them idler' (II, 439). On Postelthwayt, see Johnson 1937, 287.

7 The 1750s saw the appearance of a number of dictionaries and encyclopedias, both in Britain and in France. Dr Johnson published his *Plan for a Dictionary of the English Language* in 1747 (two years before Postelthwayt) and he produced his great work in 1755.

8 On the copy of this pamphlet in the Kress Library, H. S. Foxwell wrote: 'This is a very remarkable proposal, admirably conceived' (see Redlich, 1970). The curriculum has numerous similarities with that of the Bachelor of Commerce degree introduced by W. J. Ashley in Birmingham at the beginning of the twentieth century, the first university degree course of its kind in England.

9 The accusation of plagiarism against Postelthwayt might be unfounded or unfair. The Cantillon family seems to have had an extreme passion for secrecy and may not have wanted Richard's name mentioned or his *Essay* brought to light. On Postelthwayt, see Johnson 1937, 405–8.

10 A convenient collection of Franklin's main economic writings is available in vol. II of Spark's edition of his works (1844).

11 In his *Modest Inquiry* of 1729 (see chapter 8), Franklin had emphasized the different endowments and qualities, both of countries and individuals, and had drawn the consequences in terms of the advantages of free exchange; 'Not only different countries, but even different parts of the same country, have their particular most suitable products; and likewise ... different men have geniuses adapted to a variety of different arts and manufactures' (1844, 263–4). On this last point, regarding individual differences, Adam Smith denied that they could serve as a reason for the division of labour and specialization, maintaining that they were caused by it.

12 Josiah Tucker wrote rather abrasively about the American colonists. In

particular, he attacked an argument of Franklin about the importance of the North American trade for Britain, which he concluded was less than with Holland or Germany. Tucker also expressed 'a strong suspicion' that Franklin had 'fibbed designedly' as ambassador (see Tucker 1775a, in 1931, 386n.). The brusque exchange of letters (1774) followed an accusation by the Dean that Franklin had indulged in jobbery on behalf of his friends.

Chapter 14 Demography and Cameralism in Germany and Austria

1 The edition of Süssmilch's work referred to here is the fourth (1775).

2 Justi began his *Staatswirtschaft* (1755, 2nd ed. 1758, quoted here) by complaining of the neglect by German universities of the economic and cameral sciences: 'cameralists' were essential to the state. He maintained that a historical approach to finance and commerce was necessary, and he himself started from the Phoenicians. He put much emphasis on freedom as 'indispensable for the happiness of a monarch's subjects'. The most important means of increasing the wealth of a country was an increasing population, and he urged that immigration should be encouraged by promoting freedom of religion. On foreign trade, Justi supported most of the main mercantilist policies: the first principle must be that more gold and silver was brought in than went out; the export of raw materials should be prohibited; non-essential imports should be heavily taxed. He favoured the development of manufacturing, and especially of mining. Justi observed that saving was necessary for the increase of wealth, but it must be invested, at risk. Investment should depend on present wealth and prospective profit (an early and useful contribution to a vital subject; see 464–5). He called for censuses of population and of manufactures. On the life of Justi, see Frensdorff (1903, reprinted 1970).

3 The translation here of Justi's *System des Finanzwesens* is taken from Monroe (1924). It has been slightly modified at some points.

4 As an example for justifying progression, Justi took two merchants, Martin and Christopher:

> Martin, a merchant, has property amounting to twenty thousand dollars, and makes a profit of three thousand dollars. Christopher, another merchant, has property amounting to sixty thousand dollars, and makes, at this rate, nine thousand dollars a year. Let us assume that each of these merchants needs two thousand dollars a year for the support of his household, family, and servants; Martin, therefore, has only one thousand net earnings, while Christopher has seven thousand. Now if contributions are collected in exact proportion to property, and Martin pays two hundred dollars, while Christopher, having three times as much property, pays six hundred dollars a year, it is evident that Christopher nevertheless has to pay a much more moderate contribution than Martin; for the latter has only eight hundred dollars left to increase his property, while Christopher has six thousand four hundred dollars, that is, eight times as much, though he pays only three times as much in taxes. (391)

There seems to have been no similarly penetrating analysis of taxation by English or French writers at this time, or for some time to come.

5 The edition of Sonnenfels' *Grundsätze* referred to here is the third, of 1770–1.

Chapter 15 Italian Illumination: Subjective Utility, Money and the Mathematical Method

1 Regarding the scholastic doctrines on value and price, and the Italian contribution on utility and subjective value, see De Roover, 1967; Langholm, 1979; and

Spicciani, 1972. Langholm describes Olivi as 'one of the really brilliant economic minds of the Middle Ages' (1979, 153). As Spicciani observes, Olivi's views were censored (1972, 320). St Bernardino and St Antoninus proceeded to borrow heavily from Olivi, who expounded a synthesis of demand and labour theories of value, as based on the power of scarce labour to command a price, but only if it produced something useful. Langholm maintains that Galiani 'very obviously depended' on Olivi's ideas (1979, 156), which, in fundamental outline, anticipated the basic principles of neoclassical analysis.

2 On the life of Galiani, see Galiani (1770 [1968]). I am also much indebted to Ganzoni (1938), and Einaudi (1945).

3 Antonio Genovesi (1713–69) was an important contributor to the Italian tradition in value theory, though he was a learned rather than an original writer. His *Lezioni di commercio* was published in 1769. He claimed to be influenced by his fellow Neapolitan Giovanni Batista Vico (1668–1744), and drew on, among others, Child, Locke, Melon, Montesquieu and Galiani. He is cited as one of their predecessors by both Carl Menger and Léon Walras.

Genovesi based the value of goods on 'the power to satisfy our needs' (1769, 11–12). He combined mercantilist views, in favour of a large population and some restrictions on imports, with support for the greatest possible economic freedom internally, and with a mildly physiocratic emphasis on agriculture as the prime source of wealth.

4 Important sections of Galiani's *Della moneta* have been translated by Monroe (see Galiani, 1924). I have used Monroe's versions, as far as they go and also given the page references to the 1963 edition (ed. A. Caracciolo) of *Della moneta*.

5 For a French translation of selections from Galiani's *Della moneta*, including in particular his chapter on 'Alzamento', see Galiani (1955).

6 On Galiani's theory of economic growth, see Pier Luigi Portà (1986) to whom I am most grateful for his having shown me his paper before publication. Portà observes that Galiani saw growth as coming about mainly through the manufacturing sector, though he did not, as his Neapolitan predecessor, Antonio Serra had, explicitly contrast diminishing returns in agriculture with increasing returns in manufacturing. Galiani favoured low prices for corn as an encouragement to manufacturing, whereas the physiocrats (and Boisguilbert;) wanted high prices for corn. As Professor Portà suggests, Galiani may have found support for his theory of development in the example of England.

7 It is a pity that Galiani's remarks about England are not available in full. David Hume, in a latter to Morellet of 10 July 1769 wrote: 'The Abbé Galiani goes to Naples: he does well to leave Paris before I come thither for I should certainly put him to death for all the ills he has spoke of England' (1932, vol. II, 205). What these objectionable remarks of Galiani's were is unknown.

Certainly Hume and Galiani, perhaps the two most brilliant critical minds of the century, were closely agreed in their savage denunciation of the physiocrats. Incidentally, Nietzsche described Galiani as 'the most profound, sharply perceptive, and perhaps also the dirtiest man of his century' (*sic*, 'schmutzigste'), and as 'much more profound than Voltaire' (*Jenseits von Gut und Böse*, Aphorismen 26). Fernand Braudel describes Galiani as 'the most clear-sighted man of his century' (1979, 325).

8 The following passage, from a letter, shows the influence of Vico: 'Everything in this world follows a pendulum: seasons, empires, governments, men, happiness and unhappiness, virtue, vice; one ascends and one descends, *and no one knows how to stop in the middle*; if one could stop, one would find the good,

but the movement must go on to its end' (Galiani, 1881, vol. I, 194). On Vico, see Isaiah Berlin (1980, 111ff). Hayek has maintained that Vico, 'and his great disciple Ferdinando Galiani, constitute the only important parallel on the Continent to the anti-rationalist British tradition' (1960, 429).

Chapter 16 François Quesnay and the Rise and Fall of the Physiocratic School

1 On the life of Quesnay, see Hecht (in Quesnay, 1958); also E. Fox-Genovese (1976), to which book I am much indebted.
2 For criticism of Boisguilbert's 'agricultural enthusiasm' by a contemporary of Quesnay, see Pinto's *Traité de la circulation et du crédit* (1773, English translation, 1774). Pinto also attacked the physiocrats (1773, 156–70).
3 On Quesnay's theory of economic growth, see Eltis (1984, chapter 2, 39ff).
4 With regard to Quesnay's views on saving and spending Schumpeter noted: 'the similarity with Keynesian views is striking: in itself, saving is sterile and a disturber; it must always be offset' (1954, 287).
5 Quesnay's knowledge of China was derived from J. P. Rousselot de Surgy's *Mélange interessant et curieux, ou abrégé d'histoire de l'Asie, de l'Afrique, de l'Amerique, etc.* (ten vols, 1763–5). Quesnay copied out passages from this work (see Quesnay, 1946, 27).
6 Some 200 years later, long after the empire so admired by Quesnay had dissolved and passed away, some western economists were again to look to the régime in China as the embodiment of politico-economic wisdom and success. A Chinese 'Cultural Revolution' was hailed as marking the dawn of a great new age of human history, in the course of which 'even upon cautious estimates, the rate of growth of industrial capacity is probably the most rapid the world has ever seen' (Robinson, 1960, 409–10). Of course, this claim did not express a Quesnaysian concept of economic objectives, in terms of which it was extolling record rates of growth in 'sterility'. See also *The Cultural Revolution in China* (1969), by Joan Robinson. For the views of intellectuals in France 200 years after Quesnay, during the Cultural Revolution, see P. J. Bruckner (1987).
7 On Mercier's life, see the excellent study by Richner (1931).
8 On Mercier's conversation with Catherine the Great, see Robbins (1952, 35). Robbins describes Mercier as a specimen of 'extreme individualism'. The conversation went as follows:

Catherine: Sir, can you tell me the best way to govern a state?
Mercier: There is only one way, Madame. Be just, that is to say, uphold the constitution and observe the laws.
C: But on what basis should laws be made?
M: On one basis, only, Your Majesty, on the nature of things and of men.
C: Most certainly: but when one wishes to make these laws, what rules should be observed?
M: Madame, to give laws to mankind is God's prerogative. How can mere man venture on such a task? By what right would he dictate to those whom God has not placed in his hands?
C: To what then do you reduce the science of government?
M: To study the laws which God has so manifestly engraven in human society from the time of its creation. To seek to go beyond this would be a great mistake and a disastrous undertaking.
C: Sir, it has been a great pleasure to meet you. I wish you good day.

To impart this guidance Mercier travelled for many weeks across Europe, together with his wife and mistress, in the same carriage. See also Oncken (1920, 421).

9 Dupont's pamphlet (1763) was entitled *Réflexions sur l'écrit intitulé Richesse de l'état*, which criticized a work by Roussel de la Tour.

10 Abbé Nicolas Baudeau (1730–92), besides first editing the *Éphémérides*, was the author of *Première introduction à la philosophie économique ou analyse des état policés* (1771). Like Mercier, Baudeau supported an absolute monarchy. His most important theoretical contribution was to the physiocrats' rather subtle concept of 'luxury'. As Meek put it: 'The physiocrats' theory of luxury was in effect an attempt to evaluate the various ways of spending the net product according to the effect which they might be expected to have on the size of future net products, and thus on the size of future national incomes' (1962, 316). According to this analysis what would often be described as 'luxury' spending by the rich, though less directly productive than investment in agriculture, might be more 'productive' than hoarding, if it promoted demand for primary or agricultural products. Sumptuary laws were opposed. See Baudeau (1767).

Guillaume F. Le Trosne (1728–80) argued the case for free trade in grain in his work of 1765. His later writings (*De l'ordre social* and *De l'interêt social*, both 1777), discussed the legal framework of society, including taxation and (in the second volume) the analysis of value.

11 See *Effet des assignats sur le prix du pain* (1790, in E. Daire, translated by E. E. Lincoln, 1950, as *Dupont de Nemours on the Dangers of Inflation*). See also Dupont's *Rapport fait à l'Assemblée Nationale* (1790).

12 According to theoreticians, whether the failure has been one of socialist planning, or of some over-enthusiastic free-market experiment, when things have gone wrong, it has almost always been the fault of the politicians, often for not pressing on with sufficient determination. Very seldom, apparently, has it been the fault of any inadequacies in the theoretical models, but rather of the less than Utopianly patient and intelligent handling on the political side.

13 On Graslin see chapter 18, note 5.

14 Galiani was first answered by the Abbé Morellet (1727–1819), who was a friend of Turgot and disciple of Gournay. He supported the policy of free trade in grain internally, and, to some extent, externally. He was the author of *Fragment d'une lettre sur la policé des grains* (1764). He drafted a prospectus for *A New Dictionary of Commerce* (1769) (for which Turgot wrote his very important, but unfinished article 'Valeurs et Monnaie'). The project, however, was never completed. Morellet also introduced Beccaria's work into France. In 1774, when Turgot came to power in Paris, Morellet acted as his secretary, and his answer to Galiani's *Dialogues* was published: *Réfutation de l'ouvrage qui a pour titre Dialogues sur le commerce des blés* (written 1770).

15 As Tocqueville put it of the *économistes*: 'Though most of them were amiable, well-meaning persons, men of substance, conscientious public servants or able administrators, such was their enthusiasm for the cause they sponsored that they carried their theories to fanatical lengths. Our economists had a vast contempt for the past' (159).

Chapter 17 The Milanese Enlightenment: Utility, Liberty and Mathematics

1 When he met Pietro Verri, Beccaria was twenty-three, and in trouble with his father, who disapproved of his marriage. Verri at once helped to reconcile the young Beccaria with his father. There followed a few years of intense intellectual

cooperation, ended by a savage break on Beccaria's return from his disastrous visit to Paris with Verri's brother Alessandro in October 1766. According to Morellet, in the French capital Beccaria was so moody and depressed that 'one could hardly get a word out of him' (see Bouvy, 1889, and the introduction by H. Paolucci to his English translation, *On Crimes and Punishments* 1963). It appears that Beccaria's wife may have been heavily involved in the quarrel between her husband and Pietro Verri.

2 Jeremy Bentham hailed Beccaria as 'my master, first evangelist of reason ... You have made so many useful excursions into the path of utility, what is there left for us to do?' (Halévy, 1928, 21; and Beccaria, 1963, x).

3 The intellectual relationship between Beccaria and Verri has been described in Paolucci's introduction to his English translation of Beccaria's masterpiece. In a letter to Morellet, Beccaria acknowledged that Verri 'gave me the strength to write; and I owe it to him that the manuscript of *On Crimes and Punishments* ... which he generously transcribed for me in his own hand, did not end up in the flames' (1963, xiii). Verri claimed that he suggested the topic to Beccaria and added that 'writing is so laborious for him, and costs him so much effort that after an hour he collapses and 'can't go on. When he had amassed the materials, I wrote them out, arranged them in order, and thus made a book out of them' (quoted by Paolucci in Beccaria, 1963, xiii–xiv). Paolucci added, regarding Beccaria's later career:

> Enjoying the patronage of the Austrian government, he lapsed into Epicurean indolence. From 1768 until his death in 1794, he occupied a series of public offices that were all more or less sinecures; but isolated as he was from his old friend he was not able, in all that time, to produce a single writing worthy of public attention. (xvi)

Paul Hazard confirms, or accepts, this contradiction of 'the Beccaria myth'. He describes Pietro Verri as 'the moving spirit' in the Milanese Enlightenment, and continues, regarding Beccaria, that he

> had more time on his hands than he knew what to do with ... To look at him, you would have taken him for more of a loafer than he really was, the sort of individual who might well have spent a completely useless sort of life had it not been for the people he had about him, and for the prevailing temper of the times.

Eventually, thanks to Pietro Verri and the group around *Il Caffè*, he discovered 'his true line ... and somewhere between his indolent youth and his barren old age he produced a masterpiece' (1965, 174).

4 I have used mainly the Custodi edition of Beccaria's economic writings, *Scrittori classici Italiani di economia politica* (1804, vols XI and XII); except for his paper *Tentativo analitico sui contrabandi*, which is included in *Opere* (vol. II, 1822, 427ff).

5 Perhaps not too much should be expected of inaugural lectures. Anyhow, according to Verri, Beccaria's discourse 'did not contain a single luminous and new idea on the subject' (see Venturi, 1965). But the journal of the physiocrats, the *Éphémérides du citoyen* paid Beccaria's appointment and inaugural lecture in Milan an enthusiastic tribute.

6 On Ustariz and Ulloa, see note 8 below.

7 Beccaria's analysis of value elaborated the utility and scarcity theory which he and Verri had inherited from their Italian predecessors and the scholastics, and which had contained a markedly subjectivist emphasis. A recognition of the role of utility in value does not necessarily imply a subjectivist approach. Beccaria and Verri were pioneers of utilitarian ideas which were to be based mainly on a significantly measurable, objective concept of utility. Indeed, after the decline and fall of the English labour-and-cost-of-production theory, around

1870, several of the neo-classicals went on to pursue some kind of objectively measurable utility concept, or attempted a justification of inter-personal comparisons of utility, or the notion of social utility. A century before, however, at the time of Beccaria and Verri, such questions as those of measurable, or inter-personally comparable utility had only been very vaguely formulated. Certainly, phrases like that of Beccaria about 'the greatest happiness shared by the greatest number' might suggest an attempt to 'objectify' the utility concept. It is not clear how far Beccaria and Verri were prepared to depart from the subjective utility concept of their predecessors, which must be sharply contrasted both with later utilitarian concepts and with classical attempts to replace the traditional utility and scarcity approach to value theory with a pseudo-objective cost-of-production theory, together with the Smithian 'realist' concept of value in use.

8 Joseph Schumpeter managed to discern very close and significant similarities between Beccaria and Adam Smith. Together with Turgot, they apparently formed a great 'triumvirate' (1954, 248). Schumpeter maintained that 'the similarity between the two men is indeed striking. There is even some similarity in their social backgrounds and locations. There is similarity in their lives' (1954, 179–80). Of course there are *some* similarities in their ages and interests. But the dissimilarities surely far outweigh the similarities between the Glasgow professor and the Milanese marquis. To observe that 'neither was merely an economist' is not to observe very much. Very few people were *merely* economists when Smith and Beccaria were writing. Moreover, there seems to be no basis in biographical fact for Schumpeter's statement that 'the main difference, from the standpoint of their scientific achievement is that A. Smith expended very little of his energies on non-scientific work, Beccaria very much'; and that this difference 'explains all there is to explain' about the different degrees to which their writings 'were finished works at all' (248).

Other questions regarding Schumpeter's comparison between Smith and Beccaria, and his claims about a triumvirate with Turgot, are raised by the numerous less-than-favourable judgements pronounced on Smith, in the great *History of Economic Analysis*. For example, as to 'the wooden hands of the Scottish professor' (was Beccaria 'the wooden-handed Milanese marquis'?); also as to there being 'no single original contribution' in *The Wealth of Nations* (which surely does not apply to *Of Crimes and Punishments*); or regarding Smith, or 'the Scottish Beccaria', having been 'far below' Galiani on the subject of value (188); and that 'the blame is at his [Smith's] door for much that is unsatisfactory in the economic theory of the subsequent hundred years' (308). *Some* of these judgements (incidentally) are quite acceptable to the present writer. But, acceptable or unacceptable, just where do such strictures leave Schumpeter's description of Beccaria as 'the Italian Adam Smith'? (179). Moreover, Schumpeter goes on, surely quite correctly, to place Beccaria and Smith on opposite sides of the division, then about to develop, with regard to the theory of value, as between subjective or utility theories, and the cost-of-production or labour theories – a division in which *The Wealth of Nations* played a crucial role (see chapter 20). It goes against the grain to have to disagree so strongly with the great master of the history of economic thought, even on such a narrowly personal or biographical point. We would emphasize that insofar as Schumpeter's remarks on Beccaria are concerned with stressing the value and importance of the Italian contribution to political economy at this time, alongside those of Scotland and France, they are certainly and strongly to be supported. One may agree also with Schumpeter's enthusiastic eulogy of Verri, as ranking with 'the greatest economists' (1954, 178).

9 The Spanish writers cited by Verri were the two mercantilists, Geronimo de Ustariz (1670–1732) and Bernardo de Ulloa (d.1740). They were both concerned with reviving the economy and trade of Spain. Ustariz, an official of Phillip V, urged that Spain must recover the gold and silver which had flowed out to other countries by restricting imports and encouraging exports. See his *Theory and Practice of Commerce* (1724; 2nd ed., 1742; English translation by J. Kippax, 1751). Ulloa, from Seville, in his work entitled *The Revival of the Manufactures and Commerce of Spain* (1740), called for the removal of internal barriers to trade, the reduction of taxation, and the revival of the textile industry. See Wirminghaus (1886), and Grice-Hutchinson (1978).

10 I was only able to see Professor Groenewegen's English edition after I had already drafted this section. This valuable edition and translation has, however, enabled me to make several improvements and additions. The page references are to the edition of Verri's writings edited by R. de Felice, 1964, *Del piacere e del dolore*.

11 Verri's attempt at a mathematical formulation of a quantity theory of money appeared in the sixth edition of the *Meditazioni sulla economia politica* (1772), edited by the mathematician Paolo Frisi (1728–84), a member of the *Il Caffè* group. Frisi added notes and a review of Henry Lloyd's *Essay on the Theory of Money* (1771). (See Theocharis, 1961, 27–35; and Einaudi, 1953, 185.)

12 On the writing of Verri's *Meditazioni*, see Venturi (1978, 531), who states that the book was written in less than a month.

13 Henry Lloyd served in various armies in most parts of Europe, from Portugal to Russia and from Scotland to Italy. He first joined the French army and served in military intelligence, being sent to Scotland in 1745 to assist the Jacobite cause. Later he fought in the Austrian army, obtaining the rank of Major-General, and subsequently served Catherine the Great of Russia. He also travelled in Italy. He was never in the British army, though he received a pension from the British government. He was the author of *A History of the Wars between the King of Prussia and the Empress of Germany* (1766), with *A Continuation* (1781); and of *A Political and Military Rhapsody* (1779), which was concerned with the decline of Britain, and went through several editions. Liddell Hart has written of Lloyd: 'Few British soldiers know the name of Major-General Henry Lloyd. Yet his name was better known in this country during the 18th century than that of any British soldier save Marlborough.' Michael Howard has stated that 'it can almost be said that he opened a new age in the history of military thought'. (For these quotations, see Venturi, 1979, 430, n. 261.)

Jevons discovered a copy of Lloyd's *Essay on the Theory of Money*, accidentally in a bookshop. There is a very enlightening study of Lloyd by Franco Venturi (1979). I am indebted to Professor P. D. Groenewegen for referring me to Venturi's work; and to Venturi's paper for the reference to the Lloyd papers at the Fitzwilliam Museum, Cambridge. I am grateful to the librarians at the Fitzwilliam for permission and assistance. Lloyd's papers contain a number of manuscript essays in English and in French, including *Essai sur l'homme*, which contains a chapter on 'De l'origine des sociétés', together with *Essais philophiques sur les gouvernements*, and some writings on military subjects. There is also a *Memoir* by his son, Hannibal Evans Lloyd (1842).

14 Giammaria Ortes also applied mathematics to economic and social problems. A Venetian monk, Ortes (1713–90) was the author of *Economia nazionale* (1774), which was a survey of industries and occupations. In his most important work,

Riflessioni sulla populazione, he anticipated Malthus in estimating that, in the absence of checks, population would double every thirty years, while subsistence would increase more slowly. Perhaps optimistically, Ortes maintained that the increase of population would be held back by human reason.

Chapter 18 French Pre-eminence: Saving and Investment: Subjective Utility and Expectations

1 As Turgot wrote in a letter of 1770: 'It is ironic that I, who have all my life detested sects, who have never been either an *encyclopédiste* or an *économiste*, have more than any other person borne the double reproach of being both the one and the other' (quoted and translated by Rogers, 1971, 159).

2 Ronald Meek (1973b; 79), long a staunch supporter of the labour theory of value, suggested that Turgot's work 'Value and Money' was left unfinished because he found insuperable difficulties in constructing a satisfactory theory of value based on utility. There are no valid grounds for such a suggestion. On the other hand, there are ample grounds for believing that Turgot had to leave his paper uncompleted because of the pressure of his work as a conscientious administrator, and/or because the volume, to which it was intended as a contribution, was cancelled by the editor or publisher. Turgot's unfinished paper was first published in the edition of his works edited by Dupont (1808–11).

3 See Smith (1776, 89–90). Smith wrote of the Quesnaysian Utopia in China: 'The poverty of the lower ranks of people in China far surpasses that of the most beggarly nations in Europe'. Relative conditions were probably much the same roughly 200 years later at the time of the Maoist Utopia brought about by the Cultural Revolution.

4 An indication of the difficulty of striking a right balance regarding Turgot's philosophical views is provided by Hayek in his *Counter-Revolution of Science* (1952). Hayek describes Turgot as having been one of the original exponents of positivist ideas, with 'a strong tinge of French rationalism', and as having 'unwittingly started trains of thought which produced views on social matters very different from their own' (190–1). It is sometimes very difficult to judge how far a great thinker should be held responsible for the subsequent objectionable development of his ideas by others.

5 Another writer who contributed at this time to the development of a subjective theory of value was J. J. F. Graslin (1727–90), who was referred to in chapter 16 as a critic of the physiocrats. Graslin was a high official in Nantes. His most important work was his *Essai analytique sur la richesses et sur l'impot* (1767). Graslin emphasized the subjective element as follows: 'The attribute of value does not belong to the nature of a thing; its principle is uniquely in man; it increases and decreases with the needs of man, and disappears with him' (51). Graslin stressed that needs which may seem far from natural 'are, when they exist, the necessary cause of value'. Graslin clearly stated both the idea of a scale of needs, which will be satisfied in order of intensity, and the idea of diminishing utility, explaining that 'the value of any unit of a good diminishes in proportion as the quantity of that kind of good becomes greater' (43).

6 Jean Barbeyrac (1674–1744) edited and translated into French Pufendorf's *De officio hominis et civis*, and his *De jure naturae et gentium*. Any influence of Barbeyrac on the history of economic thought must presumably have come through Burlamaqui.

7 Burlamaqui's *Élémens* first appeared in Latin in 1754. The French edition of 1783 is used here.

8 I am much indebted to the distinguished monograph by Dr Paul Meyer (1944).

9 'For Condillac value is not a quality belonging to the object valued, but exists only in our judgment of it and varies as our judgment varies. This notion precisely parallels his theory of knowledge, in which the material characteristics of a body likewise do not reside in the body . . . but exist in our perception of them. Economic value, then, like the material world, is a subjective phenomenon' (Knight, 1968, 237).

10 Another point on which Condillac flatly contradicted Quesnay was with regard to China and the quality of the Chinese government and political order. Condillac, like Adam Smith, emphasized the extreme poverty of the Chinese people, which he took as no recommendation for their government – regarded by the physiocrats as supremely wise.

11 Daniel Klein (1985) has attributed to Condillac 'a deductive economic methodology', explaining that 'what is meant by the deductivist methodology of economics is the establishing of economic laws by deductions from first principles (or axioms) (51). But the fundamentally important question remains as to how Condillac regarded the initial principles, or propositions, from which the deductions start. 'Deductivism' is not the same thing as *a priorism*. Fundamentally, Condillac was a thoroughgoing empiricist (as much as, or more so, than John Locke), who, however important the scope he envisaged for deduction in economic theory, would have insisted that the foundations from which he started were empirical.

12 See chapter 15 of Meyer (1944). One difficulty in tracing the history of subjectivist ideas in economic theory is that even the greatest names in the history of economic individualism were sometimes less than consistently and consequentially subjective with regard to certain concepts (e.g. Adam Smith on utility). Meyer observes that, unlike Condillac, Carl Menger was not consequentially subjective in his definition of scarce, 'economic' goods (1944, 248–9).

Chapter 19 History and Political Economy in Scotland: Alternative 'Inquiries' and Scottish Ascendancy

1 Lehmann (1960, 3) emphasizes how the thought of the Scottish Enlightenment

> stands in sharp contrast with many, though by no means all the tendencies of the French Enlightenment from Descartes to Voltaire, Rousseau and Condorcet. To see in the Enlightenment of the eighteenth century only a modified Cartesianism, a restatement of the earlier ideas of 'natural law' in terms of 'natural rights' and of physical naturalism, the *a priorism* of many of the *philosophes*, a blind faith in progress and in man's ability to make man, society and all political institutions over, unhistorically, on an abstract rational model – this would be to reveal, at least so far as Scottish thought is concerned, either a vast lacuna in one's knowledge of the facts, or an excessively romantic bias in their evaluation.

2 In a letter to Hume (mid-1776) Millar wrote of *The Wealth of Nations*:

> . . . notwithstanding all the pains he has taken, there are many of his positions which I find great difficulty in admitting – and somewhere I am not sure in what latitude he means to establish them. In particular, his great leading opinion concerning the unbounded freedom of trade. I have but a vague notion how far it is true, or how far he meant to say it ought to be carried.

Millar continued: 'I doubt whether there be not some branches of trade, very profitable to the merchant, which are hurtful to the public . . . If this be true, then a regulation of trade must often be highly expedient' (quoted by Lehmann, 1960, 398).

3 Professor D. C. Coleman (1987, 14) points out that in Millar's *An Historical View of the English Government* (1787) there are to be found 'chapters which are the closest approximation to economic history amongst all the writings of the Scottish Enlightenment'.

4 As Professor Coleman maintains of James Mill's historical work, 'there was hardly a sign' of 'what might then have been regarded as historical political economy, let alone of what might today be called economic history' (1987, 21). As regards the other 'southbound Scot', 'far from continuing the tradition of the Scottish Enlightenment, McCulloch helped to debase and undermine it' (28). Professor Coleman continues: 'Such an absence of interest in the economic past dovetailed exactly with the structure of Ricardo's own thought . . . So, by the mid-nineteenth century, the combined efforts of Mill, Ricardo, and McCulloch had gone far to remove the historical elements from the formulation of economic theory' (27–8). The efforts of Nassau Senior, in the same direction, who emphasized that political economy was a science 'not avid of facts', should also be remembered.

5 On Steuart's life see Skinner's 'Biographical Sketch', in vol. I of his edition of Steuart's *Inquiry*, 1966, xxi. See also S. R. Sen's stimulating work (1957).

6 See Davie's article 'Anglophobe and Anglophile' (1967).

7 I have used mainly Andrew Skinner's edition (1966) of Steuart's *Inquiry*, and this is the edition referred to unless otherwise indicated. When citing chapters not included in Skinner's edition, I refer to the three-volume edition of 1770. Steuart's other writings are cited from the six-volume edition of his works edited by his son in 1805.

8 See chapter 8, section IV and appendix.

9 Steuart might well have hoped that in describing his discussion of the economy of the Spartan military dictatorship as a farcical interlude in his serious examination of economic policy, that he had made it clear that he himself was not advocating such a system and that in describing such an economy as embodying 'a perfect plan', he was simply presenting it as an ultra-extreme case – that is, as 'a system uniform and consistent in all its parts' (225), based on the political requirements of a perfect war-making machine (the dangers to Europe of which he presciently warned). Evidently, however, Steuart was insufficiently explicit. For he has, in fact, been accused by some supporters of Adam Smith of *actually advocating* the totalitarian *dirigisme* of the Spartans. (See Anderson and Tollison, 1984, 466.)

10 See Skinner (1966, vol. I, lxxvii) on Steuart on 'infant trades'.

11 The more recent judgment of a distinguished historian and critic of the Scottish Enlightenment may be compared with that of Sir Leslie Stephen: Professor Lehman writes of Steuart's *Inquiry*: 'It is a more systematic and rounded treatise than *The Wealth of Nations*, is based on a scholarship scarcely less broad, and certainly not less sound; and reveals an insight into human nature, the psychology of living-standards and of consumption and into economic processes, generally scarcely less penetrating' (1960, 98).

For a vigorous defence of Steuart against Smith, from a Marxian point of view, see Perelman (1983); and, from the opposite pole, denouncing Steuart as a totalitarian planner, eager to bring about a Spartan dictatorial régime, whose 'vision was of society as a closely regimented military camp', see Anderson and Tollison (1984).

Chapter 20 Adam Smith and *The Wealth of Nations*

1 The chapter on Smith in my book of 1978 was first written as a bicentenary lecture. I do not want to alter the general emphasis of the judgements it contains. As a result, however, of having devoted much of a decade to the study of Smith's predecessors, I feel that a certain shift in the general balance is desirable.

2 See Lapidus (1986, 60ff).

3 For comprehensive accounts of *The Wealth of Nations*, see the general introduction by R. H. Campbell and A. S. Skinner to Smith (1976a); also Blaug (1985, chapter 2), Hollander (1973), O'Brien (1975) and Schumpeter (1954, 181–94).

4 Many writers have recognized that Smith was primarily a social philosopher. For example, James Bonar: 'Adam Smith undoubtedly started with the purpose of giving to the world a complete social philosophy' (1922, 149); A. L. Macfie: 'He himself would not have regarded his work as primarily economic. For him it was broadly social, fitting into that title the political as well as the psychological and ethical aspects of individuals living in societies' (1967, 13–16); Glen Morrow on *The Wealth of Nations*: 'This an economic work? It is far more than that; it is a history and criticism of all European civilisation . . . a philosophical work' (1928, 157). As J. R. Lindgren has insisted: 'All who are familiar with Smith's life and writings recognize that he was a philosopher by profession and that all his writings were conceived and executed as works of philosophy' (1973, ix).

5 See Smith's letter to the Duc de la Rochefoucauld (1895), and both the preliminary advertisement and the closing paragraph of *The Theory of Moral Sentiments* (1976b).

6 See Duncan Forbes (1954, 643–70). Though, as T. D. Campbell has observed (1971, 80n.), the theme of progress is not so prominent in *The Theory of Moral Sentiments*, it is present there to a significant extent.

7 Political Economy Club (1876, 32). Thorold Rogers' successors as economic historians have also laid methodological claim to *The Wealth of Natons*. George Unwin: 'Adam Smith was the first great economic historian, and I do not scruple to add that he is still the greatest. There is scarcely a page of *The Wealth of Nations* where history and theory are sundered from each other' (1908). According to R. H. Tawney (1932, 39 and 91): 'It is a truism that the central theme of *The Wealth of Nations* is historical.' In his bicentennial tribute H. M. Robertson suggested that 'the reader himself has to be something of an economic historian fully to appreciate *The Wealth of Nations*, whilst *other economists, who are without a true historical bent, somehow truncate it in their own minds*' (1976, 383, italics added).

8 See H. J. Bitterman (1940, 504): 'Smith's work is not deductive in the sense that could be applied to, say, the major works of Ricardo and Senior. The bulk of Smith's text consists of descriptive, historical, and statistical data, with a few inferences from "conjectural history".' On the other hand the views of a distinguished dissenter should be recorded: 'Smith's frame of mind was on the whole essentially unhistorical . . . historical narration and inductive reasoning were with him subordinate to a deductive movement of thought' (Ashley, 1900, 310). The answer to Ashley is twofold: (a) whether 'subordinate' or not, the input of historical narration and inductive reasoning is incomparably larger and more important than in any other comprehensive treatment of economic principles by a classical economist; and (b) Smith himself maintained: 'The

general maxims of morality are formed, like all other maxims, from experience and induction' '... by induction from experience, we establish those general rules' (*Theory of Moral Sentiments*, 1976b, 319).

9 On 'the man of system', see *Theory of Moral Sentiments* (1976b, 233):

> The man of system ... is apt to be very wise in his own conceit; and is often so enamoured with the supposed beauty of his own ideal plan of government, that he cannot suffer the smallest deviation from any part of it. He goes on to establish it completely and in all its parts, without any regard either to the great interests, or to the strong prejudices which may oppose it.

10 Smith's readiness to use different methods was not accompanied by any pretentious professional over-confidence regarding results. On the question of quantitative methods, Schumpeter castigated Smith for remarking that he placed 'no great faith in political arithmetic', or in the exactness of its computations: 'It was the inspiring message, the suggestive programme which wilted in the wooden hands of the Scottish professor ... A. Smith took the safe side' (1954, 212). After the considerable over-confidence of 'the quantitative revolution' to be brought about by the methods of econometrics, which took place after Schumpeter was writing, with such marvellous results for economic policies, it may be possible to discern more intellectual merit in the sobering attitude of someone who was ready 'to take the safe side'. Without, however, placing great faith in their estimates, Smith made considerable use of the work of Gregory King and Fleetwood (see 1976a, 534; and chapter 4 in this volume).

On the other hand, unlike Petty and the quantitative writers of the seventeenth century, and unlike Cantillon, Adam Smith, with his lavish use of the ambiguous adjective 'natural', did not assist the recognition of the vital distinction between the moral and the technical, or between normative and positive.

11 On the methodological revolution of James Mill, Ricardo and Senior, see chapter 2 of Hutchison (1978).

12 See Viner's essay on 'Adam Smith and *Laissez-Faire*' (1928, 116ff).

13 Smith returned to the comparison with the laws of Solon in *The Wealth of Nations* on the vital controversial questions of the corn laws and the prohibition of wheat exports, when the price had risen to a certain level. Again there is some contrast with the views of Quesnay: 'With all its imperfections ... we may perhaps say that [this law] though not the best in itself, it is the best which the interests, prejudices and temper of the times would admit of' (1976a, 543). As the editors note regarding this passage, Smith had observed:

> Some general, and even systematical, idea of the perfection of policy and law, may no doubt be necessary for directing the views of the statesman. But to insist upon establishing, and upon establishing all at once, and in spite of all opposition, every thing which that idea may seem to require, must often be the highest degree of arrogance. It is to erect his own judgment into the supreme standard of right and wrong. (*Theory of Moral Sentiments*, 1976b, 234)

14 Smith did not employ the concept of *perfect* competition (see Richardson, 1976, 350–60). Smith explicitly took account of the pervasiveness of ignorance, for example with regard to the prime motivator: 'Profit is so very fluctuating, that the person who carries on a particular trade cannot always tell you what is the average of his annual profit' (1976a, 105).

15 'Smith may be understood as a writer who advocated capitalism for the sake of freedom, civil and ecclesiastical' (Cropsey, 1957, 95).

16 The point about Smith is well put by D. A. Reisman:

> On the one hand, he *appears* to have been a commodity-utilitarian concerned with free trade, economic growth, the ending of restrictive practices and other ways of providing 'a plentiful revenue or subsistence for the people'; while on the other hand, he seems to have been determined to prove that higher material standards of living do not, except for the poor, represent a significant change in human happiness. (1976, 102)

As Reisman shows, there is no contradiction here.

17
> The difference of natural talents in different men is, in reality, much less than we are aware of; and the very different genius which appears to distinguish men of different professions, when grown up to maturity, is not upon many occasions so much the cause, as the effect of the division of labour. The difference between the most dissimilar characters, between a philosopher and a common street porter, for example, seems to arise not so much from nature, as from habit, custom, and education. (1976a, 28)

Other writers, such as Tucker and Franklin make differencs of natural talents a main reason for specialization and the division of labour.

18 As Odd Langholm has observed (1979, 144):

> The success of the value theory which was to be developed in the line extending from Montanari through Galiani to the Italian and French economists of the eighteenth centuries is in no small part explained by its emphasis on utility as a psychological experience, playing down considerations of the properties in goods which cause men to desire them, a preoccupation which is sure to take theorists away from the main point.

Langholm remarks that the main medieval source of value theory in Italy was based on Buridan's version of the concept of *indigentia*, which comprised 'every desire which moves us to set store by things'.

19 See Dmitriev (1902, 182), quoted in chapter 15.

20 According to R. L. Meek in his history of the subject, 'the most advanced statement of the labour theory of value prior to the publication of *The Wealth of Nations*' (1973, 42) appeared in the anonymous pamphlet by William Pulteney, *Some Thoughts on the Interest of Money in General, and Particularly in the Public Funds. With Reasons for Fixing the same at a lower rate* ... (1738). Pulteney's statement of the labour theory does not seem to go very significantly further than the *obiter dicta* of Petty, to whom, probably, Pulteney was indebted. William Pulteney, Earl of Bath (1684–1764), an aristocratic Whig politician, was a fluent, prolific, and versatile pamphleteer. His writings on political economy were mainly concerned with problems of the national debt. See the reprint of Pulteney's pamphlet introduced by P. D. Groenewegen (1982). Another eighteenth-century pamphleteer who mentioned the labour theory of value was W. Temple, in his *A Vindication of Commerce and the Arts* (1758). We have mentioned in chapter 8 Benjamin Franklin's brief statement, which followed Petty very closely.

21 The alleged schism between two main lines of thought on value and price is the theme of Baranzini and Scazzieri (1986). Such a schism could hardly have been claimed to exist before *The Wealth of Nations*. According to R. L. Meek: 'It cannot be too strongly emphasised that any approach to the problem of the determination of value from the side of utility and demand (as opposed to that of cost and supply) would have been regarded by him [Smith] as quite alien to the general outlook of *The Wealth of Nations*' (1973, 73). From a non-Marxian point of view M. L. Myers claims that Smith 'will never let go of a labour theory of value' (1983, 117).

22 Though they make their point in rather categorical black-and-white terms, one can understand the conclusions of Schumpeter and De Roover. According to Schumpeter, Smith was 'far below' Galiani on the subject of value and price

(1954, 188); while De Roover, the distinguished authority on scholastic economics, concluded: 'The Doctors, especially the members of the school of Salamanca, made one of their main contributions in developing a theory of value, based on utility and scarcity, which is more in line with modern thinking than that of Adam Smith' (1955, 186).

23 See Hutchison (1953b, 52ff; and 1958, 393ff).

24 There have been two forms of the doctrine that 'money doesn't matter': that of modern Keynesian opponents of the quantity theory, and that of Smithian-classical anti-mercantilists. On the latter, see Eagly (1974), who describes the doctrine 'the underlying theme of classical monetary economics'. Eagly also contrasts the monetary analysis of Hume with that of Smith, and maintains that 'Hume's analysis is not that of classical economics', but is 'worked out in an essentially mercantilist theoretical framework' (71).

25 In an earlier paper (of 1929) Schumpeter complained that 'the arguments of the classicals were much too inadequate to be reliable . . . they overshot the target and arrived at propositions which, in their full generality, were hardly more correct than the errors they were opposing' (1985, 229).

Chapter 21 Postscript

1 On the classical version of the history of economic thought, see Hutchison (1978, 217ff).

2 It should be recognized that McCulloch made a number of important contributions to the serious study of the history of economic thought. He continued, however, to republish the version propagated in his *Discourse* (1824) for many decades.

3 Regarding the treatment by J. Mill, Ricardo, and McCulloch of the historical dimension and approach to political economy, see Coleman (1987, 20–8).

4 Also writing at the turn of the century, A. Dubois remarked regarding the analysis of value of Galiani, Turgot and Condillac: 'The radiant glory of Adam Smith and his pleiad of disciples rejected their advances, consigning them to the shadows of oblivion, although their own notion of value constituted not progress but regress. Today [1897] it is abandoned and the doctrine currently triumphant is the psychological theory put forward by Galiani, Turgot and Condillac' (1897, 864).

5 It is not quite clear what thinkers J. S. Mill was referring to in making his remarkable claim that not only political economy but 'the philosophy of society' had 'advanced many steps beyond the point at which he [i.e. Adam Smith] left it' (1848 [1909], xxviii). Presumably Mill had Bentham and Comte in mind. One may, however, beg leave to doubt whether the political element in Mill's political economy should be considered 'many steps' in advance of the political element in *The Wealth of Nations*, and not rather quite a few steps in arrears, not only of Smith's politics, but of those of Mandeville, Hume and Galiani. We are, of course, concerned here with positive, political analysis and discernment, rather than with political valuations or normative attitudes.

6 In a recent discerning judgement, Professor Milton Friedman has stated:

> Keynes's heritage was twofold – to technical economics and to politics. I have no doubt that Keynes's bequest to technical economics was extremely beneficial, and that historians of economic thought will continue to regard him as one of the greatest economists of all time, in the direct line of succession to his famous British predecessors, Adam Smith, David Ricardo, J. S. Mill, Alfred Marshall, and W. Stanley Jevons.

> The situation is very different with respect to Keynes's bequest to politics, *which has had far more influence on the shape of the world today than his bequest to technical economics*. In particular, it has contributed substantially to the proliferation of overgrown governments, increasingly concerned with every aspect of the daily lives of their citizens. (1986, 47, italics added)

Let us note first how, at least in this case, the influence of one of the great exponents of political economy is held to have been *far* greater through his politics than his technical economics. It is interesting to compare Adam Smith with Keynes in terms of Friedman's contrast. Perhaps the judgement might be ventured that both the supreme influence and – in contrast with the case of Keynes – the supreme *quality* of Adam Smith's contribution is owing, to a very large extent, to its *politics* – together with its historical and social-psychological component. On the other hand, in spite of many important contributions to technical economics, there are one or two highly original and fundamental points, on which Smith's contributions to economic theory – in particular, regarding utility and money – may be seriously questioned, when they are compared with the contributions on those subjects of his contemporaries and immediate predecessors.

7 It is vital, of course, to distinguish a valid orthodoxy, or consensus, and the way this has been established, from an orthodoxy which is scientifically invalid, or brought about by invalid means, such as selective hiring and firing of researchers, or political pressures or censorship. Regarding precise questions – which might be described as 'scientific questions' – to which only one correct answer can be given, *at least* (n−1), out of *n* answers currently put forward, *must* be false, and it is presumably a prime aim of scientific endeavour to eliminate by testing as many as possible of the candidates. Since, however, as is well known, adequate testing which would justify the elimination of an answer, is often practically impossible to achieve, the discipline of withholding judgement ought to be practised on a much more massive scale than seems acceptable to many economists. Moreover, the leading orthodoxies in the history of economic thought have embraced not only 'single-answer' questions, but questions to which a number of answers might be valid, however thorough and decisive the available testing procedures might be.

References and Literature

Primary sources are listed under 'I' and secondary sources under 'II'.

1 The Period and its Starting-point

I

Boisguilbert, P. de: 1966: *Boisguilbert ou la naissance de l'économie politique*, INED.
Cantillon, R.: 1931: *Essay on the Nature of Commerce in General*, ed. H. Higgs.
——: 1952: *Essai sur la nature du commerce en générale*, INED.
Hume, D.: 1955: *Economic Writings*, ed. E. Rotwein.
Mandeville, B.: 1924: *The Fable of the Bees*, ed. F. B. Kaye, 2 vols.
Marx, K.: 1951: *Theories of Surplus Value*, trans. G. A. Bonner and E. Burns.
Petty, W.: 1899: *Economic Writings*, ed. C. H. Hull, 2 vols.
Quesnay, F.: 1958: *François Quesnay et la Physiocratie*, INED, 2 vols.
Steuart, J.: 1967: *The Principles of Political Economy*, ed. A. S. Skinner, 2 vols.

II

Ashton, T.S.: 1955: *The Eighteenth Century*.
Blaug, M.: 1985: *Economic Theory in Retrospect*, 4th ed.
Bliss, C.: 1986: 'Progress and Anti-Progress in Economic Science', in *Foundations of Economics*, eds M. Baranzini and R. Scazzieri.
Bowley, M.: 1973: *Studies in the History of Economic Theory before 1870.*
Heckscher, E.: 1955: *Mercantilism*, 2nd ed., 2 vols.
Hutchison, T. W.: 1985: 'On the Interpretation and Misinterpretation of Economists', in *Gli Economisti e la politica economia*, ed. P. Roggi, 323ff.
Johnson, E. A. J.: 1937: *Predecessors of Adam Smith*.
Letwin, W.: 1963: *The Origins of Economic Science*.
Mill, J. S. : 1844: *Essays on Some Unsettled Questions in Political Economy*.
Peach, T.: 1986: 'David Ricardo's Treatment of Wages', in *Ideas in Economics*, ed. R. D. C. Black, 104ff.
Roscher, W.: 1851: *Zur Geschichte der englischen Volkswirtschaftslehre im sechzehnten und siebzehnten Jahrhundert*.
Say, J. B.: 1841: *Traité d'économie politique*, 6th ed.
Schumpeter, J. A.: 1954: *History of Economic Analysis*.
Sewall, H.: 1901: *Theories of Value before Adam Smith*.

Spiegel, H. W.: 1983: *The Growth of Economic Thought*, 2nd edn.
Vickers, D.: 1959: *Studies in the Theory of Money, 1690–1776.*
Viner, J.: 1937: *Studies in the Theory of International Trade.*

2 The Century before Petty: Some Outstanding Writings

I

Bodin, J.: 1576: *Les six livres de la république*, parts translated in A. E. Monroe (1924).
Botero, G.: 1588: *A Treatise concerning the Causes of the Magnificence and Greatness of Cities*, trans. R. Peterson, ed. D. Waley, 1956.
Copernicus, N.: 1526: *Monetae cudendae ratio*, French translation in L. Wolowski (1864).
Covarruvias, D.: *c.*1550: *Variarum resolutionum* etc., parts translated in M. Grice-Hutchinson (1952).
Culpeper, T.: 1621: *A Tract against Usury* (republished by his son, 1668).
Davanzati, B.: 1588: *Discourse upon Coins*, trans. John Toland, 1696.
De La Calle, L. S.: 1544: *Instrucción de mercarderes ...* part trans. in M. Grice-Hutchinson (1952).
Grotius, H.: 1625: *De jure belli et pacis*, trans. F. W. Kelsey, 1925.
Hobbes, T.: 1642: *De Cive*, ed. H. Warrender, 1983.
——: 1651: *Leviathan*, Everyman ed., 1914.
Lee, J.: 1656: *A Vindication of Regulated Enclosure.*
Malynes, G. de: 1601: *A Treatise of the Canker of England's Commonwealth.*
——: 1603: *England's View in the Unmasking of Two Paradoxes.*
——: 1622: *The Maintenance of Free Trade.*
Misselden, E.: 1622: *Free Trade, or the Means to Make Trade Flourish.*
——: 1623: *The Circle of Commerce or the Balance of Trade.*
Montchrétien, A. de: 1615: *Traité de l'économie politique.*
Mun, T.: 1621: *A Discourse of Trade from England unto the East–Indies.*
——: 162?: *England's Treasure by Foreign Trade*, ed. by his son, 1664.
Navarro, M. de A.: 1556: *Commentario resolutorio de usuras*, trans. in M. Grice-Hutchinson (1952).
Serra, A.: 1613: *A Brief Treatise on the Causes which can make Gold and Silver Plentiful where there are No Mines*, trans. in A. E. Monroe (1924).
[Smith, T.]: 1581: *A Discourse of the Commonweal of this Realm of England*, ed. M. Dewar, 1969.
Vaughn, R.: 162?: *A Discourse of Coin and Coinage.*

II

Appleby, J.: 1978: *Economic Thought and Ideology in Seventeenth-Century England.*
Chalk, A. F.: 1951: 'Natural Law and the Rise of Economic Individualism in England', *Journal of Political Economy*, **59**, 332ff.
Grice-Hutchinson, M.: 1952: *The School of Salamanca: Readings in Spanish Monetary Theory, 1544–1605.*
——: 1978: *Early Economic Thought in Spain.*
Langholm, O.: 1979: *Price and Value in the Aristotelian Tradition.*
Monroe, A.E.: 1924: *Early Economic Thought.*
Roover, R. de: 1955: 'Scholastic Economics: Survival and Lasting Influence'. *Quarterly Journal of Economics*, **69**, 161ff.
Supple, B. E.: 1959: *Commercial Crisis and Change in England, 1600–1642..*

Schumpeter, J. A.: 1954: *History of Economic Analysis.*
Wolowski, L.: 1864: *Traité de la première invention des monnaies.*

3 Petty on Policy, Theory and Method

I

Petty, W.: 1662 et seq.: *Economic Writings*, ed. C. H. Hull, 2 vols, 1899.
——: 1927: *The Petty Papers*, ed. H. Lansdowne.

II

Aubrey, J.: 1669–96: *Brief Lives*, ed. R. Barber, 1982.
Endres, A. M.: 1985: 'The Functions of Numerical Data in the Writings of Graunt, Petty and Davenant'. *History of Political Economy*, **17** (2), 245ff.
Fitzmaurice, E.: 1895: *The Life of Sir William Petty.*
Furniss, E. S.: 1920: *The Position of the Labourer in a System of Nationalism.*
Hull, C. H.: 1900: 'Petty's Place in the History of Economic Theory'. *Quarterly Journal of Economics*, **14**, 307ff.
Letwin, W. L.: 1963: *The Origins of Economic Science.*
Marx, K.: 1951: *Theories of Surplus Value*, trans. G. A. Bonner and E. Burns.
Matsukawa, S.: 1977: 'Sir William Petty, an Unpublished Manuscript'. *Hitotsubashi Journal of Economics*, **17** (2), 33ff.
Roncaglia, A.: 1985: *Petty: the Origins of Political Economy.*
Schumpeter, J.A.: 1954: *History of Economic Analysis.*
Sewall, H.: 1901: *The Theory of Value before Adam Smith.*
Strauss, E.: 1954: *Sir William Petty: Portrait of a Genius.*

4 English Pioneers of Social and Economic Statistics

I

Cantillon, R.: n.d.: *Essai sur la nature du commerce*, ed. H. Higgs, 1931.
Davenant, C.: 1695–6: *Two Manuscripts*, ed. A. P. Usher, 1942.
——: 1771: *The Political and Commercial Works*, ed. C. Whitworth, 5 vols.
Derham, W.: 1713: *Physico-Theology.*
Fleetwood, W.: 1707: *Chronicon Preciosum.*
Graunt, J.: 1662: *Natural and Political Observations made upon the Bills of Mortality*, ed. W. F. Willcox, reprinted 1939.
Halley, E.: 1693: *Two Papers on the Degrees of Mortality of Mankind*, ed. L. J. Reed, 1942.
Jevons, W. S.: 1871: *The Theory of Political Economy.*
King, G.: 1936: *Two Tracts*, ed. G. E. Barnett.
Petty, W.: 1899: *Economic Writings*, ed. C. H. Hull, 2 vols, 1899.
Süssmilch, J. P.: 1741–2: *Die Göttliche Ordnung.*

II

Ashley, W. J.: 1900: 'The Tory Origins of Free Trade Policy', in *Surveys, Historic and Economic*, 268ff.
Aubrey, J.: 1669–96: *Brief Lives*, ed. R. Barber, 1982.
Benjamin, B.: 1968: 'John Graunt', in *International Encyclopedia of the Social Sciences*, vol. 6, 253.

Cantillon, R.: n.d.: *Essay on the Nature of Commerce in General*, ed. H. Higgs, 1931.
Creedy, J.: 1986: 'On the King–Davenant Law of Demand'. *Scottish Journal of Political Economy*, **33** (3), 193ff.
Deane, P.: 1968: 'Gregory King' in *International Encyclopedia of the Social Sciences*, vol. 8, 385.
Endres, A. M.: 1985: 'The Functions of Numerical Data in the Writings of Graunt, Petty and Davenant'. *History of Political Economy*, **17** (2), 245ff.
Evans, G. H.: 1967: 'The Law of Demand: the Roles of Gregory King and Charles Davenant'. *Quarterly Journal of Economics*, **81**, 483ff.
Fitzmaurice, E.: 1895: *The Life of Sir W. Petty*.
Holmes, G.: 1986: *Politics, Religion and Society in England, 1679–1742*.
Keynes, J. M.: 1930: *Treatise on Money*, 2 vols.
Myers, M. L.: 1983: *The Soul of Modern Economic Man*.
Petty, W.: 1927: *The Petty Papers*, ed. H. Lansdowne.
Schumpeter, J. A.: 1954: *History of Economic Analysis*.
Smith, A.: 1776: *The Wealth of Nations*, ed. R. H. Campbell, A. S. Skinner and W. B. Todd, 2 vols, 1976.
Strauss, E.: 1954: *Sir William Petty: Portrait of a Genius*.
Sutherland, I.: 1963: 'John Graunt, a Tercentenary Tribute'. *Journal of the Royal Statistical Society*, **A126**, 537ff.
Thomas, P. J.: 1926: *Mercantilism and the East India Trade*.
Viner, J.: 1937: *Studies in the Theory of International Trade*.
Waddell, D. A. G.: 1958: 'Charles Davenant (1658–1714) – a Biographical Sketch'. *Economic History Review*, 2nd series, **11**, 279ff.
Willey, B.: 1940: *The Eighteenth Century Background*.

5 John Locke and the 1690s

I

Anon.: 1677: *England's Great Happiness*, in *A Select Collection of Early English Tracts on Commerce*, ed. J. R. McCulloch, 1856, reprinted 1952.
Barbon, N.: 1685: *An Apology for the Builder*.
——: 1690: *Discourse of Trade*, reprinted 1934.
——: 1696: *Discourse concerning Coining the New Money Lighter*.
Child, J.: 1668: *Brief Observations concerning Trade and Interest of Money*, reprinted in Letwin (1959).
——: 1693: *A New Discourse of Trade*.
Culpeper, T.: 1621: *A Tract against Usury*.
Locke, J.: 1812: *The Works of John Locke*, 11th ed., 10 vols, vol. V.
——: 1954: *Essays on the Law of Nature*, ed. W. van Leyden.
Lowndes, W.: 1695: *Essay for the Amendment of the Silver Coin*.
Martyn, H.: 1701: *Considerations on the East-India Trade*, in *A Select Collection of Early English Tracts on Commerce*, ed. J. R. McCulloch, 1856, reprinted 1952.
North, D.: 1691: *Discourses upon Trade*, ed. J. H. Hollander, 1907.
Temple, W.: 1672: *Observations upon the United Provinces*.

II

Appleby, J.: 1978: *Economic Thought and Ideology in Seventeenth-Century England*.
Ashley, W. J.: 1900: 'The Tory Origins of Free Trade Policy', in *Surveys, Historic and Economic*, 268ff.

Bowley, M.: 1973: *Studies in the History of Economic Theory before 1870.*
Cranston, M.: 1957: *John Locke, a Biography.*
Dunn, J.: 1969: *The Political Thought of John Locke.*
Feavyearyear, A. E.: 1963: *The Pound Sterling*, 2nd ed.
Fox-Bourne, H. R.: 1876: *The Life of John Locke.*
Grampp, W. D.: 1965: *Economic Liberalism*, 2 vols.
Hayek, F. A.: 1949: *Individualism and Economic Order.*
——: 1969: *The Counter-revolution of Science*, 2nd ed.
Heckscher, E.: 1955: *Mercantilism*, 2 vols.
Keynes, J. M.: 1936: *The General Theory of Employment, Interest and Money.*
Leigh, A. H.: 1974: 'John Locke and the Quantity Theory of Money'. *History of Political Economy*, **6**, 200ff.
Letwin, W. L.: 1963: *The Origins of Economic Science.*
MacLeod, C.: 1983: 'Henry Martin and the Authorship of the Considerations upon the East India Trade'. *Bulletin of the Institute of Historical Research*, **56**, 134, 222ff.
Marx, K.: 1951: *Theories of Surplus Value*, trans. G. A. Bonner and E. Burns.
Raffel, F.: 1905: *Englische Freihändler vor Adam Smith.*
Schumpeter, J. A.: 1954: *History of Economic Analysis.*
Thomas, P. J.: 1926: *Mercantilism and the East India Trade.*
Vaughn, K.: 1980: *John Locke, Economist and Social Scientist.*
Vickers, D.: 1959: *Studies in the Theory of Money, 1690–1776.*
Viner, J.: 1937: *Studies in the Theory of International Trade.*
Winch, D.: 1978: *Adam Smith's Politics.*

6 Continental Alternatives: Colbertism and Cameralism: Natural Law and Moral Philosophy

I

Becher, J.J.: 1668: *Politische Discours von den eigentlichen Ursachen des Auf- und Abnehmens der Städte, Länder und Republiken* (reprinted 1972).
Colbert, J. B.: 1859–82: *Lettres, Instructions et Memoires*, ed. P. Clement, 7 vols.
Domat, J.: 1689: *Lois civiles dans leur ordre naturel*, trans. W. Strahan, 1722.
Hörnigk, P. von: 1684: *Oesterreich über alles, wenn es nur will*, trans. in Monroe (1924).
Nicole, P.: 1671 and 1675: *Essais morales*, vols I and III, 1715 ed.
Pufendorf, S.: 1660: *Elementorum jurisprudentiae universalis*, trans. W. A. Oldfather, 1931.
——: 1672: *De jure naturae et civis*, trans. C. H. and W. A. Oldfather, 1934.
——: 1675: *De officio hominis et civis*, trans. F. G. Moore, 1927.
Schröder (*or* Schrötter), W. von: 1686: *Fürstliche Schatz- und Rent-Kammer*, 1737 ed.
Smith, A.: 1776: *The Wealth of Nations*, eds R. H. Campbell, A. S. Skinner and W. B. Todd, 2 vols, 1976.

II

Bonar, J.: 1922: *Philosophy and Political Economy.*
Clapham, J. H.: 1940: 'Review of *Colbert and French Mercantilism*, by C. W. Cole'. *Economic History Review*, **10**, 389ff.
Cole, C. W.: 1939: *Colbert and French Mercantilism*, 2 vols, reprinted 1964.
Faccarello, G.: 1983a: 'L'equilibre économique chez Pierre de Boisguilbert'. *Oeconomia*, *1*, 35ff.

——: 1983b: *Information, anticipations et équilibre macroéconomique chez P. de Boisguilbert* (typescript).
——: 1986: *Aux origines de l'économie politique libérale: Pierre de Boisguilbert.*
Gerstenberg, H.: 1930: 'Philipp von Hörnigk', *Jahrbücher für Nationalökonomie und Statistik*, **78**, 813ff.
Hamilton, E. J.: 1969: 'The Political Economy of France at the Time of John Law'. *History of Political Economy*, **1**, 123ff.
Hasbach, W.: 1891: *Untersuchungen über Adam Smith.*
Hassinger, H.: 1951: *Johann Joachim Becher.*
Heckscher, E.: 1955: *Mercantilism*, 2nd ed.
Horne, T. A. : 1978: *The Social Thought of Bernard de Mandeville.*
James, E. D.: 1972: *Pierre Nicole, Jansenist and Humanist.*
Kauder, E.: 1924: 'Johann Joachim Becher als Wirtschafts- und Sozialpolitiker'. *Schmollers Jahrbuch*, **4**, 811f.
Keohane, N. O.: 1980: *Philosophy and the State in France: the Renaissance to the Enlightenment.*
Keynes, J. M.: 1936: *The General Theory of Employment, Interest and Money.*
Langholm, O.: *Price and Value in the Aristotelian Tradition.*
Monroe, A. E.: 1924: *Early Economic Thought.*
Pascal, B.: 1670: *Pensées*, trans. W. F. Trotter, Everyman ed., 1931.
Roscher, W.: 1874: *Geschichte der Nationalökonomik in Deutschland.*
Rothkrug, L.: 1965: *Opposition to Louis XIV: the Political and Social Origin of the French Enlightenment.*
Saether, A.: 1984: 'Ludvig Holberg: the First Dano-Norwegian Economist' in *Proceedings of the Conference of American History of Economic Thought Society, Pittsburgh.*
Schumpeter, J. A.: 1954: *History of Economic Analysis.*
Small, A. W.: 1909: *The Cameralists.*
Sommer, L.: 1920–5: *Die Oesterreichischen Kameralisten*, 2 vols.
Tribe, K.: 1984: 'Cameralism and the Science of Government'. *Journal of Modern History*, **56**, 263ff.
Viner, J.: 1953: Introduction to *A Letter to Dion*, by B. Mandeville, in *The Long View and the Short*, 1958, 332ff.
——: 1978: 'Religious Thought and Economic Society'. *History of Political Economy*, **10**, 1ff.

Chapter 7 Economic Harmonies, Equilibriating Tendencies and Freedom of Trade

I

Boisguilbert, P. de: 1695–1707: *Boisguilbert ou la naissance de l'économie politique* (collected works), 2 vols, ed. J. Hecht and A. Sauvy, 1966.
——: 1695: *Le Détail de la France.*
——: 1704: *Traité de la nature, culture, commerce et intérêt des grains.*
——: 1705: *Memoire sur l'assiette de la taille.*
——: 1707a: *Factum de la France*, vol. 1.
——: 1707b: *Dissertation de la nature des richesses.*
——: 1725: *The Life of Mary Stewart, Queen of Scotland and of France*, trans. James Freebairn (from original French ed. 1674).
Gervaise, I.: 1720: *The System or Theory of the Trade of the World*, ed. J. M. Letiche, foreword by J. Viner, 1954.
Decker, M.: 1743: *Serious Considerations on the Several High Duties, etc.*

Decker, M.: 1744: *An Essay on the Causes of the Decline of Foreign Trade.*
Mandeville, B. de: 1714–29: *The Fable of the Bees*, ed. F. B. Kaye, 1924.
——: 1714: *The Fable of the Bees*, ed. P. Harth, 1970.
——: 1720: *Free Thoughts on Religion.*
——: 1732: *A Letter to Dion*, introduction by J. Viner.
Pinto, I. de: 1773: *Traité de la circulation et du crédit.*
Rochefoucauld, F. de la: 1665: *Maximes.*
Souligné, D.: 1697: *The Desolation of France Unmasked.*
Vanderlint, J.: 1734: *Money Answers All Things.*
Vauban, S.: 1707: *Projet d'une Dîme royale.*

II

Boswell, J.: 1791: *Life of Samuel Johnson*, Everyman ed., 2 vols, 1906.
Dumont, L.: 1977: *From Mandeville to Marx.*
Faccarello, G.: 1983a: 'L'équilibre économique chez P. de Boisguilbert'. *Oeconomia*, **1**, 35ff.
——: 1983b: *Information, anticipations et équilibre économique chez P. de Boisguilbert.*
——: 1986: *Aux origines de l'économie politique libérale: Pierre de Boisguilbert.*
Grampp, W. D.: 1965: *Economic Liberalism.* 2 vols.
Hamilton, E. J.: 1969: 'The Political Economy of France at the Time of John Law'. *History of Political Economy*, **1**, *123ff.*
Hayek, F. A.: 1978: 'Dr Bernard de Mandeville', in *New Studies in Philosophy, Politics, Economics and the History of Ideas.*
Heckscher, E.: 1955: *Mercantilism*, revised ed., 2 vols.
Horne, T. A.: 1978: *The Social Thought of Bernard de Mandeville.*
Keynes, J. M.: 1936: *General Theory of Employment, Interest and Money.*
Landreth, H.: 1975: 'The Economic Thought of Bernard de Mandeville'. *History of Political Economy*, **7**, 193ff.
Letiche, J. M.: 1952: 'Isaac Gervaise on the International Mechanism of Adjustment'. *Journal of Political Economy*, **60**, 34ff.
McDonald, S. L.: 1954: 'Boisguilbert, a Neglected Precursor of Aggregate Demand Theorists'. *Quarterly Journal of Economics*, **68**, 407ff.
Marx, K.: 1859: *A Contribution to the Critique of Political Economy*, ed. M. H. Dobb, 1969.
——: 1867: *Capital*, vol. I, Moscow ed., n.d.
——: n.d.: *Theories of Surplus Value*, translated by E. Burns, Moscow ed., 3 vols.
Meek, R. L.: 1962: *The Economics of Physiocracy.*
Morize, A.: 1909: *L'Apologie du luxe au XVIIIe siècle.*
Murphy, A.: 1986: *Richard Cantillon, Entrepreneur and Economist.*
Raffel, F.: 1905: *Englische Freihändler vor Adam Smith.*
Roberts, H. v. D.: 1935: *Boisguilbert, Economist of the Reign of Louis XIV.*
Rosenberg, N.: 1963: 'Mandeville and Laissez Faire'. *Journal of the History of Ideas*, **24**, 183ff.
Schatz, A. and Caillemer, R.: 1906: 'Le mercantilisme liberal à la fin du XVIIe siècle'. *Revue d'économie politique*, **20**, 29ff., 387ff., 559ff., 630ff., and 791ff.
Schumpeter, J. A.: 1954: *History of Economic Analysis.*
Stephen, L.: 1876: *History of English Thought in the Eighteenth Century*, 2 vols.
Vickers, D.: 1959: *Studies in the Theory of Money, 1690–1776.*
Viner, J.: 1937: *Studies in the Theory of International Trade.*
——: 1953: Introduction to *A Letter to Dion*, by B. de Mandeville, reprinted in *The Long View and the Short*, 1958, 332ff.

Chapter 8: Paper Money, Employment and the Increase of Wealth

I

Berkeley, G.: 1733: *Alciphron, or the Minute Philosopher.*
——: 1735–7: *The Querist*, 3 vols, ed. J. H. Hollander, 1910.
——: 1910: *Works*, ed. A. C. Fraser, 4 vols.
——: 1948–57: *Works*, ed. A. Luce and T. E. Jessop, vol. IV, 1951, and vol. VI, 1953.
Franklin, B.: 1844: *The Works of B. Franklin*, ed. J. Sparks, vol. II.
——: 1964: *Papers*, vol. 7, ed. L. W. Labaree.
——: 1972: *Papers*; vol. 16, ed. W. B. Willcox.
Law, J.: 1705: *Money and Trade Considered*, reprinted in *Œuvres de John Law*, 3 vols, ed. P. Harsin, 1931, vol. 1.
Petty, W.: 1662 et seq.: *The Economic Writings of Sir William Petty*, 2 vols, ed. C. H. Hull, 1899.
Smith, A.: 1776: *The Wealth of Nations*, ed. R. H. Campbell, A. S. Skinner and W. B. Todd, 2 vols, 1976.

II

Ashton, T. S.: 1959: *Economic Fluctuations in England, 1700–1800.*
Dewey, D. R.: 1900: 'Franklin, B.', in *Dictionary of Political Economy*, ed. R. H. I. Palgrave.
Furniss, E. S.: 1920: *The Position of the Laborer in a System of Nationalism.*
Hayek, F. A.: 1966: *Dr Bernard Mandeville.*
——: 1978: *New Studies in Philosophy, Politics, Economics and the History of Ideas.*
Heckscher, E.: 1955: *Mercantilism*, 2 vols, 2nd ed.
Hildebrand, R.: 1863: 'Benjamin Franklin als Nationalökonom'. *Jahrbücher für Nationalökonomie und Statistik*, **1**, 577ff and 643ff.
Hutchison, T. W.: 1953: 'Berkeley's *Querist* and its Place in the Economic Thought of the Eighteenth Century'. *British Journal for the Philosophy of Science*, **4**, 13 and 52ff.
——: 1960: 'George Berkeley as an Economist, a Comment'. *Journal of Political Economy*, **68**, 302ff.
——: 1978: *On Revolutions and Progress in Economic Knowledge.*
Hyde, H. M.: 1948: *John Law, the History of an Honest Adventurer.*
Iremonger, F. A.: 1948: *Life of William Temple.*
Johnston, J.: 1939: 'Commercial Restriction and Monetary Deflation in Eighteenth-Century Ireland'. *Hermathena*, **53**, 79ff.
Leyburn, E. D.: 1937: 'Bishop Berkeley: *The Querist*'. *Proceedings of the Royal Irish Academy*, Dec. 1937.
Marx, K.: 1859: *A Contribution to the Critique of Political Economy*, ed. M. H. Dobb, 1969.
Menger, C.: 1871: *Grundsätze der Volkswirtschaftslehre.*
Nicholson, J. S.: 1893: 'John Law of Lauriston', in *Essays on Monetary Problems*, 2nd ed., 109ff.
Schumpeter, J. A.: 1954: *History of Economic Analysis.*
Ward, I. D. S: 1959 and 1960: 'George Berkeley: Precursor of Keynes or Moral Economist on Underdevelopments'. *Journal of Political Economy*, **67**, 31.
Wetzel, W. A.: 1895: *Benjamin Franklin as an Economist.*

Appendix to Chapter 8

Ashton, T. S.: 1955: *The Eighteenth Century*.
——: 1959: *Economic Fluctuations in England, 1700–1800.*
Blaug, M.: 1964: 'Economic Theory and Economic History in Britain 1650–1776'. *Past and Present*, **28**, 111ff.
Clark, G. N.: 1947: *The Seventeenth Century*.
Furniss, E. S.: 1920: *The Position of the Laborer in a System of Nationalism.*
Grampp, W. D.: 1952: 'The Liberal Elements in English Mercantilism', *Quarterly Journal of Economies*, 66, 465ff.
——: 1965: *Economic Liberalism*, 2 vols.
Hale, Sir M: 1805: *Works: Moral and Religious*, 2 vols.
Harrod, R. F.: 1951: *Life of J. M. Keynes.*
Heckscher, E. F.: 1955: *Mercantilism*, 2nd ed., 2 vols.
Hinton, R. W. K.: 1955: 'The Mercantile System in the Time of Thomas Mun'. *Economic History Review*, **7** (3), 277ff.
Hutchison, T. W.: 1978: *On Revolutions and Progress in Economic Knowledge.*
Keynes, J. M.: 1936: *The General Theory of Employment, Interest and Money.*
——: 1973: *Collected Writings*, vol. 13.
Muchmore, L.: 1969: 'G. de Malynes and Mercantile Economics'. *History of Political Economy*, **1**, 336ff.
Supple, B. E.: 1959: *Commercial Crisis and Change in England 1600–1642.*
Suviranta, B.: 1923: *The Theory of the Balance of Trade in England.*
Van Klaveren, J.: 1969: 'Fiscalism, Mercantilism and Corruption', in *Revisions in Mercantilism*, ed. D. C. Coleman.
Vickers, D. W.: 1959: *Studies in The Theory of Money 1690–1776.*
Viner, J.: 1964: 'Comment', in *Keynes' General Theory*, ed. R. Lekachman, 253ff.
Wilson, C. H.: 1967: *Economic History and the Historian.*
Wood, J.: 1972: *Money and Output: Keynes and Friedman in Historical Perspective.*

Chapter 9 Fundamental Ideas and Concepts: The Emergence of Systematic Theories

I

Bernoulli, D.: 1738: *Specimen theoriae novae de mensura sortis*, trans. L. Sommer, in *Econometrica*, 1954, **22**, 23ff.
Cantillon, R.: 1931: *Essai sur la nature du commerce en général*, ed. H. Higgs.
——: 1952: *Essai sur la nature du commerce en général*, ed. A. Sauvy et al.
——: 1979: *Essai sur la nature du commerce en général*, ed. T. Tsuda.
Carl, E. L.: 1722–3: *Traité de la richesse des princes et de leur états*, 3 vols.
Ceva, G.: 1711: *De re numaria* . . . reprinted in Masé-Dari (1935).

II

Bianchini, M.: 1982: *Alle origini della scienza eocnomica: felicità pubblica e matematica sociale negli economisti Italiani del settecento.*
Bordo, M. D.: 1983: 'Some Aspects of the Monetary Economics of Richard Cantillon'. *Journal of Monetary Economics*, **12**, 235ff.
Diderot, D. and D'Alembert, J.: 1755: *Encyclopédie ou dictionnaire raisonné des sciences des arts et des métiers.*
Hayek, F. A.: 1931: Introduction and Notes to R. Cantillon's *Abhandlung über die*

Natur des Handels im Allgemeinen, trans. H. Hayek.
Hofmann, F.: 1943: 'Die Leistung von Ernst Ludwig Carl ...'. *Weltwirtschaftliches Archiv*, **58** (2), 245ff.
Hone, J.: 1944: 'R. Cantillon, Economist – a Biographical Note'. *Economic Journal*, **54**, 96.
Hyse, R.: 1971: 'Richard Cantillon, Financier to Amsterdam'. *Economic Journal*, **81**, 324 and 812ff.
Katscher, L.: 1901: 'Bibliographical Discovery in Political Economy'. *Journal of Political Economy*, **9**, *423ff*.
Kauder, E.: 1965: *A History of Marginal Utility Theory*.
Masè–Dari, E.: 1935: 'Un precursore della econometrica'. *Modena*.
Murphy, A.: 1984: 'Richard Cantillon, an Irish Banker in Paris', in *Economists and the Irish Economy*, ed. A. Murphy, 45ff.
——: 1986: *Richard Cantillon: Entrepreneur and Economist*.
Pringsheim, A.: 1896: *Die Grundlage der modernen Wetlehre: Daniel Bernoulli, Versuch einer neuen Theorie der Wertbestimmung von Glücksfallen*.
Schumpeter, J. A.: 1954: *History of Economic Analysis*.
Shirras, G. F. and Craig, J. H.: 1945: 'Sir Isaac Newton and the Currency'. *Economic Journal*, **55**, 217ff.
Spengler, J. J.: 1954: 'Richard Cantillon, the First of the Moderns'. *Journal of Political Economy*, **62**, 281ff and 406ff.
Stigler, G. J.: 1965: *Essays in the History of Economics*, 109ff.
Tautscher, A.: 1939: *Ernst Ludwig Carl (1682–1743), der Begründer der Volkswirtschaftslehre*.
——: 1940: 'Der Begründer der Volkswirtschaftslehre – ein Deutscher?'. *Schmollers Jahrbuch*, **63**, 79ff.
——: 1941: 'Die Arbeitsteilung als Grundproblem der Nationalökonomie bei Ernst Ludwig Carl'. *Zeitschrift für Nationalökonomie*, **10**, 1ff.
——: 1941: 'Ernst Ludwig Carol und Adam Smith'. *Weltwirtschaftsliches Archiv*, **56**, 13ff.
Theocharis, R. D.: 1961: *Early Developments in Mathematical Economics*.
Vickers, D.: 1959: *Studies in the Theory of Money, 1690–1776*'.
Viner, J.: 1937: *Studies in the Theory of International Trade*.
——: 1965: *Guide to John Rae's Life of Adam Smith*.

Chapter 10 Mid-Century Efflorescence, French Enlightenment and the Thirty-year Boom

Acquaviva, D. P.: 1984: *Il pensiero economico classico in Italia (1750–1860)*
Coleman, D. C.: 1987: *History and the Economic Past*.
Einaudi, L.: 1953: *Saggi bibliografici e storici intorno alle dottrine economiche*.
Gay, P.: 1969: *The Enlightenment*, vol. II.
Higgs, H.: 1935: *Bibliography of Economics, vol. I, 1751–1775*.
Tocqueville, A.: 1856: *The Old Régime and the French Revolution*, trans. S. Gilbert, 1955.
Tribe, K.: 1984: 'Cameralism and the Science of Government'. *Journal of Modern History*, **56**, 263ff.

Chapter 11 Moral Philosophy and Political Economy in Scotland

I

Carmichael, G.: 1724: Annotations, in revised ed. of *De officio hominis et civis* by S. Pufendorf.

Hume, D.: 1739: *A Treatise of Human Nature*, Everyman ed., 1911, 2 vols.

——: 1751: 'An Inquiry concerning the Principles of Morals', in *Essays and Treatises on Several Subjects*, vol. II, 1800, 213ff.

——: 1752: 'Of Civil Liberty' in *Essays and Treatises on Several Subjects*, vol. I, 1800, 91ff.

——: 1932: *Letters of David Hume*, ed. J. Y. Greig, 2 vols.

——: 1955: *Writings on Economics*, ed. E. Rotwein.

Hutcheson, F.: 1725–7: *Remarks upon the Fable of the Bees*.

——: 1747: *A Short Introduction to Moral Philosophy*.

——: 1755: *A System of Moral Philosophy*, 3 vols.

Smith, A.: 1976: *The Wealth of Nations* 3rd ed., 1784, ed. R. H. Campbell, A. S. Skinner and W. B. Todd.

——: 1978: *Lectures on Jurisprudence*, ed. R. L. Meek, D. D. Raphael and P. G. Stein.

II

Arkin, M.: 1956: 'The Economic Writings of David Hume, a Reassessment'. *South African Journal of Economics*, **24** (3), 204ff.

Bagehot, W.: 1879: 'Adam Smith and Our Modern Economy', in *Economic Studies*, ed. R. H. Hutton, new ed. 1895, 125ff.

—— 1881: 'Adam Smith as a Person', in *Biographical Studies*, ed. R. H. Hutton, 247ff.

Bonar, J.: 1922: *Philosophy and Political Economy*.

Bryson, G.: 1945: *Man and Society: the Scottish Inquiry of the Eighteenth Century*.

Burton, J. H.: 1895: *Life and Correspondence of David Hume*, 2 vols.

Campbell, T. D.: 1982: 'Francis Hutcheson' in *The Origin and Nature of the Scottish Enlightenment*, ed. R. H. Campbell and A. S. Skinner.

Clark, G. N.: 1932: 'The Study of Economic History', in *The Study of Economic History*, ed. N. B. Harte, 1971.

Duke, M. I.: 1979: 'David Hume and Monetary Adjustment'. *History of Political Economy*, **11**, 572ff.

Forbes, D.: 1954: 'Scientific Whiggism: Adam Smith and John Millar'. *Cambridge Journal*, **7** (11), 643ff.

——: 1975: *Hume's Philosophical Politics*.

Hamilton, W.: 1872: Introduction to *Works of Thomas Reid*, 2nd ed.

Heckscher, E.: 1955: Mercantilism, 2 vols, 2nd ed.

Hill, J. B.: 1846: *Life and Correspondence of David Hume*.

Hont, I.: 1983: 'The Rich-Country–Poor-Country Debate in Scottish Classical Political Economy', in *Wealth and Virtue*, ed. I. Hont and M. Ignatieff, 271ff.

Hutchison, T. W.: 1953: 'Berkeley's *Querist* and its Place in the Economic Thought of the Eighteenth Century'. *British Journal for the Philosophy of Science*, **4**, 13.

——: 1978: *Revolutions and Progress in Economic Knowledge*.

Johnson, E. A. J.: 1937: *Predecessors of Adam Smith*.

Keynes, J. M.: 1936: *General Theory of Employment, Interest and Money*.

Low, J. M.: 1952: 'An Eighteenth-Century Controversy in the Theory of Economic Progress'. *Manchester School*, **20**, 311ff.

Medick, H.: 1973: *Naturzustand und Naturgeschichte der bürgerlichen Gesellschaft*.

Meek, R. L. and Skinner, A. S.: 1973: 'The Development of Adam Smith's Ideas

on the Division of Labour'. *Economic Journal*, **83**, 1094ff.
Moore, J. and Silverthorne, M.: 1983: 'Gershom Carmichael and Natural Jurisprudence', in *Wealth and Virtue*, ed. I. Hont and M. Ignatieff, 73ff.
Mossner, E. C.: 1980: *Life of David Hume*.
Perlman, M.: 1987: 'Of a Controversial Passage in Hume'. *Journal of Political Economy*, **95**, 274ff.
Rae, J.: 1895: *Life of Adam Smith*.
Robbins, L. C.: 1952: *The Theory of Economic Policy in English Classical Political Economy*.
Schatz, A.: 1902: *L'Œuvre économique de David Hume*.
Scott, W. R.: 1900: *Francis Hutcheson*.
——: 1937: *Adam Smith as Student and Professor*.
Semmel, B.: 1965: 'The Hume–Tucker Debate and Pitt's Trade Proposals'. *Economic Journal*, **75**, 759ff.
Stewart, D.: 1811: *Memoir of Adam Smith*.
Taylor, W. L.: 1955: 'Gershom Carmichael: a Neglected Figure in British Political Economy'. *South African Journal of Economics*, **23**, 251ff.
——: 1965: *Francis Hutcheson and David Hume as Predecessors of Adam Smith*.
Thomson, J.: 1859: *An Account of the Life, Lectures and Writings of William Cullen M.D.*, 2 vols.
Vickers, D.: 1959: *Studies in the Theory of Money, 1690–1776*.

Chapter 12 Between Boisguilbert and Quesnay

I

Child, Sir J.: 1754: *Traités sur le commerce et sur les avantages qui résultent de la reduction de l'interest de l'argent* ... Traduit de l'Anglois [by Gournay].
Dutot, C. de F.: 1738: *Réflexions politiques sur les finances et le commerce*, trans anon, 1739.
Forbonnais, F. L. V.: 1754: *Eléments du commerce*.
Melon, J. F. : 1734: *Essai politique sur le commerce*, trans.
——: 1767: *Principes et observations économiques*.
Montesquieu, C. L. de: 1748: *L'Esprit des lois*, trans. T. Nugent ed. F. Neumann, 1949.
——: 1734: *Considérations sur les causes de la grandeur des Romains et de leur decadence*, trans. J. Baker, 1882.

II

Fletcher, F. T. H.: 1939: *Montesquieu and English Politics*.
Grice-Hutchinson, M.: 1978: *Early Economic Thought in Spain*.
Higgs, H.: 1897: *The Physiocrats*.
Keynes, J. M.: 1973: *The Collected Writings*, ed. D. E. Moggridge, vol. VII.
Morize, A.: 1909: *L'Apologie du luxe au XVIII*ième siècle.
Murphy, A.: 1986: *Richard Cantillon: Entrepreneur and Economist*.
Morrisson, C. and Goffin, R.: 1967: *Questions financières aux XVII*ième et XIXième siècle.
Oncken, A.: 1886: *Die maxime Laissez-faire et Laissez-passer*.
Weulersse, G.: 1910: *Le mouvement physiocratique en France*.

Chapter 13 Josiah Tucker and the English Contribution

I

Cantillon, R.: 1931: *Essai sur la nature du commerce en général*, ed. Higgs.
Franklin, B.: 1844: *Works*, vol. II, ed. J. Sparks.
Harris, J.: 1757–8: *Essay upon Money and Coins*, 2 vols.
Massie, J.: 1750: *The Natural Rate of Interest.*
——: 1760: *A Representation concerning the Knowledge of Commerce as a National Concern, pointing out the proper means of promoting such knowledge in this kingdom.*
Postelthwayt, M.: 1749: *A Dissertation on the Plan, Use and Importance of the Universal Dictionary of Trade and Commerce.*
——: 1751: *The Universal Dictionary of Trade and Commerce*, 2 vols, (further editions, 1766 and 1774).
——: 1757: *Great Britain's True System.*
Royston, J.: 1750: *The British Mercantile Academy: or the Accomplished Merchant.*
Tucker, J.: 1749: *A Brief Essay on the Advantages and Disadvantages which Respectively Attend* France *and Great Britain with regard to Trade.*
——: 1751–2: *Reflections on the Expediency of a Law for the Naturalization of Foreign Protestants*, parts I and II.
——: 1753: *A brief Essay on the Advantages and Disadvantages which Respectively Attend France and Great Britain with regard to trade* (2nd edn).
——: 1755: *The Elements of Commerce and Theory of Taxes*, see Tucker (1931).
——: 1758: *Instructions for Travellers*, see Tucker (1931).
——: 1763: *The Case of Going to War*, see Tucker (1931).
——: 1766: *A Letter from a Merchant in London to his Nephew in North America, see Tucker (1931).*
——: 1770: *Considerations upon American Colonies.*
——: 1772: *Six Sermons on Important Subjects.*
——: 1774a: *Four Tracts Together with Two Sermons.*
——: 1774b: *The True Interest of Great Britain Set Forth with regard to Colonies*, see Tucker (1931).
——: 1775a: *A Letter to Edmund Burke*, see Tucker (1931).
——: 1775b: *An Humble Address and an Earnest Appeal.*
——: 1776a: *Seventeen Sermons.*
——: 1776b: *A Series of Answers.*
——: 1779: *Further Thoughts on the Present Posture of Affairs.*
——: 1780: *Dispassionate Thoughts on the American War.*
——: 1781: *Cui Bono?*
——: 1931: *A Selection from the Economic and Political Writings*, ed. R. L. Schuyler.
Turgot, A. R. J.: 1808–11: *Œuvres*, 9 vols, ed. Dupont de Nemours, vol. 9.

II

Boswell, J.: 1791: *Life of Johnson*, Everyman ed., 2 vols, 1906.
Bryson, G.: 1945: *Man and Society: the Scottish Inquiry of the Eighteenth Century.*
Clark, W. E.: 1903: *Josiah Tucker, Economist.*
Dewey, D. R.: 1900: 'Franklin, B.', in Palgrave's *Dictionary of Political Economy.*
Einaudi, L.: 1953: *Saggi bibliografici e storici intorno alle dottrine economiche.*
Furniss, E. S.: 1920: *The Position of the Laborer in a System of Nationalism* (reprinted 1957).

Hildebrand, R.: 1863: 'Benjamin Franklin als Nationalökonom'. *Jahrbücher für Nationalökonomie und Statistik*, **1**, 577ff and 643ff.
Johnson, E. A. J.: 1937: *Predecessors of Adam Smith.*
Low, J. M.: 1954: 'The Rate of Interest: British Opinion in the Eighteenth Century'. *Manchester School*, **22**, 115ff.
Marx, K.: 1867: *Capital*, vol. I, Moscow ed., n.d.
Raffel, F.: 1905: *Englische Freihändler vor Adam Smith.*
Rashid, S.: 1986: 'Adam Smith and the Division of Labour: A Historical View'. *Scottish Journal of Political Economy*, **33**, 292ff.
Redlich, F.: 1970: 'The Earliest English Attempt at Theoretical Training for Business'. *History of Political Economy*, **2**, 199ff.
Rotwein, E.: 1955: *David Hume: Writings on Economics*, Introduction.
Semmel, B.: 1965: 'The Hume–Tucker Debate and Pitt's Trade Proposals'. *Economic Journal,* **75**, 759ff.
Shelton, G.: 1981: *Dean Tucker and Eighteenth-Century Economic and Political Thought.*
Smith, A.: 1776: *The Wealth of Nations*, eds R. H. Campbell, A. S. Skinner and W. B. Todd, 1976.
Tucker, G. S. L.: 1960: *Progress and Profits in British Economic Thought.*
Viner, J.: 1937: *Studies in the Theory of International Trade.*
Wetzel, W. A.: 1895: *Benjamin Franklin as an Economist.*

Chapter 14 Demography and Cameralism in Germany and Austria

I

Justi, J. H. G. von: 1755: *Staatswirtschaft oder systematische Abhandlung aller ökonomischen- und Cameralwissenschaften*, 2nd ed., 1758.
——: 1766: *System des Finanzwesens*, (reprinted 1969).
Sonnenfels, J. von: 1765: *Grundsätze der Polizei, Handlung und Finanzwissenschaft*, 3rd ed., 1770–1.
Süssmilch, J. P.: 1741–2: *Die Göttliche Ordnung* 4th ed., 1775.

II

Frensdorff, F.: 1903: *Über das Leben und die Schriften der Nationalökonom J. H. G. von - Justi,* reprinted 1970.
Monroe, A. E.: 1924: *Early Economic Thought.*
Riha, T.: 1985: *German Political Economy: The History of an Alternative Economics.*

Chapter 15 Italian Illumination: Subjective Utility, Money and the Mathematical Method

I

Galiani, F.: 1751: *Della moneta*, introduced by A. Caracciolo, 1963.
——: 1770: *Dialogues sur le commerce des blés*, ed. F. Nicolini, 1958.
——: 1770: *Dialogues* (Galiani's original text), ed. P. Koch, *Analecta Romanica*, 21, 1968.
——: 1881: *Correspondance,* ed. L. Perey and G. Maugras, 2 vols.
——: 1924: *Ancient Economic Thought*, chapter 12, extracts from *Della moneta* in English translation by A. E. Monroe.
——: 1955: *De la monnaie*, ed. and trans. G. H. Bousquet and J. Crisafulli.

——: 1979: *La Bagarre: Galiani's 'Lost' Parody*, ed. S. L. Kaplan.
Genovesi, A.: 1769: *Lezioni di commercio o sia economia civile.*
Montanari, G.: 1680: *Breve trattato del valore delle monete in tuttigli stati*, in *Scrittori classici Italiani di economia politica*, vol. III, ed. P. Custodi, 1804.
——: 1683–4: *Della Moneta*, ibid.

II

Berlin, I.: 1980: *Against the Current: Essays in the History of Ideas*, 111ff.
Braudel, F.: 1979: *The Perspective of the World*, trans. S. Reynolds.
Cesarano, F.: 1976: 'Monetary Theory in Ferdinando Galiani's *Della moneta*'. *History of Political Economy*, **8** (3), 380ff.
De Roover, R.: 1967: *San Bernardino of Siena and San Antonino of Florence, the Two Great Thinkers of the Middle Ages.*
Dmitriev, V. K.: 1902: 'The Theory of Marginal Utility', in *Economic Essays on Value, Competition and Utility*, trans. D. Fry, ed. D. M. Nuti, 1974.
Einaudi, L.: 1945: 'Ferdinando Galiani'. *Schweizerische Zeitschrift für Volkswirtschaft und Statistik*, **81**, 1ff. Partly translated in *The Development of Economic Thought*, ed. H. W. Spiegel, 1952, 62ff.
——: 1953: *Saggi bibliografici e storici intorno alle dottrine economiche.*
Ganzoni, E.: 1938: *Ferdinando Galiani: ein verkannter Nationalökonom des 18te Jahrhunderts.*
Grice-Hutchinson, M.: 1978: *Early Economic Thought in Spain.*
Hayek, F. A.: 1960: *The Constitution of Liberty.*
Hume, D.: 1932: *Letters*, ed. J. Y. T. Greig, 2 vols.
Kaplan, S. L.: 1976: *Bread, Politics and Political Economy in the Reign of Louis XIV.*
Kauder, E.: 1965: *A History of Marginal Utility Theory.*
Langholm, O.: 1979: *Price and Value in the Aristotelian Tradition.*
Nietzsche, F.: 1886: *Jenseits von gut und böse.*
Portà, P. L.: 1986: 'From Subjective Value to Population and Economic Growth: Ferdinando Galiani' (typescript).
Ruben, M.: 1936: *Ferdinando Galiani: der politische Ökonom des Ancien Régimes.*
Schumpeter, J. A.: 1954: *History of Economic Analysis.*
Spicciani, A.: 1972: *Sant' Antonino, San Bernardino e Pier di Giovanni Olivi nel pensiero economico medioevale.*
Tocqueville, A.: 1856: *The Old Régime and the French Revolution*, trans. S. Gilbert, 1955.
Viner, J.: 1972: *The Role of Providence in the Social Order.*

Chapter 16 François Quesnay and the Rise and Fall of the Physiocratic School

I

Baudeau, N.: 1767: *Principles de la science morale et politique sur le luxe et les loix somptuaires*, ed. Dubois, 1912.
Dupont de Nemours, P. S.: 1763: *Réflexions sur l'écrit intitulé Richesse de l'état.*
——: 1768: *De l'origine et des progrès d'une science nouvelle.*
——: 1774: *On Economic Curves*, trans. and ed. H. W. Spiegel, 1955.
——: 1790: *Dupont de Nemours on the Dangers of Inflation*, trans. E. E. Lincoln, 1950.
Galiani, F.: 1979: *La Bagarre*, ed. S. L. Kaplan.
Hume, D.: 1932: *Letters of David Hume*, ed. J. Y. T. Greig, 2 vols.

Le Trosne, G. F.: *La liberté du commerce des grains, toujours utile et jamais nuisible.*
Mercier de la Rivière, P.: 1767: *L'Ordre naturel et essentiel des sociétés politiques*, 2 vols.
——: 1770: *L'interêt général de l'état ou la liberté du commerce des blé.*
Mirabeau, V. R., Marquis de: 1756: *L'Ami des hommes.*
——: 1760: *Théorie de l'impôt.*
Pinto, I.: 1773: *Traité de la circulation et du crédit*, trans. S. Bagges, 1774.
Quesnay, F.: 1888: *Œuvres économiques et philosophiques de F. Quesnay*, ed. A. Oncken, reprinted 1969.
——: 1946: *China, a Model for Europe*, vol. II; translation of *Le despotisme de la Chine*, by L. A. Maverick.
——: 1958: *François Quesnay et la Physiocratie*, INED, 2 vols.
——: 1962: *The Economics of Physiocracy*, trans. and ed. R. L. Meek.
——: 1972: *Quesnay's Tableau Économique*, ed. M. Kuczynski and R. L. Meek.

II

Brocard, L.: 1902: *Les doctrines économiques et sociales du Marquis de Mirabeau.*
Bruckner, P. J.: 1987: *The Tears of the White Man*, trans. W. R. Beer.
Eltis, W. A.: 1984: *The Classical Theory of Economic Growth.*
Foley, V.: 1973: 'The Origins of the *Tableau Économique*', *History of Political Economy*, **5**, 121ff.
Fox-Genovese, E.: 1976: *The Origins of Physiocracy.*
Gay, P.: 1969: *The Enlightenment*, vol. II.
Gide, C. and Rist, C.: 1948: *A History of Economic Doctrines*, trans. R. Richards, 2nd ed.
Hayek, F. A.: 1949: *Individualism and Economic Order.*
Higgs, H.: 1897: *The Physiocrats.*
Kaplan, S. L.: 1976: *Bread, Politics and Political Economy in the Reign of Louis XIV.*
Knies, K.: 1892: *Carl Friedrich von Baden: Brieflicher Verkehr mit Mirabeau und Dupont.*
McLain, J. J.: 1977: *The Economic Writings of Du Pont de Nemours.*
Meek, R. L.: 1962: *The Economics of Physiocracy.*
——: 1973: *Precursors of Adam Smith.*
Neill, T. P.: 1949: 'The Physiocrats' Concept of Economics'. *Quarterly Journal of Economics*, **63**, 532ff.
Oncken, A.: 1920: *Geschichte des Nationalökonomie*, vol. 1.
Richner, E.: 1931: *Le Mercier de la Rivière.*
Robbins, L. C.: 1952: *The Theory of Economic Policy in English Classical Political Economy.*
Robinson, J.: 1960: Review of The Economic Development of Communist China, by T. J. Hughes and D. E. T. Luard, *Economic Journal*, **70**, 409ff.
Rogers, J. W.: 1971: *The Opposition to the Physiocrats.*
Ruben, M.: 1936: *Ferdinando Galiani: der politische Ökonom des Ancien Régimes.*
Samuels, W. J.: 1961: 'The Physiocratic Theory of Property and the State'. *Quarterly Journal of Economics*, **75**, 96ff.
——: 1962: 'The Physiocratic Theory of Economic Policy'. *Quarterly Journal of Economics*, **76**, 145ff.
Schumpeter, J. A.: 1954: *History of Economic Analysis.*
Smith, A.: 1776: *The Wealth of Nations*, ed. R. H. Campbell, A. S. Skinner and W. B. Todd, 1976.
Tocqueville, A.: 1856: *The Old Régime and the French Revolution*, trans. S. Gilbert, 1955.

Vaggi, G.: 1987: *The Economics of François Quesnay.*
Ware, N. J.: 1931: 'The Physiocrats: a Study in Rationalization'. *American Economic Review*, **21** (4), 607ff.
Woog, H.: 1950: *The Tableau Économique of François Quesnay.*

Chapter 17 The Milanese Enlightenment: Utility, Liberty and Mathematics

I

Beccaria, C.: 1762: *De disordine e de rimedi delle monete nello stato di Milano*, in *Scrittori classici Italiani di economia politica*, ed. P. Custodi, vol. XI, 1804.
——: 1764: *Tentative analitico sui contrabandi*, in *Opere*, vol. 2, 1822, 427ff. (translated in *Precursors in Mathematical Economics*, ed. W. J. Baumol and S. Goldfield, 1968).
——: 1769: *A Discourse on Public Economy and Commerce*, trans. anon. 1769.
——: 1804: *Elementi di economia pubblica*, ed. P. Custodi, vol. XII, 1804.
——: 1963: *On Crimes and Punishments*, ed. and trans. H. Paolucci.
Lloyd, H.: 1771: *An Essay on the Theory of Money.*
Verri, P.: 1762: *Dialogo sul disordine delle monete nello stato di Milano*, in *Scrittori classici Italiani di economia politica*, vol. XVI, ed. P. Custodi, 1803.
——: 1763: *Discorso sulla felicità*, in *Del piacere e del dolore e altri scritti*, ed. R. de Felice, 1964.
——: 1769: *Riflessioni sulle legge vincolanti principalmente nel commercio de grani*, ed. R. de Felice, 1964.
——: 1771: *Meditazioni sulla economia politica*, ed. R. de Felice, 1964: also 6th ed. 1772.
——: 1986: *Reflections on Political Economy*, trans. B. McGilvray and ed. P. D. Groenewegen.

II

Bouvy, E.: 1889: *Le Comte Pietro Verri, 1728–1797.*
Chichester, H. M.: 1909: 'Henry Lloyd', in *Dictionary of National Biography*, vol. IX.
Einaudi, L.: 1953: *Saggi bibliografici e storici intorno alle dottrine economiche.*
Grice-Hutchinson, M.: 1978: *Early Economic Thought in Spain.*
Halévy, E.: 1928: *The Growth of Philosophic Radicalism.*
Hazard, P.: 1965: *European Thought in the Eighteenth Century*, trans. J. L. May, Pelican ed.
Jevons, W. S.: 1911: *Theory of Political Economy*, 4th ed.
Schumpeter, J. A.: 1954: *History of Economic Analysis.*
Theocharis, R. D.: 1961: *Early Developments in Mathematical Economics.*
Venturi, F.: 1965: 'Beccaria', *Dizionario Biografico degli Italiani.*
——: 1978: 'Le *Meditazioni* di Pietro Verri'. *Rivista storica Italiana*, **90**, 530ff.
——: 1979: 'Le avventure del Generale Henry Lloyd'. *Rivista storica Italiana*, **91**, 369ff.
Wirminghaus, K.: 1886: *Zwei Spanische Merkantilisten.*

Chapter 18 French Pre-eminence: Saving and Investment: Subjective Utility and Expectations

I

Burlamaqui, J. J.: 1773: *Elémens du droit naturel*, 1783 ed.
Condillac, E. B. de: 1749: *Traité des systèmes*, 2 vols.
——: 1776: *Le commerce et le gouvernement considérés relativement l'un à l'autre* in *Œuvres de Condillac*, 21 vols, 1821–2, vol. 4.
——: 1798: *Cours d'études pour l'instruction du Prince de Parme*.
Graslin, J. J. F.: 1767: *Essai analytique sur la richesse et sur l'impot*.
Menger, C.: 1871: *Grundsätze der Volkswirtschaftslehre*.
Turgot, A. R. J.: 1769: *Réflexions sur la formation et la distribution des richesses*, ed. and trans. W. J. Ashley, 1898.
——: 1808–11: *Œuvres*, 9 vols, ed. Dupont de Nemours, 1808–11.
Walras, A.: 1831: *De la nature de la richesse et de l'origine de la valeur*.
Walras, L.: 1954: *Elements of Pure Economics*, trans. W. Jaffé.

II

Bourinnet, J.: 1966: 'Les prodromes de l'équilibre économique'. *Revue d'économie politique*, **86**, 255ff.
Dakin, D.: 1939: *Turgot and the Ancien Régime in France*.
Feilbogen, S.: 1892: *Smith and Turgot*.
Gillespie, C. C.: 1980: *Science and Polity in France at the End of the Old Régime*.
Groenewegen, P. D.: 1969: 'Turgot and Adam Smith'. *Scottish Journal of Political Economy*, **16**, 271ff.
——: 1970: 'A Reappraisal of Turgot's Theory of Value, Exchange and Price Determination'. *History of Political Economy*, **2**, 177ff.
——: 1977: *The Economics of Turgot*.
——: 1981: 'Turgot's Place in the History of Economic Thought', Paper at Conference on History of Economic Thought, Oxford.
Hayek, F. A.: 1949: *Individualism and Economic Order*.
——: 1952: *The Counter-Revolution of Science*.
Hutchison, T. W.: 1981: 'Turgot and Smith', in *Turgot, économiste et administrateur*, ed. C. Bordes et Jean Morange.
Kaplan, S. L.: 1976: *Bread, Politics and Political Economy in the Reign of Louis XIV*.
Klein, D.: 1985: 'Deductive Economic Methodology in the French Enlightenment'. *History of Political Economy*, **17**, 51ff.
Knight, I. F.: 1968: *The Geometric Spirit: the Abbé de Condillac and the French Enlightenment*.
Meek, R. L.: 1973a: *Turgot on Progress, Sociology and Economics*.
——: 1973b: *Precursors of Adam Smith*.
Meyer, P.: 1944: *Etienne Bonnot de Condillac*.
Rogers, J.W., Jr.: 1971: *The Opposition to the Physiocrats: a Study of the Economic Thought and Policy in the Ancien Régime, 1750–1780*.
Schumpeter, J. A.: 1954: *History of Economic Analysis*.
Smith, A.: 1776: *The Wealth of Nations*, ed. R. H. Campbell, A. S. Skinner and W. B. Todd, 2 vols, 1976.

Chapter 19 History and Political Economy in Scotland

I

Ferguson, A.: 1767: *A History of Civil Society.*
Hume, D.: 1742: *Essays Moral and Political.*
Millar, J.: 1771: *Observations concerning the Distinction of Ranks in Society.*
——: 1787: *An Historical View of the English Government.*
Steuart, J.: 1767: *An Inquiry into the Principles of Political Economy*, 1770, 3 vols.
——: 1966: *An Inquiry into the Principles of Political Economy*, ed. A. S. Skinner.
——: 1805: *Works*, 6 vols.

II

Akhtar, M. A.: 1978: 'Sir J. Steuart on Economic Growth'. *Scottish Journal of Political Economy*, **25**, 57ff.
——: 1979: 'An Analytical Outline of Sir J. Steuart's Macroeconomic Model'. *Oxford Economic Papers*, **26**, 283ff.
Anderson, G. M. and Tollison, R. D.: 1984: 'Sir James Steuart as the Apotheosis of Mercantilism', *Southern Economic Journal*, **51**, 456ff.
Bryson, G.: 1945: *Man and Society.*
Chamley, P.: 1963a: 'Sir J. Steuart: Inspirateur de la Théorie Générale de Lord Keynes' *Revue d'économie politique'*, vol. 3.
——: 1963b: *Économie politique et philosophie chez Steuart et Hegel.*
——: 1965: *Documents relatifs à Sir J. Steuart.*
Coleman, D. C.: 1987: *History and the Economic Past*,
Davie, G. E.: 1967: 'Anglophobe and Anglophil'. *Scottish Journal of Political Economy*, **14**, 291ff.
Eagly, R. V.: 1961: 'Sir J. Steuart and the Aspiration Effect'. *Economica* (NS) **18**, 53ff.
Eltis, W.: 1986: 'Sir James Steuart's Corporate State, in *Ideas in Economics*, ed. R. D. C. Black, 43ff.
Hayek, F. A.: 1949: *Individualism and Economic Order.*
Lehmann, W. C.: 1960: *John Millar of Glasgow.*
McCulloch, J. R.: 1845: *The Literature of Political Economy.*
Pascal, R.: 1938: 'Property and Society: the Scottish Historical School of the 18th Century'. *Modern Quarterly*, **3**, 167ff.
Perelman, M.: 1983: *Classical Political Economy.*
Rae, J.: 1895: *Life of Adam Smith.*
Robbins, L. C.: 1963: *Politics and Economics.*
Schatz, A.: 1902: *L'œuvre économique de David Hume.*
Sen, S. R.: 1957: *The Economics of Sir J. Steuart.*
Skinner, A.: 1962: 'Sir James Steuart: Economics and Politics'. *Scottish Journal of Political Economy*, **9**, 17ff.
——: 1965: 'Economics and History – the Scottish Enlightenment'. *Scottish Journal of Political Economy*, **12**, 1ff.
Stephen, L.: 1876: *A History of English Thought in the 18th Century*, 2 vols.
Vickers, D.: 1959: *Studies in the Theory of Money*, 1690–1776.
——: 1970: Review Article of *The Works, Political Metaphysical and Chronological of Sir James Steuart. Journal of Economic Literature*, **8**, 1190ff.

Chapter 20 Adam Smith and *The Wealth of Nations*

I

Hutcheson, F.: 1755: *A System of Moral Philosophy*.

Pufendorf, S.: 1660: *Elementorum jurisprudentiae universalis*, trans. W. A. Oldfather, 1931.

Pulteney, W.: 1738: *Some Thoughts on the Interest of Money in general and particularly in the Public Funds*, ed. P. D. Groenewegen, 1984.

Smith, A.: 1896: *Letter to the Duc de la Rochefoucauld* (of 1 November 1785), see *Economic Journal*, **6**, 165.

Smith, A.: 1976a: *The Wealth of Nations*, 3rd ed., 1784, ed. R. H. Campbell, A. S. Skinner and W. B. Todd.

——: 1976b: *The Theory of Moral Sentiments*, 6th ed., 1790, ed. D. D. Raphael and A. L. Macfie.

——: 1978: *Lectures on Jurisprudence*, ed. R. L. Meek, D. D. Raphael, and P. G. Stein.

——: 1983: *Lectures on Rhetoric and Belles Lettres*, ed. J. C. Bryce.

Steuart, Sir J.: 1966: *Priciples of Political Economy*, ed. A. Skinner (1767).

Temple, W.: 1758: *A Vindication of Commerce and the Arts*.

II

Ashley, W. J.: 1900: 'The Historical School of Economists', in *Dictionary of Political Economy*, ed. R. H. I. Palgrave, vol. I, 310.

Bagehot, W.: 1881: 'Adam Smith as a Person', in *Biographical Studies*, ed. R. H. Hutton, 247ff.

——. 1895: 'Adam Smith and our Modern Economy', in *Economic Studies*, ed. R. H. Hutton, 125ff.

Baranzini, M. and Scazzieri, R.: 1986 eds: *Foundations of Economics*.

Bitterman, H. J.: 1940: 'Smith's Empiricism and the Law of Nature'. *Journal of Political Economy*, **47**, 487ff and 703ff.

Blaug, M.: 1985: *Economic Theory in Retrospect*, 4th ed.

Bonar, J.: 1922: *Philosophy and Political Economy*.

Bowley, M.: 1973: *Studies in the History of Economic Theory before 1870:*

Buchanan, J. M.: 1976: 'Public Goods and Natural Liberty', in *The Market and the State*, ed. T. Wilson and A. Skinner, 271ff.

Campbell, T. D.: 1971: *Adam Smith's Science of Morals*.

Checkland, S. G.: 1976: 'Adam Smith and the Bankers', in *Essays on Adam Smith*, ed. T. Wilson and A. Skinner, 271ff.

Clark, G. N.: 1932: 'The Study of Economic History', in *The Study of Economic History*, ed. N. B. Harte, 1971.

Cropsey, J.: 1957: *Polity and Economy*.

De Roover, R.: 1955: 'Scholastic Economics: Survival and Lasting Influence' *Quarterly Journal of Economics*, **69**, 161ff.

Dmitriev, V. K.: 1902: *Economic Essays on Value, Competition and Utility*, trans. D. Fry, 1974.

Douglas, P. H.: 1928: 'Smith's Theory of Value and Distribution', in *Adam Smith 1776–1926*, ed. J. H. Hollander et al., 77ff.

Eagly, R. V.: 1974: *The Structure of Classical Economic Theory*.

Fay, C. R.: 1956: *Adam Smith and the Scotland of his Day*.

Forbes, D.: 1954: '"Scientific" Whiggism: Adam Smith and John Millar'. *Cambridge Journal*, **7**, 643ff.

Hayek, F. A.: 1952: *The Counter-Revolution of Science.*
Hicks, Sir John: 1965: *Capital and Growth.*
Hollander, S.: 1973: *The Economics of Adam Smith.*
Hutchison, T. W.: 1953a: *A Review of Economic Doctrines 1870–1929.*
——: 1953b: 'Berkeley's *Querist* and its Place in the Economic Thought of the Eighteenth Century'. *British Journal for the Philosophy of Science*, **4**, 13ff and 52ff.
——: 1958: 'Keynes und die Geschichte der klassischen Nationalökonomie'. *Zeitschrift für Nationalökonomie*, **8**, 393ff.
——: 1978: *On Revolutions and Progress in Economic Knowledge.*
Keynes, J. M.: 1938: Review of W. R. Scott, *Adam Smith as Student and Professor*, *Economic History*, **3**, 33ff.
Keynes, J. N.: 1917: *Scope and Method of Political Economy*, 4th ed.
Langholm, O.: 1979: *Price and Value in the Aristotelian Tradition.*
Lapidus, A.: 1986: *Le detour de valeur.*
Leslie, C.: n.d.: *Essays in Political and Moral Philosophy* , 4th ed.
Lindgren, J. R.: 1973: *The Social Philosophy of Adam Smith.*
Macfie, A. L.: 1967: *The Individual in Society.*
Marshall, A.: 1975: *The Early Writings*, ed. J. K. Whittaker.
Meek, R. L.: 1971: 'Smith, Turgot and the Four Stages Theory'. *History of Political Economy*, **3**, 9ff.
——: 1973: *Studies in the Labour Theory of Value*, 2nd ed.
Morrow, G.: 1928: 'Adam Smith: Moralist and Philosopher', in *Adam Smith, 1776–1926*, ed. J. H. Hollander, 156ff.
Myers, M. L.: 1983: *The Soul of Modern Economic Man.*
O'Brien, D.: 1975: *The Classical Economists.*
Pigou, A. C.: 1929: *Economics of Welfare*, 3rd ed.
Political Economy Club: 1876: *Revised Report of the proceedings at the Dinner of 31st May, 1876.*
Rae, J.: 1895: *Life of Adam Smith.*
Reisman, D. A.: 1976: *Adam Smith's Sociological Economics.*
Richardson, G. B.: 1976: 'Adam Smith on Competition and Increasing Returns', in *Essays on Adam Smith*, ed. T. Wilson and A. Skinner, 350ff.
Robertson, H. M.: 1976: 'Euge! Belle! Dear Mr Smith'. *South African Journal of Economics*, 44, 378ff.
Schumpeter, J. A.: 1954: *History of Economic Analysis.*
——: 1985: *Aufsätze zur Wirtschaftspolitik.*
Scott, W. R.: 1937: *Adam Smith as Student and Professor.*
——: 1938: *Adam Smith, an Oration.*
Senior, N. W.: 1928: *Industrial Efficiency and Social Economy*, ed. S. L. Levy, 2 vols.
Small, A. W.: 1907: *Adam Smith and Modern Sociology.*
Stigler, G. J.: 1950: *Five Lectures on Economic Problems.*
Tawney, R. H.: 1932: 'The Study of Economic History', in *The Study of Economic History*, ed. N. B. Harte, 1971.
Thomson, J.: 1859: *An Account of the Life, Lectures and Writings of W. Cullen, M.D.*, 2 vols.
Unwin, G.: 1908: 'The Aims of Economic History', in *The Study of Economic History*, ed. N. B. Harte, 1971.
Viner, J.: 1928: 'Adam Smith and Laissez-faire', in *Adam Smith, 1776–1926*, ed. J. H. Hollander, 116ff.
——: 1965: *Guide to John Rae's Life of Adam Smith.*
——: 1968: 'Adam Smith'. *Encyclopedia of the Social Sciences*, **14**.
Wilson, C. H.: 1958: *Mercantilism.*

Winch, D.: 1978: *Adam Smith's Politics.*
Young, A. A.: 1928: 'Increasing Returns and Economic Progress'. *Economic Journal*, **38**, 527ff.

Chapter 21 Postscript

Coleman, D. C.: 1987: *History and the Economic Past.*
Dubois, A.: 1897: 'Les théories psychologiques de la valeur au XVIIIe siècle'. *Revue d'économie politique*, **11**, 849.
Friedman, M.: 1986: 'Keynes's Political Legacy', in *Keynes's General Theory, Fifty Years On*, ed. J. Burton, 47ff.
Hicks, Sir John: 1965: *Capital and Growth.*
Hutchison, T. W.: 1953: *Review of Economic Doctrines, 1870–1929.*
——: 1978: *On Revolutions and Progress in Economic Knowledge.*
Keynes, J. M.: 1937: 'The General Theory of Employment'. *Quarterly Journal of Economics*, **51**, 209ff.
Leslie, C.: n.d.: *Essays in Political and Moral Philosophy.*
Link, R. G.: 1959: *English Theories of Economic Fluctuations 1815–1848.*
McCulloch, J. R.: 1824: *A Discourse on the Rise, Progress, Peculiar Objects and Importance of Political Economy.*
Meek, R.: 1973: *Studies in the Labour Theory of Value*, 2nd ed.
Mill, J.: 1836: 'Whether Political Economy is Useful', in *Selected Writings*, ed. D. Winch, 1966, 371ff.
Mill, J. S.: 1844: *Essays on Some Unsettled Questions of Political Economy.*
——: 1848: *Principles of Political Economy*, ed. W. J. Ashley, 1909.
Mitchell, W.: 1927: *Business Cycles.*
Sewall, H.: 1901: *The Theory of Value before Adam Smith.*
Walras, A.: 1831: *De la nature de la richesse et de l'origine de la valeur.*
Winch, D.: 1978: *Adam Smith's Politics.*

Chronology

NOTE

In drawing up the chronology of 'Other Events' I have been much indebted to the volumes by Neville Williams: *Chronology of the Expanding World* (1969) and *Chronology of the Modern World* (1969); also to *The Timetables of History* by Bernard Grun, 1982.

	Works in English	Works in other languages	Births and deaths	Other events
1660		Pufendorf: *Elementorum jurisprudentiae*		Restoration of the Monarchy in England: Charles II reigns
1661				Louis XVI begins personal rule: Colbert becomes finance minister – 1683
1662	Petty: *Treatise of Taxes and Contributions* Graunt: *Observations on the Bills of Mortality*			Last silver pennies minted in England. Royal Society receives charter from Charles II
1664	Mun: *England's Treasure by Foreign Trade* (written 1625–30). Petty: *Verbum Sapienti*			
1665		La Rochefoucauld: *Maximes*		Great Plague in London Anglo-Dutch naval war
1666				Great Plague and Great Fire in London.
1668	Child: *Brief Observations concerning trade, and interest of money.* Culpeper: *A Tract against Usury* (1621, reprinted)	Becher: *Politische Discours*	Vico b. (d. 1744)	East India Company takes over Bombay.

	Locke: *Some of the Consequences that are likely to follow upon Lessening of Interest to 4 per cent* (unpublished MS).			
1670			Mandeville b. (d. 1733)	Hudson Bay Co. incorporated by Royal Charter
1671		Nicole: *Essais Morales*		Law b. (d. 1729)
1672:	Petty: *Political Anatomy of Ireland* (published 1691) Temple: *Observations upon the United Provinces of the Netherlands*	Pufendorf: *De jure naturae et gentium*	Carmichael b. (d. 1729)	Britain declares war on Holland
1673				Mitsui trading and banking house founded
1674			Graunt d. (b. 1620) Barbeyrac b. (d. 1744)	
1675		Pufendorf: *De officio hominis et civis*	Melon b. (d. 1738).	Wren rebuilds St Paul's (1675–1710)
1676	Petty: *Political Arithmetic* (published 1690)			Leibniz discovers infinitesimal calculus
1679	Petty: *Treatise of Taxes and Contributions* (new ed.)		Hobbes d. (b. 1588) Decker b. (d. 1749)	
1680		Montanari: *Breve tratto del valore delle monete*		

1681				Royal Charter for Pennsylvania
1682	Petty: *Quantulumcunque concerning Money* (published 1695)		E. L. Carl b. (d. 1743) Becher d. (b. 1635)	
1683		Montanari: *Della moneta*	Colbert d. (b. 1619)	
1684		Hörnigk: *Oesterreich über alles*	Holberg b. (d. 1754)	
1685	Barbon: *Apology for the Builder*		Berkeley b. (d. 1753) Cantillon b. ? (d. 1734)	Charles II d.: succeeded by James II Revocation of Edict of Nantes: Protestant refugees flee to England
1686		Schröder: *Fürstliche Schatz- und Rentkammer*		
1687	Petty: *Essays in Political Arithmetic*		Montanari d. (b. 1633) Petty d. (b. 1623)	Newton's *Philosophiae naturalis principia mathematica* published
1688	King: *Scheme of the Income and Expense of several Families of England*		Schröder d. (b. 1640)	James II escapes to France
1689		Domat: *Les lois civiles dans leur ordre naturel*	Montesquieu b. (d. 1755)	Glorious Revolution in England

Year	British works	Other works	Births and deaths	Events
1690	Locke: *Two Treatises of Civil Government* Barbon: *A Discourse on Trade* Child: *A New Discourse of Trade*			William III defeats James II at Battle of the Boyne
1691	Locke: *Consequences of the Lowering of Interest* Petty: *Several Essays in Political Arithmetic* North: *Discourses upon Trade*		North d. (b. 1644)	
1692				William and Mary College, Virginia, founded.
1693	Halley: *Degrees of Mortality of Mankind*			National debt established in England
1694			Pufendorf d. Quesnay b. (d. 1774) Hutcheson b. (d. 1746) Burlamaqui b. (d. 1748)	Bank of England founded
1695	Lowndes: *An Essay for the Amendment of the Silver Coin* Locke: *Further Considerations concerning raising the value of money*	Boisguilbert: *Détail de la France*	Nicole d. (b. 1625)	Bank of Scotland founded

1696	King: *Natural and Political Observations . . .*	Domat d. (b. 1625)	Recoinage of English silver money
1697	Davenant: *Essay on the East India Trade* English translation of Davanzati: *Discourse upon Coins*		
1698	Davenant: *Discourses on the Public Revenues and on Trade*		
1699		Child d. (b. 1630) Temple d. (b. 1628)	
1700			Approximate populations: France 19 million; England and Scotland 7½ million; Spain 6 million
1701	Martyn: *Considerations on the East-India Trade*		War of Spanish Succession (–1714) Yale College founded
1702		Harris b. (d. 1764)	Death of William III, succeeded by Anne
1703			Methuen Treaty between England and Portugal

1704			Locke d. (b. 1632)	Victory of Marlborough at Blenheim
1705	Law: *Money and Trade Considered* Mandeville: *The Grumbling Hive*	Boisguilbert: *Factum de la France*	Justi b. (d. 1771)	
1706			Franklin b. (d. 1790)	
1707	Fleetwood: *Chronicon Preciosum*	Vauban: *Dîme royale* Boisguilbert: *Dissertation de la nature des richesses . . .*	Vauban d. (b. 1633) Süssmilch b. (d. 1767) Postelthwayt b. (d. 1767)	Union of England and Scotland
1710	Berkeley: *A Treatise concerning the Principles of Human Knowledge*			South Sea Co. founded
1711		Ceva: *De re numaria*	Hume b. (d. 1776)	
1712			Gregory King d. (b. 1648) Hörnigk d. (b. 1638) Genovesi b. (d. 1769) Gournay b. (d. 1759) Steuart b. (d. 1780)	
1713			Tucker b. (d. 1799) Ortes b. (d. 1790)	Peace of Utrecht
1714	Mandeville: *Fable of the Bees*		Davenant d. (b. 1656) Boisguilbert d. (b. 1646)	Death of Queen Anne: George I succeeds

Year				
1715			Condillac b. (d. 1780) Mirabeau b. (d. 1789)	Death of Louis XIV Regency follows of great grandson, Louis XV
1716				Law establishes Banque générale in Paris
1717				Law's Mississippi Co. obtains a monopoly of trade with Louisiana
1719			Mercier de la Rivière b. (d. 1801)	
1720	Gervaise: *The System or Theory of the Trade of the World*		Lloyd b. (d.)	South Sea Bubble bursts in London John Law flees from France after collapse of Mississippi Co. and financial panic
1721		Montesquieu: *Lettres Persanes*		
1722		Carl: *Traité de la richesses des princes*	Forbonnais b. (d. 1800)	
1723			Fleetwood d. (b. 1656) Smith b. (d. 1790) Ferguson b. (d. 1816)	

Year	British works	Foreign works	Births and deaths	Events
1725	Hutcheson: *Enquiry into Beauty and Virtue*	Vico: *Scienza nuova*		
1727			Newton d. (b. 1642) Turgot b. (d. 1781)	George I dies: accession of George II
1728			Galiani b. (d. 1787) Pietro Verri b. (d. 1797)	
1729	Mandeville: *Fable of the Bees, Part II* Franklin: *Modest Inquiry into Paper Currency* Gee: *Trade and Navigation of Great Britain Considered*		Carmichael d. (b. 1672) Law d. (b. 1671)	
1732	Berkeley: *Alciphron, or the Minute Philosopher*		Sonnenfels b. (d. 1817)	
1733			Mandeville d. (b. 1670)	
1734	Vanderlint: *Money Answers All Things*	Melon: *Essai politique sur le commerce*	Cantillon d. (b. ?)	
1735	Berkeley: *Querist*, Part I		Millar b. (d. 1801)	
1736	Berkeley: *Querist*, Part II			
1737	Berkeley: *Querist*, Part III			
1738		Dutot: *Refléxions politiques sur les finances et le commerce* Bernoulli: *Specimen theoriae novae de mensura sortis*	Melon d. (b. 1675) Beccaria b. (d. 1794)	

1739	Hume: *Treatise on Human Nature* Decker: *Serious Considerations or the several high duties*		Dupont de Nemours b. (d. 1817)	
1740				Frederick the Great launches first Silesiasn war against Maria Theresa
1742		Süssmilch: *Die Göttliche Ordnung*	Halley d. (b. 1656)	
1743			Carl d. (b. 1682)	
1744	Decker: *Essay on the Causes of the Decline of the Foreign Trade ...*		Barbeyrac d. (b. 1674) Vico d. (b. 1668)	
1745				Jacobite rebellion
1746		Condillac: *Essai sur l'origine des connaissances humaines*	Hutcheson d. (b. 1694)	Battle of Culloden: defeat of Jacobites
1747	Hutcheson: *Introduction to Moral Philosophy*			
1748		Montesquieu: *Esprit des lois*	Burlamaqui d. (b. 1694) Bentham b. (d. 1832)	Peace of Aix la Chapelle

1749	Tucker: *Essay on Trade . . .*			
1750	Massie: *Natural Rate of Interest*			
1751	Tucker: *Naturalization of Foreign Protestants*, Part I Hume: *Enquiry concerning the Principles of Morals* Postelthwayt: *Universal Dictionary of Trade and Commerce*	Galiani: *Della moneta* *Encyclopédie*, vols I–III		Adam Smith appointed to chair of Logic at Glasgow University
1752	Hume: *Political Discourses* Tucker: *Naturalization of Foreign Protestants*, Part II			Adam Smith appointed to chair of Moral Philosophy at Glasgow University Franklin invents lightning conductor
1753			Berkeley d. (b. 1685)	English Parliament permits naturalization of Jews
1754	Hume: *History of Great Britain*, vol. I	Hume's *Political Discourses* translated into German Forbonnais: *Eléments du Commerce* Child's *Discourse on Trade*, translated into French, with notes by Gournay	Holberg d. (b. 1684)	

1755	Hutcheson: *System of Moral Philosophy* Tucker: *Elements of Commerce* Franklin: *Observations concerning the Increase of Mankind* Johnson's *Dictionary of the English language*	Justi: *Staatswirtschaft* Tucker's *Naturalization of Foreign Protestants*, translated into French by Turgot Cantillon, *Essai sur la nature du commerce en genéral* (published)	Montesquieu d. (b. 1689)	
1756		Quesnay: *Fermiers* Mirabeau: *Ami des Hommes, ou Traité de la population*		Seven Years War begins
1757	Harris: *Essay upon Money and Coins*, part I Hume: *History of Great Britain*, vol. II Postelthwayt: *Great Britain's True System*			Battle of Plassey
1758	Tucker: *Instructions for Travellers*	Quesnay: *Tableau Économique*		
1759	Smith: *Theory of Moral Sentiments* Hume: *History of Great Britain*, vols 3 and 4	Turgot: *Éloge de Gournay*		British capture Quebec
1760		Mirabeau: *Théorie de l'impôt*		Death of George II: accession of George III

Year				
1762		Beccaria: *De disordine e de rimedi delle monete nello stato di Milano* Verri: *Dialogo sul disordine delle monete nello stato di Milano*		
1763		Sonnenfels: *Grundsätze der Polizei-, Handlungs- und Finanzwissenschaft*		Peace of Paris ends Seven Years War
1764		Beccaria: *Dei delitti e delle pene*	Harris d. (b. 1702)	
1765		Quesnay: '*Droit naturel*' *Éphémérides* founded in Paris by Baudeau		Stamp Act taxing American colonies
1766		Turgot: *Réflexions* (published 1769–70) Justi: *System des Finanzwesens*	Malthus b. (d. 1834)	
1767	Steuart: *Principles of Political Economy* Ferguson: *History of Civil Society*	Mercier: *Ordre naturel et essentiel des sociétés politiques* Graslin: *Essai analytique sur la richesse et sur l'impôt*	Süssmilch d. (b. 1707) Say b. (d. 1832) Postelthwayt d. (b. 1707)	
1768		Dupont: *De l'origine et de progrès d'une science nouvelle*		

1769	English translation (anon.) of Beccaria: *A Discourse on Public Economy and Commerce* Franklin: *Concerning National Wealth*	Beccaria: *Elementi di economia politica* (published 1804) Turgot: *Valeurs et monnaie* (published 1808–11)	Genovesi d. (b. 1712)
1770		Galiani: *Dialogues sur le commerce des blé* Mercier: *L'intérêt générale de l'Etat*	Hegel b. (d. 1831)
1771		Verri: *Meditazioni sulla economia politica*	Justi d. (b. 1705)

1772			Ricardo b. (d. 1723)	Bridgwater Canal constructed
1773		Pinto: *Traité de la circulation et du crédit*	J. Mill b. (d. 1836) Sismondi b. (d. 1842)	Boston Tea Party
1774	English translation of Pinto, 1773	Ortes: *Economia nazionale* Burlamaqui: *elémens du droit naturel*	Quesnay d. (b. 1694)	Louis XV d. Turgot reintroduces free trade in France
1775				American War of Independence begins Watt's steam engine perfected
1776	Smith: *Wealth of Nations* Gibbon: *Decline and Fall of the Roman Empire* Bentham: *Fragment on Government*	Condillac: *Le commerce et le gouvernement*	Hume d. (b. 1711)	American Declaration of Independence Turgot dismissed as Minister of Finance

Index of Names

Pages of main references given in bold

Index of Subjects

In order to clarify the historical development of ideas, the names of writers in the sub-headings are set out in chronological order and not alphabetically.